Conflict and Consensus

in American History

Volume 2

Ninth Edition

Edited by

Allen F. Davis

Temple University

Harold D. Woodman

Purdue University

Houghton Mifflin Company   Boston   New York

For Gregory and Paul
&
Allan and David

Senior Sponsoring Editor: Patricia A. Coryell
Assistant Editor: Jeanne Herring
Associate Project Editor: Elena Di Cesare
Editorial Assistant: Angela Schoenherr
Senior Designer: Henry Rachlin
Associate Production Coordinator: Deb Frydman
Director of Manufacturing: Michael O'Dea
Marketing Manager: Clint Crockett

Cover image and design by Minko Dimov.

Photo Credits

Chapter 1: © Archive Photos; Chapter 2: © Archive Photos; Chapter 3: © Corbis-Bettmann; Chapter 4: © Archive Photos; Chapter 5: © Museum of the City of New York; Chapter 6: © Theodore Roosevelt Collection, Harvard College Library; Chapter 7: © The Granger Collection; Chapter 8: © UPI/Bettmann; Chapter 9: © Lambert/Archive; Chapter 10: © AP/Wide World Photos; Chapter 11: © P. Jones GRIFFITHS/Magnum Photos, Inc.; Chapter 12: David Young-Wolff/Photo Edit.

Excerpts from *The Robber Barons: The Great American Capitalists 1861–1901,* copyright 1934 and renewed 1962 by Matthew Josephson, reprinted by permission of Harcourt Brace & Company.

Printed in the U.S.A.

Library of Congress Catalog Card Number: 96-76888

ISBN: 0-669-41697-5

456789-DOC-05 04 03 02 01

Contents

10. *The Turbulent 1960s* 435

11. *Vietnam: Crisis in United States Foreign Policy* 494

12. *Unity or Disunity: The Multicultural Debate* 552

Preface

We are pleased that the continued success of *Conflict and Consensus in American History* has warranted publication of this ninth edition. Those familiar with earlier editions will note that we have not changed the basic organization. We seek to keep the book useful for the introductory course and, therefore, have retained the traditional periodization found in most of the popular survey texts. But, like the best of these texts, we have given considerable attention to social history, to the history of women and minorities, and to the contributions of ordinary people to the history of the United States. Our goal has been to suggest, whenever possible, how events that have been traditionally viewed from the elite white male perspective often take on new and richer meaning when women, blacks, and common folk are integrated into the story.

In this latest edition, we have also retained our emphasis on the theme of conflict and consensus. Our experience and the experiences of those who have used the book have persuaded us that the presentation of conflicting views of particular periods and problems, when shown within the context of general interpretations, allows students to deepen their understanding of the historical details and provides them with the means to interpret the broad sweep of the country's history. We remain convinced that the theme of conflict and consensus remains viable and valuable more than a generation after the first so-called consensus historians challenged prevailing views. If the issues are not always as starkly presented as they once were, they nevertheless remain important sources of disagreement among historians, as the selections in this volume make clear.

In this edition, as in the previous ones, we have avoided presenting only two extreme positions on each problem raised. Such an either/or approach is artificial, and forces students to choose between extremes or to conclude, without adequate evidence, that the truth must be midway between the two extremes. We have, therefore, included three selections dealing with each problem and have chosen selections that illustrate the subtleties of interpretation rather than stark and rigid presentations of either point of view. Although we have sought to be up to date by choosing selections illustrating the most recent scholarship, we reject the idea that the newest is always the best and therefore have retained older work we deemed important, influential, and of high quality.

In the third edition we added a general introduction designed to help the beginning student understand why historians disagree. We found that students were often confused rather than enlightened when presented with conflicting interpretations of the same events. Too often they lacked the skills needed to discern the bases of disagreements. Perhaps because of their experience in memorizing details and answering multiple-choice questions, they concluded that when historians disagreed, one must be right and the others wrong. Instead of seeing a variety of interpretations as a means to enrich and broaden their understanding of the nation's past, many students concluded that the inclusion of a variety of interpretations was a little trick designed to force them to discover the "right" answer. Because of the favorable response to this brief introduction to historical methods and philosophy, we have retained it with some revisions, including a brief discussion of the most recent developments in historical scholarship. As a further aid to students, we have provided a brief introduction to each chapter in which we set the general historical context, discuss the particular selections included in the chapter, and raise a series of questions and suggestions to help readers understand the evidence, the arguments, and the methods the authors use.

Our main concern has not been with historiography, although we do direct interested students to relevant historiographical discussions. Beginning students are not especially interested in tracing shifting interpretations, nor should they be at this stage. They should be stimulated to learn *what* happened and *why* it happened by seeing how different historians, viewing the same event, have attempted to answer these questions. We have therefore concentrated not on the evolution of historical writing but on the historical problems themselves. We hope to leave students with a heightened understanding of how various issues in American history are interpreted and at the same time to provide the ammunition for thoughtful and spirited discussions. The brief, annotated bibliographies provided at the end of each chapter are not designed to be exhaustive, but they will help those who might wish to do further reading on a particular interpretation.

A. F. D.

H. D. W.

Acknowledgments

We wish to thank the various publishers and authors for permission to reprint copyrighted material. This book had its origin in our introductory course in American history at the University of Missouri; our former teaching assistants and students will recognize many of the ideas, as will those with whom we have worked at Temple University and Purdue University. We are grateful for their aid and recognize that in a real sense they have been collaborators.

We would also like to thank the many teachers and students who have made useful comments on this and earlier editions. Their candid evaluations and suggestions have been invaluable. We are especially grateful to Maria A. Brown of El Camino College; Luis Flores of Longview Community College; Thomas L. Powers of the University of South Carolina, Sumter; Harry Hewitt of Midwestern State University; Roger D. Launius of Louisiana State University; Robert C. McMath, Jr., of the Georgia Institute of Technology; William E. Pemberton of the University of Wisconsin—La Crosse; Thomas L. Powers of the University of South Carolina—Sumter; Don Hansdorff of the College of Staten Island, City University of New York; Gerald R. Gill of Tufts University; Bennett H. Wall of the University of Georgia; S. J. Adams of Lake Tahoe Community College; Hyman Berman of the University of Minnesota; C. Yuan of Worcester State College; Steven R. Boyd of the University of Texas at San Antonio; Robert L. Branyan and Lawrence H. Larsen of the University of Missouri, Kansas City; Franklin Mitchell of the University of Southern California; Lyle Dorsett of Wheaton College; James F. Watts of the City College of the City University of New York; John Burnham of Ohio State University; J. Stanley Lemons of Rhode Island College; William Cutler, Herbert Ershkowitz, and Howard Ohline of Temple University; Richard S. Kirkendall of the University of Washington; Alonzo Hamby of Ohio University; William O. Wagnon, Jr., of Washburn University of Topeka; Alice Kessler-Harris of Rutgers University; Kenneth Wayne Mixon and Henry R. Warnock of Mercer University; Ross Webb of Winthrop College; Joe P. Dunn of Converse College; Alton Hornsby of Morehouse College; Juliet Walker of the University of Illinois at Urbana-Champaign; Anita Goodstein of the University of the South; Sharon Alter of William Rainey Harper College; Jess Flemion of San Diego State University; Ruth W. Towne of Northeast Missouri State University; Jean S. Hunt of Loop College; James M. Morris of Christopher Newport College; S. L. Silberman of Connecticut College; Michel Dahlin of the University of Colorado at Colorado Springs; Bryan LeBeau of Creighton University; Gerald W. Wolff of the University of South Dakota; Cynthia K. Morrongiello of Garden City Senior High School, Garden City, New York; Mark Pittenger of Grand Valley State College; Roger P. Davis of the University of Nevada/Las Vegas; and Charles Hardy of Westchester State University.

A. F. D.

H. D. W.

Conflict and Consensus
in American History

Introduction:
History and Historians

Most students are usually introduced to the study of history by way of a fat textbook and become quickly immersed in a vast sea of names, dates, events, and statistics. The students' skills are then tested by examinations that require them to show how much of the data they remember; the more they remember, the higher their grades. From this experience a number of conclusions seem obvious: the study of history is the study of "facts" about the past; the more "facts" you know, the better you are as a student of history. The professional historian, whether teacher or textbook writer, is simply one who brings together a very large number of "facts."

Of course, only the most naive of students fail to see that the data of history, the "facts," are presented in an organized manner. Textbooks describe not only what happened, but also why it happened. For example, students learn that Puritans began coming from England to the Massachusetts Bay Colony in the New World in 1630, but they also learn why the Puritans came when they read about the religious persecutions in seventeenth-century England. Similarly, they read of the steady trek of people westward during the nineteenth century; however, at the same time they learn details that explain this movement of people—the availability of fertile lands in the West, the discovery of gold in California, the improvement of roads and other transportation facilities.

But beginning students, even as they come to recognize that their teacher and their textbook are explaining as well as describing events in the past, still have no reason to alter their notion of what history is all about. They are still working in the realm of "fact." The "fact" of the movement of people into Ohio is explained by the "fact" that fertile land was available there. They may learn more details about the event—how many people went to Ohio, when they arrived, where they settled—and about the explanation—the cost of land in Ohio, the availability of credit, the exhaustion of soils in the eastern states. Or they may be introduced to a fuller explanation when they read that some people came to Ohio to escape their creditors or to seek adventure or to speculate in land. In either case, they are simply learning more "facts." An advanced course in American history in high school differs from the sixth-grade course in American history in that it gives more detail; the older students must remember more "facts."

Students who have been introduced to history in this way may become confused upon discovering in a book like this one that historians often disagree sharply. To be sure, historians present their material in familiar ways; they tell us what happened and why it happened by presenting a mass of historical data. But students soon discover that two or three or more historians dealing with the same event may come to quite different conclusions about it. Sometimes two historians will use two very different sets of "facts" in describing an event, and this leads them to different conclusions. At other times, however, the same "facts" are given different meanings by different historians, and their conclusions therefore differ.

Experience and common sense might lead students to conclude that when historians disagree, one must be right while the others must be wrong. Just as students remember being marked down on their exams when they presented incorrect or inadequate information, they conclude that some historians are wrong because they have their "facts" wrong. But in this case, both common sense and experience can be profoundly misleading. Not only do students find that all historians argue reasonably and persuasively, but they also discover that the "facts" historians present—the names, dates, events, figures—usually turn out to be correct. Moreover, complicating matters even further, they often find that contending historians often agree on the facts and that they regularly use much the same data to come to different conclusions. To state that all are right when they say different things seems irrational; in any case, such an approach is often unacceptable to teachers who expect their students to take a position. The only way out for the baffled students is to choose one point of view for reasons they cannot fully explain. History, which had seemed to be a cut-and-dried matter of memorizing "facts," now becomes a matter of choosing one good interpretation from among many. Historical truth becomes a matter of personal preference, like the choice of one brand-name item over another in a supermarket.

This position is hardly satisfying. And when their teachers inform them that the controversy over historical interpretations is what lends excitement to the study of history, students can only respond that they feel more confusion than excitement. They cannot help but feel that two diametrically opposed points of view about an event cannot both be right; yet they lack the ability to decide between them.

Obviously, there is no easy solution to this problem. Historians do not disagree in order to spread confusion or to provide the raw material for "problems" books such as this one. Historians disagree because they view the past from different perspectives and because they ask different questions and therefore get different answers. Once students grasp this, they have taken the first step toward being able to evaluate the work of various historians. But before pursuing this matter, we must consider a problem that we have more or less taken for granted: What is history?

The word *history* has several meanings. In its broadest sense, it denotes the whole of the human past. More restricted is the notion that history is the *recorded* past, that is, that part of human life which has left some sort of record such as folk tales, artifacts, or written documents. Finally, history may be defined as that which historians write about the past.

Of course, the three meanings are related. Historians writing about the past base their accounts on the remains of the past, on the artifacts and documents left by people. Obviously they cannot know everything for the simple reason that not every event, every happening, was fully and completely recorded. And the further back one goes in time, the fewer are the records that remain. In this sense, then, the historian can only approximate history in the first meaning above—that is, history as the entire human past.

But this does not say enough. If historians cannot know everything because not everything was recorded, neither do they use all the records that are available to them. Rather, historians *select* from the total those records they deem most significant. Moreover, to complicate matters a bit more, they also recreate parts of the past for which they have no recorded evidence. Like detectives, they piece together evidence to fill in the gaps in the available records.

Historians are able to select evidence and to create evidence by using some theory or idea of human motivation and behavior. Sometimes this appears to be easy, requiring very little sophistication and subtlety. Thus, for example, historians investigating America's entry into World War I would probably find that the sinking of American merchant ships on the high seas by German submarines was relevant to their discussion. At the same time, they would most likely not use evidence that President Woodrow Wilson was dissatisfied with a new hat he bought during the first months of 1917. The choice as to which fact to use is based on a theory—admittedly, in this case a rather crude theory, but a theory nonetheless. It would go something like this: National leaders contemplating war are more likely to be influenced by belligerent acts against their countries than by their unhappiness with their haberdashers.

The choice, of course, is not always so obvious. But, before pursuing the problem further, it is important to note that a choice must be made. Historians do not just present facts; they present *some* facts and not others. They choose those facts that seem significant and reject others. This is one of the reasons that historians disagree: they have different views or different theories concerning human behavior and therefore find different kinds of information significant.

Perhaps it might appear that the subject matter being investigated, rather than any theory held by the historian, dictates which facts are significant. But this is not really so. With a little imagination—and poetic license—one could conceive of a psychological explanation for Wilson's actions that would include mounting frustration and anger fed in part, at least, by his strong disappointment with his new hat. In this case the purchase of a new hat would be a relevant fact in explaining Wilson's decision to ask Congress for a declaration of war. If readers find this outlandish, it is only because their notions of presidential motivation do not include this kind of personal reaction as an influence in determining matters of state.

If the choices were always as simple as choosing between German submarines and President Wilson's new hat, the problem would be easily resolved. But usually the choices are not so easy to make. Historians investigating the United States's entry into World War I will find in addition to German submarine warfare a whole series of other facts that could be relevant to the event under study. For instance, they will find that the British government had a propaganda machine at work in the United States that did its best to win public support for the British cause. They will discover that American bankers had made large loans to the British, loans that would not be repaid in the event of a British defeat.

They will read of the interception of the "Zimmermann Note," in which the German foreign secretary ordered the German minister in Mexico, in the event of war, to suggest an alliance between Germany and Mexico whereby Mexico, with German support, could win back territory taken from Mexico by the United States in the Mexican War. They will also find among many American political leaders a deep concern over the balance of power in Europe, a balance that would be destroyed—to America's disadvantage—if the Germans were able to defeat the French and the British and thereby emerge as the sole major power in Europe.

What, then, are the historians investigating America's entry into World War I to make of these facts? One group could simply conclude that America entered the war for several reasons and then list the facts they have discovered. By doing so, they would be making two important assumptions: (1) those facts they put on their list—in this case, German submarine warfare, British propaganda, American loans, the Zimmermann Note, and concern over the balance of power—are the main reasons, while those they do not list are not important; and (2) those things they put on their list are of equal importance in explaining the United States's role. But another group of historians might argue that the list is incomplete in that it does not take into account the generally pro-British views of Woodrow Wilson, views that stemmed from the President's background and education. The result will be a disagreement among the historians. Moreover, because the second group raise the question of Wilson's views, they will find a number of relevant facts that the first group would ignore. They will concern themselves with Wilson's education, with the influence of his teachers, with the books he read, and with the books he wrote. In short, although both groups of historians are dealing with the same subject—America's entry into World War I—they will come to different conclusions and use different facts to support their points of view. The facts selected, and those ignored, will depend not on the problem studied but on the points of view of the historians.

Similarly, a third group of historians might maintain that the various items on the list should not be given equal weight, that one of the reasons listed—say bankers' loans—was most important and that the others seemed to be significant only because of the overwhelming power of the bankers to influence American policy. The theory here would be that economic matters are the key to human motivation and that a small number of wealthy bankers have a disproportionate ability to influence government. Again, these historians will disagree with the first two groups, and they will find relevant certain facts that the others overlook—for example, bankers' opinions, the lobbying activities of bankers, financial and political connections between bankers and politicians, and the like.

In the examples given, historians disagree and use different facts or give different emphasis to the same facts because they begin from different premises; in other words, they have different theories of human motivation. But to put the matter in this way is somewhat misleading. It makes it appear that historical scholarship is merely a matter of deduction, as in Euclidean geometry, where conclusions are deduced from a set of given premises termed axioms and postulates. If this were so, historians would have it very easy. They would begin with a premise—for example, human beings are primarily motivated by selfish economic interests—and then they would seek whatever evidence they could find that showed people acting in that manner. They would ignore contrary evidence as unimportant or explain it away as being mere rhetoric designed to hide real motivations. The results of such efforts would be foreordained; the actors and the details might be different, but in the end the explanations would always be the same.

Historians term this approach or method "determinism," and most modern historians reject it. They argue that the premises cannot be merely assumed but must be proved or at least supported by concrete historical information. Nevertheless, historians cannot even begin their investigations without adopting some theory, even if it is expressed vaguely and held tentatively. In the course of their investigations they might alter or refine the original theory or replace it with another. But their final product will always rest upon some kind of theoretical base. Thus, if two historians become convinced by their evidence that different factors motivated the behavior of the people involved in a particular event, they will disagree, presenting different facts and giving different meanings to the same facts.

But there is still another realm of disagreement that, although it often appears similar to that just discussed, in fact stems from something rather different. Historians sometimes disagree because they are not really discussing the same thing. Often they are merely considering different levels of cause and effect. A few examples will illustrate this point.

The simplest level of analysis of cause and effect is to recognize what may be called proximate cause. "I was late for class," you explain, "because I overslept." Or, to use a historical example, "The Civil War began because South Carolina shore batteries under the command of General Beauregard opened fire on the federal garrison at Fort Sumter on April 12, 1861." Neither statement can be faulted on the grounds that it is inaccurate; at the same time, however, neither is sufficient as an explanation of the event being considered. The next question is obvious: Why did you oversleep, or why did relations between one state and the federal government reach the point where differences had to be settled by war? To this you may answer that you were out very late last night at a party, and the historian may respond that the authorities in South Carolina concluded that the election of Abraham Lincoln and his subsequent actions in threatening to supply the federal garrison at Fort Sumter were a clear menace to the well-being of South Carolina.

We have now dug more deeply into the problems, but the answers may still not be sufficient to satisfy us. Again we ask the question why and the answer takes us more deeply into the causes of the events under consideration. As we probe further, of course, the answers become more difficult and more complex. The problems discussed earlier—a theory of motivation and the selection of facts—begin to become increasingly important, and disagreements among historians will begin to emerge. But the potential for another kind of disagreement also arises. The further back or the deeper the historian goes, the more factors there are to be considered and the more tenuous the connection between cause and effect becomes. Historians may disagree about the point at which to begin their analysis—that is, about the location of a point beyond which the causal connection becomes so tenuous as to be meaningless. You might argue that the

ultimate cause of your being late to class was the fact that you were born, but obviously this goes back too far to be meaningful. That you were born is, of course,
a *necessary* factor—unless that had happened, you could not have been late—but
is not a *sufficient* factor; it does not really tell enough to explain your behavior
today. Similarly, we could trace the cause of the Civil War back to the discovery
of America, but again, this is a necessary but not a sufficient cause.

The point at which causes are both necessary and sufficient is not self-evident.
In part, the point is determined by the theoretical stance of historians. If they decide that slavery is the key to understanding the coming of the Civil War, the
point will be located somewhere along the continuum of the history of slavery in
the United States. But even those historians who agree that slavery is the key to
the war will not necessarily agree at what point slavery becomes both necessary
and sufficient. The historians who believe that slavery was a constant irritant
driving the North and South apart might begin their discussion with the introduction of blacks into Virginia in 1619. They would find relevant the antislavery
attitudes of Northerners during the colonial period, the conflict over slavery in
the Constitutional Convention, the Missouri Compromise, the militant abolitionist movement of the 1830s, and the Compromise of 1850. But other historians
might argue that the slavery issue did not become really significant until it was
associated with the settlement of the western lands. They would probably begin
their discussion with the Missouri Compromise, and the facts they would find
most relevant would be those that illustrated the fear many people had of the expansion of slavery into the new western lands.

Ostensibly, both groups of historians would be discussing the role of slavery
in the coming of the Civil War, but actually they would be discussing two different things. For the first group, the expansion of slavery to the West would be
only part of a longer and more complex story; for the second group, slavery and
the West would be the whole story. Sometimes the same facts would be used by
both, with each giving them different weight and significance; at other times one
group would find some facts relevant that the other would not.

An important variant of this kind of disagreement among historians may be
illustrated by returning to our earlier example of the causes of American entry
into World War I. Some historians might set out to discover the effects of British
propaganda efforts in molding public and official views toward the war. German
submarine warfare, the Zimmermann Note, bankers' loans, and other matters
would enter the discussion, but they would all be seen from the perspective of the
ways in which the British propaganda machine used them to win American support for the British side.

Historians emphasizing the role of British propaganda would disagree with
those emphasizing the influential role of bankers, although both groups of historians would be using many of the same facts to support their points of view. In reality, of course, the disagreement arises at least in part from the fact that the two
groups of historians are not really discussing the same things.

The reader should now be in a position to understand something of the
sources of disagreement among historians. Historians arrive at different conclusions because they have different notions about human motivation and different
ideas about what constitutes necessary and sufficient cause, and because they

seek to investigate different aspects of the same problems. All supply their readers with data and information—that is, with "facts"—to support their arguments. And, with rare exceptions, all of the facts presented are accurate.

Clearly, then, historical facts as such have no intrinsic meaning; they take on meaning and significance only when they are organized and presented by historians with a particular point of view. The well-used phrase "let the facts speak for themselves" therefore has no real meaning. The facts do *not* speak for themselves; historians use the facts in a particular way and therefore they, and not the facts, are doing the speaking. In other words, historians give meaning to facts by assessing their significance and by presenting them in a particular manner. In short, they *interpret*. Because different historians use different facts or use the same facts in different ways, their interpretations differ.

Once we understand the sources of differences among historians we are in a better position to evaluate their work. To be sure, our ability to understand why historians disagree will not make it possible to eliminate all disagreement. Only if we could devise a model of unquestioned validity that completely explained human behavior would it be possible for us to end disagreement. Any analysis that began by assuming a different model or explanation would be wrong.*

But we do not have such a complete and foolproof explanatory model. Nor can we expect to find one. Human life is too complicated to be so completely modeled; different problems require different explanatory models or theories. And because historians cannot agree as to which is the best model to employ for any given problem and because they are constantly devising new models, disagreements are destined to remain.

For the readers who have been patient enough to follow the argument to this point, the conclusions stated here may appear somewhat dismal and unrewarding. In convincing them that evaluating a historical interpretation is not like picking an item off a supermarket shelf, have we done more than move them to another store with a different stock on its shelves? If there are many explanatory models to choose from, and if no one of them is complete, foolproof, and guaranteed true, then it would appear that we are simply in another store with different merchandise on display.

Such a conclusion is unwarranted. In the first place, students who are able to understand the premises from which historians begin will be able to comprehend the way historians work and the process by which they fashion interpretation. Moreover, this understanding will enable them to evaluate the work of the historians. For at this stage students are no longer simply memorizing details; nor are they attempting to evaluate a historical essay by trying to discover whether each of the facts presented is true. They can now ask more important questions of the material before them. Are the premises from which historians begin adequate

---

*It should be noted in passing that even if we had such a theory, there would be much room for disagreement because we would often lack the required data. Some essential information would be lost through deliberate or accidental destruction. Other information might leave no record. Records of births, deaths, income, and so forth are now required by law, but in earlier days these records were not kept or were kept only sporadically. And telephone and personal conversations might leave no concrete record even though they could have a profound influence on behavior.

explanations of human behavior? Do the facts they present really flow from their premises and support their conclusions? Are there other data that would tend to undermine their arguments and throw doubt on the adequacy of their premises?

As students attempt to answer these questions, they begin to learn history by thinking and acting like historians; they begin to accumulate knowledge, understanding, and insight in much the same ways that historians do. And they begin to understand more fully how historians gain new information, how they reassess information others have used, and how they come to new and different conclusions.

Historians are constantly getting new information that had been unavailable to their predecessors. Diaries, letters, business records, and family Bibles are always being found in attics, in basements, and even in remote corners of large research libraries; and government agencies, private organizations, and individuals regularly make their letters, reports, and other papers available to historians. This new information sometimes supports and enriches earlier interpretations by providing more concrete details about matters that earlier writers merely suggested or surmised because they lacked the newly available information. Often, however, the new information leads historians to revise earlier interpretations by revealing actions, thoughts, and behavior that were unknown to earlier historians because the documents were unavailable to them.

But the availability of new information does not fully explain the sources of disagreement among historians and the regular process of revision of older interpretations. Much of the "new" information that later writers use is not new in the sense of being newly discovered or made available. The information was in the archives and libraries all the time, but historians did not use it, or they used it in very different ways. In short, the "facts" were there, but until historians asked different questions, the facts had no meaning or relevance, and historians ignored them.

Historians ask new questions and therefore seek new facts to answer the questions for a variety of reasons. They often gain new insights from the research of social scientists such as economists, political scientists, sociologists, and psychologists. Investigations by these scholars into such problems as family relationships, the influence of propaganda on behavior, the effects of the money supply on economic change, the relationship between voting patterns and racial and ethnic origin, and the psychological effects of racism all suggest new questions that historians might find valuable in investigating the past and in turn new kinds of data—facts—that they should seek in answering the new questions. In seeking such answers, historians also master and use new techniques and methods. For example, modern statistical methods and the computer permit the historian to handle huge masses of data quickly and accurately.

Historians also learn from one another. For example, when one historian discovers the existence of certain political, social, and economic relationships in a given city at a certain time, he or she provides other historians studying other cities, either at the same or different times, with what may be important and enlightening insights. International comparisons of similar events and institutions can also reveal important features that will be invisible or obscure when these events and institutions are viewed from the perspective of a single nation's history.

Finally, and perhaps most important, their own experiences often help historians to relate the past to the present; that is, they interpret the past through a frame of reference that is influenced by the world in which they live. During World War II, for instance, historians reexamined the causes and consequences of World War I, just as the war in Vietnam provided a new perspective on the Cold War years. The civil rights movement and black radicalism in the 1960s inspired a number of historians to reinterpret the role of abolitionists in the events leading up to the Civil War and to give more attention to race and racism in American life. In a similar way the feminist movement spurred them to reexamine the role of women and the family in the American past, while urban violence, the black revolution, and increasing ethnic identity led them to reassess the importance of violence, slavery, and ethnicity in American history.

When historians use the insights and techniques of the social scientists and when they make comparisons over time and place, the results may be enlightening and valuable. But they may also be misleading. By mechanically applying one or another theory of human behavior taken from the social sciences or by using behavior patterns in one place or time to explain behavior in another place or time, historians run the twin risks of determinism and anachronism. The attitudes, perceptions, and outlooks of people in one area or time in the past may differ considerably from those of another area or time. Therefore, for example, evidence that would explain certain kinds of behavior in the United States in the 1990s would not necessarily explain similar behavior in an earlier time.

A concrete example will illustrate the point. In recent years, some historians have provided evidence that in the pre–Civil War decades Southerners who owned slaves and grew cotton earned a rate of profit that equaled or exceeded that of investments in other enterprises elsewhere in the nation. From this evidence, some conclude that Southerners continued to invest primarily in slaves and cotton production (rather than in commerce and industry) because of the high rate of return earned in such investment. Others add that Southerners were willing to go to war to protect this profitable enterprise. A crucial assumption concerning behavior underlies this reasoning: Southerners acted like modern businessmen, making their investment decisions based upon the highest expected rate of return. That assumption may indeed be valid, but students should be aware first, that it *is* an assumption, and second, that the assumption is not necessarily supported by the evidence that Southerners continued to invest in slaves and cotton production. Southerners might have continued to buy slaves and grow cotton for reasons other than expected high rates of profit; social or political benefits that came with being a slaveowning cotton planter may have been their primary motivation.

In short, then, insights from the social sciences as well as those from other times and places are invaluable—indeed, essential—for historians. But they must be used with care, because they carry assumptions about behavior that may not be appropriate when applied to other times and places. By recognizing the theories and assumptions that guide historians when they formulate questions to investigate and then gather, evaluate, and present the evidence to answer these questions, students may more readily understand how historians work and why they disagree, and will thus be able to evaluate more accurately the work of the historians they read.

At first it may seem frustrating to realize that there is no one easy answer to the problems historians raise and that "truth" is but an elusive yet intriguing goal in a never-ending quest. But when students realize this, they have *begun* their education. At that point, they will find the study of history to be a significant, exhilarating, and useful part of their education. For coming to grips with conflicting interpretations of the past is more than an interesting classroom game; it is part of a larger process of coming to terms with the world around us. Every day we are asked to evaluate articles in newspapers and magazines or reports of events provided by friends or media commentators. A knowledge of history provides a background for interpreting these accounts; but more than that, the past and the present are so interconnected that one's interpretation of the American Revolution, slavery, the progressive movement, or American foreign policy after World War II are intimately related to one's views toward civil rights and domestic and foreign policy today.

The discussion thus far has emphasized the element of disagreement among historians and has attempted to show beginning students how these disagreements arise and how they should deal with them. But if disagreements arise because historians often start their analyses from different perspectives, it does not follow that there is no agreement at all among historians. On the contrary, groups of historians have tended to assume similar theoretical postures, and the result has been the emergence of "schools" of historical writing. All differences among members of a particular school do not disappear, but their approaches remain similar enough to differentiate them from members of other schools.

Identifying schools and placing historians in them is seldom easy and is always somewhat arbitrary. The reasons are obvious enough: the amount and complexity of work about America's past are so great that it is possible to identify a large number of schools. Moreover, because few historians begin with an explicit ideology or philosophy of history, their work may fit into a number of possible schools. Finally, most good historians do not cling dogmatically to a particular approach. As their research and writing proceeds, as they learn more, or as contemporary events alter their perspectives, their interpretations tend to change.

In organizing this book we have chosen two recurrent and important schools, or interpretive themes, in the writings on American history: conflict and consensus. Admittedly, the choice, in one sense at least, is arbitrary; we could have chosen from a number of other unifying themes. On the other hand, the choice has not been completely arbitrary in that these themes—conflict and consensus—expressed either explicitly or implicitly, may be found in virtually all major interpretations of our country's past. The student who reads the following pages and attempts to evaluate the arguments presented will be faced with two real and meaningful ways to understand the American past and, indeed, to judge the contemporary American scene.

Stripped to its essentials, the task of historians is to deal with change. And nowhere do historians find change more manifest than when they study the United States. Almost in the twinkling of an eye, a vast, scarcely populated continent was transformed into a major industrial power of phenomenal complexity. Overnight, virgin forests became fertile farms; Indian trails became roads, highways, and railroads; and empty spaces became bustling cities. Matching this transformation of the physical face of the continent were equally momentous changes in politics, social relations, ideas, and attitudes. For most Americans, constant and rapid change was inevitable if only because it was so obvious. "Ten years in America are like a century in Spain," wrote the German immigrant Francis Leiber soon after his arrival in the United States early in the nineteenth century. "The United States really changes in some respects more within ten years than a country like Spain has within a hundred."

But who could argue that Europe was static and unchanging? True enough, Europe had little in the way of trackless wilderness to be discovered, settled, and transformed; and, true also, Europe was crowded with the remnants of what might appear to be an unchanging past—cathedrals and monuments, aristocratic and royal institutions, and ways of doing things that seemed to have existed time out of mind. But at the same time, Europe periodically exploded into change. Indeed, time after time, Americans saw Europe swept by rebellion and war as one group after another sought, often successfully, to revolutionize European lives and institutions.

Generations of American historians have tried to describe and to explain the vast alterations that have taken place on the North American continent. As they did so, many kept one eye on the changes in European institutions, seeking to compare and to contrast the nature of changes in Europe with those of North America. But even as they read the historical documents, often in the light of European history and experience, the historians themselves were living through vast and rapid changes taking place around them in the United States, changes that often influenced their historical scholarship. From the rich and varied work by American historians two rather distinct traditions or interpretive themes have emerged, each of which has sought to provide a general explanation for American historical development.

One tradition stresses conflict, finding American history to be similar in this respect to that of Europe. Historians within this tradition often speak of revolutionary changes and emphasize the importance of conflict in bringing these changes. They stress the class, ethnic, racial, and political *differences* among Americans and the fundamental nature of the conflicts these differences created: democrats versus aristocrats, debtors versus creditors, workers versus businessmen, North versus South, farmers versus railroads, blacks versus whites. Change, they argue, is a result of this never-ending conflict; it arises from the efforts of particular groups and classes to impose their hegemony over American society, or at least to increase their influence over that society.

The other tradition stresses the uniqueness of the American experience by finding a basic consensus in American society. According to this tradition, all Americans of whatever class or station shared what was essentially a common outlook. To be sure, Americans did not all live alike nor did they always agree with one another. But their disagreements, especially when compared with the dissensions that divided European society, were not fundamental. Consensus historians do not ignore class and sectional differences, and they do not deny conflicts between groups such as workers and employers; but they do deny that these conflicts were basic. Americans, they argue, achieved a consensus on fundamentals; if they disagreed, their disagreements were minor differences within an underlying consensus. Change, then, is the result of a fundamental agreement that change is required and does not arise from a struggle for power.

Although both these themes can be found in the earliest writings on American history, they became dominant interpretive themes only during the twentieth century. The theme of conflict was central to the writings of those Richard Hofstadter has called the "Progressive Historians": Frederick Jackson Turner, Charles A. Beard, and Vernon L. Parrington. Growing up in the midst of the nation's rapid industrialization and living in a time of increasing protest against the problems created by that industrialization, these historians saw the past in terms of bitter conflict. Their influence, as the reader of the following pages will discover, was profound.

The theme of consensus, with its roots in the nationalistic histories of the nineteenth century, became especially important beginning in the early 1950s, in part as a reaction to what some considered to be the overstatements of the conflict school and in part as a reaction to world conditions. For many American historians at the time, European revolutionary and ideological conflicts seemed strangely alien to the United States, making historical interpretations cast in the European mold completely inappropriate. Looking at the past, these historians discovered that America had always been different from Europe. For the most part, the United States had been spared the bitter conflicts that divided European countries, because Americans from the beginning had agreed on fundamentals. Consensus historians therefore stressed the uniqueness of the American experience and sought to explain the origins of this uniqueness.

Like the conflict historians of an earlier generation, the new consensus historians had a great influence on American historical thought. An especially important part of the consensus school was the American Studies movement, an interdisciplinary effort to combine history, literature, and the social sciences to describe and explain the special and unique American experience and to define an American "character" that was molded by that experience.

But the consensus historians were not without their critics. John Higham argued that they were "homogenizing" American history; he accused them of "carrying out a massive grading operation to smooth over America's social convulsions." He and other critics did not simply call for a return to the history of the progressive historians. They argued that the consensus historians had made the American past bland and meaningless because they ignored real and significant differences that produced sharp conflicts. Even some of the consensus historians began to have second thoughts about the interpretation. Richard Hofstadter, who had been a sharp critic of the conflict historians, felt that the consensus interpretation had gone too far. "Americans may not have quarreled over profound ideological matters, as these are formulated in the history of political thought, but they quarreled consistently enough over issues that had real pith and moment," he wrote in 1967 in a new introduction to his book *The American Political Tradition.* He added that "an obsessive fixation on the elements of consensus that do undoubtedly exist strips the story of the drama and the interest it has."

The responses to the concern over the seeming domination of the consensus school and the homogenization of American history were not long in coming. Indeed, many were already under way. Sometimes the responses became little more than arguments over the meaning given to the words *conflict* and *consensus* or were simply reassertions of the old conflict interpretations. Most historians, however, did far more. They used new techniques, often drawing upon the scholarship of other disciplines. They adopted fresh approaches, asking new questions that led to the discovery of new sources and the reevaluation of existing evidence. The result was not only new interpretations of the nation's past but also a considerable redefinition of what constituted that past, that is, a redefinition of what kinds of questions historians should ask about the past.

Quantitative historians, aided by the computer and modern statistical methods and using theories borrowed from economics, sociology, political science, linguistics, anthropology, and psychology, conducted massive investigations of such matters as economic growth patterns, voting behavior, family life, social mobility, changes in standards of living, and fashions. Social historians, using both quantitative and more traditional methods, attempted to write what they called history "from the bottom up," seeking to investigate and even emphasize the lives of ordinary people rather than members of the political and economic elite. Labor historians who had traditionally concentrated on organized labor gave increasing attention to the culture and ideology of workers in unorganized shops and factories. Many social historians, as well as political and economic historians argued that most Americans, especially in the years before the changes in technology allowed for the rapid dissemination of news and information, experienced history on a local level. Hence they studied local developments in great detail, concerning themselves with small communities, villages and towns, and neighborhoods within larger cities; they also gave considerable attention to local religious and political institutions.

Intellectual and cultural historians, investigating ideology and the use of language to discover how people perceived and made sense of the world in which they lived, described what they called "republican" and "liberal" syntheses. The republican synthesis, essentially a consensus interpretation with its emphasis on all Americans united in a quest for republican virtue, was sharply challenged by historians who found that many Americans, even as they mouthed the words of republicanism, gave these words very different meanings. Indeed, some Americans used republican language to attack republicanism. Other historians argued that the republican synthesis was never universal, that it always found itself challenged by liberalism, that is, by the ideas and practices of the modern free market. Some intellectual and cultural historians began to give increasing attention to popular culture, insisting that the concentration on the study of "high culture" was elitist, unrepresentative, and therefore misleading.

Another sign of change came with the appearance of a group calling themselves "new western historians." These historians broke sharply with Frederick Jackson Turner, arguing that the frontier experience was not the whole of American western history and that even the frontier experience was more diverse and complicated than Turner had argued. Indians and Mexicans, miners and environmentalists, ranchers and urbanities, and women along with men were some of the diverse groups of people who became important actors in the new western history.

The work of the new western historians reveals what perhaps has been the most significant change in the writing of American history: the increasing attention historians began to give to gender, race, and ethnicity.

Fueled in part by the feminist movement and in part by the belated recognition of the absence of women in so much of the writings on American history, historians began to investigate the parts played by women in events and areas—for example, the Revolution, the Civil War, and the West—that they had traditionally studied as male dominated. This added a new dimension to the study of traditional subjects by showing that the role of women was often an important part of the story. Sometimes such investigations led historians to challenge the traditional periodization of history as marked by wars, elections, and political movements. While some historians sought to overcome the neglect of women's voices in traditionally studied areas, others began to look into matters involving women—for example, courtship, the family, and the household economy—that had received little or no attention previously, but that, their studies showed, were important factors in historical development.

Another area experiencing a rush of new and innovative scholarship was that of African-American history. In addition to more subtle and meaningful discussions of traditional areas of race relations, racism, and race conflict, the new work dealt with the development of a distinctive African-American culture and ideology. Much of this new work in such diverse areas as, for example, slavery, the transition from slavery to freedom after the Civil War, the fight for integration, black political action, and South to North migration told the story from the black perspective and stressed the importance of blacks as actors rather than as powerless victims.

Much of the same perspective marked the new studies of other racial and ethnic groups. Historians no longer viewed Indian history as simply the story of wars, defeat, and historical oblivion on the reservations as told from the perspective of the victorious and "civilized" whites; new work emphasized Indian culture and indigenous religious and social practices. Historians studying other racial and ethnic groups gave similar emphasis to cultural persistences as well as to changes over time, sharply calling into question older notions of the melting pot and providing evidence of significant differences among ethnic groups that earlier historians had ignored.

What much of this new work has in common is its emphasis on diversity, on differences among Americans that usually led to conflict rather than consensus. Americans, it suggests, have always been divided by race, class, gender, and ethnicity, and these differences are significant enough to mean that it is wrong and misleading to speak of an American history that is shared by all who reside within the nation's borders. There is not *an* American mind or *an* American culture, but many American minds and cultures, and this diversity has often—indeed, has usually—led to significant conflicts.

This new work, which mounts a strenuous attack on the consensus history that critics such as John Higham charged had homogenized American history, has not been universally accepted. Critics, although they do not deny the differences among Americans, nevertheless argue that those who emphasize diversity, that is, the differences among Americans, create a history without a central synthesis, without a general unifying theme that would give meaning to American history. Those who emphasize diversity usually find the lack of a general synthesis to be a virtue, not a problem; diversity aims at inclusiveness, they insist, and inclusiveness is closer to reality than a general synthesis that could only be artificial. But their opponents insist with equal vigor that recognition of diversity and inclusiveness does not preclude the existence of a general synthesis; indeed, they argue, giving exclusive attention to differences hides underlying themes and cultural features that unite Americans within their diversity.

In sum, then, new work has enriched historical writing and has often provided a more subtle and complex story of the nation's past. Nevertheless, the themes of conflict and consensus, although significantly altered in emphasis and content, continue to be relevant and therefore continue to be important ways to view the complexities of American history.

The lines that divide the conflict from the consensus historians are not as sharp as they once were. If many contemporary historians draw from both in their analyses of America's past, the emphasis on one or the other remains, both in studies of particular movements and periods as well as in general assessments of the course of American history. Differences in interpretation will persist even as historians continue their work, and, although their efforts will never end the debate, they will give us a richer understanding of our nation's past. This ongoing quest for understanding gives historical scholarship its interest and excitement. The readings that follow, by introducing students to the two traditions of conflict and consensus and their variations through the words of some of their most able proponents, will also introduce students to some of that interest and excitement.

SUGGESTIONS FOR FURTHER READING

When historians seek to determine how to evaluate evidence, they are really attempting to answer a whole set of very complicated questions. Is their goal to achieve fairness, objectivity, and balance? If so, what exactly do these words mean when applied to historical scholarship? Is it possible to find truth in history? Can the study of the past be made scientific? Are all conclusions by historians relative because historians cannot escape bias and because they make assumptions that they cannot support with adequate evidence? A few volumes on the theory and practice of history have been written specifically for the beginning student; examples are Walter T. K. Nugent, *Creative History* (Philadelphia, 1967) and Allan J. Lichtman and Valerie French, *Historians and the Living Past* (Arlington Heights, Ill., 1978). More sophisticated but eminently readable are four classic studies: Marc Bloch, *The Historian's Craft* (New York, 1953); Allan Nevins, *The Gateway to History* (Garden City, N.Y., 1962); Louis Gottschalk, *Understanding History* (New York, 1963); and E. H. Carr, *What Is History?* (New York, 1964). Several more recent studies deserve attention. Joyce Appleby, Lynn Hunt, and Margaret Jacob, *Telling the Truth About History* (New York, 1994) is a clearly written and sensible survey that

---

*Available in paperback edition.

provides a fine review of current debates about "history's relationship to scientific truth, objectivity, postmodernism and the politics of identity." Gene Wise, *American Historical Explanations* (Minneapolis, 1980) is also a very valuable discussion of these and other matters. Peter Novick, *That Noble Dream: The "Objectivity Question" and the American Historical Profession* (New York, 1988) is a fascinating and valuable account of history writing in the United States. An illuminating and superbly written guide to historical research and writing is Jacques Barzun and Henry F. Graff, *The Modern Researcher,* 5th ed. (Fort Worth, 1992).

For an introduction to the controversy over the value of quantitative history, see Robert William Fogel and G. R. Elton, *Which Road to the Past? Two Views of History* (New Haven, Conn., 1983), a friendly, but sharp, debate between a "new" and a "traditional" historian. Quantitative history is difficult for the uninitiated, but for those who want a taste of it, a good introduction is William O. Adydelotte, Allan G. Bogue, and Robert William Fogel, eds., *The Dimensions of Quantitative Research in History* (Princeton, N.J., 1972).

A brief, very accessible introduction to the postmodern approach to history, or at least one historian's view of this approach, is Keith Jenkins, *Re-thinking History* (New York, 1991). For those interested in further exploring the mysteries of postmodernism as well as the new historicism, deconstructionism, and other concepts that are influencing some historians, good places to start are the following: Madan Sarup, *An Introductory Guide to Post-Structuralism and Postmodernism* (Athens, Ga., 1989); Bryan D. Palmer, *Descent into Discourse: The Reification of Language and the Writing of Social History* (Philadelphia, 1990); and John E. Toews, "Intellectual History After the Linguistic Turn," *American Historical Review,* 92 (October 1987), 879–907.

Students wishing to pursue the historiography (that is, the history of historical writing) of the conflict-consensus theme should begin with the progressive historians. Charles A. Beard was a prolific writer, but the best approach to him is through Charles and Mary Beard, *The Rise of American Civilization* (New York, 1927, 1930), a lively and interesting interpretation of the whole course of American history, with an emphasis on class and economic conflict. Beard's *An Economic Interpretation of the Constitution* (New York, 1913, 1935) must be read by any serious student. Vernon Parrington's three-volume *Main Currents in American Thought* (New York, 1927, 1930) complements Beard's work and deals with the relationship of literature and ideas to society and social movements. Frederick Jackson Turner's essays may be found in *The Frontier in American History* (New York, 1920) and *The Significance of Sections in American History* (New York, 1932). There are many discussions of the work and influence of these historians; the reader can do no better than to begin with Richard Hofstadter, *The Progressive Historians* (New York, 1968), the work of a perceptive and sensitive critic. This book's great value is enhanced by an outstanding "bibliographical essay" that will lead the student deep into the literature on the subject.

Any serious student of the consensus historians must read and study Louis Hartz, *The Liberal Tradition in America* (New York, 1955) and the key works of Daniel J. Boorstin: *The Genius of American Politics* (Chicago, 1953); *The Americans: The Colonial Experience* (New York, 1958); *The Americans: The Democratic Experience* (New York, 1973); and *The Americans: The National Experience* (New York, 1965). A perceptive discussion of these books as well as of the entire consensus school along with good bibliographical information may be found in the Hofstadter volume cited above. An important and provocative critique of the consensus approach is John Higham, "The Cult of the American Consensus," *Commentary,* 27 (February 1959), 93–100. See also Gene Wise, "Political 'Reality' in Recent American Scholarship: Progressives Versus Symbolists," *American Quarterly,* 22, Part 2 (Summer 1967), 303–28.

John Higham, *History: Professional Scholarship in America* (Baltimore, 1983) is a concise overview of American historiography that places the conflict-consensus debate in perspective. Ernst A. Breisach, *American Progressive History: An Experiment in Modernization* (Chicago, 1993) is a useful summary that describes the rise and decline of the progressive "conflict" interpretation and places the story in the context of European historiography. David W. Noble, *The End of American History* (Minneapolis, 1985) is especially interested in the theory and meaning of historical scholarship after the "collapse of the Progressive paradigm." Bernard Sternsher, *Consensus, Conflict and American Historians* (Bloomington, Ind., 1975) examines the theme in great detail.

The literature on women's history is vast; a good place to start is Gerda Lerner, *The Majority Finds Its Past: Placing Women in History* (New York, 1979). There are many collections of articles on women's history that include valuable bibliographies. See, for examples, Linda K. Kerber and Jane Sherron DeHart, eds., *Women's America*, 3rd ed. (New York, 1991); Jean E. Friedman and William G. Shade, eds., *Our American Sisters: Women in American Life and Thought,* 2nd ed. (Boston, 1976); and Bernice A. Carroll, ed., *Liberating Women's History: Theoretical and Critical Essays* (Urbana, Ill., 1976).

Drew Gilpin Faust, *Mothers of Invention: Women of the Slaveholding South in the American Civil War* (Chapel Hill, N.C., 1996) is a recent example of how our understanding of traditional subjects such as the Confederacy, the Civil War, and Southern slavery is enhanced by a consideration of the role of women. Work on women's history has spurred an interest in men's history—or, more accurately, in the history of masculinity in America. A good recent survey is Michael Kimmel, *Manhood in America: A Cultural History* (New York, 1995).

Important and influential examples of the American Studies approach are Henry Nash Smith, *Virgin Land* (Cambridge, Mass., 1950); R. W. B. Lewis, *The American Adam* (Chicago, 1955); and Leo Marx, *The Machine in the Garden: Technology and the Pastoral Idea in America* (New York, 1964). A study of the American Studies approach is Cecil F. Tate, *The Search for a Method in American Studies* (Minneapolis, 1973). Changing emphases in American Studies may be followed in the articles in the *American Quarterly,* the journal of the American Studies Association

Good general introductions to the new western history by two of its leading practitioners are Patricia Nelson Limerick, *The Legacy of Conquest: The Unbroken Past of the American West* (New York, 1987); and Richard White, *'It's Your Misfortune and None of My Own': A New History of the American West* (Norman, Okla., 1991). A very brief discussion of recent trends in Indian history along with a good introductory bibliography is Donald Parman, "Twentieth Century Indian History: Achievements, Needs, and Problems," *OAH Magazine of History* (Fall 1994), 9, 10–16.

Important contributions to the republican synthesis are Bernard Bailyn, *The Ideological Origins of the American Revolution* (Cambridge, Mass., 1967); J. G. A. Pocock, "Machiavelli, Harrington, and English Political Ideologies in the Eighteenth Century," *William and Mary Quarterly,* 3rd series, 22 (October 1965), 549–83; and Gordon Wood, *The Creation of the American Republic, 1776–1787* (Chapel Hill, N.C., 1969). Critics of republicanism are Isaac Kramnick, "Republican Revisionism Revisited," *American Historical Review,* 87 (June 1982), 629–64; Joyce Appleby, *Capitalism and a New Social Order: The Republican Vision of the 1790s* (New York, 1984); and John Patrick Diggins, *The Lost Soul of American Politics: Virtue, Self-Interest and the Foundations of Liberalism* (New York, 1985). These and other works on the republican synthesis are reviewed in two articles by Robert E. Shalhope, "Toward a Republican Synthesis: The Emergence of an Understanding of Republicanism in American Historiography," *William and Mary Quarterly,* 3rd series, 29 (January 1972), 49–80; and "Republicanism and Early American Historiography," *William and Mary Quarterly,* 3rd series, 39 (April 1982), 334–56. A special issue of the *American Quarterly,* 37 (Fall 1985) contains a half-dozen articles on "Republicanism in the History and Historiography of the United States." *Reviews in American History,* 10 (December 1982) contains articles surveying the state of scholarship in some twenty subdisciplines in American history. A more recent survey and evaluation of the new histories is Eric Foner, ed., *The New American History* (Philadelphia, 1990), a collection of thirteen essays on the scholarship of the last twenty years that "shattered the 'consensus' vision that had dominated historical writing."

The debate over diversity has created lively controversy. In December 1988 at a meeting of the American Historical Association, five historians with varying points of view concerning the state of historical scholarship presented papers that illustrated some of the sharp differences that divide the profession. These papers, which were published in the *American Historical Reviews,* 94 (June 1989), 654–98, under the general title "The Old History and the New," provide a convenient introduction to the debate: Theodore S. Hamerow, "The Bureaucratization of History"; Gertrude Himmelfarb, "Some Reflections on the New History"; Lawrence W. Levine, "The Unpredictable Past: Reflections on Recent American Historiography"; Joan Wallach Scott, "History in Crisis? The Others' Side of the Story," and John E. Toews, "Perspectives on 'The Old History and the New': A Comment." Lawrence W. Levine, who welcomes the emphasis on diversity because of what he considers to be the need for inclusiveness, expanded on his argument in the *American Historical Review* in a volume of essays, *The Unpredictable Past: Explorations in American Cultural History* (New York, 1993). Gertrude Himmelfarb, a sharp critic of those who emphasize diversity and see no unifying synthesis in American history, presents her views in more detail in her book *The New History and the Old: Critical Essays and Reappraisals* (Cambridge, Mass., 1987). John Higham, who earlier had been critical of the consensus historians, has more recently raised some doubts about the later emphasis on diversity in his essay "Multiculturalism and Universalism: A History and a Critique," *American Quarterly,* 45 (1993), 195–219. In light of the debate, Michael Kammen finds an old interpretation worthy of refinement and reconsideration in "The Problem of American Exceptionalism: A Reconsideration," *American Quarterly,* 45 (March 1993), 1–43.

Reconstruction

The Civil War has had an endless fascination for Americans, who usually see it as a time of great heroism and idealism on the part of both sides in the conflict. But no such rosy aura surrounds the years after the war, the years when an attempt was made to reconstruct the nation and heal the wounds of war. If the Civil War made heroes, Reconstruction produced villains; if the war was marked by tragic idealism, Reconstruction was characterized by venal corruption. Even those historians who find much that was beneficial in Reconstruction conclude that the period ended in dismal failure.

The basic problem facing Northern leaders after the war was how to restore national unity after a bitter and bloody sectional conflict. But there was sharp disagreement as to the best approach. Should the Confederacy be treated as a conquered province, or should the Southern states be welcomed back into the

19

Union as wayward but repentant members of the family? What kinds of changes should the former Confederate states accept before being allowed to participate once again in the political process?

Even during the war there was disagreement between President Lincoln, who favored treating the seceded states leniently, and some congressional leaders, who argued for harsher peace terms. This executive-legislative battle continued after the assassination of Lincoln, but the mid-term elections of 1866, favorable to the so-called radicals, made it possible for Congress to pass legislation concerning the South over the opposition and vetoes of President Andrew Johnson. Congress quickly passed the Civil Rights Act, the Freedman's Bureau Act, and, finally, the Reconstruction Acts of 1867. The Southern states were put under military rule until they approved new constitutions guaranteeing black suffrage, ratified the Fourteenth Amendment, and in other ways satisfied the radical majority in Congress.

Only after each Southern state organized a new government under congressional tutelage was it declared reconstructed and its representatives and senators admitted to Congress. For the first time, blacks voted and held state and local office; some even served as their states' senators and representatives in Congress. The new Republican-dominated state governments were often marked by corruption and inefficiency, but in this they differed little from state legislatures elsewhere in the nation and, indeed, from the national government. But radical Southern state legislatures also instituted significant and needed reforms in education and welfare for blacks and whites alike. These reforms, along with the resentment many Southern whites felt toward being ruled by governments in which blacks participated, elicited sharp and often violent opposition, and one by one the radical Republican governments fell from power. The victors termed themselves "redeemers," because they promised to redeem the states and return them to those who, they said, had the necessary talent and education and, therefore, deserved to rule. None of the radical governments remained when the last Federal troops were removed from the South in 1877.

The conflicts of the Reconstruction era were a continuation of the bitter antebellum struggles made even more bitter by the Northern victory and emancipation. Slavery may not have been the cause of the Civil War, as some have argued, but emancipation was clearly its key result. And emancipation raised a myriad of social, economic, and political questions, the answers to which would have profound effects on the future of the blacks, the South, and the entire nation. What exactly did freedom mean for the blacks? Did freedom carry with it the rights that free whites in the country enjoyed—the right to vote, to hold office, to own property, to use all public facilities, for example? Did the nation have any obligations to the former slaves—for example, to compensate them for the two centuries in which they were enslaved by granting them land and equipment to help them gain economic independence to match their freedom?

The answers given to these questions obviously affected Southern whites. Were those who had participated in rebellion to be punished by having their land confiscated and distributed to former slaves? Were whites who had ruled the South to be allowed to continue to do so, or were they to be forced to share political power with enfranchised blacks?

The answers to these questions would, of course, affect the future of the nation. Were Southern political and economic interests to be subordinated to those of the North?

These were the questions that politicians and the people hotly debated. As blacks sought to give meaning to their newly won freedom, their former masters sought to limit their losses and maintain as much of their political and economic power as they could. As Republican politicians and those who supported the Republican economic and political programs sought to maintain their dominance, Democrats and those who supported their programs saw the return of the South to the Union as an opportunity to increase their following.

Invariably the debate centered on the future of the blacks. For former abolitionists and those who came to see the Civil War as a moral crusade to rid the nation of slavery and for former slaves seeking to become free citizens, granting civil and economic rights to blacks became crucial. Conversely, for those who reluctantly accepted emancipation and continued to believe that the blacks were innately inferior and incapable of assuming the rights and obligations of a free people, limiting the civil and political rights of blacks became necessary. Even those who cared little about the blacks but were concerned mainly with national politics and future legislation could not avoid the debate on the future of the blacks because granting or denying civil and economic rights to blacks would affect the outcome of elections and, therefore, votes in Congress.

This furious debate among contemporaries and the answers that finally emerged have sharply influenced historians' interpretations of Reconstruction and its results. No period has evoked more impassioned and opinionated historical writing. Some historians, seeing the South as victim, have called it a "tragic era," a period during which the defeated South was "put to the torture" by a vindictive conqueror. Others, sensitive to the position and aspirations of the black population, have depicted Reconstruction as a time of real opportunity to right the wrongs of generations of slavery, and they see the end of Reconstruction as a betrayal by opportunistic Northerners who abandoned the blacks to racist violence and a life of discrimination and fear that lasted for a century.

Some of this debate among contemporaries and among modern historians who consider this debate in their interpretations may be seen in the selections that follow. In the first selection, Eric Foner writes that for the newly emancipated slaves freedom meant more than simply the absence of slavery. The freedmen's efforts to order their own lives, to determine their own religious practices, family life, and work regimes and their efforts to enter politics all reflected their "desire for independence from white control, for autonomy both as individuals and as members of a community being transformed by emancipation." The freedmen's aspirations for equality as individuals and as a community met with violent opposition from Southern whites who refused to accept those rights that blacks deemed essential to make their newly won freedom meaningful.

In the second selection, Thomas C. Holt compares the emancipation experience in the British West Indies with that in the United States and concentrates on the transformation of slaves into free workers. He shows that freedom had very different meanings for former slaves, for former slaveowners, and for emancipators, and, as a result, each group looked to a different kind of free labor system in the future. The differing views of the meaning of freedom led to sharp conflicts among the three groups. In the end, Holt concludes that repression, buttressed by racism, forced the blacks into a free labor system producing commercial crops for the market.

La Wanda Cox, in the third selection, centers her attention on the national policymakers. She argues that one of their goals was to guarantee civil rights for the freed slaves, and she considers some of the possible alternatives open to the politicians attempting to reach that goal. She finds that some actions, such as the distribution of land to former slaves, would not have had the desired results. She notes that there were some realistic opportunities available that the politicians ignored, but argues that historical conditions set limits to what could be accomplished. To assume that Reconstruction following the Civil War could have achieved the consensus that the civil rights movement of the 1960s achieved, she concludes, is to ignore the political realities of the time.

The Reconstruction era witnessed sharp political conflict that often turned into physical violence as the Ku Klux Klan and other groups intimidated, harassed, beat, and killed blacks. Obviously, former slaveholders and their supporters used such tactics in their attempt to maintain their accustomed control, and, just as obviously, such actions often met determined and armed resistance by blacks, many of them former Federal soldiers, who sought to give meaning to their newly won freedom. Less obvious are the reasons that the victorious North permitted this violence and then allowed the conflict in the South to be resolved in a manner so detrimental to the former slaves. What were the victorious Northerners trying to achieve in the South? If preservation of the Union, emancipation, and a return to the commercial production of the South's staple crops were their goals, then the North succeeded, and the way in which Reconstruction ended revealed a large measure of consensus, at least among the nation's white population.

But if, as some have argued, civil rights for the emancipated blacks was also a Northern goal, then why did Northerners abandon that goal? Did they lack the power? The will? Or did they face problems that really could not be solved in the mid-nineteenth century? In short, did racism create a new consensus that led most whites to accept the subordination of blacks? How did blacks respond to the conditions in which they found themselves? Did they continue their struggle to make freedom real? In what ways?

All decisions made in the past affect the future in one way or another. But the settlement made during Reconstruction had repercussions that have lasted to this day, as all of the selections here suggest. What have been some of those effects? And how might a different settlement have affected the course of history in the United States?

ERIC FONER

The Meaning of Freedom

Freedom came in different ways to different parts of the South. In large areas, slavery had disintegrated long before Lee's surrender, but elsewhere, far from the presence of federal troops, blacks did not learn of its irrevocable end until the spring of 1865. Despite the many disappointments that followed, this generation of blacks would always regard the moment when "de freedom sun shine out" as the great watershed of their lives. Houston H. Holloway, who had been sold three times before he reached the age of twenty in 1865, later recalled with vivid clarity the day emancipation came to his section of Georgia: "I felt like a bird out of a cage. Amen. Amen. Amen. I could hardly ask to feel any better than I did that day. . . . The week passed off in a blaze of glory."

"Freedom," said a black minister, "burned in the black heart long before freedom was born." But what did "freedom" mean? "It is necessary to define that word," Freedmen's Bureau Commissioner O. O. Howard told a black audience in 1865, "for it is most apt to be misunderstood." Howard assumed a straightforward definition existed. But "freedom" itself became a terrain of conflict, its substance open to different and sometimes contradictory interpretations, its content changing for whites as well as blacks in the aftermath of the Civil War.

Blacks carried out of bondage an understanding of their new condition shaped both by their experience as slaves and by observation of the free society around them. What one planter called their "wild notions of rights and freedom" encompassed, first of all, an end to the myriad injustices associated with slavery. Some, like black minister Henry M. Turner, stressed that freedom meant the enjoyment of "our rights in common with other men." "If I cannot do like a white man I am not free," Henry Adams told his former master in 1865. "I see how the poor white people do. I ought to do so too, or else I am a slave."

But underpinning the specific aspirations lay a broader theme: a desire for independence from white control, for autonomy both as individuals and as members of a community being transformed by emancipation. Before the war, free blacks had created churches, schools, and mutual benefit societies, while slaves had forged a culture centered on the family and church. With freedom, these institutions were consolidated, expanded, and liberated from white supervision, and new ones—particularly political organizations—joined them as focal points of black life. In stabilizing their families, seizing control of their churches, greatly expanding their schools and benevolent societies, staking a claim to economic independence, and forging a political culture, blacks during Reconstruction laid the foundation for the modern black community, whose roots lay deep in slavery but whose structure and values reflected the consequences of emancipation.

From Slavery to Freedom

Long after the end of the Civil War, the experience of bondage remained deeply etched in blacks' collective memory. The freedmen resented not only the brutal incidents of slavery but the fact of having been held as slaves at all. During a visit to Richmond, Scottish minister David Macrae was surprised to hear a former slave complain of past mistreatment, while acknowledging he had never been whipped. "How were you cruelly treated then?" asked Macrae. "I was cruelly treated," answered the freedman, "because I was kept in slavery."

In countless ways, the newly freed slaves sought to overturn the real and symbolic authority whites had exercised over every aspect of their lives. Blacks relished opportunities to flaunt their liberation from the innumerable regulations, significant and trivial, associated with slavery. Freedmen held mass meetings and religious services unrestrained by white surveillance, acquired previously forbidden dogs, guns, and liquor, and refused to yield the sidewalks to whites. They dressed as they pleased, black women sometimes wearing gaudy finery, carrying parasols, and replacing the slave kerchief with colorful hats and veils. Whites complained of "insolence" and "insubordination" among the freedmen, by which they meant any departure from the deference and obedience expected under slavery. On the Bradford plantation in Florida, one untoward incident followed another. First, the family cook told Mrs. Bradford "if she want any dinner she kin cook it herself." Then the former slaves went off to a meeting with Northern soldiers to discuss "our freedom." Told that she and her daughter could not attend, one woman replied "they were now free and if she saw fit to take her daughter into that crowd it was nobody's business." "Never before had I a word of impudence from any of our black folk," recorded nineteen-year-old Susan Bradford, "but they are not ours any longer."

Among the most resented of slavery's restrictions was the rule, enforced by patrols, that no black could travel without a pass. With emancipation, it seemed that half the South's black population took to the roads. Southern towns and cities experienced an especially large influx of freedmen during and immediately after the Civil War. In the cities, many blacks believed, "freedom was free-er." Here were schools, churches, and fraternal societies, as well as the army (including, in 1865, black soldiers) and the Freedmen's Bureau, offering protection from the violence so pervasive in much of the rural South. Between 1865 and 1870, the black population of the South's ten largest cities doubled, while the number of white residents rose by only ten percent. Smaller towns, from which blacks had often been excluded as slaves, experienced even more dramatic increases.

Black migrants who hoped to find urban employment often encountered severe disappointment. The influx from the countryside flooded the labor market, consigning most urban blacks to low-wage, menial employment. Unable to obtain decent housing, black migrants lived in squalid shantytowns on the outskirts of Southern cities, where the incidence of disease and death far exceeded that among white city dwellers. The result was a striking change in Southern urban living patterns. Before the war, blacks and whites had lived scattered throughout Southern cities. Reconstruction witnessed the rise of a new, segregated, urban geography.

No aspect of black mobility was more poignant than the effort to reunite families separated during slavery. "In their eyes," wrote a Freedmen's Bureau agent, "the work of emancipation was incomplete until the families which had been dispersed by slavery were reunited." One freedman, writing from Texas, asked the Bureau's aid in locating "my own dearest relatives," providing a long list of sisters, nieces, nephews, uncles, and in-laws, none of whom he had seen since his sale in Virginia twenty-four years before. A typical plea for help appeared in the Nashville *Colored Tennessean*:

During the year 1849, Thomas Sample carried away from this city, as his slaves, our daughter, Polly, and son. . . . We will give $100 each for them to any person who will assist them . . . to get to Nashville, or get word to us of their whereabouts.

Although vulnerable to disruption, strong family ties had existed under slavery. Emancipation allowed blacks to solidify their family connections, and most freedmen seized the opportunity. Many families, in addition, adopted the children of deceased relatives and friends rather than see them apprenticed to white masters or placed in Freedmen's Bureau orphanages. By 1870, a large majority of blacks lived in two-parent households.

But while emancipation strengthened the preexisting black family, it also transformed the roles of its members and relations among them. One common, significant change was that slave families, separated because their members belonged to different owners, could now live together. More widely noticed by white observers in early Reconstruction was the withdrawal of black women from field labor.

Beginning in 1865, and for years thereafter, Southern whites throughout the South complained of the difficulty of obtaining female field laborers. Planters, Freedmen's Bureau officials, and Northern visitors all ridiculed the black "female aristocracy" for "acting the *lady*" or mimicking the family patterns of middle-class whites. White employers also resented their inability to force black children to labor in the fields, especially after the spread of schools in rural areas.

Contemporaries appeared uncertain whether black women, black men, or both were responsible for the withdrawal of females from agricultural labor. There is no question that many black men considered it manly to have their wives work at home and believed that, as head of the family, the male should decide how its labor was organized. But many black women desired to devote more time than under slavery to caring for their children and to domestic responsibilities like cooking, sewing, and laundering.

The shift of black female labor from the fields to the home proved a temporary phenomenon. The rise of renting and sharecropping, which made each family responsible for its own plot of land, placed a premium on the labor of all family members. The dire poverty of many black families, deepened by the depression of the 1870s, made it essential for both women and men to contribute to the family's income. Throughout this period, a far higher percentage of black than white women and children worked for wages outside their homes. Where women continued to concentrate on domestic tasks, and children attended school, they frequently engaged in seasonal field labor. Thus, emancipation did not eliminate labor outside the home by black women and children, but it fundamentally altered control over their labor. Now blacks themselves, rather than a white owner or overseer, decided where and when black women and children worked.

For blacks, liberating their families from the authority of whites was an indispensable element of freedom. But the family itself was in some ways transformed by emancipation. Although historians no longer view the slave family as matriarchal, it is true that slave men did not function as economic breadwinners and that their masters wielded authority within the household. In a sense, slavery had imposed on black men and women the rough "equality" of powerlessness. With freedom came developments that strengthened patriarchy within the black family and consigned men and women to separate spheres.

Outside events strongly influenced this development. Service in the Union Army enabled black men to participate more directly than women in the struggle for freedom. The Freedmen's Bureau designated the husband as head of the black household, insisting that men sign contracts for the labor of their entire families and establishing lower wage scales for women. After 1867 black men could serve on juries, vote, hold office, and rise to leadership in the Republican party, while black women, like their white counterparts, could not. And black preachers, editors, and politicians emphasized women's responsibility for making the home "a place of peace and comfort" for men and urged them to submit to their husbands' authority.

Not all black women placidly accepted the increasingly patriarchal quality of black family life. Indeed, many proved more than willing to bring family disputes before public authorities. The records of the Freedmen's Bureau contain hundreds of complaints by black women of beatings, infidelity, and lack of child support. Some black women objected to their husbands signing labor contracts for them, demanded separate payment of their wages, and refused to be liable for their husbands' debts at country stores. Yet if emancipation not only institutionalized the black family but also spawned tensions within it, black men and women shared a passionate commitment to the stability of family life as the solid foundation upon which a new black community could flourish.

Building the Black Community

Second only to the family as a focal point of black life stood the church. And, as in the case of the family, Reconstruction was a time of consolidation and transformation for black religion. With the death of slavery, urban blacks seized control of their own churches, while the "invisible institution" of the rural slave church emerged into the light of day. The creation of an independent black religious life proved to be a momentous and irreversible consequence of emancipation.

In antebellum Southern Protestant congregations, slaves and free blacks had enjoyed a kind of associate membership. Subject to the same rules and discipline as whites, they were required to sit in the back of the church or in the gallery during services and were excluded from Sabbath schools and a role in church governance. In the larger cities, the number of black members often justified the organization of wholly black congregations and the construction of separate churches, although these were legally required to have white pastors. In the aftermath of emancipation, the wholesale withdrawal of blacks from biracial congregations redrew the religious map of the South. Two causes combined to produce the independent black church: the refusal of whites to offer blacks an equal place within their congregations and the black quest for self-determination.

Throughout the South, blacks emerging from slavery pooled their resources to purchase land and erect their own churches. Before the buildings were completed, they held services in structures as diverse as a railroad boxcar, where Atlanta's First Baptist Church gathered, or an outdoor "bush arbor," where the First Baptist Church of Memphis congregated in 1865. The first new building to rise amid Charleston's ruins was a black church on Calhoun Street; by 1866 ten more had been constructed. In the countryside, a community would often build a single church, used in rotation by the various black denominations. By the end of Reconstruction in 1877, the vast majority of Southern blacks had withdrawn from churches dominated by whites. On the eve of the war, 42,000 black Methodists worshipped in biracial South Carolina churches; by the 1870s, only 600 remained.

The church was "the first social institution fully controlled by black men in America," and its multiple functions testified to its centrality in the black community. Churches housed schools, social events, and political gatherings. In rural areas, church picnics, festivals, and excursions often provided the only opportunity for fellowship and recreation. The church served as an "Ecclesiastical Court House," promoting moral values, adjudicating family disputes, and disciplining individuals for adultery and other illicit behavior. In every black community, ministers were among the most respected individuals, esteemed for their speaking ability, organizational talents, and good judgment on matters both public and private.

Inevitably, too, preachers played a central role in Reconstruction black politics. Many agreed with Rev. Charles H. Pearce, who held several Reconstruction offices in Florida, that it was "impossible" to separate religion and politics: "A man in this State cannot do his whole duty as a minister except he looks out for the political interests of his people." Even those preachers who lacked ambition for political position sometimes found it thrust upon them. Often among the few literate blacks in a community, they were called on to serve as election registrars and candidates for office. Over 100 black ministers, hailing from North and South, from free and slave backgrounds, and from every black denomination from African Methodist Episcopal to Primitive Baptist, would be elected to legislative seats during Reconstruction.

Throughout Reconstruction, religious convictions shaped blacks' understanding of the momentous events around them, the language in which they voiced aspirations for justice and autonomy. Blacks inherited from slavery a distinctive version of Christian faith, in which Jesus appeared as a personal redeemer offering solace in the face of misfortune, while the Old Testament suggested that they were a chosen people, analogous to the Jews in Egypt, whom God, in the fullness of time, would deliver from bondage. "There is no part of the Bible with which they are so familiar as the story of the deliverance of the Children of Israel," a white army chaplain reported in 1866.

Emancipation and the defeat of the Confederacy strongly reinforced this messianic vision of history. Even nonclerics used secular and religious vocabulary interchangeably, as in one 1867 speech recorded by a North Carolina justice of the peace:

He said it was not now like it used to be, that . . . the negro was about to get his equal rights. . . . That the negroes owed their freedom to the courage of the negro soldiers and to God. . . . He made frequent references to the II and IV chapters of Joshua for a full accomplishment of the principles and destiny of the race. It was concluded that the race have a destiny in view similar to the Children of Israel.

The rise of the independent black church was accompanied by the creation of a host of fraternal, benevolent, and mutual aid societies. In early Reconstruction, blacks created literally thousands of such organizations; a partial list includes burial societies, debating clubs, Masonic lodges, fire companies, drama societies, trade associations, temperance clubs, and equal rights leagues. Offering social fellowship, sickness and funeral benefits, and, most of all, a chance to manage their own affairs, these voluntary associations embodied a spirit of collective self-improvement. Robert G. Fitzgerald, who had been born free in Delaware, served in both the U.S. Army and Navy, and came to Virginia to teach in 1866, was delighted to see rural blacks establishing churches, lyceums, and schools. "They tell me," he recorded in his diary, "before Mr. Lincoln made them free they had nothing to work for, to look up to, now they have everything, and will, by God's help, make the best of it." Moreover, the spirit of mutual self-help extended outward from the societies to embrace destitute nonmembers. In 1865 and 1866, blacks in Nashville, Jackson, New Orleans, and Atlanta, as well as in many rural areas, raised money to establish orphanages, soup kitchens, employment agencies, and poor relief funds.

Perhaps the most striking illustration of the freedmen's quest for self-improvement was their seemingly unquenchable thirst for education. Before the war, every Southern state except Tennessee had prohibited the instruction of slaves, and although many free blacks had attended school and a number of slaves became literate through their own efforts or the aid of sympathetic masters, over ninety percent of the South's adult black population was illiterate in 1860. Access to education for themselves and their children was, for blacks, central to the meaning of freedom, and white contemporaries were astonished by their "avidity for learning." Adults as well as children thronged the schools. A Northern teacher in Florida reported how one sixty-year-old woman, "just beginning to spell, seems as if she could not think of any thing but her book, says she spells her lesson all the evening, then she dreams about it, and wakes up thinking about it."

Northern benevolent societies, the Freedmen's Bureau, and, after 1868, state governments provided most of the funding for black education during Reconstruction. But the initiative often lay with blacks themselves. Urban blacks took immediate steps to set up schools, sometimes holding classes temporarily in abandoned warehouses, billiards rooms, or, in New Orleans and Savannah, former slave markets. In rural areas, Freedmen's Bureau officials repeatedly expressed surprise at discovering classes organized by blacks already meeting in churches, basements, or private homes. And everywhere there were children teaching their parents the alphabet at home, laborers on lunch breaks "poring over the elementary pages," and the "wayside schools" described by a Bureau officer:

A negro riding on a loaded wagon, or sitting on a hack waiting for a train, or by the cabin door, is often seen, book in hand delving after the rudiments of knowledge. A group on the platform of a depot, after carefully conning an old spelling book, resolves itself into a class.

Throughout the South, blacks in 1865 and 1866 raised money to purchase land, build schoolhouses, and pay teachers' salaries. Some communities voluntarily taxed themselves; in others black schools charged tuition, while allowing a number of the poorest families to enroll their children free of charge. Black artisans donated their labor to construct schoolhouses, and black families offered room and board to teachers to supplement their salaries. By 1870, blacks had expended over $1 million on education, a fact that long remained a point of collective pride. "Whoever may hereafter lay claim to the honor of 'establishing' . . . schools," wrote a black resident of Selma in 1867, "I trust the fact will never be ignored that Miss Lucy Lee, one of the emancipated, was the pioneer teacher of the colored children, . . . without the aid of Northern societies."

Inevitably, the first black teachers appeared incompetent in Northern eyes, for a smattering of education might place an individual in front of a class. One poignantly explained, "I never had the chance of goen to school for I was a slave until freedom. . . . I am the only teacher because we can not doe better now." Yet even an imperfect literacy, coupled with the courage often required to establish a rural school in the face of local white opposition, marked these teachers as community leaders. Black teachers played numerous roles apart from education, assisting freedmen in contract disputes, engaging in church work, and drafting petitions to the Freedmen's Bureau, state officials, and Congress. Like the ministry, teaching frequently became a springboard to political office. At least seventy black teachers served in state legislatures during Reconstruction. And many black politicians were linked in other ways to the quest for learning, like Alabama Congressman Benjamin S. Turner, an ex-slave "destitute of education," who financed a Selma school.

Not surprisingly, the majority of black teachers who held political office during Reconstruction had been free before the Civil War. Indeed the schools, like the entire institutional structure established by blacks during Reconstruction, symbolized the emergence of a community that united the free and the freed, and Northern and Southern blacks. The process occurred most smoothly in the Upper South, where the cultural and economic gap between free blacks and slaves had always been less pronounced than in the urban Deep South. While generally lighter in color than slaves, most Upper South free blacks were poor urban workers or farm laborers, often tied to the slave community through marriage and church membership. In cities like New Orleans, Mobile, Savannah, and Charleston, however, affluent mulatto elites responded with deep ambivalence to the new situation created by emancipation. Even in New Orleans, where politically conscious free blacks had already moved to make common cause with the freedmen, a sense of exclusivity survived the end of slavery. The Freedmen's Bureau found many free blacks reluctant to send their children to school with former slaves.

After New Orleans, the South's largest and wealthiest community of free blacks resided in Charleston, although the free elite there was neither as rich nor as culturally distinct as its Louisiana counterpart. Arriving in Charleston in November 1865, Northern journalist John R. Dennett found some members of the free elite cultivating their old exclusiveness. Others, however, took the lead in organizing assistance for destitute freedmen and in teaching the former slaves. Sons and daughters of prominent free families, mostly young people in their twenties, fanned out into the South Carolina countryside as teachers and missionaries. Several thereby acquired positions of local political leadership and later returned to Charleston as constitutional convention delegates and legislators. Thus the children of the Charleston elite cast their lot with the freedmen, bringing, as they saw it, modern culture to the former slaves. This encounter was not without its tensions. But in the long run it hastened the emergence of a black community stratified by class rather than color, in which the former free elite took its place as one element of a new black bourgeoisie, instead of existing as a separate caste as in the antebellum port cities.

In the severing of ties that had bound black and white families and churches to one another under slavery, the coming together of blacks in an explosion of institution building, and the political and cultural fusion of former free blacks and former slaves, Reconstruction witnessed the birth of the modern black community. All in all, the months following the end of the Civil War were a period of remarkable accomplishment for Southern blacks. Looking back in January 1866, the Philadelphia-born black missionary, Jonathan C. Gibbs could only exclaim: "we have progressed a century in a year."

The Economics of Freedom

Nowhere were blacks' efforts to define their freedom more explosive for the entire society than in the economy. Freedmen brought out of slavery a conception of themselves as a "Working Class of People" who had been unjustly deprived of the fruits of their labor. To white predictions that they would not work, blacks responded that if any class could be characterized as lazy, it was the planters, who had "lived in idleness all their lives on stolen labor." It is certainly true that many blacks expected to labor less as free men and women than they had as slaves, an understandable aim considering the conditions they had previously known. "Whence comes the assertion that the 'nigger won't work'?" asked an Alabama freedman. "It comes from this fact: . . . the freedman refuses to be driven out into the field two hours before day, and work until 9 or 10 o'clock in the night, as was the case in the days of slavery."

Yet freedom meant more than shorter hours and payment of wages. Freedmen sought to control the conditions under which they labored, end their subordination to white authority, and carve out the greatest measure of economic autonomy. These aims led them to prefer tenancy to wage labor, and leasing land for a fixed rent to sharecropping. Above all, they inspired the quest for land. Owning land, the freedmen believed, would "complete their independence."

To those familiar with the experience of other postemancipation societies, blacks' "mania for owning a small piece of land" did not appear surprising. Freedmen in Haiti, the British and Spanish Caribbean, and Brazil all saw ownership of land as crucial to economic independence, and everywhere former slaves sought to avoid returning to plantation labor. Unlike freedmen in other countries, however, American blacks emerged from slavery convinced that the federal government had committed itself to land distribution. Belief in an imminent division of land was most pervasive in the South Carolina and Georgia lowcountry, but the idea was shared in other parts of the South as well, including counties that had never been occupied by federal troops. Blacks insisted that their past labor entitled them to at least a portion of their owners' estates. As an Alabama black convention put it: "The property which they hold was nearly all earned by the sweat of *our* brows."

In some parts of the South, blacks in 1865 did more than argue the merits of their case. Hundreds of freedmen refused either to sign labor contracts or to leave the plantations, insisting that the land belonged to them. On the property of a Tennessee planter, former slaves not only claimed to be "joint heirs" to the estate but, the owner complained, abandoned the slave quarters and took up residence "in the rooms of my house." Few freedmen were able to maintain control of land seized in this manner. A small number did, however, obtain property through other means, squatting on unoccupied land in sparsely populated states like Florida and Texas, buying tiny city plots, or cooperatively purchasing farms and plantations. Most blacks, however, emerged from slavery unable to purchase land even at the depressed prices of early Reconstruction and confronted by a white community unwilling to advance credit or sell them property. Thus, they entered the world of free labor as wage or share workers on land owned by whites. The adjustment to a new social order in which their persons were removed from the market but their labor was bought and sold like any other commodity proved in many respects difficult. For it required them to adapt to the logic of the economic market, where the impersonal laws of supply and demand and the balance of power between employer and employee determine a laborer's material circumstances.

Most freedmen welcomed the demise of the paternalism and mutual obligations of slavery and embraced many aspects of the free market. They patronized the stores that sprang up throughout the rural South, purchasing "luxuries" ranging from sardines, cheese, and sugar to new clothing. They saved money to build and support churches and educate their children. And they quickly learned to use and influence the market for their own ends. The early years of Reconstruction witnessed strikes or petitions for higher wages by black urban laborers, including Richmond factory workers, Jackson washerwomen, New Orleans and Savannah stevedores, and mechanics in Columbus, Georgia. In rural areas, too, plantation freedmen sometimes bargained collectively over contract terms, organized strikes, and occasionally even attempted to establish wage schedules for an entire area. Blacks exploited competition between planters and nonagricultural employers, seeking work on railroad construction crews and at turpentine mills and other enterprises offering pay far higher than on the plantations.

Slavery, however, did not produce workers fully socialized to the virtues of economic accumulation. Despite the profits possible in early postwar cotton farming, many freedmen strongly resisted growing the "slave crop." "If ole massa want to grow cotton," said one Georgia freedman, "let him plant it himself." Many freedmen preferred to concentrate on food crops and only secondarily on cotton or other staples to obtain ready cash. Rather than choose irrevocably between self-sufficiency and market farming, they hoped to avoid a complete dependence on either while taking advantage of the opportunities each could offer. As A. Warren Kelsey, a representative of Northern cotton manufacturers, shrewdly observed:

The sole ambition of the freedmen at the present time appears to be to become the owner of a little piece of land, there to erect a humble home, and to dwell in peace and security at his own free will and pleasure. If he wishes, to cultivate the ground in cotton on his own account, to be able to do so without anyone to dictate to him hours or system of labor, if he wishes instead to plant corn or sweet potatoes—to be able to do that free from any outside control. . . . That is their idea, their desire and their hope.

Historical experience and modern scholarship suggest that acquiring small plots of land would hardly, by itself, have solved the economic plight of black families. Without control of credit and access to markets, land reform can often be a hollow victory. And where political power rests in hostile hands, small landowners often find themselves subjected to oppressive taxation and other state policies that severely limit their economic prospects. In such circumstances, the autonomy offered by land ownership tends to be defensive, rather than the springboard for sustained economic advancement. Yet while hardly an economic panacea, land redistribution would have had profound consequences for Southern society, weakening the land-based economic and political power of the old ruling class, offering blacks a measure of choice as to whether, when, and under what circumstances to enter the labor market, and affecting the former slaves' conception of themselves.

Blacks' quest for economic independence not only threatened the foundations of the Southern political economy, it put the freedmen at odds with both former owners seeking to restore plantation labor discipline and Northerners committed to reinvigorating staple crop production. But as part of the broad quest for individual and collective autonomy, it remained central to the black community's effort to define the meaning of freedom. Indeed, the fulfillment of other aspirations, from family autonomy to the creation of schools and churches, all greatly depended on success in winning control of their working lives and gaining access to the economic resources of the South.

Origins of Black Politics

If the goal of autonomy inspired blacks to withdraw from religious and social institutions controlled by whites and to attempt to work out their economic destinies for themselves, in the polity, "freedom" meant inclusion rather than separation. Recognition of their equal rights as citizens quickly emerged as the animating impulse of Reconstruction black politics. In the spring and summer of 1865, blacks organized a seemingly unending series of mass meetings, parades, and petitions demanding civil equality and suffrage as indispensable corollaries of emancipation. By midsummer, "secret political Radical Associations" had been formed in Virginia's major cities. Richmond blacks first organized politically to protest the army's rounding up of "vagrants" for plantation labor, but soon expanded their demands to include the right to vote and the removal of the "Rebel-controlled" local government.

Statewide conventions held throughout the South in 1865 and early 1866 offered the most visible evidence of black political organization. Several hundred delegates attended these gatherings, some selected by local meetings, others by churches, fraternal societies, Union Leagues, and black army units, still others simply appointed by themselves. The delegates "ranged all colors and apparently all conditions," but urban free mulattoes took the most prominent roles, and former slaves were almost entirely absent from leadership positions. But other groups also came to the fore in 1865. In Mississippi, a state with few free blacks before the war, ex-slave army veterans and their relatives comprised the majority of the delegates. Alabama and Georgia had a heavy representation of black ministers, and all the conventions included numerous skilled artisans.

The prominence of free blacks, ministers, artisans, and former soldiers in these early conventions foreshadowed black politics for much of Reconstruction. From among these delegates emerged such prominent officeholders as Alabama Congressman James T. Rapier and Mississippi Secretary of State James D. Lynch.

In general, however, what is striking is how few of these early leaders went on to positions of prominence. In most states, political mobilization had advanced far more rapidly in cities and in rural areas occupied by federal troops during the war than in the bulk of the plantation counties, where the majority of the former slaves lived. The free blacks of Louisiana and South Carolina who stepped to the fore in 1865 remained at the helm of black politics throughout Reconstruction; elsewhere, however, a new group of leaders, many of them freedmen from the black belt, soon superseded those who took the lead in 1865.

The debates at these conventions illuminated conflicting currents of black public life in the immediate aftermath of emancipation. Tensions within the black community occasionally rose to the surface. One delegate voiced resentment that a Northern black had been chosen president of North Carolina's convention. By and large, however, the proceedings proved harmonious, the delegates devoting most of their time to issues that united blacks rather than divided them. South Carolina's convention demanded access to all the opportunities and privileges enjoyed by whites, from education to the right to bear arms, serve on juries, establish newspapers, assemble peacefully, and "enter upon all the avenues of agriculture, commerce, [and] trade."

The delegates' central preoccupation, however, was equality before the law and the suffrage. In justifying their demand for the vote, the delegates invoked America's republican traditions, especially the Declaration of Independence—"the broadest, the deepest, the most comprehensive and truthful definition of human freedom that was ever given to the world." The North Carolina freedmen's convention portrayed the Civil War and emancipation as chapters in the onward march of "progressive civilization," embodiments of "the fundamental truths laid down in the great charter of Republican liberty, the Declaration of Independence." Such language was not confined to the convention delegates. Eleven Alabama blacks, who complained of contract frauds, injustice before the courts, and other abuses, concluded their petition with a revealing masterpiece of understatement: "This is not the persuit of happiness."

Like their Northern counterparts during the Civil War, Southern blacks proclaimed their identification with the nation's history, destiny, and political system. The abundance of letters and petitions addressed by black gatherings and ordinary freedmen to military officials, the Freedmen's Bureau, and state federal authorities, as well as the decision of a number of conventions to send representatives to Washington to lobby for black rights, revealed a belief that the political order was at least partially open to their influence. "We are Americans," declared a meeting of Norfolk blacks, "we know no other country, we love the land of our birth." Their address reminded white Virginians that in 1619, "our fathers as well as yours were toiling in the plantations on James River" and that a black man, Crispus Attucks, had shed "the first blood" in the American Revolution. And, of course, blacks had fought and died to save the Union. America, resolved one meeting, was "now *our* country—made emphatically so by the blood of our brethren."

Despite the insistence on equal rights, the convention resolutions and public addresses generally adopted a moderate tone, offering "the right hand of fellowship" to Southern whites. Even the South Carolina convention, forthright in claiming civil and political equality and in identifying its demand with "the cause of millions of oppressed men" throughout the world, took pains to assure the state's white minority of blacks' "spirit of meekness," their consciousness of "your wealth and greatness, and our poverty and weakness."

To some extent, this cautious tone reflected a realistic assessment of the political situation at a time when Southern whites had been restored to local power by President Johnson and Congress had not yet launched its own Reconstruction policy. But the blend of radicalism and conciliation also mirrored the indecision of an emerging black political leadership still finding its own voice in 1865 and 1866 and dominated by urban free blacks, ministers, and others who had in the past enjoyed harmonious relations with at least some local whites and did not always feel the bitter resentments of rural freedmen.

Nor did a coherent economic program emerge from these assemblies. Demands for land did surface at local meetings that chose convention delegates. Yet such views were rarely expressed among the conventions' leadership. By and large, economic concerns figured only marginally in the proceedings, and the addresses and resolutions offered no economic program apart from stressing the "mutual interest" of capital and labor and urging self-improvement as the route to personal advancement. The ferment rippling through the Southern countryside found little echo at the state conventions of 1865, reflecting the paucity of representation from plantation counties and the prominence of political leaders more attuned to political equality and self-help formulas than to rural freedmen's thirst for land.

Nonetheless, these early black conventions both reflected and advanced the process of political mobilization. Some Tennessee delegates, for example, took to heart their convention's instruction to "look after the welfare" of their constituents. After returning home, they actively promoted black education, protested to civil authorities and the Freedmen's Bureau about violence and contract frauds, and struggled against unequal odds to secure blacks a modicum of justice in local courts. Chapters of the Georgia Equal Rights and Educational Association, established at the state's January 1866 convention, became "schools in which the colored citizens learn their rights." Spreading into fifty counties by the end of the year, the Association's local meetings attracted as many as 2,000 freedmen, who listened to speeches on issues of the day and readings from Republican newspapers.

All in all, the most striking characteristic of this initial phase of black political mobilization was unevenness. In some states, organization proceeded steadily in 1865 and 1866; in others, such as Mississippi, little activity occurred between an initial flurry in the summer of 1865 and the advent of black suffrage two years later. Large parts of the black belt remained untouched by organized politics, but many blacks were aware of Congressional debates on Reconstruction policy and quickly employed on their own behalf the Civil Rights Act of 1866. "The negro of today," remarked a correspondent of the New Orleans *Tribune* in September 1866, "is not the same as he was six years ago. . . . He has been told of his rights, which have long been robbed." Only in 1867 would blacks enter the "political nation," but in organization, leadership, and an ideology that drew on America's republican heritage to demand an equal place as citizens, the seeds that flowered then were planted in the first years of freedom.

Violence and Everyday Life

The black community's religious, social, and political mobilization was all the more remarkable for occurring in the face of a wave of violence that raged almost unchecked in large parts of the postwar South. In the vast majority of cases freedmen were the victims and whites the aggressors.

In some areas, violence against blacks reached staggering proportions in the immediate aftermath of the war. "I saw white men whipping colored men just the same as they did before the war," testified ex-slave Henry Adams, who claimed that "over two thousand colored people" were murdered in 1865 in the area around Shreveport, Louisiana. In some cases, whites wreaked horrible vengeance for offenses real or imagined. In 1866, after "some kind of dispute with some freedmen," a group near Pine Bluff, Arkansas, set fire to a black settlement and rounded up the inhabitants. A man who visited the scene the following morning found "a sight that apald me 24 Negro men women and children were hanging to trees all round the Cabbins."

The pervasiveness of violence reflected whites' determination to define in their own way the meaning of freedom and to resist black efforts to establish their autonomy, whether in matters of family, church, labor, or personal demeanor. Georgia freedman James Jeter was beaten "for claiming the right of whipping his own child instead of allowing his employer and former master to do so." Black schools, churches, and political meetings also became targets. Conduct deemed manly or dignified on the part of whites became examples of "insolence" and "insubordination" in the case of blacks. One North Carolina planter complained bitterly to a Union officer that a black soldier had "bowed to me and said good morning," insisting blacks must never address whites unless spoken to first. In Texas, Bureau records listed the "reasons" for some of the 1,000 murders of blacks by whites between 1865 and 1868: One victim "did not remove his hat"; another "wouldn't give up his whiskey flask"; a white man "wanted to thin out the niggers a little"; another wanted "to see a d—d nigger kick." Gender offered no protection—one black woman was beaten by her employer for "using insolent language," another for refusing to "call him master," a third "for crying because he whipped my mother." Probably the largest number of violent acts stemmed from disputes arising from blacks' efforts to assert their freedom from control by their former masters. Freedmen were assaulted and murdered for attempting to leave plantations, disputing contract settlements, not laboring in the manner desired by their employers, attempting to buy or rent land, and resisting whippings.

The pervasive violence underscored what might be called the politicization of everyday life that followed the demise of slavery. A seemingly insignificant incident reported to the state's governor in 1869 by black North Carolinian A. D. Lewis graphically illustrates this development:

Please allow me to call your kine attention to a transaction which occurred to day between me and Dr. A. H. Jones. . . . I was in my field at my own work and this Jones came by me and drove up to a man's gate that live close by . . . and ordered my child to come there and open that gate for him`. . . . while there was children in the yard at the same time not more than twenty yards from him and jest because they were white and mine black he wood not call them to open the gate. . . . I spoke gently to him that [the white children] would open the gate. . . . He got out of his buggy . . . and walked nearly hundred yards rite into my field where I was at my own work and double his fist and strick me in the face three times . . . cursed me [as] a dum old Ratical. . . . Now governor I wants you to please rite to me how to bring this man to jestus.

No record exists of the disposition of this complaint, but Lewis's letter conveys worlds of meaning about Reconstruction: his powerful sense of place, his quiet dignity in the face of assault, his refusal to allow his son to be treated differently from white children or to let a stranger's authority be imposed on his family, the way an everyday encounter rapidly descended into violence and acquired political meaning, and Lewis's assumption (reflecting the situation after 1867) that blacks could expect justice from the government under which they lived. Most of all, it illustrates how day-to-day encounters between the races became infused with the tension inevitable when a social order, with its established power relations and commonly understood rules of conduct, has been swept away and a new one has not yet come into being. As David L. Swain, former governor of North Carolina, remarked in 1865, "With reference to emancipation, we are at the beginning of the war."

Thomas C. Holt

Emancipation, Race, and Ideology

The first half of the nineteenth century was preeminently an era of revolutions—in social and political thought, in social and economic relations. We now know that the problem of slavery was a vital nexus for the ideological transformation of the era and that slave emancipation figured prominently in its political and military upheavals. Beginning with Haiti at the turn of the century and ending with Cuba and Brazil during its final decades, slave-labor systems in the Western Hemisphere were eroded and finally swept away in successive waves of slave revolt, wars of national liberation, and internal conflicts between social classes. Concurrent with and linked to the dramatic transition from slavery to free labor was the maturing of industrial capitalism and the liberal democratic ideology that purported to explain and justify the new bourgeois economic order.

But while antislavery agitation was closely intertwined with the rise of bourgeois ideology in the early decades of the century, actual emancipation exposed the difficulty of applying that ideology to radical transformations in the social relations of culturally different populations. In the wake of these developments, the late nineteenth century witnessed the rise of an explicitly racist ideology that gained a hitherto unprecedented intellectual and social legitimacy, clashed with critical premises of liberal democratic thought, and undermined the promise of black emancipation. Indeed, there appear to have been subtle relationships and interactions between the social transformations occasioned by slave emancipation and this subsequent racist reaction. Early social reformers had posed the problem of slavery in a way that justified a particular concept of freedom in the emerging capitalist social order; by the late nineteenth century what one might call "the problem of freedom" in former slave societies confronted many of these same thinkers with difficulties inherent in liberal democratic thought. Racism appears to have been, in part, a means of evading that confrontation.

The confrontation was most compelling in the British and the American emancipation experiences. In ideological as well as diplomatic terms, abolition in the British West Indies and in the southern United States were major turning points in the international antislavery struggle. The emancipation of approximately three-quarters of a million British West Indian and four million American blacks eliminated well over half the entire slave population in the Western Hemisphere. Furthermore, only in Haiti was the emancipation process more rapid than that under British and American auspices; in both places the process was completed over a four-year period. Of course, in the British West Indies this "gradualism" was by design, while in the United States it was caused by the vicissitudes of war. Hundreds of thousands of American slaves fled to Union lines from the commencement of the Civil War in 1861; their quest for freedom was accelerated by the Emancipation Proclamation in 1863 and completed with the Thirteenth Amendment in 1865. British West Indian planters, however, were paid compensation totaling £20 million sterling for their slave property and enjoyed an official four-year transition period between the abolition of legal slavery on August 1, 1834, and the complete emancipation of their workers on August 1, 1838. During this so-called apprenticeship period, the freedmen were required to remain on the plantations and to work much as they had before. They could not be subjected to corporal punishment by their former masters, however, and part of their week was reserved for their own use, preferably to work for wages. Special magistrates, whose duties and recruitment were similar to those of the American Freedmen's Bureau agents, were appointed to supervise the transition and to protect the freedmen from abuse; however, they could and did order physical punishment to force recalcitrant freedmen to work.

It was not simply the size and political significance of emancipation in the British possessions and the United States that affected other slaveholding powers; American and British policy debates shaped the terms of discussion if not the actual policies pursued elsewhere. For example, in July 1839, Alexis de Tocqueville completed a study of the British West Indian experience and recommended an emancipation plan for the French islands to the Chamber of Deputies. Following the British precedent, he suggested that a special transition period separate the ending of formal slavery and complete emancipation. This period, he thought, was "the most favorable moment to found that empire over the minds and habits of the black population" that was essential to preserving social order. Moreover, he proposed that during this transition period the French must be prepared, if necessary, to "compel the laborious and manly habits of liberty." Drawing attention to Tocqueville's remarks, C. Vann Woodward has observed that the problem of reconciling force with freedom, and liberty with necessity, represented a "paradox that lay at the heart of the problem of emancipations and reconstructions everywhere in the world."

The political systems of Great Britain and the United States differed radically, and the British West Indies and the American South were politically, economically, and demographically distinct. Nevertheless, policymakers at the White

House and in Whitehall posed the problem of emancipation in strikingly similar political and philosophical terms and wrestled with the same paradoxical issues. These similarities exist no doubt because the terms of their policy discussions were derived from the broader ideological presuppositions that British and American policymakers shared. The task of compelling the "voluntary" transformation of slaves into wage laborers, the crux of the problem of formulating emancipation policy everywhere, found precedents in the ongoing transformation of white agricultural workers into an industrial working class. Yet, the fact that such a transformation would pose an intellectual "problem" is comprehensible only in the context of the prevailing liberal democratic ideology of the emancipators, that is, the paradoxical situation of having to compel people to be "free" was rooted in the character of the "freedom" espoused.

Defining freedom was the beginning of the difficulty. David Brion Davis has revealed how social reformers used slavery as a curious negative referent with which to define the otherwise elusive concept of freedom. For none was this difficulty more poignant than for English Quakers, the vanguard of British industrial development as well as of the abolitionist movement. For them slavery helped define the meaning of freedom within a capitalist economy and a liberal political state. Slavery, being clearcut and concrete, could be used to symbolize "all the forces that threatened the true destiny of man." Freedom, being abstract and liable to misuse, was more difficult to define in substance. Thus slavery helped locate the outer boundaries of freedom; it was the antithesis of freedom. Slavery meant subordination to the physical coercion and personal dominion of an arbitrary master; freedom meant submission only to the impersonal forces of the marketplace and to the rational and uniform constraints of law. Slavery meant involuntary labor for the master's benefit; freedom meant voluntary contracts determined by mutual consent, which theoretically should guarantee that one received the value of one's labor. Slavery meant little, if any, legal protection of property, person, or family; freedom meant equal protection of the laws. Historians might empirically determine that slavery and capitalism were compatible, but to contemporaries of the reform era, slavery was logically synonymous with irrational monopoly power in both labor markets and commodity markets. The power of the abolition movement in this era derived in large part from the fact that slavery was such a convenient foil for free markets, free labor, and free men.

Moreover, the abolitionists and those men who fashioned and implemented emancipation policies were all heirs to a historically unique set of concepts about human behavior, about the sources of social action, and about the nature of political and economic justice. First, there was a materialist assumption regarding man's nature: man is a creature of insatiable material appetites, and all humans share an innate desire for self-improvement and personal gain. Second, it was assumed that in general men have a natural aversion to labor and that therefore material incentives are necessary to make them work. From these unquestioned assumptions was deduced a coherent view of political economy. Its key axiom was the notion C. B. Macpherson has called "possessive individualism"—namely, that society consists of an aggregation of individuals each of whom is proprietor of his own person and capacities, for which he owes nothing to society. Consequently, social action (at least beyond the bounds of the family) is reducible to exchange relations between these individual proprietors. The mainspring of the entire socioeconomic and political system is "that men do calculate their most profitable courses and do employ their labour, skill, and resources as that calculation dictates." Political order exists merely as "a calculated device for the protection of this property and for the maintenance of an orderly relation of exchange." In such a social order human freedom is defined as autonomy from the will of others, except in relations entered into voluntarily with a view to one's own interest, that is, self-interested contractual relations. But autonomy also means that whether one eats or starves depends solely on one's individual will and capacities. In the liberal democratic state, social relations—in their political as well as their economic dimensions—are ultimately self-regulating, impersonal, and therefore just.

The efforts of British and American policymakers to define a framework for the transition from slavery to freedom reveal the force of these ideas. The essential difference between freedom and slavery, as Viscount Howick lectured the members of Parliament during the debate on British West Indian emancipation in 1833, was that free men worked "because they are convinced that it is in their interest to do so." Theirs was a rational calculation of the relative advantages to be gained from industry over the privation to be expected if they "indulge in their natural inclination for repose." Slaves worked out of fear of punishment and for the benefit of others.

Three decades later, Americans echoed Howick's sentiments. "The incentive to faithful labor," advised the Boston *Advertiser* in 1865, "is self-interest." This pithy rule confirmed sentiments articulated earlier by the men and women who had gathered at Port Royal, South Carolina, to conduct the first experiment with black free labor in the American South. One of them, William Gannett, declared, "Let all the natural laws of labor, wages, competition, &c come into play—and the sooner will habits of responsibility, industry, self-dependence & manliness be developed." His colleague Edward Philbrick added, "Negro labor has got to be employed, if at all, because it is *profitable,* and it has got to come into the market like everything else, subject to the supply and demand." Upon returning from Port Royal in May 1862, John Murray Forbes, a pre–Civil War abolitionist and postwar investor in Southern cotton, assessed the South Carolina situation for readers of the Boston *Advertiser*: "All those engaged in the experiment will testify that the negro has the same selfish element in him which induces other men to labor, and that with a fair prospect of benefit . . . he will work like other human beings." Elsewhere Forbes put the matter more bluntly: "The necessity of getting a living is the great secret of providing for sheep, negroes and humans generally."

It was not so simple as all that, however. While it was true that "sheep, negroes and humans generally" work to keep from starving, it did not follow that freedmen would apply themselves to the production of plantation staples or that their labor would be disciplined and reliable. The problem was not merely to make ex-slaves work, but to make them into a working class, that is, a class that would submit to the market because it adhered to the *values* of a bourgeois society: regularity, punctuality, sobriety, frugality, and economic rationality.

One of the more thoughtful examinations of this central problem of freedom, from the liberal point of view, was written in 1833 by Henry Taylor, a middle-level bureaucrat in the British Colonial Office. In colonies like Jamaica, wrote Taylor, where the population density was low and large areas of the interior had not been devoted to plantation staples, the problem of getting the freedmen to work on the sugar estates would be formidable. Jamaican planters had encouraged their slaves to grow foodstuffs on interior lands to supplement their weekly rations of salt fish and corn. They allocated garden plots either on the plantation itself or on land leased from others. By custom, Jamaican slaves had come to treat these so-called provision grounds as their private property. They sold their surplus produce in the weekend markets of nearby villages and towns and retained the profits for themselves. Taylor noted that testimony before the House of Commons had shown conclusively that freedmen could earn their accustomed subsistence needs by working these provision grounds for little better than one day a week. The key question, therefore, was "What, except compulsion, shall make them work six?"

Taylor brushed aside abolitionist testimony that the slaves' industry on their provision grounds showed they would continue to work on plantations after emancipation. Slaves who worked one or two days to purchase necessities would not necessarily work five or six more days for superfluous luxuries. They could be expected to expand their workweek sixfold only if their needs and wants were likewise expanded; this was an "extremely improbable" occurrence in the foreseeable future. "It is true that the wants and desires of mankind are indefinitely expansive," wrote Taylor, echoing a basic premise of Adam Smith's *Wealth of Nations,* "but when the habits of a whole population are concerned, the expansion must be necessarily gradual. Their habits cannot be suddenly changed." For the moment, one had to expect that the freedmen would strive merely for the possessions they were accustomed to, or for those which persons of slightly higher status—that is, the black headmen and estate artisans—possessed. It would be reasonable to assume that "it will only be in the long course of years and progress of society that their wants will creep up the scale of luxury, and be characterized by that exigency in the higher degrees of it which might suffice to animate and prolong their labours."

Taylor thought that the dangers implicit in the proposed West Indian emancipation and the subsequent needs of the colonial economy would not permit such delay. It was necessary that industrious habits be inculcated in some manner; work discipline must be internalized by the freedmen without the normal spur of necessity or desire. The problem, therefore, was to overcome the legacy of slavery. "The state of slavery if it implies much injustice, implies also much ignorance and want of moral cultivation," Taylor concluded. Being "ignorant, destitute of moral cultivation, and . . . habituated to dependence," slaves required "both a sense of subordination in themselves, and the exercise by others over them of a strict and daily discipline." But there was reason to believe that under "disinterested instructors" they would advance in civilization. Once it had been thought that blacks were intellectually inferior, but the preponderant evidence presented to Parliament revealed striking cultural progress. Under the tutelage of missionaries, the slaves showed a strong desire to learn and were "a quick and intelligent race of people." Of course, some racial differences remained. Taylor rejected one witness's testimony that the blacks possessed "shrewd" intellects; he thought their mental character might be better described as rash, volatile, and somewhat shallow, "the intelligence, in short, of minds which had neither discipline nor cultivation, and nothing but natural vivacity to enlighten them."

Given their character and the absence of sufficient incentives to work for wages, freedmen were likely to relapse "into a barbarous indolence" if suddenly or completely emancipated. Experience showed that where population density was low, people have a "strong propensity to scatter themselves" and to live in the wild as hunter-gatherers. A society must be "condensed" to be civilized, otherwise a situation develops wherein "capitalists [will be] shorn of their profits by the want of labour, and . . . those who *should be* labourers, turning squatters and idlers, and living like beasts in the woods.". . .

The problem that Taylor's memorandum highlights is that the necessity that leads men to work is culturally defined and therefore varies from culture to culture. Thus Taylor recognized that the remaking of slaves into a working class involved remaking the slaves' culture. As long as the freedmen limited their material aspirations to goods they had received as slaves, their interest in working for wages would be insufficient to maintain the production of plantation staples. Therefore, the physical coercion of slavery must be replaced by more subtle stimuli. Those insatiable material appetites that all humans were alleged to be blessed with needed to be awakened in the freed slaves. . . .

Americans were also aware of the connection between black consumer desires and the larger economic and social order. John Miller McKim returned to Philadelphia in 1862 from Port Royal, waxing eloquent about the greatly expanded market for Northern goods in the South in the postwar period. "They [the Negroes] begin to demand articles of household use also such as pots, kettles, pans, brushes, brooms, knives, forks, spoons, soap, candles, combs, Yankee clocks, etc." In 1866 the New York *Herald* praised the role of business-minded people in managing freedmen's affairs in the South and made explicit the links between material consumption, education, and the preservation of social order. "Negroes will unquestionably be made better members of society, less subject to the influences of the enemies of social order, more industrious, because more ambitious to have the comforts and luxuries of life, if they can be thoroughly educated, than if they were allowed to remain in ignorance. A negro with no needs beyond a slave's allowance and a couple of suits of osnaburg a year, has far less motive to exert himself than one who sports a gold watch and fine clothes." The New York *Independent* expanded upon this theme. "Families that once fed out of the pot in which their hominy was cooked—the pot being their only utensil, and the hominy the only article of food—now breakfast, dine and sup as do other people, sitting down at a table, with food before them varying in character and decently served.". . .

The state papers produced by Americans—though generally less full or articulate than Taylor's memorandum—expressed identical propositions about human behavior, the principles of social action, and the significance of race. In the spring of 1863, Secretary of War Edwin M. Stanton assigned three social reformers—Robert Dale Owen, Samuel Gridley Howe, and James McKaye—the task of studying the problems involved in the transition from slavery to free labor and recommending appropriate policies and programs. The report of this Freedmen's

Inquiry Commission formed the basis for the establishment two years later of the U.S. Freedmen's Bureau, which like the British Special Magistracy was charged with overseeing the immediate transition from slavery.

Although the commissioners specifically rejected the unsuccessful British apprenticeship system as a model for American policy, they strongly recommended a very similar "guided" transition from slavery to free labor, during which the federal government would act as the temporary guardian, protector, and educator of the freedmen. In the first instance, they felt, the freedmen had to be taught that "emancipation means neither idleness nor gratuitous work, but fair labor for fair wages." The commissioners urged that the freedmen be given "a fair chance," but no more than that. There should be no compulsory contracts to labor, no statutory rate of wages, no interference between the hirer and the hired, and, except for antivagrancy legislation, no regulation of workers' movements. Thus freedom was defined in terms of wage labor, and wage labor meant competition in a market regulated only by "the natural laws of supply and demand."

Freedom to compete did not imply equality, however. The commissioners were confident that "the African race . . . lacks no essential aptitude for civilization," but they did not expect blacks in general to equal whites in the race of life. Like Henry Taylor, they found blacks intelligent but different. They were "a knowing rather than a thinking race"; their intelligence was that of "quick observation rather than comprehensive views or strong sense." It was not, the commissioners felt, "a race that will ever take a lead in the material improvement of the world; but it will make for itself, whenever it has fair play, respectable positions, [and] comfortable homes." The freedman would become "a useful member of the great industrial family of nations. Once released from the disabilities of bondage, he will somewhere find, and will maintain, his own appropriate social position."

The commissioners made clear that freedom of opportunity was not expected to lead to equality of condition, and they made racist assessments of black character and ability. But these should not distract us from the essential thrust of their report. Blacks were judged to have the same innate nature and potential desires and appetites as whites and were expected, therefore, to respond to the same market incentives. Consequently, they required neither perpetual guardianship nor special privileges. The import of such propositions and the subtlety of the distinctions were not lost on George King, a South Carolina freedman. "The Master he says we are all free, but it don't mean we is white. And it don't mean we is equal. Just equal for to work and earn our living and not depend on him for no more meat and clothes."

The Freedman's Bureau was established to implement the policy recommendations of the Inquiry Commissioners. Bureau officials carefully instructed freedmen and planters alike in the principles of a market economy. First of all, labor power—rather than the laborer—was now the commodity to be exchanged for wages. The rates of exchange would vary solely according to supply and demand. Neither the bureau nor combinations of planters would be allowed to set wage prices artificially. Accordingly, General Clinton B. Fisk, the Bureau Commissioner for Tennessee, declared in a circular that labor would be "free to compete with other commodities in an open market." Similarly in Florida, T. W. Osborn, in later years a radical Republican politician, declared that "labor is a commodity in the market and that the possessor of it is entitled to the highest market value."

Other Bureau officials expressed confidence in the freedmen's successful adoption of market values. Wages would induce thrift, J. W. Alvord, the Bureau's inspector of schools, assured General Oliver O. Howard. "The wants and opportunities of freedom show the worth of money, and what can be done with it." The South Carolina Bureau commissioner Rufus Saxton, after urging the freedmen to grow more cotton, the "regal crop," explained in phrases reminiscent of Special Magistrate Chamberlain the transformation he expected to observe in them. "In slavery you only thought of to-day. Having nothing to hope for beyond the present, you did not think of the future, but, like the ox and horse, thought only of food and work for the day. In freedom you must have an eye to the future, and have a plan and object in life."

But it was clear to British and American authorities that the re-education and resocialization of the freedmen would require more formal institutions than the Freedmen's Bureau or the British Special Magistracy. In both instances religious and secular missionaries seemed best suited to achieve the desired transformation in ex-slave cultures and characters. Education seemed to offer the paradoxical possibility of encouraging greater material and moral aspirations as well as inculcating social restraint and acceptance of the status quo in social relations. "It was education which made us free, progressive, and conservative," declared the Boston cotton merchant Edward Atkinson in 1861, "and it is education alone which can keep us so." In a field report to President Andrew Johnson, Carl Schurz reiterated the conservative role of education. "The education of the lower orders is the only reliable basis of the civilization as well as of the prosperity of a people." Moreover, it was "the true ground upon which the efficiency and the successes of free labor society grows"; it was the means for making the freedman "an intelligent cooperator in the general movements of society." Similarly, a special magistrate reporting to the Jamaican governor insisted that "in infant schools we at once get over the obstacle to regulated thought and action in the negro's cottage.". . .

Thus it was that missionaries and schoolmasters were dispatched to the British West Indies and the defeated Confederacy. Ex-slaves had to be taught to internalize the discipline and materialist psychology required in a free, but not equal, society. One should not lose sight of the fact, however, that fundamental to these emancipation policies was the belief that blacks shared the innate nature, desires, and psychology of white men. This is not to say that the emancipators were without racial bias; the point is that those biases were less salient in shaping their policies than were other propositions about human behavior which constituted their larger ideological commitments.

Ideally the freedmen would have access to economic, political, and social opportunities on the same basis as whites, as long as they conformed to the behavior patterns of whites. Should they fail to imbibe these cultural values and adhere to these norms, should education, religion, and consumerism fail to take, the freedmen would be remanded to the same types of social institutions used to discipline white deviants. In the harsh words of Henry Taylor, those who did not conform to the new order would be considered "an idle and spendthrift residue, whose liberation from arbitrary control would be duly retarded." In the liberal democratic state, when the market failed to achieve the appropriate discipline, these "arbitrary controls" were exercised by penal and reformatory institutions in various guises—workhouses, asylums, poorhouses, and penitentiaries.

Of course, the emancipators assumed that such deviance would be the exception rather than the rule and that these institutions would act not simply to coerce but to reform their inmates. They were prepared for the fact that slavery had unfitted both the planter and the freedmen for the roles they would have to play in the new economy, and they anticipated the need to re-educate the master as well as the slave. But nowhere were they prepared for the depth and breadth of the resistance actually encountered from both former masters and ex-slaves.

A major obstacle to the attempt to transform slave societies into liberal states was the planter. In his 1865 tour of the Southern states, Carl Schurz found uniform and pervasive among white Southerners the belief that blacks would not work without physical compulsion. The planters rejected the free-labor system, one student of the period concludes, "not because it had been tried and failed, but because it contradicted fundamental assumptions." Clearly, the defense of slavery had left a legacy of racism that would not be easily surrendered. A Southern planter summarized the viewpoint of his class succinctly: "Northern laborers are like other men, [but] southern laborers are nothing but niggers, and you can't make anything else out of them. They're not controlled by the same motives as white men, and unless you have power to compel them, they'll only work when they can't beg or steal enough to keep from starving." A Louisiana planter declared that "the nature of the negro cannot be changed by the offer of more or less money, all he desires is to eat, drink and sleep, and perform the least possible amount of labor." The Alabamian Hugh J. Davis, Jr., declared, "Negroes will not work for pay, the lash is all I feel that will make them."

That the planters clung to racist views of their black work force is clear, but the extent to which racial perceptions as opposed to perceptions of the requirements of the plantation regime governed their behavior is yet unclear. Putative racial deficiencies provided a justification for maintaining a highly coercive labor discipline, but the crux of the problem was the need for labor discipline regardless of the racial character of the work force. "Authority and control," George Beckford reminds us, "are inherent in the plantation system." After all, the raison d'être of slavery in the first place was the plantation's need for a docile, subservient, and immobile labor force. Arguing against free labor, Hugh W. Pugh, a Louisiana sugar planter, insisted that he needed "thorough control of ample and continuous labor." During the Civil War, planters in Union-occupied Jefferson Parish, Louisiana, expressed their willingness to accept "free" labor but wanted one or two military guards stationed on each plantation to "compel the negroes to work." Alabama planters meeting in 1867 resolved "that when we hire freedmen they concede to us the right to control their labor as our time and convenience requires." Historian Lawrence Powell has observed with appropriate sarcasm that "when the old masters talked of free labor, they really meant slave labor, only hired not bought."

The freedmen also proved reluctant to accept the new economic order as defined by the emancipators. In the British West Indies as well as in the American

South, most blacks had been born into slavery and few had experienced freedom. Nevertheless, ex-slaves had their own ideas about the meaning of freedom. They shared with their emancipators the notion that freedom involved some measure of personal autonomy, the ability to make choices about one's life and destiny. Initially, autonomy and control seemed to refer primarily to limitations on white action against them. They wished to be free from physical abuse, especially whipping. They wished to maintain the integrity of their families against forced separation by slave owners. In Jamaica and America freed women and children abandoned field labor for other economic endeavors and education, respectively. It was of such matters as these that they sang during the days of jubilee: no more "peck o'corn," "no more mistress' call," no more stocks and chains, no more driver's lash, no more auction block. But the act of singing itself points up the fact that autonomy was not simply personal, that it embraced familial and community relationships as well. In the American South freedmen withdrew from white churches and formed their own; in Jamaica they expanded their Christian congregations but returned to African rituals and beliefs.

But the freedmen clearly recognized the bearing that economic relationships had on other social arrangements. When informed that the federal government would return to the planters lands temporarily confiscated during the war, a Georgia freedman declared, "Damn such freedom as that." After the war Southern freedmen everywhere resisted the Union policy of evicting them from those confiscated plantations, even when resistance brought them musket to musket against veteran federal troops. Freedmen in Edisto Island, South Carolina, expressed their incredulity at a government policy that rewarded its erstwhile enemies and punished its loyal supporters; in the process they also revealed their understanding of the essence of freedom.

[W]e are at the mercy of those who are combined to prevent us from getting land enough to lay our Fathers bones upon. We Have property In Horses, cattle, carriages, & articles of furniture, but we are landless and homeless, from the Homes we Have lived In In the past we can only do one of three things Step Into the public road or the sea or remain on them working as In former time and subject to their will as then. We can not resist It In any way without being driven out Homeless upon the road. You will see this Is not the condition of really freemen[.]

Other Afro-Americans and Afro-Jamaicans were jealous of their rights as they understood them and quick to defend against any infringement of those rights, even when defense required violence against planters and legal authorities. For example, efforts by planters and special magistrates in Jamaica to impose extra work on the apprentices or to reduce their compensation were met by determined resistance. There were work stoppages, sit-down strikes, and arson on Jamaican plantations. Likewise, in Louisiana during the Civil War, General Nathaniel Banks's forced-labor policies were resisted with strikes and work stoppages by black field hands.

In certain ways the freedmen learned their new economic roles too well, in the view of some whites. They learned to bargain with and to discriminate among potential employers. They learned quickly to place a money value on their time and to demand overtime pay for work beyond normal hours. As one exasperated planter described the situation, "If he goes to the house for an axe he is to be paid extra for it. It's well enough to pay a man for all he does, but who can carry on a farm in such a way as that?" Jamaican planters voiced similar complaints about the freedmen's allegedly overscrupulous attention to the monetary value of time.

The dramatic increase in market activity and thrift among Jamaican and American freedmen immediately following emancipation encouraged missionaries, Bureau officials, and special magistrates to report favorably on their apparent adjustment to the new order. As one American Missionary Association agent reported from the South Carolina Sea Islands: "In temporal things, the colored people of these islands, are mainly doing well. I do not think it would be for their good, at the present time, to increcis [sic] their facilities for getting money. Most of them have ample means for gaining property fast, by their industry & shrewdness; they have become owners of land to a considerable extent, & are raizing [sic] cotton, as they say for 'old nigger himself,' & not fo 'massa.' "

Despite this evidence, however, metropolitan authorities were disturbed by the tendency of freedmen everywhere to devote themselves to economic activities other than the cultivation of plantation staples. Both in Jamaica and in the American South many blacks showed a preference for raising food crops rather than cotton or sugar, just as Henry Taylor had feared they might. No doubt this was due in part to the fact that the labor requirements were much less rigorous for food gardening than for staples, especially for sugar. And on occasion, particularly in Jamaica, provision crops could be more remunerative than plantation wages. But there probably existed more profound causes than these. Jamaicans were not averse to growing sugar, and American blacks grew cotton—on their own account. It was not the crop but the mode of labor organization that they seemed to object to. In both societies freedmen strongly resisted working for wages, preferring task systems and tenant arrangements that left them in apparent, and sometimes substantial, control of their labor.

Of course, the freedmen's views of political economy are less accessible than are those of their emancipators and the planters; we can only infer their "ideology" or world view from their behavior. But one might begin with the hypothesis that because they issued from a radically different set of social relations, they embraced a radically different vision of what man, work, and society should be. In both the British West Indies and the American South many slaves had participated in a market economy, hiring their "own time" and keeping part of the proceeds of their labor, raising and marketing food crops, and so forth. In Jamaica, slave provision grounds fed an extensive and well-developed internal marketing system. But this market experience had to be very different from that envisioned by classical economists, simply because slaves were not subject to the market's full rigor. One needs to distinguish between mere participation in exchange relationships, as in the case of peasants and small landowners who sell their surpluses to buy "luxuries," and complete absorption in and loss of autonomy to the market, as in the case of planters, wage workers, and others whose *primary* purpose is to produce for exchange.

In an attempt to clarify the inherent difficulties in liberal democratic thought, C. B. Macpherson describes a hypothetical simple market society, which he contrasts with a possessive market society like that of nineteenth-century Britain and America. In the former there is an exchange of goods and services that is regulated by the market (supply and demand, etc.), but labor itself is not a commodity. It is presumed that productive resources, such as land, are available to all in such a society. All members of the society retain control over their own resources, including their labor, and exchange only goods and services; consequently no person's gain comes at the expense of another. No person can accumulate more than he produces with his own hand. Although there can be a division of labor in a simple market economy and people are motivated by gain, according to Macpherson one maximizes gains only by greater exertion and more product exchanges and not by converting another man's labor power to one's own use. The difference between what one would earn as a dependent wage laborer and one's earnings as an independent producer—raising subsistence crops and selling the surplus in the market—is likely to be less than "the satisfaction of retaining control of one's labour," that is, one's autonomy. Presumably any inequities that might develop in such a society arise only because of differences in individual will and effort and not because of an unequal distribution of productive resources.

Macpherson defines a possessive market society as one in which labor itself is a commodity. One man's conversion of another's labor power to his own use quickly leads to a society divided by class—one group controlling the means of production and another left without resources. Ultimately such a division undercuts the ostensible benefits of a free economy and liberal democratic political order, argues Macpherson, as one class loses its "powers" and its freedom of action not only in the marketplace but in political and social spheres as well.

It would appear that the ex-slaves, by their own lights, of course, recognized this danger. In Jamaica many withdrew into the hills and raised food crops, laboring on the sugar estates only during the time they could spare from their provision grounds or when natural and man-made disasters forced them back to the plantations. In the American South, given the relative lack of access to land, freedmen made the best deal they could to avoid the wage system—sharecropping. In retrospect, of course, we recognize that sharecropping degenerated into a system of in-kind wages, but this was not self-evident as the system evolved. Indeed, such a development was probably less the result of inevitable economic tendencies than a consequence of the collapse of black political power.

In whatever way one might interpret the freedmen's behavior, it is clear that it disappointed many of the emancipation advocates and played an as yet uncharted role in the racial backlash of the late nineteenth century. It was not so simple a matter as racist ideas appearing where there had been none before. Racist ideas had been there all along; what was new was the willingness to express them, the use to which they were put, and the policies they appeared to justify. People like Henry Taylor, Carl Schurz, and Samuel Gridley Howe had always believed that blacks were inferior to whites in some respects, but their somewhat contradictory belief that blacks had the same basic innate character as whites had leeched their racism of many of its most poisonous consequences. But when released from slavery, blacks did not appear to respond in the ways predicted by the emancipators' other, more powerful ideas about human behavior. Thus racial explanations of the freedmen's behavior—by placing them in a different category of humankind—allowed the reformers to maintain their faith in their liberal democratic ideology which justified the bourgeois world they had created.

The irony, of course, is that the ex-slaves' response to freedom was in accord with many of the tenets of the liberal reformers as to "rational" self-interested behavior. Freedmen were motivated by gain. They worked hard, saved their money, built churches and schools, and tried to improve themselves materially and morally. But as long as they had choices—and possession of or access to land was the major factor creating choice—freedmen resisted working for wages on the plantations. It could be argued, of course, that higher pay, better working conditions, and greater security could have overcome this resistance (or as economists would put it, their "high reserve price" for plantation work). But plantations have traditionally, if not inherently, required cheap and docile labor forces. In any case, to improve conditions was not the way most planters dealt with the situation. American cotton planters adopted sharecropping, which along with crop liens and political coercion helped insure a subservient labor force. Sugar planters turned to indentured workers and mechanization. Where they monopolized the land and controlled the political system, the retooling of their industry proceeded without undue strain on themselves and often with indirect subsidies from their laborers.

The pattern of events following emancipation, then, should have alerted the emancipators to the inconsistencies in their own ideology—namely, that inequality was a precondition for the economic and social system they envisioned. Given their three centuries of experience, the planter class saw this clearly. As long as they were unable to monopolize resources and alternatives, especially land, plantations required slavery or something very much like it. To give, sell, or allow freedmen to squat on land to any significant degree was to surrender the whole plantation system. Furthermore, conceding effective political power to ex-slaves, whereby they might redirect society's resources, threatened a similar disaster. . . .

By the late 1860s and 1870s disillusionment with the progress of the freedmen was pervasive among emancipation advocates and policymakers of the preceding decades. The sighs of despair of an A.M.A. missionary in Jamaica, reflecting on the poverty and irreligion of his congregants, summed up the sentiments of many of his British and American colleagues:

In speaking thus of the straitened circumstances of our people, I cannot in truthfulness attribute it to causes altogether independent of themselves. For while they are not given to vicious habits which tend to impoverish those who indulge them, yet they lack qualities of heart & mind which are essential to success in undertakings of any kind. They are not indolent, yet they are not industrious after the manner of our countrymen, making the most of precious time. They are not extravagant, but neither are they wisely economical. They lack forethought, reflection & practical wisdom in the management of their affairs. They possess little or nothing of the spirit of enterprise & are especially lacking in that indomitable pluck which grapples with difficulties & scorns to succumb to adverse circum-stances....

In America many of the liberal reformers of the 1860s formed the core of the Liberal Republican movement in the 1870s and the Mugwumps of the 1880s and 1890s. Having urged a thorough reconstruction of Southern society earlier, one including civil and political rights for blacks, they came to revise their assess-ments of blacks and of the policies to be pursued. They now expressed disap-pointment with black progress since emancipation, opposed legislation favorable to the civil and political rights of blacks, and urged that such matters be returned to the control and discretion of Southern whites.

One could interpret these reversals of racial attitudes as mere expressions of personal idiosyncrasies or group pathologies. But the strange ideological career of British and American emancipators suggests a different interpretation. Their racial attitudes and beliefs were not autonomous, discrete entities unrelated to other ideas and events; during the emancipation era racial attitudes were shaped by events even as they shaped events in turn. Thus these beliefs must be treated as a part of, and not abstracted from, the broader ideological and historical context in which they occurred.

Perhaps there are implications here for the general treatment of race and racism in American history. Historians often tend to treat racism as more or less constant in effect over time, undifferentiated in content, and disconnected from other developments—in short, as unresponsive to the processes and forces of his-tory itself. Given such treatment, racism becomes a phenomenon that is *a*histori-cal or, as another author has written, "*trans*historical." As such, racial phenom-ena are almost beyond the scope of historical analysis. It might be more fruitful to approach such ideas as integral to the larger world view of the protagonists we study and to evaluate them in the context of their ideas about human behavior generally.

And, perhaps, it is precisely at this juncture that contemporary historians confront the difficulty that we are also heirs to the broader nineteenth-century ideology, even if not necessarily to its particular racist component. Our notions of the responsibilities of freedom and of appropriate human behavior are no less experientially and historically unique than were those of the nineteenth-century emancipators. Most of us would have difficulty defining innate human character and aspirations in other than our own Western cultural terms. The question of what terms ex-slaves would have used—their world view—is yet to be fully ex-plored. But while we await that exploration, we must recognize the nature and limitations of our own presuppositions and resist imposing them upon people whose experience was by definition quite different. We are heirs of nineteenth-century liberal democratic thought; often we are its prisoners as well.

LA WANDA COX

Reflections on the Limits
of the Possible

The victory for equal civil and political rights inaugurated by national legislation and the southern state conventions of 1868 was tragically temporary, but it should not be deprecated. Opportunities were opened to former slaves and antebellum free blacks for participation in political power, opportunities they pursued with vigor. However brief and episodic their role in political decision-making and their enjoyment of public facilities formerly denied them, free blacks had defied old taboos and left an imprint upon the institutions of the South—political, social, and economic—which the resurgence of white supremacy never completely annihilated. Some native white southerners not only had supported them out of expediency or loyalty to the Union but had come to accept as valid concepts of racial equity alien to their own past. Yet there can be no question but that the equality of citizenship embodied in national and state law during the 1860s lay shattered and apparently unmendable as the South entered the twentieth century. Most former slaves and their children still lived in agrarian dependence and poverty, poorly educated, increasingly disfranchised and segregated, with little protection against a new surge of white violence.

All accounts of Reconstruction recognize the intensity of white southern resistance to the new status of blacks imposed by Republicans upon the defeated South. Curiously, in explaining the outcome, generally characterized by modern historians as the failure of Reconstruction (though with qualification and some dissent), they tend to place major responsibility not upon the South but upon "the North." By "the North" they usually mean the Republican party, which held national political power, and sometimes say as much. Their explanation is not free of moral stricture, often patently implicit when not expressly stated. Since the mid-1960s there has seldom been missing from accounts of the "First

Reconstruction" the pejorative term "betrayal." Present-day scholars do not indulge in "moral discourse" on black slavery, for as David Donald observed "in the middle of the twentieth century there are some things that do not need to be said." Even less likely is an echo of antebellum abolitionist strictures upon slaveholders as "sinners," though there has been lively debate as to whether or not planters harbored a sense of guilt about their peculiar institution. In terms of the moral judgment of history, the vanquished hold an advantage over the victors. Little restraint or understanding has been extended to the latter. Yet few historians would question the statement that those who won the military contest lost the peace. They have not considered the implications. To lose a battle is not to betray a cause; to retreat in the face of a seemingly weak but relentless and resourceful foe is not the equivalent of treachery; to put an end to a bruising fight that has been lost is not without a certain moral justification of its own. In a self-governing nation the will to persevere indefinitely in a just cause, subordinating all else both of interest and conviction, is beyond the realm of reasonable expectation. If Republican politicians and their constituencies of the 1860s and '70s have received little charity, the one professionally acceptable defense of the opprobrium cast upon them is that the political leaders had viable alternatives—viable in the sense that other policies would have changed the outcome, viable also in the sense that such measures could have been perceived and implemented. . . .

If the success of Republicans in reconstructing the South rested upon the precondition of an absence of race prejudice, the limits of the possible were so narrow as to have foreordained failure. Modern scholarship has recognized and amply documented the pervasiveness and persistence of racial prejudice. In some form it contaminated almost all white Americans. Had mid-nineteenth-century America constituted a society utopian in its freedom from "racism," the obstacles to successful reordering of southern society would have been immensely lessened, though European experience suggests that they would not have been completely removed. It does not follow, however, that race prejudice precluded an equality of civil and political rights. Differences in the quality and priority of prejudice, not only between individuals but between the two major parties, provided a significant opening for political action. By the 1860s many northerners who did not find objectionable discrimination against blacks in private and social relationships had come to view an unacceptable discrimination against blacks in public matters. Most of them were Republicans. Prejudices existed among Republicans, but they did not prevent the party from making equal citizenship the law of the land. To explain the breakdown of that law by pointing to the racial bias of Republicans is unconvincing unless one assumes that a commitment to civil and political equality can be met only by men who accept and seek to realize the more far-reaching twentieth-century concept of racial equality, a highly questionable premise.

Neither can it be taken for granted that a racism so strong as to reject an equality of basic rights is impervious to change. There is no question but that racial attitudes affect behavior, but it is also recognized that behavior affects racial attitudes, though more slowly. Furthermore, a belief in racial inferiority or an emotional revulsion against accepting one of a different race as an equal does not necessarily result in discriminatory action. That may be held in check by a whole range of countervailing forces—by self-interest or a common goal, by institutions such as law with courts that enforce the law, by a perception of discrimination as unwarranted because it conflicts with other norms of societal behavior. And the experience gained by foregoing discrimination can result in changed views and changed emotional responses. Even when it does not, nondiscriminatory practices may continue. Logically, equality may be indivisible; in practice, it has never been a seamless web.

Failure to enforce black civil and political rights in the South is often attributed to a lack of will on the part of Republican leaders and their constituencies due to their racial views. The explanation may not be susceptible of definite disproof, but it has not been proven and probably cannot be. Many factors entered into the abandonment of the cause of the black man in the South, and Republicans gave up neither quickly or easily. The voting record of regular Republicans in Congress through 1891 remained remarkably consistent and cohesive behind efforts to strengthen federal enforcement of Reconstruction legislation. Democratic party obstruction was equally consistent and created a major roadblock. Republicans enacted a drastic enforcement law in 1870 and another in 1871. For most of the twenty years after the elections of 1870 they did not have the power in Congress to pass additional legislation supportive of black rights but they kept the issue alive. It is true that as early as 1872 some Republicans, notably those who joined the Liberal Republican movement, broke with the policy of national action in support of black rights. But race prejudice was neither a conscious nor a major determinant of their new attitude toward federal intervention in the South. Indeed, the Liberal Republican platform of 1872 tried to reconcile a policy of national retreat with loyalty to the Reconstruction amendments. When Republicans regained control of both houses of Congress in 1890–1891 by only a narrow margin, they passed in the House an enforcement bill to protect black voters but narrowly lost it in the Senate by the perfidy of a few who broke ranks to gain support for silver legislation. On the local front in the northern states, in keeping with party tradition, the Republican record on black rights remained better than that of their opponents.

In 1877 when President Hayes withdrew federal troops and acquiesced to "home rule" for the South, racism was not the key to presidential decision. No critical causal connection has been established between the "betrayal" and race attitudes. There is no doubt but that Hayes' action was related to a general lessening of northern support for intervention in the South. The erosion had been going on for several years, and for that there were a number of reasons. The will to continue the battle was undermined by growing doubt of the wisdom of immediate universal black enfranchisement, increasingly seen as the source of corruption. There was revulsion against the turmoil of disputed elections and the force used to settle them. Many Republicans were discouraged as state after state came under "Redeemer" control, or distracted by the pressure of problems closer at home. There was a general desire in the North for the peace and national reconciliation that Grant had invoked but could not attain as president. Whatever part race prejudice played in weakening Republican support for continuing military intervention, its role was peripheral rather than central. . . .

Race prejudice played a larger role in the obstructionist tactics of northern Democrats than in weakening the will of Republicans. During and after the Civil War, appeal to the race prejudice of their constituencies was a standard procedure in election battles. Yet when it failed to yield decisive political profit, northern Democratic leaders changed tactics. By the mid-1870s they had retreated from public avowals to overturn Reconstruction. By the 1880s in northern states they were wooing black voters by helping to enact local civil rights laws and by giving blacks recognition in patronage appointments. Prejudice had bowed to political advantage. Within little more than a decade, an equal right to the ballot was accepted and institutionalized in both northern parties. Continuing support by northern Democrats in Congress for their southern colleagues in opposing federal enforcement of the right to vote rested upon party advantage in maintaining solidarity with the Democratic South.

Racism linked to southern resistance was more politically formidable. As events developed after Congress repudiated Johnsonian Reconstruction and prescribed its own plan, the appeal to white prejudice was critically important. It enabled Democrats to recapture political ascendancy and to cripple the projected operational arm of congressional policy, the Republican party in the South, as an effective contestant for political power. To attain victory the "Redeemers" mobilized a racism whose many faces were evident about them—conviction that white superiority and black incapacity were nature's law, revulsion against accepting the black man on an equal basis in any capacity as both distasteful and insulting, umbrage at being confronted with violations of the race etiquette to which whites had been conditioned by slavery. Racial hostility was used to organize and to justify terror, intimidation, and fraud, particularly in election contests but also in more mundane activities when freedom led blacks beyond "their place."

Even so, racism alone does not explain southern intransigence. It was strongly reinforced by other factors—by the psychological need of white southerners to avoid "dishonor" in defeat, by fears of economic chaos and race warfare, by shock and outrage at the congressional peace terms of 1867, by a perception of Republican demand for black civil and political equality as punitive. Increased taxation at a time of economic stress helped inflame emotions. The result was resistance, sometimes open and sometimes covert, often violent but also subtle. A guerrilla warfare outmaneuvered and overwhelmed Republican forces in the South and gave way before federal military force only to regroup and strike again. It was a resistance strengthened by a sense of right in safeguarding a social order in which blacks were subordinate to whites. If racism was a crucial element in the failure to establish securely black civil and political rights, it was not because racial prejudice permeated both sections, both parties, and all classes. It was because prejudice in the South was deeply rooted, intrinsic to the social and economic structure, and effectively mobilized for political combat. To induce a change in southern white racial behavior to the extent of accepting the black man as an equal in the courts and at the ballot box and as a free laborer entitled to choose, to move about, to better his condition—that task was not in theory beyond the power of Congress and president but it was an uncertain undertaking that would have tested the political skill of any party and president. Fortuitous circumstances, both political and economic, may well have precluded success.

Lincoln's assassination changed the direction of presidential policy, and the downward slide of the postbellum cotton economy of the South reinforced white resistance to change.

A critical question needs to be addressed. Could a greater use of force have brought white southerners to accept civil and political rights for blacks? Neither history nor theory can answer this question with certainty. A number of historians have implied that direct coercion could have effected a fundamental change, that Reconstruction was the nation's great missed opportunity. Few would go so far as Eugene Genovese, who has written that there was no prospect of a better future for blacks unless several thousand leaders of the Lost Cause had been summarily killed. Michael Perman would have had the political and economic power of the southern elite eliminated by means less Draconian and more nearly representative of recent historiographic opinion. He suggests an immediate "edict of the conqueror" enforced by occupying troops to exclude the elite from political power, give suffrage to blacks, confiscate plantations, and divide their lands among the freedmen. Far too good an historian to argue that such an edict had been a practical postwar possibility, he nonetheless believes that had it been possible, it would have worked. William Gillette has taken a more historically realistic approach to the problem. Recognizing that Republicans were not in a position to enforce their Reconstruction program until 1869 when they obtained control of the presidency as well as of Congress, he examines closely the southern record of the Grant years. While he comes to the conclusion that Republicans might have succeeded, or at least achieved a great deal, his analysis of the requirements for success is not reassuring. The skill he sees lacking but needed by Grant might have overtaxed even a Lincoln. According to Gillette, Grant should have been cautious where he was bold, bold where he was timid. He had to be both master politician and resolute soldier. The situation required his effective direction of an expert bureaucracy and an overwhelming military muscle, neither of which was at his disposal. Grant should have overpowered militarily southern white resistance yet come to terms with the fact that "in the long run coercion could not replace a sanctioned consensus." Given the nation's traditional commitment to civilian control and majority rule, "the use of force was self-defeating."

Force *and* consent, how to achieve the one by use of the other, posed a dilemma which by the 1870s strained the bounds of the possible. The outcome would have been only a little less problematic had Reconstruction been formulated in early 1865 and backed by force, i.e., by force alone. Particularly vulnerable is the assumption that by eliminating the power of the landed aristocracy, resistance would have been broken and a new order of equal rights for blacks securely established. There would still have remained for the South as a whole a white majority with prejudices and interests inimical to the advancement of blacks. A stunned acceptance in the despondency of defeat of such peace terms as Perman has outlined would have been no guarantee of their permanent observance by white southerners. Here theory is of some help to speculation. It lends support to Gillette's perception of the need to reconcile the seemingly irreconcilable. Historians have tended to approach the concepts of coercion/consent, or conflict/consensus, as coercion vs. consent or conflict vs. consensus, and not without precedent in political and sociological thought. There exist, however, theoretical analyses that see coercion and consensus as compatible, even complementary. They suggest that the problem, both in theory and practice, is one of interrelationship. Even theorists identified with the view that conflict and coercion are essential to the creation of a new and better social order seldom argue that force alone is sufficient to bring about the change desired. Nor do they overlook the danger that coercion can be self-defeating. The more consensus oriented see force as unable to operate alone over any length of time. The concern to identify "authority," to examine the sources of its "legitimacy," to distinguish authority from "power," to establish the noncoercive forms of power and the nonphysical forms of coercion—these continuing efforts indicate the importance attached to means other than direct force in effecting and maintaining social change. And there is a long tradition of political thought that admonishes caution in trying to force change contrary to traditional convictions lest it provoke deep and bitter reaction. From an approach either through theory or history, it would seem reasonable to conclude that a policy of force *plus* some form and degree of consent—even if the consent, to borrow from P. H. Partridge, were only "a patchwork of divergent and loosely adjusted values, norms, and objectives"—would have had a better chance of success in reordering the South than force alone. Lincoln was capable of a "patchwork" design in implementing policy.

Certainly by the mid-1870s the use of coercion had intensified a deep and bitter reaction. Instead of passive resignation, coercion led to a "negative consensus" that rejected the legitimacy of national authority over the status of blacks, fed resistance, and united white southerners to an unprecedented degree. It is well to be reminded that the coercion used had been considerable. Whatever the formality of consent in the ratification of the Fourteenth Amendment, Congress had left the recalcitrant secession states no effective choice. In the initial enfranchisement of blacks, white southerners were allowed not even the formality of consenting; enfranchisement was mandated by Congress and implemented by military authority and presence. The military also intervened in the reorganization of the South's labor system and in the operation of its local courts. The presence of an occupying army preceded the interim period of military rule set up by Congress in 1867 and did not disappear with the restoration of state authority. Violent resistance to the new order was answered not only by the passage of drastic congressional legislation in 1870 and 1871 but also by the use under these laws of federal armed forces, notably in Mississippi, South Carolina, North Carolina, and Alabama. Troops helped make arrests, guarded prisoners, protected court proceedings, and maintained order at the polls. Over a thousand military arrests were made in three counties of South Carolina in 1871–1872. Federal attorneys obtained 540 criminal convictions in Mississippi in 1872–1873 and 263 in North Carolina in 1873. The district attorney for the northern and middle districts of Alabama obtained indictments of more than 350 persons from two grand juries, one in the fall of 1871 and the other in the spring of 1872. From 1870, when the first enforcement law was passed, through 1874, 3,382 cases under the acts were adjudicated in federal courts in the southern states. In addition, under Grant's direction federal troops in effect decided disputes over who rightfully held elective office in Louisiana, Arkansas, and Mississippi.

The force employed in the 1870s was grossly insufficient for the task at hand. Too often local officials and courts sidestepped justice for blacks without interference. Troops stationed in the South were woefully inadequate in number to contain violent resistance wherever it erupted. Relatively few of the men arrested in South Carolina were brought to trial. In general, indictments were difficult to obtain and even in the federal courts many cases were dismissed. By the end of 1874 little vitality was left in the federal enforcement program. Southern resistance turned increasingly to intimidation and more subtle, less legally vulnerable means than the earlier violence. Democratic power in Congress deprived the executive of resources needed to enforce the laws and prevented legislative action to strengthen them.

Nonetheless, the direct coercion mobilized by the national government in the 1860s and 1870s was substantial, far greater than any similar action in support of desegregation and black voting in the 1950s and '60s. It was large enough to give strong support to the contention that a century ago the amount of force necessary to realize equal civil and political rights in the South was impossible to sustain in a nation whose democratic tradition and constitutional structure limited the use of power, exalted the rule of law, and embodied the concept of government by the consent of the governed. Neither national institutions nor public opinion could be expected to have sustained a military intervention of indefinite length and of sufficient strength to crush all local resistance. And by the mid-1870s, the issue at stake no longer appeared clear-cut, even to northern Republicans. Popular government at the South seemed to have become "nothing but a sham."

Assumptions regarding the potency of national power to effect social change, largely valid for the "Second Reconstruction," may inadvertently have biased historical judgment concerning the earlier period. By the 1950s the capacity for resistance in the South, although still strong, was markedly less than in the post–Civil War decades. Race prejudice remained formidable, but in the wake of Hitler's holocaust and advances in the social sciences, psychology, and biology, prejudice could no longer command arguments of scientific or moral respectability. Despite shocking episodes of violence, white terror never reached the epidemic proportions of the 1860s and '70s. Apparently it was no longer condoned by majority white opinion in the South. Moreover, in the 1950s and '60s not Congress but the judiciary took the initiative in forcing change and remained a vital mechanism for implementing it. The aura of legitimacy created by supportive judicial decisions, lacking in the earlier period, greatly lessened the necessity for direct physical coercion. With a few exceptions, notably at Little Rock in 1957, federal enforcement of court decisions and civil rights legislation proceeded without a show of force. Nor were federal criminal prosecutions numerous. A total of only 323 criminal cases were filed by the newly established civil rights division of the Justice Department from 1958 through mid-1972, only a tenth of the number that had been brought by the attorney general's office in the first five years of the 1870s. Other methods of coercion were available, both more effective and more consonant with the traditional primacy of civil over military authority, of persuasion over force. Civil cases initiated or assisted by the Justice Department far outnumbered criminal ones, and the department was active in negotiating voluntary agreements of compliance and in community counseling. With the great increase in the functions undertaken by the federal government to meet the needs of a mature industrial society, there were at hand powerful monetary and administrative sanctions, and a bureaucracy to use them.

In contrast to the 1870s, during the "Second Reconstruction" votes and time were available to pass a whole array of acts, progressively more comprehensive in scope and more resourceful in their enforcement provisions. What made this achievement possible, according to authorities in the field, was the existence of a national consensus. Although it did not encompass majority white opinion in the South, elsewhere it found support in both major parties, quite unlike the situation in the Civil War era when consensus, on a much more limited program of black rights, existed only within the Republican party. Presidential leadership by the second President Johnson, in contrast to that of the first, was exerted to expand civil rights. In the creation of the national consensus of the 1950s blacks themselves played a key role beyond that open to them a century earlier. Their political influence in the North was considerable because of the numbers who had moved out of the South to fill northern labor needs. The distance from slavery allowed their leaders, South as well as North, to operate with formidable resources, skills, and organization and to present a case that could no longer be evaded by a show of scientific or social justification. They made inescapably visible to white America the injustices piled high during the postemancipation decades.

In short, the "Second Reconstruction" is a false model from which to project in retrospect the limits of the possible a century earlier. As an analogy, however, it suggests the need for far more than direct force to attain success. Its loss of momentum by the 1970s also indicates the difficulty of sustaining a national moral purpose, even with a task recognized as unfinished. In November 1971, the United States Commission on Civil Rights wrote "that the American people have grown somewhat weary, that the national sense of injustice, which was the foundation on which the legislative victories of the 1960s were built, has dimmed." And a few years later other informed analysts agreed. They attributed the fuel for the engine of change during the two previous decades in part to the deceptive clarity of the problems seen through the lens of the New Frontier and the New Society. There had been a naive public faith that new programs of government intervention would quickly bear fruit. Results failed to meet expectations. Advance slowed as injustices were reduced to ones less shockingly visible, as moral issues became clouded by the complexity of problems, as economic conditions turned less favorable, and as conflicts of interest intensified. Analysts concluded that the future was not sanguine. The circumstances of the 1960s had been unusually conducive to change and were not apt to be duplicated. . . .

A fatal weakness of Reconstruction, constitutional historians have argued, arose from the constitutional conservatism of Republican lawmakers, particularly their deference to the traditional federal structure embodied in the Constitution. This led them to preserve the primacy of state responsibility for the rights of citizens, thereby denying to the national government effective power to protect the rights of blacks. It has been contended that Reconstruction required "a major constitutional upheaval," that it "could have been effected only by a revolutionary destruction of the states and the substitution of a unitary constitutional system." Part of the argument is unassailable. The new scholarship has demolished the old stereotype of Republican leaders as constitutional revolutionaries. They had, indeed, been waging a war for constitution as well as for nation with every intent of maintaining both. And the concern of Republicans for state and local government was no superficial adulation of the constitution; it was deeply rooted in their commitment to self-government. Yet unlike Democrats who denounced as unconstitutional any amendment to the constitution that enlarged federal authority at the expense of the states, Republicans did not uphold state rights federalism without qualification. They believed that they had found a way to protect freedmen in their new citizenship status by modifying, rather than destroying, the traditional federal structure. . . .

Similarly circumscribed was any potential role for Lincoln in helping shape economic developments to assure freedmen an escape from poverty and dependence. No explanation for the tragic outcome of the postwar decades for black America has been more generally accepted in modern scholarship than that Reconstruction failed because the national government did not provide land for the freedmen. The thesis has been sharply challenged, and the challenge has not been met. The work of historians and economists in exploring afresh the roots of poverty, particularly of black poverty, in the postbellum South afford some relevant perspectives. Between 1974 and 1979 six book-length studies appeared with significant bearing on the problem of black poverty, and others were in progress; conference papers and published articles also reflected the vigor of scholarly interest in the question.

No consensus has developed either as explanation for the continuing dependence and poverty of southern blacks or as an analysis of the potential economic effect of land distribution. However, four of five econometricians who addressed the latter question concluded that grants of land, while desirable and beneficial, would not have solved the predicament of the freedmen and their children. Robert Higgs has written that "historians have no doubt exaggerated the economic impact of such a grant." Gavin Wright holds that "the tenancy systems of the South cannot be assigned primary blame for Southern poverty," that a more equitable distribution of land "would not have produced dramatic improvements in living standards" or "generated sustained progress." In their book, *One Kind of Freedom,* Roger Ransom and Richard Sutch appear to accept what Heman Belz has characterized as the "new orthodoxy" of the historians, but they dramatically qualified that position in a subsequent paper. They argued that confiscation and redistribution would have resulted in little improvement in the postbellum situation, which they characterize as one of economic stagnation and exploitation, unless accompanied by federally funded compensation for landowners thereby providing liquid capital for reinvigorating agriculture and possibly developing manufactures. This retrospective prescription is restrained as compared to the requirements outlined by twentieth-century experts who seek land distribution as an avenue out of rural poverty. They see successful land reform as requiring supplementary government programs providing credit, seed and fertilizer distribution, marketing facilities, rural and feeder transportation, pricing mechanisms affecting both what the farmer buys and what he sells, technical research, and agricultural education.

More than a land program was needed to insure the freedman's economic future. Although areas of land with high fertility prospered, it seems doubtful that income from cotton between the close of the war and the turn of the century, even if equitably distributed, could have sustained much beyond a marginal level of existence for those who worked the cotton fields whether as wage earner, cropper, tenant, or small owner. And the lower South because of its soils and climate, as Julius Rubin has convincingly shown, had no viable alternative to cotton as a commercial crop until the scientific and technological advances of the twentieth century. Nor could nonmarket subsistence farming offer much by way of material reward. The "more" that was needed can be envisaged in retrospect, and was glimpsed by contemporaries, but it is not clear how it could have been achieved. Gavin Wright has concluded that the postbellum South "required either a massive migration away from the region or a massive Southern industrial revolution." Both in the North and the South there was enthusiasm for promoting southern industry, but only the future could reveal how elusive would be that "New South" of ever-renewed expectations. Despite scholarship, new and old, there is no certain explanation of why the South failed to catch up with the North. If historians and economists should agree upon a diagnosis, it is unlikely that they will uncover a remedy that could have been recognized and implemented a century ago. The heritage of slavery most certainly will be part of the diagnosis. It left behind an underdeveloped, overwhelming rural economy tied to the world market and bereft of adequate foundations for rapid economic growth. Recovery and growth had to be attempted in a period of initial crop disasters, of disadvantage for primary products in terms of world trade, and by the mid-1870s of prolonged and recurrent economic crises. There were high hopes for southern industrialization in the 1880s, but the effort substantially failed. With opportunity drastically limited in the South and industry expanding in the North, there was yet no great out-migration of blacks until the twentieth century. The reasons for this also are not altogether clear. Neither the restraints placed on southern agricultural labor by law and custom nor the discrimination blacks faced in the North is sufficient explanation. The ways in which European immigrants blocked black advance deserve further study, as does the attitude of blacks themselves both toward leaving the South and toward the unskilled, menial labor which alone might have afforded them large-scale entry into the northern labor market. . . .

There were limits to the possible. Yet the dismal outcome for southern blacks as the nation entered the twentieth century need not have been as unrelieved as it was in fact. More than a land program, the civil and political rights Republicans established in law, had they been secured in practice, could have mitigated the discrimination that worsened their condition and constricted whatever opportunities might otherwise have existed for escape from poverty. Moreover, the extraordinary effort black men made to vote—and to vote independently in the face of white cajolery, intimidation, and economic pressure—strongly suggests that for the emancipated to cast a ballot was to affirm the reality of freedom and the dignity of black manhood.

The priority Republicans gave to civil and political rights in their fight to establish a meaningful new status for ex-slaves has been too readily discounted by historians. Small landholdings could not have protected blacks from intimidation, or even from many forms of economic coercion. They would not have brought economic power. In the face of overwhelming white opposition, they could not have safeguarded the new equality of civil and political status. Where blacks voted freely, on the other hand, there was always the potential for sharing political power and using it as a means to protect and advance their interests. There is considerable evidence that this did happen. Local officials elected by black votes during the years of Republican control upheld blacks against planters, state legislators repealed Black Codes, shifted the burden of taxation from the poor, granted agriculture laborers a first lien on crops, increased expenditures for education. Eric Foner has concluded that at least in some areas Republican Reconstruction resulted in subtle but significant changes that protected black labor and prevented planters from using the state to bolster their position. Harold D. Woodman's study of state laws affecting agriculture confirms the generalization that a legislative priority of the Redeemer governments was passage of measures to give landowners greater control over the labor force. By the end of the century legal bonds had been so tightened that as prosperity returned to cotton culture neither cropper nor renter but only their employer was in a position to profit. In a study of rural Edgefield County, South Carolina, Vernon Burton has found that black voting made possible real gains in economic position and social status between 1867 and 1877. Howard Rabinowitz's examination of the urban South discloses that Republican city governments brought blacks a greater share of elected and appointed offices, more jobs in construction work, in fire and police departments. And beyond immediate gains, black votes meant support for educational facilities through which blacks could acquire the literacy and skills essential for advancement.

Security for black civil and political rights required acceptance by white southerners. An acquiescence induced by a judicious combination of force and consent needed for its perpetuation reinforcement by self-interest. The most effective vehicle of self-interest would have been a Union-Republican party able to command substantial continuing support from native whites. The Republican party that gained temporary dominance through the congressional legislation of 1867 enfranchising blacks failed to meet the test of substantial white support. Despite a strong white following in a few states, its scalawag component from the start was too limited to offset the opposition's attack on it as the party of the black man and the Yankee. And white participation diminished as appeals to race prejudice and sectional animosity intensified.

The potential for a major second party among southern whites existed in the aftermath of Confederate defeat. The Democratic party was in disarray, discredited for having led the South out of the Union and having lost the war. Old Whig loyalists subsumed by the slavery issue had nonetheless endured; southern unionism had survived in varying degrees from wartime adherence to the Union to reluctant support of the Confederacy. Opposition to Jefferson Davis's leadership and willingness to accept northern peace terms had grown as the hope for southern victory diminished. Such sources of Democratic opposition overlapped with the potential for ready recruits to Union-Republicanism from urban dwellers, from men whose origins had been abroad or in the North, from those whose class or intrasectional interests created hostility to the dominant planter leadership of the Democracy. A "New South" of enterprise and industry presented an attractive vision to many a native son. And there were always those who looked to the loaves and the fishes dispensed from Washington.

Had party recruitment and organization, with full presidential support, begun at the end of hostilities and escaped the period of confusion and bitterness that thinned the ranks of the willing during the conflict between Johnson and Congress, the result could have been promising. Greater white support and the accession of black voters by increments might have eased racial tension and lessened deadly factionalism within the party. Lincoln's political skill and Whig background would certainly have served party-building well, as would the perception of presidential policy as one of moderation and reconciliation. The extent to which southern whites did in fact support the Republican party after 1867 despite its image as Radical, alien, and black-dominated, an image that stigmatized and often ostracized them, suggests the potency of a common goal, or a common enmity, in bridging the chasm between the races.

Even under the guidance of a Lincoln, the building of a permanent biracial major party in the South was by no means assured. A broad enduring coalition of disparate elements would face the necessity of reconciling sharply divergent economic interests. Agricultural workers sought maximum autonomy, more than bare necessities, and an opportunity for land ownership while planter-merchants strove to control labor and maximize profit. The burden of increased taxation to meet essential but unaccustomed social services, particularly for blacks, meant an inescapable clash of class and racial interests. Concessions by the more privileged were especially difficult in a South of limited available resources and credit, impoverished by war and enmeshed in inflated costs, crop disasters, and falling cotton prices. By the mid-1870s a nationwide depression intensified regional problems. Efforts to promote a more varied and vigorous economy by state favor, credit, and appropriation became a political liability as the primary effect appeared to be the proliferation of civic corruption and entrepreneurial plunder.

Outside the South a vigorous Republican party and two-party system managed to endure despite the clash of intraparty economic interests. A similar development in the South faced the additional and more intractable conflict inherent in the new black-white relationship. Within the Republican party that took shape after 1867, factionalism often cut between blacks and carpetbaggers, on the one hand, and scalawags on the other; but there was also a considerable amount of accommodation, not all of it from blacks. A study of the voting record of 87 Republicans, 52 of them native whites, who served in the North Carolina House of Representatives in the 1868 to 1870 session shows scalawags trailing carpetbaggers and blacks in voting on issues of Negro rights and support for public schools, yet compiling a positive overall record, a score of 61.2 and 55.9 respectively. On the few desegregation questions that came to a roll call, however, only a small minority of native whites voted favorably. In Mississippi when the black-carpetbagger faction gained control, they quietly ignored the platform calling for school integration even though black legislators were sufficiently numerous and powerful to have pressed the issue. Black office-holding was a similar matter where fair treatment held danger, and black leaders often showed restraint. Such issues were explosive. They not only threatened the unity of the party but undermined its ability to attract white votes or minimize opposition demagoguery and violence. A Lincolnian approach to building an interracial party would have diminished the racial hazard, but could hardly have eliminated it.

The years of political Reconstruction, to borrow an apt phrase from Thomas B. Alexander's study of Tennessee, offered no "narrowly missed opportunities to leap a century forward in reform." Not even a Lincoln could have wrought such a miracle. To have secured something less, yet something substantially more than blacks had gained by the end of the nineteenth century, did not lie beyond the limits of the possible given a president who at war's end would have joined party in an effort to realize "as nearly as we can" the fullness of freedom for blacks.

SUGGESTIONS FOR FURTHER READING

Howard K. Beale, *The Critical Year: A Study of Andrew Johnson and Reconstruction* (Baton Rouge, La., 1947) and William B. Hesseltine, "Economic Factors in the Abandonment of Reconstruction," *Mississippi Valley Historical Review,* 22 (September 1935), 191–220, argue that Radical Republicans were primarily concerned with efforts to perpetuate Republican political control and to advance the economic interests of the Northern industrialists. Claude G. Bowers, *The Tragic Era: The Revolution After Lincoln* (Boston, 1929) argues that during Reconstruction "the Southern people literally were put to the torture" by a "brutal, hypocritical, and corrupt" leadership in the North. E. Merton Coulter argues along much the same lines in *The South During Reconstruction* (Baton Rouge, La., 1947). The "father" of the antiradical school is William A. Dunning. See, especially, his *Reconstruction, Political and Economic* (New York, 1907).

W. E. B. Du Bois, *Black Reconstruction in America* (New York, 1935) is a vigorous direct attack on the position taken by Dunning and his many students, which dominated work on Reconstruction for a half-century. Where Dunning found only unrelieved corruption and evil in the Radical Republican state governments in the South, Du Bois points to their many accomplishments. Du Bois was the first of those historians who have been termed "revisionists"—that is, those who have sought to revise the uniformly negative picture of Reconstruction painted by Dunning and his followers. But it took a quarter-century before the new interpretation suggested by Du Bois became widely accepted. Among the many important revisionist interpretations are the following: John Hope Franklin, *Reconstruction After the Civil War* (Chicago, 1961); Kenneth M. Stampp, *The Era of Reconstruction* (New York, 1965); James M. McPherson, *The Struggle for Equality: Abolitionists and the Negro in the Civil War and Reconstruction* (Princeton, N.J., 1964); Willie Lee Rose, *Rehearsal for Reconstruction: The Port Royal Experiment* (Indianapolis, 1964); Leon Litwack, *Been in the Storm So Long: The Aftermath of Slavery* (New York, 1979); Michael Perman, *Emancipation and Reconstruction, 1862–1879* (Arlington Heights, Ill., 1987); and Eric Foner, *Reconstruction: America's Unfinished Revolution, 1863–1877* (New York, 1988), a portion of which is reprinted here. These works not only give a more positive picture of radical governments in the South; they also avoid the unconcealed racism in the work of Dunning and many of his students.

---

*Available in paperback edition.

Although C. Vann Woodward's monumental study, *The Origins of the New South, 1877–1913* (Baton Rouge, La., 1951, 1971) deals with the post-Reconstruction years in the South, it offers important insights into the meaning of Reconstruction and has exerted an enormous influence on studies of what may be called economic and social Reconstruction in the South, the effects of emancipation and the postwar settlement on the life and labor of the Southern landlords, the yeomen, and the freed slaves. Woodward argues that the Civil War and emancipation marked a fundamental turning point in Southern history. Woodward writes of "new men" taking control and creating a new South on the ruins of the old. This view, when applied more generally, is in line with the "second American revolution" interpretation of Charles and Mary Beard in Chapter 9 of *Conflict and Consensus in American History,* Volume 1.

Studies that tend to offer support for Woodward's argument include Michael Wayne, *The Reshaping of Plantation Society: The Natchez District, 1860–1880* (Baton Rouge, La., 1983); Ronald L. F. Davis, *Good and Faithful Labor: From Slavery to Sharecropping in the Natchez District, 1860–1890* (Westport, Conn., 1982); Willie Lee Rose, *Slavery and Freedom* (New York, 1982); and Thavolia Glymph and John J. Kushma, eds., *Essays on the Postbellum Southern Economy* (College Station, Tex., 1985).

Other studies tend to disagree with Woodward and see considerable continuity in Southern history although they disagree with one another in substantial ways: Jonathan M. Wiener, *Social Origins of the New South: Alabama, 1860–1885* (Baton Rouge, La., 1978); Jay R. Mandle, *The Roots of Black Poverty* (Durham, N.C., 1978); Roger L. Ransom and Richard Sutch, *One Kind of Freedom* (Cambridge, Eng., 1977); Robert Higgs, *Competition and Coercion* (Cambridge, Eng., 1977); Gerald David Jaynes, *Branches Without Roots: Genesis of the Black Working Class in the American South, 1862–1882* (New York, 1986); and Gavin Wright, *Old South, New South: Revolutions in the Southern Economy Since the Civil War* (New York, 1986). A broader study that emphasizes continuity and includes a valuable discussion of the literature is Carl Degler, *Place over Time: The Continuity of Southern Distinctiveness* (Baton Rouge, La., 1977). J. Morgan Kousser and James M. McPherson, eds., *Region, Race, and Reconstruction: Essays in Honor of C. Vann Woodward* (New York, 1982) contains a number of important essays reflecting the most recent scholarship (the Holt essay reprinted here is taken from this book). The essays are all by Woodward's former students, but not all agree with his emphasis on discontinuity.

In recent years historians have attempted to provide fuller explanations of how the freedpersons understood the meaning of freedom and their efforts to set goals for the future that gave meaning to their perceptions. Important examples of this work are Julie Saville, *The Work of Reconstruction: From Slave to Wage Laborer in South Carolina, 1860–1870* (Cambridge, Eng., 1994) and Barbara Jeanne Fields, *Slavery and Freedom on the Middle Ground: Maryland During the Nineteenth Century* (New Haven, Conn., 1985).

Studies of the life and policies of Andrew Johnson reveal some of the controversy among historians. He has been depicted as a racist who worked to block equal rights for blacks, as a Jacksonian democrat who despised the planter aristocracy as much as he hated the thought of black equality, and as an inept politician who unnecessarily fomented radical opposition. For examples of studies of Johnson, see Eric McKitrick, *Andrew Johnson and Reconstruction* (Chicago, 1960); Hans L. Trefousse, *Andrew Johnson: A Biography* (New York, 1989); and David Warren Bowen, *Andrew Johnson and the Negro* (Knoxville, Tenn., 1989).

The bitter conflicts over Reconstruction policy left little room for moderate middle-of-the-roaders. A recent study that shows the difficulties faced by moderate Southerners attempting to lead the reconstruction of their states immediately after the Civil War is Dan

T. Carter, *When the War Was Over: The Failure of Self-Reconstruction in the South, 1865–1867* (Baton Rouge, La., 1985). The moderate position, Carter argues, could not survive the conflicts generated by the goals and attitudes of blacks, the masses of former Confederates, and the political aims of the Republicans. Political conflicts among radicals, conservatives, and moderates on the national level may be followed in books by Franklin and Stampp noted above and in David Herbert Donald, *The Politics of Reconstruction, 1863–67* (Baton Rouge, La., 1965); Michael Les Benedict, *A Compromise of Principle: Congressional Republicans and Reconstruction, 1865–69* (New York, 1974); and William Gillette, *Retreat from Reconstruction, 1869–1879* (Baton Rouge, La., 1979).

The literature on Reconstruction is enormous and varied. Students who desire to follow changing interpretations or to find books and articles relating to any aspect of the period might look into the following surveys of the historical literature: Bernard A. Weisberger, "The Dark and Bloody Ground of Reconstruction Historiography," *Journal of Southern History,* 25 (November 1959), 427–47; Richard O. Curry, "The Civil War and Reconstruction, 1861–1877: A Critical Overview of Recent Trends and Interpretations," *Civil War History,* 20 (September 1974), 215–28; Eric Foner, "Reconstruction Revisited," *Reviews in American History,* 10 (November 1982), 82–100; and La Wanda Cox, "From Emancipation to Segregation: National Policy and Southern Blacks" and Harold D. Woodman, "Economic Reconstruction and the Rise of the New South, 1865–1900," both in John B. Boles and Evelyn Thomas Nolen, eds., *Interpreting Southern History: Historiographical Essays in Honor of Sanford W. Higginbotham* (Baton Rouge, La., 1987), 199–253 and 254–307.

An outstanding collection of documents from the Freedmen's Bureau papers and other records in the National Archives, along with splendid introductions and bibliographic references, is the series of volumes appearing under the general title *Freedom: A Documentary History of Emancipation, 1861–1867,* edited by Ira Berlin et al. (Cambridge, Eng., 1982, 1985, 1991). Several volumes are already published, and more are under way.

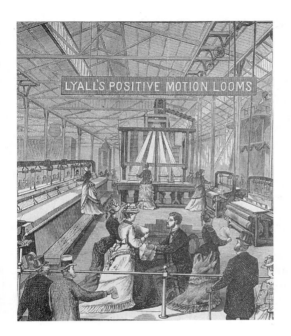

Business in an Industrial Age

Most historians and economists agree that America's industrial revolution—or, to use W. W. Rostow's striking phrase, "the take-off into sustained growth"—began in the early nineteenth century. But it was the massive industrial expansion in the late nineteenth century that transformed the United States into the world's leading industrial power. Older industries such as textiles and meat packing expanded, and new industries such as oil, electricity, steel, and automobile manufacturing began and grew into giants by the early decades of the twentieth century. Industrialism became more pervasive, spreading from the Northeast to the Midwest and beyond. Heavy industry became more important, as measured by the value of its products and by the number of workers employed. Although many small firms remained, large-scale production dominated in most areas of manufacturing.

The results were profound. Developments in one area had what economists call "linkages"; that is, they produced changes in other areas. Large manufacturers' voracious appetites for raw materials stimulated the growth of mining, the drilling of oil, the output of farms, and the exploitation of timber and other natural resources. The capital needs of large firms fostered the expansion of banking and security markets in which large firms bought and sold stocks and bonds and financed the expansion of old companies and the creation of new companies. Giant firms required skilled leadership and a disciplined and efficient working class, resulting in the expansion of educational institutions and changes in factory organization. Supplying manufacturers with the necessary raw materials and distributing their output necessitated the expansion of facilities for transportation, warehousing, and wholesaling. And, finally, selling the growing array of consumers' goods, increasingly under brand names, brought the growth of large retailing chains and an expansion of the advertising business and of inexpensive, large circulation newspapers and magazines financed by such advertising.

As the output of goods and services soared, many Americans celebrated their nation's growing industrial might and the endless variety of goods available to them in the stores and in mail-order catalogs from Sears, Roebuck; Montgomery Ward; and other firms. Americans began to proclaim their high standard of living, which they measured by the availability of goods and services, and they proudly compared American standards with those of other, less fortunate nations.

But some Americans were less enthusiastic. They pointed to serious problems created by the nation's industrial expansion. Smaller firms found it increasingly difficult to compete with the larger, richer, and more highly mechanized firms. Thousands of small businesses went bankrupt or were absorbed into the larger firms. In industry after industry, monopoly or oligopoly (control by a very few firms) seemed to be replacing competition. A relatively few men, the leaders of the new industrial and financial empires, seemed to be dominating American life by controlling output, prices, wages, and working conditions; and their wealth allowed them to exert undemocratic influence on politics.

Critics complained of corruption and venality in public and private life and traced the cause to the materialism of the business classes. "Society, in these states, is canker'd, crude, superstitious, and rotten," charged Walt Whitman in his "Democratic Vistas." He decried the "depravity of the business classes" and the "corruption, bribery, falsehood, maladministration" in government on all levels. In 1873 Mark Twain and Charles D. Warner published a long and rambling novel in which they described corruption and decay behind the glittering facade of progress, a novel aptly entitled *The Gilded Age.*

For such critics, the period was one of conflict. Rapacious business leaders, often termed "robber barons," supported by a corrupt government, enriched themselves at the expense of less fortunate businessmen and of the public at large. The results were high prices, shoddy merchandise, poor service, and the rule of a business elite that ignored the well-being of the people.

Others deny that this is an accurate portrayal of the age of industrial expansion. They call the business leaders "industrial statesmen," energetic leaders who were innovators, organizers, and risk takers with the foresight, the talent, and the courage necessary to industrialize the nation. They invested their money and their talents in the organization of modern enterprise, always seeking new methods to expand production, to lower costs, and to make more goods and services available to the people. Although these men were motivated by a desire for wealth and power, the net result of their efforts was substantial progress for the entire nation. In a word, then, there was no basic conflict between the aims and methods of the business community and the needs and desires of the entire nation.

Some of these differences are illustrated in the selections that follow. In assessing the different interpretations, readers should note that, at least in part, the historians pose different questions and therefore arrive at different answers. Is the question raised one of morality, that is, the ethical behavior of the industrialists? Or is the most important problem an assessment of efficiency and organization? Is it possible to condemn the industrialists as robber barons while commending them for being innovators and leaders who provided the American people with more and better goods and therefore with a higher standard of living? Do critics accept the value of industrial expansion but condemn the ways in which it occurred? Or do critics question the benefits of large-scale industrial growth because of the social costs it entailed?

In the first selection, Alan Trachtenberg describes the ambivalent response to the growing mechanization of production in the late nineteenth century. The machine seemed to represent progress, but at the same time it appeared menacing. It promised increasing prosperity and well-being for all, but it also brought hard times, wretched working conditions, and violent labor upheavals. However, critics and supporters alike agreed that the mechanization of production was inevitable and unstoppable. Therefore, Trachtenberg concludes, the changes brought by mechanization of production required adaptation, the creation of a new consensus.

In the second selection, Matthew Josephson discusses John D. Rockefeller and the Standard Oil Company, which he organized and led. For Josephson, industrialists such as Rockefeller were robber barons. Granting the ability and energy of men such as Rockefeller, Josephson finds them often to have been ruthless exploiters who brought hardship and difficulty to many. Any positive contributions they made were merely inadvertent by-products of their greedy and predatory quest for wealth and power.

Alfred D. Chandler, Jr., in the final selection, approaches the rise of big business in a very different way. He does not discuss the morality of the tactics used by business leaders. Instead, he considers how such leaders recognized and seized opportunities to expand their enterprises by moving into distribution and by consolidating with competitors. If their goal was higher profits, the achievement of that goal meant increased efficiency, expanded output at lower costs, and, therefore, more and cheaper goods for consumers.

Interpretations of the growth of big business often raise the question of morality. Are business leaders to be condemned for their moral lapses, for their greed, their unfair and often violent tactics? If so, is it possible to criticize them on these grounds and find other classes in society less guilty?

Perhaps the moral question is not the most important one to ask. Perhaps we would do better to judge the industrialists by their contribution to the economic growth and well-being of the nation, that is, not by the means they adopted but by the ends they achieved. This approach raises a wide range of different questions: Was *big* business essential for the great industrial expansion in the nation? Did the development of monopolies and oligopolies help or hinder economic development? Did the unrestrained activities of the big business leaders create more problems than they solved?

As we shall see in later chapters, some reformers insisted that big business, by restraining competition, slowed economic growth and put too much power in the hands of a few. Other reformers, however, insisted that although bigness was essential for efficiency, the power of businessmen had to be restrained by government regulation. They argued, in other words, that it was possible to have the advantages of big business without suffering from all of the negative consequences.

Some critics refused to accept the assumption that large-scale industrial production was good because it provided an increasing array of goods and services for the people. These critics insist that big business created a crass, materialistic culture that undermined traditional American ways. They argued that a good life, a high standard of living, is better measured by the *quality* of life than by the *quantity* of goods available. Do you agree or disagree with this assessment?

ALAN TRACHTENBERG

Mechanization Takes Command

I

Even before the Civil War, the westward trails were destined to be lined with tracks; the pony express and the covered wagon, like the mounted Plains Indian, would yield to the Iron Horse. For if the West of "myth and symbol," in Henry Nash Smith's apt terms, provided one perspective by which Americans might view their society, the machine provided another. The two images fused into a single picture of a progressive civilization fulfilling a providential mission. As John Kasson has shown, many Americans before the Civil War believed that industrial technology and the factory system would serve as historic instruments of republican values, diffusing civic virtue and enlightenment along with material wealth. Factories, railroads, and telegraph wires seemed the very engines of a democratic future. Ritual celebrations of machinery and fervently optimistic prophecies of abundance continued throughout the Gilded Age, notably at the two great international expositions, in Philadelphia in 1876 and in Chicago in 1893.

The image of the machine, like the image of the West, proved to be a complex symbol, increasingly charged with contradictory meanings and implications. If the machine seemed the prime cause of the abundance of new products changing the character of daily life, it also seemed responsible for newly visible poverty, slums, and an unexpected wretchedness of industrial conditions. While it inspired confidence in some quarters, it also provoked dismay, often arousing hope and gloom in the same minds. For, accompanying the mechanization of industry, of transportation, and of daily existence, were the most severe contrasts yet visible in American society, contrasts between "progress and poverty" (in Henry

George's words), which seemed to many a mockery of the republican dream, a haunting paradox. Each act of national celebration seemed to evoke its opposite. The 1877 railroad strike, the first instance of machine smashing and class violence on a national scale, followed the 1876 Centennial Exposition, and the even fiercer Pullman strike of 1894 came fast on the heels of the World's Columbian Exposition of 1893.

It is no wonder that closer examination of popular celebrations discloses bewilderment and fear. In fiction and poetry, as Leo Marx has shown in his seminal *Machine in the Garden* (1964), serious writers before the Civil War had fastened on the image of a mechanical intrusion on a pastoral setting as a characteristic expression of a deeply troubled society. In the language of literature, a machine (railroad or steamship) bursting on a peaceful natural setting represented a symbolic version of the trauma inflicted on American society by unexpectedly rapid mechanization. The popular mode of celebration covered over all signs of trauma with expressions of confidence and fulsome praise. But confidence proved difficult to sustain in the face of the evidence.

Current events instilled doubt at the very site of celebration. A period of great economic growth, of steadily rising per capita wealth, and new urban markets feeding an expanding industrial plant, the Gilded Age was also wracked with persisting crises. An international "great depression" from 1873 to 1896 afflicted all industrial nations with chronic overproduction and dramatically falling prices, averaging one-third on all commodities. "It was," writes David Landes, "the most drastic deflation in the memory of man." A severe Wall Street crash in 1873 triggered a round of bankruptcies and failures in the United States, six thousand businesses closing in 1874 alone, and as many as nine hundred a month folding in 1878. A perilously uneven business cycle continued for more than twenty years, affecting all sections of the economy: constant market uncertainties and stiffening competition at home and abroad for business; inexplicable surpluses and declining world prices, together with tightening credit for farmers; wage cuts, extended layoffs and irregular employment, and worsening conditions, even starvation, for industrial workers. Recurrent cycles of boom and collapse seemed as inexorable as the quickening pace of technological innovation. Thus, even in the shadow of glorious new machines displayed at the fairs, the public sense of crisis deepened.

No wonder modern machinery struck observers, especially those associated with the business community, as in Charles Francis Adams, Jr.'s words, "an incalculable force." The tempo of crisis accelerated in the 1870's. Farmers agitated through Granger clubs and the Greenback Party against the government's policy of supporting business through deflationary hard money and the gold standard. Industrial unrest reached a climax and a momentary catharsis in July 1877, when fears of a new civil war spread across the country during the great railroad strike. Provoked by a 10 percent wage cut announced without warning by the Baltimore and Ohio line, a measure to halt a declining rate of profit, the strike spread like wildfire to other lines, reaching from Baltimore to Pittsburgh, Chicago, St. Louis, Kansas City, and San Francisco. The apparently spontaneous work stoppages met with approval and support from local merchants, farmers, clergy, and politicians, tapping reserves of anger and wrath against the railroad companies. Workers in other industries joined the walkout, and for a short spell it seemed that the United States faced a mass rebellion, a recurrence of the Paris Commune of 1871 on an even vaster scale. In some communities (St. Louis, for example) committees of strikers briefly assumed control of government and railroad services.

The strike turned bloody and destructive, arousing a vehemence of response from big business and the national government even surpassing the wrath vented by strikers against railroad yards and equipment. The companies recruited local police and militia to protect their property, and pitched battles raged along the lines, although many militiamen refused to fire on the strikers, among whom they recognized relatives and friends. Finally, the newly inaugurated President, Rutherford Hayes, invoked his powers of military intervention and called out federal troops to protect "by force" (as he noted in his diary) the property of the railroad companies, among whose leaders he counted many of his closest friends and supporters. In the end, the strike left more than a hundred dead, millions of dollars of property destroyed, and a toughened company and government stand against unions. Strikers were very often fired and blacklisted, their leaders fined and jailed. The War Department issued a pamphlet on "riot duty" and constructed for the first time a system of armories in major cities to house a standing "national guard." Industrialization of the state's military force seemed a necessary adjunct to the mechanization of production.

The very extremes of effect lent to the machine an aura of supreme power, as if it were an autonomous force that held human society in its grip. In *The First Century of the Republic*, a book of essays published by *Harper's* magazine in celebration of the nation's centennial in 1876, the economist David Wells observed that "like one of our mighty rivers," mechanization was "beyond control." And indeed the display in Machinery Hall in Philadelphia that summer gave credence to the image of a flood, though without Wells's ominous note. Here, in an exposition of machines removed from their working location, a profusion of mechanisms seduced the eye: power looms, lathes, sewing machines, presses, pumps, toolmaking machines, axles, shafts, wire cables, and locomotives. The Remington Arms Company, declaring its versatility, displayed one of its newest products: Christopher Schole's new "typewriter," an astonishing device for producing neat, legible messages at the touch of a finger. The twenty-nine-year-old Thomas A. Edison, already the wunderkind of invention, disclosed his "multiplex" telegraph, capable of carrying several messages on the same slender wire. And, most memorably, Alexander Graham Bell here gave the world first notice of the greatest wonder of electrical communication: the telephone. For sheer grandeur and sublimity, however, the mechanisms of communication could not compete with the two most imposing structures in the Hall: the thirty-foot-high Corliss Double Walking-Beam Steam Engine, which powered the entire ensemble from a single source, and its counterpart, a 7,000-pound electrical pendulum clock which governed, to the second, twenty-six lesser "slave" clocks around the building. Unstinted but channeled power and precisely regulated time: that combination seemed to hold the secret of progress. . . .

II

The idea of an autonomous and omnipotent machine, brooking no resistance against its untold and ineluctable powers, became an article of faith. The image implied a popular social theory: the machine as a "human benefactor," a "great emancipator of man from the bondage of labor." Modern technology was mankind's "civilizing force," driving out superstition, poverty, ignorance. "Better morals, better sanitary conditions, better health, better wages," wrote Carroll D. Wright, chief of the Massachusetts Bureau of Statistics of Labor, in 1882; "these are the practical results of the factory system, as compared with what preceded it, and the results of all these have been a keener intelligence." Wright's paper, originally given as an address before the American Social Science Association, bore the title "The Factory System as an Element in Civilization."

The events of the 1870's and 1880's, however, also elicited less sanguine accounts of what the factory system had wrought. Even Wright adopted a defensive tone, warning against the seductive "poetry" and "idyllic sentiment" of many critics: "I am well aware that I speak against popular impression, and largely against popular sentiment when I assert that the factory system in every respect is vastly superior as an element in civilization to the domestic system which preceded it." Wright failed to acknowledge, however, that his account of the superior benefits of the system did not include the opportunity of workers to change their status within it; his defense assumes a permanent class of wage earners, a prospect abhorrent to believers in republican enlightenment and progress. Not surprisingly, a growing number of Americans openly questioned whether industrialization was in fact, in Henry George's words, "an unmixed good." As if in pointed rebuke of Wright's arguments and images, George observed the following year, in *Social Problems* (1883), that so-called labor-saving inventions, the "greater employment of machinery," and "greater division of labor," result in "positive evils" for the working masses, "degrading men into the position of mere feeders of machines." Machines employed in production under the present system are "absolutely injurious," "rendering the workman more dependent; depriving him of skill and of opportunities to acquire it; lessening his control over his own condition and his hope of improving it; cramping his mind, and in many cases distorting and enervating his body." True, George found the source of such evils not in machines themselves but in unjust concentrations of land ownership. In the end, he shared Wright's vision of the potential benefits of machinery, though not his conception of a permanent class of "operatives." George plainly perceived the process of degradation in factory labor as strictly mechanical, experienced as an *effect* of machinery. To a wider public than Wright had addressed, George's views seemed irrefutable. . . .

III

If Americans seemed especially intense in their response to mechanization, especially obsessed with alternating images of mechanical plenitude and devastation, an explanation lies in the special circumstances of native industrialization, its speed, its scale, its thoroughness within a brief period. Suffering fewer social barriers, possessing the largest domestic region convertible to a national market without internal restriction, by the end of the century American industry rapidly surpassed its chief European rivals, England and Germany. Figures of absolute increase signified the triumph: the production of raw steel rising from 13 thousand tons in 1860 to near 5 million in 1890, and of steel rails multiplying ten times in the same years; total agricultural output tripling between 1870 and 1900. Agriculture showed the most dramatic and immediate evidence. A single mechanized farmer in 1896 was able to reap more wheat than eighteen men working with horses and hand equipment sixty years earlier. As output increased, more land came under cultivation (increasing almost fivefold between 1850 and 1900, from about 15 to 37 percent of the total area of the country), and the proportion of the agricultural work force (including owners, tenants, and managers) declined precipitously from its height of 44 percent in 1880. In the critical decade of the 1880's, the balance began its historic shift in favor of nonfarm labor; heavy Northern investment, in machines to produce cash crops such as cotton, tobacco, grain, and cattle (their steep profits flowing as capital into industrial expansion), stimulated this process of displacement into crowded cities already bursting with rural immigrants from overseas.

But such figures of expansion tell only the outside story. The inner story concerned not only absolute increase but a revolutionary rise in *productivity*. "We have increased the power of production with a given amount of personal effort throughout the country," observed David Wells in 1885, "probably at least twenty-five, and possibly forty percent." In such figures the American propensity for mechanical improvement seemed to bear its most impressive fruit.

Of course, that propensity characterized the entire industrial world, but it had been a special mark of American manufacturing since its beginnings. With a scarcity of skilled labor, of craftsmen and artisans with accumulated experience in nascent industrial processes such as spinning, weaving, and milling, American circumstances placed a premium on mechanical invention and improvement. Scarcity of skills together with cheapness of land had maintained a relatively high cost of labor in the young United States. Moreover, as H. J. Habakkuk has explained, the relative absence of customary work processes and of formal engineering and scientific academies provided incentives for invention, for the devising of machines and techniques to compensate for labor scarcity. Without an inherited aristocratic social order, the new country held out more hope to entrepreneurs for social acceptance as well as material rewards. Many early industrial entrepreneurs had begun their working lives as craftsmen, mechanics with a knack for invention, and had risen to wealth and status as a result of their mechanical skill and entrepreneurial expertise. With mechanical efficiency a greater economic need in the United States than in Europe, and with business a freer field of endeavor, American inventor-manufacturers such as Eli Whitney and Elias Howe developed and refined the practice of interchangeable parts (originally in the making of small arms) considerably before their European counterparts. By the 1850's, the practical Yankee inventor-entrepreneur, the tinkerer with an eye on profit, had come to seem an American type, proof of the republican principle that self-taught men of skill and ingenuity might rise to wealth and social position.

The prominence of mechanical skill made it seem to many that the dramatic increases in productivity during the years of explosive growth after the Civil War arose from the logic of invention, of mechanical improvement itself. But new economic conditions in fact marked a radical discontinuity with the past difficult for many Americans to grasp. The new breed of business leaders were often skilled in finance, in market manipulation, in corporate organization: entrepreneurial skills on a scale unimaginable to most manufacturers before the war. Moreover, they conducted their daily business through a growing system of managers, accountants, supervisors, lawyers: a burgeoning structure of business offices increasingly removed from the machines and labor in the factory itself. The process of invention and technological change lay increasingly in the hands of university-trained engineers and applied scientists, representing an entire new institutional formation which had mushroomed during and after the war. And industrial laborers now tended to be men and women without traditional skills, operators and machine tenders, with little hope of significant social improvement through their own talents and efforts. In short, the increasingly rigid social stratification that accompanied the dramatic rise in industrial productivity confused, angered, and frustrated masses of Americans, a growing percentage of them recent immigrants recruited into the very industrial system which seemed destined to dash their hopes of social improvement.

Technological determinism implied that machines demanded their own improvement, that they controlled the forms of production and drove their owners and workers. Americans were taught to view their machines as independent agencies of power, causes of "progress." Machines seemed fixed in shape, definite self-propelled objects in space. In fact, however, machinery underwent constant change in appearance, in function, in design. Machines were working parts of a dynamic system. And the motives for change, the source of industrial dynamism, lay not in the inanimate machine but in the economic necessities perceived by its owners. Higher rates of productivity through economies of scale and velocity, through greater exploitation of machinery and reorganization of both factory labor and corporate structures, were deliberate goals chosen by business leaders out of economic need. "Goaded by necessity and spurred by the prospect of higher returns," as David Landes writes, industrialists undertook a concerted quest for higher productivity. That quest proved the inner engine of mechanization. . . .

In these years the mighty river of industrial expansion threatened to take dominion everywhere, converting all labor to mechanical labor, to the production of commodities for distant markets. The spread of the machine meant the spread of the market: more of the continent and the society brought under the domain of political economy and its unconscious logic Wells explicated so vividly. Along with regional and local autonomy, age-old notions of space and time felt the impact of mechanization as a violent wrenching of the familiar. As more efficient machine production required greater attention to uniform parts and units of measurement, standardization of basic perceptions infiltrated the society. And the chief agent of such cultural changes was, of course, the most conspicuous machine of the age: the steam-driven locomotive, with its train of cars.

It is not difficult to account for the prominence of the railroad as the age's symbol of mechanization and of economic and political change. Railroad companies were the earliest giant corporations, the field of enterprise in which first appeared a new breed of men—the Cookes, Stanfords, Huntingtons, and Hills—of unprecedented personal wealth and untrammeled power. Not only did the railroad system make modern technology visible, intruding it as a physical presence in daily life, but it also offered means of exercising unexampled ruthlessness of economic power. In railroad monopolies, combinations, conspiracies to set rates and control traffic, lobbies to bribe public officials and buy legislatures, the nation had its first taste of robber barons on a grand scale.

At the same time the railroad system provided the age with fundamental lessons in physical and economic coordination. Its physical plant in these years represented the very best mechanical invention and improvement: greater load-bearing capabilities, higher speeds, and longer trains, following from air brakes, automatic couplers, block-signaling apparatus, standard-gauge tracks. Although often overcapitalized in the 1860's (through "watered stock," a favorite device of Wall Street speculators), the railroad system expanded into several national networks, providing major stimulation to basic industries like steel, construction, and machine making. In its corporate organization the system stressed coordination and interdependence, the railroad companies being the first to rationalize their business offices into central- and regional-sales, freight, passenger, and legal divisions. Resolutely private entities, even though they thrived on outlays of public funds and privileges through government agencies, the companies organized themselves along strict military lines; indeed, former Civil War generals often served as presidents and directors of operations. They emerged by the 1870's as competing private structures employing hundreds of thousands of citizens as managers, civil and mechanical engineers, lawyers, firemen and conductors, yard and gang laborers. Models of a new corporate world, they seemed the epitome of the modern machine.

Their prominence in America also followed from unique geographical conditions: the vast spaces to be traversed as cheap land, before the Civil War, encouraged far-flung settlements. As George Taylor has shown, a revolution in transportation proved necessary before "the almost explosive rush of industrial expansion which characterized the later decades of the century." Unlike the European situation, where mechanized transport appropriated existing roads and horse tracks as it overturned an older society and culture, here the railroad seemed to "open" places for settlement, for raw materials and transport to markets. As Wolfgang Schivelbusch observes about the American difference: "The mechanization of transport is not seen, as in Europe, as the destruction of a traditional culture, but as a means to gaining a new civilization from a hitherto worthless (because inaccessible) wilderness." The American railroad seemed to create new spaces, new regions of comprehension and economic value, and finally to incorporate a prehistoric geological terrain into historical time.

The exact economic value of this massive process has been a matter of some controversy among economic historians, Robert Fogel arguing that the "net benefit" of the displacement of the canal system by the railroad being "much less than is usually presumed." But there is no doubt that the railroad "increased the *economic accessibility*" of raw material. The railroads proved decisive in this area in facilitating that "interchange of matter" from one location to another (as

Karl Marx put it), essential to industrial production. This change of location of raw materials and then of goods represented a radical breaking of spatial barriers, barriers of local and regional terrain and cultural difference. Thus, the external economy provided by the railroad in its increased velocity of transport included the incorporation of space and time as factors among the elements of production: the necessary act of overcoming barriers, of virtually annihilating space or distance by reconceiving it as time (places becoming identified as scheduled moments of departure and arrival), emerging as the major capital industry in the age of steam.

The necessity of pushing aside old concepts asserted itself especially in the establishment of standard time zones in 1883. Until that year, "local mean time" ruled across the continent, as it did throughout the world. Each locale assumed responsibility for setting its own time by tested methods of solar readings. Bells and clocks struck noon, for example, when the sun stood directly overhead: never exactly the same moment from place to place or week to week. Local life arranged itself in relation to the most influential community timepieces: church bells and steeple clocks, and after the 1840's, the cupolas and stark brick bell towers of mills and factories. The latter testified to a new importance assigned to time by the factory system, to promptness, regularity of work habits, and most of all, to the conversion of work into time-wages occurring within factory walls. But stubborn local standards persisted, and overlappings of regional times set by the larger cities and local times in the hinterlands formed a crazy-quilt pattern across the nation.

The necessity of regulating times appeared with the railroad; especially after the first transcontinental hookup in 1869, the situation seemed increasingly eccentric, to the point of danger and economic loss. Obviously, a railroad passing from New York to Chicago could not adjust itself to the dozens of local times different from each other by fractions of minutes (11 minutes 45 seconds, between Boston and New York, for example). Railroad corporations set their own times. By early 1883, there were about fifty such distinct private universes of time, each streaming on wheels through the countryside, oblivious of the others. Railroad stations, which quickly became the most influential source of time in the larger cities, often displayed several clocks, each indicating the time on specific lines, and one declaring the presumed local time.

The issue came to a head in these years: not coincidentally, years of increasingly destructive competition in which the smallest factors of technical innovation in production or distribution might make the difference between success and failure. It seemed in everyone's interest to eliminate the disadvantage of eccentric time. The American Society of Civil Engineers joined with the American Association for the Advancement of Science and similar groups to give the approval of science to standard time zones. In 1882 the engineers reported: "Mistakes in the hour of the day are frequent. In every city or town, in every State, discrepancies are met which produce great aggregate inconvenience. Thousands of engagements are broken. Innumerable disappointments and losses result." In 1883 the railroads acted and, by joint decision, placed the country—without act of Congress, President, or the courts—under a scheme of four "standard time zones." This, of course, was "railroad time." Most communities adjusted their clocks at the railroad's behest (Chicago held out for a brief spell), and where local time did not immediately fall before the rush of the industrial machine, it remained only as a kind of twitch of residual "nervousness." . . .

IV

In the quest for greater productivity, more efficient machines, more output per unit of cost, calculation of several kinds played an increasingly significant role. With the enlarged role of the accounting office in decisions relevant to materials and labor, transportation, advertising, and sales, mathematical considerations entered the business world in a major way. At an opposite pole to commerce, another kind of abstract calculation appeared in an enlarged and more systematic role for science, for basic research as well as applied science and engineering. Professional, white-collar personnel expanded the size and influence of office and laboratory, both increasingly distant from the shop floor but increasingly pertinent to the daily arrangements and pace of factory life. Calculations of economy and of science developed into professional processes with their own skills and rules, but in the end their effects were felt in the changing relations between human labor and machines, in the steady encroachment of mechanization on the forms of work, of everyday life, and social transactions throughout America.

The enhanced importance of refined and reliable calculations implied a position of new significance for knowledge, a critical role for trained abstract thought within the productive system. This development appeared in an intricate process of institutional change: the appearance of new schools, of new relations between formal education and corporate industries, and greater accessibility of science to industry. Events in the 1870's and 1880's prepared the way for the turn-of-the-century research laboratory as an integral component of the electrical and chemical industries. The role of scientific method and knowledge within industries expanded, however, not primarily from schools and laboratories themselves, but from new perceptions on the part of industrial managers of the advantages of scientific calculation in their quest for greater productivity, a quest itself spurred by more systematic and rationalized methods of economic calculation.

The incorporation of basic science and formal technological training with industrial production quickened dramatically during these decades of economic uncertainty. During the earlier stages of industrialization, science and technology had seemed wholly separate and often antagonistic fields, theoretical scientists (often gentlemen amateurs) holding themselves aloof from either direct mechanical application or entrepreneurship. Even as late as the early nineteenth century, craftsmen-inventors such as Elias Howe and Oliver Evans ruled over technological innovation, using an on-the-job cut-and-try technique of experimentation. Such figures predominated especially in America, where formal science bore the onus of impracticality and remoteness from human need. In fact, however, practical innovators were less ignorant and disdainful of basic principles than the popular notion recognized, and trained university scientists, particularly geologists, served as consultants for mining and railroad companies even before the Civil War. Even as the image of the self-taught cut-and-try inventor remained uppermost in popular thought as more distinctly American than the "gentleman scientist" or pure experimentalist, the currents began to converge. Graduate programs in science developed at major universities, and specialized schools of engineering supported by private funds, such as Massachusetts Institute of Technology (1866), proliferated; by 1900, the list of technical institutes included Case, Carnegie, Stevens, and Worcester Polytechnical Institute. With their close ties to private industries, their willingness to design their curricula to meet industrial needs, such schools fostered specialization of functions, a process reflected in the new professional societies splitting off from the original American Society of Civil Engineers (founded in 1852): mining, mechanical, electrical, and naval engineers all forming distinct societies with their own journals and meetings in these years.

Engineering thus transformed itself from its earlier empiricism and artisanship in order to mediate the vast structural changes in mechanical production compelled by economic need. "The artisan was replaced in the vanguard of technological progress by a new breed," writes Edwin Layton. "In place of oral traditions passed from master to apprentice, the new technologist substituted a college education, a professional organization, and a technical literature patterned on that of science." The schools, the professional societies, the new roles of responsibility within corporate hierarchies, fostered a new quality of mind and outlook: disciplined, systematic, administrative. Trained to combine the findings of formal science with economic, legal, and logistical considerations, the new engineers brought into industry an apparently detached, objective, and highly specialized approach to solving problems. But whether designing the flow of work in factories or rating the output of machines, the engineer served finally a chronic need of the industrial system: to impose system and order, through improved machinery, for the sake of assuring a reliable return on investments. As David Noble has argued, the new institutional ties between engineering and industry served that need of capitalists, more dire in time of crisis, "routinely to anticipate the future in order to survive."

The consequences were felt throughout the society and culture: most notably in the increasing specialization of knowledge, its fragmentation into arcane regions of technique and learning, and in the growing concentration of the power accompanying specialized knowledge and skills within private corporations. In the 1870's and 1880's, however, this process remained fairly hidden from view. With public attention focused on severe economic fluctuations, rising tensions between capital and labor, and the colorful if morally dubious lives of captains of industry, the steady incorporation of institutionalized rationality into the system went generally unnoticed. Moreover, persisting popular images of business success through self-help, luck and pluck, and venturesome risk taking, left little room for the concept of controlled and systematic anticipation of the future.

It remained a common belief that the system owed its dynamism and innovations to the personal "genius" of prominent individuals like Thomas A. Edison. One of the most popular Americans of his own time and since, Edison in his public guise represented a form of knowledge starkly at odds with new realities; indeed, at odds even with the truth about his own activities. Like the image of the isolated machine with its alternating demonic and Promethean currents, popular perceptions of Edison distorted the underlying logic of events, making "progress" seem both more accidental and more innocent.

Already renowned by the 1876 exposition for his multiflex telegraph, his improved ticker tape, his many patented devices, and his success as a manufacturer of his own stock-quotation printer, Edison rose to genuine fame with the invention of the phonograph in 1877 (he was then thirty years old). With his talking machine and, in 1879, the electric light bulb, Edison attracted perhaps the widest attention of the age in the press, journals, and popular books. In these years, the Edison legend took shape: the stories of his childhood experiments in rural Ohio with chemistry and electricity, his exploits as a trainboy on the Grand Trunk Railroad of Canada and Central Michigan, the newspaper he published on board the train, his self-taught mastery of mechanics and electricity, his years of study, wandering, working at odd jobs, until his arrival in New York in 1868 and his invention of a stock-quotation printer which won the attention of Western Union and launched his career. The periodical literature stressed two key elements of Edison's success: his natural genius, flourishing without formal school training, and his instinctual entrepreneurship which led him unerringly to *useful,* that is to say, marketable, inventions. Thus, the public Edison seemed to embody in perfect combination precisely what many at the time felt America to be losing, its rural Protestant virtues of the self-made man, and what it was gaining in the way of material improvements. Edison seemed to hold together the old and new, the world of the tinkerer and the world of modern industry; the age of steam (his youth on the railroad) and the coming age of electricity. He made the new America of cities and complicated machinery seem to evolve in an orderly fashion from the old America of country towns and youthful high jinks on country railroads.

As a form of popular knowledge and a version of the new industrial realities, the most critical feature of the Edison image concerned the origins of invention. In 1876, Edison had sold his manufacturing business in Newark and withdrew with a small group of helpers to Menlo Park, a quiet New Jersey town about an hour by railroad from New York, where he established the first significant industrial-research laboratory in America. After five years he moved to larger, better-equipped buildings in Orange, New Jersey, but the period at Menlo Park from 1876 to 1881 proved the most fertile of his career, yielding the most dramatic products of his labors: the phonograph, the improved telephone, the incandescent lamp, and the basic elements of a central power-generating system. It was during these years, too, that Edison assumed his best-known role, as "Wizard of Menlo Park." And in their accounts of the wizard, popular stories in the press and journals portrayed a character part Prometheus, bringing light, and part Faust, tainted with satanic association. The setting itself—the mysterious fire-lit laboratories in wooden buildings within a peaceful rural landscape—enhanced the demonic aura. But demonism was no more than a whiff, dissolved by descriptions of the guileless, open-faced, wry and salty Midwestern boy-man Edison turned out to be. Instead, the wizard image served another primary function: to account for the origins of Edison's inventions as personal "genius," out of the thin air of a fertile imagination and heroic persistence. "His inventions were calling to him with a sort of siren voice," wrote *Scribner's* in 1879. Moreover, as wizard and natural genius, Edison had no need of formal science, of mathematics and theory; the press played up his superiority to the schools, which on occasion issued scornful pronouncements upon him as a mere "mechanic."

Thus, Edison offered a reassurance that the old routes to personal success were still open, that the mass of inventions and improvements profoundly altering industry and reshaping personal lives truly emerged from a heroic wresting of the secrets of nature for human betterment. The phonograph especially, the inanimate made animate, inspired rhapsodies of technological fantasy. " 'If this can be done,' we ask, 'what is there that cannot be?' " exclaimed the writer in *Scribner's*. "We feel that there may, after all, be a relief for all human ills in the great storehouse of nature," he continued, adding pointedly: "There is an especial appropriateness, perhaps, in its occurring in a time of more than usual discontent."

With his eye to publicity, and no doubt his bemused enjoyment of so much attention, Edison seemed glad to collaborate in the image of the wizard, the wunderkind. In fact, however, Menlo Park and the later laboratories were testing grounds for the full-scale industrial research organizations which would develop within private industries such as General Electric and the American Telephone and Telegraph Company by the turn of the century. Edison hired university-trained scientists among his staff, including Francis R. Upton, a specialist in mathematical physics. Menlo Park was a team operation, the earliest research and development laboratory in America; Edison established the place as an "invention factory," a place where invention might be made to order for private industry. He differed from much of his public by having no illusions on that score. Invention was his business. . . .

Whether acts of wizardry or genius, or sheer luck, Edison's work belonged to the evolving structure of experimental science and its alliance with industrial capitalism. To stress this obvious fact is not to debunk the myth but to place it in perspective: to see it as a myth which disguises the radical changes occurring in the origins and uses of knowledge in these years. The new relations of science to industrial technology ultimately represented a new relation of human labor to the process of production. Separated by increasingly complex and dense institutions, the shop floor and the research laboratory belonged to the same universe of production. With machines performing more of the work previously performed by people, workers themselves were required to *know* less in order to perform their tasks—to know less because their machines know more. Mechanization entailed, then, the transference of technical knowledge from workers to machines, a process mediated by a new corps of trained engineers. The rise of specialized skills and arcane knowledge corresponded precisely to the obliteration of traditional knowledge among skilled manual laborers. The growing numbers of trained technologists on one hand and unskilled workers on the other were two faces of the same process.

As if called forth by this prime economic motive, Frederick W. Taylor, a foreman at the Midvale Steel Company in Pennsylvania, inaugurated in the 1880's his famous "time-study" experiments, aimed at elimination of waste, inefficiency, and what he called "soldiering" on the part of workers. With his stopwatch—a further encroachment of time on physical movement—Taylor proposed to systematize exactly that process Wells had described as production through destruction: the absolute subordination of "living labor" to the machine. He envisioned a complete renovation of the production process, with standardization of tools and equipment, replanning of factories for greater efficiency, and "piece-rate" method of payment as incentive for workers. In *The Principles of Scientific Management* (1911), Taylor made explicit the heart of his program: to take possession for management of the "mass of traditional knowledge" once possessed by the workers themselves, "knowledge handed down to them by word of mouth, through the many years in which their trade has been developed from the primitive condition." For Taylor the stopwatch and flowchart were basic instruments whereby management might reduce that knowledge to measurable motions, eradicating their workers' autonomy at one stroke while enhancing their productivity.

Thus, the social distribution of knowledge begins a major shift, a transference (as far as technology and technique are concerned) from bottom to top, in these years of extensive and intensive mechanization. Just as important, and as a symbol of the process, *thought* now appears often in the dumb, mystifying shapes of machines, of standing and moving mechanical objects as incapable of explaining themselves to the unknowing eye as the standing stones of ancient peoples. The momentous event of mechanization, of science and technology coming to perform the labor most significant to the productivity of the system, reproduced itself in ambivalent cultural images of machines and inventors, and in displacements running like waves of shock through the social order.

The Robber Barons

In John D. Rockefeller, economists and historians have often seen the classic example of the modern monopolist of industry. It is true that he worked with an indomitable will, and a faith in his star à la Napoleon, to organize his industry under his own dictatorship. He was moreover a great innovator. Though not the first to attempt the plan of the pool—there were pools even in the time of Cicero—his South Improvement Company was the most impressive instance in history of such an organism. But when others had reached the stage of the pool, he was building the solid framework of a monopoly.

Rockefeller's problems were far more difficult than those for instance of Carnegie, who quickly won special economies through constructing a very costly, well-integrated, technically superior plant upon a favored site. In the oil-refining business, a small still could be thrown up in the '70's for manufacturing kerosene or lubricating oil at a tenth the cost of the Edgar Thomson steel works. The petroleum market was mercurial compared to iron, steel and even coal; there were thousands of petty capitalists competing for advantage in it. Hence the tactics of Rockefeller, the bold architecture of the industrial edifice he reared, have always aroused the liveliest interest, and he himself appeals to us for many reasons as the greatest of the American industrialists. In no small degree this interest is owing to the legend of "Machiavellian" guile and relentlessness which has always clung to this prince of oil.

After the dissolution of the South Improvement Company, Rockefeller and Flagler had come to a conference of the irate diggers of petroleum with mild proposals of peaceful coöperation, under the heading of the "Pittsburgh Plan." The two elements in the trade, those who produced the raw material from the earth and those who refined it, were to combine forces harmoniously. "You misunderstand us," Rockefeller and Flagler said. "Let us see what combination will do."

There was much suspicion. One of Titusville's independent refiners (one of those whom Standard Oil tried to erase from the scene) made a rather warlike speech against the plan, and he recalls that Rockefeller, who had been softly swinging back and forth in a rocking chair, his hands over his face, through the conference, suddenly stopped rocking, lowered his hands and looked straight at his enemy. His glance was fairly terrifying.

You never saw such eyes. He took me all in, saw just how much fight he could expect from me, and then up went his hands and back and forth went his chair.

At this very moment, Rockefeller was arranging anew the secret rebates with the leading railroads of the country, which had been so loudly decried in 1872. Upon the refined oil he shipped from Cleveland he received a rebate of 50 cents a barrel, giving him an advantage of 25 percent over his competitors. Once more the railroads continued a form of espionage for his company. But all arrangements were now effected in a more complete secrecy.

Equally secret was the campaign Rockefeller pursued to amalgamate with his own company the strongest refineries in the country. According to Miss Tarbell's "History," he now constantly "bent over a map of the refining interests of the country," or hurried from one secret conference to another, at Cleveland, New York, or at Saratoga, "the Mecca of schemers," where long hours of nocturnal debate in a certain pavilion brought into his plan the refineries of Pittsburgh and Philadelphia. Look at what combination has done in one city, Cleveland, he would say. The plan now was for all the chosen ones to become the nucleus of a private company which should gradually acquire control of all the refineries everywhere, become the only shippers, and have the mastery of the railroads in the matter of freight rates. Those who came in were promised wealth beyond their dreams. The remarkable economies and profits of the Standard were exposed to their eyes. "We mean to secure the entire refining business of the world," they were told. They were urged to dissemble their actions. Contracts were entered into with the peculiar secret rites which Mr. Rockefeller habitually preferred. They were signed late at night at his Euclid Avenue home in Cleveland. The participants were besought not to tell even their wives about the new arrangements, to conceal the gains they made, not to drive fast horses or put on style, or buy new bonnets, or do anything to let people suspect there were unusual profits in oil-refining, since that might invite competition.

In this campaign perhaps fifteen of the strongest firms in the country, embracing four-fifths of the refining trade, were brought into alliance with the Standard Oil Company by 1875–78. Among them were individuals who had opposed Rockefeller most strenuously a season before: the ablest of these, J. J. Vandergrift and John Archbold of the Pennsylvania oil regions, Charles Pratt and Henry Rogers of New York, entering the family of Standard Oil as partners by exchange of stock. They continued under their own corporate identity as "Acme Oil Company," or "Pratt & Rogers," but shared the same freight advantages as Standard Oil, used the same sources of information and surveillance, the common organization of agents and dealers in the distributing field.

"I wanted able men with me," Rockefeller said later. "I tried to make friends with these men. I admitted their ability and the value of their enterprise. I worked to convince them that it would be better for both to cooperate."

In the meantime a campaign no less elaborate and bold was pursued to eliminate from the field those firms whose existence was considered superfluous. Rockefeller did not "confiscate" his opponents outright. In the interests of his great consolidation he measured the value of their properties without sentiment, and gave his terms. Thus a plant which had cost $40,000 might in the future, after his own plans had matured, be worth little more than $15,000, or 37½ cents on the dollar. Such an offer he would make and this only. The victim, as the case might be, would surrender if timid, or attempt resistance in trade, or practice blackmail upon him, or fight him to the finish and have resort to the highest courts.

Where a "deal" across the table could not be effected, Rockefeller might try a variety of methods of expropriation. With his measured spirit, with his organized might, he tested men and things. There were men and women of all sorts who passed under his implacable rod, and their tale, gathered together reverently by Miss Tarbell, has contributed to the legend of the "white devil" who came to rule over American industry.

A certain widow, a Mrs. Backus of Cleveland, who had inherited an oil refinery, had appealed to Mr. Rockefeller to preserve her, "the mother of fatherless children." And he had promised "with tears in his eyes that he would stand by her." But in the end he offered her only $79,000 for a property which had cost $200,000. The whole story of the defenseless widow and her orphans, the stern command, the confiscation of two-thirds of her property, when it came out made a deep stir and moved many hearts.

In another instance a manufacturer of improved lubricating oils set himself up innocently in Cleveland, and became a client of the Standard Oil for his whole supply of residuum oils. The Rockefeller company encouraged him at first, and sold him 85 barrels a day according to a contract. He prospered for three years, then suddenly when the monopoly was well launched in 1874, his supply was cut down to 12 barrels a day, the price was increased on some pretense, and the shipping cost over the railroads similarly increased. It became impossible to supply his trade. He offered to buy of Rockefeller 5,000 barrels and store it so that he might assure himself of a future supply. This was refused.

"I saw readily what that meant," the man Morehouse related to the Hepburn Committee in 1879. "That meant squeeze you out—Buy out your works.... They paid $15,000 for what cost me $41,000. He [Rockefeller] said that he had facilities for freighting and that the coal-oil business belonged to them; and any concern that would start in that business, they had sufficient money to lay aside a fund and wipe them out—these are the words."

In the field of retail distribution, Rockefeller sought to create a great marketing machine delivering directly from the Standard Oil's tank wagons to stores in towns and villages throughout the United States. But in the laudable endeavor to wipe out wasteful wholesalers or middlemen, he would meet with resistance again, as in the producing fields. Where unexpectedly stout resistance from competing marketing agencies was met, the Standard Oil would simply apply harsher weapons. To cut off the supplies of the rebel dealer, the secret aid of the railroads and the espionage of their freight agents would be invoked again and again. A message such as the following would pass between Standard Oil officials:

We are glad to know you are on such good terms with the railroad people that Mr. Clem [handling independent oil]gains nothing by marking his shipments by numbers instead of by names.

Or again:

Wilkerson and Company received car of oil Monday 13th—70 barrels which we suspect slipped through at the usual fifth class rate—in fact we might say we know it did—paying only $41.50 freight from here. Charges $57.40. Please turn another screw.

The process of "Turning the Screw" has been well described by Henry D. Lloyd. One example is that of a merchant in Nashville, Tennessee, who refused to come to terms and buy from Standard Oil; he first found that all his shipments were reported secretly to the enemy; then by a mysterious coincidence his freight rates on shipments of all kinds were raised 50 percent, then doubled, even tripled, and he felt himself under fire from all parts of the field. He attempted to move his merchandise by a great roundabout route, using the Baltimore & Ohio and several other connecting roads, but was soon "tracked down," his shipments lost, spoiled. The documents show that the independent oil-dealers' clients were menaced in every way by the Standard Oil marketing agency; it threatened to open competing grocery stores, to sell oats, meat, sugar, coffee at lower prices. "If you do not buy our oil we will start a grocery store and sell goods at cost and put you out of business."

By this means, opponents in the country at large were soon "mopped up"; small refiners and small wholesalers who attempted to exploit a given district were routed at the appearance of the familiar red-and-green tank wagons, which were equal to charging drastically reduced rates for oil in one town, and twice as much in an adjacent town where the nuisance of competition no longer existed. There were, to be sure, embittered protests from the victims, but the marketing methods of Standard Oil were magnificently efficient and centralized; waste and delay were overcome; immense savings were brought directly to the refining monopoly.

But where the Standard Oil could not carry on its expansion by peaceful means, it was ready with violence; its faithful servants knew even how to apply the modern weapon of dynamite.

In Buffalo, the Vacuum Oil Company, one of the "dummy" creatures of the Standard Oil system, became disturbed one day by the advent of a vigorous competitor who built a sizable refinery and located it favorably upon the water front. The offices of Vacuum conducted at first a furtive campaign of intimidation. Then emboldened or more desperate, they approached the chief mechanic of the enemy refinery, holding whispered conferences with him in a rowboat on Lake Erie. He was asked to "do something." He was urged to "go back to Buffalo and construct the machinery so it would bust up . . . or smash up," to fix the pipes and stills "so they cannot make a good oil. . . . And then if you would give them a little scare, they not knowing anything about the business. You know how . . . ." In return the foreman would have a life annuity which he might enjoy in another part of the country.

So in due time a small explosion took place in the independent plant, as Lloyd and Miss Tarbell tell the tale, from the records of the trial held several years later, in 1887. The mechanic, though on the payrolls of the Vacuum Oil Company, led a cursed existence, forever wandering without home or country, until in complete hysteria he returned to make a clean breast of the whole affair. The criminal suit against high officials of the Standard Oil monopoly included Henry Rogers and John Archbold, but the evil was laid by them to the "overenthusiasm" of underlings. Evidence of conspiracy was not found by the court, but heavy damages were awarded to the plaintiff, who thereafter plainly dreaded to reenter the dangerous business.

These and many other anecdotes, multiplied, varied or even distorted, spread through the Oil Regions of Pennsylvania and elsewhere through the country (as ogre-tales are fed to children), and were accumulated to make a strange picture of Mr. Rockefeller, the baron of oil. Miss Tarbell in her "History," written in her "muck-raking" days, has dwelt upon them with love. She has recorded them in rending tones with a heart bleeding for the petty capitalists for whom alone "life ran swift and ruddy and joyous" before the "great villain" arrived, and with his "big hand reached out from nobody knew where to steal their conquest and throttle their future."

But if truth must be told, the smaller capitalists, in the producing field especially, were themselves not lacking in predatory or greedy qualities; as Miss Tarbell herself admits, they were capable of hurrying away from church on Sundays to tap enemy tanks or set fire to their stores of oil. What they lacked, as the Beards have commented, was the discipline to maintain a producers' combination equal in strength to that of the refiners. The other factors in the industry engaged in individualistic marketing or refining ventures were very possibly "mossbacks," as one of the Standard Oil chieftains growled, "left in the lurch by progress."

The campaigns for consolidation, once launched, permitted Rockefeller little rest, and engaged his generalship on many fronts at once. In a curious interview given while he was in Europe, cited by Flynn, he himself exclaimed:

How often I had not an unbroken night's sleep, worrying about how it was all coming out. . . . Work by day and worry by night, week in and week out, month after month. If I had foreseen the future I doubt whether I would have had the courage to go on.

With unblinking vigilance he conducted throughout his company an eternal war against waste. We have spoken of his unequaled efficiency and power of organization. There is a famous note to his barrel factory in his careful bookkeeper's hand which has been cited with amused contempt by his critics, to show how attention to small details absorbed his soul. It reads:

Last month you reported on hand, 1,119 bungs. 10,000 were sent you beginning this month. You have used 9,527 this month. You report 1,092 on hand. What has become of the other 500?

It is not a laughing matter, this affair of 500 barrel bungs, worth at the most a dollar or two in all. Rockefeller's hatred of waste told him that in a large-scale industry the rescued pennies multiplied a million times or more represented enormous potential gains. This was to be true of all the great industrial leaders after Rockefeller's time; the spirit regarded as parsimony is a large-visioned conception of technical efficiency in handling big machines. Thus the feeding of horses, the making of his own glue, hoops, barrels, all was carefully supervised and constantly reduced in cost. Barrels were cut $1.25 apiece, saving $4,000,000 a year, cans were reduced 15 cents, saving $5,000,000 a year, and so forth. In absorbing the services of J. J. Vandergrift, in 1872, Rockefeller had acquired as an ally to his enterprise a combination of small pipe lines called the United Pipe Lines. His lieutenants then constructed more pipes; and by 1876 he controlled almost half the existing pipe lines, some running 80 to 100 miles, to the railroad terminals and shipping points. At this time the largest pipe-line interest in competition with Standard Oil's was the Empire Transportation Company, headed by Colonel Joseph Potts, but dominated by the officers of the Pennsylvania Railroad, which held an option over the entire property.

Himself an aggressive entrepreneur, Potts soon found that he must expand or suffer extinction. To the alarm of the Rockefeller organization, he purchased several big refineries in New York and proceeded to pipe crude oil from the oil fields and over the railroad to seaboard. Rockefeller vehemently petitioned the railroad to withdraw from his domain. Refused at an interview, he promised that he would take his own measures, and left his adversaries with expressions of sanctimonious regret, the form in which his most deadly threats were usually offered.

It was war, a war of rates. He moved with lightning speed. At once the other railroads, Erie and New York Central, were ordered to stand by, lowering their freight rates for him while he slashed the price of refined oil in every market which Potts reached.

But Potts, a stubborn Presbyterian, fought back harder than anyone Rockefeller had ever encountered. He replied in kind by further price cuts; he then began to build large refineries at the coast ports, lined up independent oil-producers behind him, and reserves in quantities of tank cars, in barges, ships, dock facilities. During the bitter conflict, with which, as Flynn relates, the hills and fields of Pennsylvania resounded, both sides, and the railroads supporting them as well, suffered heavy wounds. Yet Rockefeller would not desist, since Standard Oil's whole system of organization was endangered.

In the midst of this furious engagement a great blow fell upon the enemies of John D. Rockefeller, as if given by the hand of God to whom he constantly prayed. During the summer of 1877 the workers of the Baltimore & Ohio Railroad struck against wage cuts and their strike spread quickly to adjacent railroads, raging with especial violence in the Pennsylvania system. The most destructive labor war the nation had ever known was now seen in Baltimore and Pittsburgh, with militant mobs fighting armed troops and setting in flames property of great value in revenge for the many deaths they suffered. During this storm which the railroad barons had sown by cutting wages 20 percent and doubling the length of freight trains, the Pennsylvania interests quickly came to terms with Standard Oil, so that they might be free to turn and crush the rebellious workers. The entire business of Empire Transportation was sold out to the oil combination at their own terms, while Potts was called off. In Philadelphia, Rockefeller and his partners, quietly jubilant, received the sword of the weeping Potts.

The oil industry as a whole was impressed with the victory of Standard Oil over a railroad ring which had seemed invincible in the past. In a movement of fear many other interests hastened to make terms with Rockefeller. By the end of 1878 he controlled all the existing pipe-line systems; through a new freight pool he directed traffic or quantities of supplies to the various regions or cities as he pleased.

By 1876 this industry had assumed tremendous proportions. Of the annual output of nearly 10,000,000 barrels, the Standard Oil Company controlled approximately 80 percent, while exports of petroleum products to the value of $32,000,000 passed through their hands. But in 1877 the great Bradford oil field was opened with a wild boom, the uproarious coal-oil scenes of '59 were enacted anew, crowds rushed to the new fields, acreage values boomed, oil gushed out in an uncontrollable flood—half again as much oil as existed before came forth almost overnight. The markets grew demoralized again, just when Rockefeller seemed to have completed his conquest of the old Oil Regions.

What was he to do? In the two years that followed he directed his organization at the high tension of an ordnance department in wartime, so that piping, refining and marketing capacity might be expanded in time, and the almost untenable supply handled without faltering. With utmost energy a huge building program was carried on and further millions were staked on the hazardous business. Then holding down the unruly producers, he imposed harsh terms through his pipe lines, refusing storage, forcing them to sell the oil they drilled "for immediate shipment" at the depressed prices of 64 to 69 cents a barrel, or have it run into the ground.

The overproduction could not be stopped. The oil men raged at the great machine which held them in bonds. Once more the independents gathered all their forces together to form a protective combination of their own. They founded the Parliament of Petroleum. They raised funds to construct an immense "free" pipe line running over the mountains to the seaboard, and ridding them at last of the railroads which hemmed them in. The new Tidewater Pipe Line would break Standard's control over railroad rates and bring crude oil to the sea.

Rockefeller's agents now lobbied in the state legislature of Pennsylvania to have the proposed pipe line banned. Failing of this his emissaries were thrown out over the state to buy up right of way in the path of the enemy's advance. But the Tidewater's engineers moved with equal speed and secrecy, eluded the defense which Rockefeller threw in their way and by April, 1879, completed their difficult project.

From successive stations, the great pumps were to drive oil over the very top of the Alleghenies, and down to Williamsport, touching the Reading Railroad, which had joined forces with the independents. Amid picturesque celebration— while the spies of the Standard Oil looked on incredulously—the valves were opened, the oil ran over the mountain and down toward the sea! Rockefeller was checkmated—but to whom would the producers and their free pipe line sell the crude oil at the seaboard? They had no inkling, though they berated him, of the extent of his control at the outlet.

The opposition to the Rockefeller "conspiracy" now rose to its climax of enthusiasm. The hundreds of petty oil men who fought to remain "independent" and keep their sacred right to flood the market or "hold up" consumers at their own pleasure, won sympathy everywhere; and with the aid of local politicians in New York and Pennsylvania they also had their day in court. Their tumult had grown so violent that at long last the lawmakers of Pennsylvania moved to prosecute the monopolists for "conspiracy in restraint of trade." Writs were served and on April 29, 1879, a local Grand Jury indicted John D. Rockefeller, William Rockefeller, J. A. Bostwick, Henry Flagler, Daniel O'Day, J. J. Vandergrift and other chieftains of Standard Oil for criminal conspiracy, to "secure a monopoly of the oil industry, to oppress other refiners, to injure the carrying trade, to extort unreasonable railroad rates, to fraudulently control prices," etc. Simultaneously in New York State, the legislature appointed a committee of investigation of railroads, headed by the young lawyer A. Barton Hepburn. Forced to look at all the facts which were brought out by the Hepburn Committee, the nation was shocked. The railroad interests, as archconspirators, were at once under heavy fire. But no one understood the scope and meaning of the new phase reached in industrial life at this stage, save perhaps Mr. Chauncey Depew, who in a moment of illumination exclaimed on behalf of the railroad interests he so gallantly championed: "Every manufacturer in the state of New York existed by violence and lived by discrimination. . . . By secret rates and by deceiving their competitors as to what their rates were and by evading all laws of trade these manufacturers exist." This was God's truth and certainly true of all the other states in the Union. And of course under the prevailing circumstances there was nothing to be done, save recommend certain "regulative" laws.

With Rockefeller, there had arisen the great industrial combination in colossal and "sinister" form; he was the mighty bourgeois who was to expropriate all the petty bourgeois and his name was to be the rallying cry of parties and uprisings. The outlook for monopoly seemed dark, yet the trial, in the name of a democratic sovereignty which held "sacred" the property of the "conspirators," whatever the means by which they may have preëmpted or confiscated such property—was to be simply a comedy, and was to be enacted again and again. Before the bar of justice, Rockefeller and his brilliant lieutenants would appear, saying, "I refuse to answer on the advice of counsel." A Henry Rogers, a Flagler, would use every shift which such philosophers of the law as Joseph Choate or Samuel C. T. Dodd might counsel. They would "refuse to incriminate themselves" or evade reply on a point of technicality, or lie pointblank. Or, as in the case of the terribly cynical Archbold, they would simply jest, they would make mock of their bewildered prosecutors.

It was Rockefeller who made the most profound impression upon the public. He seemed distinguished in person; with his tall stooping figure, his long well-shaped head, his even jaw. His long, fine nose, his small birdlike eyes set wide apart, with the narrowed lids drooping a little, and the innumerable tiny wrinkles, made up a remarkable physiognomy. But his mouth was a slit, like a shark's. Rockefeller, impeccably dressed and groomed, thoroughly composed, pretendedly anxious to please, foiled his accusers with ease. Every legal subterfuge was used by him with supreme skill. Certain of his denials were legally truthful, as Flynn points out, since stockownership concerning which he was questioned was often entrusted temporarily (in time for such trials) to mere clerks or bookkeepers in his employ.

But the moment came when he was asked specifically about his connection with the notorious refiners' pool of 1872.

"Was there a Southern Improvement Company?"

"I have heard of such a company."

"Were you not in it?"

"I was not."

His hearers were amazed at the apparent perjury he made pointblank with even voice and an inscrutable movement of the eyes. But no! He had been only a director of the *South Improvement Company,* and not of the "Southern Improvement Company," as the prosecutor had named it by mistake.

If Rockefeller was embittered by the cruel fame he won, he never showed it. The silence he preserved toward all reproaches or questions may have been a matter of clever policy; yet it suggested at bottom a supreme contempt for his critics and accusers alike.

"We do not talk much—we saw wood!"

There were times when his movements were hampered, times when he dared not enter the State of Pennsylvania though the authorities there called for him impatiently; times when it was equally convenient to remain almost in hiding at his New York headquarters in Pearl Street, while the world at large howled against him. Yet he moved with unequaled agility and force against all serious attacks upon his industrial barony.

The menace of the Tidewater Pipe Line which cut through his network of railroads and refineries he must crush at all costs. This was far more important than any impeachment of his character. Fertile in expedients at a crisis, he could also be infinitely patient. It used to be said: "To Mr. Rockefeller a day is as a year, and a year as a day. He can wait, but he never gives up." Now when he perceived that the Tidewater's line to the sea was a reality, he besieged it from all sides. On the one hand he offered to buy all the oil it ran, a tempting offer which would have made the affair most profitable to the stockholders. Rebuffed here he proceeded to use the inventions of his rivals and build a long pipe line of his own to the sea. Night and day his engineers and gangs labored in the mountains, to connect the Bradford fields with the Standard Oil terminal at Bayonne. Then before the walls of Bayonne, where lay his great coastal refineries and storage tanks, his pipe line was stopped by an interested railroad from which he would have removed his freight business. The Town Council of Bayonne was induced to be friendly and grant a franchise; the Mayor who resisted for a time was suddenly won over; and in all secrecy, because of the need of haste to prevent a blocking franchise by the railroad, his gangs assembled. There were 300 men ready in the night of September 22, 1879, with all materials, tools, wagons gathered, waiting for the signal—the swift passage of an ordinance by the Town Council and its signing by the Mayor. Then with mad speed the trench across the city was dug, the pipes laid, jointed and covered, before the dawn. The National Transit Company was completed as the largest pipe-line system in the field.

His own line of communications was now secured against the enemy. But he also pursued a campaign of secret stock purchase for control, gaining a minority interest in the Tidewater company, creating dissensions within, damaging its credit, detaching its officials, instigating suits for receivership, serving writs, injunctions, and more writs, until the managers seemed to struggle for their very sanity. Day by day these blows fell mysteriously, until in 1882 the adversary surrendered and effected the best agreement possible under the circumstances. By this a minor part of the oil-transporting business was apportioned to itself and it yielded up its independence after four years of fighting an unresting, infinitely armed master. All the pipe lines were now amalgamated under Standard Oil control; the great railroads, notably the Pennsylvania, were forced by agreement and in return for a stipulated yearly ransom to retire from the business of oil transportation forever. John D. Rockefeller at the age of forty-four had accomplished his ambition—he was supreme in the oil industry, "the symbol of the American monopolist."

Up to 1881 the forty-odd companies controlled by Rockefeller and his partners formed a kind of *entente cordiale* bound by interchange of stock. This form of union being found inadequate or impermanent, the counsel of the Standard Oil Company, Samuel C. T. Dodd, came forward with his idea of the Trust. By a secret agreement of 1882, all the existing thirty-seven stockholders in the divers enterprises of refining, piping, buying or selling oil conveyed their shares "in trust" to nine Trustees: John and William Rockefeller, O. H. Payne, Charles Pratt, Henry Flagler, John Archbold, W. G. Warden, Jabez Bostwick and Benjamin Brewster. The various stockholders then received "trust certificates" in denominations of $100 in return for the shares they had deposited; while the Trustees, controlling two-thirds of all the shares, became the direct stockholders of all the companies in the system, empowered to serve as directors thereof, holding in their hands final control of all the properties. The Trustees could dissolve any corporations within the system and organize new ones in each state, such as the Standard Oil of New Jersey, or the Standard Oil of New York. Nor could any outsiders or newly arrived stockholders have any voice in the affairs of the various companies. The Trustees formed a kind of supreme council giving a centralized direction to their industry. Such was the first great Trust; thus was evolved the harmonious management of huge aggregations of capital, and the technique for large-scale industry.

Dodd, the resourceful philosopher of monopoly, defended his beautiful legal structure of the "Standard Oil Trust" both in a pamphlet of 1888 and in an argument before a Congressional committee of that year. It was but the outcome of a crying need for centralized control of the oil business, he argued. Out of disastrous conditions had come "coöperation and association among the refiners, resulting eventually in the Standard Oil Trust [which] enabled the refiners so coöperating to reduce the price of petroleum products, and thus benefit the public to a very marked degree." In these arguments, learned economists of the time, such as Professor Hadley, supported Dodd. The Trust, as perfected monopoly, pointed the way to the future organization of all industry, and abolished "ruinous competition."

From their headquarters in the small old-fashioned building at 140 Pearl Street the supreme council of an economic empire sat together in conference like princes of the Roman Church. Here in utmost privacy confidential news brought by agents or informers throughout the world was discussed, and business policies determined. The management and responsibility was skillfully divided among committees: there was a committee on Crude Oil, a committee on Marketing, on Transportation, and numerous other departments. By these new processes markets or developments everywhere in everybody's business were followed or acted upon.

Every day the astute leaders rounded together by Rockefeller lunched together in Pearl Street, and later in a large and famous office building known as 26 Broadway. No one questioned the pre-eminence of John D. Rockefeller, though Charles Pratt usually sat at the head of the table. The aggressive Archbold was closest to John D. Rockefeller. His brother William Rockefeller, an amiable mediocrity, but immensely rich as well, and long trained in the use of money, depended most upon Henry H. Rogers. Rogers took a more dominant place in the management with the passing years. He is described by Thomas Lawson as "one of the most distinguished-looking men of the time, a great actor, a great fighter, an intriguer, an implacable foe."

These, together with Brewster, Barstow, J. H. Alexander and Bostwick, were the leaders who carried on their industrial operations throughout the world like a band of conspiratorial revolutionists. But "there was not a lazy bone nor a stupid head" in the whole organization, as Miss Tarbell has said. Behind them were the active captains, lieutenants, followers and workers, all laboring with the pride, the loyalty, the discipline and the enthusiasm born of the knowledge that "they can do no better for themselves" anywhere than under the "collar" of the Standard Oil. Freed of all moral scruples, curiously informed of everything, they were prompted by a sense of the world's realities which differed strangely from that of the man in the street. They were a major staff engaged in an eternal fight; now they scrapped unprofitable plants, acquiring and locating others; or now they gathered themselves for tremendous mobilizing feats during emergencies in trade. They found ways of effecting enormous economies; and always their profits mounted to grotesque figures: in 1879, on an invested capital of $3,500,000, dividends of $3,150,000 were paid; the value of the congeries of oil companies was then estimated at $55,000,000. Profits were overwhelmingly reinvested in new "capital goods" and with the formation of the Trust capitalization was set at $70,000,000. By 1886 net earnings had risen to $15,000,000 per annum.

"Hide the profits and say nothing!" was the slogan here. To the public prices had been reduced, it was claimed. But after 1875, and more notably after 1881, despite the fluctuations of crude oil a firm tendency set in for the markets of refined oil products. Upon the charts of prices the rugged hills and valleys of oil markets turn into a nearly level plain between 1881 and 1891. Though raw materials declined greatly in value, and volume increased, the margin of profit was consistently controlled by the monopoly; for the services of gathering and transporting oil, the price was not lowered in twenty years, despite the superb technology possessed by the Standard Oil. Questioned on this, that "frank pirate" Rogers replied, laughing: *"We are not in business for our health, but are out for the dollar."*

While the policy of the monopoly, as economists have shown, might be for many reasons to avoid *maximum* price levels—such as invited the entrance of competition in the field—it was clearly directed toward keeping the profit margin stable during a rising trend in consumption and falling "curve" in production cost. Similarly in perfecting its technology the Trust was guided by purely pecuniary motives, as Veblen points out, and it remains always a matter of doubt if the mightier industrial combinations improved their service to society at large in the highest possible degree. As often as not it happened that technical improvements were actually long delayed until, after a decade or more, as in the case of Van Syckel's pipe line of 1865, their commercial value was proved beyond a doubt. It was only after rivals, in desperation, contrived the pumping of oil in a two-hundred-mile-long pipe line that Rockefeller followed suit. So it was with the development of various by-products, the introduction of tank cars, etc.

The end in sight was always, as Veblen said, increase of ownership, and of course pecuniary gain rather than technical progress in the shape of improved workmanship or increased service to the community. These latter effects were also obtained. But to a surprising degree they seem accidental by-products of the long-drawn-out struggles, the revolutionary upheavals whence the great industrial coalitions sprang.

The greatest service of the industrial baron to business enterprise seemed to lie elsewhere, as Veblen contended. "The heroic role of the captain of industry is that of a deliverer from an excess of business management." It is a "sweeping retirement of business men as a class from service . . . a casting out of business men by the chief of business men."

John D. Rockefeller said that he wanted in his organization "only the big ones, those who have already proved they can do a big business. As for the others, unfortunately they will have to die."

The obscure tumult in the Oil Regions in 1872, the subsequent exposures of the railroad rebate and the oil monopoly in 1879, made a lively though unclear impression upon the public mind. Now the more imaginative among the mass of consumers felt fear course through them at the thought of secret combinations ranged against them, the loud demagogue was roused from his slumbers, the reformer set off upon his querulous and futile searches. But among the alert entrepreneurs of all the money marts an entirely different response must have been perceptible. With envious lust the progress of the larger, more compact industrial organizations, like that of Carnegie Brothers & Company, or the associations formed by a Rockefeller, was now studied. Ah-ha! there was the way to profits in these confused and parlous times. How quickly and abundantly those fellows accumulated cash and power! "I was surprised," confessed William Vanderbilt before a committee of New York legislators in 1878, "at the amount of ready cash they were able to provide." He referred to the oil-refiners' combination. In the twinkling of an eye they had put down 3,000,000 to buy out Colonel Potts' pipe-line company. And in the following year Vanderbilt, commenting to the Hepburn Committee at Albany on the shrewdness of the Standard Oil ring, said:

There is no question about it but these men are smarter than I am a great deal. . . . I never came in contact with any class of men as smart and alert as they are in their business. They would never have got into the position they now are. And one man could hardly have been able to do it; it is a combination of men.

The storms of public indignation, as we have seen, vented themselves chiefly upon the railroad heads who "discriminated against the little fellow" by the re-bate and freight pool. But far from being frightened at such protests the money-changers hastened to throw their gold at the feet of him who promised them crushing, monopolistic advantages. So Villard, in 1881, by whispering his plans to conquer all the Northwest overnight, attracted instantly a powerful following of capitalists to his "blind pool." So the lawyers or undertakers who came for-ward with plans for secret trade associations or pools in salt, beef, sugar or whiskey, were heard with intense excitement by men who yesterday were busy ambushing or waylaying each other in the daily routine of their business.

They would say to each other, as in the Salt Association, formed earliest of all, "In union there is strength. . . ." Or, *"Organized we have prospered; unor-ganized not."* "Our combination has not been strong enough; the market is de-moralized." And others would murmur fearsomely: "But we will be prosecuted for 'restraint of trade.' There are state laws in Maryland, Tennessee and else-where which hold that 'monopolies are odious.' There is the common law against trade conspiracy. . . ."

Then a bolder voice among the plotters would say: "How much did you make last year? Not a cent? Are you making anything now? Well, what do you propose to do? Sit here and lose what capital you have got in the business? There is only one way to make any money in a business like the—business and that is to have a pool."

Thus the trail would be blazed. The industrialists, like the railroad barons before them, came together in furtive conferences, much mistrusting each other, but lamenting together the bad times and owning to the folly of competition among themselves; while those who made pools, as they heard by rumor, in oil or salt flourished. After much bickering and jockeying, the lawyers would draw up binding agreements by which the amount of output would be fixed, quotas and territories would be assigned to each member, and business orders proportionally allotted, with fines levied upon those who broke the rules. These planning agree-ments the members of the pool would promise faithfully to live by.

The first pools, crude experiments in a "federalism" of industry, were as in-ept as the first weak devices for union among laborers. Their tactics and results differed widely. By 1880, certain pools such as the salt pool had got the margin of profit much higher by "pegging" the market price of a barrel of salt at about double what it was formerly, and holding steadily to this level. Their procedure usually avoided raising the market price too high. This would beget fresh competition. However, they kept prices "moderately" firm, although supply might actually be abundant. The essential object in view was "to increase the margins between the cost of materials and the price of the finished product," and this was effected, according to Ripley, "in almost every case."

A variety of economies were gained by pooling, depending upon the firmness of the association. Railroads were forced to give rebates; inefficient or badly located plants were closed down; excess sales forces and labor were reduced, a "war chest" was accumulated and competitors were driven out. To intruders the cost of necessary machinery might be made more burdensome. Thus in connection with the Wire Nail Pool, independents declared to government investigators:

We found the market in which we could buy machines [to manufacture nails] was very limited, most of the machine manufacturers having entered into an agreement with the combination to stop making them for outside parties.

In some cases the pool might, as in the case of salt in 1881, decide to "slaughter the market" for a reason, giving the *coup de grâce* to overstocked competitors in some areas, then resume the even tenor of their ways. Or they would sell low in one section which was pestered by competition, and recoup off the general market. The pools, in short, claimed to represent the party of "modernity," of progress by specializing machinery, buying raw materials cheaper, utilizing more by-products, research units, export development, advertising and selling in common. While "not wishing to take the position of posing before the public as benefactors to any extent," yet they claimed that industry was more stabilized, prices were seldom raised inordinately, and labor was paid higher wages—though here one famous manufacturer, John Gates, admitted that this was done on demand, in periods of affluence, when it was seen they had high profits and desired to avoid labor troubles. Generally they assumed a marvelous command over the labor situation—here was one of their surest gains. The workman became truly their commodity; for in time of a strike, orders could be shifted to other factories in a different section of the country and these kept running full blast.

In other cases, it was also notable that a technique of central control, extremely rigid and absolute, was developed. Immediately upon formation of the Distilling & Cattle Feeding Association, as Ripley relates, prices were cut sharply to force competitors into the pool, rivals were bought up or forced out, sometimes by negotiations and sometimes by intimidation or violence. Then by 1889, from twelve to twenty whiskey distilleries were operated on behalf of eighty-three plants previously existing, great savings were effected, and profits were steady and high enough to "accumulate a surplus for purpose of contest with outsiders." Thus the "whiskey ring," as Henry Lloyd wrote at the time, regulated the liquor traffic as no government could up to then or ever since effectively do, decreeing where and how much liquor should be made, and enforcing their decree, controlling alcohol, hence the sciences, medicine, even the arts and poetry. By February, 1888, only two large independents out of eighty distilleries resisted the combination. These were in Chicago, and one of them in April of that year published in the *Chicago Tribune* the fact that they had caught a spy of the combination in their works; later, tampering with the valves of their vats was discovered; then offers of large bribes if they would sell out their plants. In December, according to Lloyd's account, this distillery became the scene of an awful explosion:

All the buildings in the neighborhood were shaken and many panes of glass were broken. . . . There were 15,000 barrels of whiskey stored under the roof that was torn open, and if these had been ignited a terrible fire would have been added to the effect of the explosion. A package of dynamite which had failed to explode, though the fuse had been lighted, was found on the premises by the Chicago police. . . .

In the meantime, the years of depression after 1893 had wrought no less signal changes in the nature of the Standard Oil Company. This industrial empire, which continued to conquer markets and sources of supply in Russia and China as well as at the frontiers of the two Americas, was in no way checked by the period of general hardship. Nor had prohibitive laws, or condemnation of the company in certain regions such as the State of Ohio, hampered its progress in any degree. The order of dissolution in Ohio had simply been resisted by every legal subterfuge conceivable to its counsels; and then after seven years the Standard Oil had simply sloughed off its skin, and appeared as a New Jersey holding corporation.

But after 1893 the Standard Oil Company had a dual character. It was no longer simply an industrial monopoly, composed of men who simply owned and managed their oil business; it became, in great part, a reservoir of money, a house of investment bankers or absentee owners. So rapid had been the increase in annual profits, from $15,000,000 per annum in 1886 to $45,000,000 in 1899, that there was always more cash than could be used as capital in the oil and kindred trades. It became inevitable that the Standard Oil men make reinvestments regularly and extensively in new enterprises which were to be carried on under their absentee ownership. By a coincidence these developments came at a time when John D. Rockefeller announced his "retirement" from active business.

Moody in his "Masters of Capital" relates:

The Rockefellers were not the type of investors who were satisfied with five or six percent. . . . They meant to make, if possible, as large profits in the investment of their surplus cash as they had been accustomed to make in their own line of business. But to make money at so rapid a pace called for the same shrewd, superior business methods. . . . To discerning men it was clear that ultimately these other enterprises into which the Standard Oil put its funds must be controlled or dominated by Standard Oil. William Rockefeller had anticipated this development to some extent years before when he had become active in the financial management of the Chicago, Milwaukee and St. Paul Railroad. But it was not until after the panic of 1893 that he and his associates began to reach out aggressively to control the destinies of many corporations.

John D. Rockefeller at this time possessed a fortune that has been estimated at two hundred millions; his brother William owned probably half as much, while his associates who usually moved in conjunction with him or his brother,

Rogers, Flagler, Harkness, Payne, and various others combined now to form a capital of a size probably unprecedented in history. Soon the money markets felt the entrance of the Standard Oil "gang" in strange ways, as they began buying and selling pieces of capital, industries, men and material. This omnipotent group had brought a "new order of things" into the world of high finance. They had introduced into Wall Street operations, according to Henry Clews, "the same quiet, unostentatious, but resistless measures that they have always employed heretofore in their corporate affairs." Where a Gould might sometimes face the chance of failure, or a Commodore Vanderbilt have to fight for his life, Clews continued wonderingly, these men seemed to have removed the element of chance:

Their resources are so vast that they need only to concentrate on any given property in order to do with it what they please . . . that they have thus concentrated . . . is a fact well known. . . . They are the greatest operators the world has ever seen, and the beauty of their method is the quiet and lack of ostentation . . . no gallery plays . . . no scare heads in the newspapers . . . no wild scramble or excitement. With them the process is gradual, thorough, and steady, with never a waver or break.

In the conduct of these far-flung undertakings the Standard Oil family had always the loyal cooperation of the captains and lieutenants who wore their "collar" so contentedly, and who sent confidential news every day from all parts of the world. The "master mind" in these investment operations nowadays would seem to have been Henry Rogers; while important alliances . . . were effected with Stillman, the astute commander of the National City Bank, and Harriman, the rising giant of railroads.

After the headquarters of Standard Oil had been removed from Pearl Street to the high building at 26 Broadway, the active leaders of The System, as Thomas W. Lawson termed it, would go upstairs every day at eleven o'clock, to the fifteenth floor, and gather together around a large table. It was the high council of a dynasty of money, and men everywhere now spoke with bated breath of the commands which went forth from this council, and of the power and relentlessness of The System. In his romantic history, "Frenzied Finance," the stock-market plunger Lawson seems to blubber at the stupendous holdings of the Standard Oil "gang" toward 1900—"its countless miles of railroads . . . in every state and city in America, and its never-ending twistings of snaky pipe lines . . . its manufactories in the East, its colleges in the South, and its churches in the North." The guarded headquarters of Standard Oil aroused and have always aroused an awe which Lawson accurately reflects:

At the lower end of the greatest thoroughfare in the greatest city of the New World is a huge structure of plain gray-stone. Solid as a prison, towering as a steeple, its cold and forbidding facade. . . . Men point to its stern portals, glance quickly up at the rows of unwinking windows, nudge each other, and hurry onward, as the Spaniards used to do when going by the offices of the Inquisition. The building is No. 26 Broadway.

The Coming of the Modern Industrial Corporation

Reasons for Integration

Integration of mass production with mass distribution offered an opportunity for manufacturers to lower costs and increase productivity through more effective administration of the processes of production and distribution and coordination of the flow of goods through them. Yet the first industrialists to integrate these two basic sets of processes did not do so to exploit such economies. They did so because existing marketers were unable to sell and distribute products in the volume they were produced. The new mass producers were keenly aware of the national and international markets opened up by the new transportation and communication infrastructure. The potential of that market had impelled them to adopt the mass production machinery. However, as long as merchandising enterprises were able to sell their goods, they saw little reason to build marketing organizations of their own. Once the inadequacies of existing marketers became clear, manufacturers integrated forward into marketing.

In the 1880s two types of mass producers embarked on such a strategy of vertical integration. One set was composed of those who adopted new continuous-process machinery that swiftly expanded the output of their industrial establishments. Such entrepreneurs found that the existing marketers were unable to move their goods quickly enough or to advertise them effectively enough to keep their high-volume production facilities operating steadily. Most of these manufacturers continued to distribute through wholesalers, but they assumed responsibility for the coordination of the flow from the factory to the customer.

The second set of pioneers were manufacturers who required specialized distribution and marketing services which wholesalers, mass retailers, manufacturers' agents, and other middlemen were unable to provide. These manufacturers were, in turn, of two sorts. One included a small number of processors who had adopted refrigerated or temperature-controlled techniques for the distribution of perishable products in the national market. The other included the makers of new complex, high-priced machines that required specialized marketing services—demonstration, installation, consumer credit, after-sales service and repair—if they were to be sold in volume. The marketing of these latter products demanded a continuing after-sales contact with the customer. Existing middlemen had neither the interest nor the facilities to maintain a continuing relationship. Nearly all of the firms in this last group manufactured standardized machines that were or could be mass produced through the fabrication and assembling of interchangeable parts.

Those manufacturers who found existing marketers inadequate to meet these needs created multiunit marketing organizations of their own. They set up branch offices headed by salaried managers in major commercial centers of the country and the world. Next, to assure a high-volume continuing flow of materials into their factories, they built large purchasing establishments and smaller traffic departments and often began to supply and transport their own materials.

Because they integrated production, marketing, and purchasing, the activities of the new firms were far more varied than those of other business enterprises of their day. Whereas the railroad, telegraph, marketing, financial, or existing manufacturing firms carried on a single basic economic function, the new integrated enterprise carried on several. Because they came to own and operate many factories, many sales offices, many purchasing units, mines, forest lands, and transportation lines, their operation required even more full-time salaried managers than did the railroad and telegraph companies of the late nineteenth century. These managers handled a far wider variety of tasks and faced even greater challenges in coordinating the flow of materials through their enterprises than did those in transportation, communication, or mass marketing. With the rise of the integrated industrial enterprise, the salaried manager became a major figure in the operation of the American economy.

The new administrative hierarchies, extending as they did from the supplier of raw materials to the ultimate consumer, were from their beginning national enterprises; many soon became multinational. The railroads by the 1890s covered large regions, but there was no single nationwide railroad enterprise. The mass marketers concentrated on local urban and larger rural regional markets. Before 1880, Western Union and Montgomery Ward were among the few large firms to operate on a national scale. By the end of the 1880s, however, a number of industrial enterprises were beginning to serve the entire nation. By 1900 the names of many integrated, multifunctional enterprises had become household words. By then they were beginning to play a significant role in the transformation of the nation from what Robert Wiebe had termed a distended society of "island communities" into a far more homogeneous and integrated community.

As the twentieth century opened, the new integrated multifunctional, often multinational, enterprise was becoming the most influential institution in the American economy. It surpassed the railroad in size and in complexity and diversity of operations. The decisions of its managers affected more businessmen, workers, consumers, and other Americans than did those of railroad executives. It soon replaced the railroad as the focus for political and ideological controversy. In fact, in the first decade of the twentieth century the control of the new industrial corporations became the central domestic political issue of the day. Of more lasting importance, the techniques and procedures perfected in the first years of the century to manage these integrated enterprises have remained the foundation of modern business administration.

Integration by Users of Continuous-Process Technology

The most dramatic examples of the integration of mass production and mass distribution came in those industries adopting continuous-process machinery during the decade of the 1880s. Such machinery was, it will be recalled, invented almost simultaneously for making cigarettes, matches, flour, breakfast cereals, soup and other canned products, and photographic film. These innovations in mechanical continuous-process machinery and plant became the basis for a number of the first of the nation's giant industrial corporations. The creation of such enterprises drastically and permanently altered the structure of the industry in which they operated. . . .

As has been suggested, innovation in these industries was in part a response to the rise of the mass market which emerged with the completion of the nation's basic transportation and communication infrastructure. By the 1880s railroad, steamship, and telegraphic networks were fully integrated. By then belt lines, standard gauges and equipment, and interroad administrative arrangements permitted the movement of goods in nearly all parts of the nation with the minimum of transshipment. And almost instantaneous communication existed between Western Union's 12,000 offices.

The potential of the national market was further enlarged by two new types of ancillary business institutions that had already become widely used by the mass marketers. The credit agency, operating on a national scale after the Civil War, permitted manufacturers to check the reliability of jobbers and retailers in all parts of the country. The advertising agency, which purchased advertising space for clients in newspapers, journals, and periodicals circulating throughout the nation, was of even more value to mass producers. Until after the Civil War such agencies concentrated on writing copy and buying space in their local communities. Until the 1870s their major customers were department stores and jobbers and wholesalers selling traditional lines of dry goods, hardware, groceries, jewelry, furniture, cards, and stationery in local and regional markets. In that decade only books, journals, and patent medicines were advertised on more than a regional basis. Nearly all other manufacturers left advertising to the wholesalers who marketed their goods.

The manufacturers adopting the new continuous-process technology differed from the producers of books, journals, and patent medicines in that the unit output of their factories was much higher. To enlarge and maintain a market for these goods, they embarked on massive advertising campaigns carried out through these advertising agencies. They learned soon, too, that the wholesaler could not be relied upon to order and maintain inventory so that the customer could be always sure of obtaining the product. So the manufacturer took charge of scheduling the flow of finished products from the factory to the customer and then of raw and semi-finished materials from the suppliers to the factories.

The story of James Buchanan Duke effectively illustrates these general practices. Duke's dominance in the cigarette industry rested on his appreciation of the potential of the Bonsack cigarette machine. Duke, a manufacturer of smoking tobacco in Durham, North Carolina, had decided in 1881 to produce cigarettes because he was having difficulty in competing with a well-established neighbor, Blackwell and Company. At that date cigarettes were still a new and exotic product just beginning to find favor in the growing urban markets. Cigarette smoking was only starting to take the place of pipe smoking, chewing tobacco, cigars, or snuff. In 1881 four cigarette firms produced 80 percent of the output, primarily for nearby markets.

As a newcomer, Duke was searching for a way to break into the market. In 1884, shortly after a sharp reduction in taxes on cigarettes permitted a major price cut to consumers, Duke installed two Bonsack machines. With each machine producing 120,000 cigarettes a day, he could easily saturate the American market. To test the world market, Duke had sent a close associate, Richard M. Wright, on a nineteen-month tour overseas. In June, 1885, Duke signed a contract with Bonsack to use the machine exclusively to make all his cigarettes, high-quality as well as cheap, in return for a lower leasing charge.

Duke's gamble paid off. Output soared. Selling became the challenge. Even before Duke had made his basic contract with Bonsack, he built a factory in New York City, the nation's largest urban market, and set up his administrative offices there. He immediately intensified a national advertising campaign. Not only did Duke rely on advertising agencies but also his own staff distributed vast quantities of cards, circulars, and handbills—all proclaiming the virtues of his products.

He then began to build extensive sales organizations. Duke followed up the contacts Wright had made on his trip abroad by signing marketing agreements with wholesalers and dealers in all parts of the globe. At the same time, he and one or two other associates established a network of sales offices in the larger American cities. These offices, headed by salaried managers, became responsible for both the marketing and distributing of the product. The office kept an eye on local advertising. Its salesmen regularly visited tobacco, grocery, drug, and other jobbers, and a few large retailers to obtain orders. Duke's local sales managers worked closely with New York headquarters to assure the effective scheduling of the high-volume flow of cigarettes to jobbers and a few large retailers.

At the same time that Duke and his close associates were building their sales organization, they were creating an extensive purchasing network in southeastern United States, where bright-leaf tobacco—that used in cigarettes—was grown. Tobacco, after its annual harvest, was normally dried and cured before being sold to manufacturers. The timing of the process varied from several months to two or three years, according to the leaf and the quality desired. Because the supply of cured tobacco depended on both the size of the crop and the availability of curing facilities, prices fluctuated widely. By building its own buying, storing, and curing facilities, Duke's company was able to purchase directly from the farmers, usually at auctions, and so reduce transactions costs and uncertainties. What counted more was that the company was also assured of a steady supply of cured tobacco for its mass-producing factories in Durham and New York City.

By combining mass production with mass distribution Duke was able to maintain low prices and reap high profits. By 1889 Duke was by far the largest manufacturer in the industry, producing 834 million cigarettes with sales of over $4.5 million and profits of $400,000 annually, despite heavy advertising costs. To compete, other cigarette manufacturers had little choice but to follow Duke's strategy. They quickly turned to machine production and began to build and enlarge their sales and purchasing organizations. As packages of cigarettes were priced in 5 cent increments—5 cents for the standard package and 10 cents to 25 cents for the better brands—there was little room for price cutting, particularly in the all-important cheaper brands. The manufacturers concentrated on advertising instead. In 1889 Duke's advertising cost rose to $800,000 a year. Here his high volume and resulting cash flow gave him an advantage, for he had a larger cash surplus than the others to spend on advertising. But the cost of these sales campaigns reduced profits.

The desire to control this competition caused Duke and his four competitors to merge in 1890, forming the American Tobacco Company. For a brief time the constituent companies continued to operate independently; but after 1893 their functional activities were consolidated into the Duke manufacturing, sales, and leaf (purchasing) departments. As had been the case with the railroads and would be again in manufacturing, the largest of the early enterprises became the core organization for continuing growth. The enlarged centralized departmentalized company, operating from its New York corporate central office, proved extraordinarily profitable even during the economically depressed years of the 1890s. Profits from cigarettes allowed Duke to install new methods of production and distribution in other branches of the tobacco trade. By 1900 the American Tobacco Company had come to dominate that industry completely, except for the making of cigars. . . .

During a very short period in the 1880s, new processes of production and distribution had transferred the organization of a number of major American industries—tobacco, matches, grain milling, canning, soap, and photography. These changes were revolutionary, and they were permanent. The enterprises that pioneered in adopting and integrating the new ways of mass production and mass distribution became nationally known. By 1900, they were household words. Three-quarters of a century later the names American Tobacco, Diamond Match, Quaker Oats, Pillsbury Flour, Campbell Soup, Heinz, Borden, Carnation, Libby, Procter & Gamble, and Eastman Kodak are still well known.

These enterprises were similar in that they used new continuous-process machinery to produce low-priced packaged consumer goods. Their new processes of production were so capital-intensive (that is, the ratio of workers to the quantity of units produced was so small) that production for the national and global market became concentrated in just a few plants, often only one or two. In all cases it was the massive increase in output made possible by the new continuous-process, capital-intensive machinery that caused the manufacturers to build large marketing and purchasing networks.

The national and international network of sales offices took over from the wholesaler the functions of branding and advertising. Although advertising agents continued to be used to reach the national and world markets, the sales department became increasingly responsible for the content, location, and volume of advertising. As many of these products, like cigarettes, cereals, canned milk, and canned meat, were relatively new, advertising was important to enlarge demand. It was also a major competitive weapon because a relatively low unit price per package (usually 5 cents or 10 cents) made demand inelastic. It was difficult to increase demand by reducing prices. Although in most cases, jobbers continued to be used to distribute goods to the retailers, the sales offices took over scheduling and coordinating the flow of goods from factories to jobbers and often to retailers. (At Eastman this involved the flow of exposed film for printing as well.) They also worked closely with the manufacturing departments to coordinate the flow from the suppliers of the raw material through the process of production and distribution to the final consumers. A few of these firms, including Campbell Soup and Eastman Kodak, were soon selling and delivering directly to retailers. By the early twentieth century Eastman Kodak began to build its own retail stores in major cities.

In all these cases the high volume of output permitted by the integration of mass production with mass distribution generated an impressive cash flow that provided these enterprises with most of their working capital, as well as funds to expand capital equipment and facilities. These enterprises relied on local businessmen and commercial banks for both short-term and long-term loans. None, however, needed to go to the capital markets for funds to finance the expansion that so quickly placed them among the largest business enterprises in the world. For this reason the entrepreneurs, their families, and the associates who created these enterprises continued to control them. They personally held nearly all the voting stock in a company. Thus, although day-to-day operations had to be turned over to full-time salaried managers, long-term decisions as to investment, allocation of funds, and managerial recruitment remained concentrated in the hands of a small number of owners.

The administrative networks built to integrate the new processes of production and distribution gave the pioneering enterprises their greatest competitive advantage. Although capital-intensive in terms of the ratio of capital to labor inputs, the new machinery was not that expensive. The absolute cost of entry was not high, nor in most industries were patents a barrier to entry. The makers of cigarette, milling, canning, and soap-making machinery were eager to sell their products to as many manufacturers as possible. Nor was branding or advertising a barrier. Advertising agencies were just as intent as machinery manufacturers on finding new clients.

The most imposing barrier to entry in these industries was the organization the pioneers had built to market and distribute their newly mass-produced products. A competitor who acquired the technology had to create a national and often global organization of managers, buyers, and salesmen if he was to get the business away from the one or two enterprises that already stood astride the major marketing channels. Moreover, where the pioneer could finance the building of the first of these organizations out of cash flow, generated by high volume, the newcomer had to set up a competing network before high-volume output reduced unit costs and created a sizable cash flow. In this period of building he had to face a competitor whose economies of speed permitted him to set prices low and still maintain a margin of profit. Newcomers, of course, did appear. Kellogg and Postum in breakfast cereals and Colgate and Babbitt in soaps are examples. But all these industries were highly concentrated from the moment mass production methods were adopted. Except for flour milling, the industries in which these integrated industrial enterprises first appeared immediately became oligopolistic and have so remained.

Integration by Processors of Perishable Products

Whereas many of the mass producers of semiperishable packaged products continued to use the wholesaler to handle the physical distribution of their goods—even after they had taken over that middleman's advertising and scheduling functions—the makers of more perishable products such as meat and beer, in building their marketing networks, began to sell and distribute directly to the retailers. The market for perishable products expanded as the railroad and telegraph networks grew. As early as the 1850s crude refrigerator cars were used to bring milk, butter, and meat to urban markets. In the 1870s, when the direct movement of cars over long distances became possible, western meat packers began to ship fresh meat to the eastern cities. Then, in 1881 the modern refrigerated car made its appearance. Gustavus F. Swift hired Andrew J. Chase, a leading refrigeration engineer, to design a car to carry Swift's dressed beef from Chicago to Boston. Again, the 1880s were the crucial years.

The refrigerator car, however, was not the reason Swift became the innovator in high-volume, year-round production of perishable products. He became the first modern meat packer because he was the first to appreciate the need for a distribution network to store meat and deliver it to the retailers. He was the first to build an integrated enterprise to coordinate the high-volume flow of meat from the purchasing of cattle through the slaughtering or disassembling process and through distribution to the retailer and ultimate consumer.

When Gustavus Swift, a New England wholesale butcher, moved to Chicago in 1875, nearly all meat went east "on the hoof." Western cattle were shipped alive by rail in cattle cars to local wholesalers who butchered and delivered to retailers. The economies of slaughtering in the West and shipping the dressed meat east were obvious. Sixty percent of an animal was inedible and cattle lost weight and often died on the trip east. Moreover, the concentration of butchering in Chicago and other western cities permitted a high-volume continuous operation which not only lowered unit cost but also made possible fuller use of by-products.

To carry out his strategy, Swift, who had begun winter shipments in 1878, not only concentrated on improving the refrigerated car but also built a network of branch houses, first in the northeast and then after 1881 in the rest of the country. Each house included refrigerated storage space, a sales office, and a sales staff to sell and deliver the meat to the retail butchers, grocers, and other food shops. Swift soon supplemented this distributing and marketing network with "peddler car routes" which distributed dressed meat in small lots by refrigerator car to towns and villages.

In executing his plan, Swift met with most determined opposition. Railroads, startled by the prospect of losing their livestock business, which was an even greater producer of revenue than grain on the west to east routes, refused to build refrigerated cars. When Swift began to construct his own, the Eastern Trunk Line Association refused to carry them. Only by using the Grand Trunk, then outside of the association, was Swift able to bring his cars east. At the same time he had to combat boycotts by local wholesalers, who in 1886 formed the National Butchers' Protective Association to fight "the trust." These butchers attempted to exploit a prejudice against eating fresh meat that had been killed days or even weeks before, more than a thousand miles away.

High quality at low prices soon overcame this opposition. Though Swift did rely on advertising to counter prejudice against his product, it was clearly the prices and quality made possible by high-volume operations and the speed and careful scheduling of product flow that won the market. Once the market was assured, Swift had to expand his production facilities to keep up with demand. He increased his speed of throughput by subdividing the processes of butchering and by using moving "disassembling" lines. In the 1880s and early 1890s, Swift & Company built new packing plants in six cities along the cattle frontier. The company then bought into adjoining stockyards where men from its purchasing department became experts in buying cattle in volume.

Other packers realized that if they were to compete with Swift in the national market they must follow his lead. By the end of 1882, Philip D. Armour of Chicago and George H. Hammond of Detroit were beginning to build comparable networks of branch houses and to compete with Swift for the best locations along the railroad lines. Nelson Morris of Chicago and the two Cudahy brothers of Omaha constructed similar networks in the mid-1880s. The oligopoly was rounded out when the New York firm of Swartschild and Sulzberger completed a comparable integrated national enterprise in the early 1890s. Except for Hammond who died in 1886, all these entrepreneurs enlarged their processing facilities, built new packing plants in other western cities, bought into the stockyards, and expanded their fleet of refrigerated cars. Well before the end of the eighties a small number of very large meat-packing firms dominated the dressed meat business, and they continued to do so until well into the twentieth century. . . .

Integration by Machinery Makers Requiring Specialized Marketing Services

The other manufacturers to by-pass the wholesalers were the makers of recently invented machines that were produced in volume through the fabrication and assembling of interchangeable parts. The marketing needs of these machinery makers were even greater than those of the meat packers and brewers. They found that the volume sale of their products required more than centralized advertising and coordinated flows. Their new and relatively complex products had to be demonstrated before they could be sold. Mechanical expertise was needed to service and repair them after they had been sold. And because the machines were relatively costly, buyers often could only purchase them on credit. Independent wholesalers were rarely able or willing to provide such demonstrations, maintenance and repair, and consumer credit.

The machines requiring these close and continuing services to the customer were of two sorts. Sewing machines, agriculture equipment, and office machinery were similar to present-day consumer durables, even though they were sold primarily to produce goods and services and not for consumption by the final consumer. They were produced at a high rate, often many thousands a week, and sold to individuals as well as to business firms. The second type—elevators, pumps, boilers, printing presses, and a variety of electrical equipment—were clearly producers' goods. They were complex, large, standardized machines that required specialized installation as well as sales and repair and long-term credit. In the eighties the makers of both sorts of machines began to expand output by pioneering in or adopting the new ways of systematic factory management. Both sold their products in national and world markets and created or reorganized extensive marketing organizations in that same decade.

The first mass producers of machinery to build their own sales organizations were the makers of sewing machines. These machines could be produced commercially in the early 1850s, but the manufacturers could not begin to make them in quantity until the legal battle over patents was settled in 1854 and a patent pool formed. The winner of the court trials, Elias Howe, insisted that the pooled patents be released to twenty-four manufacturers. Nevertheless, the industry was dominated within a short time by the three firms that first acquired marketing networks—Wheeler & Wilson Co., Grover and Baker, and I. M. Singer Company. These manufacturers at first relied on full-time but independent agents who, though receiving a small salary, were paid primarily on a commission basis and were solely responsible for marketing activities within their territories. But these agents had little technical knowledge of the machines and were unable to demonstrate them properly or service and repair them. Nor were the agents able to provide credit, an important consideration if customers were to pay for these relatively expensive goods in installments.

As an alternative, Grover and Baker began to set up a company owned and operated store or branch office to provide such services. By 1856 Grover and Baker had already established such branch offices, as they were called, in ten cities. In that year Isaac Merritt Singer decided to follow suit. So, almost immediately, did Wheeler & Wilson. By 1859 Singer had opened fourteen branches, each with a female demonstrator, a mechanic to repair and service, and a salesman or canvasser to sell the machine, as well as a manager who supervised the others and handled collections and credits. Nevertheless, because finding and training personnel took time, these three enterprises continued to rely heavily on commission agents to market their goods. The swift selection of these agents and the building of branch stores permitted these three to dominate the trade. By 1860 they already produced three-fourths of the industry's output, with Wheeler & Wilson manufacturing 85,000 machines in that year and the other two 55,000 apiece.

After 1860 Singer moved more aggressively than the other two in replacing regional distributors with branch stores supervised by full-time, salaried regional agents. Edward Clark, Singer's partner and the business brains of the partnership, had become even more convinced as time passed of the value of relying on his own sales force. The independent agents had difficulty in supplying the necessary marketing services, and they failed to maintain inventories properly. They waited until their stocks were low and then telegraphed large orders, requesting immediate delivery. They seemed to be always either understocked or overstocked. Moreover, the agents were frustratingly slow in returning payments made on the machines to the central office.

Therefore, Clark was constantly on the outlook for men he could hire as salaried "general agents" or regional managers of geographical districts to supervise existing branch stores and to set up new ones. Where such men could not be found, Clark continued to rely on independent agents; but he insisted that such dealers set up branch offices similar to those in a company-managed district.

When Clark became president in 1876, a year after Singer's death, he decided to eliminate the independent agencies altogether, at home and abroad. Singer's central offices in New York and London had as yet little control over the branch stores of the independent distributors and, in fact, relatively little control over their own salaried agents. Scarcely any effort had been made to sell in any systematic or standardized way. Uniformity in sales, accounting, credit policies, and procedures was lacking. The techniques of administrative coordination had not yet been perfected. Moreover, in 1877 the last patents of the 1856 pool were to expire. After that year Singer would have to compete at home, as it had long done abroad, without patent protection.

Working closely with George Ross McKenzie, a Scotsman who helped to build Singer's overseas organization and succeeded him as president, Clark gradually reorganized and rationalized Singer's marketing and distribution network. First he completed the replacement of the independent distributors with regional offices manned by salaried executives. Then he installed everywhere similar branch offices with teams of canvassers as well as repairmen and accountants. Such offices had proved particularly successful in Great Britain, an area where Singer had never enjoyed patent protection. The network made possible aggressive marketing, reliable service and repair, and careful supervision of credits and collections; it also assured a steady cash flow from the field to the headquarters in London, Hamburg, and New York.

In the period immediately after 1878, Clark and McKenzie perfected the procedures and methods needed to supervise and evaluate this branch office network. In the United States twenty-five different regional "general agencies" reported to the central office in New York. In the United Kingdom, twenty-six regional sales offices reported to a London office. In northern and central Europe the managers of fifty-three more reported to headquarters in Hamburg. Nine others in the rest of Europe, Africa, and the Near East reported to London, while those in Latin America, Canada, and the Far East were supervised by the central New York office.

The expansion and then reformation of the marketing organization resulted in a constant increase in Singer's sales and, therefore, the daily output of its factories, and the overall size of the enterprise. In 1874 the company built by far the largest sewing machine factory in the world at Elizabethport, New Jersey. During the 1880s it grew in size; but its capacity was surpassed when the company constructed a plant in 1885 in Kilbowie, Scotland (a suburb of Glasgow). That plant, with a rated capacity of 10,000 machines a week, was constructed to replace a smaller Scottish plant built in 1867. Both plants were constructed to improve coordination between production and distribution. The filling of hundreds and then thousands of orders in Europe from the American factory became more and more difficult. Delays became the major cause for losing orders. In 1866, for example, the head of Singer's London office complained that the inability to deliver machines had "utterly ruined" the company's business in Britain. All Singer's capital facilities—its two great factories, a small cabinetmaking plant in South Bend, Indiana, and a foundry in Austria—were financed out of current earnings.

Increased demand in these years caused Singer to expand and systematize its purchasing operations. By the 1890s the company had obtained its own timberlands, an iron mill, and some transportation facilities. These purchases were also paid for from the ample cash flow provided by sale of the machines. Indeed, the company often had a surplus which it invested in railroad and government bonds, and even in other manufacturing firms. Both insiders and outsiders credited Singer's business success to its marketing organization and abilities. . . .

As the experience of all the new mass-produced machinery companies emphasizes, they could sell in volume only if they created a massive, multiunit marketing organization. All their products were new, all were relatively complicated to operate and maintain, and all relatively costly. No existing marketer knew the product as well as the manufacturer. None had the facilities to provide after-sales service and repair. Few were willing to take the risk of selling on installment, a marketing device which these machinery makers had to invent. Nor were outsiders able to maintain close control over collections, essential to assure a continued cash flow on which the financial health of the enterprise rested. Finally, by using uniform sales techniques, bringing together regularly members of a nationwide sales force, and comparing the activities and performances of the many different sales offices, the single, centrally controlled sales department was able to develop more effective marketing techniques. It was also able to obtain a constant flow of information on the changing shifts in demands and customer requirements.

Close and constant communication between the branch sales offices, the factory, and its purchasing organization made it possible to schedule a high-volume flow of goods from the suppliers of raw materials to the ultimate consumer, and so to keep the manufacturing facilities relatively full and running steadily. It also assured a steady flow of cash to the central office. Such coordination would have been exceedingly difficult if independent enterprises handled each stage of the processes of supplying, manufacturing, and marketing. The regular and increasing demand made possible in part by an aggressive sales force in turn created pressures to speed up the processes of production through improved machinery, plant design, and management. Increased speed of production in its turn reduced unit costs. The economies of speed and scale, and their national, often global, marketing organizations gave the pioneering firms an impressive competitive advantage and so made it easy for them to continue to dominate their industries.

All this was also true for the makers of new, technologically advanced, relatively standardized machinery that was sold to other manufacturers to be used in their production processes. Because these goods were even more complex and more costly, they required specialized installation as well as closer attention to after-sales service and repair. The sales force for such manufacturers required more professional training than persons selling light machines in mass markets. Salesmen often had degrees in mechanical engineering. Again, it was the decade of the 1880s when enterprises in these industries began to build or rationalize their national and global sales forces.

An excellent example of enterprises producing and marketing in volume for global markets were the makers of recently invented machinery to generate, transmit, and use electricity for power and light. The salesmen at Westinghouse, Thompson-Houston, and Edison General Electric (the last two combined into General Electric in 1892) all knew more about the technical nature of their equipment than did most of their customers. Moreover, few independent distributors could obtain a firm grasp of the rapidly changing new technology. Because of the dangers of electrocution and fire, trained salaried employees of these companies had to install and service and repair their products. Financing involved large sums, often requiring extensive credit, which independent distributors were unable to supply. Thompson-Houston and Edison Electric, and, to a lesser extent, Westinghouse, began to finance new local central power stations in order to build the market for their machinery.

In these pioneering years of the electrical equipment business, technology was developing fast. Coordination between the sales, production, and purchasing departments thus involved more than scheduling flows of material. It meant that salesmen, equipment designers, and the manufacturing executives had to be in constant touch to coordinate technological improvements with market needs so that the product could be produced at the lowest possible unit cost. It also lessened even more the opportunities for independent sales agencies to acquire the necessary skills to market the product. . . .

All of the pioneering machinery firms continued to dominate their industries for decades. Administrative coordination brought lower costs and permitted manufacturers to have a more direct contact with markets. The technological complexities of their products, particularly those selling producers' goods, made their marketing organizations of trained engineers and other technical specialists even more powerful competitive weapons than were the sales departments of makers of consumer goods purchased for immediate consumption. The nature of their processes as well as products, led to the assigning of technicians to concentrate on improving both product and process and so to the formation of the first formal industrial research departments. As in the case of the first integrated manufacturers of perishable and semiperishable products, the machinery firms soon had competitors. But to compete with the established enterprise demanded the creation of a comparable national and often international marketing network. And in competing, the new enterprise had to win customers before its organization could generate the volume necessary to provide low prices and high cash flow or develop its staffs of expert marketing and research technicians. Rarely did more than a handful of competitors succeed in obtaining a significant share of the national and international markets. These industries quickly became and remained oligopolistic or monopolistic.

Makers of volume-produced standardized machinery, processors of perishable products, and those that mass produced low-priced packaged goods, internalized the activities of the wholesaler or other middlemen when these distributors were unable to provide the marketing services needed if the goods were to be manufactured in the unprecedented volume permitted by the new technologies of production and distribution. The resulting enterprises, clustered in the food and machinery industries, were then the first industrial corporations to coordinate administratively the flow of goods on a national, indeed a global, scale. They were among the world's first modern multinationals. Their products were usually new. This was true not only for sewing, agricultural, and office machinery but also for cigarettes, matches, breakfast cereals, canned milk and soup, roll film and Kodak cameras, and even fresh meat that had been butchered a thousand miles away. In all these new industries the pioneers remained dominant enterprises. Because they were the first big businesses in American industry, they defined many of its administrative practices and procedures. Their formation, organization, and growth, therefore, have significant implications for the operation and structure of American industry and the economy as a whole.

SUGGESTIONS FOR FURTHER READING

Good surveys of economic change are Stuart Bruchey, *Growth of the Modern Economy* (New York, 1975); Edward C. Kirkland, *Industry Comes of Age: Business, Labor, and Public Policy, 1860–1897* (Chicago, 1961); and Robert Higgs, *The Transformation of the American Economy, 1865–1914* (New York, 1971). Robert McCloskey, *Conservatism in the Age of Enterprise* (New York, 1951) and Sidney Fine, *Laissez Faire and the General-Welfare State* (Ann Arbor, Mich., 1956) discuss the political, economic, and social conservatism that accompanied the rise of big business, and Matthew Josephson discusses the politics during the age of the robber barons in *The Politicos* (New York, 1938).

Samuel P. Hays, *The Response to Industrialism* (Chicago, 1957), argues that "the desire to create wealth possessed all Americans." Industrialism created new problems, but Americans welcomed it as they sought to adjust by creating a new consensus. Robert Wiebe, *The Search for Order* (New York, 1967) shows how economic change broke down the old order based upon local authority and created a new one based upon growing centralization of authority. He describes how Americans had to adjust to these changed conditions.

Olivier Zunz, *Making America Corporate, 1870–1920* (Chicago, 1990) focuses on the role of a new middle class in designing the corporate world. A discussion of the middle class in a longer perspective is Stuart M. Blumin, *The Emergence of the Middle Class: Social Experience in the American City, 1790–1900* (Cambridge, Eng., 1989).

Gustavus Myers, *History of the Great American Fortunes* (New York, 1907), like Josephson's *The Robber Barons* (New York, 1934), is a blistering attack on the businessmen. Henry Demarest Lloyd, *Wealth Against Commonwealth* (New York, 1894) is

---

*Available in paperback.

sharply critical of John D. Rockefeller, as is Ida M. Tarbell, *The History of Standard Oil Company* (New York, 1904; abridged version in paperback). The opposite approach is taken by Allan Nevins in his long biography of Rockefeller: *John D. Rockefeller: The Heroic Age of American Enterprise,* 2 vols. (New York, 1940), and *Study in Power: John D. Rockefeller, Industrialist and Philanthropist,* 2 vols. (New York, 1953). Like Nevins, Ralph W. and Muriel E. Hidy, *Pioneering in Big Business, 1882–1911: History of Standard Oil Company (New Jersey)* (New York, 1955), stress the importance of Rockefeller in organizing the oil business. Louis M. Hacker, *The Triumph of American Capitalism* (New York, 1940) places the contributions of the post–Civil War industrialists in the context of earlier economic history; although often critical of them, Hacker concludes by praising their accomplishments.

As famous (or infamous) as Rockefeller was J. P. Morgan. Two very different pictures of the great banker may be found in Frederick Lewis Allen, **The Great Pierpont Morgan* (New York, 1949), and Lewis Corey, *The House of Morgan* (New York, 1930).

Useful interpretive surveys of the vast literature on the "robber barons" may be found in Edward C. Kirkland, "The Robber Barons Revisited," *American Historical Review,* 66 (October 1960), 68–73; Hal Bridges, "The Robber Baron Concept in American History," *Business History Review,* 32 (Spring 1958), 1–13; Thomas C. Cochran, "The Legend of the Robber Barons," *The Pennsylvania Magazine of History and Biography,* 74 (July 1950), 307–21; and Gabriel Kolko, "The Premises of Business Revisionism," *Business History Review,* 33 (Autumn 1959), 330–44.

The selection by Alfred D. Chandler, Jr., illustrates a different approach toward the rise of big business that has been adopted by some scholars in recent years. Discounting the personalities of the business leaders and avoiding the question of whether they were right or wrong, these historians give emphasis instead to problems such as management, markets, organization, and structure. A good discussion of this work, its assumptions, and its methods is Louis Galambos, "The Emerging Organizational Synthesis in Modern American History," *Business History Review,* 44 (Autumn 1970), 279–90. Brief discussions of the emergence of big business are David G. Bunting, *The Rise of Large American Corporations, 1889–1919* (New York, 1987) and Glen Porter, **The Rise of Big Business, 1860–1920,* 2nd ed. (Arlington Heights, Ill., 1992). Porter's book concludes with a splendid "Bibliographic Essay" that provides additional references and puts his and other studies of big business in an insightful historical context.

The serious student should read Chandler's **The Visible Hand* in its entirety, as well as Chandler's earlier book, **Strategy and Structure* (Cambridge, Mass., 1962), and his later, comparative study, *Scale and Scope: The Dynamics of Industrial Capitalism* (Cambridge, Mass., 1990). A valuable comparative study that considers the political actions of business is Michael Useem, *The Inner Circle: Large Corporations and the Rise of Business Political Activity in the U.S. and U.K.* (New York, 1984).

Farmers in
an Industrial Age

Those who labor in the earth are the chosen people of God," wrote Thomas Jefferson. Virtue resides in the hearts of the agriculturists, he explained. "Corruption of morals in the mass of cultivators is a phenomenon of which no age nor nation has furnished an example." To this day many Americans have the vague feeling that farming is the most natural, the most virtuous occupation, that somehow those who work the land are especially important to the survival of American democracy.

Yet farmers are rarely mentioned in history textbooks except in discussions of their problems. And, indeed, over the years the American farmer has had many serious problems. In the colonial period, when most of the nation's citizens tilled the soil, the small farmers along the frontier bore the brunt of the Indian raids and lamented the lack of adequate protection for their families and lands. They complained that they were underrepresented in the assemblies, overtaxed, and given too few of the bridges and roads that they demanded. Occasionally, when they felt that their problems had gone unheeded too long, they rebelled against colonial authorities.

Independence did not end the small farmers' difficulties. Shays's Rebellion in Massachusetts and the Whiskey Rebellion in Pennsylvania, both put down quickly, represented the unhappiness and the discontent of some farmers.

Working the land may have seemed an ideal occupation to those living in the cities, but many farmers knew better. The everyday struggle to eke out a living from the soil, often without the cooperation of the elements, was hard and frequently frustrating. Nor did the passage of time solve the farmers' problems; more often new problems were added to the old.

From the colonial period to the early nineteenth century, most of those who worked the land were subsistence farmers; that is, they consumed the greatest part of what they grew. A few had a cash crop—grain (often distilled into whiskey), cotton, or tobacco, depending on the area—but most sold only their surplus that remained after they consumed what they needed for their own use. The opening of new lands in the West, improvements in transportation, innovations in farm equipment, and growing urban markets combined to transform growing numbers of subsistence farmers into commercial producers. Increasingly, farmers concentrated on cash crops such as wheat, corn, cotton, or pork, and used the proceeds to buy tools, clothing, household equipment, and other manufactured goods. As they commercialized, farmers lost their economic independence. They became increasingly dependent on the bankers, who lent them money to buy more land and machinery needed to increase production; on the railroad, which provided the means to get crops to market; on manufacturers, who supplied the necessary tools and equipment; and on a host of middlemen who handled their crops and arranged for sales in distant markets. The farmers' incomes, and hence their well-being, depended upon the cost of goods and services they needed and upon the vicissitudes of the worldwide market for their crops.

The spread of commercial farming and the expansion of industrialism, especially in the years after the Civil War, raised the standard of living of many farmers, who were able to purchase some of the luxuries enjoyed by the city dweller. Often, however, the price of higher living standards was great. Many went deeply in debt as they sought to increase production by purchasing new lands and more machinery. As production rose, prices went down; efforts to increase income through further increases in production compounded the problem. Fluctuations of the business cycle, as well as the natural disasters of droughts, floods, hail, and wind, added to the farmers' woes. Increasingly in the years after the Civil War, farmers felt victimized, and often they blamed the railroads, the bankers, the manufacturers, or the middlemen for their plight.

In an effort to improve their situation, farmers attempted to organize, in part for self-help, but, increasingly, to get government action to solve their problems. They joined the Patrons of Husbandry, more commonly known as the Grange. At first primarily a social organization, inevitably the Grange became involved in politics, and in several midwestern states successfully pressured for laws regulating railroads. When most of the laws proved inadequate, farmers continued to agitate, joining societies like the Agricultural Wheel in Arkansas, the Farmers' Union in Louisiana, and the Farmers' Alliances in various other states. All this organizing came to a climax in 1892 when many farmers bolted the two regular parties and formed the People's or Populist party.

The Populists regarded their movement as a weapon in their struggle against what they termed "the interests," a massive conspiracy of bankers, railroads, and big businessmen seeking to exploit the farmers. Their only defense, they concluded, was organization and struggle. For many of their opponents, the movement was a threat, for it smacked of revolution. Some historians, accepting this evaluation, have concluded that the farmers' movements represented a fundamental class conflict in American society. According to this view, farmers resisted the encroachment of big business and sought to retain their economic independence and their political influence. Some scholars add that what made the farmers' movement really revolutionary was that they were proposing an alternative path for the country to follow; they opposed the growth of big business and the centralized corporate state, favoring instead decentralized production with local controls.

Other scholars disagree, insisting that the farmers were not revolutionary; indeed, they were not even particularly radical. Most farmers, according to this view, had become modern businessmen who welcomed economic changes and the growth of large-scale, highly mechanized agriculture. Their complaint was that they were not sharing equitably with other businessmen in the benefits of change; their goal was simply to get a bigger slice of the economic pie.

Still other historians argue that the Populists were in a very real sense counterrevolutionaries. Unwilling or unable to adapt to changing economic conditions, they longed to turn back the clock, to return to the age of subsistence agriculture, the small family farm, and the pastoral village.

Examples of these very different interpretations are presented in the following selections. Readers should keep a number of questions in mind as they seek to sort out the various interpretations. What exactly were the farmers asking for? Did all farmers seek essentially the same reforms or did farmers in different areas and with different problems demand different changes? Were the demands radical or revolutionary? If the farmers had gotten all they asked for, would the result have been a revolutionary change in American society?

In the first selection, John D. Hicks spells out the farmers' grievances against the railroads, big business, bankers, and middlemen. Farmers complained that the prices they received for the goods they sold were low and falling, while prices they had to pay for transportation, credit, storage, sales, and machinery were high and rising. Unconvinced that the problem was overproduction of farm commodities, the farmers blamed a conspiracy of eastern businessmen for their plight. The picture that emerges from Hicks's discussion is one of sharp class conflict, with agrarians—West and South—arrayed against eastern capitalists.

Richard Hofstadter, in the next selection, notes that in some ways the Populists were progressive reformers who recognized that the federal government had the responsibility to help solve some of the problems of industrialism. But Hofstadter argues that the rhetoric that accompanied their demands indicates that the Populists "were nurtured by the traditions of the agrarian myth," a backward-looking ideology that saw a vision of an agrarian "golden age" in the past. Instead of attempting to adapt to the modern world, the Populists, unable to understand the real problems they faced, looked backward toward what seemed to be better days; instead of realistically assessing their problems, they viewed themselves as the victims of an eastern Jewish banker conspiracy.

Lawrence Goodwyn, in the final selection, completely disagrees. He finds the farmers' grievances to be real and their solutions realistic. They were attacking the growth and consolidation of the "corporate state" and proposing an alternative, more democratic path for America to follow. "Heretics in a land of true believers and recent converts, they saw the coming society and they did not like it." The Populists failed not because their goals were unrealistic but because they proposed a future for the nation that went counter to the newly created consensus that accepted and promoted a less-democratic corporate state.

There can be no doubt that farmers' lives were often difficult and that they faced real problems. But what was the source of those problems? Were the farmers victims of a conspiracy of eastern businessmen and bankers who controlled the country? Did their efforts to improve their conditions signal class war between farmers and businessmen for control? Or were the farmers merely victims of their own efficiency, which led to overproduction and falling prices? If so, and if they recognized the real problem, then perhaps their proposals for reform were realistic efforts to adapt to the new industrial age. If the farmers failed to see the real source of the problems they faced and instead blamed a nonexistent conspiracy, then their proposals were nostalgic, reactionary yearnings for a past that could not be recaptured—or, perhaps, never existed. But if the farmers sought the solution to their problems in proposals that rejected the ideology of the new age, then their demands and their rhetoric were forward looking, proposing an alternative, more democratic future for the nation.

JOHN D. HICKS

The Farmers' Grievances

In the spring of 1887 a North Carolina farm journal stated with rare accuracy what many farmers in all sections of the United States had been thinking for some time.

There is something radically wrong in our industrial system. There is a screw loose. The wheels have dropped out of balance. The railroads have never been so prosperous, and yet agriculture languishes. The banks have never done a better or more profitable business, and yet agriculture languishes. Manufacturing enterprises never made more money or were in a more flourishing condition, and yet agriculture languishes. Towns and cities flourish and "boom" and grow and "boom," and yet agriculture languishes. Salaries and fees were never so temptingly high and desirable, and yet agriculture languishes.

Nor was this situation imputed to America alone. Once in an unguarded burst of rhetoric a high priest of the Alliance movement pointed out that similar conditions prevailed in all thickly populated agricultural countries, "high tariff and low tariff; monarchies, empires, and republics; single gold standard, silver standard or double standard." It was true indeed that the blessings of civilization had not fallen upon all mankind with equal bounty. To the upper and middle classes more had been given than to the lower; to the city dweller far more than to his country kinsman. The farmer had good reason to believe, as he did believe, that he worked longer hours, under more adverse conditions, and with smaller compensation for his labor than any other man on earth.

For this condition of affairs the farmer did not blame himself. Individual farmers might be lacking in industry and frugality, but farmers as a class were devoted to these virtues. Those who gave up the struggle to win wealth out of the land and went to the cities so generally succeeded in the new environment that a steady migration from farm to city set in. Why should the same man fail as a farmer and succeed as a city laborer? More and more the conviction settled down upon the farmer that he was the victim of "some extrinsic baleful influence." Someone was "walking off with the surplus" that society as a whole was clearly building up and that in part at least should be his. He was accustomed to regard himself as the "bone and sinew of the nation" and as the producer of "the largest share of its wealth." Why should his burdens be "heavier every year and his gains . . . more meager?" Why should he be face to face with a condition of abject servility? Not himself, certainly, but someone else was to blame.

The farmer never doubted that his lack of prosperity was directly traceable to the low prices he received for the commodity he had to sell. The period from 1870 to 1897 was one of steadily declining prices. As one writer put it, the farmer's task had been at the beginning of this era "to make two spears of grass grow where one grew before. He solved that. Now he is struggling hopelessly with the question how to get as much for two spears of grass as he used to get for one." Accurate statistics showing what the farmer really received for his crops are almost impossible to obtain, but the figures given by the Department of Agriculture for three major crops, given in the table below, will at least reveal the general downward trend of prices.

These prices are subject to certain corrections. They are as of December 1, whereas the average farmer had to sell long before that time, often on a glutted market that beat down the price to a much lower figure. They make no allowance, either, for commissions to dealers, for necessary warehouse charges, nor for deductions made when the produce could not be regarded as strictly first class. They fail to show, also, the difference in prices received along the frontier, where the distance to market was great, and in the eastern states, where the market was near at hand. In 1889, for example, corn was sold in Kansas for as low a price as ten cents a bushel and was commonly burned in lieu of coal. In 1890 a farmer in Gosper County, Nebraska, it was said, shot his hogs because he could neither sell nor give them away.

Average Market Prices of Three Crops, 1870–1897

Years	Wheat (per bushel)	Corn (per bushel)	Cotton (per pound)
1870–1873	106.7	43.1	15.1
1874–1877	94.4	40.9	11.1
1878–1881	100.6	43.1	9.5
1882–1885	80.2	39.8	9.1
1886–1889	74.8	35.9	8.3
1890–1893	70.9	41.7	7.8
1894–1897	63.3	29.7	5.8

So low did the scale of prices drop that in certain sections of the country it was easy enough to prove, statistically at least, that farming was carried on only at an actual loss. It was generally agreed that seven or eight cents of the price received for each pound of cotton went to cover the cost of production; by the later eighties, moreover, many cotton growers were finding it necessary to market their crops for less than they had been getting. The average price per bushel received by northwestern wheat growers dropped as low as from forty-two to forty-eight cents, whereas the cost of raising a bushel of wheat was variously estimated at from forty-five to sixty-seven cents. Statisticians held that it cost about twenty-one cents to produce a bushel of corn, but the western farmer sometimes had to take less than half that sum. Quoth one agitator:

We were told two years ago to go to work and raise a big crop, that was all we needed. We went to work and plowed and planted; the rains fell, the sun shone, nature smiled, and we raised the big crop that they told us to; and what came of it? Eight cent corn, ten cent oats, two cent beef and no price at all for butter and eggs—that's what came of it. Then the politicians said that we suffered from overproduction.

Not politicians only but many others who studied the question held that overproduction was the root of the evil. Too many acres were being tilled, with the result that too many bushels of grain, too many bales of cotton, too many tons of hay, too many pounds of beef were being thrown upon the market each year. As the population increased, the number of consumers had advanced correspondingly, but the increase in production had gone on even more rapidly. It was a fact that the per capita output of most commodities had risen with each successive year. The markets of the world were literally broken down. With the supply so far in excess of the demand, prices could not possibly be maintained at their former levels. . . .

But the farmers and their defenders refused to place much stock in the overproduction theory. Admitting that the output from the farm had increased perhaps even more rapidly than population, they could still argue that this in itself was not sufficient to account for the low prices and the consequent agricultural depression. They pointed out that, with the general improvement of conditions among the masses, consumption had greatly increased. Possibly the demand attendant upon this fact alone would be nearly, if not quite, sufficient to offset the greater yearly output. There would be, moreover, even heavier consumption were it possible for those who needed and wanted more of the products of the farm to buy to the full extent of their ability to consume. In spite of all the advances of the nineteenth century the world was not yet free from want. "The makers of clothes were underfed; the makers of food were underclad." Farmers used corn for fuel in the West because the prices they were offered for it were so low, while at the same moment thousands of people elsewhere faced hunger and even starvation because the price of flour was so high. Why should the Kansas farmer have to sell his corn for eight or ten cents a bushel when the New York broker could and did demand upwards of a dollar for it? Were there not certain "artificial barriers to consumption"? Were there not "certain influences at work, like thieves in the night," to rob the farmers of the fruits of their toil?

Many of the farmers thought that there were; and they were not always uncertain as to the identity of those who stood in the way of agricultural prosperity. Western farmers blamed many of their troubles upon the railroads, by means of which all western crops must be sent to market. There was no choice but to use these roads, and as the frontier advanced farther and farther into the West, the length of the haul to market increased correspondingly. Sometimes western wheat or corn was carried a thousand, perhaps even two thousand, miles before it could reach a suitable place for export or consumption. For these long hauls the railroads naturally exacted high rates, admittedly charging "all the traffic would bear." The farmers of Kansas and Nebraska and Iowa complained that it cost a bushel of corn to send another bushel of corn to market, and it was commonly believed that the net profit of the carrier was greater than the net profit of the grower. The farmers of Minnesota and Dakota were accustomed to pay half the value of their wheat to get it as far towards its final destination as Chicago. Small wonder that the farmer held the railroads at least partly responsible for his distress! He believed that if he could only get his fair share of the price for which his produce eventually sold he would be prosperous enough. "How long," a Minnesota editor queried, "even with these cheap and wonderfully productive lands, can . . . any agricultural community pay such enormous tribute to corporate organization in times like these, without final exhaustion?"

Local freight rates were particularly high. The railroads figured, not without reason, that large shipments cost them less per bushel to haul than small shipments. The greater the volume of traffic the less the cost of carrying any portion of that traffic. Accordingly, on through routes and long hauls where there was a large and dependable flow of freight the rates were comparatively low—the lower because for such runs there was usually ample competition. Rates from Chicago to New York, for example, were low in comparison with rates for similar distances from western points to Chicago, while between local points west of Chicago the rates were even more disproportionate. Sometimes the western local rate would be four times as great as that charged for the same distance and the same commodity in the East. The rates on wheat from Fargo to Duluth were nearly double those from Minneapolis to Chicago—a distance twice as great. It cost as much as twenty-five cents a bushel to transport grain from many Minnesota towns to St. Paul or Minneapolis, while for less than as much more it could be transported all the way to the seaboard. Indeed, evidence was at hand to show that wheat could actually be sent from Chicago to Liverpool for less than from certain points in Dakota to the Twin Cities. Iowa farmers complained that it cost them about as much to ship in corn from an adjoining county for feeding purposes as it would have cost to ship the same corn to Chicago; and yet the Iowa rates seemed low to the farmers of Nebraska, who claimed that they paid an average of fifty percent more for the same service than their neighbors across the Missouri River.

Undoubtedly it cost the railroads more to haul the sparse freight of the West than it cost them to haul the plentiful freight of the East. Railway officials pointed out that western traffic was nearly all in one direction. During one season of the year for every car of wheat hauled out an empty car had to be hauled in, while the rest of the time about ninety percent of the traffic went from Chicago westward. They asserted that the new roads were often in thinly settled regions and were operated at a loss even with the highest rates. James J. Hill maintained that the roads were reducing rates as fast as they could, and to prove it he even declared himself "willing that the state make any rates it see fit," provided the state would "guarantee the roads six percent on their actual cost and a fund for maintenance, renewal and other necessary expenditures." President Dillon of the Union Pacific deplored the ingratitude of the farmers who grumbled about high rates. "What would it cost," he asked, "for a man to carry a ton of wheat one mile? What would it cost for a horse to do the same? The railway does it at a cost of less than a cent." Moreover, he thought that unreasonable rates could never long survive, for if a railroad should attempt anything of the sort competition would come immediately to the farmers' aid, and a parallel and competing line would be built to drive the charges down.

But critics of the railroads saw little that was convincing in these arguments. As for the regulation of rates by competition, it might apply on through routes, providing the roads had no agreement among themselves to prevent it, but competition could scarcely affect the charges for local hauls for the simple reason that the average western community depended exclusively upon a single road. Only rarely did the shipper have a choice of two or more railway companies with which to deal, and even when he had this choice there was not invariably competition. The roads reached agreements among themselves; more than that, they consolidated. "The number of separate railroad companies operating distinct roads in Minnesota was as high as twenty, three years ago," wrote the railway commissioner of that state in 1881. "Now the number is reduced to substantially one-third that number." Nor did Minnesota differ particularly in this respect from any other frontier state. Throughout the eighties as the number of miles of railroad increased, the number of railroad companies tended to decrease. Communities that prided themselves upon a new "parallel and competing line" were apt to discover "some fine morning that enough of its stock had been purchased by the older lines to give them control." Thus fortified by monopoly, the railroads, as the farmer saw it, could collect whatever rates they chose. . . .

It was commonly believed also that the practice of stock-watering had much to do with the making of high rates. The exact extent to which the railroads watered their stock, or to which a particular railroad watered its stock, would be a difficult matter to determine, but that the practice did exist in varying degrees seems not to be open to question. A writer in Poor's *Manual* for 1884 stated that the entire four billion dollars at which the railways of the United States were capitalized represented nothing but so much "water." So sweeping a statement seems rather questionable, but the belief was general that railroad companies got their actual funds for investment from bond issues and passed out stocks to the shareholders for nothing. The roads, indeed, did not deny the existence of a certain amount of stock-watering. They argued that their property was quite as likely to increase in value as any other property—farm lands, for example—and that they were justified in increasing their capital stock to the full extent that any increase in value had taken place. Some of their apologists held also that the value of the road was determined by its earning power rather than by the amount actually invested in the enterprise. It followed, therefore, that new capital stock should be issued as fast as the earnings of the road showed that the old valuation had been outgrown.

But to those who suffered from the high rates all these arguments seemed like so many confessions of robbery. The governor of Colorado, considering especially the sins of the Denver and Rio Grande, declared it "incredible that the legitimate course of business can be healthfully promoted by any such inflated capitalization. There must be humbug, if not downright rascality, behind such a pretentious array of figures." The *Kansas Alliance* saw in the prevalent custom of stock-watering an evil "almost beyond comprehension." It placed the total amount of railway overcapitalization at a sum far in excess of the national debt and described these inflated securities as "an ever present incubus upon the labor and land of the nation." Jerry Simpson of Kansas figured that the 8,000 miles of road in his state cost only about $100,000,000, whereas they were actually capitalized at $300,000,000 and bonded for $300,000,000 more. "We who use the roads," he argued, "are really paying interest on $600,000,000 instead of on $100,000,000 as we ought to." Such statements could be multiplied indefinitely. The unprosperous farmers of the frontier saw nothing to condone in the practice of stock-watering. Honest capitalization of railroad property would, they felt, make possible a material reduction in rates. And, in spite of the assertion of one who defended the practice of stock-watering that a citizen who questioned "the right of a corporation to capitalize its properties at any sum whatever committed an 'impertinence'," the farmers had no notion that the matter was none of their business.

High rates due to overcapitalization and other causes were not, however, the sole cause of dissatisfaction with the railways. It was commonly asserted that the transportation companies discriminated definitely against the small shipper and in favor of his larger competitors. The local grain merchant without elevator facilities or the farmer desirous of shipping his own grain invariably had greater and graver difficulties with the roads than did the large elevator companies. These latter, the farmers contended, were favored by "inside rates," by rebates, and by preferential treatment with regard to cars. . . .

The indictment against the railroads was the stronger in view of their political activities. It is not unfair to say that normally the railroads—sometimes a single road—dominated the political situation in every western state. In Kansas the Santa Fe was all-powerful; in Nebraska the Burlington and the Union Pacific shared the control of the state; everywhere the political power of one or more of the roads was a recognized fact. Railway influence was exerted in practically every important nominating convention to insure that no one hostile to the railways should be named for office. Railway lobbyists were on hand whenever a legislature met to see that measures unfavorable to the roads were quietly eliminated. Railway taxation, a particularly tender question, was always watched with the greatest solicitude and, from the standpoint of the prevention of high taxes, usually with the greatest of success. How much bribery and corruption and intrigue the railroads used to secure the ends they desired will never be known. For a long time, however, by fair means or foul, their wishes in most localities were closely akin to law. Beyond a doubt whole legislatures were sometimes bought and sold. . . .

But from the standpoint of the western pioneer the crowning infamy of the railroads was their theft, as it appeared to him, of his lands. Free lands, or at least cheap lands, had been his ever since America was. Now this "priceless heritage" was gone, disposed of in no small part to the railroads. To them the national government had donated an area "larger than the territory occupied by the great German empire," land which, it was easy enough to see, should have been preserved for the future needs of the people. For this land the railroads charged the hapless emigrant from "three to ten prices" and by a pernicious credit system forced him into a condition of well-nigh perpetual "bondage." "Only a little while ago," ran one complaint, "the people owned this princely domain. Now they are *starving for land*—starving for an opportunity to labor—starving for the right to create from the soil a subsistence for their wives and little children." To the western farmers of this generation the importance of the disappearance of free lands was not a hidden secret to be unlocked only by the researches of some future historian. It was an acutely oppressive reality. The significance of the mad rush to Oklahoma in 1889 was by no means lost upon those who observed the phenomenon. "These men want *free* land," wrote one discerning editor. "They want *free* land—the land that Congress squandered . . . the land that should have formed the sacred patrimony of unborn generations." Senator Peffer of Kansas understood the situation perfectly. "Formerly the man who lost his farm could go west," he said, "now there is no longer any west to go to. Now they have to fight for their homes instead of making new." And in no small measure, he might have added, the fight was to be directed against the railroads.

Complaints against the railways, while most violent in the West, were by no means confined to that section. Practically every charge made by the western farmers had its counterpart elsewhere. In the South particularly the sins that the roads were held to have committed differed in degree, perhaps, but not much in kind, from the sins of the western roads. Southern railroads, like western railroads, were accused of levying "freight and fares at their pleasure to the oppression of the citizens" and of making their rates according to the principle, "take as much out of the pocket of the farmers as we can without actually taking it all." Southerners believed, in fact, that the general decline in freight rates that had accompanied the development of the railroads throughout the country was less in the South than anywhere else and that their section was for this reason worse plagued by high rates than any other. . . .

These common grievances of South and West against the railroads promised to supply a binding tie of no small consequences between the sections. Whether they were westerners or southerners, the orators of revolt who touched upon the railway question spoke a common language. Moreover, the common vocabulary was not used merely when the malpractices of the railroads were being enumerated. Any eastern agitator might indeed have listed many of the same oppressions as typical of his part of the country. But the aggrieved easterner at least suffered from the persecutions of other easterners, whereas the southerner or the westerner was convinced that he suffered from a grievance caused by outsiders. In both sections the description of railway oppression was incomplete without a vivid characterization of the wicked eastern capitalist who cared nothing for the region through which he ran his roads and whose chief aim was plunder. This deep-seated antagonism for a common absentee enemy was a matter of the utmost importance when the time came for bringing on joint political action by West and South. . . .

If the farmer had little part in fixing the price at which his produce sold, he had no part at all in fixing the price of the commodities for which his earnings were spent. Neither did competition among manufacturers and dealers do much in the way of price-fixing, for the age of "big business," of trusts, combines, pools, and monopolies, had come. These trusts, as the farmers saw it, joined with the railroads, and if necessary with the politicians, "to hold the people's hands and pick their pockets." They "bought raw material at their own price, sold the finished product at any figure they wished to ask, and rewarded labor as they saw fit." Through their machinations "the farmer and the workingman generally" were "overtaxed right and left."

One western editor professed to understand how all this had come about. The price-fixing plutocracy, he argued, was but the "logical result of the individual freedom which we have always considered the pride of our system." The American ideal of the "very greatest degree of liberty" and the "very least legal restraint" had been of inestimable benefit to the makers of the trusts. Acting on the theory that individual enterprise should be permitted unlimited scope, they had gone their way without let or hindrance, putting weaker competitors out of business and acquiring monopolistic privileges for themselves. At length the corporation "had absorbed the liberties of the community and usurped the power of the agency that created it." Through its operation "individualism" had congealed into "privilege."

The number of "these unnatural and unnecessary financial monsters" was assumed to be legion. An agitated Iowan denounced the beef trust as "the most menacing" as well as the most gigantic of "about 400 trusts in existence." A Missouri editor took for his example the "plow trust. As soon as it was perfected the price of plows went up 100 percent . . . who suffers? . . . Who, indeed, but the farmer?" Senator Plumb of Kansas held that the people of his state were being robbed annually of $40,000,000 by the produce trust. Southern farmers complained of a fertilizer trust, a jute-bagging trust, a cottonseed oil trust. Trusts indeed there were: trusts that furnished the farmer with the clothing he had to wear; trusts that furnished him with the machines he had to use; trusts that furnished him with the fuel he had to burn; trusts that furnished him with the materials of which he built his house, his barns, his fences. To all these he paid a substantial tribute. Some of them, like the manufacturers of farm machinery, had learned the trick of installment selling, and to such the average farmer owed a perpetual debt. . . .

It was the grinding burden of debt, however, that aroused the farmers, both southern and western, to action. The widespread dependence upon crop liens in the South and farm mortgages in the West has already been described. In the

South as long as the price of cotton continued high and in the West as long as the flow of eastern capital remained uninterrupted, the grievances against the railroads, the middlemen, and the tariff-protected trusts merely smouldered. But when the bottom dropped out of the cotton market and the western boom collapsed, then the weight of debt was keenly felt and frenzied agitation began. The eastern capitalists were somehow to blame. They had conspired together to defraud the farmers—"to levy tribute upon the productive energies of West and South." They had made of the one-time American freeman "but a tenant at will, or a dependent upon the tender mercies of soulless corporations and of absentee landlords." . . .

As one hard season succeeded another the empty-handed farmer found his back debts and unpaid interest becoming an intolerable burden. In the West after the crisis of 1887 interest rates, already high, rose still higher. Farmers who needed money to renew their loans, to meet partial payments on their land, or to tide them over to another season were told, truly enough, that money was very scarce. The flow of eastern capital to the West had virtually ceased. The various mortgage companies that had been doing such a thriving business a few months before had now either gone bankrupt or had made drastic retrenchments. Rates of seven or eight percent on real estate were now regarded as extremely low; and on chattels ten or twelve percent was considered very liberal, from eighteen to twenty-four percent was not uncommon, and forty percent or above was not unknown. Naturally the number of real estate mortgages placed dropped off precipitately. Instead of the six thousand, worth nearly $5,500,000, that had been placed in Nebraska during the years 1884 to 1887, there were in the three years following 1887 only five hundred such mortgages, worth only about $650,000, while only one out of four of the farm mortgages held on South Dakota land in 1892 had been contracted prior in 1887. When the farmer could no longer obtain money on his real estate, he usually mortgaged his chattels, with the result that in many localities nearly everything that could carry a mortgage was required to do so. In Nebraska during the early nineties the number of these badges of "dependence and slavery" recorded by the state auditor averaged over half a million annually. In Dakota many families were kept from leaving for the East only by the fact that their horses and wagons were mortgaged and could therefore not be taken beyond the state boundaries.

Whether at the old rates, which were bad, or at the new, which were worse, altogether too often the western farmer was mortgaged literally for all he was worth, and too often the entire fruits of his labor, meager enough after hard times set in, were required to meet impending obligations. Profits that the farmer felt should have been his passed at once to someone else. The conviction grew on him that there was something essentially wicked and vicious about the system that made this possible. Too late he observed that the money he had borrowed was not worth to him what he had contracted to pay for it. As one embittered farmer-editor wrote,

There are three great crops raised in Nebraska. One is a crop of corn, one a crop of freight rates, and one a crop of interest. One is produced by farmers who by

sweat and toil farm the land. The other two are produced by men who sit in their offices and behind their bank counters and farm the farmers. The corn is less than half a crop. The freight rates will produce a full average. The interest crop, however, is the one that fully illustrates the boundless resources and prosperity of Nebraska. When corn fails the interest yield is largely increased.

What was the fair thing under such circumstances? Should the farmer bear the entire load of adversity, or should the mortgage-holder help? Opinions varied, but certain extremists claimed that at the very least the interest should be scaled down. If railroads were permitted to reorganize, reduce their interest rates, and save their property when they got into financial straits, why should the farmer be denied a similar right?

The only reorganization to which the farmer had recourse, as a rule, was through foreclosure proceedings, by which ordinarily he could expect nothing less than the loss of all his property. Usually the mortgagor was highly protected by the terms of the mortgage and could foreclose whenever an interest payment was defaulted, whether the principal was due or not. In the late eighties and the early nineties foreclosures came thick and fast. Kansas doubtless suffered most on this account, for from 1889 to 1893 over eleven thousand farm mortgages were foreclosed in this state, and in some counties as much as ninety percent of the farm lands passed into the ownership of the loan companies. It was estimated by one alarmist that "land equal to a tract thirty miles wide and ninety miles long had been foreclosed and bought in by the loan companies of Kansas in a year." Available statistics would seem to bear out this assertion, but the unreliability of such figures is notorious. Many farmers and speculators, some of them perfectly solvent, deliberately invited foreclosure because they found after the slump that their land was mortgaged for more than it was worth. On the other hand, many cases of genuine bankruptcy were settled out of court and without record. But whatever the unreliability of statistics the fact remains that in Kansas and neighboring states the number of farmers who lost their lands because of the hard times and crop failures was very large.

In the South the crop-lien system constituted the chief mortgage evil and the chief grievance, but a considerable amount of real and personal property was also pledged for debt. Census statistics, here also somewhat unreliable because of the numerous informal and unrecorded agreements, show that in Georgia about one-fifth of the taxable acres were under mortgage, and a special investigation for the same state seemed to prove that a high proportion of the mortgage debt was incurred to meet current expenditures rather than to acquire more land or to make permanent improvements. Similar conditions existed throughout the cotton South. Chattel mortgages were also freely given, especially by tenants, but frequently also by small proprietors. Interest rates were as impossibly high as in the West, and foreclosures almost as inevitable. Evidence of foreclosures on chattels could be found in the "pitiful heaps of . . . rubbish" that "commonly disfigured the court house squares." Foreclosures on land, or their equivalent, were numerous, serving alike to accelerate the process of breaking down the old plantations and of building up the new "merchant-owned 'bonanzas.' " Many small farmers lapsed into tenantry; indeed, during the eighties the trend was unmistakably in the direction of "concentration of agricultural land in the hands of merchants, loan agents, and a few of the financially strongest farmers."

Taxation added a heavy burden to the load of the farmer. Others might conceal their property. The merchant might underestimate the value of his stock, the householder might neglect to list a substantial part of his personal property, the holder of taxable securities might keep his ownership a secret, but the farmer could not hide his land. If it was perhaps an exaggeration to declare that the farmers "represent but one-fourth of the nation's wealth and they pay three-fourths of the taxes," it was probably true enough that land bore the chief brunt of taxation, both in the South and in the West. Tax-dodging, especially on the part of the railroads and other large corporations, was notorious. Some North Carolina railroads had been granted special exemptions from taxation as far back as the 1830's, and they still found them useful. In Georgia the railroads paid a state tax but not a county tax. Nearly everywhere they received special treatment at the hands of assessors, state boards of equalization, or even by the law itself. Western land-grant railroads avoided paying taxes on their huge holdings by delaying to patent them until they could be sold. Then the farmer-purchaser paid the taxes. Meantime the cost of state and local government had risen everywhere, although most disproportionately in the West, where the boom was on. In the boom territory public building and improvement projects out of all proportion to the capacity of the people to pay had been undertaken, and railways, street-car companies, and other such enterprises had been subsidized by the issuing of state or local bonds, the interest and principal of which had to be met by taxation. For all this unwise spending the farmers had to pay the greater part. The declaration of one Kansas farmer that his taxes were doubled in order "to pay the interest on boodler bonds and jobs voted by nontaxpayers to railroad schemes and frauds and follies which are of no benefit to the farmer" was not without a large element of truth. The farmer was convinced that he was the helpless victim of unfair, unreasonable, and discriminatory taxation. Here was another reason why he was "gradually but steadily becoming poorer and poorer every year."

Beset on every hand by demands for funds—funds with which to meet his obligations to the bankers, the loan companies, or the tax collectors and funds with which to maintain his credit with the merchants so that he might not lack the all-essential seed to plant another crop or the few necessities of life that he and his family could not contrive either to produce for themselves or to go without—the farmer naturally enough raised the battle cry of "more money." He came to believe that, after all, his chief grievance was against the system of money and banking, which now virtually denied him credit and which in the past had only plunged him deeper and deeper into debt. There must be something more fundamentally wrong than the misdeeds of railroads and trusts and tax assessors. Why should dollars grow dearer and dearer and scarcer and scarcer? Why, indeed, unless because of the manipulations of those to whom such a condition would bring profit?

Much agitation by Greenbackers and by free-silverites and much experience in the marketing of crops had made clear even to the most obtuse, at least of the debtors, that the value of a dollar was greater than it once had been. It would buy two bushels of grain where formerly it would buy only one. It would buy twelve pounds of cotton where formerly it would buy but six. The orthodox retort of the creditor to such a statement was that too much grain and cotton were being produced—the overproduction theory. But, replied the debtor, was this the whole truth? Did not the amount of money in circulation have something to do with the situation? Currency reformers were wont to point out that at the close of the Civil War the United States had nearly two billions of dollars in circulation. Now the population had doubled and the volume of business had probably trebled, but the number of dollars in circulation had actually declined! Was not each dollar overworked? Had it not attained on this account a fictitious value?

Whatever the explanation, it was clear enough that the dollar, expressed in any other terms than itself, had appreciated steadily in value ever since the Civil War. The depreciated greenback currency, in which all ordinary business was transacted until 1879, reached by that year a full parity with gold. But the purchasing power of the dollar still continued its upward course. For this phenomenon the quantity theory may be—probably is—an insufficient explanation, but in the face of the figures from which the accompanying chart has been drawn, the fact of continuous appreciation can hardly be denied.

For those farmers who were free from debt and were neither investors nor borrowers such a condition might have had little meaning. The greater purchasing power of the dollar meant fewer dollars for their crops, but it meant also fewer dollars spent for labor and supplies. Conceivably, the same degree of prosperity could be maintained on the smaller income. But in the West and in the South the number of debt-free farmers was small indeed, and for the debtor the rising value of the dollar was a serious matter. The man who gave a long-term mortgage on his real estate was in the best position to appreciate how serious it was. Did he borrow a thousand dollars on his land for a five-year term, then he must pay back at the end of the allotted time a thousand dollars. But it might well be that, whereas at the time he had contracted the loan a thousand dollars meant a thousand

The Appreciating Dollar, 1865–1895

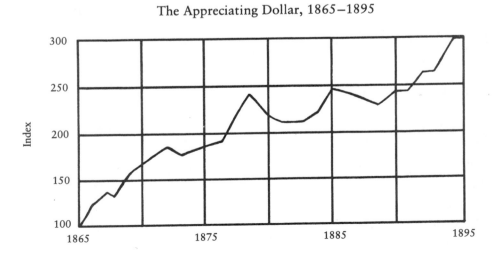

bushels of wheat or ten thousand pounds of cotton, at the time he must pay it the thousand dollars meant fifteen hundred bushels of wheat or fifteen thousand pounds of cotton. Interest, expressed likewise in terms of produce, had mounted similarly year by year so that the loss to the borrower was even greater than the increase in the value of the principal. What it cost the debtor to borrow under such circumstances has been well expressed by Arnett in the [following] table . . . , which is based on statistics taken from the census of 1890.

Add to this the unreasonably high interest rates usually exacted and the commissions and deductions that were rarely omitted and the plight of the debtor farmer becomes painfully clear. He was paying what would have amounted to about a twenty or twenty-five percent rate of interest on a non-appreciating dollar.

It was, moreover, far from comforting to reflect that in such a transaction what was one man's loss was another's gain. Nor was it surprising that the harassed debtor imputed to the creditor, to whose advantage the system worked, a deliberate attempt to cause the dollar to soar to ever greater and greater heights. Had not the creditor class ranged itself solidly behind the Resumption Act of 1875, by which the greenback dollar had been brought to a parity with gold? Was not the same class responsible for the "crime of 1873," which had demonetized silver and by just so much had detracted from the quantity of the circulating medium? Was there not, indeed, a nefarious conspiracy of creditors—eastern creditors, perhaps with English allies—to increase their profits at the expense of the debtors—western and southern—by a studied manipulation of the value of the dollar? "We feel," said Senator Allen of Nebraska, "that, through the operation of a shrinking volume of money, which has been caused by Eastern votes and influences for purely selfish purposes, the East has placed its hands on the throat of the West and refused to afford us that measure of justice which we, as citizens of a common country, are entitled to receive." And the grievance of the West against the East was also the grievance of the South.

Nor was this grievance confined to resentment against the steadily mounting value of the dollar. There was in addition an undeniable and apparently unreasonable fluctuation in its purchasing power during any given year. At the time of crop movements, when the farmers wished to sell—indeed, had to sell, in most cases—the dollar was dear and prices were correspondingly depressed. When, on the other hand, the crop had been marketed and the farmers' produce had passed to other hands, the dollar fell in value and prices mounted rapidly. Wall Street

Debt Appreciation, 1865–1890

Average Five-year Debt Contracted in	Appreciation (in terms of dollar's purchasing power)
1865–1869	35.2
1870–1874	19.7
1875–1879	4.5
1880–1884	11.7
1885–1890	11.6

speculators and others bought heavily when prices were low and sold later when prices were high at handsome profits—profits which, the farmers firmly believed, should have gone to the original producer. . . .

Such were the grievances of which the farmers complained. They suffered, or at least they thought they suffered, from the railroads, from the trusts and the middlemen, from the money-lenders and the bankers, and from the muddled currency. These problems were not particularly new. Always the farmer had had to struggle with the problem of transportation. He had never known a time when the price of the things he had to buy was not as much too high as the price of the things he had to sell was too low. He had had his troubles with banks and bankers. But those earlier days were the days of cheap lands, and when things went wrong the disgruntled could seek solace in a move to the West. There was a chance to make a new start. Broader acres, more fertile fields, would surely bring the desired results. And with the restless ever moving to the West, the more stable elements of society left behind made pleasing progress. Now with the lands all taken and the frontier gone, this safety valve was closed. The frontier was turned back upon itself. The restless and discontented voiced their sentiments more and fled from them less. Hence arose the veritable chorus of denunciation directed against those individuals and those corporations who considered only their own advantage without regard to the effect their actions might have upon the farmer and his interests.

RICHARD HOFSTADTER

Populism: Nostalgic Agrarianism

The Two Nations

For a generation after the Civil War, a time of great economic exploitation and waste, grave social corruption and ugliness, the dominant note in American political life was complacency. Although dissenting minorities were always present, they were submerged by the overwhelming realities of industrial growth and continental settlement. The agitation of the Populists, which brought back to American public life a capacity for effective political indignation, marks the beginning of the end of this epoch. In the short run the Populists did not get what they wanted, but they released the flow of protest and criticism that swept through American political affairs from the 1890's to the beginning of the first World War.

Where contemporary intellectuals gave the Populists a perfunctory and disdainful hearing, later historians have freely recognized their achievements and frequently overlooked their limitations. Modern liberals, finding the Populists' grievances valid, their programs suggestive, their motives creditable, have usually spoken of the Populist episode in the spirit of Vachel Lindsay's bombastic rhetoric:

> Prairie avenger, mountain lion,
> Bryan, Bryan, Bryan, Bryan,
> Gigantic troubadour, speaking like a siege gun,
> Smashing Plymouth Rock with his boulders from the West.

There is indeed much that is good and usable in our Populist past. While the Populist tradition had defects that have been too much neglected, it does not follow that the virtues claimed for it are all fictitious. Populism was the first modern political movement of practical importance in the United States to insist that the federal government has some responsibility for the common weal; indeed, it was the first such movement to attack seriously the problems created by industrialism. The complaints and demands and prophetic denunciations of the Populists stirred the latent liberalism in many Americans and startled many conservatives into a new flexibility. Most of the "radical" reforms in the Populist program proved in later years to be either harmless or useful. In at least one important area of American life a few Populist leaders in the South attempted something profoundly radical and humane—to build a popular movement that would cut across the old barriers of race—until persistent use of the Negro bogy distracted their following. To discuss the broad ideology of the Populists does them some injustice, for it was in their concrete programs that they added most constructively to our political life, and in their more general picture of the world that they were most credulous and vulnerable. Moreover, any account of the fallibility of Populist thinking that does not acknowledge the stress and suffering out of which that thinking emerged will be seriously remiss. But anyone who enlarges our portrait of the Populist tradition is likely to bring out some unseen blemishes. In the books that have been written about the Populist movement, only passing mention has been made of its significant provincialism; little has been said of its relations with nativism and nationalism; nothing has been said of its tincture of anti-Semitism.

The Populist impulse expressed itself in a set of notions that represent what I have called the "soft" side of agrarianism. These notions, which appeared with regularity in the political literature, must be examined if we are to re-create for ourselves the Populist spirit. To extract them from the full context of the polemical writings in which they appeared is undoubtedly to oversimplify them; even to name them in any language that comes readily to the historian of ideas is perhaps to suggest that they had a formality and coherence that in reality they clearly lacked. But since it is less feasible to have no labels than to have somewhat too facile ones, we may enumerate the dominant themes in Populist ideology as these: the idea of a golden age; the concept of natural harmonies; the dualistic version of social struggles; the conspiracy theory of history; and the doctrine of the primacy of money. The last of these I will touch upon in connection with the free-silver issue. Here I propose to analyze the others, and to show how they were nurtured by the traditions of the agrarian myth.

The utopia of the Populists was in the past, not the future. According to the agrarian myth, the health of the state was proportionate to the degree to which it was dominated by the agricultural class, and this assumption pointed to the superiority of an earlier age. The Populists looked backward with longing to the lost agrarian Eden, to the republican America of the early years of the nineteenth century in which there were few millionaires and, as they saw it, no beggars, when the laborer had excellent prospects and the farmer had abundance, when statesmen still responded to the mood of the people and there was no such thing as the money power. What they meant—though they did not express themselves in such terms—was that they would like to restore the conditions prevailing before the development of industrialism and the commercialization of agriculture. It should not be surprising that they inherited the traditions of Jacksonian democracy, that they revived the old Jacksonian cry: "Equal Rights for All, Special Privileges for None," or that most of the slogans of 1896 echoed the battle cries of 1836. General James B. Weaver, the Populist candidate for the presidency in 1892, was an old Democrat and Free-Soiler, born during the days of Jackson's battle with the United States Bank, who drifted into the Greenback movement after a short spell as a Republican, and from there to Populism. His book, *A Call to Action,* published in 1892, drew up an indictment of the business corporation which reads like a Jacksonian polemic. Even in those hopeful early days of the People's Party, Weaver projected no grandiose plans for the future, but lamented the course of recent history, the growth of economic oppression, and the emergence of great contrasts of wealth and poverty, and called upon his readers to do "All in [their]power to arrest the alarming tendencies of our times."

Nature, as the agrarian tradition had it, was beneficent. The United States was abundantly endowed with rich land and rich resources, and the "natural" consequence of such an endowment should be the prosperity of the people. If the people failed to enjoy prosperity, it must be because of a harsh and arbitrary intrusion of human greed and error. "Hard times, then," said one popular writer, "as well as the bankruptcies, enforced idleness, starvation, and the crime, misery, and moral degradation growing out of conditions like the present, being unnatural, not in accordance with, or the result of any natural law, must be attributed to that kind of unwise and pernicious legislation which history proves to have produced similar results in all ages of the world. It is the mission of the age to correct these errors in human legislation, to adopt and establish policies and systems, in accord with, rather than in opposition to divine law." In assuming a lush natural order whose workings were being deranged by human laws, Populist writers were again drawing on the Jacksonian tradition, whose spokesmen also had pleaded for a proper obedience to "natural" laws as a prerequisite of social justice.

Somewhat akin to the notion of the beneficence of nature was the idea of a natural harmony of interests among the productive classes. To the Populist mind there was no fundamental conflict between the farmer and the worker, between the toiling people and the small businessman. While there might be corrupt individuals in any group, the underlying interests of the productive majority were the same; predatory behavior existed only because it was initiated and underwritten by a small parasitic minority in the highest places of power. As opposed to the idea that society consists of a number of different and frequently clashing interests—the social pluralism expressed, for instance, by Madison in the *Federalist*—the Populists adhered, less formally to be sure, but quite persistently, to a kind of social dualism: although they knew perfectly well that society was composed of a number of classes, for all practical purposes only one simple division need be considered. There were two nations. "It is a struggle," said Sockless Jerry Simpson, "between the robbers and the robbed." "There are but two sides in the conflict that is being waged in this country today," declared a Populist manifesto. "On the one side are the allied hosts of monopolies, the money power, great trusts and railroad corporations, who seek the enactment of laws to benefit them and impoverish the people. On the other are the farmers, laborers, merchants, and all other people who produce wealth and bear the burdens of taxation. . . . Between these two there is no middle ground." "On the one side," said Bryan in his famous speech against the repeal of the Sherman Silver Purchase Act, "stand the corporate interests of the United States, the moneyed interests, aggregated wealth and capital, imperious, arrogant, compassionless. . . . On the other side stand an unnumbered throng, those who gave to the Democratic party a name and for whom it has assumed to speak." The people versus the interests, the public versus the plutocrats, the toiling multitude versus the money power—in various phrases this central antagonism was expressed. From this simple social classification it seemed to follow that once the techniques of misleading the people were exposed, victory over the money power ought to be easily accomplished, for in sheer numbers the people were overwhelming. "There is no power on earth that can defeat us," said General Weaver during the optimistic days of the campaign of 1892. "It is a fight between labor and capital, and labor is in the vast majority."

The problems that faced the Populists assumed a delusive simplicity: the victory over injustice, the solution for all social ills, was concentrated in the crusade against a single, relatively small but immensely strong interest, the money power. "With the destruction of the money power," said Senator Peffer, "the death knell of gambling in grain and other commodities will be sounded; for the business of the worst men on earth will have been broken up, and the mainstay of the gamblers removed. It will be an easy matter, after the greater spoilsmen have been shorn of their power, to clip the wings of the little ones. Once get rid of the men who hold the country by the throat, the parasites can be easily removed." Since the old political parties were the primary means by which the people were kept wandering in the wilderness, the People's Party advocates insisted, only a new and independent political party could do this essential job. As the silver question became more prominent and the idea of a third party faded, the need for a monolithic solution became transmuted into another form: there was only one *issue* upon which the money power could really be beaten and this was the money issue. "When we have restored the money of the Constitution," said Bryan in his Cross of Gold speech, "all other necessary reforms will be possible; but . . . until this is done there is no other reform that can be accomplished."

While the conditions of victory were thus made to appear simple, they did not always appear easy, and it would be misleading to imply that the tone of Populistic thinking was uniformly optimistic. Often, indeed, a deep-lying vein of anxiety showed through. The very sharpness of the struggle, as the Populists experienced it, the alleged absence of compromise solutions and of intermediate groups in the body politic, the brutality and desperation that were imputed to the plutocracy—all these suggested that failure of the people to win the final contest peacefully could result only in a total victory for the plutocrats and total extinction of democratic institutions, possibly after a period of bloodshed and anarchy. "We are nearing a serious crisis," declared Weaver. "If the present strained relations between wealth owners and wealth producers continue much longer they will ripen into frightful disaster. This universal discontent must be quickly interpreted and its causes removed." "We meet," said the Populist platform of 1892, *in the midst of a nation brought to the verge of moral, political, and material ruin. Corruption dominates the ballot-box, the Legislatures, the Congress, and touches even the ermine of the bench. The people are demoralized. . . . The newspapers are largely subsidized or muzzled, public opinion silenced, business prostrated, homes covered with mortgages, labor impoverished, and the land concentrating in the hands of the capitalists. The urban workmen are denied the right to organize for self-protection, imported pauperized labor beats down their wages, a hireling standing army, unrecognized by our laws, is established to shoot them down, and they are rapidly degenerating into European conditions. The fruits of the toil of millions are boldly stolen to build up colossal fortunes for a few, unprecedented in the history of mankind; and the possessors of these, in turn, despise the Republic and endanger liberty.*

Such conditions foreboded "the destruction of civilization, or the establishment of an absolute despotism." . . .

History as Conspiracy

There was . . . a widespread Populist idea that all American history since the Civil War could be understood as a sustained conspiracy of the international money power.

The pervasiveness of this way of looking at things may be attributed to the common feeling that farmers and workers were not simply oppressed but oppressed deliberately, consciously, continuously, and with wanton malice by "the interests." It would of course be misleading to imply that the Populists stand alone in thinking of the events of their time as the results of a conspiracy. This kind of thinking frequently occurs when political and social antagonisms are sharp. Certain audiences are especially susceptible to it—particularly, I believe, those who have attained only a low level of education, whose access to information is poor, and who are so completely shut out from access to the centers of power that they feel themselves completely deprived of self-defense and subjected to unlimited manipulation by those who wield power. There are, moreover, certain types of popular movements of dissent that offer special opportunities to agitators with paranoid tendencies, who are able to make a vocational asset out of their psychic disturbances. Such persons have an opportunity to impose their own style of thought upon the movements they lead. It would of course be misleading to imply that there are no such things as conspiracies in history. Anything that partakes of political strategy may need, for a time at least, an element of secrecy, and is thus vulnerable to being dubbed conspiratorial. Corruption itself has the character of conspiracy. In this sense the Crédit Mobilier was a conspiracy, as was the Teapot Dome affair. If we tend to be too condescending to the Populists at this point, it may be necessary to remind ourselves that they had seen so much bribery and corruption, particularly on the part of the railroads, that they had before them a convincing model of the management of affairs through conspiratorial behavior. Indeed, what makes conspiracy theories so widely acceptable is that they usually contain a germ of truth. But there is a great difference between locating conspiracies *in* history and saying that history *is*, in effect, a conspiracy, between singling out those conspiratorial acts that do on occasion occur and weaving a vast fabric of social explanation out of nothing but skeins of evil plots.

When conspiracies do not exist it is necessary for those who think in this fashion to invent them. Among the most celebrated instances in modern history are the forgery of the Protocols of the Elders of Zion and the grandiose fabrication under Stalin's regime of the Trotzkyite-Bukharinite-Zinovievite center. These inventions were cynical. In the history of American political controversy there is a tradition of conspiratorial accusations which seem to have been sincerely believed. Jefferson appears really to have believed, at one time, that the Federalists were conspiring to re-establish monarchy. Some Federalists believed that the Jeffersonians were conspiring to subvert Christianity. The movement to annex Texas and the war with Mexico were alleged by many Northerners to be a slaveholders' conspiracy. The early Republican leaders, including Lincoln, charged that there was a conspiracy on the part of Stephen A. Douglas to make slavery a nationwide institution. Such pre-Civil War parties as the Know-Nothing and Anti-Masonic movements were based almost entirely upon conspiratorial ideology. The Nye Committee, years ago, tried to prove that our entry into the first World War was the work of a conspiracy of bankers and munitions-makers. And now not only our entry into the second World War, but the entire history of the past twenty years or so is being given the color of conspiracy by the cranks and political fakirs of our own age.

Nevertheless, when these qualifications have been taken into account, it remains true that Populist thought showed an unusually strong tendency to account for relatively impersonal events in highly personal terms. An overwhelming sense of grievance does not find satisfactory expression in impersonal explanations, except among those with a well-developed tradition of intellectualism. It is the city, after all, that is the home of intellectual complexity. The farmer lived in isolation from the great world in which his fate was actually decided. He was accused of being unusually suspicious, and certainly his situation, trying as it was, made thinking in impersonal terms difficult. Perhaps the rural middle-class leaders of Populism (this was a movement of farmers, but it was not led by farmers) had more to do than the farmer himself with the cast of Populist thinking. At any rate, Populist thought often carries one into a world in which the simple virtues and unmitigated villainies of a rural melodrama have been projected on a national and even an international scale. In Populist thought the farmer is not a speculating businessman, victimized by the risk economy of which he is a part, but rather a wounded yeoman, preyed upon by those who are alien to the life of folkish virtue. A villain was needed, marked with the unmistakable stigmata of the villains of melodrama, and the more remote he was from the familiar scene, the more plausibly his villainies could be exaggerated.

It was not enough to say that a conspiracy of the money power against the common people was going on. It had been going on ever since the Civil War. It was not enough to say that it stemmed from Wall Street. It was international: it stemmed from Lombard Street. In his preamble to the People's Party platform of 1892, a succinct, official expression of Populist views, Ignatius Donnelly asserted: "A vast conspiracy against mankind has been organized on two continents, and it is rapidly taking possession of the world. If not met and over-thrown at once it forebodes terrible social convulsions, the destruction of civilization, or the establishment of an absolute despotism." A manifesto of 1895, signed by fifteen outstanding leaders of the People's Party, declared: "As early as 1865–66 a conspiracy was entered into between the gold gamblers of Europe and America. . . . For nearly thirty years these conspirators have kept the people quarreling over less important matters while they have pursued with unrelenting zeal their one central purpose. . . . Every device of treachery, every resource of statecraft, and every artifice known to the secret cabals of the international gold ring are being made use of to deal a blow to the prosperity of the people and the financial and commercial independence of the country."

The financial argument behind the conspiracy theory was simple enough. Those who owned bonds wanted to be paid not in a common currency but in gold, which was at a premium; those who lived by lending money wanted as high a premium as possible to be put on their commodity by increasing its scarcity. The panics, depressions, and bankruptcies caused by their policies only added to their wealth; such catastrophes offered opportunities to engross the wealth of others through business consolidations and foreclosures. Hence the interests actually relished and encouraged hard times. The Greenbackers had long since popularized this argument, insisting that an adequate legal-tender currency would break the monopoly of the "Shylocks." Their demand for $50 of circulating medium per capita, still in the air when the People's Party arose, was rapidly replaced by the less "radical" demand for free coinage of silver. But what both the Greenbackers and free-silverites held in common was the idea that the contraction of currency was a deliberate squeeze, the result of a long-range plot of the "Anglo-American Gold Trust." Wherever one turns in the Populist literature of the nineties one can find this conspiracy theory expressed. It is in the Populist newspapers, the proceedings of the silver conventions, the immense pamphlet literature broadcast by the American Bimetallic League, the Congressional debates over money; it is elaborated in such popular books as Mrs. S. E. V. Emery's *Seven Financial Conspiracies which have Enslaved the American People* or Gordon Clark's *Shylock: as Banker, Bondholder, Corruptionist, Conspirator.*

Mrs. Emery's book, first published in 1887, and dedicated to "the enslaved people of a dying republic," achieved great circulation, especially among the Kansas Populists. According to Mrs. Emery, the United States had been an economic Garden of Eden in the period before the Civil War. The fall of man had dated from the war itself, when "the money kings of Wall Street" determined that they could take advantage of the wartime necessities of their fellow men by manipulating the currency. "Controlling it, they could inflate or depress the business of the country at pleasure, they could send the warm life current through the channels of trade, dispensing peace, happiness, and prosperity, or they could check its flow, and completely paralyze the industries of the country." With this great power for good in their hands, the Wall Street men preferred to do evil. Lincoln's war policy of issuing greenbacks presented them with the dire threat of an adequate supply of currency. So the Shylocks gathered in convention and "perfected" a conspiracy to create a demand for their gold. The remainder of the book was a recital of a series of seven measures passed between 1862 and 1875 which were alleged to be a part of this continuing conspiracy, the total effect of which was to contract the currency of the country further and further until finally it squeezed the industry of the country like a hoop of steel.

Mrs. Emery's rhetoric left no doubt of the sustained purposefulness of this scheme—described as "villainous robbery," and as having been "secured through the most soulless strategy." She was most explicit about the so-called "crime of 1873," the demonetization of silver, giving a fairly full statement of the standard greenback-silverite myth concerning that event. As they had it, an agent of the Bank of England, Ernest Seyd by name, had come to the United States in 1872 with $500,000 with which he had bought enough support in Congress to secure the passage of the demonetization measure. This measure was supposed to have greatly increased the value of American four percent bonds held by British capitalists by making it necessary to pay them in gold only. To it Mrs. Emery attributed the panic of 1873, its bankruptcies, and its train of human disasters: "Murder, insanity, suicide, divorce, drunkenness and all forms of immorality and crime have increased from that day to this in the most appalling ratio."

"Coin" Harvey, the author of the most popular single document of the whole currency controversy, *Coin's Financial School,* also published a novel, *A Tale of Two Nations,* in which the conspiracy theory of history was incorporated into a melodramatic tale. In this story the powerful English banker Baron Rothe plans to bring about the demonetization of silver in the United States, in part for his own aggrandizement but also to prevent the power of the United States from outstripping that of England. He persuades an American Senator (probably John Sherman, the *bête noire* of the silverites) to co-operate in using British gold in a campaign against silver. To be sure that the work is successful, he also sends to the United States a relative and ally, one Rogasner, who stalks through the story like the villains in the plays of Dion Boucicault, muttering to himself such remarks as "I am here to destroy the United States—Cornwallis could not have done more. For the wrongs and insults, for the glory of my own country, I will bury the knife deep into the heart of this nation." Against the plausibly drawn background of the corruption of the Grant administration, Rogasner proceeds to buy up the American Congress and suborn American professors of economics to testify for gold. He also falls in love with a proud American beauty, but his designs on her are foiled because she loves a handsome young silver Congressman from Nebraska who bears a striking resemblance to William Jennings Bryan!

One feature of the Populist conspiracy theory that has been generally overlooked is its frequent link with a kind of rhetorical anti-Semitism. The slight current of anti-Semitism that existed in the United States before the 1890's had been associated with problems of money and credit. During the closing years of the century it grew noticeably. While the jocose and rather heavy-handed anti-Semitism that can be found in Henry Adams's letters of the 1890's shows that this prejudice existed outside Populist literature, it was chiefly Populist writers who expressed that identification of the Jew with the usurer and the "international gold ring" which was the central theme of the American anti-Semitism of the age. The omnipresent symbol of Shylock can hardly be taken in itself as evidence of anti-Semitism, but the frequent references to the House of Rothschild make it clear that for many silverites the Jew was an organic part of the conspiracy theory of history. Coin Harvey's Baron Rothe was clearly meant to be Rothschild; his Rogasner (Ernest Seyd?) was a dark figure out of the coarsest anti-Semitic tradition. "You are very wise in your way," Rogasner is told at the climax of the tale, "the commercial way, inbred through generations. The politic, scheming, devious way, inbred through generations also." One of the cartoons in the effectively illustrated *Coin's Financial School* showed a map of the world dominated by the tentacles of an octopus at the site of the British Isles, labeled: "Rothschilds." In Populist demonology, anti-Semitism and Anglophobia went hand in hand.

The note of anti-Semitism was often sounded openly in the campaign for silver. A representative of the New Jersey Grange, for instance, did not hesitate to warn the members of the Second National Silver Convention of 1892 to watch out for political candidates who represented "Wall Street, and the Jews of Europe." Mary E. Lease described Grover Cleveland as "the agent of Jewish bankers and British gold." Donnelly represented the leader of the governing Council of plutocrats in *Caesar's Column*, one Prince Cabano, as a powerful Jew, born Jacob Issacs; one of the triumvirate who led the Brotherhood of Destruction is also an exiled Russian Jew, who flees from the apocalyptic carnage with a hundred million dollars which he intends to use to "revive the ancient splendors of the Jewish race, in the midst of the ruins of the world." One of the more elaborate documents of the conspiracy school traced the power of the Rothschilds over America to a transaction between Hugh McCulloch, Secretary of the Treasury under Lincoln and Johnson, and Baron James Rothschild. "The most direful part of this business between Rothschild and the United States Treasury was not the loss of money, even by hundreds of millions. It was the resignation of the country itself INTO THE HANDS OF ENGLAND, as England had long been resigned into the hands of HER JEWS."

Such rhetoric, which became common currency in the movement, later passed beyond Populism into the larger stream of political protest. By the time the campaign of 1896 arrived, an Associated Press reporter noticed as "one of the striking things" about the Populist convention at St. Louis "the extraordinary hatred of the Jewish race. It is not possible to go into any hotel in the city without hearing the most bitter denunciation of the Jews as a class and of the particular Jews who happen to have prospered in the world." This report may have been somewhat overdone, but the identification of the silver cause with anti-Semitism did become close enough for Bryan to have to pause in the midst of his campaign to explain to the Jewish Democrats of Chicago that in denouncing the policies of the Rothschilds he and his silver friends were "not attacking a race; we are attacking greed and avarice which know no race or religion."

It would be easy to misstate the character of Populist anti-Semitism or to exaggerate its intensity. For Populist anti-Semitism was entirely verbal. It was a mode of expression, a rhetorical style, not a tactic or a program. It did not lead to exclusion laws, much less to riots or pogroms. There were, after all, relatively few Jews in the United States in the late 1880's and early 1890's, most of them remote from the areas of Populist strength. It is one thing, however, to say that this prejudice did not go beyond a certain symbolic usage, quite another to say that a people's choice of symbols is of no significance. Populist anti-Semitism does have its importance—chiefly as a symptom of a certain ominous credulity in the Populist mind. It is not too much to say that the Greenback-Populist tradition activated most of what we have of modern popular anti-Semitism in the United States. From Thaddeus Stevens and Coin Harvey to Father Coughlin, and from Brooks and Henry Adams to Ezra Pound, there has been a curiously persistent linkage between anti-Semitism and money and credit obsessions. A full history of modern anti-Semitism in the United States would reveal, I believe, its substantial Populist lineage, but it may be sufficient to point out here that neither the informal connection between Bryan and the Klan in the twenties nor Thomas E. Watson's conduct in the Leo Frank case were altogether fortuitous. And Henry Ford's notorious anti-Semitism of the 1920's, along with his hatred of "Wall Street," were the foibles of a Michigan farm boy who had been liberally exposed to Populist notions.

Populism: Democratic Promise

A large number of people in the United States discovered that the economic premises of their society were working against them. These premises were reputed to be democratic—America after all was a democratic society in the eyes of most of its citizens and in the eyes of the world—but farmers by the millions found that this claim was not supported by the events governing their lives.

The nation's agriculturalists had worried and grumbled about "the new rules of commerce" ever since the prosperity that accompanied the Civil War had turned into widespread distress soon after the war ended. During the 1870s they did the kinds of things that concerned people generally do in an effort to cope with "hard times." In an occupation noted for hard work they worked even harder. When this failed to change things, millions of families migrated westward in an effort to enlist nature's help. They were driven by the thought that through sheer physical labor they might wring more production from the new virgin lands of the West than they had been able to do in their native states of Ohio and Virginia and Alabama. But, though railroad land agents created beguiling stories of Western prosperity, the men and women who listened, and went, found that the laws of commerce worked against them just as much in Kansas and Texas as they had back home on the eastern side of the Mississippi River.

So in the 1870s, the farmers increasingly talked to each other about their troubles and read books on economics in an effort to discover what had gone wrong. Some of them formed organizations of economic self-help like the Grange and others assisted in pioneering new institutions of political self-help like the Greenback Party. But as the hard times of the 1870s turned into the even harder times of the 1880s, it was clear that these efforts were not really going anywhere. Indeed, by 1888 it was evident that things were worse than they had been in

1878 or 1868. More and more people saw their farm mortgages foreclosed. As everyone in rural America knew, this statistic inexorably yielded another, more ominous one: the number of landless tenant farmers in America rose steadily year after year. Meanwhile, millions of small landowners hung on grimly, their unpaid debts thrusting them dangerously close to the brink of tenantry and peonage. Hard work availed nothing. Everywhere the explanation of events was the same: "Times were hard."

Then gradually, in certain specific ways and for certain specific reasons, American farmers developed new methods that enabled them to try to regain a measure of control over their own lives. Their efforts, halting and disjointed at first, gathered form and force until they grew into a coordinated mass movement that stretched across the American continent from the Atlantic coast to the Pacific. Millions of people came to believe fervently that a wholesale overhauling of their society was going to happen in their lifetimes. A democratic "new day" was coming to America. This whirlwind of effort, and the massive upsurge of democratic hopes that accompanied it, has come to be known as the Populist Revolt. . . .

For a number of reasons, all of them rather fundamental to historical analysis, the Populist moment has proved very difficult for Americans to understand. Under the circumstances, it is probably just as well to take these reasons up one at a time at the very outset in an effort to clear as much underbrush as possible before turning our attention to the protesting farmers of the 1890s.

There are three principal areas of interpretive confusion that bear directly on the Populist experience. First, very little understanding exists as to just what mass democratic movements are, and how they happen. Second, there are serious problems embedded in the very language of description modern Americans routinely employ to characterize political events. These problems particularly affect commonly held presumptions about how certain "classes" of people are supposed to "act" on the stage of history. Finally, and by all odds most importantly, our greatest problem in understanding protest is grounded in contemporary American culture. In addition to being central, this cultural difficulty is also the most resistant to clear explanation: we are not only culturally confused, our confusion makes it difficult for us even to imagine our confusion. Obviously, it is prudent, then, to start here.

The reigning American presumption about the American experience is grounded in the idea of progress, the conviction that the present is "better" than the past and the future will bring still more betterment. This reassuring belief rests securely on statistical charts and tables certifying the steady upward tilt in economic production. Admittedly, social problems have persisted—inequities of income and opportunity have plagued the society—but these, too, have steadily been addressed through the sheer growth of the economy. For all of its shortcomings, the system works.

This is a powerful assumption. It may be tested by reflecting upon the fact that, despite American progress, the society has been forced to endure sundry movements of protest. In our effort to address the inconvenient topic of protest, our need to be intellectually consistent—while thinking within the framework of continuous progress—has produced a number of explanations about the nature of dissent in America. Closely followed, these arguments are not really explanations at all, but rather the assertion of more presumptions that have the effect of defending the basic intuition about progress itself. The most common of these explanations rests upon what is perceived to be a temporary malfunction of the economic order: people protest when "times are hard." When times stop being "hard," people stop protesting and things return to "normal"—that is to say, progress is resumed.

Unfortunately, history does not support the notion that mass protest movements develop because of hard times. Depressed economies or exploitive arrangements of power and privilege may produce lean years or even lean lifetimes for millions of people, but the historical evidence is conclusive that they do not produce mass political insurgency. The simple fact of the matter is that, in ways that affect mind and body, times have been "hard" for most humans throughout human history and for most of that period people have not been in rebellion. Indeed, traditionalists in a number of societies have often pointed in glee to this passivity, choosing to call it "apathy" and citing it as a justification for maintaining things as they are.

This apparent absence of popular vigor is traceable, however, not to apathy but to the very raw materials of history—that complex of rules, manners, power relationships, and memories that collectively comprise what is called culture. "The masses" do not rebel in instinctive response to hard times and exploitation because they have been culturally organized by their societies not to rebel. They have, instead, been instructed in deference. Needless to say, this is the kind of social circumstance that is not readily apparent to the millions who live within it.

The lack of visible mass political activity on the part of modern industrial populations is a function of how these societies have been shaped by the various economic or political elites who fashioned them. In fundamental ways, this shaping process (which is now quite mature in America) bears directly not only upon our ability to grasp the meaning of American Populism, but our ability to understand protest generally and, most important of all, on our ability to comprehend the prerequisites for democracy itself. This shaping process, therefore, merits some attention.

Upon the consolidation of power, the first duty of revolutionaries (whether of the "bourgeois" or "proletarian" variety) is obviously to try to deflect any further revolutions that necessarily would be directed against them. Though a strong central police or army has sometimes proved essential to this stabilizing process, revolutionaries, like other humans, do not yearn to spend their lives fighting down counterrevolutions. A far more permanent and thus far more desirable solution to the task of achieving domestic tranquillity is cultural—the creation of mass modes of thought that literally make the need for major additional social changes difficult for the mass of the population to imagine. When and if achieved, these conforming modes of thought and conduct constitute the new culture itself. The ultimate victory is nailed into place, therefore, only when the population has been persuaded to define all conceivable political activity within the limits of existing custom. Such a society can genuinely be described as "stable." Thenceforth, protest will pose no ultimate threat because the protesters will necessarily conceive of their options as being so limited that even should they be successful, the resulting "reforms" will not alter significantly the inherited modes of power and privilege. Protest under such conditions of cultural narrowness is, therefore, not only permissible in the eyes of those who rule, but is, from time to time, positively desirable because it fortifies the popular understanding that the society is functioning "democratically." . . .

The principal hazard to a clear understanding of the meaning of American Populism exists in this central anomaly of contemporary American culture. Reform movements such as Populism necessarily call into question the underlying values of the larger society. But if that society is perceived by its members to be progressive and democratic—and yet is also known to have resisted the movement of democratic reform—the reigning cultural presumption necessarily induces people to place the "blame" for the failure of protest upon the protesters themselves. Accordingly, in the case of the Populists, the mainstream presumption is both simple and largely unconscious: one studies Populism to learn where the Populists went wrong. The condescension toward the past that is implicit in the idea of progress merely reinforces such complacent premises.

Further, if the population is politically resigned (believing the dogma of "democracy" on a superficial public level but not believing it privately), it becomes quite difficult for people to grasp the scope of popular hopes that were alive in an earlier time when democratic expectations were larger than those people permit themselves to have today. By conjoining these two contradictory features of modern culture—it is at once evident that modern people are culturally programmed, as it were, to conclude that past American egalitarians such as the Populists were "foolish" to have had such large democratic hopes. Again, our "progressive" impulse to condescend to the past merely reinforces such a presumption. In a society in which sophisticated deference masks private resignation, the democratic dreams of the Populists have been difficult for twentieth-century people to imagine. Contemporary American culture itself therefore operates to obscure the Populist experience.

A second obstacle to a clear perception of Populism is embedded in the language of description through which contemporary Americans attempt to characterize "politics." A central interpretive tool, derived from Marx but almost universally employed today by Marxists and non-Marxists alike, is based upon concepts of class: that is, that the intricate nature of social interaction in history can be rendered more intelligible by an understanding of the mode and extent of class conflict that was or was not at work during a given period. Needless to say, many psychological, social, and economic ingredients are embedded in concepts of class, and, when handled with care, they can, indeed, bring considerable clarity to historical events of great complexity. Nevertheless, as an interpretive device, "class" is a treacherous tool if handled casually and routinely—as it frequently is. For example, offhand "class analysis," when applied to the agrarian revolt in America, will merely succeed in rendering the Populist experience visible. While classes in agricultural societies contain various shadings of "property-consciousness" on the part of rich landowners, smallholders, and landless laborers ("gentry," "farmers," and "tenants," in American terminology), these distinctions create more problems than they solve when applied to the agrarian revolt. It is a long-standing assumption—not so thoroughly tested in America by sustained historical investigation as some might believe—that "landowners" must perforce behave in politically reactionary ways. The political aspirations of the landless are seen to deserve intense scrutiny, but the politics of "the landed" cannot be expected to contain serious progressive ideas. The power of this theoretical assumption can scarcely be understated. It permits the political efforts of millions of human beings to be dismissed with the casual flourish of an abstract category of interpretation. One can only assert the conviction that a thoroughgoing history of, for example, the Socialist Party of the United States, including the history of the recruitment of its agrarian following in early twentieth-century America, will not be fully pieced together until this category of political analysis is successfully transcended. The condition of being "landed" or "landless" does not, *a priori,* predetermine one's potential for "progressive" political action: circumstances surrounding the ownership or non-ownership of land are centrally relevant, too. The Populist experience in any case puts this proposition to a direct and precise test, for the agrarian movement was created by landed *and* landless people. The platform of the movement argued in behalf of the landless because that platform was seen as being progressive for small landowners, too. Indeed, from beginning to end, the chief Populist theoreticians—"landowners" all—stood in economic terms with the propertyless rural and urban people of America.

In consequence, neither the human experiences within the mass institutions generated by the agrarian revolt nor the ideology of Populism itself can be expected to become readily discernible to anyone, capitalist or Marxist, who is easily consoled by the presumed analytical clarity of categories of class. The interior life of the agrarian revolt makes this clear enough. While the economic and political threads of populism did not always mesh in easy harmony (any more than the cultural threads did), the evolution of the political ideology of the movement proceeded from a common center and a common experience and thus possessed an instructive degree of sequential consistency.

The use of the word "sequential" provides an appropriate introduction to the final hazard confronting the student of the agrarian revolt—the rather elementary problem of defining just what "mass movements" are and how they happen. The sober fact is that movements of mass democratic protest—that is to say, coordinated insurgent actions by hundreds of thousands or millions of people—represent a political, an organizational, and above all, a cultural achievement of the first magnitude. Beyond this, mass protest requires a high order not only of cultural education and tactical achievement, it requires a high order of *sequential* achievement. These evolving stages of achievement are essential if large numbers of intimidated people are to generate both the psychological autonomy and the practical means to challenge culturally sanctioned authority. A failure at any stage of the sequential process aborts or at the very least sharply limits the growth of the popular movement. Unfortunately, the overwhelming nature of the impediments to these stages of sequential achievement are rarely taken into account. The simple fact of the matter is that so difficult has the process of movement-building proven to be since the onset of industrialization in the Western world that all democratic protest movements have been aborted or limited in this manner prior to the recruitment of their full natural constituency. The underlying social reality is, therefore, one that is not generally kept firmly in mind as an operative dynamic of modern society—namely, that mass democratic movements are overarchingly difficult for human beings to generate.

How does mass protest happen at all, then—to the extent that it does happen?

The Populist revolt—the most elaborate example of mass insurgency we have in American history—provides an abundance of evidence that can be applied in answering this question. The sequential process of democratic movement-building will be seen to involve four stages: (1) the creation of an autonomous institution where new interpretations can materialize that run counter to those of prevailing authority—a development which, for the sake of simplicity, we may describe as "the movement forming"; (2) the creation of a tactical means to attract masses of people—"the movement recruiting"; (3) the achievement of a heretofore culturally unsanctioned level of social analysis—"the movement educating"; and (4) the creation of an institutional means whereby the new ideas, shared now by the rank and file of the mass movement, can be expressed in an autonomous political way—"the movement politicized."

Imposing cultural roadblocks stand in the way of a democratic movement at every stage of this sequential process, causing losses in the potential constituencies that are to be incorporated into the movement. Many people may not be successfully "recruited," many who are recruited may not become adequately "educated," and many who are educated may fail the final test of moving into autonomous political action. The forces of orthodoxy, occupying the most culturally sanctioned command posts in the society, can be counted upon, out of self-interest, to oppose each stage of the sequential process—particularly the latter stages, when the threat posed by the movement has become clear to all. In the aggregate, the struggle to create a mass democratic movement involves intense cultural conflict with many built-in advantages accruing to the partisans of the established order.

Offered here in broad outline, then, is a conceptual framework through which to view the building process of mass democratic movements in modern industrial societies. The recruiting, educating, and politicizing methods will naturally vary from movement to movement and from nation to nation, and the relative success in each stage will obviously vary also. The actions of both the insurgents and the defenders of the received culture can also be counted upon to influence events dramatically.

Within this broad framework, it seems helpful to specify certain subsidiary components. Democratic movements are initiated by people who have individually managed to attain a high level of personal political self-respect. They are not resigned; they are not intimidated. To put it another way, they are not culturally organized to conform to established hierarchical forms. Their sense of autonomy permits them to dare to try to change things by seeking to influence others. The subsequent stages of recruitment and of internal economic and political education (steps two, three, and four) turn on the ability of the democratic organizers to develop widespread methods of internal communication within the mass movement. Such democratic facilities provide the only way the movement can defend itself to its own adherents in the face of the adverse interpretations certain to emanate from the received culture. If the movement is able to achieve this level of internal communication and democracy, and the ranks accordingly grow in numbers, and in political consciousness, a new plateau of social possibility comes within reach of all participants. In intellectual terms, the generating force of this new mass mode of behavior may be rather simply described as "a new way of looking at things." It constitutes a new and heretofore unsanctioned mass folkway of autonomy. In psychological terms, its appearance reflects the development within the movement of a new kind of collective self-confidence. "Individual self-respect" and "collective self-confidence" constitute, then, the cultural building blocks of mass democratic politics. Their development permits people to conceive of the idea of acting in self-generated democratic ways—as distinct from passively participating in various hierarchical modes bequeathed by the received culture. In this study of Populism, I have given a name to this plateau of cooperative and democratic conduct. I have called it "the movement culture." Once attained, it opens up new vistas of social possibility, vistas that are less clouded by inherited assumptions. I suggest that all significant mass democratic movements in human history have generated this autonomous capacity. Indeed, had they not done so, one cannot visualize how they could have developed into significant mass democratic movements.

Democratic politics hinge fundamentally on these sequential relationships. Yet, quite obviously the process is extremely difficult for human beings to set in motion and even more difficult to maintain—a fact that helps explain why genuinely democratic cultures have not yet been developed by mankind. Self-evidently, mass democratic societies cannot be created until the components of the creating process have been theoretically delineated and have subsequently come to be understood in practical ways by masses of people. This level of political analysis has not yet been reached, despite the theoretical labors of Adam Smith, Karl Marx, and their sundry disciples and critics. As a necessary consequence, twentieth-century people, instead of participating in democratic cultures, live in hierarchical cultures, "capitalist" and "socialist," that merely call themselves democratic.

All of the foregoing constitutes an attempt to clear enough cultural and ideological landscape to permit an unhampered view of American Populism. The development of the democratic movement was sequential. The organizational base of the agrarian revolt was an institution called the National Farmers Alliance and Industrial Union. Created by men of discernible self-possession and political self-respect, the Alliance experimented in new methods of economic self-help. After nine years of trial and error, the people of the Alliance developed a powerful mechanism of mass recruitment—the world's first large-scale working class cooperative. Farmers by the hundreds of thousands flocked into the Alliance. In its recruiting phase, the movement swept through whole states "like a cyclone" because, easily enough, the farmers joined the Alliance in order to join the Alliance cooperative. The subsequent experiences of millions of farmers within their cooperatives proceeded to "educate" them about the prevailing forms of economic power and privilege in America. This process of education was further elaborated through a far-flung agency of internal communication, the 40,000 lecturers of the Alliance lecturing system. Finally, after the effort of the Alliance at economic self-help had been defeated by the financial and political institutions of industrial America, the people of the movement turned to independent political action by creating their own institution, the People's Party. All of these experiences, stretching over a fifteen-year period from 1877 to 1892, may be seen as an evolutionary pattern of democratic organizing activity that generated, and in turn was generated by, an increasing self-awareness on the part of the participants. In consequence, a mass democratic movement was fashioned.

Once established in 1892, the People's Party challenged the corporate state and the creed of progress it put forward. It challenged, in sum, the world we live in today. Though our loyalty to our own world makes the agrarian revolt culturally difficult to grasp, Populism may nevertheless be seen as a time of economically coherent democratic striving. Having said this, it is also necessary to add that Populists were not supernatural beings. As theoreticians concerned with certain forms of capitalist exploitation, they were creative and, in a number of ways, prescient. As economists, they were considerably more thoughtful and practical than their contemporary political rivals in both major parties. As organizers of a huge democratic movement, Populists learned a great deal about both the power of the received hierarchy and the demands imposed on themselves by independent political action. As third party tacticians, they had their moments, though most of their successes came earlier in the political phase of their movement than later. And, finally, as participants in the democratic creed, they were, on the evidence, far more advanced than most Americans, then or since. . . .

Out of their cooperative struggle came a new democratic community. It engendered within millions of people what Martin Luther King would later call a "sense of somebodiness." This "sense" was a new way of thinking about oneself and about democracy. Thus armed, the Populists attempted to insulate themselves against being intimidated by the enormous political, economic, and social pressures that accompanied the emergence of corporate America. . . .

Populism in America was not the sub-treasury plan, not the greenback heritage, not the Omaha Platform. It was not, at bottom, even the People's Party. The meaning of the agrarian revolt was its cultural assertion as a people's movement of mass democratic aspiration. Its animating essence pulsed at every level of the ambitious structure of cooperation: in the earnest probings of people bent on discovering a way to free themselves from the killing grip of the credit system ("The suballiance is a schoolroom."); in the joint-notes of the landed, given in the name of themselves and the landless ("The brotherhood stands united."); in the pride of discovery of their own legitimacy ("The merchants are listening when the County Trade Committee talks."); and in the massive and emotional effort to save the cooperative dream itself ("The Southern Exchange Shall Stand."). The democratic core of Populism was visible in the suballiance resolutions of inquiry into the patterns of economic exploitation ("find out and apply the remedy"); in the mile-long Alliance wagon trains ("The Fourth of July is Alliance Day."); in the sprawling summer encampments ("A pentecost of politics"); and, perhaps most tellingly, in the latent generosity unlocked by the culture of the movement itself, revealed in the capacity of those who had little, to empathize with those who had less ("We extend to the Knights of Labor our hearty sympathy in their manly struggle against monopolistic oppression," and "The Negro people are part of the people and must be treated as such.").

While each of these moments occurred in the 1890s, and have practical and symbolic meaning because they did occur, Populism in America was not an egalitarian achievement. Rather, it was an egalitarian attempt, a beginning. If it stimulated human generosity, it did not, before the movement itself was destroyed, create a settled culture of generosity. Though Populists attempted to break out of the received heritage of white supremacy, they necessarily, as white Americans, did so within the very ethos of white supremacy. At both a psychological and political level, some Populists were more successful than others in coping with the pervasive impact of the inherited caste system. Many were not successful at all. This reality extended to a number of pivotal social and political questions beside race—sectional and party loyalties, the intricacies of power relationships embedded in the monetary system, and the ways of achieving a politics supportive of popular democracy itself. In their struggle, Populists learned a great truth: cultures are hard to change. Their attempt to do so, however, provides a measure of the seriousness of their movement.

Populism thus cannot be seen as a moment of triumph, but as a moment of democratic promise. It was a spirit of egalitarian hope, expressed in the actions of two million beings—not in the prose of a platform, however creative, and not, ultimately, even in the third party, but in a self-generated culture of collective dignity and individual longing. As a movement of people, it was expansive, passionate, flawed, creative—above all, enhancing in its assertion of human striving. That was Populism in the nineteenth century. . . .

However they were subsequently characterized, Populists in their own time derived their most incisive power from the simple fact that they declined to participate adequately in a central element of the emerging American faith. In an age of progress and forward motion, they had come to suspect that Horatio Alger was not real. In due course, they came to possess a cultural flaw that armed them with considerable critical power. Heretics in a land of true believers and recent converts, they saw the coming society and they did not like it. It was perhaps inevitable that since they lost their struggle to deflect that society from its determined path of corporate celebration, they were among the last of the heretics. Once defeated, they lost what cultural autonomy they had amassed and surrendered their progeny to the training camps of the conquering army. All Americans, including the children of Populists, were exposed to the new dogmas of progress confidently conveyed in the public school system and in the nation's history texts. As the twentieth-century recipients of this instruction, we have found it difficult to listen with sustained attention to the words of those who dissented at the moment a transcendent cultural norm was being fashioned.

In their own era, the agrarian spokesmen who talked of the "coming revolution" turned out to be much too hopeful. Though in the months of Populist collapse and for successive decades thereafter prosperity eluded those the reformers called the "producing classes," the growing industrial society preserved the narrowed boundaries of political dialogue substantially intact, as roughly one-third of America's urban workers moved slowly into the middle class. The mystique of progress itself helped to hold in muted resignation the millions who continued in poverty and other millions who, for reasons of the exclusiveness and white supremacy of the progressive society, were not permitted to live their lives in dignity.

As the first beneficiary of the cultural consolidation of the 1890s, the new Republican orthodoxy, grounded in the revolutionary (and decidedly anti-Jeffersonian) political methods of Mark Hanna, provided the mores for the twentieth century without ever having to endure a serious debate about the possibility of structural change in the American forms of finance capitalism. Political conservatives nevertheless endured intermittent periods of extreme nervousness—such as was produced in 1933 by the nation's sudden and forced departure from the gold standard. Given the presumed centrality of a metallic currency, it took a while for cultural traditionalists, including bankers, to realize that the influence of the banking community had not suffered organic disturbances—J. Laurence Laughlin to the contrary notwithstanding. Though the pattern of interest rates during and after World War II continued to transfer measurable portions of the national income from both business and labor to bankers—in the process burdening the structure of prices with an added increment of cost as well as changing the very structure of industrial capitalism—disputes over the distribution of income within the whole society did not precipitate serious social contentions as long as America maintained a favorable international trade and investment balance. It remained clear, however, that unresolved questions about the inherited financial system might well make a sudden and unexpected reappearance if, at any time in the second half of the twentieth century, shifts in world trade and the cost of imported raw materials placed severe forms of competitive pressure on the American economy and on the international monetary system. At such a moment the cultural consolidation fashioned in the Gilded Age would undergo its first sustained re-evaluation, as the "financial question" once again intruded into the nation's politics and the issues of Populism again penetrated the American consciousness. That time, while pending, has not yet come.

For their part, Gilded Age traditionalists did not view the conclusive triumph of the corporate ethos as a foregone conclusion. Themselves insecure in an era of real and apparent change, they were unable to distinguish between authentic signs of economic dislocation and the political threat represented by those who called attention to those signs. On this rather primitive level the politics of the era resolved itself, and the progressive society was born. As an outgrowth of its insularity and complacency, industrializing America wanted uncritical voices of celebration. The agrarian radicals instead delivered the warning that all was not well with the democracy. They were not thanked.

Today, the values and the sheer power of corporate America pinch in the horizons of millions of obsequious corporate employees, tower over every American legislature, state and national, determine the modes and style of mass communications and mass education, fashion American foreign policy around the globe, and shape the rules of the American political process itself. Self-evidently, corporate values define modern American culture.

It was the corporate state that the People's Party attempted to bring under democratic control.

SUGGESTIONS FOR FURTHER READING

John D. Hicks, *The Populist Revolt* (Minneapolis, 1931) deserves to be read in its entirety. Broader in scope and sympathetic to the farmers is Fred A. Shannon's outstanding work, *The Farmers' Last Frontier: Agriculture, 1860–1897* (New York, 1945). Excellent introductions to Southern Populism are C. Vann Woodward, *The Origins of the New South, 1877–1913* (Baton Rouge, 1951, 1971) and Theodore Saloutos, *Farmer Movements in the South, 1865–1933* (Lincoln, Neb., 1960).

Especially useful examples of the vast literature dealing with farmers' problems are Allan G. Bogue, *Money at Interest: The Farm Mortgage on the Middle Border* (Ithaca, N.Y., 1955) and *From Prairie to Cornbelt: Farming on the Illinois and Iowa Prairies in the Nineteenth Century* (Chicago, 1963); Paul W. Gates, *Fifty Million Acres: Conflicts over Kansas Land Policy, 1854–1890* (Ithaca, N.Y., 1954); Theodore Saloutos and John D. Hicks, *Twentieth Century Populism* (Lincoln, Neb., 1951); and Earl W. Hayter, *The Troubled Farmer, 1850–1900: Rural Adjustment to Industrialism* (DeKalb, Ill., 1968).

In the 1950s, Richard Hofstadter's *The Age of Reform* (a portion of which is reprinted here) began a reexamination of the Populists. He and others charged the Populists with some degree of responsibility for the anti-Semitism, isolationism, and anti-intellectualism in American life. C. Vann Woodward discusses some of this anti-Populist literature in "The Populist Heritage and the Intellectual," *American Scholar,* 29 (Winter 1959–1960), 55–72, also reprinted in C. Vann Woodward, *The Burden of Southern History* (Baton Rouge, La., 1960). The attack on the Populists has also produced a vigorous defense. Walter T. K. Nugent denies that the Populists were anti-Semitic and xenophobic in *The Tolerant Populists* (Chicago, 1963). Norman Pollack, *The Populist Response to Industrial America* (Cambridge, Mass., 1962), finds them to be realistic radicals, who looked not to the past but to a future when businessmen would no longer be able to exploit farmers and workers. For Pollack, the Populists posed a kind of socialist answer, a view that he has modified in his more recent books, *The Just Polity: Populism, Law, and Human Welfare* (Urbana, Ill., 1987) and *The Humane Economy: Populism, Capitalism, and Democracy* (New Brunswick, N.J., 1990).

Robert C. McMath, Jr., *American Populism: A Social History, 1877–1898* is a splendid, recent synthesis that contains a good bibliography. Michael Kazin, *The Populist Persuasion: An American History* (New York, 1995) traces a populist impulse in reformist politics over a hundred years, finding a rightist tendency that gains predominance in the twentieth century.

A number of studies center on the South. Lawrence Goodwyn, *The Populist Moment: A Short History of the Agrarian Revolt in America* (a portion of which is reprinted here) denies that the Populist alternative was socialistic and argues that the radical farmers posed a realistic alternative to developing big business in America. (*The Populist Moment* is an abridgement of Goodwyn's more detailed study, *Democratic Promise* [New York, 1976].) A similar point of view is found in Robert C. McMath, Jr., *Populist Vanguard: A History of the Southern Farmers' Alliance* (Chapel Hill, N.C., 1975) and in Bruce Palmer, * "Man over Money": The Southern Populist Critique of American Capital-

---

*Available in paperback edition.

ism (Chapel Hill, N.C., 1980). Steven Hahn, *The Roots of Southern Populism* (New York, 1983) finds the source of Populism in the conflict between yeoman farmers who resisted the modernizing efforts of the large planters and their urban allies. Michael Schwartz, *Radical Protest and Social Structure: The Southern Farmers' Alliance and Cotton Tenancy, 1880–1890* (New York, 1976), argues that the Alliance was a radical people's movement and that it was diverted from its radicalism when it was taken over by politicians whose main goal was election to office rather than real reform. A different perspective of Southern Populism may be found in Gerald H. Gaither, *Blacks and the Populist Revolt: Ballots and Bigotry in the "New South"* (University, Ala., 1977).

Useful recent studies of western Populism are Scott G. McNall, *The Road to Rebellion: Class Formation and Kansas Populism, 1865–1900* (Chicago, 1988); Karel D. Bicha, *Western Populism: Studies in an Ambivalent Conservatism* (Lawrence, Kans., 1976); and Jeffrey Ostler, *Prairie Populism: The Fate of Agrarian Radicalism in Kansas, Nebraska and Iowa* (Lawrence, Kans., 1993).

4

Workers in
an Industrial Age

I n the long run, industrialization provided the nation's workers with added opportunities, increased wages, improved working conditions, and the ability to purchase more goods and services. But these long-term improvements exacted a cost. Behind the cold statistics of economic growth, growing incomes, and increasing efficiency were serious problems brought by the rapid and often chaotic economic and social changes. Workers found themselves crowded into urban slums that were marked by unspeakable filth and grossly inadequate public services. In the shops and factories hours were usually long, conditions dangerous and unhealthy, and wages woefully low. Periodic economic crises threw people out of work, giving employers a powerful weapon to force down the wages and to lengthen the working hours of those who remained employed. Equally significant were massive alterations in the nature and organization of work. Employers, in their quest for efficiency and cost cutting, replaced skilled with unskilled workers by introducing machinery to replace workers and by dividing the work into small, easily learned tasks, and they constantly speeded the pace of work. Workers found themselves as interchangeable as the parts they produced, and the work itself became mindless, boring, and increasingly dangerous because of the hectic pace at which it was conducted.

In order to protect themselves, workers often united, sometimes in trade unions but often in less formal and structured organizations. When organized and determined workers used the strike in their struggle against organized and equally determined employers, the results were bitter and, at times, violent. Striking workers were often greeted at plant gates by armed guards hired by factory owners intent upon dispersing the pickets and maintaining production with unorganized labor. Workers regularly armed themselves, equally resolved to keep the struck factory closed by preventing "scabs" from entering the shops. When these two determined and armed groups met, the result was invariably a bloody clash.

Every labor history bristles with these accounts of violent struggles between labor and management, leading some historians to conclude that conflict, rather than consensus, best characterizes the history of labor in America. The workers, these historians argue, in their fight to raise wages and improve working conditions, found themselves locked in bitter class conflict with their employers.

Yet other historians, without attempting to ignore these conflicts, insist that they do not signify that workers had adopted a radical or revolutionary outlook. These historians argue that only a small minority of American union members and leaders have been radicals and that the trade-union movement never adopted a program designed to overthrow the existing social and economic system. The major portion of organized labor has consistently repudiated the few radical sections of the trade-union movement whenever they appeared.

In a word, then, these historians point to consensus as the basic theme in American labor history. Labor and management, they argue, have often disagreed over wages and working conditions, and these disagreements often led to strikes and conflicts; but, behind these disagreements, there existed an underlying unity based upon an acceptance of the sanctity of private property as well as the most important features of American democratic government. American workers, they insist, never developed a class consciousness such as existed among their European counterparts; they sought merely to increase their wages and improve their working and living conditions and sought to climb the economic and social ladder rather than change the economic and social system.

If those historians who emphasize consensus cannot ignore the violent conflicts that often characterized labor-management relations, those who stress conflict cannot ignore the fact that the majority of American workers and, with only a few exceptions, most of the trade unions never adopted revolutionary socialist goals. A few argue that American workers will eventually learn from their struggles, as did European workers, that socialism provides the only real solution to their problems. Others who stress conflict insist that although the labor movement has never been socialistic, it has often fought for goals that would fundamentally alter the social and economic system. Indeed, some note that the organized efforts of workers have resulted in significant reforms, making it unnecessary for the labor movement to become more radical.

Some of these disagreements among historians may be followed in the selections that follow. Readers should keep in mind that evaluations of the labor movement, including the many instances of strikes and violence, rest upon an assessment of the workers' goals as well as the methods they used to attempt to reach these goals. In short, what exactly did the workers want?

One answer to this question is provided by Herbert G. Gutman in the first selection. Gutman finds sharp and bitter conflict as workers—both men and women, from rural and artisan backgrounds—were forced to modernize—that is, to adapt to the new industrial society. Workers resisted, but the ensuing conflict was not revolutionary or socialistic. Workers resisted changes being forced upon them by the demands of expanding industrialism; they sought to retain many of their old ways and traditions.

Leon Fink, in the second selection, contends that the workers during the early stages of industrialism were far more radical in their ideology and their goals. Although they accepted many of the traditional American values and did not, for the most part, become socialists, they drew radical conclusions from these traditional values: ". . . the labor movement in the Gilded Age turned the plowshares of a consensual political past into a sword of class conflict." New conditions widened the gulf between employer and employee as the same words took on different meanings for workers and their employers. The workers, Fink concludes, did not look backward to some kind of golden age; they looked forward to a different future that would be a "kind of workingmen's democracy."

Thus, both Gutman and Fink find sharp class conflict to be characteristic of the early labor movement, and both find the workers resisting the changes being forced upon them by their employers. But Gutman insists that workers were attempting to hold on to traditional values, while Fink argues that workers were using traditional values in new and radical ways. In either case, could the conflict be said to be revolutionary in that it challenged the fundamentals of the economic and social system? Or were the workers merely adopting different tactics to reach their main goal of increasing their share of the nation's wealth?

A somewhat different view of matters appears in the final selection, where Alice Kessler-Harris considers problems from the perspective of women workers. To improve their working conditions and wages, women had to fight not only their employers but also the traditions that defined their proper role and the unions that were often antagonistic. Employers who wanted a cheap and docile labor force hired increasing numbers of women workers, while the unions felt that women workers took jobs that were rightly men's and that they kept wages low. In the end, women remained in the labor force, but they found themselves segregated into what was considered "women's work."

The goals of the workers as discussed in these three selections do not seem to be revolutionary. Although the workers often adopted militant tactics that sometimes led to violent confrontations with their employers, they did not call for a socialist revolution. But does it therefore follow that working men and women simply accepted the ideas and outlook of their employers, thereby becoming conservative and acquiescent? Is the demand for socialism, in other words, the only sign of true radicalism?

If not, then what other demands might constitute a radical response by workers? Were the demands of late-nineteenth-century workers "radical" by some other definition of the term?

A different set of questions concerns the results of the workers' actions. What, if anything, did the workers achieve by their organized activities? Were they compelled to give in completely to their employers? Or were they able to force an accommodation between labor and capital, and, if so, what was the nature of this accommodation?

Herbert G. Gutman

Work, Culture, and Society in
Industrializing America, 1815–1919

With a few significant exceptions, for more than half a century American labor history has continued to reflect both the strengths and the weaknesses of the conceptual scheme sketched by its founding fathers, John R. Commons and others of the so-called Wisconsin school of labor history. Even their most severe critics, including the orthodox "Marxist" labor historians of the 1930s, 1940s, and 1950s and the few New Left historians who have devoted attention to American labor history, rarely questioned that conceptual framework. Commons and his colleagues asked large questions, gathered important source materials, and put forth impressive ideas. Together with able disciples, they studied the development of the trade union as an institution and explained its place in a changing labor market. But they gave attention primarily to those few workers who belonged to trade unions and neglected much else of importance about the American working population. Two flaws especially marred this older labor history. Because so few workers belonged to permanent trade unions before 1940, its overall conceptualization excluded most working people from detailed and serious study. More than this, its methods encouraged labor historians to spin a cocoon around American workers, isolating them from their own particular subcultures and from the larger national culture. An increasingly narrow "economic" analysis caused the study of American working-class history to grow more constricted and become more detached from larger developments in American social and cultural history and from the writing of American social and cultural history itself. . . .

The focus in these pages is on free white labor in quite different time periods: 1815–43, 1843–93, 1893–1919. The precise years serve only as guideposts to mark the fact that American society differed greatly in each period. Between

"Work, Culture, and Society in Industrializing America, 1815–1919," by Herbert G. Gutman, from *American Historical Review*, LXXVIII (June 1973). Used by permission.

1815 and 1843 the United States remained a predominantly preindustrial society and most workers drawn to its few factories were the products of rural and village preindustrial culture. Preindustrial American society was not premodern in the same way that European peasant societies were, but it was, nevertheless, premodern. In the half century after 1843 industrial development radically transformed the earlier American social structure, and during this Middle Period (an era not framed around the coming and the aftermath of the Civil War) a profound tension existed between the older American preindustrial social structure and the modernizing institutions that accompanied the development of industrial capitalism. After 1893 the United States ranked as a mature industrial society. In each of these distinctive stages of change in American society, a recurrent tension also existed between native and immigrant men and women fresh to the factory and the demands imposed upon them by the regularities and disciplines of factory labor. That state of tension was regularly revitalized by the migration of diverse premodern native and foreign peoples into an industrializing or a fully industrialized society. The British economic historian Sidney Pollard has described well this process whereby "a society of peasants, craftsmen, and versatile labourers became a society of modern industrial workers." "There was more to overcome," Pollard writes of industrializing England,

than the change of employment or the new rhythm of work: there was a whole new culture to be absorbed and an old one to be traduced and spurned, there were new surroundings, often in a different part of the country, new relations with employers, and new uncertainties of livelihood, new friends and neighbors, new marriage patterns and behavior patterns of children within the family and without.

That same process occurred in the United States. Just as in all modernizing countries, the United States faced the difficult task of industrializing whole cultures, but in this country the process was regularly repeated, each stage of American economic growth and development involving different first-generation factory workers. The social transformation Pollard described occurred in England between 1770 and 1850, and in those decades premodern British cultures and the modernizing institutions associated primarily with factory and machine labor collided and interacted. A painful transition occurred, dominated the ethos of an entire era, and then faded in relative importance. After 1850 and until quite recently, the British working class reproduced itself and retained a relative national homogeneity. New tensions emerged but not those of a society continually busy (and worried about) industrializing persons born out of that society and often alien in birth and color and in work habits, customary values, and behavior. "Traditional social habits and customs," J. F. C. Harrison reminds us, "seldom fitted into the patterns of industrial life, and they had . . . to be discredited as hindrances to progress." That happened regularly in the United States after 1815 as the nation absorbed and worked to transform new groups of preindustrial people, native whites among them. The result, however, was neither a static tension nor the mere recurrence of similar cycles, because American society itself changed as did the composition of its laboring population. But the source of the tension remained the same, and conflict often resulted. It was neither the conflict emphasized by the older Progressive historians (agrarianism versus capitalism, or sectional disagreement) nor that emphasized by recent critics of that early twentieth-century synthesis (conflict between competing elites). It resulted instead from the fact that the American working class was continually altered in its composition by infusions, from within and without the nation, of peasants, farmers, skilled artisans, and casual day laborers who brought into industrial society ways of work and other habits and values not associated with industrial necessities and the industrial ethos. Some shed these older ways to conform to new imperatives. Others fell victim or fled, moving from place to place. Some sought to extend and adapt older patterns of work and life to a new society. Others challenged the social system through varieties of collective associations. But for all—at different historical moments—the transition to industrial society, as E. P. Thompson has written, "entailed a severe restructuring of working habits—new disciplines, new incentives, and a new human nature upon which these incentives could bite effectively." . . .

Men and women who sell their labor to an employer bring more to a new or changing work situation than their physical presence. What they bring to a factory depends, in good part, on their culture of origin, and how they behave is shaped by the interaction between that culture and the particular society into which they enter. Because so little is yet known about preindustrial American culture and subcultures, some caution is necessary in moving from the level of generalization to historical actuality. What follows compares and contrasts working people new to industrial society but living in quite different time periods. First, the expectations and work habits of first-generation predominantly native American factory workers before 1843 are compared with first-generation immigrant factory workers between 1893 and 1920. Similarities in the work habits and expectations of men and women who experienced quite different premodern cultures are indicated. Second, the work habits and culture of artisans in the industrializing decades (1843–93) are examined to indicate the persistence of powerful cultural continuities in that era of radical economic change. Third, evidence of premodern working-class behavior that parallels European patterns of premodern working-class behavior in the early phases of industrialization is briefly described to suggest that throughout the entire period (1815–1920) the changing composition of the American working class caused the recurrence of "premodern" patterns of collective behavior usually only associated with the early phases of industrialization. And, finally, attention is given to some of the larger implications resulting from this recurrent tension between work, culture, and society.

The work habits and the aspirations of men and women new to factory life and labor are examined first. Common work habits rooted in diverse premodern cultures (different in many ways but nevertheless all ill fitted to the regular routines demanded by machine-centered factory processes) existed among distinctive first-generation factory workers all through American history. We focus on two quite different time periods: the years before 1843 when the factory and machine were still new to America and the years between 1893 and 1917 when the country had become the world's industrial colossus. In both periods workers new to factory production brought strange and seemingly useless work habits to the factory gate. The irregular and undisciplined work patterns of factory hands before 1843 frustrated cost-conscious manufacturers and caused frequent complaint among them. Textile factory work rules often were designed to tame such rude customs. A New Hampshire cotton factory that hired mostly women and children forbade "spirituous liquor, smoking, nor any kind of amusement . . . in the workshops, yards, or factories" and promised the "immediate and disgraceful dismissal" of employees found gambling, drinking, or committing "any other debaucheries." A Massachusetts firm nearby insisted that young workers unwilling to attend church stay "within doors and improve their time in reading, writing, and in other valuable and harmless employment." Tardy and absent Philadelphia workers paid fines and could not "carry into the factory nuts, fruits, etc.; books or paper." A Connecticut textile mill owner justified the twelve-hour day and the six-day week because it kept "workmen and children" from "vicious amusements." He forbade "gaming . . . in any private house." Manufacturers elsewhere worried about the example "idle" men set for women and children. Massachusetts family heads who rented "a piece of land on shares" to grow corn and potatoes while their wives and children labored in factories worried one manufacturer. "I would prefer giving constant employment at some sacrifice," he said, "to having a man of the village seen in the streets on a rainy day at leisure." Men who worked in Massachusetts woolen mills upset expected work routines in other ways. "The wool business requires more man labour," said a manufacturer, "and this we study to avoid. Women are much more ready to follow good regulations, are not captious, and do not clan as the men do against the overseers." Male factory workers posed other difficulties, too. In 1817 a shipbuilder in Medford, Massachusetts, refused his men grog privileges. They quit work, but he managed to finish a ship without using further spirits, "a remarkable achievement." An English visitor in 1832 heard an American complain that British workers in the Paterson cotton and machine shops drank excessively and figured as "the most beastly people I have ever seen." Four years later a New Jersey manufacturer of hats and caps boasted in a public card that he finally had "4 and 20 good, permanent workmen," not one infected with "the brutal leprosy of blue Monday habits and the moral gangrene of 'trades union' principles." Other manufacturers had less good fortune. Absenteeism occurred frequently among the Pennsylvania iron workers at the rural Hopewell Village forge: hunting, harvesting, wedding parties, frequent "frolicking" that sometimes lasted for days, and uproarious Election and Independence Day celebrations plagued the mill operators. In the early nineteenth century, a New Jersey iron manufacturer filled his diary with notations about irregular work habits: "all hands drunk"; "Jacob Ventling hunting"; "molders all agree to quit work and went to the beach"; "Peter Cox very drunk and gone to bed. Mr. Evans made a solemn resolution any person or persons bringing liquor to the work enough to make drunk shall be liable to a fine"; "Edwrd Rutter off a-drinking. It was reported he got drunk on cheese."

Employers responded differently to such behavior by first-generation factory hands. "Moral reform" as well as what Sidney Pollard calls carrot-and-stick policies meant to tame or to transform such work habits. Fining was common. Hopewell Furnace managers deducted one dollar from Samuel York's wages "for getting intoxesitated [*sic*] with liquer [*sic*] and neglecting hauling 4 loads wash Dird at Joneses." Special material rewards encouraged steady work. A Hopewell Village blacksmith contracted for nineteen dollars a month, and "if he does his work well we are to give him a pair of coarse boots." In these and later years manufacturers in Fall River and Paterson institutionalized traditional customs and arranged for festivals and parades to celebrate with their workers a new mill, a retiring superintendent, or a finished locomotive. Some rewarded disciplined workers in special ways. When Paterson locomotive workers pressed for higher wages, their employer instructed an underling: "Book keeper, make up a roll of men . . . making *fulltime;* if they can't support their families on the wages they are now getting, they must have more. But the other men, who are drunk every Monday morning, I don't want them around the shop under any circumstances." Where factory work could be learned easily, new hands replaced irregular old ones. A factory worker in New England remembered that years before the Civil War her employer had hired "all American girls" but later shifted to immigrant laborers because "not coming from country homes, but living as the Irish do, in the town, they take no vacations, and can be relied on at the mill all year round." Not all such devices worked to the satisfaction of workers or their employers. Sometime in the late 1830s merchant capitalists sent a skilled British silk weaver to manage a new mill in Nantucket that would employ the wives and children of local whalers and fishermen. Machinery was installed, and in the first days women and children besieged the mill for work. After a month had passed, they started dropping off in small groups. Soon nearly all had returned "to their shore gazing and to their seats by the sea." The Nantucket mill shut down, its hollow frame an empty monument to the unwillingness of resident women and children to conform to the regularities demanded by rising manufacturers.

First-generation factory workers were not unique to premodern America. And the work habits common to such workers plagued American manufacturers in later generations when manufacturers and most native urban whites scarcely remembered that native Americans had once been hesitant first-generation factory workers. To shift forward in time to East and South European immigrants new to steam, machinery, and electricity and new to the United States itself is to find much that seems the same. American society, of course, had changed greatly, but in some ways it is as if a film—run at a much faster speed—is being viewed for the second time: primitive work rules for unskilled labor, fines, gang labor, and subcontracting were commonplace. In 1910 two-thirds of the workers in twenty-one major manufacturing and mining industries came from Eastern and Southern Europe or were native American blacks, and studies of these "new immigrants" record much evidence of preindustrial work habits among the men and women new to American industry. According to Moses Rischin, skilled immigrant Jews carried to New York City town and village employment patterns, such as the *landsmannschaft* economy and a preference for small shops as opposed to larger factories, that sparked frequent disorders but hindered stable trade unions until 1910. Specialization spurred anxiety: in Chicago Jewish glovemakers resisted the subdivision of labor even though it promised better wages.

"You shrink from doing either kind of work itself, nine hours a day," said two observers of these immigrant women. "You cling to the variety . . . , the mental luxury of first, fingersides, and then, five separate leather pieces, for relaxation, to play with! *Here* is a luxury worth fighting for!" American work rules also conflicted with religious imperatives. On the eighth day after the birth of a son, Orthodox Jews in Eastern Europe held a festival, "an occasion of much rejoicing." But the American work week had a different logic, and if the day fell during the week the celebration occurred the following Sunday. "The host . . . and his guests," David Blaustein remarked, "know it is not the right day," and "they fall to mourning over the conditions that will not permit them to observe the old custom." . . . Slavic and Italian immigrants carried with them to industrial America subcultures quite different from that of village Jews, but their work habits were just as alien to the modern factory. Rudolph Vecoli had reconstructed Chicago's South Italian community to show that adult male seasonal construction gangs as contrasted to factory labor were one of many traditional customs adapted to the new environment, and in her study of South Italian peasant immigrants Phyllis H. Williams found among them men who never adjusted to factory labor. After "years" of "excellent" factory work, some "began . . . to have minor accidents" and others "suddenly give up and are found in their homes complaining of a vague indisposition with no apparent physical basis." Such labor worried early twentieth-century efficiency experts, and so did Slavic festivals, church holidays, and "prolonged merriment." "Man," Adam Smith wisely observed, "is, of all sorts of luggage, the most difficult to be transported." That was just as true for these Slavic immigrants as for the early nineteenth-century native American factory workers. A Polish wedding in a Pennsylvania mining or mill town lasted between three and five days. Greek and Roman Catholics shared the same jobs but had different holy days, "an annoyance to many employers." The Greek Church had "more than eighty festivals in the year," and "the Slav religiously observes the days on which the saints are commemorated and invariably takes a holiday." . . .

More than irregular work habits bound together the behavior of first-generation factory workers separated from one another by time and by the larger structure of the society they first encountered. Few distinctive American working-class populations differed in so many essentials (their sex, their religions, their nativity, and their prior rural and village cultures) as the Lowell mill girls and women of the Era of Good Feelings and the South and East European steel workers of the Progressive Era. To describe similarities in their expectations of factory labor is not to blur these important differences but to suggest that otherwise quite distinctive men and women interpreted such work in similar ways. The Boston Associates, pioneer American industrialists, had built up Lowell and other towns like it to overcome early nineteenth-century rural and village prejudices and fears about factory work and life and in their regulation of working-class social habits hoped to assure a steady flow of young rural women ("girls") to and from the looms. "The sagacity of self-interest as well as more disinterested considerations," explained a Lowell clergyman in 1845, "has led to the adoption of a strict system of moral police." Without "sober, orderly, and moral" workers, profits would be "absorbed by cases of irregularity, carelessness, and neglect." The Lowell capitalists thrived by hiring rural women who supplemented a distant family's income, keeping them a few years, and then renewing the process. Such steady labor turnover kept the country from developing a permanent proletariat and so was meant to assure stability. Lowell's busy cotton mills, well-ordered boarding houses, temples of religion and culture, factory girls, and moral police so impressed Anthony Trollope that he called the entire enterprise a "philanthropic manufacturing college." John Quincy Adams thought the New England cotton mills "palaces of the Poor," and Henry Clay marveled over places like the Lowell mills. "Who had not been delighted with the clock-work movements of a large cotton factory?" asked the father of the American System. The French traveler Michel Chevalier had a less sanguine reaction. He found Lowell "neat and decent, peaceable and sage," but worried, "Will this become like Lancashire? Does this brilliant glare hide the misery and suffering of the working girls?"

Historians of the Lowell mill girls find little evidence before 1840 of organized protest among them and attribute their collective passivity to corporation policing policies, the frequent turnover in the labor force, the irregular pace of work (after it was rationalized in the 1840s, it provoked collective protest), the freedom the mill girls enjoyed away from rural family dominance, and their relatively decent earnings. The women managed the transition to mill life because they did not expect to remain factory workers too long. Nevertheless frequent inner tension revealed itself among the mobile mill women. In an early year, a single mill discharged twenty-eight women for such reasons as "misconduct," "captiousness," "disobedience," "impudence," "levity," and even "mutiny." The difficult transition from rural life to factory work also caused tensions outside the mills. . . .

Even the *Lowell Offering* testified to the tensions between mill routines and rural rhythms and feelings. Historians have dismissed it too handily because the company sponsored it and refused to publish prose openly critical of mill policies. But the fiction and poetry of its contributors, derivative in style and frequently escapist, also often revealed dissatisfactions with the pace of work. Susan, explaining her first day in the mill to Ann, said the girls awoke early and one sang, "Morning bells, I hate to hear. / Ringing dolefully, loud and clear." . . . Ellen Collins quit the mill, complaining about her "obedience to the ding-dong of the bell—just as though we were so many living machines." In "A Weaver's Reverie," Ella explained why the mill women wrote "so much about the beauties of nature."

Why is it that the delirious dreams of the famine-stricken are of tables loaded with the richest viands? . . . Oh, tell me why this is, and I will tell you why the factory girl sits in the hours of meditation and thinks, not of the crowded, clattering mill, nor of the noisy tenement which is her home.

Contemporary labor critics who scorned the *Lowell Offering* as little more than the work of "poor, caged birds," who "while singing of the roses . . . forget the bars of their prison," had not read it carefully. Their attachment to nature was the concern of persons working machines in a society still predominantly "a garden," and it was not unique to these Lowell women. In New Hampshire five hundred men and women petitioned the Amoskeag Manufacturing Company's proprietors in 1853 not to cut down an elm tree to allow room for an additional mill: "It was a beautiful and goodly tree" and belonged to a time "when the yell of the red man and the scream of the eagle were alone heard on the banks of the Merrimack, instead of two giant edifices filled with the buzz of busy and well-remunerated industry." Each day, the workers said, they viewed that tree as "a connecting link between the past and the present," and "each autumn [it] remind[s] us of our own mortality."

Aspirations and expectations interpret experience and thereby help shape behavior. Some Lowell mill girls revealed dissatisfactions, and others made a difficult transition from rural New England to that model factory town, but that so few planned to remain mill workers eased that transition and hampered collective protest. Men as well as women who expect to spend only a few years as factory workers have little incentive to join unions. That was just as true of the immigrant male common laborers in the steel mills of the late nineteenth and early twentieth centuries (when multi-plant oligopoly characterized the nation's most important manufacturing industry) as in the Lowell cotton mills nearly a century earlier. David Brody has explained much about the common laborers. In those years, the steel companies successfully divorced wages from productivity to allow the market to shape them. Between 1890 and 1910, efficiencies in plant organization cut labor costs by about a third. The great Carnegie Pittsburgh plants employed 14,359 common laborers, 11,694 of them South and East Europeans. Most, peasant in origin, earned less than $12.50 a week (a family needed fifteen dollars for subsistence). A staggering accident rate damaged these and other men: nearly twenty-five per cent of the recent immigrants employed at the Carnegie South Works were injured or killed each year between 1907 and 1910, 3,723 in all. But like the Lowell mill women, these men rarely protested in collective ways, and for good reason. They did not plan to stay in the steel mills long. Most had come to the United States as single men (or married men who had left their families behind) to work briefly in the mills, save some money, return home, and purchase farm land. Their private letters to European relatives indicated a realistic awareness of their working life that paralleled some of the Lowell fiction: "if I don't earn $1.50 a day, it would not be worth thinking about America"; "a golden land so long as there is work"; "here in America one must work for three horses"; "let him not risk coming, for he is too young"; "too weak for America." Men who wrote such letters and avoided injury often saved small amounts of money, and a significant number fulfilled their expectations and quit the factory and even the country. Forty-four South and East Europeans left the United States for every one hundred that arrived between 1908 and 1910. . . . Immigrant expectations coincided for a time with the fiscal needs of industrial manufacturers. The Pittsburgh steel magnates had as much good fortune as the Boston Associates. But the stability and passivity they counted on among their unskilled workers depended upon steady work and the opportunity to escape the mills. When frequent recessions caused recurrent unemployment, immigrant expectations and behavior changed. What Brody calls peasant "group consciousness" and "communal loyalty" sustained bitter wildcat strikes after employment picked up. The tenacity of these immigrant strikes for higher wages amazed contemporaries, and brutal suppression often accompanied them (Cleveland, 1899; East Chicago, 1905; McKees Rock, 1909; Bethlehem, 1910; and Youngstown in 1915 where, after a policeman shot into a peaceful parade, a riot caused an estimated one million dollars in damages). The First World War and its aftermath blocked the traditional route of overseas outward mobility, and the consciousness of immigrant steel workers changed. They sparked the 1919 steel strike. The steel mill had become a way of life for them and was no longer the means by which to reaffirm and even strengthen older peasant and village life-styles.

Let us sharply shift the time perspective from the years before 1843 and those between 1893 and 1919 to the decades between 1843 and 1893 and also shift our attention to the artisans and skilled workers who differed so greatly in the culture and work-styles they brought to the factory from men and women bred in rural and village cultures. The focus, however, remains the same—the relationship between settled work habits and culture. This half century saw the United States (not small pockets within it) industrialize as steam and machinery radically transformed the premodern American economic structure. That so much attention has been given to the Civil War as a crucial divide in the nation's history (and it was, of course, for certain purposes) too frequently has meant neglect by historians of common patterns of behavior that give coherence to this period. . . . In the year of Abraham Lincoln's election as President, the United States ranked behind England, France, and Germany in the value of its manufactured product. In 1894 the United States led the field: its manufactured product nearly equalled in value that of Great Britain, France, and Germany together. But such profound economic changes did not entirely shatter the older American social structure and the settled cultures of premodern native and immigrant American artisans. "There is no such thing as economic growth which is not, at the same time, growth or change of a culture," E. P. Thompson has written. Yet he also warns that "we should not assume any automatic, or overdirect, correspondence between the dynamic of economic growth and the dynamic of social or cultural life." That significant stricture applies as much to the United States as to England during its Industrial Revolution and especially to native and immigrant artisans between 1843 and 1893.

It is not surprising to find tenacious artisan work habits before the Civil War, what Thompson calls "alternate bouts of intense labour and of idleness wherever men were in control of their working lives." An English cabinetmaker shared a New York City workplace with seven others (two native Americans, two Germans, and one man each from Ireland, England, and France), and the readers of *Knight's Penny Magazine* learned from him that "frequently . . . after several weeks of real hard work . . . a simultaneous cessation from work took place." "As if . . . by tacit agreement, every hand" contributed "loose change," and an apprentice left the place and "speedily returned laden with wine, brandy, biscuits, and cheese." Songs came forth "from those who felt musical," and the same near-ritual repeated itself two more times that day. Similar relaxations, apparently self-imposed, also broke up the artisans' work day in the New York City shipyards, and a ship carpenter described them as "an indulgence that custom had made as much of a necessity in a New York shipyard as a grind-stone". . . .

Despite the profound economic changes that followed the American Civil War, Gilded Age artisans did not easily shed stubborn and time-honored work habits. Such work habits and the life-styles and subcultures related to them retained a vitality long into these industrializing decades. Not all artisans worked in factories, but some that did retained traditional craft skills. Mechanization came in different ways and at different times to diverse industries. Samuel Gompers recollected that New York City cigarmakers paid a fellow craftsman to read a newspaper to them while they worked, and Milwaukee cigarmakers struck in 1882 to retain such privileges as keeping (and then selling) damaged cigars and leaving the shop without a foreman's permission. "The difficulty with many cigarmakers," complained a New York City manufacturer in 1877, "is this. They come down to the shop in the morning; roll a few cigars and then go to a beer saloon and play pinnocio or some other game, . . . working probably only two or three hours a day." Coopers felt new machinery "hard and insensate," not a blessing but an evil that "took a great deal of joy out of life" because machine-made barrels undercut a subculture of work and leisure. Skilled coopers "lounged about" on Saturday (the regular pay day), a "lost day" to their employers. . . . Such traditions of work and leisure . . . angered manufacturers anxious to ship goods as much as it worried sabbatarians and temperance reformers. Conflicts over life- and work-styles occurred frequently and often involved control over the work process and over time. The immigrant Staffordshire potters in Trenton, New Jersey, worked in "bursts of great activity" and then quit for "several days at a time." "Monday," said a manufacturer, "was given up to debauchery." . . . Hand coopers (and potters and cigarmakers, among others) worked hard but in distinctly preindustrial styles. Machine-made barrels pitted modernizing technology and modern habits against traditional ways. To the owners of competitive firms struggling to improve efficiency and cut labor costs, the Goose Egg and Blue Monday proved the laziness and obstinacy of craftsmen as well as the tyranny of craft unions that upheld venerable traditions. To the skilled cooper, the long weekend symbolized a way of work and life filled with almost ritualistic meanings. Between 1843 and 1893, compromise between such conflicting interests was hardly possible. . . .

The persistence of such traditional artisan work habits well into the nineteenth century deserves notice from others besides labor historians, because those work habits did not exist in a cultural or social vacuum. If modernizing technology threatened and even displaced such work patterns, diverse nineteenth-century subcultures sustained and nourished them. "The old nations of the earth creep on at a snail's pace," boasted Andrew Carnegie in *Triumphant Democracy* (1886), "the Republic thunders past with the rush of an express." The articulate steelmaster, however, had missed the point. The very rapidity of the economic changes occurring in Carnegie's lifetime meant that many, unlike him, lacked the time, historically, culturally, and psychologically, to be separated or alienated from settled ways of work and life and from relatively fixed beliefs. Continuity not consensus counted for much in explaining working-class and especially artisan behavior in those decades that witnessed the coming of the factory and the radical transformation of American society. Persistent work habits were one example of that significant continuity. But these elements of continuity were often revealed among nineteenth-century American workers cut off by birth from direct contact with the preindustrial American past, a fact that has been ignored or blurred by the artificial separation between labor history and immigration history. In Gilded Age America (and afterwards in the Progressive Era despite the radical change in patterns of immigration), working-class and immigration history regularly intersected, and that intermingling made for powerful continuities. . . .

As early as the 1830s, the theme that industrialism promised to make over the United States into a "European" country had its artisan and working-class advocates. Seth Luther then made this clear in his complaint about "gentlemen" who "exultingly call LOWELL the Manchester of America" and in his plea that the Bunker Hill monument "stand *unfinished,* until the time passes away when aristocrats talk about mercy to mechanics and laborers, . . . until our rights are acknowledged." The tensions revealed in labor rhetoric between the promises of the Republic and the practices of those who combined capital and technology to build factories continued into the 1890s. In 1844 New England shoemakers rewrote the Declaration of Independence to protest that the employers "have robbed us of certain rights," and two years later New England textile workers planned without success a general strike to start on July 4, 1846, calling it "a second Independence Day." The great 1860 shoemakers' strike in Lynn started on George Washington's birthday, a celebration strikers called "sacred to the memory of one of the greatest men the world has ever produced." Fear for the Republic did not end with the Civil War. The use of state militia to help put down a strike of Northeastern Pennsylvania workers in 1874 caused *Equity,* a Boston labor weekly, to condemn the Erie Railroad as "the George III of the workingman's movement" and "the Government of Pennsylvania" as "but its parliament." ("Regiments," it added, "to protect dead things.")

Such beliefs, not the status anxieties of Progressive muckrakers and New Deal historians, gave rise to the pejorative phrase "robber baron." Discontented Gilded Age workers found in that phrase a way to summarize their worries about dependence and centralization. "In America," exploded the *National Labor Tribune* in 1874, "we have realized the ideal of republican government at least in form." "America," it went on, "was the star of the political Bethlehem which shone radiantly out in the dark night of political misrule in Europe. The masses of the old world gazed upon her as their escape." Men in America could be "their own rulers"; "no one could or should become their masters." But industrialization had created instead a nightmare: "These dreams have not been realized. . . . The working people of this country . . . suddenly find capital as rigid as an absolute monarchy." Two years later, the same Pittsburgh labor weekly asked, "Shall we let the gold barons of the nineteenth century put iron collars of ownership around our necks as did the feudal barons with their serfs in the fourteenth century?" The rhetoric surrounding the little-understood 1877 railroad strikes and riots summed up these fears. Critics of the strikes urged repressive measures such as the building of armories in large cities and the restriction of the ballot, and a few, including Elihu Burritt, even favored importing "British" institutions to the New World. But the disorders also had their defenders, and a strain in their rhetoric deserves notice. A radical Massachusetts clergyman called the strikers "the lineal descendants of Samuel Adams, John Hancock, and the Massachusetts yeomen who began so great a disturbance a hundred years ago . . . only now the kings are money kings and then they were political kings." . . .

Quite diverse patterns of collective working-class behavior (some of them disorderly and even violent) accompanied the industrialization of the United States, and certain of them (especially those related to artisan culture and to peasant and village cultures still fresh to factory labor and to the machine) deserve brief attention. Characteristic European forms of "premodern" artisan and lower-class protest in the United States occurred before (prior to 1843), during (1843–93), and after (1893–1919) the years when the country "modernized." The continuing existence of such behavior followed from the changing composition of the working-class population. Asa Briggs' insistence that "to understand how people respond to industrial change it is important to examine what kind of people they were at the beginning of the process" and "to take account of continuities as well as new ways of thinking," poses in different words the subtle interplay between culture and society that is an essential factor in explaining working-class behavior. Although their frequency remains the subject for much further detailed study, examples of premodern working-class behavior abound for the entire period from 1815 to 1919, and their presence suggests how much damage has been done to the past American working-class experiences by historians busy, as R. H. Tawney complained more than half a century ago, "dragging into prominence forces which have triumphed and thrusting into the background those which have been swallowed up." Attention is briefly given to three types of American artisan and working-class behavior explored in depth and with much illumination by European social historians ("church-and-king" crowds, machine-breaking, and food riots) and to the presence in quite different working-class protests of powerful secular and religious rituals. These occurred over the entire period under examination, not just in the early phases of industrial development.

Not much is yet known about premodern American artisan and urban lower-class cultures, but scattered evidence suggests a possible American variant of the European church-and-king phenomenon. Although artisan and lower-class urban cultures before 1843 await their historians, popular street disorders (sometimes sanctioned by the established authorities) happened frequently and increasingly caused concern to the premodern elite classes. Street gangs, about which little is yet known except the suggestion that some had as members artisans (not just casual or day laborers) and were often organized along ethnic lines, grew more important in the coastal and river towns after 1830. New York City, among other towns, had its Fly Boys, Chichesters, Plug Uglies, Buckaroos, and Slaughterhouse Gangs, and their violence against recent immigrants provoked disorderly counterthrusts. Political disorders on election days, moreover, were apparently well-organized and may have involved such gangs. The recurrence of such disorders through the pre-Civil War decades (including the nativist outbursts in nearly all major Northern and Southern cities in the 1850s) may have meant that local political parties, in their infancy, served as the American substitute for the King and the Church, a third party "protecting" artisans and even day laborers from real and imagined adversaries and winning clanlike loyalty. . . .

Available evidence does not yet indicate that machine-breaking of the "Luddite" variety was widespread in the United States. There are suggestive hints in reports that Ohio farm laborers burnt and destroyed farm machinery in 1878 and that twenty years later in Buffalo a crowd of Polish common day laborers and their wives rioted to break a street-paving machine, but the only clear evidence found of classic machine-breaking occurred early in the Civil War among rural blacks in the South Carolina Sea Islands, who resisted Yankee missionary and military efforts to make them plant cotton instead of corn and therefore broke up cotton gins and hid the iron work. "They do not see the use of cotton," said a Northern female school teacher, and a Yankee entrepreneur among them added that "nothing was more remote from their shallow pates than the idea of planting cotton for 'white-folks' again." (Some time later, this same man ordered a steam-run cotton gin. "This engine," he confided, "serves as a moral stimulus to keep the people at work at their hand-gins, for they want to gin all the cotton by hand, and I tell them if they don't by the middle of January I shall get it by steam.") If white workers rarely broke machines to protest their introduction, they sometimes destroyed the product of new technology. In the early 1830s Brooklyn ropemakers paraded a "hated machine" through town and then "committed to the flames" its product. Theirs was not an irrational act. They paid for the destroyed hemp, spun "a like quantity" to allow the machine's owner to "fulfill his engagement for its delivery," and advertised their product in a newspaper, boasting that its quality far surpassed machine-made rope "as is well known to any practical ropemaker and seaman." Silk weavers in the Hudson River towns of New Jersey broke looms in 1877 but only to prevent production during a strike. A more common practice saw the destruction of the product of labor or damage to factory and mining properties to punish employers and owners. Paterson silk weavers regularly left unfinished warps to spoil in looms. Crowds often stoned factories, burned mine tipples, and did other damage to industrial properties (as in the bitter Western Pennsylvania coke strikes between 1884 and 1894) but mostly to protest the hiring of new hands or violence against them by "police." . . .

"Luddism" may have been rare, but classic "European" food riots occurred in the United States, and two in New York City—the first in 1837 and the second in 1902—that involved quite different groups of workers are briefly examined to illustrate the ways in which traditional cultural forms and expectations helped shape working-class behavior. (Other evidence of similar disorders, including the Confederate food riots led by white women in Mobile, Savannah, and Richmond, await careful study.) In February, 1837, thousands gathered in City Hall Park to protest against "monopolies" and rising food prices. Some months before, that park had witnessed yet another demonstration against the conspiracy trial of twenty-five striking journeymen tailors. In their rhetoric the protesters identified the trial with the betrayal of the premodern "Republic." "Aristocrats" had robbed the people of "that liberty bequeathed to them, as a sacred inheritance by their revolutionary sires" and "so mystified" the laws that "men of common understanding cannot unravel them." "What the people thought was liberty, bore not a semblance to its name." Resolutions compared the tailors to that "holy combination of that immortal band of Mechanics who . . . did throw into Boston Harbor the Tea." In 1837 a crowd dumped flour, not tea, and in its behavior revealed a commonplace form of premodern protest, a complaint against what Thompson calls "the extortionate mechanisms of an unregulated market economy." The crowd in City Hall Park heard protests about the high price of rent, food, and especially flour and denunciations of "engrossers," and the New York *Herald* called the gathering "a flour meeting—a fuel meeting—a rent meeting—a food meeting—a bread meeting—every kind of a meeting except a political meeting." But a New York newspaper had printed advice from Portland, Maine, that "speculating" flour dealers be punished with "some mark of public infamy," and after the meeting adjourned a crowd (estimates range from two hundred to several thousand) paraded to Eli Hart's wholesale flour depot. A speaker advised it to "go to the flour stores and offer a fair price, and if refused take the flour." Crowd members dumped two hundred barrels of flour and one thousand bushels of wheat in the streets, broke windows, did other minor damage, and chased the city's mayor with stones and "balls of flour." At first, little looting occurred, and when wagons finally appeared to carry home sacks of flour "a tall athletic fellow in a carman's frock" shouted: "No plunder, no plunder; destroy as much as you please. Teach these monopolists that we know our rights and will have them, but d—n it don't rob them." The crowd moved on to other flour wholesalers and continued its work. It smashed the windows of B. S. Herrick and Son, dumped more flour, and finally stopped when "a person of respectable appearance" came from inside the building to promise that what remained untouched would be distributed gratis the next day to the "poor." The crowd cheered and melted away. More than twenty-eight persons were arrested (among them "mere boys," a few "black and ignorant laborers," a woman, and as yet unidentified white men), but the *Herald* found "mere humbug . . . the unholy cry of 'It's the foreigners who have done all this mischief.'" The daily press, including the *Herald,* denounced the crowd as "the very canaille of the city," but the *Herald* also pleaded for the reimposition of the assize of bread. "Let the Mayor have the regulation of it," said the *Herald.* "Let the public authorities regulate the price of such an essential of life." (In 1857, incidentally, New Yorkers again filled the City Hall Park to again demand the restoration of the assize of bread and to ask for public works.)

More than half a century later different New York City workers reenacted the 1837 food "riot." Unlike the rioters of 1837 in origins and rhetoric, the later rioters nevertheless displayed strikingly similar behavior. In 1902, and a few years before Upton Sinclair published *The Jungle,* orthodox New York City Jews, mostly women and led by a woman butcher, protested the rising price of kosher meat and the betrayal of a promised boycott of the Meat Trust by retail butchers. The complaint started on the Lower East Side and then spontaneously spread among Jews further uptown and even among Jews in Brooklyn, Newark, and Boston. The Lower East Side Jews demanded lower prices. Some called for a rabbi to fix for the entire New York Jewish community the price of meat, as in the East European *shtetl.* Others formed a cooperative retail outlet. But it is their behavior that reveals the most. The nation's financial metropolis saw angry immigrant women engage in seemingly archaic traditional protest. Outsiders could not understand its internal logic and order. These women did not loot. Like the

1837 demonstrators, they punished. Custom and tradition that reached far back in historical time gave a coherence to their rage. The disorders started on a Wednesday, stopped on Friday at sundown, and resumed the following evening. The women battered butcher shops but did not steal meat. Some carried pieces of meat "aloft on pointed sticks . . . like flags." Most poured kerosene on it in the streets or in other ways spoiled it. "Eat no meat while the Trust is taking meat from the bones of your women and children," said a Yiddish circular apparently decorated with a skull and crossbones. . . .

The perspective emphasized in these pages tells about more than the behavior of diverse groups of American working men and women. It also suggests how larger, well-studied aspects of American society have been affected by a historical process that has "industrialized" different peoples over protracted periods of time. Fernand Braudel reminds us that "victorious events come about as the result of many possibilities," and that "for one possibility which actually is realized, innumerable others have drowned." Usually these others leave "little trace for the historian." "And yet," Braudel adds, "it is necessary to give them their place because the losing movements are forces which have at every moment affected the final outcome." Contact and conflict between diverse preindustrial cultures and a changing and increasingly bureaucratized industrial society also affected the larger society in ways that await systematic examination. Contemporaries realized this fact. Concerned in 1886 about the South's "dead"—that is, unproductive—population, the Richmond *Whig* felt the "true remedy" to be "educating the industrial morale of the people." The *Whig* emphasized socializing institutions primarily outside of the working class itself. "In the work of inculcating industrial ideas and impulses," said the *Whig,* "all proper agencies should be enlisted—family discipline, public school education, pulpit instruction, business standards and requirements, and the power and influence of the workingmen's associations." What the *Whig* worried over in 1886 concerned other Americans before and after that time. And the resultant tension shaped society in important ways. Some are briefly suggested here. In a New York *Times* symposium ("Is America by Nature a Violent Society?") soon after the murder of Martin Luther King, the anthropologist Clifford Geertz warned: "Vague references to the frontier tradition, to the unsettledness of American life, to our exploitative attitude toward nature or to our 'youthfulness' as a nation, provide us with prefabricated 'explanations' for events we, in fact, not only do not understand, but do not want to understand." More needs to be said than that Americans are "the spiritual descendants of Billy the Kid, John Brown, and Bonnie and Clyde." It has been suggested here that certain recurrent disorders and conflicts relate directly to the process that has continually "adjusted" men and women to regular work habits and to the discipline of factory labor. The British economic historian Sidney Pollard reminds us that this "task, different in kind" is "at once more subtle and more violent from that of maintaining discipline among a proletarian population of long standing."

The same process has even greater implications for the larger national American culture. Hannah Arendt has brilliantly suggested that the continual absorption of distinctive native and foreign "alien" peoples has meant that "each time the law had to be confirmed anew against the lawlessness inherent in all up-rooted people," and that the severity of that process helps explain to her why the United States has "never been a nation-state." The same process also affected the shaping and reshaping of American police and domestic military institutions. We need only realize that the burning of a Boston convent in 1834 by a crowd of Charlestown truckmen and New Hampshire Scotch-Irish brickmakers caused the first revision of the Massachusetts Riot Act since Shays' Rebellion, and that three years later interference by native firemen in a Sunday Irish funeral procession led to a two-hour riot involving upwards of fifteen thousand persons (more than a sixth of Boston's population), brought militia to that city for the first time, and caused the first of many reorganizations of the Boston police force. The regular contact between alien work cultures and a larger industrializing or industrial so-ciety had other consequences. It often worried industrialists, causing C. E. Perkins, the president of the Chicago, Burlington, and Quincy Railroad to confide in a friend in the late nineteenth century, "If I were able, I would found a school for the study of political economy in order to harden men's hearts." It affected the popular culture. A guidebook for immigrant Jews in the 1890s advised how to make it in the New World: "Hold fast, this is most necessary in America. Forget your past, your customs, and your ideals. . . . A bit of advice to you: do not take a moment's rest. Run, do, work, and keep your own good in mind." Cultures and customs, however, are not that easily discarded. So it may be that America's extraordinary technological supremacy—its talent before the Second World War for developing labor-saving machinery and simplifying complex mechanical pro-cesses—depended less on "Yankee know-how" than on the continued infusion of prefactory peoples into an increasingly industrialized society. The same process, moreover, may also explain why movements to legislate morality and to alter habits have lasted much longer in the United States than in most other industrial countries, extending from the temperance crusades of the 1820s and the 1830s to the violent opposition among Germans to such rules in the 1850s and the 1860s and finally to formal prohibition earlier in this century. Important relationships also exist between this process and the elite and popular nativist and racist social movements that have ebbed and flowed regularly from the 1840s until our own time, as well as between this process and elite political "reform" movements be-tween 1850 and the First World War. . . .

These pages have fractured historical time, ranging forward and backward, to make comparisons for several reasons. One has been to suggest how much re-mains to be learned about the transition of native and foreign-born American men and women to industrial society, and how that transition affected such per-sons and the society into which they entered. "Much of what gets into American literature," Ralph Ellison has shrewdly observed, "gets there because so much is left out." That has also been the case in the writing of American working-class history, and the framework and methods suggested here merely hint at what will be known about American workers and American society when the many transitions are studied in detail. Such studies, however, need to focus on the particularities of both the group involved and the society into which they enter. Transitions differ and depend upon the interaction between the two at specific historical moments. But at all times there is a resultant tension. Thompson writes:

There has never been any single type of "the transition." The stress of the transition falls upon the whole culture: resistance to change and assent to change arise from the whole culture. And this culture includes the systems of power, property-relations, religious institutions, etc., inattention to which merely flattens phenomena and trivializes analysis.

Enough has been savored in these pages to suggest the particular importance of these transitions in American social history. And their recurrence in different periods of time indicates why there has been so much discontinuity in American labor and social history. The changing composition of the working population, the continued entry into the United States of nonindustrial people with distinctive cultures, and the changing structure of American society have combined together to produce common modes of thought and patterns of behavior. But these have been experiences disconnected in time and shared by quite distinctive first-generation native and immigrant industrial Americans. It was not possible for the grandchildren of the Lowell mill girls to understand that their Massachusetts literary ancestors shared a great deal with their contemporaries, the peasant Slavs in the Pennsylvania steel mills and coal fields. And the grandchildren of New York City Jewish garment workers see little connection between black ghetto unrest in the 1960s and the Kosher meat riots seventy years ago. A half century has passed since Robert Park and Herbert Miller published W. I. Thomas's *Old World Traits Transplanted*, a study which worried that the function of Americanization was the "destruction of memories."

LEON FINK

Working-Class Radicalism in the Gilded Age

The labor movement of the Gilded Age, not unlike its nineteenth-century British counterpart, spoke a "language of class" that was "as much political as economic." In important ways an eighteenth-century republican political inheritance still provided the basic vocabulary. The emphasis within the movement on equal rights, on the identity of work and self-worth, and on secure, family-centered households had informed American political radicalism for decades. A republican outlook lay at the heart of the protests of journeymen-mechanics and women millworkers during the Jacksonian period; it likewise inspired abolitionist and the women's suffrage and temperance movements and even contributed to the common school crusade. Within the nineteenth-century political mainstream this tradition reached its height of influence in the free labor assault of the Radical Republicans against slavery. . . .

Certain tendencies of the Gilded Age, however, heralded for some an alarming social regression. The permanency of wage labor, the physical and mental exhaustion inflicted by the factory system, and the arrogant exercise of power by the owners of capital threatened the rational and progressive march of history. "Republican institutions," the preamble to the constitution of the Knights of Labor declared simply, "are not safe under such conditions." "We have openly arrayed against us," a Chicago radical despaired in 1883, "the powers of the world, most of the intelligence, all the wealth, and even law itself." The lament of a Connecticut man that "factoryism, bankism, collegism, capitalism, insurance-ism and the presence of such lump-headed malignants as Professor William Graham Sumner" were stultifying "the native genius of this state" framed the evil in more homespun terms. In 1883 cigarmakers' leader Samuel Gompers, not yet accepting the inevitability of capitalist industry, bemoaned the passing of the

From Leon Fink, *Workingmen's Democracy: The Knights of Labor and American Politics,* © 1985 by the Board of Trustees of the University of Illinois. Used with the permission of the author and University of Illinois Press.

day of "partners at the work bench" that had given way to "the tendency . . . which makes man, the worker, a part of the machine." The British-born journalist Richard J. Hinton, an old Chartist who had commanded black troops during the Civil War, also reflected on the sudden darkening of the social horizon. The "average, middle-class American," he complained, simply could not appreciate the contemporary position of American workers: "They all look back to the days when they were born in some little American village. . . . They have seen their time and opportunity of getting on in the world, and they think that is the condition of society today, when it is totally a different condition."

In response the labor movement in the Gilded Age turned the plowshares of a consensual political past into a sword of class conflict. "We declare," went the Knights' manifesto, "an inevitable and irresistible conflict between the wage-system of labor and republican system of government." To some extent older demons seemed simply to have reappeared in new garb, and, as such, older struggles beckoned with renewed urgency. A Greenback editor in Rochester, New Hampshire, thus proclaimed that "patriots" who overturn the "lords of labor" would be remembered next to "the immortal heroes of the revolution and emancipation." Labor rhetoric in the period rings with a variety of appeals to an extended republican heritage. "If you lose this fight," Michigan Knights' leader Thomas B. Barry exhorted striking lumbermen in 1885, "you have nothing to do but get a collar and chain and hammer and staple, and tell your employers to fasten you to a block." Others similarly denounced unorganized railroad workers as "Corbin's chattel" or assailed Pinkerton agents as "Hessians." After the deployment of Pinkertons by Chicago meatpacking firms in 1886, a pro-labor Catholic newspaper pointedly warned that "the Roman republic was free until the patricians gathered around them their armed clients." Knights' national officer Ralph Beaumont's description of New York corporation directors who "walk around with pug dogs, while their offspring follow behind in their nurses' arms" and a Michigan labor orator's denunciation of Congressmen as "pot-bellied millionaires, who live on porterhouse steaks, drink champagne, smoke 15 cent cigars . . . who will ride out with their wives, or more likely other peoples' wives" represented the invective of latter-day Tom Paines.

Unlike Tom Paine, however, late nineteenth-century American radicals had the advantage of being able to rely on rather than abandon historical experience. A philosophical Ohio farmer, Donn Piatt, thus offered the contrast that "in Europe labor is accustomed to oppression, and it is a hard part of God's destiny for them, to be borne patiently as long as they can get enough to hold body and soul together." Americans, however, were different: "Our people have been carefully educated to consider themselves the best on earth, and they will not patiently submit to privation such as this system is leading to. They not only feel that they are the best of the earth, but there is no power, no standing army, no organized iron rule to hold them down."

Piatt was not alone in his nationalistic pride. To many other outside observers in the 1880s, the American working class—in terms of organization, militancy, and collective self-consciousness—appeared more advanced than its European counterparts. A leader of the French Union des Chambres Syndicales Ouvrières compared the self-regarding, individualist instincts of the French workers to those of the Americans enrolled in the Knights of Labor (Ordre des Chevaliers du Travail):

Unfortunately, the French worker, erratic as he is enthusiastic, of an almost discouraging indolence when it is a question of his own interests, does not much lend himself to organization into a great order like yours. He understands nevertheless their usefulness, even cites them as an example each time that he has the occasion to prove the possibility of the solidarity of workers; but when it comes to passing from the domain of theory to that of practice, he retreats or disappears. Thirsty for freedom he is always afraid of alienating any one party while contracting commitments toward a collectivity; mistrustful, he is afraid of affiliating with a group whose positions might not correspond exactly to those inscribed on his own flag; undisciplined, he conforms with difficulty to rules which he has given to himself. . . . He wants to play it safe and especially will not consent to any sacrifice without having first calculated the advantages it will bring to him.

Eleanor Marx and Edward Aveling returned from an 1886 American tour with a glowing assessment of the workers' mood. Friedrich Engels, too, in the aftermath of the eight-hour strikes and the Henry George campaign, attached a special preface to the 1887 American edition of *The Condition of the Working Class in England in 1844*:

In European countries, it took the working class years and years before they fully realized the fact that they formed a distinct and, under the existing social conditions, a permanent class of modern society; and it took years again until this class-consciousness led them to form themselves into a distinct political party, independent of, and opposed to, all the old political parties, formed by the various sections of the ruling classes. On the more favored soil of America, where no medieval ruins bar the way, where history begins with the elements of the modern bourgeois society as evolved in the seventeenth century, the working class passed through these two stages of its development within ten months.

Nor was it only in the eyes of eager well-wishers that the developments of the 1880s seemed to take on a larger significance. Surveying the map of labor upheaval, the conservative Richmond *Whig* wrote in 1886 of "socialistic and agrarian elements" threatening "the genius of our free institutions." The Chicago *Times* went so far in its fear of impending revolution as to counsel the use of hand grenades against strikers.

Revolutionary anticipations, pro or con, proved premature. That was true at least partly because both the movement's distant boosters as well as its domestic detractors sometimes misrepresented its intentions. Gilded Age labor radicals did not self-consciously place themselves in opposition to a prevailing economic system but displayed a sincere ideological ambivalence toward the capitalist marketplace. On the one hand, they frequently invoked a call for the "abolition of the wage system." On the other hand, like the classical economists, they sometimes spoke of the operation of "natural law" in the marketplace, acknowledged the need for a "fair return" on invested capital, and did not oppose profit per se.

Employing a distinctly pre-Marxist economic critique that lacked a theory of capital accumulation or of surplus value, labor leaders from Ira Steward to Terence Powderly tried nevertheless to update and sharpen the force of received wisdom. The Knights thus modified an earlier radical interpretation of the labor-cost theory of value, wherein labor, being the source of all wealth, should individually be vested with the value of its product, and demanded for workers only an intentionally vague "proper share of the wealth they create." In so doing they were able to shift the weight of the analysis (not unlike Marx) to the general, collective plight of the laboring classes. In their eyes aggregation of capital together with cutthroat price competition had destroyed any semblance of marketplace balance between employer and employee. Under the prevailing economic calculus labor had been demoted into just another factor of production whose remuneration was determined not by custom or human character but by market price. In such a situation they concluded, as Samuel Walker has noted, that "the contract was not and could not be entered into freely. . . . The process of wage determination was a moral affront because it degraded the personal dignity of the workingman." This subservient position to the iron law of the market constituted "wage slavery," and like other forms of involuntary servitude it had to be "abolished."

Labor's emancipation did not, ipso facto, imply the overthrow of capitalism, a system of productive relations that the Knights in any case never defined. To escape wage slavery workers needed the strength to redefine the social balance of power with employers and their allies—and the will and intelligence to use that strength. One after another the Knights harnessed the various means at their disposal—education, organization, cooperation, economic sanction, and political influence—to this broad end: "To secure to the workers the full enjoyment [note, not the full return] of the wealth they create, sufficient leisure in which to develop their intellectual, moral and social faculties, all of the benefits of recreation, and pleasures of association; in a word to enable them to share in the gains and honors of advancing civilization."

A wide range of strategic options was represented within the counsels of the labor movement. One tendency sought to check the rampant concentration of wealth and power with specific correctives on the operation of the free market. Radical Greenbackism (with roots in Kelloggism and related monetary theories), Henry George's single tax, and land nationalization, each of which commanded considerable influence among the Knights of Labor, fit this category. Another important tendency, cooperation, offered a more self-reliant strategy of alternative institution-building, or, as one advocate put it, "the organization of production without the intervention of the capitalist." Socialism, generally understood at the time as a system of state as opposed to private ownership of production, offered a third alternative to wage slavery. Except for a few influential worker-intellectuals and strong pockets of support among German-Americans, however, Socialism . . . carried comparatively little influence in the 1880s. The argument of veteran abolitionist and labor reformer Joseph Labadie—"To say that state socialism is the rival of co-operation is to say that Jesus Christ was opposed to Christianity"— met a generally skeptical reception. Particularly in the far West, self-identified anarchists also agitated from within the ranks of the Order.

If Gilded Age labor representatives tended to stop short of a frontal rejection of the political-economic order, there was nevertheless no mistaking their philosophic radicalism. Notwithstanding differences in emphasis, the labor movement's political sentiments encompassed both a sharp critique of social inequality and a broad-based prescription for a more humane future. Indeed, the labor representative who shrugged off larger philosophical and political commitments in favor of a narrow incrementalism was likely to meet with incredulity. One of the first, and most classic, enunciations of business unionism, for example, received just this response from the Senate Committee on Labor and Capital in 1883. After taking testimony from workers and labor reformers across the country for six months, the committee, chaired by New Hampshire Senator Henry Blair, interviewed Adolph Strasser, president of the cigarmakers' union. Following a disquisition on the stimulating impact of shorter working hours on workers' consumption patterns, Strasser was asked if he did not contemplate a future beyond the contemporary exigencies of panic and overproduction, "some time [when] every man is to be an intelligent man and an enlightened man?" When Strasser did not reply, Senator Blair interceded to elaborate the question. Still, Strasser rebuffed the queries, "Well, our organization does not consist of idealists . . . we do [not] control the production of the world. That is controlled by employers, and that is a matter for them." Senator Blair was taken aback.

> BLAIR I was only asking you in regard to your ultimate ends.
>
> WITNESS We have no ultimate ends. We are going on from day to day. We are fighting only for immediate objects—objects that can be realized in a few years. . . .
>
> BLAIR I see that you are a little sensitive lest it should be thought that you are a mere theorizer. I do not look upon you in that light at all.
>
> WITNESS Well, we say in our constitution that we are opposed to theorists, and I have to represent the organization here. We are all practical men.
>
> blair Have you not a theory upon which you have organized?
>
> WITNESS Yes, sir: our theory is the experience of the past in the United States and in Great Britain. That is our theory, based upon actual facts. . . .
>
> BLAIR In other words you have arrived at the theory which you are trying to apply?
>
> WITNESS We have arrived at a practical result.
>
> BLAIR But a practical result is the application of a theory is it not?

On a cultural level, labor's critique of American society bore the same relation to Victorian respectability that its political radicalism bore to contemporary liberalism. In both cases the middle-class and working-class radical variants derived from a set of common assumptions but drew from them quite different, even opposing, implications. No contemporary, for example, took more seriously than the Knights of Labor the cultural imperatives toward productive work, civic responsibility, education, a wholesome family life, temperance, and self-improvement. The intellectual and moral development of the individual, they would have agreed with almost every early nineteenth-century lyceum lecturer, was a precondition for the advancement of democratic civilization. In the day of Benjamin Franklin such values may well have knit together master craftsmen, journeymen, and apprentices. In the age of the factory system, however, the gulf between employer and employee had so widened that the lived meanings of the words were no longer the same.

No phrase was more frequently invoked in the litany of Knights' rhetoric and elaborate ritual than "nobility of toil." Like labor reformers in previous decades the Knights appropriated the classical economic labor theory of value to shower a sentimental glory on the toiler. No doubt the Knights' sanctification of work carried multiple meanings. In part labor drew on nostalgia or a preindustrial past, in part on a defense of devalued craft skills, but in part also on a transcendent vision of a cooperative industrial future. They dreamed of a day when even the enterprise of a Cornelius Vanderbilt or Jay Gould might be harnessed to "a different social system," which would replace the possession of "wealth" with "industrial and moral standard[s] of worth." For the Knights, in short, celebration of the work ethic came to serve as both a political and cultural badge of honor and even, as in the following news item, as a certificate of health:

A physician has lately written a work on the hay fever, in which he claims to have discovered for it a complete remedy. He has found a season of farm work a sure cure for the disease. He suggests that the susceptivity to that malady comes from eating too much in proportion to the physical labor one performs. It is a remarkable fact, that workingmen are not subject to the malady. It only appears to attack the idlers. The loafers will come eventually to understand that they must labor, if only to keep themselves in health. "Labor is the law of life."

For the Knights the concept of the producing classes indicated an ultimate social division that they perceived in the world around them. Only those associated with idleness (bankers, speculators), corruption (lawyers, liquor dealers, gamblers), or social parasitism (all of the above) were categorically excluded from membership in the Order. Other social strata such as local merchants and manufacturers were judged by their individual acts, not by any inherent structural antagonism to the workers' movement. Those who showed respect for the dignity of labor (i.e., who sold union-made goods or employed union workers at union conditions) were welcomed into the Order. Those who denigrated the laborer or his product laid themselves open to the righteous wrath of the boycott or strike. Powderly characteristically chastised one ruthless West Virginia coal owner. "Don't die, even if you do smell bad. We'll need you in a few years as a sample to show how *mean* men used to be."

This rather elastic notion of class boundaries on the part of the labor movement was reciprocated in the not inconsequential number of shopkeepers and small manufacturers who expressed sympathy and support for the labor movement. An exchange between John Keogh, a Fall River, Massachusetts, job printer and the Senate Committee on Labor and Capital is illustrative:

Q Conducting business for yourself?

A Yes, sir.

Q Are you a capitalist?

A No, sir. I was an operative for eleven years in the mills in Fall River.

Q But you have a little establishment of your own now?

A Yes.

Q You are a capitalist then, to that extent you control yourself and your own money, and do your own business as you please?

A Yes, but I do not consider myself a capitalist.

In part, what "being considered a capitalist" implied was disregard for the workers' self-respect, the open defense of the laws of classical political economy, the working assumption of labor as a commodity.

If honest labor fulfilled moral and physical imperatives, too much of it not only damaged the individual physically but also interfered with the equally important imperatives of moral and intellectual development. The conditions of industrial life all too often made impossible the original bourgeois ideal of cultivated self-fulfillment. "That man who passes yonder with heavy footstep, hair unkempt, person dirty, dinner bucket in hand, and a general air of desolation," thus protested a Pittsburgh glass-blower, "is a 12 hour a day wage slave." The New York City tailors' union based its indictment of sweated labor on answers to the following circular sent to its members—"Are you compelled to work on Sunday to support your family? . . . Have you got time and means to visit Central Park or any other places of pleasure? Does your family or you go to hear public lectures?" A Saginaw Knight of Labor argued that lumbermen who toiled fourteen or fifteen hours a day were "not free men—[they] had no time for thought, no time for home." Petersburg, Virginia, streetcar workers justified their strike for shorter hours on grounds that they could not get to the theatre on time.

Such public appeals were well calculated to appeal to middle-class sympathies, but workers' organizations took such concerns quite seriously too. Fall River spinners' leaders and workingmen's state representative Robert Howard approached the movement's instructional role with a missionary zeal: "We must get our people to read and think, and to look for something higher and more noble in life than working along in that wretched way from day to day and from week to week and from year to year." A Detroit Knight worried that long hours were rendering workers "incapable of doing anything requiring thought. . . . They will read trashy novels, or go to a variety theatre or a dance, but nothing beyond amusements." Through a network of reading rooms, traveling lecturers, dramatics societies, and the labor press, radical labor leadership hoped to awaken the masses of working people to a sense of their rights and responsibilities. Richard Powers, for instance, who had passed from cabin boy to ship's mate to president of the 7,000-member [Great] Lake Seamen's Union, measured his union's achievements by an educational standard. "Morally and intellectually the men we have out West have gained a good deal. For instance when they come off a vessel they have got a reading-room to go to, and they read now and study questions and know what is going on; they argue questions too." Boston typographers' leader Frank Foster boasted that "reading rooms and the various places provided for intellectual gratification were taken advantage of by printers more than any other trade." Perhaps nowhere was intellectual discourse within the Knights more highly valued than within the Socialist-led New York City District Assembly 49. "If you could hear our members quoting Spencer, Mill, Recardo, Walter, Mar, Laselles, Prouddon and other political economists," reported District Master Workman T. B. McGuire, "you would think you had struck a convention of teachers of the science which has enslaved us." Finally in Atlanta in 1885 approximately 800 people a week made use of the workers' Union Hall and Library Association, whose 350 to 400 daily and weekly newspapers made it one of the best-supplied reading rooms in the South.

Idealization of hearth and home, a mainstay of familial sentimentality in the Gilded Age, also enjoyed special status within the labor movement. For here, as clearly as anywhere in the radicals' world view, conventional assumptions had a critical, albeit ambivalent, edge in the context of changing social circumstances. Defense of an idealized family life as both moral and material mainstay of society served as one basis of criticism of capitalist industry. Machinist John Morrison argued before the Senate investigating committee that the insecurities of the unskilled labor market were so threatening family life as to make the house "more like a dull prison instead of a home." A self-educated Scottish-born leader of the type-founders, Edward King, associated trade union morality with the domestic "sentiments of sympathy and humanity" against the "business principles" of the age. Almost unanimously, the vision of the good life for labor radicals included the home. Grand Secretary of the Knights of Labor Robert Layton defined the relative success of skilled trade unionists like Pittsburgh rollers and puddlers by a domestic standard: "They often occupy an entire house themselves and have it neatly furnished; and if they have children that can play the piano, or if they have an ear for music, they will in many instances have a piano in the house, and generally they enjoy life pretty well." By the same rationale Knights' raffles would usually consist of small items to increase the comforts of domestic life. And when the Knights sought to reward grand old labor warrior Richard Trevellick for decades of service in abolitionist and labor circles, they found the ultimate gift in the provision of a cottage house, "to which he may retreat in the intervals of the conflict, and in the decline of life for that rest, that solace and refreshment which he has so nobly earned and so richly deserves."

The importance of the domestic moral order to the late nineteenth-century radical vision also translated into an unparalleled opening of the labor movement to women. As Susan Levine has recently documented, the Knights of Labor beckoned both to wage-earning women and workingmen's wives to join in construction of a "cooperative commonwealth," which, without disavowing the Victorian ideal of a separate female sphere of morality and domestic virtue, sought to make that sphere the center of an active community life.

Both their self-improving and domestic commitments converged in the working-class radicals' antipathy to excessive drinking. The Knights' oath of temperance, which became known as "the Powderly pledge," appealed in turn to intellectual development and protection of the family as well as to the collective interests of the labor movement. Like monopoly, the bottle lay waiting to fasten a new form of slavery upon the free worker. In another sense, as David Brundage has suggested, the growing capitalization of saloons together with expansion of saloon-linked variety theatre directly threatened a family-based producers' community. While most radicals stopped short of prohibition, exhortations in behalf of temperance were commonplace. In part it was a matter of practical necessity. Tension between the mores of traditional plebian culture and the need for self-discipline by a movement striving for organization and power were apparent in Thomas Barry's appeal to Saginaw Valley general strikers. "My advice has always been in favor of sobriety. . . . If a man wants a glass of beer he should take it, but it is this going to extremes that is dangerous. The danger that would threaten us on the [picnic] grounds would be the system of treating. . . . If you are invited often drink pop. When you don't want to drink pop drop your pipe and smoke a cigar for a change. . . . I expect you all to act as deputy marshalls."

In general, then, the labor movement of the late nineteenth century provided a distinct arena of articulation and practice for values that crossed class lines. Two aspects of this use of inherited values for radical ends merit reemphasis. First, to the extent that labor radicalism shared in the nineteenth century's cult of individualism, it established a social and moral framework for individual achievement. The culture of the labor movement stressed the development of individual capacity, but not competition with other individuals; while striving to elevate humanity, it ignored what S. G. Boritt has identified as the essence of the Lincoln-sanctified American Dream—the individual's "right to rise." The necessary reliance by the labor movement upon collective strength and community sanction militated against the possessive individualism that anchored the world of the workers' better-off neighbors. By its very nature, the labor movement set limits to the individual accumulation of wealth extracted from others' efforts and represented, in Edward King's words, "the graduated elimination of the personal selfishness of man."

Second, in an age of evolutionary, sometimes even revolutionary, faith in progress and the future (a faith generally shared by labor radicals), the movement made striking use of the past. Without renouncing the potential of industrialism for both human liberty and material progress, radicals dipped selectively into a popular storehouse of memory and myth to capture alternative images of human possibility. The choice of the name "Knights of Labor" itself presented images of chivalry and nobility fighting the unfeeling capitalist marketplace. Appeals to the "nobility of toil" and to the worker's "independence" conjured up the proud village smithy—not the degradation of labor in the factory system. Finally, celebrations of historic movements of human liberation and political advancement challenged a political-economic orthodoxy beholden to notions of unchanging, universal laws of development. Indeed, so conspicuously sentimental were the celebrations of Independence Day and Memorial Day that Powderly had to defend the Order from taunts of "spread-eagleism" and "Yankee doodleism."

This sketch of working-class radicalism in the Gilded Age raises one final question. Whose movement—and culture—was it? In a country as diverse as the United States, with a labor force and labor movement drawn from a heterogeneous mass of trades, races, and nationalities, any group portrait runs the risk of oversimplification. . . . Nevertheless, the Knights of Labor did provide a vast umbrella under which practically every variety of American worker sought protection. As such, the dynamic of the Order itself offers important clues to the general social context in which working-class radicalism as defined here flourished. . . .

The articulate leadership of the Knights of Labor and the political movement that sprang from it included brainworkers (especially the editors of the labor press), skilled craftworkers, and shopkeepers who looked to the labor movement as a source of order in a disorderly age. The self-conception of the radical labor leadership as a middle social stratum, balanced between the very rich and very poor, was evident in Powderly's 1885 characterization of his own ancestors— "they did not move in court circles; nor did they figure in police courts." Likewise the Union Labor party, heavily influenced by the Knights, was described by its national chairman, John W. Breidenthal, in 1887 as representing "the middle class of society . . . not the extremely rich or extremely poor. We stand on the middle ground. We have come here to organize and save this Government from the extremes of the one and the robbery of the other."

This dominant stream within the labor movement included people who had enjoyed considerable control over their jobs, if not also economic autonomy, men who often retained claim to the tools as well as the knowledge of their trade. They had taken seriously the ideal of a republic of producers in which hard work would contribute not only to the individual's improved economic standing but also to the welfare of the community. So long as they could rely on their own strength as well as their neighbors' support, this skilled stratum organized in an array of craft unions showed economic and political resilience. But the spreading confrontations with national corporate power, beginning in the 1870s, indicated just how much erosion had occurred in the position of those who relied on custom, skill, and moral censure as ultimate weapons. Industrial dilution of craft skills and a direct economic and political attack on union practices provided decisive proof to these culturally conservative workingmen of both the illegitimacy and ruthlessness of the growing power of capital. It was they, according to every recent study of late nineteenth-century laboring communities, who formed the backbone of local labor movements. The Knights were, therefore, first of all a coalition of reactivating, or already organized, trade unions.

In expressing the ideology of skilled workers, the Knights indicated that skilled workers in the early and mid-1880s were responding to their social predicament in an expansive and affirmative fashion. Instead of using their existing status as a badge of exclusion, the aristocrats of labor in communities all over the country offered their ideals as well as their power as a shield for all those below them. The teacherish invocations of the radical labor leaders toward the rank and file thus represented, in part, a measure of the real social distance among the members of the Order, despite a simultaneous (and sincere) egalitarianism of principle.

For reasons of their own masses of workers who had not lost full and equal citizenship—for they had never possessed it—joined the skilled workers within the Knights. Wherever the Order achieved political successes, it did so by linking semiskilled and unskilled industrial workers to its base of skilled workers and leaders. The special strength of the Knights, noted the Boston *Labor Leader* as-tutely, lay "in the fact that the whole life of the community is drawn into it, that people of all kinds are together . . . , and that they all get directly the sense of each others' needs."

Lydia Drake of Battle Creek, Michigan, might therefore experience the Or-der as a schoolhouse of democratic virtues. "I have learned to love and honor it for the instructions it is ever ready to impart; the anxious care it sustains in be-half of justice and individual rights; the desire it expresses not only in words but in deeds to advance the cause of moral and intellectual culture; the hope it cher-ishes of harmonizing discordant factions; for the determined efforts it has already made to elevate the standard of labor, distribute more equally the profits thereof, and unite the interests of humanity in one common brotherhood." . . .

The Knights of Labor envisioned a kind of workingmen's democracy. The or-ganized power of labor was capable of revitalizing democratic citizenship and safeguarding the public good within a regulated marketplace economy. Through vigilant shop committees and demands such as the eight-hour day, organized workers—both men and women—would ensure minimal standards of safety and health at the industrial workplace, even as they surrounded the dominant corpo-rate organizational model of business with cooperative models of their own. A pride in honest and useful work, rational education, and personal virtue would be nurtured through a rich associational life spread out from the workplace to meeting hall to the hearth and home. Finally, the integrity of public institutions would be vouchsafed by the workingmen in politics. Purifying government of party parasitism and corruption, cutting off the access to power that allowed an-tilabor employers to bring the state apparatus to their side in industrial disputes, improving and widening the scope of vital public services, and even contemplat-ing the takeover of economic enterprises that had passed irreversibly into mo-nopoly hands—by these means worker-citizens would lay active claim to a repub-lican heritage.

The dream was not to be. At the workplace management seized the initiative toward the future design and control of work. A managerial revolution overcom-ing the tenacious defenses of the craft unions transferred autonomy over such matters as productivity and skill from custom and negotiation to the realm of corporate planning. Except for the garment trades and the mines, the national trade unions had generally retreated from the country's industrial heartland by 1920. In the local community as well, the differences, even antagonisms, among workers often stood out more than did the similarities. Segmentation of labor markets, urban ethnic and socioeconomic residential segregation, cultural as well as a protectionist economic disdain for the new immigrants, and the depoliticiza-tion of leisure time (i.e., the decline of associational life sponsored by labor or-ganizations) all contributed toward a process of social fragmentation. In such cir-cumstances working-class political cooperation proved impossible. The Socialist party and the Progressive slates could make little more than a dent in the hold of the two increasingly conservative national parties over the electorate. Only with the repolarization of political life beginning in 1928 and culminating in the New Deal was the relation of labor and the party system again transformed. By the late 1930s and 1940s a revived labor movement was beginning, with mixed success, to play the role of a leading interest group and reform conscience within the Democratic party.

This impressionistic overview permits one further observation of a quite general nature. One of the favorite tasks of American historians has been to explain why the United States, alone among the nations of the Western world, passed through the industrial revolution without the establishment of a class consciousness and an independent working-class political movement. Cheap land, the cult of individualism, a heterogeneous labor force, social mobility, and the federal separation of powers comprise several of the numerous explanations that have been offered. While not directly denying the importance of any of the factors listed above, this study implicitly suggests a different approach to the problem of American exceptionalism.

The answer appears to lie less in a permanent structural determinism—whether the analytic brace be political, economic, or ideological—than in a dynamic and indeed somewhat fortuitous convergence of events. To understand the vicissitudes of urban politics, we have had to keep in mind the action on at least three levels: the level of working-class social organization (i.e., the nature and strength of the labor movement), the level of business response, and the level of governmental response. During the Gilded Age each of these areas took an incendiary turn, but only briefly and irregularly and most rarely at the same moment. The 1880s, as R. Laurence Moore has recently reiterated, were the international seedtime for the strong European working-class parties of the twentieth century. In America, too, the momentum in the 1880s was great. Indeed, examined both at the level of working-class organization and industrial militancy, a European visitor might understandably have expected the most to happen here first. At the political level, as well, American workers were in certain respects relatively advanced. In the 1870s and in the 1880s they established independently organized local labor regimes well before the famous French Roubaix or English West Ham labor-Socialist town councils of the 1890s. Then, a combination of forces in the United States shifted radically away from the possibilities outlined in the 1880s. The labor movement fragmented, business reorganized, and the political parties helped to pick up the pieces. The initiatives from without directed at the American working class from the mid-1890s through the mid-1920s—part repression, part reform, part assimilation, and part recruitment of a new labor force—at an internationally critical period in the gestation of working-class movements may mark the most telling exceptionalism about American developments.

It would in any case be years before the necessary conditions again converged and labor rose from the discredited icons of pre-Depression America with a new and powerful political message. Workplace, community, and ballot box would all once again be harnessed to a great social movement. But no two actors are ever in quite the same space at the same time. The choices open to the CIO, it is fair to say, were undoubtedly influenced both by the achievement and failure of their counterparts a half-century earlier.

ALICE KESSLER-HARRIS

Technology, Efficiency, and Resistance

By the late nineteenth century there was nearly universal agreement on two scores. Women's expanding labor force participation was an unfortunate necessity that threatened to interfere with their more desirable work at home. And nothing that happened at work could be allowed to hinder the capacity of wage-earning women to resume or assume home roles at some future time. . . . Such ideas channeled women's entrance into the work force, and . . . instead of providing them with safe, clean, unpressured jobs, notions of women's place in fact reduced them to the poorest levels. Unskilled, largely unorganized, and crowded into few occupations, women found themselves subject to some of the worst conditions of any wage workers.

The pattern, once established, encouraged employers to hire women because they were said to have characteristics such as docility, attachment to family, little expectation of advancement, and no trade union consciousness. It led employers to assign women to jobs that matched their expectations of women's possibilities and performance. But in the late 1800s and early 1900s, new technology and new forms of industrial organization altered the structure of work, promising new opportunities to women. The struggle to take advantage of these jobs placed women in direct competition with male workers. To protect themselves, male workers, who were rapidly unionizing, drew on the ideology of woman's place to create obstacles for women. These efforts, along with managerial attempts to order the labor market, cemented the existing segmentation in place, defining the boundaries of men's and women's work for more than half a century.

The rapidity of Gilded Age industrialization created turmoil in male and female jobs. Since only minimal respect remained for custom and ideology—

---

traditionally the barriers inhibiting substitution of white women for more expensive male workers—employers felt free to experiment with the sexual division of labor. As they did so, the contributions of women seemed increasingly threatening to male workers. Worry began early and got worse by the turn of the century. The federal government had provoked hostility when it hired women for some clerical jobs in 1862. Until then there had been no more than a few women scattered in an occasional federal office, employed largely as copyists and low-grade clerks. Under pressure of the war, the Treasury hired some women to cut currency. And in 1862 the Post Office hired eight women among twenty-five new employees to sort mail. The new employees were ridiculed and insulted by male colleagues who "stared, blew smoke in the women's faces, spat tobacco juice, and gave cat-calls or made obnoxious remarks." The women, who earned an average of $300 a year less than men for precisely the same job, were discovered to be as productive as their colleagues, and the department promptly hired more women at the reduced rate. Though some federal officials objected on principle to hiring women, others appreciated the money saved by paying lower salaries. The end of the war brought predictable outcries. The *Workingmen's Advocate* deplored the fact that even the "government of the United States, which squanders millions uselessly every year, has stooped to the hiring of female clerks to do the work of its Departments because they could be got for a smaller sum than males."

But new machinery constituted the most typical reason to substitute women for men. Each time women entered an occupation for which training had become unnecessary, men saw it as an attack. In the pottery industry, skilled jiggermen feared, as they testified in 1900, that female labor operating new machinery would cut their wages in half and drive them out of the trade. It had happened, they said, in Great Britain, where the jobs of Englishmen had already been destroyed. The 1910 government report on the glass industry concluded that not only had certain parts of the work been readjusted so that women could be employed, but "new methods and new machines were devised with this end in view." The resulting reorganization of the work force broke up processes previously performed by skilled men into smaller tasks that "ceased to require skill. Machinery was adapted to women and much of it was and is advertised as being so adapted."

Changes in machinery, of course, had variable results. Sometimes jobs were created for women; but frequently a change had the opposite result. The textile industry witnessed both kinds of changes in the nineteenth century. In 1850, spinning jennies, operated by women in cotton mills, were widely replaced by spinning mules, heavy machines that called for physical strength and lent themselves to a male work force, according to the custom of the day. By the 1890s, when mule spinners, who then earned the relatively high wage of twelve to fourteen dollars a week, began seeking even more pay, several mills took advantage of new ring-spinning machinery to replace these demanding craftsmen with women at from six to eight dollars per week. One mill superintendent described the replacement process in his mill as follows: "A few years ago they were giving us trouble . . . so one Saturday afternoon, after they had gone home, we started right in and smashed up a room full of mules with sledge hammers. When the men came back on Monday morning, they were astonished to find that there was no work for them. That room is now full of ring frames run by girls." . . .

After the first breach of the office walls during the labor shortage of the Civil War, women moved quickly into most clerical positions. Their place was assured when the typewriter came into general use in the 1890s. The machine required nimble fingers—presumably an attribute of women. Its operators exercised no initiative. They were expected simply to copy. And the work was clean. Attracted by the new jobs, large numbers of women not previously employed began to look for work. These were native-born daughters of native parents, who had consistently refused jobs next to immigrant women in factories. For them, office work brought only minimal loss of dignity and offered the chance to earn decent incomes. The best-paid office workers—those who worked for the federal government, for example—might earn $900 a year in the 1870s. Though less than male wages for similar jobs, this compared favorably with other women's jobs. A teacher could make $500 a year. A stellar "typewriter" could make $7 a week, and an ordinary office clerk earned $6. A competent cap maker might earn $7 a week, but seasonal unemployment reduced her wages to less than $250 for a year's work.

Women's entry into the labor force accompanied a transition in the structure of offices. Unlike the men they replaced, women did not work primarily as personal secretaries. Rather, they found themselves doing tasks that were subdivided to produce maximal efficiency with minimal training. A year of secretarial training could turn a woman into a competent typist and stenographer. Lesser amounts were required for file clerks, telephone operators, and receptionists. But her ability to perform tasks constituted only part of a woman employee's attraction. Her personality weighed heavily. In 1916, a writer in the *Ladies' Home Journal* attributed 50 percent of the stenographer's value to her personality, quoting an employer who declared, "I expect from my stenographer the same service I get from the sun, with this exception: the sun often goes on a strike and it is necessary for me to use artificial light, but I pay my stenographer to work six days out of every seven and I expect her all the while to radiate my office with sunshine and sympathetic interest in the things I am trying to do."

The office worker's job might have made consistent sunshine difficult. Expected to possess all the sympathetic and nurturing characteristics of a good wife, she often performed tasks as routine as those of any factory worker. In the interests of efficiency, managers pooled their labor so that women might be called upon to perform their assigned job for any number of bosses. Even in this early period, managers simplified jobs, reducing tasks to the level of petty detail. One office manager declared women to be more "temperamentally reconciled" to the new jobs than ambitious men. By the 1920s attempts to systematize and control the office led to experiments with scientific management techniques. Creating systems for filing, keeping records, and corresponding became the tasks of an office manager. In a scientifically managed office the clerk or typist could no longer work according to her own methods, but according to methods and at times specified by the manager. Detailed studies were expected to reveal optimal speeds for each task and to break down the work into its simplest components. Though these techniques were never widely adopted, they influenced perceptions of systematic work and affected the tasks of numerous female office clerks.

In the given-out trades the transition first to factory work and then to efficiency techniques produced different results. As long as women made hats, garments, paper flowers, and feathers in the context of a rural family environment, they could trade off their small wages against the advantages of flexible work schedules. Supported by home-grown products, they might get through hard times without work, and they benefited from community sanction against those who cheated or did not pay as promised. These favorable conditions changed as the production of most goods shifted to factories in the 1850s, 1860s, and 1870s. During the transition, home work competed with factory products, forcing middlemen to demand a speedup in manufacture at the cost of quality. And centralization of the manufacturing process meant that even the paid work that remained in the home tended to gravitate from rural to urban environments, where community sanctions had less force and women had fewer resources to fall back on. . . . Contractors who distributed work from a shop in an impersonal urban environment succumbed to temptations to cheat and to offer the lowest possible wages. They ushered in some of the worst abuses of the sweating system.

In the garment industry, the rapid spread of the sewing machine after 1860 meant that for a while women, whether they sewed at home or in a shop, had to bear the increased costs of buying a piece of equipment. But its long-run effect was to encourage the slow movement of the work force into factories, where centralized production rationalized the garment-making process.

For a while, garment manufacturers distinguished sharply between "inside" and "outside" shops. In both, manufacturers distributed cut garments to contractors who bid against each other. The lowest bid got the bundle, and the contractor who won it hired his own operators to make up the pieces. Those who worked "inside" normally supervised the work process under the roof of the manufacturer himself. Others took the bundles "outside" to their own tenement flats, or to cheaply rented quarters. Since a contractor's income depended directly on how cheaply he could get people to finish the garments, he paid as little as he possibly could, and charged for thread, heat, light, and power, if he could get away with it. The system encouraged the use of family labor—which could be employed for endless hours—and of women. Though immigrant men were sometimes as much as 40 percent of the machine operators, the core of the labor force consisted of young, often immigrant women. Whether a woman worked inside or outside, she was most often paid directly by the contractor to whom she was responsible. That contractor—perhaps a tailor—in turn got his bundles from a foreman who coordinated the work of finishing and pressing completed garments. In inside shops this relationship left the subcontracting tailor less control than might otherwise seem possible. Becky Stein, a Philadelphia garment worker, recounted to the Commission on Industrial Relations in 1916 her sense of grievance at foremen who could compel a tailor to discharge a finisher against his will by threatening, "If you won't discharge her, you can't get no work."

The sewing machine, agitation from reformers who feared the spread of disease from tenement-made goods, and a desire for close supervision of the work process all encouraged manufacturers to bring their contractors inside, and by the early 1900s some branches of the industry began to eliminate the contractor altogether. As among telephone operators later, the increasing similarity of work and close association of workers stimulated unionization. Female sewing machine operators employed in the shirtwaist industry led the series of strikes that breathed life into the moribund International Ladies' Garment Workers' Union between 1909 and 1911. Shirtwaist manufacture—the newest branch of the garment industry—was organized in fairly large inside shops with relatively decent working conditions. The young female labor force sought freedom from the erratic decisions and often harassing behavior of foremen and supervisors. To get it, they fought for and finally won union recognition.

Not surprisingly, manufacturers, interested in rationalizing their industry, used the young union to institute some efficiency techniques that the union agreed would benefit workers as well as manufacturers. Their agreements are embodied in the Protocols of Peace—a series of compacts negotiated from 1910 to 1917 between local unions and manufacturers' associations representing various branches of the women's garment industry. The protocols normally included provisions for minimum wages, maximum hours, sanitary conditions, and arbitration mechanisms. But some went further. In New York's dress and waist industry, for example, the protocol guaranteed union cooperation in raising worker efficiency and holding manufacturers' costs down in return for guaranteed prices, mutually negotiated and agreed upon by the two parties in advance. The Board of Protocol Standards created under this industry's 1913 agreement set up union/employer time-and-motion study teams that would recommend appropriate wages and standard procedures and accounting methods. Since efficiency systems were then anathema to organized trade unionists, who were largely skilled, white males, the ILGWU leadership acted cautiously. But, for its semiskilled female membership, notions of efficiency and negotiated prices had tangible benefits. The union acquired a voice in the labor process. Women experienced relatively less harassment by amorous foremen and received designated and attainable tasks at prescribed prices. The ILGWU's rationale earned the support of Sidney Hillman, president of the newly formed Amalgamated Clothing Workers' Union, which organized workers in the men's clothing industry. The Amalgamated, 40 percent of whose members were female in 1920, cooperated with employers who tried to increase efficiency on the grounds that it subjected employees to less irrational behavior.

As it encouraged employers to turn to female labor for some jobs, the movement to increase worker productivity and to rationalize the work process produced an upsurge of resistance on the part of both men and women. But whereas men involved in the de-skilling process could and did unionize to defend their status, women discovered that their attempts to do so ran counter to assumptions about their social roles.

When the Knights of Labor flourished in the 1880s, women took advantage of its open membership policy to organize in large numbers. But the American Federation of Labor, founded in 1886, represented relatively privileged workers, willing to sacrifice the larger issue of working-class solidarity for the immediate gain of higher wages. In the creation of what economist Selig Perlman called "a joint partnership of organized labor and organized capital," the Federation cooperated extensively with corporation-dominated government agencies, sought to exclude immigrants, and supported an imperialist foreign policy. Its mechanisms for dealing with the huge numbers of women entering the labor force are an integral part of the puzzle surrounding the interaction of ideological and economic forces in regulating labor–market participation.

In the period from 1897 to 1920, the AFL underwent dramatic expansion. It consolidated and confirmed its leadership over a number of independent unions, including the dying Knights of Labor. Membership increased from about 265,000 in 1897 to more than four million by 1920, and included four-fifths of all organized workers. In the same period, the proportion of women working in the industrial labor force climbed by about 20 percent. Rapid and heady expansion offered a golden opportunity for organizers. That they did not take advantage of it is one of the most important facts in the history of labor organizing in America.

Figures for union membership are notoriously unreliable, and estimates fluctuate widely. But something like 3.3 percent of the women who were engaged in industrial occupations in 1900 were organized into trade unions. As low as that figure was, it began to decrease around 1902 and 1903, reaching a low of 1.5 percent in 1910. Then, a surge of organization among garment workers raised it. A reasonable estimate might place 6.6 percent of wage-earning women in trade unions by 1920—nearly half of them in the clothing trades and another 25 percent in printing. The rest belonged to a variety of unions, including meat packers, electrical workers, railway clerks, textile workers, boot and shoe workers, and hotel employees. In a decade that saw little change in the relative proportion of female and male workers, the proportion of women who were trade union members quadrupled, increasing at more than twice the rate for trade union members in general. Even so, the relative numbers of wage-earning women who were trade union members remained tiny. One in every five men in the industrial work force belonged to a union, compared to one in every fifteen women. Although more than 20 percent of the labor force was female, less than 8 percent of organized workers were women.

The dearth of women in unions had historic roots. These are readily located in the personality and behavioral patterns that derived from traditional family expectations. The young, unskilled workers who looked to marriage to escape the shop or factory were not ideal candidates for unionization. At the turn of the century, 87 percent of female workers were unmarried and nearly half were under twenty-five. Wage-earning women often came from groups without a union tradition: about half were immigrants or daughters of immigrants who shared rural backgrounds. In the cities, the figure sometimes rose to 90 percent. Like immigrant and black men, women formed a large reservoir of unskilled workers. Because they offered employers the advantage of low pay and exploitative working conditions, employers had a special incentive to resist unionization among women. As John Andrews, writing in the 1911 Report on the Condition of Woman and Child Wage Earners, put it: "The moment she organizes a union and seeks by organization to secure better wages she diminishes or destroys what is to the employer her chief value."

Women who wished to unionize had to fight on two fronts: against the weight of tradition and expectation, and against employers.

There was yet a third battle front—the trade union itself—and it might have been the most important of all. Instead of recognizing women as workers and encouraging them to join in organizational struggles, male unionists insisted on women's primary function in the home and remained stubbornly ambivalent about their efforts. They understood that employers had an important economic incentive for hiring women, and so their rhetoric, reflecting fears of being undercut, affirmed a commitment to unionize women wage earners and to extract equal pay for them. Yet in practice trade unionists remained locked into patriarchal attitudes that valued women's contributions to the home. Women's duties as mothers and wives, most felt, echoing the arguments of the preceding generation, were so valuable that women ought not to be in the labor force at all. This was unfortunate for women who wished to organize because it deprived them of help from the largest body of collective working-class opinion.

"The great principle for which we fight," said the AFL's treasurer in 1905, "is opposed to taking . . . the women from their homes to put them in the factory and the sweatshop." "We stand for the principle," said another AFL member, "that it is wrong to permit any of the female sex of our country to be forced to work, as we believe that the man should be provided with a fair wage in order to keep his female relatives from going to work. The man is the provider and should receive enough for his labor to give his family a respectable living." And yet a third proclaimed, "Respect for women is apt to decrease when they are compelled to work in the factory or the store. . . . More respect for women brings less degeneration and more marriages . . . if women labor in factories and similar institutions they bring forth weak children who are not educated to become strong and good citizens." No language was too forceful or too dramatic. "The demand for female labor," wrote an official of the Boston Central Labor Union in 1897, is "an insidious assault upon the home . . . it is the knife of the assassin, aimed at the family circle." The AFL journal, *American Federationist,* romanticized women's jobs at home, extolling the virtues of refined and moral mothers, of good cooking, and even of beautiful needlework and embroidery.

These arguments from home and motherhood had several effects. They sustained women's sense of themselves as temporary workers—a self-image on which their exploitation rested. In so doing they inadvertently aided employers, who relied on the notion that women were marginal to the work force to pay low wages and limit training. Trade unionists thus contributed to segmenting the labor force and crowding women into a few areas. Perhaps worst of all, the notion that women constituted a different kind of worker created barriers between the sexes that inhibited cooperation in a common struggle with employers.

The perception that women belonged in the home translated into the desire that they be eliminated from the work force entirely. "Every woman employed," wrote an editor in *American Federationist,* "displaces a man and adds one more to the idle contingent that are fixing wages at the lowest limit." "It is the so-called competition of the unorganized defenseless woman worker, the girl and the wife, that often tends to reduce the wages of the father and husband," proclaimed Samuel Gompers. . . .

These sentiments did not entirely prevent the AFL from attempting to unionize women. Although the grim realities of exploitative working conditions and the difficulties of caring for children while working ten or more hours a day sustained the argument for eliminating women from the work force, this goal was impossible to achieve. So the AFL, supported by well-intentioned social reformers, continued to organize women and to demand equal pay for equal work. Gompers editorialized on the subject frequently: "We . . . shall bend every energy for our fellow workmen to organize and unite in the trade unions; to federate their effort without regard to . . . sex." He and others conceded the "full and free opportunity for women to work whenever and wherever necessity requires," but Gompers did not address himself to the problem of how to determine which women were admissible by this standard, and his actions revealed that he thought their numbers relatively few. . . .

A strong union could simply cut women out of the kinds of jobs held by unionized men, a form of segmenting the labor market that sometimes contradicted the interests of employers who would have preferred cheap labor. A Binghamton, New York, printing establishment, for example, could not hire women Linotype operators because "the men's union would not allow it." This tactic excluded racial minorities as often as it restricted women; and, like appeals to racist beliefs, arguments based on the natural weakness of women worked well as a rationale. Mary Dreier, then president of the New York Chapter of the Women's Trade Union League, recalled a union of tobacco workers whose leaders refused to admit women because "they could only do poor sort of work . . . because women had no colour discrimination." A Boston metal polishers' union refused to admit women. "We don't want them," an official told an interviewer. "Women can only do one kind of work while men can polish anything from iron to gold and frame the smallest part to the largest." Besides, he added, "metal polishing is bad for the health."

Less direct methods excluded women from unions equally effectively. The International Retail Clerk's Union charged an initiation fee of three dollars and dues of fifty cents a month. Hilda Svenson, a local organizer in 1914, complained that she had been unable to negotiate a compromise with the International. "We want to be affiliated with them," she commented, "but on account of the dues and initiation fee we feel it is too high at the present time for the salaries that the girls in New York are getting." Sometimes union pay scales were set so high that the employer would not pay the appropriate wage to women. Joining the union could mean that a female printer would lose her job; so women simply refused to join.

But even membership in a union led by men guaranteed little to women. Unions often deliberately sabotaged their female members. Detroit's Amalgamated Association of Street Railway and Electrical Employees had agreed under wartime duress to admit women who were to be employed as conductors into their union in 1918. Just as their probationary period ended, men began returning from overseas and the union refused 250 women regular cards. Only an appeal to the National Labor Board, which ruled in the women's favor, saved their jobs. Supporting union men was not likely to benefit women either. Mary Anderson, newly appointed head of the U.S. Department of Labor's Women's Bureau, got a frantic telegram from a WTUL organizer in Joliet, Illinois, early in 1919. The women in a Joliet steel plant who, in return for the promise of protection, had supported unionized men in a recent strike were fighting desperately for jobs that the union now insisted they give up. The company wanted to retain the women, but union men argued that the work was too heavy for them.

In addition, such well-known tactics as holding meetings in saloons, scheduling them at late hours, and ridiculing women who dared to speak deprived women of full participation. Italian and southern families disliked their daughters going out in the evenings. Married and self-supporting women and widows had household duties at which they spent after-work hours. Women who attended meetings usually participated reluctantly. They found the long discussions dull and were often intimidated by the preponderance of men. Men, for their part, resented the indifference of the women and further excluded them from leadership roles, thereby discouraging more women from attending. Even fines failed to spark attendance. Some women preferred to pay them rather than go to the meetings.

Cultural patterns that derived from a patriarchal society joined ethnic ties in hindering unionization. Wage-earning women, anxious to marry, were sometimes reluctant to join unions for what they felt would be a temporary period. The role conflict implicit in a young wage-earning woman's assumptions about future family life emerged in ambivalence toward unions. "No nice girl would belong to one," said one young woman. An ILGWU organizer commented that the reluctance of most women who did not want to unionize reflected the obedience they owed to fathers. "The boss is good to us" they claimed; "we have nothing to complain about and we don't want to join the union." A woman who resisted unionization told an organizer that she knew "$6 a week is not enough pay but the Lord helps me out. He always provides. . . . I won't ever join a union. The Lord doesn't want me to." A recent convert to unionism apologized for her former reluctance. She had always scabbed because church people disapproved of unions. Moreover, she and her sister, she admitted to an organizer, had only with difficulty overcome their fear of the Italian men who were organizing their factory.

For all their initial reluctance women could be devoted and successful union members, convinced that unionism would serve them as it seemed to be serving their brothers. In the words of a seventeen-year-old textile worker, "We all work hard for a mean living. Our boys belong to the miners' union so their wages are better than ours. So I figure that girls must have a union. Women must act like men, ain't?" Such attitudes occurred most often among women whose ethnic backgrounds encouraged both wage labor and a high level of social consciousness, as in the American Jewish community, for example. Young Jewish women constituted the bulk of the membership of the International Ladies' Garment Workers' Union in the period from 1910 to 1920. Their rapid organization and faithful tenure was responsible for at least one-quarter of the increased number of unionized women in those years. And yet they were unskilled and semiskilled workers, employed in small, scattered shops, theoretically among the least organizable. These women, having unionized at their own initiative, formed the backbone of the ILGWU, which had originally sought to organize the skilled male cutters in the trade. They often served as shop "chairladies" and reached positions of minor importance in the union structure. Faige Shapiro recalled that her union activity began at the insistence of a business agent but quickly became an absorbing interest. The commitment of some women was such that when arrested on picket lines, they offered to spend the night in jail in order to save the union bail costs before returning to the line in the morning.

Whether in mixed unions or segregated by sex, women often outdid men in militancy. Once organized, they could more easily rely on the families they lived with to support them in a pinch. Since women as a group tended to have fewer dependents than men, they could hold out longer in a strike. Examples abound. Iowa cigar makers reported in 1899 that striking men had resumed work, while the women stood fast. Boot and shoe workers in Massachusetts were reported in 1905 to be tough bargainers. "It is harder to induce women to compromise," said their president; "they are more likely to hold out to the bitter end . . . to obtain exactly what they want." The great 1909 uprising in which 20,000 women walked out of New York's garment shops occurred over the objections of the male leadership, striking terror into the hearts of Jewish men afraid "of the security of their jobs." Protesting a rate cut in the textile mills of Chicopee, Massachusetts, Polish "spool girls" refused their union's suggestion that they arbitrate and won a resounding victory. Swedish women enrolled in a Chicago Custom Clothing Makers local lost a battle against employers' attempts to subdivide and speed up the sewing process when the largely male United Garment Workers' Union agreed to the new conditions. The management promptly locked out the women, forcing many to come to terms and others to seek new jobs. These militant characteristics enabled women who overcame the initial barriers to organization to run highly successful sex-segregated unions. They account for the early success of such turn-of-the-century unions as those of female garment workers in San Francisco, of telephone operators in Boston, and of tobacco strippers, and overall and sheepskin workers elsewhere.

Militance was less effective where trade union ambivalence left women at the mercy of employers who were particularly eager to discourage organization among women. In these instances, employers pressed their advantage. Sometimes they used crude techniques familiar to men. Department store employees were commonly fired when their union membership became known. Many stores had spy systems so that employees could not trust each other. Blacklists were common. Members of the Retail Dry Goods Association refused jobs to women whose names appeared on lists of troublemakers. The Association itself kept a complete record of all employees, including where they were employed and why discharged. Records were passed on to prospective employers, with no right of appeal by the employee. For fear of retaliation, a representative of the year-old Retail Clerks' Union, testifying before a congressional committee in 1914, refused to reveal the number of members in her union. To undercut trade union activities, department stores formed their own employee associations. Filene's in Boston and Bloomingdale's in New York set up welfare funds to make loans to employees in distress or to distribute turkeys at Thanksgiving. Although these funds required employee contributions, and representatives to the boards that controlled them were technically elected by the workers, no employee had ever sat on the Filene's board when one worker described it to an investigative committee in 1916. . . .

New ideas about corporate welfare and Taylor's notions of scientific management encouraged some managers to handle disciplinary problems through personnel and welfare work. Personnel management was of course the ideal tool for intervention and control. This newly founded science purported to be able to select employees judiciously and to assign them to the work they could do most effectively. Its techniques ranged from diagnostic interviews that attempted to choose likely candidates for each job, through careful juxtaposition of workers, with due consideration for race and ethnicity, and formal procedures for promotion and termination. Welfare work promised to keep workers contented by enhancing their sense of general well-being. Plants engaged in welfare work might offer employees incentives to purchase houses, to suggest innovative techniques through formal channels, and to participate in company-sponsored recreation. As a government report on textile mills concluded: "Parks, skating rinks, baseball teams, bands, and other welfare work doubtless have as one of their objects the creation of a contented class of mill employees who will not move about."

To workers and trade union organizers, welfare work appeared as an attempt to undermine their roles. One active union organizer described welfare work as "the last stand of the intelligent employer before doing business with a trade union. . . ." The focus of such work varied, but often it seemed to workers just another form of charity. The president of the Retail Clerks' Union, employed by Bloomingdale's Department Store, complained that only married workers and male employees got turkeys at Thanksgiving. "You have got to apply for it and ask for it, say that you need it. It is given out just as a charity is handed out . . . and the turkeys are paid for out of the money of the employees." . . .

The paternalism, benevolence, and welfare employers offered in compensation for foregoing unionism proved to be particularly useful tools for diverting women from organization. They promised to alleviate some of the harsh conditions under which women worked—conditions long viewed by reformers and investigators as detrimental to the preservation of home and family. These voluntary employer programs, in conjunction with government regulation, seemed to many an adequate alternative to unionism. What was more, trade unions, by allying themselves with regulators and sometimes with employers, could use appeals to women's "natural roles" to restrict their labor force participation.

If women were not to unionize, how were they to overcome low pay and exploitation at work? Training women in the skills appropriate to their sphere seemed like a plausible answer. Such activists in women's rights as Anna Dickinson and Mary Livermore had advocated training as a solution to women's problems for years. Early commentators on female labor—Virginia Penny, Caroline Dall, and later Annie McLean—repeatedly urged vocational training for girls. These women argued that the changing sex ratio—women already made up more than 51 percent of the population in such urban states as New York, Connecticut, Massachusetts, and New Jersey—would necessitate life-long work for many women, and that widowhood, desertion, and even divorce would force still others to fend for themselves. But acceptance of their proposals turned on the critical question of whether training would break down, or contribute to, sexual segmentation in the job market.

Skilled trades had traditionally been a province of unionized craftsmen who jealously guarded access to training in their fields. Though women frequently taught each other, and occasionally managed to "steal" a trade from a willing male relative, they were rarely admitted to the requisite apprenticeships. Where they managed to acquire skills and posed a threat to male workers, craft unions sometimes grudgingly helped women to form separate, affiliated unions. . . . To allow outsiders to train men or women, but especially women, in skilled areas posed an unending threat. When, in 1872, cigar makers faced an influx of skilled female Bohemian cigar rollers into their union, they responded by excluding the women altogether, provoking their use as strikebreakers a year later.

By the late 1890s employers began to move toward manual training programs in the public schools as a way of breaking craft monopolies. Manual training—which encouraged general skills useful for industrial work—quickly gave way to vocational education, which emphasized the skills specific to particular jobs. Such developments reflected a general shift in attitude toward all education. Initially education had been seen as useless in terms of vocation. Agnes Smedley's father expressed a general prejudice when he pronounced it worthwhile "only for women and men who were dudes." But the urban and industrial nation that had emerged out of the Civil War demanded disciplined workers with positive attitudes toward their jobs. In the words of one supervisor, the best educated of his workers were "the most capable, intelligent, energetic, industrious, economical, and moral . . . they produce the best work and the most of it, with the least injury to the machinery." Youngsters, employers thought, should be taught in school to work with their hands so that when they left school they could fit easily into an industrial framework.

For men, the issue of vocational education centered on the problem of control. But for women, it became ambiguous. To some well-meaning reformers, vocational training assumed the aspect of a panacea. Teaching women a trade opened tempting possibilities of financial security for them as well as a way out of overcrowded women's fields and up in the occupational structure. "Girls do not become apprentices or learn a trade thoroughly, and consequently they lagged behind man in the race of life," argued Ernestine Rose in 1869. "Teach girls to learn a trade as well as boys," she continued, "and then they would be independent." Jennie Cunningham Croly, feminist and socialist, concurred. To a congressional committee investigating capital and labor she declared in 1883: "Wherever a person can do anything, can *do* it in a proper sense, they can always earn a living by it; they can always get a certain amount for it." Sewing women earned only 50 cents a day because they were not properly competent. Even a washerwoman, who could wash, might make $1.25 a day. Raise "the standard of useful work by education and training," Croly argued, and women would earn more. The U.S. Department of Labor added fuel to the movement in 1909 when it documented what everyone already suspected. A New York City investigative committee had discovered that the average annual wage for girls without training approximated one-third of the wage of those who were trained as stenographers, and less than half of those trained as nurses.

Training would also provide access to jobs previously closed. If women "want to do a man's work," argued New York *Tribune* publisher Whitelaw Reid, "they must prepare." She would, Croly suggested, "supplement . . . common school education with technical or industrial schools where they would be made thorough mechanical draughtsmen, engravers, modelers, designers, dressmakers, embroiderers, laundresses, cooks, and tailors." Training would provide skills for middle-aged women who had worked for years. It could even, Leonora O'Reilly proposed, "act as an incentive to unionization." O'Reilly, who would later supervise machine operators for the Manhattan Trade School for Girls, wondered in 1898 whether training might not give to "working girls" that "force of character which will secure them desirable conditions of life and work." As jobs became increasingly mechanical, she touted trade schools as a way of preventing the "numbness of mind that comes with doing rote work." A trade school taught a girl "the relation between the brain and the hands."

But in practice, vocational education for women was fraught with problems. Widespread opinion held that homemaking was sufficiently complicated that all women should train to become efficient and effective housekeepers. Women entered the labor force briefly—too briefly, some thought, to be worth the time or energy of adequate training. To provide training appropriate to rewarding jobs threatened to undermine women's investment in home roles. Female college graduates, fully half of whom never married, provided a specter of the future. Should social institutions, public or private, lend themselves to such an aberration?

Advocates of vocational education for women tried to meet this objection by praising the home-related aspects of their program and obscuring its job-training potential. "Industrial education," in the words of a noted authority, should be designed "to meet the needs of the manual wage workers in the trades and industries, and in the household." Conceptually this meant that a notion of household labor as a woman's real work underlay every aspect of her vocational training. An insistent refrain accompanied preparation for even the most difficult jobs. Training would prepare female workers "for right living and right spending" in the future, said the Women's Educational and Industrial Union, whose purpose was "the advancement of women." It could teach them to be good consumers, "intelligent, discriminating, purchasing agents for themselves and their homes," said the Federal Board for Vocational Education. Out of training for a job, in short, would come not workers prepared to cope with the job market, but better house tenders. The National Society for the Promotion of Industrial Education, a coalition of small manufacturers, educators, social workers, and representatives of organized labor, waxed eloquent on this theme. "Will not the woman who has learned to systematize, to go forth rain or shine to work an eight-hour day, to stand on her own feet, taking the consequences of her own mistakes, and expecting no indulgences, have developed a respect for method, a sense of responsibility, and a discipline that are among the best gifts she could bring into the home?"

In this conspiracy to disguise what job training could accomplish, the representatives of interest groups ranging from educators and trade unionists to feminists concurred. Every plan of education for women, the manual training committee of the National Educational Association argued, should be tested "not merely with questions of immediate expediency or of personal advantage, but always with the thought of the larger contribution to the common good, and the higher functions which women can never surrender." The committee insisted that women could not only "lead happier and richer lives and will be more successful as the future homemakers of our cities" if they had some early training, but that industrial education would provide a skill with innumerable advantages. It would raise their parents' standards of living, as well as afford them protection and support if they were to lose their own partners.

Even those who sympathized most with women's needs for saleable skills defended vocational training as an adjunct to normal expectations of marriage. A national committee on women in industry, reporting on ways to educate women at the end of the war, offered a sweeping vision: vocational education would provide training for "the period previous to marriage, or if she does not marry, for the period of her working life, or for the married woman, who, because of widowhood, desertion, childlessness, or some other deviation from normal married life, returns to industry as a wage-earner." "The qualities needed in trade," wrote Mary Woolman after five years as director of the Manhattan Trade School for Girls,

are the same as those which elevate the home. Employers ask for workers who are reliable, who respect authority, who are honest in time, in work, and in word. The development of a sense of responsibility is a difficult task to accomplish, but it is not impossible at least to lay the foundation, even though the poverty of the students necessarily limits the period of instruction. A trade school can develop character, and consequently the better homekeeper is born from the better trade worker.

Opposition to training women for exclusively wage-earning roles led to schools and curricula that appeared distinctly defensive. Those who developed trade schools played down the remunerative aspects of the skills they were teaching. Witness Florence Leadbetter, principal of Boston's Trade School for Girls: "We have always said that we would not admit to our trade school any trade which would not help the girl in her highest vocation—homemaking—but we believe that any trade, well-taught . . . will give that discipline . . . needed to make her the ideal wife, mother, sympathetic helpmate and resourceful adviser." What had begun in the 1870s as a movement to train women in saleable skills had become a major adjunct to training for the home by 1900. . . .

In accepting the condition that homemaking be part of the educational process, and in acquiescing to existing job segmentation, advocates of vocational education for women fell into a predictable trap. For the new programs perpetuated familiar characteristics among women workers. They trained women expected to stay in the labor market briefly to expect little upward mobility and to deflect their ambitions into marriage. A Women's Bureau argument illustrated the tenacious effect of old prescriptions. After making the point that women were, after all, capable of doing these jobs, the Bureau said, "The increase in the use of mechanical devices in the modern home renders a knowledge of mechanics essential, if not more so, to the average woman who eventually leaves industry to take up household duties as is a knowledge of sewing, because the manufacture of clothing has ceased practically, to be a profitable household industry." If the Woman's Bureau could resort to such logic, it was small wonder that Anna Lalor Burdick, who worked for the Federal Board of Vocational Training, found it easy to argue for training women for garment and hat work, the hosiery industry, and soap-making, on the grounds that "women's small and agile hands are especially adapted to the work of certain industries."

Despite the influx of married women into the work force, and the clear evidence that their jobs offered inadequate pay and opportunity, vocational education perpetuated the assumption that married women's work was, and would remain, peripheral. Yet for daughters of the working class, it involved a breakthrough of sorts. While denying that individual women could be permanent workers, it acknowledged a permanent role for women in general in the work force. It took women's work seriously enough to provide a few women with access to decent training and a real possibility for creative work force participation. But vocational education did not yield access to upward mobility. Rather, the skills provided more often than not led to a fixed, if slightly more comfortable, labor force position.

SUGGESTIONS FOR FURTHER READING

For many years the study of American labor was dominated by the Wisconsin school, a group of scholars working with or influenced by John R. Commons at the University of Wisconsin. They collected a great many source materials, and they emphasized in their studies organized labor, that is, the development of trade unions. They stressed the lack of class consciousness among American workers and argued that American labor organizations were primarily concerned with job consciousness—wages, hours, and working conditions—and had little interest in political radicalism. Important examples of this approach are the four-volume *History of Labor in the United States* by Commons and others (New York, 1918–1935); Selig Perlman, *A Theory of the Labor Movement* (New York, 1928); and Philip Taft's massive two-volume history of the A. F. of L.: *The A. F. of L. in the Time of Gompers* (New York, 1957) and *The A. F. of L. from the Death of Gompers to the Merger* (New York, 1959).

Strongly opposed to the Wisconsin group is Philip S. Foner, whose Marxist interpretation of the *History of the Labor Movement in the United States* (seven volumes; New York, 1947–1987) emphasizes class struggle and conflict. Violent labor conflict can be seen in studies of specific strikes: Almont Lindsay, *The Pullman Strike* (Chicago, 1942) and Henry David, *History of the Haymarket Affair* (New York, 1936). Louis Adamic's theme is expressed in the title of his book, *Dynamite; The Story of Class Violence in America* (New York, 1931).

Although labor historians continue to study organized labor, in recent years they have devoted more attention to the history of workers (rather than unions) in the context of social and economic change in the United States. These historians have been strongly influenced by a pioneer study by a British scholar, E. P. Thompson, *The Making of the English Working Class* (London, 1963). An example of this influence can be seen in the article by Herbert Gutman reprinted here. Other articles by Gutman are collected in a book, *Work,

---

*Available in paperback edition.

Culture and Society in Industrializing America (New York, 1976). David Montgomery has adopted a similar approach in his *Workers' Control in America: Studies in the History of Work, Technology, and Labor Struggles* (New York, 1979) and in his more recent book, *The Fall of the House of Labor: The Workplace, the State, and American Labor Activism, 1865–1925* (New York, 1987), which deals with the struggle for control of the workplace. For perceptive studies of class and class consciousness, see Douglas M. Eichar, *Occupations and Class Consciousness in America* (New York, 1989); Reeve Vanneman, *The American Perception of Class* (Philadelphia, 1987); Jeffrey Haydu, *Between Craft and Class: Skilled Workers and Factory Politics in the United States and Britain, 1890–1922* (Berkeley, Cal., 1988); and Kim Voss, *The Making of American Exceptionalism: The Knights of Labor and Class Formation in the Nineteenth Century* (Ithaca, N.Y., 1993).

Daniel T. Rodgers, *The Work Ethic in Industrial America, 1850–1920* (Chicago, 1978) describes how industrialism destroyed the traditional consensus concerning the work ethic, producing sharp conflict between businessmen and workers. James B. Gilbert, *Work Without Salvation* (Baltimore, 1977) considers the response of the nation's intellectuals to the same development. Gerald N. Grob, *Workers and Utopia: A Study of Ideological Conflict in the American Labor Movement, 1865–1900* (Evanston, Ill., 1961) discusses the conflict between workers and reformers in the trade-union movement. Many studies consider the myth and reality of social mobility and the effects both had on the attitudes of workers. A good place to start is with two books by Stephen Thernstrom: *Poverty and Progress: Social Mobility in a Nineteenth Century City* (Cambridge, Mass., 1964) and *The Other Bostonians* (Cambridge, Mass., 1973).

The special problems of working women can be followed in Rosiland Baxandall, Linda Gordon, and Susan Reverby, eds., *America's Working Women* (New York, 1976); David M. Katzman, *Seven Days a Week: Women and Domestic Service in Industrializing America* (New York, 1978); Leslie Woodcock Tentler, *Wage-Earning Women* (New York, 1979); Susan Porter Benson, *Counter Cultures: Saleswomen, Managers, and Customers in American Department Stores, 1890–1940* (Urbana, Ill., 1986); Patricia A. Cooper, *Once a Cigarmaker: Men, Women, and Work Culture in American Cigar Factories, 1900–1919* (Urbana, Ill., 1987); and Nancy Felice Gabin, *Feminism in the Labor Movement: Women and the United Auto Workers, 1935–1975* (Ithaca, N.Y., 1990).

Good general surveys of the problems black workers face are F. Ray Marshall, *The Negro and Organized Labor* (New York, 1965); William B. Gould, *Black Workers in White Unions: Job Discrimination in the United States* (Ithaca, N.Y., 1977); and William C. Harris, *The Harder We Run* (New York, 1982). A good collection of essays on black workers is John H. Bracey, Jr., August Meier, and Elliott Rudwick, eds., *Black Workers and Organized Labor* (Belmont, Calif., 1971). A convenient collection of documents concerning black workers is Philip S. Foner and Ronald L. Lewis, eds., *Black Workers: A Documentary Record from Colonial Times to the Present* (Philadelphia, 1989).

A perceptive general study with a good bibliography is Melvyn Dubofsky, *Industrialism and the American Worker, 1865–1920* (Arlington Heights, Ill., 1975). A collection of essays from a variety of perspectives along with a good annotated bibliography is David Brody, ed., *The American Labor Movement* (New York, 1971). A direct introduction to the words of the participants may be found in John A. Garraty, ed., *Labor and Capital in the Gilded Age* (Boston, 1968), a selection of testimony by workers, businessmen, social workers, and others in 1883 before the Senate Committee upon Relations between Labor and Capital. Melvyn Dubofsky, *The State and Labor in Modern America* (Chapel Hill, N.C., 1994) discusses the successes and the failures of organized labor to influence government policy.

5

Migrants to an Urban America

The history of modern America is in many ways a history of urbanism. "The United States was born in the country, but has moved to the city," Richard Hofstadter has written. Of course, there were cities in America from the very beginning of the nation's history; Philadelphia, with a population of about 25,000 in 1776, was one of the largest cities in the British Empire. But in the early years of the new republic, the urban population was small. In 1790 there were only twenty-four towns in the United States with a population of 2,500 or more (the census definition of an urban place); the 201,655 urban residents in that year accounted for only about 5 percent of the total population.

The growth of trade and industry in the nineteenth century brought massive urban growth. By 1860 about 20 percent of the population resided in cities, and forty years later four Americans in ten were urban dwellers. The census of 1920 revealed that more than half the American population lived in cities.

Rapid urbanization did not bring universal approval from the nation's intellectual and cultural leaders. Some, such as Frederick C. Howe, saw the city as "The Hope of Democracy," picturing the metropolis as the center of culture, business, and opportunity. But many, recalling Thomas Jefferson's warnings, distrusted the city, seeing it as a source of corruption and sin and a threat to American democracy.

Critics found much to distrust about city life. They pointed to the filth and the smoky air, to the violence and crime, and to the political corruption. But most frightening of all, the cities seemed strangely alien with their hordes of immigrants from the farms and cities of Europe. During the century after 1820, 38 million Europeans came to America; between 1902 and 1914 well over half a million immigrants arrived every year. Most of the latter came from southern and eastern Europe and settled in the cities.

Americans had always prided themselves on being a mixture of many races and nationalities and had viewed their country as a haven for the oppressed. As early as 1782, the naturalized New Yorker, J. Hector St. John Crèvecoeur, had written: "He is an American who leaving behind him all his ancient prejudices and manners, receives new ones from the new mode of life he has embraced. . . . Here individuals of all nations are melted into a new race of men. . . ." Despite the image of the melting pot, however, newly arrived immigrants were often greeted with suspicion. In the early nineteenth century, Irish and German immigrants faced resentment that occasionally boiled over into riots and violence. Antagonism toward newcomers increased as millions of eastern and southern European immigrants flocked to America during the late nineteenth and early twentieth centuries. Many Americans—including second-generation immigrants—began to question the concept of open immigration and called for restrictions.

The melting pot did not seem to be working. Contrary to expectations, the immigrants did not become Americanized overnight. Organizing their own communities and their own national societies, they held desperately to their old ways. The problems in the cities seemed to be the result of the arrival of millions of alien people who were unable and unwilling to adopt American ways. To make matters worse, in the eyes of native-born citizens, the newcomers provided the voting support for corrupt political machines in the cities or supported radical, un-American causes.

But immigrants continued to come, lured by the hope of a better life in the New World. Often they were bitterly disappointed, finding instead crowded tenements, poor jobs, and violence in the teeming streets; they lived days of struggle and nights of loneliness in an alien land. Yet, for many, America was the land of opportunity; or at least it was better than the old country. One German wrote home: "No one can give orders to anybody here, one is as good as another, no one takes off his hat to another as you have to do in Germany."

Many newcomers to America's growing cities were not foreigners, however, but native Americans who left their rural villages and farms to seek a new life and, they hoped, new opportunities in the cities. They, too, faced the problem of adjusting to new living and working conditions. Urban migrants, whatever their nationality, suffered the hardships associated with cities that had grown too fast to provide adequate housing, streets, sewers, police protection, and transportation.

African-Americans were among the most recent migrants to northern cities, although cities such as Philadelphia had a significant black community even before the American Revolution. Still, it was the massive migrations during World War I and again during World War II that brought large numbers of blacks from the South to northern cities. African-Americans faced the same problems endured by other migrants, but they suffered additionally from racism, which limited their job and housing opportunities and generally made it more difficult for them to assimilate into the life of the city. The result was sometimes turmoil that led to race riots such as those in Chicago in 1919 and in Detroit in 1943. At the same time, however, blacks found jobs, established institutions and neighborhoods, and became an integral part of the ethnic mix in northern cities.

There can be no doubt that the great migration to American cities in the nineteenth and twentieth centuries produced tensions and conflicts that often erupted into bloody violence. For many historians, this is the proper emphasis to give to the experience. But other historians have argued that despite the conflict, the newcomers were usually integrated into American society. The cities, they argue, offered new opportunities; the bewildered newcomers of one year became the solid citizens of the next. Still other historians, even if they accept the view that the melting pot was effective, maintain that there is one conspicuous exception. Black Americans, they argue, were prevented from seizing the opportunities available to other migrants. While antagonism against foreigners and rural whites eventually faded, racism remained an all but insurmountable obstacle blocking the progress of the blacks.

In the following selections the reader is introduced to some of the ways in which the problems of urban migration have been evaluated. In the first selection, Oscar Handlin discusses the alienation of the immigrants both from their native land and from the new world that they had entered. "Uprooted" from their own culture, they found it difficult to sink roots in a new and alien culture. They were expected to assimilate, to give up all that they understood and held dear, and they were condemned when they could not do so. But their children, Handlin concludes, had less trouble; they were "natives."

In the second selection, Darlene Clark Hine discusses the black migration into the cities of the Midwest. She considers the racist antagonism faced by all black migrants to the cities but focuses on the special problems faced by women. She weighs the relative importance of the "push" factors that led blacks to leave the South and the "pull" factors that enticed migrants to northern cities and compares and contrasts the experiences of men and women. She argues that a "hidden motivation" for migration among black women was their desire "to escape from sexual exploitation" and "domestic violence."

In the final selection, Richard C. Wade surveys urban violence in broad historical perspective, arguing that while violence had always characterized American urban life, its causes have over the years been largely mitigated. As a result, "the level of large-scale disorder and violence is less ominous today than it has been during much of the past." The one major exception to this generalization is the violence associated with racial antagonism. Denying that race conflict is mainly class conflict, Wade argues that racism created the ghetto, limited opportunities for the blacks, and left the nation with "a growingly alienated and embittered group" in its midst.

In judging the urban experience in America, should we emphasize the violence, the riots, the crime, and the corruption, or should we stress the cultural and economic achievements of our cities? Should we stress the urban melting pot, where many ethnically diverse people came together and found an opportunity to improve themselves, or should we emphasize the alienation, the pathos, and the conflict?

Was the migration experience different for women? Was their adjustment to urban life in America more difficult than it was for men? Is discrimination against the blacks simply the result of their being the last group to enter the cities? Or is racism a special problem that other migrants never had to face?

Oscar Handlin

The Uprooted

Letters bring the low voices across the sea. The unfamiliar pens grope for the proper words. When you ask somebody to write for you, you must go and treat him. Therefore you try yourself. In the store are printed forms. Sometimes they will do to transmit information. But you wish through this lifeless paper to do more than send news. With painful effort and at the sacrifice of precious time, you express the solidarity you still feel with those who stayed behind. The sheet is then the symbol of the ties that continue to bind.

Ceremonial salutations, *to my dearest* . . . to every him and her who filled the days of the old life and whom I will never see again. By this letter I kiss you. To the aged parents who bred and nurtured, who took trouble over, shed tears for me and now have none to comfort them; to the brother who shared my tasks and bed; to my comrades of the fields; to all the kin who joined in festivals; to the whole visible communion, the oneness, of the village that I have forfeited by emigration; to each I send my greetings. And with my greetings go wishes that you may have the sweet years of life, of health and happiness, alas elusive there and here.

They are wanderers to the wide world and often yearn toward the far direction whence they have come. Why even the birds who fly away from their native places still hasten to go back. Can ever a man feel really happy condemned to live away from where he was born? Though by leaving he has cut himself off and knows he never will return, yet he hopes, by reaching backward, still to belong in the homeland.

It is to that end that the husband and wife and older children gather to assist in the composition; it is to that end that they assemble to read the reply. Little enough occurs to them that is worth recording, certainly not the monotonous struggle of getting settled. Instead their lines go to reminiscence, to the freshening of memories, to the commemoration of anniversaries. Later, when the art spreads and photographs are available at low cost, these are exchanged with great frequency.

Other acts of solidarity also absorbed the attention of the immigrants. Vivid recollections of the suffering they had left behind spurred them on in the effort to set aside from their own inadequate earnings enough to aid the ones who had not come. By 1860 the Irish alone were sending back four or five million dollars a year; a half-century later, the total remitted by all groups was well over one hundred and forty million for a twelve-month period. Often, in addition, some unusual disaster evoked a special sympathetic response—the church burned down, or famine appeared, or war. Such contributions recognized the continued connectedness with the old place. In time, that was further strengthened by involvement in nationalistic movements which established a political interest in the affairs of the Old Country, an interest the peasants had not had while they were there.

As the passing years widened the distance, the land the immigrants had left acquired charm and beauty. Present problems blurred those they had left unsolved behind; and in the haze of memory it seemed to these people they had formerly been free of present dissatisfactions. It was as if the Old World became a great mirror into which they looked to see right all that was wrong with the New. The landscape was prettier, the neighbors more friendly, and religion more efficacious; in the frequent crises when they reached the limits of their capacities, the wistful reflection came: *This would not have happened there.*

The real contacts were, however, disappointing. The requests—that back there a mass be said, or a wise one consulted, or a religious medal be sent over—those were gestures full of hope. But the responses were inadequate; like all else they shrank in the crossing. The immigrants wrote, but the replies, when they came, were dull, even trite in their mechanical phrases, or so it seemed to those who somehow expected these messages to evoke the emotions that had gone into their own painfully composed letters. Too often the eagerly attended envelopes proved to be only empty husks, the inner contents valueless. After the long wait before the postman came, the sheets of garbled writing were inevitably below expectations. There was a trying sameness to the complaints of hard times, to the repetitious petty quarrels; and before long there was impatience with the directness with which the formal greeting led into the everlasting requests for aid.

This last was a sore point with the immigrants. The friends and relatives who had stayed behind could not get it out of their heads that in America the streets were paved with gold. *Send me for a coat. . . . There is a piece of land here and if only you would send, we could buy it. . . . Our daughter could be married, but we have not enough for a dowry. . . . We are ashamed, everyone else gets . . . much more frequently than we.* Implicit in these solicitations was the judgment that the going-away had been a desertion, that unfulfilled obligations still remained, and that the village could claim assistance as a right from its departed members.

From the United States it seemed there was no comprehension, back there, of the difficulties of settlement. It was exasperating by sacrifices to scrape together the remittances and to receive in return a catalogue of new needs, as if there were not needs enough in the New World too. The immigrants never shook off the sense of obligation to help; but they did come to regard their Old Countrymen as the kind of people who depended on help. The trouble with the Europeans was, they could not stand on their own feet.

The cousin green off the boat earned the same negative appraisal. Though he be a product of the homeland, yet here he cut a pitiable figure; awkward manners, rude clothes, and a thoroughgoing ineptitude in the new situation were his most prominent characteristics. The older settler found the welcome almost frozen on his lips in the face of such backwardness.

In every real contact the grandeur of the village faded; it did not match the immigrants' vision of it and it did not stand up in a comparison with America. When the picture came, the assembled family looked at it beneath the light. This was indeed the church, but it had not been remembered so; and the depressing contrast took some of the joy out of remembering.

The photograph did not lie. There it was, a low building set against the dusty road, weather-beaten and making a candid display of its ill-repair. But the recollections did not lie either. As if it had been yesterday that they passed through those doors, they could recall the sense of spaciousness and elevation that sight of the structure had always aroused. *Fascination + disappointment*

Both impressions were true, but irreconcilable. The mental image and the paper representation did not jibe because the one had been formed out of the standards and values of the Old Country, while the other was viewed in the light of the standards and values of the New. And it was the same with every other retrospective contact. Eagerly the immigrants continued to look back across the Atlantic in search of the satisfactions of fellowship. But the search was not rewarded. Having become Americans, they were no longer villagers. Though they might willingly assume the former obligations and recognize the former responsibilities, they could not recapture the former points of view or hold to the former judgments. They had seen too much, experienced too much to be again members of the community. It was a vain mission on which they continued to dispatch the letters; these people, once separated, would never belong again.

Their home now was a country in which they had not been born. Their place in society they had established for themselves through the hardships of crossing and settlement. The process had changed them, had altered the most intimate aspects of their lives. Every effort to cling to inherited ways of acting and thinking had led into a subtle adjustment by which those ways were given a new American form. No longer Europeans, could the immigrants then say that they belonged in America? The answer depended upon the conceptions held by other citizens of the United States of the character of the nation and of the role of the newcomers within it.

In the early nineteenth century, those already established on this side of the ocean regarded immigration as a positive good. When travel by sea became safe after the general peace of 1815 and the first fresh arrivals trickled in, there was a general disposition to welcome the movement. The favorable attitude persisted even when the tide mounted to the flood levels of the 1840's and 1850's. The man off the boat was then accepted without question or condition.

The approval of unlimited additions to the original population came easily to Americans who were conscious of the youth of their country. Standing at the edge of an immense continent, they were moved by the challenge of empty land almost endless in its extension. Here was room enough, and more, for all who would bend their energies to its exploitation. The shortage was of labor and not of acres; every pair of extra hands increased the value of the abundant resources and widened opportunities for everyone.

The youth of the nation also justified the indiscriminate admission of whatever foreigners came to these shores. There was high faith in the destiny of the Republic, assurance that its future history would justify the Revolution and the separation from Great Britain. The society and the culture that would emerge in this territory would surpass those of the Old World because they would not slavishly imitate the outmoded forms and the anachronistic traditions that constricted men in Europe. The United States would move in new directions of its own because its people were a new people.

There was consequently a vigorous insistence that this country was not simply an English colony become independent. It was a nation unique in its origins, produced by the mixture of many different types out of which had come an altogether fresh amalgam, the American. The ebullient citizens who believed and argued that their language, their literature, their art, and their polity were distinctive and original also believed and argued that their population had not been derived from a single source but had rather acquired its peculiar characteristics from the blending of a variety of strains.

There was confidence that the process would continue. The national type had not been fixed by its given antecedents; it was emerging from the experience of life on a new continent. Since the quality of men was determined not by the conditions surrounding their birth, but by the environment within which they passed their lives, it was pointless to select among them. All would come with minds and spirits fresh for new impressions; and being in America would make Americans of them. Therefore it was best to admit freely everyone who wished to make a home here. The United States would then be a great melting pot, great enough so that there was room for all who voluntarily entered; and the nation that would ultimately be cast from that crucible would be all the richer for the diversity of the elements that went into the molten mixture.

The legislation of most of the nineteenth century reflected this receptive attitude. The United States made no effort actively to induce anyone to immigrate, but neither did it put any bars in the way of their coming. Occasional laws in the four decades after 1819 set up shipping regulations in the hope of improving the conditions of the passage. In practice, the provisions that specified the minimum quantities of food and the maximum number of passengers each vessel could carry were easily evaded. Yet the intent of those statutes was to protect the travelers and to remove harsh conditions that might discourage the newcomers.

Nor were state laws any more restrictive in design. The seaports, troubled by the burdens of poor relief, secured the enactment of measures to safeguard their treasuries against such charges. Sometimes the form was a bond to guarantee that the immigrant would not become at once dependent upon public support; sometimes it was a small tax applied to defray the costs of charity. In either case there was no desire to limit entry into the country; and none of these steps had any discernible effect upon the volume of admissions.

Once landed, the newcomer found himself equal in condition to the natives. Within a short period he could be naturalized and acquire all the privileges of a citizen. In some places, indeed, he could vote before the oath in court so transformed his status. In the eyes of society, even earlier than in the eyes of the law, he was an American.

It was not necessary that the immigrants should read deeply in the writings of political and social theorists to understand this conception of America. The idea was fully and clearly expressed in practice. The sense of being welcome gave people who had elsewhere been counted superfluous the assurance that their struggles to build a new life would be regarded with sympathy by their new neighbors. On such a foundation they could proceed to settle down in their own ways, make their own adjustments to the new conditions.

Significantly, the newcomers were not compelled to conform to existing patterns of action or to accept existing standards. They felt free to criticize many aspects of the life they discovered in the New World, the excessive concern with material goods and the inadequate attention to religion, the pushiness and restlessness of the people, the transitory quality of family relationships. The boldness of such judgments testified to the voluntary nature of immigrant adjustment. The strangers did not swallow America in one gulp; through their own associations and their own exertions they discovered how to live in the new place and still be themselves.

Until the 1880's the diverse groups in the United States got in each other's way only on very unusual occasions; generally rapid expansion made room for the unrestrained activity of all. Indeed the newcomers themselves did not then become issues; nor was there then any inclination to question the desirability of continuing the traditional open policy. But the second generation was an unstable element in the situation; as it grew in prominence, it created troublesome problems precisely because it had not a fixed place in the society. Standing between the culture of its parents and the culture of the older America, it bared the inadequacies of the assumption that the fusion of the multitude of strains in the melting pot would come about as a matter of course. The moments of revelation, though still rare, were profoundly shocking.

The discovery came most commonly in matters related to employment. However the native wage earner may have judged the effects of the immigrants upon the economy in general, he knew that these people did not directly compete with him for his job. But the children of the immigrants were Americans who were not content with the places that went to foreigners. On the labor market the offspring of the newcomers jostled the sons of well-established families. There was still no lack of space in a productive system that grew at an ever-accelerating pace. But the ambitious youngster every now and then hit upon the advertisement, NO IRISH NEED APPLY! The hurt would affect him, but also his father. It would disclose to these immigrants, and to many who came later, the limits of their belonging to America.

In politics also there were occasions on which the activities of the new citizens met the hostility of the old. If the consequences then were more striking, it was because there was less room for competition in the contest for political control. There were times when groups of men, unable to attain their own ends through government and unable to understand their own failure, sought to settle the blame on the foreign-born in their midst. In the 1850's, for instance, agitation of the slavery question and of a host of reform proposals put an intolerable strain upon the existing party structure. Years of compromise had produced no durable solution; instead they had given rise to grave forebodings of the calamitous Civil War that impended.

At the point of crisis, the stranger who stood in the way of attainment of some particular objective became the butt of attack. Abolitionists and reformers who found the conservative Irish arrayed against them at the polls, proslavery politicians who made much of the radicalism of some of the German leaders, and temperance advocates who regarded an alien hankering after alcohol as the main obstruction on the way to universal abstinence—such people were the backbone of the Know-Nothing Party that leaped to sudden prominence in the election of 1854. The oddly assorted elements that entered this political coalition had little in common; it took them only two years to come to know each other better, and once they did the party fell apart. Nothing positive had drawn such men together; they were attracted to each other rather by the fears that troubled them all. Incapable for the moment of confronting the real divisions within their society, many Americans achieved a temporary unity by cohering against the outsider in their midst.

The Know-Nothing movement disappeared as rapidly as it had appeared. In that respect it traced a course later followed by similar movements that flashed across the political horizon—the A.P.A. of the 1890's and the anti-German agitation of the First World War. These brief lapses in relationships that were generally peaceful had no enduring effects upon legislation or upon the attitudes of the mass of the native-born.

But even very brief glimpses of the hatred that might be generated against them disturbed the immigrants. The memory of charges violently made lingered long after the charges themselves were no longer a threat. They left behind a persistent uneasiness. The foreign-born could not forget that their rights as citizens had once been challenged. Could they help but wonder how fully they belonged in the United States? Occasional street fights among the boys that pitted group against group, from time to time more serious riots in which the unruly elements in the town attacked the aliens, and the more frequent slurs from press and platform kept alive that doubt.

Yet until the 1880's confidence outweighed the doubt. So long as those native to the country retained the faith that America would continue to grow from the addition of variety to its culture, the newcomers retained the hope, despite the difficulties of settlement and the discouragement of sporadic acts of hostility, that there would be here a home for the homeless of Europe.

As the nineteenth century moved into its last quarter, a note of petulance crept into the comments of some Americans who thought about this aspect of the development of their culture. It was a long time now that the melting pot had been simmering, but the end product seemed no closer than before. The experience of life in the United States had not broken down the separateness of the elements mixed into it; each seemed to retain its own identity. Almost a half-century after the great immigration of Irish and Germans, these people had not become indistinguishable from other Americans; they were still recognizably Irish and German. Yet even then, newer waves of newcomers were beating against the Atlantic shore. Was there any prospect that all these multitudes would ever be assimilated, would ever be Americanized?

A generation earlier such questions would not have been asked. Americans of the first half of the century had assumed that any man who subjected himself to the American environment was being Americanized. Since the New World was ultimately to be occupied by a New Man, no mere derivative of any extant stock, but different from and superior to all, there had been no fixed standards of national character against which to measure the behavior of newcomers. The nationality of the new Republic had been supposed fluid, only just evolving; there had been room for infinite variation because diversity rather than uniformity had been normal.

The expression of doubts that some parts of the population might not become fully American implied the existence of a settled criterion of what was American. There had been a time when the society had recognized no distinction among citizens but that between the native and the foreign-born, and that distinction had carried no imputation of superiority or inferiority. Now there were attempts to distinguish among the natives between those who really belonged and those who did not, to separate out those who were born in the United States but whose immigrant parentage cut them off from the truly indigenous folk.

It was difficult to draw the line, however. The census differentiated after 1880 between natives and native-born of foreign parents. But that was an inadequate line of division; it provided no means of social recognition and offered no basis on which the *true Americans* could draw together, identify themselves as such.

Through these years there was a half-conscious quest among some Americans for a term that would describe those whose ancestors were in the United States before the great migrations. Where the New Englanders were, they called themselves Yankees, a word that often came to mean non-Irish or non-Canadian. But Yankee was simply a local designation and did not take in the whole of the old stock. In any case, there was no satisfaction to such a title. Its holders were one group among many, without any distinctive claim to Americanism, cut off from other desirable peoples prominent in the country's past. Only the discovery of common antecedents could eliminate the separations among the really American.

But to find a common denominator, it was necessary to go back a long way. Actually no single discovery was completely satisfactory. Some writers, in time, referred to the civilization of the United States as Anglo-Saxon. By projecting its origins back to early Britain, they implied that their own culture was always English in derivation, and made foreigners of the descendants of Irishmen and Germans, to say nothing of the later arrivals. Other men preferred a variant and achieved the same exclusion by referring to themselves as "the English-speaking people," a title which assumed there was a unity and uniqueness to the clan which settled the home island, the Dominions, and the United States. Still others relied upon a somewhat broader appellation. They talked of themselves as Teutonic and argued that what was distinctively American originated in the forests of Germany; in this view, only the folk whose ancestors had experienced the freedom of tribal self-government and the liberation of the Protestant Reformation were fully American.

These terms had absolutely no historical justification. They nevertheless achieved a wide currency in the thinking of the last decades of the nineteenth century. Whatever particular phrase might serve the purpose of a particular author or speaker, all expressed the conviction that some hereditary element had given form to American culture. The conclusion was inescapable: to be Americanized, the immigrants must conform to the American way of life completely defined in advance of their landing.

There were two counts to the indictment that the immigrants were not so conforming. They were, first, accused of their poverty. Many benevolent citizens, distressed by the miserable conditions in the districts inhabited by the laboring people, were reluctant to believe that such social flaws were indigenous to the New World. It was tempting, rather, to ascribe them to the defects of the newcomers, to improvidence, slovenliness, and ignorance rather than to inability to earn a living wage.

Indeed to those whose homes were uptown the ghettos were altogether alien territory associated with filth and vice and crime. It did not seem possible that men could lead a decent existence in such quarters. The good vicar on a philanthropic tour was shocked by the moral dangers of the dark unlighted hallway. His mind rushed to the defense of the respectable young girl: *Whatever her wishes may be, she can do nothing—shame prevents her from crying out.* The intention of the reformer was to improve housing, but the summation nevertheless was, *You cannot make an American citizen out of a slum.*

The newcomers were also accused of congregating together in their own groups and of an unwillingness to mix with outsiders. The foreign-born flocked to the great cities and stubbornly refused to spread out as farmers over the countryside; that alone was offensive to a society which still retained an ideal of rusticity. But even the Germans in Wisconsin and the Scandinavians in Minnesota held aloofly to themselves. Everywhere, the strangers persisted in their strangeness and willfully stood apart from American life. A prominent educator sounded the warning: *Our task is to break up their settlements, to assimilate and amalgamate these people and to implant in them the Anglo-Saxon conception of righteousness, law, and order.*

It was no simple matter to meet this challenge. The older residents were quick to criticize the separateness of the immigrant but hesitant when he made a move to narrow the distance. The householders of Fifth Avenue or Beacon Street or Nob Hill could readily perceive the evils of the slums but they were not inclined to welcome as a neighbor the former denizen of the East Side or the North End or the Latin Quarter who had acquired the means to get away. Among Protestants there was much concern over the growth of Catholic, Jewish, and Orthodox religious organizations, but there was no eagerness at all to provoke a mass conversion that might crowd the earlier churches with a host of poor foreigners. When the population of its neighborhood changed, the parish was less likely to try to attract the newcomers than to close or sell its building and move to some other section.

Indeed there was a fundamental ambiguity to the thinking of those who talked about "assimilation" in these years. They had arrived at their own view that American culture was fixed, formed from its origins, by shutting out the great mass of immigrants who were not English or at least not Teutonic. Now it was expected that those excluded people would alter themselves to earn their portion in Americanism. That process could only come about by increasing the contacts between the older and the newer inhabitants, by sharing jobs, churches, residences. Yet in practice, the man who thought himself an Anglo-Saxon found proximity to the other folk just come to the United States uncomfortable and distasteful and, in his own life, sought to increase rather than to lessen the gap between his position and theirs.

There was an escape from the horns of this unpleasant dilemma. It was tempting to resolve the difficulty by arguing that the differences between Americans on the one hand and Italians or Jews or Poles on the other were so deep as to admit of no conciliation. If these other stocks were cut off by their own innate nature, by the qualities of their heredity, then the original breed was justified both in asserting the fixity of its own character and in holding off from contact with the aliens.

Those who wished to support that position drew upon a sizable fund of racialist ideas that seeped deep into the thinking of many Americans toward the end of the nineteenth century. From a variety of sources there had been accumulated a body of doctrine that proclaimed the division of humanity into distinct, biologically separate races.

In the bitter years of controversy that were the prelude to the Civil War, there were Southerners who had felt the urgency of a similar justification. The abolitionists had raised the issue of the moral rightness of slavery, had pronounced it sinful to hold a fellow man in bondage. Sensitive to the criticism but bound in practice to his property, the plantation owner was attracted by the notion that the blacks were not his fellow men. Perhaps, as George Fitzhugh told him, the Negroes were not really human at all, but another order of beings, condemned by their natures to a servile status.

During the tragic reconstruction that followed the peace the argument acquired additional gravity. The formal, legal marks of subordination were gone; it was the more important to hold the colored people in submission by other means. Furthermore the section was now under the control of a national authority, dominated by Northern men; the vanquished faced the task of convincing the victors of the essential propriety of the losing cause.

For years after the end of the war, Southerners directed a stream of discussion across the Mason-Dixon line. Through their writing and talking ran an unvarying theme—the Negro was inherently inferior, did not need or deserve, could not use or be trusted with, the rights of humans. It did not matter how many auditors or readers were persuaded; the very agitation of the question familiarized Americans with the conception of race.

Eastward from the Pacific Coast came a similar gospel, also the product of local exigencies. Out of the dislocating effects of depression in 1873 and of the petering-out of the mining economy, there had developed in California a violently anti-Chinese movement. Those who regarded the Oriental as the source of all the state's difficulties were not content with what discriminatory measures the legislature could enact. They wished no less than the total exclusion of the Chinese.

Satisfaction of that demand could come only from the Federal Congress; and to get Congress to act, it was necessary to persuade representatives from every section of the reality of the menace. The attack upon the little brown rice-eaters, congenitally filthy and immoral, had the same consequences as the Southern charges against the Negro; it made current the notion of ineradicable race differences.

A third problem brought the prestige of many influential names to the support of the idea. The War with Spain had given the United States substantial new overseas possessions, government of which posed troublesome problems. In the traditional pattern of American expansion, additional lands were treated as territories, held in a transitional stage until the time when they would become states. But their residents were citizens, endowed with all the rights of residents of the older part of the Union.

Substantial bodies of opinion opposed the extension of such treatment to the newly acquired islands. The proponents of navalism and of an aggressive imperialism, businessmen interested in the possibilities of profitable investments, and Protestant clergymen attracted by the possibility of converting large numbers of Catholics and heathen preferred to have the conquered areas colonies rather than territories, preferred to have the inhabitants subjects rather than citizens protected by the Constitution. To persuade the nation that such a departure from past policy was appropriate, the imperialists argued that the conquered peoples were incapable of self-government; their own racial inferiority justified a position of permanent subordination.

By 1900, the debates over the Negro, the Chinese, and the Filipino had familiarized Americans with the conception of permanent biological differences among humans. References to the "realities of race" by then had taken on a commonplace, almost casual quality. Early that year, for instance, a distinguished senator, well known for his progressive temperament and scholarly attainments, spoke exultantly of the opportunities in the Philippines and in China's limitless markets. *We will not renounce our part in the mission of our race, trustee of the civilization of the world. God has not been preparing the English-Speaking and Teutonic People for one thousand years for nothing. He has made us the master organizers to establish system where chaos reigns. He has marked the American People as the chosen nation to finally lead in the regeneration of the world.*

These ideas were unsystematic; as yet they were only the unconnected defenses of specific positions. But there were not lacking men to give these rude conceptions a formal structure, to work them up into a scientific creed.

Sociology toward the end of the century, in the United States, was only just emerging as a discipline of independent stature. The certitude with which its practitioners delivered their generalizations covered its fundamental immaturity of outlook. The American social scientists approached their subject through the analysis of specific disorders: criminality, intemperance, poverty, and disease. Everywhere they looked they found immigrants somehow involved in these problems. In explaining such faults in the social order, the scholar had a choice of alternatives: these were the pathological manifestations of some blemish, either in the nature of the newcomers or in the nature of the whole society. It was tempting to accept the explanation that put the blame on the outsiders.

From the writings of the Europeans Gobineau, Drumont, and Chamberlain, the sociologists had accepted the dictum that social characteristics depended upon racial differences. A succession of books now demonstrated that flaws in the biological constitution of various groups of immigrants were responsible for every evil that beset the country—for pauperism, for the low birth rate of natives, for economic depressions, for class divisions, for prostitution and homosexuality, and for the appearance of city slums.

Furthermore, the social scientists of this period were not content with academic analysis. They were convinced their conclusions must be capable of practical application and often became involved in the reform movements which, by planning, hoped to set right the evils of the times. The sociologist eager to ameliorate the lot of his fellow men by altering the conditions of their lives found the newcomers intractable, slow to change, obstacles in the road to progress. Since few among these thinkers were disposed to accept the possibility they might themselves be in error, they could only conclude the foreigners were incapable of improvement. From opposite ends of the country, two college presidents united in the judgment that the immigrants were *beaten men from beaten races, biologically incapable of rising, either now or through their descendants, above the mentality of a twelve-year-old child.*

The only apparent solution was in eugenics, the control of the composition of the population through selection of proper stocks based on proper heredity. A famous social scientist expressed it as his considered opinion that *race differences are established in the very blood. Races may change their religions, their form of government, and their languages, but underneath they may continue the PHYSICAL, MENTAL, and MORAL CAPACITIES and INCAPACITIES which determine the REAL CHARACTER of their RELIGION, GOVERNMENT, and LITERATURE.* Surface conformity would only conceal the insidious subtle characteristics that divided the native from the foreign-born.

The fear of everything alien instilled by the First World War brought to fullest flower the seeds of racist thinking. Three enormously popular books by an anthropologist, a eugenicist, and a historian revealed to hundreds of thousands of horrified Nordics how their great race had been contaminated by contact with lesser breeds, dwarfed in stature, twisted in mentality, and ruthless in the pursuit of their own self-interest.

These ideas passed commonly in the language of the time. No doubt many Americans who spoke in the bitter terms of race used the words in a figurative sense or in some other way qualified their acceptance of the harsh doctrine. After all, they still recognized the validity of the American tradition of equal and open opportunities, of the Christian tradition of the brotherhood of man. Yet, if they were sometimes troubled by the contradiction, nevertheless enough of them believed fully the racist conceptions so that five million could become members of the Ku Klux Klan in the early 1920's.

Well, a man who was sixty then had seen much that was new in his lifetime; and though he had not moved from the town of his birth, still his whole world had wandered away and left him, in a sense, a stranger in his native place. He too knew the pain of unfamiliarity, the moments of contrast between what was and what had been. Often he turned the corner of some critical event and confronted the effects of an industrial economy, of an urban society, of unsettled institutions, and of disorderly personal relationships. And, as he fought the fear of the unknown future, he too yearned for the security of belonging, for the assurance that change had not singled out him alone but had come to the whole community as a meaningful progression out of the past.

It was fretfully hard, through the instability of things, to recognize the signs of kinship. In anxious dread of isolation the people scanned each other in the vain quest for some portentous mark that would tell them who belonged together. Frustrated, some created a sense of community, drew an inner group around themselves by setting the others aside as outsiders. The excluded became the evidence of the insiders' belonging. It was not only, or not so much, because they hated the Catholic or Jew that the silent men marched in hoods, but because by distinguishing themselves from the foreigner they could at last discover their common identity; feel themselves part of a meaningful body.

The activities of the Klan were an immediate threat to the immigrants and were resisted as such. But there was also a wider import to the movement. This was evidence, at last become visible, that the newcomers were among the excluded. The judgment at which the proponents of assimilation had only hinted, about which the racist thinkers had written obliquely, the Klan brought to the open. The hurt came from the fact that the mouthings of the Kleagle were not eccentricities, but only extreme statements of beliefs long on the margin of acceptance by many Americans. To the foreign-born this was demonstration of what they already suspected, that they would remain as alienated from the New World as they had become from the Old.

Much earlier the pressure of their separateness had begun to disturb the immigrants. As soon as the conception of Americanization had acquired the connotation of conformity with existing patterns, the whole way of group life of the newcomers was questioned. Their adjustment had depended upon their ability as individuals in a free society to adapt themselves to their environment through what forms they chose. The demand by their critics that the adjustment take a predetermined course seemed to question their right, as they were, to a place in American society.

Not that these people concerned themselves with theories of nationalism, but in practice the hostility of the "natives" provoked unsettling doubts about the propriety of the most innocent actions. The peasant who had become a Polish

Falcon or a Son of Italy, in his own view, was acting as an American; this was not a step he could have taken at home. To subscribe to a newspaper was the act of a citizen of the New World, not of the Old, even if the journal was one of the thousand published by 1920 in languages other than English. When the immigrants heard their societies and their press described as un-American they could only conclude that they had somehow become involved in an existence that belonged neither in the old land nor in the new.

Yet the road of conformity was also barred to them. There were matters in which they wished to be like others, undistinguished from anyone else, but they never hit upon the means of becoming so. There was no pride in the surname, which in Europe had been little used, and many a new arrival was willing enough to make a change, suitable to the new country. But August Björkegren was not much better off when he called himself Burke, nor [was] the Blumberg who became Kelly. The Lithuanians and Slovenes who moved into the Pennsylvania mining fields often endowed themselves with nomenclature of the older settlers, of the Irish and Italians there before them. In truth, these people found it difficult to know what were the "American" forms they were expected to take on.

What they did know was that they had not succeeded, that they had not established themselves to the extent that they could expect to be treated as if they belonged where they were.

If he was an alien, and poor, and in many ways helpless, still he was human, and it rankled when his dignity as a person was disregarded. He felt an undertone of acrimony in every contact with an official. Men in uniform always found him unworthy of respect; the bullying police made capital of his fear of the law; the postmen made sport of the foreign writing on his letters; the streetcar conductors laughed at his groping requests for directions. Always he was patronized as an object of charity, or almost so.

His particular enemies were the officials charged with his special oversight. When misfortune drove him to seek assistance or when government regulations brought them to inspect his home, he encountered the social workers, made ruthless in the disregard of his sentiments by the certainty of their own benevolent intentions. Confident of their personal and social superiority and armed with the ideology of the sociologists who had trained them, the emissaries of the public and private agencies were bent on improving the immigrant to the point at which he would no longer recognize himself.

The man who had dealings with the social workers was often sullen and uncooperative; he disliked the necessity of becoming a case, of revealing his dependence to strangers. He was also suspicious, feared there would be no understanding of his own way of life or of his problems; and he was resentful, because the powerful outsiders were judging him by superficial standards of their own. The starched young gentleman from the settlement house took stock from the middle of the kitchen. Were there framed pictures on the walls? Was there a piano, books? He made a note for the report: *This family is not yet Americanized; they are still eating Italian food.*

The services are valuable, but taking them is degrading. It is a fine thing to learn the language of the country; but one must be treated as a child to do so. *We keep saying all the time, This is a desk, this is a door. I know it is a desk and a door. What for keep saying it all the time? My teacher is a very nice young lady, very young. She does not understand what I want to talk about or know about.*

The most anguished conflicts come from the refusal of the immigrants to see the logic of their poverty. In the office it seems reasonable enough: people incapable of supporting themselves would be better off with someone to take care of them. It is more efficient to institutionalize the destitute than to allow them, with the aid of charity, to mismanage their homes. But the ignorant poor insist on clinging to their families, threaten suicide at the mention of the Society's refuge, or even of the hospital. What help the woman gets, she is still not satisfied. Back comes the ungrateful letter. *I don't ask you to put me in a poorhouse where I have to cry for my children. I don't ask you to put them in a home and eat somebody else's bread. I can't live here without them. I am so sick for them. I could live at home and spare good eats for them. What good did you give me to send me to the poorhouse? You only want people to live like you but I will not listen to you no more.*

A few dedicated social workers, mostly women, learned to understand the values in the immigrants' own lives. In some states, as the second generation became prominent in politics, government agencies came to co-operate with and protect the newcomers. But these were rare exceptions. They scarcely softened the rule experience everywhere taught the foreign-born, that they were expected to do what they could not do—to live like others.

For the children it was not so difficult. They at least were natives and could learn how to conform; to them the settlement house was not always a threat, but sometimes an opportunity. Indeed they could adopt entire[ly] the assumption that national character was long since fixed, only seek for their own group a special place within it. Some justified their Americanism by discovery of a colonial past; within the educated second generation there began a tortuous quest for eighteenth-century antecedents that might give them a portion in American civilization in its narrower connotation. Others sought to gain a sense of participation by separating themselves from later or lower elements in the population; they became involved in agitation against the Orientals, the Negroes, and the newest immigrants, as if thus to draw closer to the truly native. Either course implied a rejection of their parents who had themselves once been green off the boat and could boast of no New World antecedents.

The old folk knew then they would not come to belong, not through their own experience nor through their offspring. The only adjustment they had been able to make to life in the United States had been one that involved the separateness of their group, one that increased their awareness of the differences between themselves and the rest of the society. In that adjustment they had always suffered from the consciousness they were strangers. The demand that they assimilate, that they surrender their separateness, condemned them always to be outsiders. In practice, the free structure of American life permitted them with few restraints to go their own way, but under the shadow of a consciousness that they would never belong. They had thus completed their alienation from the culture to which they had come, as from that which they had left.

Black Women Migrate to the Urban Midwest

The significance of temporal and spatial movement to a people, defined by and oppressed because of the color of their skin, among other things, defies exaggeration. Commencing with forced journeys from the interior of Africa to the waiting ships on the coast, over 11 million Africans began the trek to New World slave plantations that would, centuries later, land their descendants at the gates of the so-called "promised lands" of New York, Philadelphia, Chicago, Cleveland, Detroit, Milwaukee, and Indianapolis. The opening page of a privately published memoir of a black woman resident of Anderson, Indiana, captures well this sense of ceaseless movement on the part of her ancestors. D. J. Steans observed that "the backward trail of relatives spread from Indiana to Mississippi, crisscrossing diagonally through several adjoining states. Whether the descendants came ashore directly from Africa to South Carolina or were detoured by way of islands off the coast of Florida is unknown."

For half a millennium black people in the New World have been, or so it seems, in continuous motion, much of it forced, some of it voluntary and self-propelled. Determined to end their tenure in the "peculiar institution," or die trying, thousands of blacks fled slavery during the antebellum decades, as the legendary exploits of Harriet Tubman and Frederick Douglass testify. Large numbers of blacks challenged, with their feet, the boundaries of freedom in the aftermath of the Civil War. Many moved west to establish new black towns and settlements in Kansas and Oklahoma in the closing decades of the nineteenth century. Others attempted to return to Africa. To understand both the processes of black migration and the motivations of the individuals, men and women, who comprised this human tide is to approach a more illuminating portrait of American history and society. Central to all of this black movement was the compelling

From Joe William Trotter, Jr., *The Great Migration in Historical Perspective: New Dimensions of Race, Class, and Gender.* Copyright © 1991. Reprinted by permission of the publisher, Indiana University Press.

quest for that ever so elusive, but distinctly American property: freedom and equality of opportunity. *desire for American freedom*

Long a riveting topic, studies of the Great Migration abound. Indeed, recent histories of black urbanization, especially those focused on key midwestern cities and towns—Chicago, Cleveland, Detroit, Milwaukee, and Evansville, Indiana— pay considerable attention to the demographic transformation of the black population, a transformation which began in earnest in 1915 and continued through the World War II crisis. As enlightening and pathbreaking as most of these studies are, there remains an egregious void concerning the experiences of black women migrants. This brief essay is primarily concerned with the gender dimension of black migration to the urban Midwest. It raises, without providing a comprehensive answer, the question, how is our understanding of black migration and urbanization refined by focusing on the experiences (similar to men in many ways, yet often unique) of the thousands of southern black women who migrated to the Midwest between the two World Wars? A corollary question concerns the nature of the relations between those black women who migrated out of the lower Mississippi Valley states and those who stayed put. It is also important to shed light on the phenomenon of intraregional migration for there was considerable movement of women between the midwestern cities and towns.

By 1920 almost 40 percent of Afro-Americans residing in the North were concentrated in eight cities, five of them in the Midwest: Chicago, Detroit, Cleveland, Cincinnati, and Columbus, Ohio. The three eastern cities with high percentages of black citizens were New York, Philadelphia, and Pittsburgh. These eight cities contained only 20 percent of the total northern population. Two peaks characterized the first phase of the Great Black Migration: 1916–1919 and 1924–1925. These dates correspond to the passage of more stringent anti-immigration laws, and the years in which the majority of the approximately 500,000 southern blacks relocated northward.

Clearly the diverse economic opportunities in the midwestern cities served as the major pull factor in the dramatic black percentage increases registered between 1910 and 1920. Detroit's black population rose an astounding 611.3 percent. More precisely put, Detroit's Afro-Americans attracted by the jobs available at the Ford, Dodge, Chrysler, Chevrolet, and Packard automobile plants, increased from 5,741 in 1910 to 120,066 in 1930. Home of the northern terminus of the Illinois Central Railroad, the *Chicago Defender,* meat packing, and mail order enterprises, Chicago was not outdone. The Windy City's black population, which in 1910 numbered 44,103, jumped to 233,903 in 1930. . . .

Information derived from statistical and demographic data on the black midwestern migration and urbanization must be combined with the knowledge drawn from the small, but growing, numbers of oral histories, autobiographies, and biographies of twentieth century migrating women. Court records of legal encounters, church histories, black women's club minutes, scrapbooks, photographs, diaries, and histories of institutions ranging from old folks' homes, orphanages, businesses, and Phillis Wheatley Homes to local YWCAs yield considerable information on the lives of black women migrants to and within the middle western region. Actually these sources, properly "squeezed and teased" promise to light up that inner world so long shrouded behind a veil of neglect, silence, and stereotype, and will quite likely force a rethinking and rewriting of all of black urban history.

A perusal of the major studies of black urbanization reveals considerable scholarly consensus on several gender-related themes. Scholars generally acknowledge that gender did make a difference in terms of the reasons expressed for quitting the South, and affected the means by which men and women arrived at their northern destinations. Likewise, scholars concur that men and women encountered radically divergent socioeconomic and political opportunities in midwestern cities. Gender and race stereotyping in jobs proved quite beyond their control and was intransigent in the face of protest. Scholars agree that black women faced greater economic discrimination and had fewer employment opportunities than black men. Their work was the most undesirable and least remunerative of all northern migrants. Considering that their economic condition or status scarcely improved or changed, for many women migrants were doomed to work in the same kinds of domestic service jobs they had held in the South, one wonders why they bothered to move in the first place. Of course there were significant differences. A maid earning $7 a week in Cleveland perceived herself to be much better off than a counterpart receiving $2.50 a week in Mobile, Alabama. A factory worker, though the work was dirty and low status, could and did imagine herself better off than domestic servants who endured the unrelenting scrutiny, interference, and complaints of household mistresses.

It is clear that more attention needs to be directed toward the noneconomic motives propelling black female migration. Many black women quit the South out of a desire to achieve personal autonomy and to escape from sexual exploitation both within and outside of their families and from sexual abuse at the hands of southern white as well as black men. The combined influence of domestic violence and economic oppression is key to understanding the hidden motivation informing major social protest and migratory movements in Afro-American history.

That black women were very much concerned with negative images of their sexuality is graphically and most forcefully echoed in numerous speeches of the early leaders of the national organization of black women's clubs. Rosetta Sprague, the daughter of Frederick Douglass, declared in an address to the Federation of Afro-American Women in 1896:

We are weary of the false impressions sent broadcast over the land about the colored woman's inferiority, her lack of noble womanhood. We wish to make it clear in the minds of your fellow country men and women that there are no essential elements of character that they deem worthy of cultivating that we do not desire to emulate that the sterling qualities of purity, virtue, benevolence and charity are no more dormant in the breast of the black woman than in the white woman.

Sociologist Lynda F. Dickson cautions that "recognition of the major problem—the need to elevate the image of black womanhood—may or may not have led to a large scale club movement both nationally and locally." It cannot be denied, however, that "the most important function of the club affiliation was to provide a support system that could continually reinforce the belief that the task at hand—uplifting the race, and improving the image of black womanhood was possible." A study of the history of the early twentieth century black women's club movement is essential to the understanding of black women's migration to the middle western towns and cities and the critical roles they played in creating and sustaining new black social, religious, political, and economic institutions. These clubs were as important as the National Urban League and the NAACP in transforming black peasants into the urban proletariat.

This focus on the sexual and the personal impetus for black women's migration neither dismisses nor diminishes the importance of economic motives, a discussion of which I will return to later. Rather, I am persuaded by historian Lawrence Levine's reservations. He cautions, "As indisputably important as the economic motive was, it is possible to overstress it so that the black migration is converted into an inexorable force and Negroes are seen once again not as actors capable of affecting at least some part of their destinies, but primarily as beings who are acted upon—southern leaves blown North by the winds of destitution." It is reasonable to assume that many were indeed "southern leaves blown North," and that others were more likely self-propelled actors seeking respect, space in which to live, and a means to earn an adequate living.

Black men and women migrated into the Midwest in distinctive patterns. Single men, for example, usually worked their way North, leaving farms for southern cities, doing odd jobs, and sometimes staying in one location for a few years before proceeding to the next stop. This pattern has been dubbed "secondary migration." Single black women, on the other hand, as a rule, traveled the entire distance in one trip. They usually had a specific relative—or fictive kin—waiting for them at their destination, someone who may have advanced them the fare and who assisted with temporary lodging and advice on securing a job. Amanda Jones-Watson, a fifty-year-old resident of Grand Rapids, Michigan, and three-time President of the still functioning Grand Rapids Study Club, founded in 1904, migrated from Tennessee in 1936 in her 30s. She recalls asking her uncle, who had just moved to Grand Rapids, to send her a ticket. She exclaimed, "I cried when it came. I was kidding. My sister said, 'Amanda, what are you worried about? You can always come back if you don't like it.' " Jones-Watson was fortunate. Her uncle was headwaiter at the Pantlind Hotel. She continued, "I got a job as a maid and was written up in a local furniture magazine for making the best bed at the Pantlind."

For Sara Brooks, a domestic, the idea that she should leave Alabama and relocate in Cleveland in 1940 originated with her brother. He implored his sister, "Why don't you come up here? You could make more here." Brooks demurred, "Well, I hadn't heard anything about the North because I never known nobody to come no further than Birmingham, Alabama, and that was my sister-in-law June, my husband's sister." A single mother of three sons and a daughter, Brooks eventually yielded to her brother's entreaties, leaving her sons with her aging parents. She recalled, "But my brother wanted me to come up here to Cleveland with him, so I started to try to save up what little money I had. . . . But I saved what I could, and when my sister-in-law came down for me, I had only eighteen dollars to my name, and that was maybe a few dollars over enough to come up here. If I'm not mistaken it was about a dollar and fifteen cent over."

The influence and pressure of family members played a substantial role in convincing many ambivalent young women to migrate. A not so young sixty-eight year old Melinda left her home in Depression-ridden rural Alabama to assist her granddaughter in childrearing in Anderson, Indiana. Even when expressing her plans to return home once her granddaughter was up and about, somehow Melinda knew that the visit would be permanent. Grounded largely in family folklore, D. J. Steans declared that Melinda had labored hard at sharecropping, besides taking in washing and ironing. Even after her sixty-second birthday, she was still going strong. Many weeks she earned less than 50¢, but she was saving pennies a day for her one desire to travel north to visit her great-grandchildren.

Some women simply seized the opportunity to accompany friends traveling north. Fired from her nursing job at Hampton Institute, in Hampton, Virginia, Jane Edna Hunter packed her bags determined to head for Florida. She never made it. According to Hunter, "en route, I stopped at Richmond, Virginia, to visit with Mr. and Mrs. William Coleman, friends of Uncle Parris. They were at church when I arrived; so I sat on the doorstep to await their return. After these good friends had greeted me, Mrs. Coleman said, 'Our bags are packed to go to Cleveland, Jane. We are going to take you with us.' " Jane needed little persuasion. She exclaimed, "I was swept off my feet by the cheerful determination of the Colemans. My trunk, not yet removed from the station, was rechecked to Cleveland." Hunter arrived in the city on May 10, 1905 with $1.75 in her pockets, slightly more than Sara Brooks brought with her thirty-five years later.

The different migratory patterns of black males and females reflect gender conventions in the larger society. A woman traveling alone was surely at greater risk than a man. After all, a man could and did, with less approbation and threat of bodily harm, spend nights outdoors. More importantly, men were better suited to defend themselves against attackers. However, given the low esteem in which the general society held black women, even the courts and law officials would have ridiculed and dismissed assault complaints from a black female traveling alone, regardless of her social status. Yes, it was wise to make the trip all at once, and better still to have company.

Although greater emphasis has been placed on men who left families behind, black women, many of whom were divorced, separated, or widowed, too left loved ones, usually children, in the South when they migrated. Like married men, unattached or single black mothers sent for their families after periods of time ranging from a month to even several years. Actually, I suspect that a great number of women who migrated into the Midwest probably left children, the products of early marriages or romantic teenage liaisons, with parents, friends, and other relatives in the South. It would be exceedingly difficult, if not impossible to develop any statistical information on this phenomenon. Nevertheless, the oral history of Elizabeth Burch of Fort Wayne, Indiana, offers poignant testimony of a child left behind:

I was born [December 20, 1926 in Chester, Georgia] out of wedlock to Arlena Burch and John Halt. My mother went north and that's where they—all of it began in a little town called Albion, Michigan and she went back south to have me. . . . Aunt Clyde that's my mother's sister, she was the baby and that was a little town called Albion, Michigan. That's where I was conceived at. That's where my mother went when she left Georgia. My mother decided well she go back up north. She married just to get away from home to go back north and this guy was working as a sharecropper and he had made enough money that year that he was willing to marry my mother and take her back up north. . . . So they left me with Miss Burch—Miss Mattie Elizabeth Burch, namesake which was my grandmother and that's where I grew up at and years passed and years went through I was just on the farm with my grandparents.

The difficulty of putting aside enough money to send for their children placed a tremendous strain on many a domestic salary. It took Sara Brooks almost fifteen years to reconstitute her family, to retrieve her three sons left behind in Orchard, Alabama. With obvious pride in her accomplishment, Brooks explained, "The first one to come was Jerome. . . . Then Miles had to come because my father didn't wanna keep him down there no more because he wouldn't mind him. . . . Then Benjamin was the last to come." Brooks summed up her success, "So I come up to Cleveland with Vivian, (her daughter) and after I came up, the rest of my kids came up here. I was glad—I was VERY glad because I had wanted em with me all the time, but I just wasn't able to support em, and then I didn't have no place for them, either, when I left and come to Cleveland cause I came here to my brother."

Arguably, inasmuch as so many midwestern black women were absentee mothers—that is, their children remained in the South—their actual acculturation into an urban life style became a long, drawn out, and often incomplete, process. On the other hand, as historians Peter Gottlieb and Jacqueline Jones persuasively maintain, black women served as critical links in the "migration chain." They proved most instrumental in convincing family members and friends to move north. This concept of women as "links in a migration chain" begs elaboration. I suspect that it is precisely because women left children behind in the care of parents and other relatives that they contributed so much to the endurance and tenacity of the migration chain. Their attachment to the South was more than sentimental or cultural. They had left part of themselves behind.

Parental obligations encouraged many black women migrants to return south for periodic visits. Burch recalled that "My mother would come maybe once a year—maybe Christmas to visit" her in Georgia from Ft. Wayne. Still other midwestern women returned perhaps to participate in community celebrations, family reunions, and to attend religious revivals. Of course, such periodic excursions southward also permitted display of new clothes and other accoutrements of success. Before she made the journey to Cleveland, Sara Brooks admitted delight in her sister-in-law's return visits. "I noticed she had some nice-lookin little clothes when she come back to Orchard to visit. She had little nice dresses and brassieres and things, which I didn't have. . . . I didn't even have a brassiere, and she'd lend me hers and I'd wear it to church." Indeed, Brooks's recollections raise a complex question—To what extent and how does the woman's relation to the South change over the course of the migrant's life? When do migrants move from being southerners in the North to southern northerners?

Unable, or unwilling, to sever ties to or abandon irrevocably the South, black women's assimilation to urban life remained fragmented and incomplete. It was the very incompleteness of the assimilation, however, which facilitated the southernization of the Midwest. Vestiges of southern black culture were transplanted and continuously renewed and reinforced by these women in motion. The resiliency of this cultural transference is reflected in food preferences and preparation styles, reliance on folk remedies and superstitions, religious practices, speech patterns, games, family structures and social networks, and music, most notably, the blues. The southernization of urban midwestern culture was but one likely consequence of the migration chain women forged. In short, although unattached black women migrants may have traveled the initial distance to Chicago, Cleveland, Detroit, or Cincinnati, in one trip, as long as offspring, relatives, and friends remained in the south, psychological and emotional relocation was much more convoluted and, perhaps, more complicated than heretofore assumed.

Discussions of the marital status and family obligations—specifically whether the women migrants had children remaining in the South—are indirectly, perhaps, related to a more controversial topic of current interest to historians of nineteenth century black migration and urbanization. In his study of violence and crime in post–Civil War Philadelphia, Roger Lane suggests that there was a marked decline in black birthrates in the city near the turn of the century. He attributes the decline in part to the rising incidence of syphilis which left many black women infertile. He notes that, "In Philadelphia in 1890 the black-white ratio was .815 to 1,000, meaning that black women had nearly 20 percent fewer children than whites, a figure that in 1900 dropped to .716 to 1,000, or nearly 30 percent fewer." Lane concludes, "All told, perhaps a quarter of Philadelphia's black women who reached the end of their childbearing years had at some time had exposure to the diseases and habits associated with prostitution. This figure would account almost precisely for the difference between black and white fertility in the city."

Without reliance on the kinds of statistical data Lane employs in his analysis, the oral histories and autobiographies of midwestern black women migrants suggest an alternate explanation, though often overlooked, in discussions of black birth decline. Sara Brooks, mother of five children, was still in her childbearing years when she embraced celibacy. She declared, "See, after Vivian was born I didn't have no boyfriend or nothin, and I went to Mobile, I didn't still have no boyfriend in a long time. Vivian was nine years old when Eric come. . . . But after Eric came along, I didn't have no boyfriend. I didn't want one because what I wanted, I worked for it, and that was that home." Brooks had realized her dream in 1957 with the purchase of her home and the reuniting of all of her children under one roof.

For women, ignorant of effective birth control or unable to afford the cost of raising additional children alone, sexual abstinence was a rational choice. It should be pointed out that often deeply held religious convictions, disillusionment with black men, a history of unhappy and abusive marriages, adherence to Victorian ideals of morality, a desire to refute prevalent sexual stereotypes and negative images of black women as a whole, or even an earlier unplanned pregnancy may have informed many a decision to practice sexual abstinence among adult black women. Only latent acceptance of the myths concerning the alleged unbridled passions and animalistic sexuality of black women prevent serious consideration of the reality and extent of self-determined celibacy. Meanwhile, until we know more about the internal lives of black women, the suggestion of abstinence or celibacy as a factor limiting births should not be dismissed.

The fact that women who migrated north produced fewer children than their southern counterparts warrants further investigation. It is not enough to argue that prostitution, venereal disease, and infanticide account for declining black births in urban settings. Many other factors, in addition to abstinence, offer fruitful and suggestive lines of inquiry. Some scholars have asserted that children in urban as opposed to rural settings had rather insignificant economic roles and therefore their labor was not as important to family survival.

As black women became more economically sufficient, better educated, and more involved in self-improvement efforts, including participation in the flourishing black women's club movement, they would have had more access to birth control information. As the institutional infrastructure of black women's clubs, sororities, church groups, and charity organizations took hold within black communities, they gave rise to those values and attitudes traditionally associated with the middling classes. To black middle-class aspirants, the social stigma of having many children would have, perhaps, inhibited reproduction. Furthermore, over time, the gradually evolving demographic imbalance in the sex ratio meant that increasing numbers of black women in urban midwestern communities would never marry. The point is simply this, that not dating, marrying, or having children may very well have been a decision—a deliberate choice, for whatever reason—that black women made. On August 23, 1921, Sarah D. Tyree wrote tellingly about her own decision not to date. Tyree had a certificate from the Illinois College of Chiropracty, but was, at the time, taking care of aged parents and her sister's children in Indianapolis. She confided to her sister in Muskegon, Michigan:

I have learned to stay at home lots. I firmly believe in a womanly independence. Believe that a woman should be allowed to go and come where and when she pleases alone if she wants to, and so long as she knows who is right, she should not have to worry about what others think. It is not every woman who can turn for herself as I can, and the majority of women who have learned early to depend upon their male factors do not believe that their sister-woman can get on alone. So she becomes dangerously suspicious, and damagingly tongue-wagging. I have become conscious of the fact that because I am not married, I am watched with much interest. So I try to avoid the appearance of evil, for the sake of the weaker fellow. I do not therefore go out unaccompanied at night. There are some young men I would like to go out with occasionally if it could be understood that it was for the occasion and not for life that we go. I don't care to be bothered at any

time with a fellow who has been so cheap and all to himself for 5 or 6 years
I have all patients [sic] to wait for the proper one to play for my hand.

Moreover, social scientists Joseph A. McFalls, Jr., and George S. Masnick persuasively argue that blacks were much more involved in birth control than previously assumed. They contend, "The three propositions usually advanced to support the view that birth control had little, if any, effect on black fertility from 1880 to 1940—that blacks used 'ineffective' methods, that blacks did not practice birth control 'effectively,' and that blacks used birth control too late in their reproductive careers to have had much of an effect on their fertility—simply have no empirical or even a priori foundation. There is no reason now to believe that birth control had little impact on black fertility during this period." Not to be overlooked are the often chronic health problems overworked, undernourished, and inadequately-housed poor black women undoubtedly experienced, especially during the Depression. In discussing the morbidity and mortality rates of blacks in Chicago, Tuttle observes that,

Chicago's medical authorities boasted of the city's low death rate, pointing to statistics which indicated that it was the lowest of any city in the world with a population of over one million. Their statistics told another story as well, however, and it was that Chicago's blacks had a death rate which was twice that of whites. The stillbirth rate was also twice as high; and the death rate from tuberculosis and syphilis was six times as high; and from pneumonia and nephritis it was well over three times as high. . . . The death rate for the entire city was indeed commendable, but the statistics indicated that the death rate for Chicago's blacks was comparable to that of Bombay, India.

One more observation about the declining birth rate among northern black women should be made. Here it is important to note the dichotomy between black women who worked in middle- and working-class occupations. Middle-class working women, regardless of color, had fewer children than those employed in blue collar jobs. The professional and semi-professional occupations most accessible to black women during the years between the world wars included teaching, nursing, and social work, on the one hand, and hairdressing or dressmaking, on the other. In some of the smaller midwestern communities and towns, married women teachers, race notwithstanding, lost their jobs, especially if the marriage became public knowledge or the wife pregnant. At least one black woman school teacher in Lafayette, Indiana, confided that she never married, though she had been asked, because in the 1930s and 1940s to have done so would have cost her the position. The pressure on the small cadre of professional black women not to have children was considerable. The more educated they were, the greater the sense of being responsible, somehow, for the advance of the race and of black womanhood. They held these expectations of themselves and found them reinforced by the demands of the black community and its institutions. Under conditions and pressures such as these, it would be erroneous to argue that this is the same thing as voluntary celibacy. Nevertheless, the autonomy, so hard earned and enjoyed to varying degrees by both professional women and personal service workers, offered meaningful alternatives to the uncertainties of marriage and the demands of childrearing. The very economic diversity— whether real or imagined—that had attracted black women to the urban Mid- west, also held the promise of freedom to fashion socially useful and independent lives beyond family boundaries.

None of this is to be taken as a categorical denial of the existence of rampant prostitution and other criminal activity in urban midwestern ghettos. Too many autobiographies and other testimony document the place and the economic func- tions of prostitution in urban society to be denied. Indeed, Jane Edna Hunter's major contribution to improving black women's lives in Cleveland—the estab- lishment of the Phillis Wheatley boarding homes—stemmed from her commit- ment to provide training, refuge, and employment for young migrating women who were frequently enticed or tricked into prostitution as a means of survival. She remarked on her own awakening, "the few months on Central Avenue made me sharply aware of the great temptations that beset a young woman in a large city. At home on the plantation, I knew that some girls had been seduced. The families had felt the disgrace keenly—the fallen ones had been wept and prayed over. . . . Until my arrival in Cleveland I was ignorant of the wholesale organized traffic in black flesh."

Young, naive country girls were not the only ones vulnerable to the lure of seduction and prostitution. Middle-aged black women also engaged in sex for pay, but for them it was a rational economic decision. Sara Brooks did not dis- guise her contempt for women who bartered their bodies. She declared, while commenting on her own struggle to pay the mortgage on her house, "Some women woulda had a man to come and live in the house and had an outside boyfriend too, in order to get the house paid for and the bills." She scornfully added, "They meet a man and if he promises em four or five dollars to go to bed, they's grab it. That's called sellin your own body, and I wasn't raised like that."

Prostitution was not the only danger awaiting single migrating black women. Police in many midwestern towns seemed quick to investigate not only black men but women who appeared suspicious. Historian James E. DeVries records several encounters between black women and the police in Monroe, Michigan. "In January 1903, Gertie Hall was arrested after acting in a very ner- vous manner on the interurban trip from Toledo. An investigation by Monroe police revealed that Hall was wanted for larceny in Toledo, and she was soon es- corted to that city." In another incident four years later involving fifteen-year-old Ahora Ward, also from Toledo, DeVries notes that she was "picked up and taken to jail. . . . As it turned out, she had been whipped by her mother and was run- ning away from home when taken into custody."

There exists a scholarly consensus about the origins and the destinations of the overwhelming majority of black migrants throughout the period between 1915 and 1945. Before turning to a discussion of the economic impetus, or the pull factors, for black women's migrations, I would like to interject another rarely explored "push" factor, that is, the desire for freedom from sexual ex- ploitation, especially rape by white men, and to escape from domestic abuse within their own families. A full exploration of this theme requires the use of a plethora of sources including oral testimonials, autobiographies, biographies, novels, and court records. The letters, diaries, and oral histories collected by the Black Women in the Middle West Project and deposited in the Indiana Historical Society contain descriptions of domestic violence which fed the intraregional movement of black women who had migrated from southern states. Elizabeth Burch explained why she left Ft. Wayne for Detroit, "And my mother—and my stepfather—would have problems. He would hit my mother and so, you know, beat upon my mother . . . but he never did beat up on me. My mother would say—'Well you just don't put your hands on her. You better not, hear.' " To avoid these scenes Burch moved to Detroit but later returned to Ft. Wayne.

Similarly Jane Pauline Fowlkes, sister of the above-mentioned Sarah Tyree, was granted a divorce from her husband, Jess Clay Fowlkes in Muskegon, Michigan, in 1923 and returned to her family and sister in Indianapolis. Granted the degree because her husband was found "guilty of several acts of extreme cruelty," Fowlkes retained custody of all three children.

While Sara Brooks's experiences are hardly representative, they are nevertheless suggestive of the internal and personal reasons black women may have had for leaving the South. Brooks vividly described the events that led her to leave her husband for the third and final time. When she ran away from home the last time, she didn't stop running until she reached Cleveland almost a decade later. "When he hit me," she said, "I jumped outa the bed, and when I jumped outa the bed, I just ran. . . . I didn't have a gown to put on—I had on a slip and had on a short-sleeved sweater. I left the kids right there with him and I went all the way to his father's house that night, barefeeted, with that on, on the twenty-fifth day of December. That was in the dark. It was two miles or more and it was rainin. . . . I walked. And I didn't go back."

For whatever reasons Sara Brooks, Melinda, Jane Edna Hunter, and others wound up in the various midwestern cities, they expected to work and to work hard, for work was part of the definition of what it meant to be a black woman in America, regardless of region. The abundant economic opportunities, or "pull factors," especially in automobile plants and, during the War, in the defense industries, had been powerful inducements for black male migrants. The dislocation of blacks in southern agriculture, the ravages of the boll weevil, floods, and the seasonal and marginal nature of the work relegated to them in the South were powerful "push" factors. Taken together these factors help us to understand why 5 percent of the total southern black population left the South between 1916 and 1921.

Black women shared with black men a desire for economic improvement and security. They too were attracted to midwestern cities, specifically those with a greater diversity of women's jobs. The female occupational structure of Chicago, for example, held the promise of more opportunity for black women than did the much more heavy industry dependent Pittsburgh. Black men, however, were not as constrained. To be sure, the majority of neither group expected to secure white collar jobs or managerial positions. None were so naive as to believe that genuine equality of opportunity actually existed in the North or the Midwest, but occasionally black women migrants did anticipate that more awaited them in Cleveland and Chicago than an apron and domestic servitude in the kitchens of white families, segregated hotels, and restaurants. Most were disappointed. Author Mary Helen Washington recalled the disappointment and frustration experienced by her female relatives when they migrated to Cleveland:

In the 1920s my mother and five aunts migrated to Cleveland, Ohio from Indianapolis and, in spite of their many talents, they found every door except the kitchen door closed to them. My youngest aunt was trained as a bookkeeper and was so good at her work that her white employer at Guardian Savings of Indianapolis allowed her to work at the branch in a black area. The Cleveland Trust Company was not so liberal, however, so in Cleveland she went to work in what is known in the black community as "private family."

Scholars concur that, while black women secured employment in low level jobs in light industry, especially during the World War I years when overseas immigration came to a standstill, this window of opportunity quickly closed with the end of hostilities. Florette Henri calculates that "immigration dropped from 1,218,480 in 1914, to 326,700 in 1915, to under 300,000 in 1916 and 1917, and finally to 110,618 in 1918." This drop and the draft made it possible for black women to squeeze into "occupations not heretofore considered within the range of their possible activities," concluded a Department of Labor survey in 1918. Thus the percentage of black domestics declined between 1910 and 1920, from 78.4 percent to 63.8 percent in Chicago, and from 81.1 percent to 77.8 percent in Cleveland.

The study of migrations from the perspective of black women permits a close examination of the intersection of gender, class, and race dynamics in the development of a stratified work force in midwestern cities. During the war years a greater number of black women migrants found work in midwestern hotels as cooks, waitresses, and maids, as ironers in the new steam laundries, as labelers and stampers in Sears Roebuck and Montgomery Wards mail order houses, as common laborers in garment and lampshade factories, and in food processing and meat packing plants. But even in these places, the limited gains were short lived and easily erased. As soon as the War ended and business leveled off, for example, both Sears and Wards immediately fired all the black women. In 1900 black women constituted 4 percent of the labor force in commercial laundries; by 1920 this figure had climbed to 6 percent. As late as 1930 a little over 3,000 black women, or 15 percent of the black female labor force in Chicago were unskilled and semi-skilled factory operatives. Thus over 80 percent of all employed black women continued to work as personal servants and domestics. Historian Allan H. Spear points out that "negro women were particularly limited in their search for desirable positions. Clerical work was practically closed to them and only a few could qualify as school teachers. Negro domestics often received less than white women for the same work and they could rarely rise to the position of head servant in large households."

In Milwaukee, especially during the Depression decades, black women were, as historian Joe Trotter observes, "basically excluded from this narrow industrial footing; 60.4 percent of their numbers labored in domestic service as compared to only 18.6 percent of all females." To be sure, this was down from the 73.0 percent of black women who had worked as domestics in Milwaukee in 1900. A decline of 13 percent over a forty-year period—regardless of from what angle it is viewed—is hardly cause for celebration.

Many reasons account for the limited economic gains of black women as compared to black men in midwestern industries. One of the major barriers impeding a better economic showing was the hostility and racism of white women. The ceiling on black women's job opportunities was secured tight by the opposition of white women. White females objected to sharing the settings, including hospitals, schools, department stores, and offices. Now 90, Sarah Glover migrated with her family to Grand Rapids, Michigan, from Alabama in 1922, where they had jobs working in the coal mines. Although she would in later years become the first practical nurse in the city, during her first seventeen years as a maid at Blodgett Hospital, she scrubbed the floors. After completing her housekeeping chores she'd voluntarily help the nurses. She reminisced, "The nurses used to call me 'Miss Sunshine' because I would cheer up the patients. I'd come over and say you look good today or crack a joke. That used to get most of them smiling again." In spite of her good work record, excellent human relations skills, and eagerness, hospital officials deemed it a violation of racial rules and thus rejected Glover's appeal to become a nurse's aid.

Historians Susan M. Hartmann and Karen Tucker Anderson convincingly demonstrate that while white women enjoyed expanded employment opportunities, black women continued to be the last hired and first fired throughout the Depression and World War II years. Employers seeking to avert threatened walkouts, slow-downs, and violence caved into white women's objections to working beside or, most particularly, sharing restroom and toilet facilities with black women. To be sure, many employers, as was the case with the Blodgett Hospital in Grand Rapids, harbored the same racist assumptions and beliefs in black inferiority, but camouflaged them behind white women's objections.

The black media was not easily fooled by racist subterfuges and remained keenly attuned to all excuses that rationalized the denial of job opportunities to black women. In its official organ, *Opportunity,* National Urban League officials catalogued the thinly-veiled justifications white employers offered when discriminating against women:

"There must be some mistake"; "No applications have heretofore been made by colored"; "You are smart for taking the courses, but we do not employ coloreds"; "We have not yet installed separate but equal toilet facilities"; "A sufficient number of colored women have not been trained to start a separate shift"; "The training center from which you come does not satisfy plant requirements"; "Your qualifications are too high for the kind of job offered"; "We cannot put a Negro in our front office"; "We will write you . . . but my wife needs a maid"; "We have our percentage of Negroes."

Trotter did, however, discover instances when the interests of white women occasionally promoted industrial opportunities for black women. "The white women of the United Steelworkers of America Local 1527, at the Chain Belt Company, resisted the firm's proposal for a ten-hour day and a six-day week by encouraging the employment of black women." In a classic understatement, historian William Harris hesitantly asserts, "Black women apparently experienced more discrimination than black men in breaking into nonservice jobs."

In their study of labor unions in Detroit, August Meier and Elliott Rudwick reveal that more than white women's hostility accounts for the employment discrimination and the job segregation black women encountered in the automobile industries. Throughout the World War II era, the Ford Motor Company hired only a token number of black women. According to Meier and Rudwick, "Black civic leaders and trade unionists fought a sustained and energetic battle to open Detroit war production to black women, but because government manpower officials gave discrimination against Negro females low priority, the gains were negligible when compared with those achieved by the city's black male workers." By March 1943, for example, the Willow Run Ford Plant employed 25,000 women, but less than 200 were black. Apparently, Ford was not alone or atypical in these anti-black women hiring practices. Both Packard and Hudson employed a mere half dozen each at this time. Most of those employed in the plants, as was to be expected, worked in various service capacities—matrons, janitors, and stock handlers. Meier and Rudwick point out that "As late as the summer of 1943 a government report termed the pool of 25,000 available black women the city's 'largest neglected source of labor.' "

Much more work needs to be done on the migration of black women. As difficult as the task may prove, historians must begin to probe deep into the internal world and lives of these women, who not only were Detroit's largest neglected source of labor, but also remain the largest neglected, and still most obscure, component of Afro-American history. It is not enough to study black women simply because they are neglected and historically invisible. Rather it is incumbent that we examine and interpret their experiences, for what this new information yields may very well bring us closer to a comprehensive and more accurate understanding of all of American history from colonial times to the present.

Richard C. Wade

Violence in the Cities

Violence is no stranger to American cities. Almost from the very beginning, cities have been the scenes of sporadic violence, of rioting and disorders, and occasionally virtual rebellion against established authority. Many of these events resulted in only modest property damage and a handful of arrests. Others were larger in scale with deaths running into the scores and damages into the millions. This paper attempts to survey briefly some of these outbreaks and to analyze their origins and consequences. We confine ourselves, however, to the larger ones, and omit any discussion of individual acts of violence or the general level of crime. In addition, to keep these remarks relevant to the present crisis, we have confined our analysis to disorders in urban areas.

There has been, in fact, a good deal more violence and disorder in the American tradition than even historians have been willing to recognize. The violence on the frontier is, of course, well known, and in writing, movies, and television it has been a persistent theme in our culture. Indeed, one of America's favorite novelists, James Fenimore Cooper, transformed the slaughter and mayhem of Indians into heroic, almost patriotic, action. As the literary historian David Brion Davis has observed: "Critics who interpret violence in contemporary literature as a symptom of a sick society may be reassured to know that American writers have always been preoccupied with murder, rape, and deadly combat." To be sure, violence is not "as American as cherry pie," but it is no newcomer to the national scene.

Though serious scholarship on this dimension of the American past is shamefully thin, it is already quite clear that disorder and violence in our cities were not simply occasional aberrations, but rather a significant part of urban development and growth. From the Stamp Act riots of the pre-revolutionary age, to the assaults on immigrants and Catholics in the decades before the Civil War, to the grim confrontation of labor and management at the end of the nineteenth century and its sporadic reappearance after World War I and during the depression, through the long series of racial conflicts for two centuries, American cities have known the physical clash of groups, widescale breakdown of established authority, and bloody disorder.

Nor is it hard to see why this early history had more than its share of chaos. American cities in the eighteenth and nineteenth centuries were very young. They had not yet the time to develop a system of orderly government; there was no tradition of habitual consent to local authority; there was no established police system. In addition, these cities grew at a spectacular rate. In the twentieth century, we have used the term "exploding metropolis" to convey the rapid pace of urbanization. It is not often remembered that the first "urban explosion" took place more than a century ago. Indeed, between 1820 and 1860 cities grew proportionately faster than they had before or ever would again. The very speed of this urban development was unsettling and made the maintenance of internal tranquillity more difficult.

The problem was further compounded by the fact that nearly every American city was born of commerce. This meant that there was always a large transient population—seamen engaged in overseas trade, rivermen plying the inland waters, teamsters and wagonmen using the overland routes, and a constant stream of merchants and salesmen seeking customers. At any moment the number of newcomers was large and their attachments to the community slight. Hence when they hit town, there was always some liveliness. After exhausting the cities' museums and libraries, sailors and teamsters would find other things to do. In the eighteenth and nineteenth century, transients comprised a significant portion of those who engaged in rioting and civil disorders.

In addition to being young, rapidly growing, and basically commercial, American cities also had very loose social structures. Unlike the Old World, they had no traditional ruling group, class lines were constantly shifting, and new blood was persistently pumped into these urban societies. One could say that up until the last part of the nineteenth century, mercantile leaders dominated municipal government; but even that commercial leadership changed continually. Later, immigrant groups shared high offices in municipal affairs, thus underlining the shifting nature of the social structure of most cities. Within this looseness there was always a great deal of mobility, with people rising and falling in status not only from generation to generation but within a single lifetime.

This fluid social system contrasted sharply with other, older societies, yet it contained a high incidence of disorder. For it depended on the constant acceptance of new people and new groups to places of influence and importance, and their incorporation into the system on a basis of equality with others. This acceptance was only grudgingly conceded, and often only after some abrasive episodes. The American social structure thus had a large capacity to absorb revolutionary tensions and avoid convulsive upheavals. But it also bred minor social skirmishes which were not always orderly. It is significant that in the pre-Civil War South, where slavery created a more traditional social structure, there was less rioting and civil disorder than in the North (though one ought not underestimate the individual violence against the slave built into institutional bondage).

The American social structure was also unique because it was composed not only of conventional classes, but also of different ethnic, religious, and racial groups. They had at once an internal cohesion that came from a common background and a shared American experience and also a sense of sharp differences with other groups, especially with the country's older stock. These groups, the Negro excepted, were initially both part of the system and yet outside of it. The resultant friction, with the newcomers pressing for acceptance and older groups striving for continued supremacy, was a fruitful source of disorder and often violence. Since it was in the city that these groups were thrown together, became aware of their differences, and struggled for survival and advancement, it would be on the streets rather than on the countryside that the social guerrilla warfare would take place.

If the internal controls in the American social structure were loose, the external controls were weak. The cities inherited no system of police control adequate to the numbers or to the rapid increase of the urban centers. The modern police force is the creation of the twentieth century; the establishment of a genuinely professional system is historically a very recent thing. Throughout the eighteenth and nineteenth century, the force was small, untrained, poorly paid, and part of the political system. In case of any sizable disorder, it was hopelessly inadequate; and rioters sometimes routed the constabulary in the first confrontation. Josiah Quincy, for example, in Boston in the 1820's had to organize and arm the teamsters to reestablish the authority of the city in the streets. Many prudent officials simply kept out of the way until the worst was over. In New York's draft riots, to use another instance, the mayor wandered down to see what the disturbance was all about and nearly got trampled in the melee.

Moreover, since some of the rioting was political, the partisanship of the police led official force to be applied against one group, or protection to be withheld from another. And with every turnover in the mayor's office, a substantial and often a complete change occurred in the police. In Atlanta, for instance, even where there was only one party, each faction had its own men in blue ready to take over with the changes in political fortunes. In some places where the state played a role in local police appointments, the mayor might even be deprived of any control at all for the peace of the city. In New York in the 1850's there was an awkward moment when there were two police forces—the Municipals and the Metropolitans—each the instrument of opposing parties. At the point of the most massive confusion, one group tried to arrest the mayor and an armed struggle took place between the two competing forces.

The evolution toward more effective and professional forces was painfully slow. Separating the police from patronage proved difficult, the introduction of civil service qualifications and protection came only in this century, and the development of modern professional departments came even later. To be sure, after a crisis—rioting, widescale looting, or a crime wave—there would be a demand for reform, but the enthusiasm was seldom sustained and conditions returned quickly to normal. The ultimate safety of the city thus resided with outside forces that could be brought in when local police could not handle the mob.

These general considerations account in large part for the high level of disorder and violence in American cities over the past three centuries. The larger disorders, however, often stemmed from particular problems and specific conditions and resulted in widescale bloodshed and destruction. Though these situations varied from place to place and time to time, it is perhaps useful to divide them into a few categories. Some rioting was clearly political, surrounding party struggles and often occasioned by legislation or an election. Some sprang from group conflict, especially the resistance to the rising influence of immigrant groups. Still others stemmed from labor disputes. And the largest, then as now, came out of race conflict. A few examples of each will convey some of their intensity and scale.

Politics has always been a fruitful source of disorders. Indeed, one of the most significant groups of riots surrounded the colonial break with Great Britain. In Boston, Samuel Adams and other radical leaders led the otherwise directionless brawling and gang warfare around the docks and wharfs into a political roughhouse against British policy. The Stamp Tax Riots, the Townshend Duty Riots and, of course, the Boston Massacre were all part of an organized and concerted campaign by colonial leaders. The urban middle classes initially tolerated the disorders because they too opposed certain aspects of British policy; they later pulled back when they felt that radical leadership was carrying resistance beyond their own limited objectives. Yet for nearly a decade, rioting and organized physical force was a part of the politics of the colonies. . . .

Attacks against immigrants comprise another theme in the story. Often the assault by older, more established groups was against individuals or small groups. But in other cases it would be more general. The string of riots against Catholic churches and convents in the nineteenth century, for example, represented an attack on the symbols of the rise of the new groups. In the summer of 1834, for instance, a Charlestown (Mass.) convent was sacked and burned to the ground; scuffles against the Irish occurred in various parts of nearby Boston; some Irish houses were set afire. At the outset, the episode was carefully managed; then it got out of hand as teenage toughs got into action. Nor was this an isolated incident.

Characteristic of this period too was the resistance to the incorporation of immigrants into the public life of the city. "Bloody Monday" in Louisville in 1855 will perhaps serve as an illustration. Local politicians had become worried about the increase of the immigrant (German and Irish) vote. The Know-Nothings (a party built in part on anti-immigrant attitudes) determined to keep foreign-born residents away from the polls on election day. There was only a single voting place for every ward, thus numbering only eight in the entire city. Know-Nothing followers rose at dawn and occupied the booths early in the morning. They admitted their own reliables, but physically barred their opponents. The pre-election campaign had been tense and bitter with threats of force flying across party lines. By this time some on each side had armed themselves. Someone fired a shot, and the rioting commenced. When it was all through, "Quinn's Row," an Irish section, had been gutted, stores looted, and Catholic churches damaged. A newspaper which was accused of stirring up feeling only barely escaped destruction. The atrocities against the Irish were especially brutal, with many being beaten and shot. Indeed, some of the wounded were thrown back into the flames of ignited buildings. Estimates of the dead range from 14 to 100, though historians have generally accepted (albeit with slim evidence) 22 as the number killed.

Labor disputes have also often spawned widescale disorder. Indeed, at the turn of the century, Winston Churchill, already a keen student of American affairs, observed that the United States had the most violent industrial relations of any western country. Most of this rioting started with a confrontation of labor and management over the right to organize, or wages and hours, or working conditions. A large portion of these strikes found the workers in a vulnerable if not helpless position, a fact which has led most historians to come down on the side of labor in these early disputes. Moreover, unlike the disorders we have previously discussed, these were nationwide in scope—occurring at widely scattered points. There was no question of their being directed since a union was usually involved and it had some control over local action throughout the country. Yet the violence was seldom uniform or confined to strikers. It might flare up in Chicago and Pittsburgh, while St. Louis, where the issues would be the same, might remain quiescent. Often, as in the case of the railroad strike of 1877, the damage to life and property was large. In the Homestead lockout alone, 35 were killed and the damage (in 1892 dollars) ran to $2,500,000. In the 1930's the organizing steel, auto, and rubber unions brought a recrudescence of this earlier grisly process. . . .

Of all the sources of civil disorder, however, none has been more persistent than race. Whether in the North or South, whether before or after the Civil War, whether nineteenth or twentieth century, this question has been at the root of more physical violence than any other. There had been some sporadic slave uprisings before emancipation, the largest being the Nat Turner rebellion in 1831. But most which moved from plot to action occurred on the countryside rather than in the cities. Yet even the fear of a slave insurrection took its toll; in 1822, for instance, Charleston, South Carolina, officials, acting on tips and rumors, hanged 37 Negroes and deported many more for an alleged plot to capture and burn the city. Seven years later, in a free state, whites invaded Cincinnati's "Little Africa" and burned and killed and ultimately drove half the colored residents from town. In the same period mobs also assaulted abolitionists, sometimes killing, otherwise sacking buildings and destroying printing presses.

Even the New York City riot against the draft in 1863 took an ugly racial twist before it had run its course. The events themselves arose out of the unpopularity of the draft and the federal government's call for more men as Lee headed into Pennsylvania. The situation was further complicated by a crisis in the police department as a result of the conflicting claims of command by a Republican mayor and a Democratic governor. The rioting broke out July 13 and the first target was the provost marshal's office. Within a short time 700 people ransacked the building and then set it afire. The crowd would not let the firemen into the area and soon the whole block lay gutted. Later the mob began to spill over into the Negro area where many blacks were attacked and some killed.

The police were helpless as the riot spread. The few clashes with the mob saw the police retreat; the crowd wandered about almost at will. Political leaders did not want to take the consequences for action against the mob, and soon it started to head toward the business district. Slowly the police reorganized, by

Tuesday they began to win engagements with the rioters, and in a little while they were able to confine the action to the original area. The mobs were, however, better armed and organized and gave a good account of themselves in pitched battle. On the third day federal troops arrived and the control swung over to the authorities and quiet was restored. But in three days the casualties ran to at least 74 dead and many times that number wounded. The property damage was never accurately added up, but claims against the county exceeded $1,500,000 by 1865.

Emancipation freed the Negro from bondage, but it did not grant him either equality or immunity from white aggression. From the New Orleans riot of 1866, through the long list of racial disorders to the end of World War II with datelines running through Atlanta, Springfield, East St. Louis, Washington, Mobile, Beaumont, Chicago, Detroit, and Harlem, [all these riots] reveal something of the depth of the crisis and the vulnerability of American cities to racial disorders. These riots were on a large scale, involved many deaths, millions of dollars of property damage, and left behind deep scars which have never been fully erased. Most of these riots involved the resort to outside military help for containment; all exposed the thinness of the internal and external controls within our urban society.

In fact, the war had scarcely ended before racial violence erupted in New Orleans. The occasion of the outbreak was a Negro procession to an assembly hall where a debate over enfranchising the blacks was to take place. There was some jostling during the march and a shot fired; but it was only after the arrival at the convention that police and special troops charged the black crowd. In the ensuing struggle [the] Negroes were finally routed, but guns, bricks, and stones were generously used. Many Negroes fell on the spot; others were pursued and killed on the streets trying to escape. Later General Sheridan reported that "at least nine-tenths of the casualties were perpetrated by the police and citizens by stabbing and smashing in the heads of many who had already been wounded or killed by policemen." Moreover, he added that it was not just a riot but "an absolute massacre by the police . . . a murder which the mayor and police . . . perpetrated without the shadow of necessity." Federal troops arrived in the afternoon, took possession of the city, and restored order. But 34 Negroes and 4 whites were already dead and over 200 injured.

Smaller places, even in the North, were also affected with racial disorder. In August 1908, for instance, a three-day riot took its toll in Springfield, Illinois. The Negro population in the capital had grown significantly in the years after the turn of the century, and some whites sensed a political and economic threat. On August 13th a white woman claimed she had been violated by a Negro. An arrest was made and the newspapers carried an inflammatory account of the episode. Crowds gathered around the jail demanding the imprisoned black, but the sheriff quickly transferred the accused and another Negro to a prison in a nearby town without letting the public know. "The crowd outside was in an ugly mood," writes an historian of the riot, "the sun had raised tempers; many of the crowd had missed their dinners, which added to their irritation; and the authorities seemed to be taking no heed of their presence. By sundown the crowd had become an ugly mob."

The first target of the rioters was a restaurant whose proprietor presumably had driven the prisoners from jail. Within a few minutes his place was a shambles. They then headed for the Negro section. Here they hit homes and businesses either owned by or catering to Negroes. White owners quickly put white handkerchiefs in their windows to show their race; their stores were left untouched. A Negro was found in his shop and was summarily lynched. Others were dragged from streetcars and beaten. On the 15th the first of 5,000 national guardsmen reached Springfield; very quickly the mob broke up and the town returned to normal. The death toll reached six (four whites and two blacks); the property damage was significant. As a result of the attack, Springfield's Negro population left the city in large numbers hoping to find better conditions elsewhere, especially in Chicago.

A decade later the depredations in East St. Louis were much larger, with the riot claiming the lives of 39 Negroes and 9 whites. The best student of this episode points out that the 1917 riot was not a sudden explosion but resulted from "threats to the security of whites brought on by the Negroes' gains in economic, political and social status; Negro resentment of the attempts to 'kick him back in his place'; and the weakness of the external forces of constraint—the city government, especially the police department." Tensions were raised when the Aluminum Ore Company replaced white strikers with Negro workers. In addition to these factors, race had become a political issue in the previous year when the Democrats accused Republicans of "colonizing" Negroes to swing the election in East St. Louis. The kindling seemed only to lack the match.

On May 28 came the fire. A Central Trades and Labor Union delegation formally requested the Mayor to stop the immigration of Negroes to East St. Louis. As the men were leaving City Hall they heard a story that a Negro robber had accidentally shot a white man during a holdup. In a few minutes the word spread; rumor replaced fact. Now it was said the shooting was intentional; that a white woman was insulted; that two white girls were shot. By this time 3,000 people had congregated and the cry for vengeance went up. Mobs ran downtown beating every Negro in sight. Some were dragged off the streetcars, others chased down. The police refused to act except to take the injured to hospitals and to disarm Negroes. The next day the National Guard arrived to restore order.

Two days later the governor withdrew troops although tension remained high. Scattered episodes broke the peace, but no sustained violence developed. The press, however, continued to emphasize Negro crimes and a skirmish broke out between white pickets and black workers at the Aluminum Company. Then on July 1 some whites drove through the main Negro neighborhood firing into homes. The colored residents armed themselves, and when a similar car, this time carrying a plain-clothesman and reporter, went down the street the blacks riddled the passing auto with gunshot.

The next day was the worst. At about 10:00 A.M. a Negro was shot on the main street and a new riot was underway. An historian of the event asserted that the area along Collinsville Avenue between Broadway and Illinois Avenue became a "bloody half mile" for three or four hours. "Streetcars were stopped: Negroes, without regard to age or sex, were pulled off and stoned, clubbed and kicked. . . . By the early afternoon, when several Negroes were beaten and lay bloodied in the street, mob leaders calmly shot and killed them. After victims were placed in an ambulance, there was cheering and handclapping." Others headed for the Negro section and set fire to homes on the edge of the neighborhood. By midnight the South End was in flames and black residents began to flee the city. In addition to the dead, the injured were counted in the hundreds and over 300 buildings were destroyed.

Two summers later the racial virus felled Chicago. Once again, mounting tension had accompanied the migration of blacks to the city. The numbers jumped from 44,000 in 1910 to 109,000 ten years later. Though the job market remained good, housing was tight. Black neighborhoods could expand only at the expense of white ones, and everywhere the transition areas were filled with trouble. Between July 1, 1917, and March 1921, there had been 58 bombings of Negro houses. Recreational areas also witnessed continual racial conflict.

The riot itself began on Sunday, July 27, on the 29th Street Beach. There had been some stone-throwing and sporadic fighting. Then a Negro boy, who had been swimming in the Negro section, drifted into the white area and drowned. What happened is not certain, but the young blacks charged he had been hit by stones and demanded the arrest of a white. The police refused, but then arrested a Negro at a white request. When the Negroes attacked the police, the riot was on. News of the events on the beach spread to the rest of the city. Sunday's casualties were 2 dead and 50 wounded. On Monday, attacks were made on Negroes coming from work; in the evening cars drove through black neighborhoods with whites shooting from the windows. Negroes retaliated by sniping at any white who entered the Black Belt. Monday's accounting found 20 killed and hundreds wounded. Tuesday's list was shorter, a handful dead, 139 injured. Wednesday saw a further waning and a reduction in losses in life and property. Rain began to fall; the Mayor finally called in the state militia. After nearly a week a city which [had] witnessed lawlessness and warfare quieted down and began to assess the implications of the grisly week.

The Detroit riot of 1943 perhaps illustrates the range of racial disorders that broke out sporadically during World War II. There had been earlier conflicts in Mobile, Los Angeles, and Beaumont, Texas, and there would be some others later in the year. No doubt the war with its built-in anxieties and accelerated residential mobility accounted for the timing of these outbreaks. In Detroit, the wider problem was compounded by serious local questions. The Negro population in the city had risen sharply, with over 50,000 arriving in the 15 months before the riot; this followed a historical increase of substantial proportions which saw black residents increase from 40,000 to 120,000 in the single decade between 1920 and 1930. These newcomers put immense pressures on the housing market, and neighborhood turnover at the edge of the ghetto bred bitterness and sometimes violence; importantly, too, recreational areas became centers of racial abrasiveness.

On June 20 the riot broke out on Belle Isle, a recreational spot used by both races, but predominantly by Negroes. Fistfighting on a modest basis soon escalated, and quickly a rising level of violence spread across the city. The Negro ghetto—ironically called Paradise Valley—saw the first wave of looting and bloodshed. The area was, as its historians have described it, "spattered with blood and littered with broken glass and ruined merchandise. The black mob had spared a few shops owned by Negroes who had chalked COLORED on their windows. But almost every store in the ghetto owned by a white had been smashed open and ransacked." Other observers noted that "crudely organized gangs of Negro hoodlums began to operate more openly. Some looters destroyed property as if they had gone berserk."

The next morning saw the violence widen. The police declared the situation out of control and the mayor asked for state troops. Even this force was ineffective, and finally the Governor asked for federal help. Peace returned under the protection of 6,000 men; and the troops remained for more than a week. The dead numbered 34, 25 Negroes and 9 whites; property damage exceeded $2,000,000. And almost as costly was the bitterness, fear, and hate that became part of the city's legacy. . . .

This survey, which is only suggestive and not exhaustive, indicates that wide-scale violence and disorder have been man's companion in the American city from the outset. Some generalizations out of this experience might be useful in the light of the present crisis.

First, most of the rioting has usually been either limited in objective or essentially sporadic. This, of course, is not true of racial conflict, but it is characteristic of a large number of the others. In those, the event was discrete; there was no immediate violent sequel. After a labor dispute, especially if it involved union recognition, bitterness and hate persisted, but there was no annual recurrence of the violence. Attacks on immigrants seldom produced an encore, though they might have an analogue in some other city in the same month or year. In short, though there was enough disorder and mob action to create a persistent anxiety, the incidence of overt conflict was irregular enough to preclude predictions of the next "long hot summer."

Second, this sporadic quality meant that the postmortems were usually short and shallow. It was characteristic to note the large number of teenagers who got involved; to attribute the disruption to outsiders (especially anarchists and communists); to place a large responsibility on the newspapers for carrying inflammatory information and spreading unfounded rumors; to blame the local police for incompetence, for prejudice, for intervening too soon or too late, or at all. After any episode, the urge to fix blame led to all kinds of analyses. The historian of the 1877 railroad violence, for example, observes that "the riots were variously ascribed to avarice, the expulsion of the Bible from the schools, the protective tariff, the demonetization of silver, the absence of General Grant, the circulation of the *Chicago Times* and original sin." Others saw in it a labor conspiracy or a communist plot. And the *New York Times* could assert after the Chicago riot in 1919 that: "The outbreak of race riots in Chicago, following so closely on those reported from Washington, shows clearly enough that the thing is not sporadic (but has) . . . intelligent direction and management . . . (It seems probable) that the Bolshevist agitation has been extended among the Negroes."

There were a few exceptions. After the Chicago race riot, for example, an Illinois commission studied the event in some detail and also examined the deteriorating relations between the races which lay at the bottom. Others occasionally probed beneath the surface [to get] at the deeper causes of unrest. But most cities preferred to forget as soon as possible and hoped for an end to any further disorder. Indeed, even the trials that followed most riots show how rapidly popular interest faded. The number of people brought to trial was small and the number of convictions extremely small; and, most significantly, there was little clamor for sterner measures.

Third, if the analyses of the riots were shallow, the response of cities and legislatures was not very effective. After quiet was restored, there would almost certainly be a discussion of police reform. Customarily little came of it, though in Louisville the utter ineptness and obvious partisanship of the police in 1855 prompted a change from an elective to an appointive force. Legislation usually emphasized control. As early as 1721, Massachusetts responded to growing disorders with an anti-riot act. And Chicago's Commercial Club made land available for Fort Sheridan after the events in 1877 in order to have troops nearby for the protection of the city. But most cities rocked back to normal as soon as the tremors died down.

Fourth, there was a general tendency to rely increasingly on outside forces for containing riots. Partly, this resulted from the fact that in labor disorders local police and even state militia fraternized with strikers and could not be counted on to discipline the workers. Partly, it was due to inadequate numbers in the face of the magnitude of the problem. Partly, too, it stemmed from the fact that sometimes the police were involved in the fighting at the outset and seemed a part of the riot. The first resort was usually to state troops; but they were often unsatisfactory, and the call for federal assistance became more frequent.

Fifth, while it is hard to assess, it seems that the bitterness engendered by riots and disorders was not necessarily irreparable. Though the immigrants suffered a good deal at the hands of nativists, it did not slow down for long the process of their incorporation into American life. Ten years after Louisville's "Bloody Monday" the city had a German mayor. The trade unions survived the assaults of the nineteenth century and a reduction of tension characterized the period between 1900 and the depression (with the notable exception of the postwar flare-ups). And after the violence of the 1930's, labor and management learned to conduct their differences, indeed their strikes, with reduced bloodshed and violence. It is not susceptible of proof, but it seems that the fury of the defeated in these battles exacted a price on the victors that ultimately not only protected the group but won respect, however grudgingly, from the public.

At any rate, the old sources of major disorders, race excepted, no longer physically agitate American society. It has been many years since violence has been a significant factor in city elections and no widespread disorders have even accompanied campaigning. Immigrant groups have now become so incorporated in American life that they are not easily visible and their election to high offices, indeed the highest, signals a muting of old hostilities. Even when people organized on a large scale against minority groups—such as the Americans' Protective Association in the 1890's or the Ku Klux Klan in the 1920's—they have seldom been able to create major riots or disorders. And though sporadic violence occasionally breaks out in a labor dispute, what is most remarkable is the continuance of the strike as a weapon of industrial relations with so little resort to force. Even the destruction of property during a conflict has ceased to be an expectation.

Sixth, race riots were almost always different from other kinds of disorders. Their roots went deeper; they broke out with increasing frequency; and their intensity mounted rather than declined. And between major disorders the incidence of small-scale violence was always high. Until recently, the Negro has largely been the object of the riot. This was true not only in northern cities where changing residential patterns bred violence, but also in the South where this question was less pervasive. In these riots the lines were sharply drawn against the Negroes, the force was applied heavily against them, and the casualties were always highest among blacks.

Finally, in historical perspective, if racial discord be removed, the level of large-scale disorder and violence is less ominous today than it has been during much of the past. As we have seen, those problems which have produced serious eruptions in the past no longer do so. In fact, if one were to plot a graph, omitting the racial dimension, violence and disorder over a long period have been reduced. Indeed, what makes the recent rioting so alarming is that it breaks so much with this historical trend and upsets common expectations.

Yet to leave out race is to omit the most important dimension of the present crisis. For it is race that is at the heart of the present discord. Some analysts, of course, have argued that the problem is class and they emphasize the numbers caught in widening poverty, and the frustration and envy of poor people in a society of growing affluence. Yet it is important to observe that though 68 percent of the poor people in this country are white, the disorders stem almost wholly from black ghettoes. The marginal participation of a few whites in Detroit and elsewhere scarcely dilutes the racial foundations of these disorders.

In fact, a historical survey of disorders only highlights the unique character of the present problem. For the experience of the Negro in American cities has been quite different from any other group. And it is in just this difference that the crisis lies. Because the black ghetto is unlike any ghettoes that our cities have known before. Of course, other groups knew the ghetto experience too. As newcomers to the city they huddled in the downtown areas where they met unspeakably congested conditions, occupied the worst housing, got the poorest education, toiled, if fortunate enough to have a job, at the most menial tasks, endured high crime rates, and knew every facet of deprivation.

The urban slum had never been a very pleasant place, and it was tolerable only if the residents, or most of them, thought there was a way out. To American immigrants generally the ghetto was a temporary stage in their incorporation into American society. Even some of the first generation escaped, and the second and third generation moved out of the slums in very large numbers. Soon they were dispersed around the metropolitan area, in the suburbs as well as the pleasant residential city wards. Those who remained behind in the old neighborhoods did so because they chose to, not because they had to. By this process, millions of people from numberless countries, of different national and religious backgrounds, made their way into the main current of American life.

It was expected that Negroes would undergo the same process when they came to the city. Thus, there was little surprise in the first generation when black newcomers did indeed find their way into the central city, the historic staging ground for the last and poorest arrivals. But the ghetto proved to be not temporary. Instead of colored residents dispersing in the second generation, the ghetto simply expanded. Block by block it oozed out into the nearby white neighborhoods. Far from breaking up, the ghetto grew. In fact, housing became more segregated every year; and the walls around it appeared higher all the time. What had been temporary for other groups seemed permanent to Negroes.

The growth of the Negro ghetto created conditions which had not existed before and which generated the explosiveness of our present situation. In the first place, the middle-class Negroes became embittered at their exclusion from the decent white neighborhoods of the city and suburbs. These people, after all, had done what society expected of them; they got their education, training, jobs, and income. Yet even so they were deprived of that essential symbol of American success—the home in a neighborhood of their own choosing where conditions would be more pleasant and schools better for their children. For this group, now about a third of all urban Negroes, the exclusion seemed especially cruel and harsh.

As a result they comprise now a growingly alienated and embittered group. The middle-class blacks are now beginning to turn their attention to organizing among the poor in the worst parts of the ghetto. Their children make up the cadres of black militants in the colleges. And when the riots come, they tolerate the activity even though they usually do not themselves participate. In short, the fact of the ghetto forces them to identify with race, not class. When the riots break, they feel a bond with the rioters, not white society. This had not been true of the emerging middle class of any immigrant group before.

If the ghetto has new consequences for the middle class, it also creates a new situation among the poorer residents of the ghetto, especially for the young people. They feel increasingly that there is no hope for the future. For other groups growing up in the ghetto there had always been visible evidence that it was possible to escape. Many before had done it; and everyone knew it. This produced the expectation that hard work, proper behavior, some schooling, and a touch of luck would make it possible to get ahead. But the young Negro grows up in increasing despair. He asks himself—"What if I do all they say I should—stay in school, get my training, find a job, accumulate some money—I'll still be living here, still excluded from the outside world and its rewards." He asks himself, "What's the use?" Thus, the hopelessness, despair, and frustration mounts, and the temperature of the ghetto rises. Nearly all of our poverty programs are stumbling on the problem of motivation. To climb out of the slum has always required more than average incentive. Yet this is precisely what is lacking in the ghetto youth.

The present riots stem from the peculiar problems of the ghetto. By confining Negroes to the ghetto we have deprived them of the chance to enter American society on the same terms as other groups before them. And they know increasingly that this exclusion is not a function of education, training, or income. Rather, it springs from the color of their skin. This is what makes race the explosive question of our time; this is what endangers the tranquillity of our cities. In the historian's perspective, until the ghetto begins to break, until the Negro middle class can move over this demeaning barrier, until the young people can see Negroes living where their resources will carry them and hence get credible evidence of equality, the summers will remain long and hot.

SUGGESTIONS FOR FURTHER READING

The literature on urban history and the urban crisis has expanded rapidly in the past decades. General introductions are Charles N. Glaab and A. Theodore Brown, *A History of Urban America* (New York, 1967) and Sam Bass Warner, *The Urban Wilderness: A History of the American City* (New York, 1972). A valuable analysis of trends in the writing of urban history, along with bibliographic information, is Richard C. Wade, "An Agenda for Urban History," in George Athan Billias and Gerald N. Grob, eds., *American History: Retrospect and Prospect* (New York, 1971), 367–98. Arthur M. Schlesinger, *The Rise of the City* (New York, 1933) is an early effort to direct historians' attention to urban history; Schlesinger finds a developing urban consensus in the late nineteenth century. A recent survey with a good bibliography that will take the interested reader further is Zane L. Miller and Patricia M. Melvin, *The Urbanization of Modern America: A Brief History,* 2nd ed. (San Diego, 1987). D. H. Hamer, *New Towns in the New World: Images and Perceptions of the Nineteenth-Century Urban Frontier* (New York, 1990) is a comparative international study.

The antiurban tradition in America can be approached through Morton and Lucia White, *The Intellectual Versus the City* (Cambridge, Mass., 1962). On the contemporary urban crisis, Jeanne Lowe, *Cities in a Race with Time* (New York, 1967) and Mitchell Gordon, *Sick Cities: Psychology and Pathology of American Urban Life* (New York, 1965) are pessimistic, while Jane Jacobs, *The Death and Life of Great American Cities* (New York, 1961) and Robert Weaver, *The Urban Complex: Human Values in Urban Life* (New York, 1964) find more hope. There are a number of books on the problems of governing cities, problems that often led to conflicts. For the problem of law enforcement, see Robert N. Fogelson, *Big-City Police* (Cambridge, Mass., 1977). A survey of the literature is Jon C. Teaford, "Finis for Tweed and Steffens: Rewriting the History of Urban Rule," *Reviews in American History,* 10 (December 1982), 133–49. Valuable and up to date is Teaford's study, *The Twentieth Century American City,* 2nd ed. (Baltimore, 1993). On the growth of urban suburbs, see Kenneth T. Jackson, *Crabgrass Frontier: The Suburbanization of the United States* (New York, 1985). Joel Garreau, *Edge City: Life on the New Frontier* (New York, 1991) writes of the world of malls, expressways, and corporate centers in the self-contained cities on the edge of, but isolated from, the old cities.

Maldwyn Allen Jones has written two good general introductions to the history of immigration: *American Immigration* (Chicago, 1960) and *Destination America* (New York, 1976). John Bodnar, *The Transplanted: A History of Immigrants in Urban America* (Bloomington, Ind., 1985), a general survey of immigration from 1830 to 1930, with an extensive bibliography, recounts the problems the mainly rural immigrants faced in adapting to urban capitalism in America. David M. Reimers, *Still the Golden Door* (New York, 1985) discusses recent immigration to the United States.

The most convenient place to begin the study of immigration and ethnicity is Stephan Thernstrom et al., *Harvard Encyclopedia of American Ethnic Groups* (Cambridge, Mass.,

---

*Available in paperback edition.

1980), which contains a good bibliography. John Higham, *Strangers in the Land: Patterns of American Nativism, 1860–1925* (New Brunswick, N.J., 1955) describes some of the sharp conflicts between the immigrants and native Americans. On the problems of assimilation, see Nathan Glazer and Daniel Patrick Moynihan, *Beyond the Melting Pot: The Negroes, Puerto Ricans, Jews, Italians and Irish of New York City* (Cambridge, Mass., 1963). An important study of New York City blacks is Gilbert Osofsky, *Harlem: The Making of a Ghetto* (New York, 1965). Kenneth L. Kusmer, *A Ghetto Takes Shape: Black Cleveland, 1870–1930* (Champaign, Ill., 1976) and Thomas Lee Philpott, *The Slum and the Ghetto: Neighborhood Deterioration and Middle-Class Reform, Chicago, 1880–1930* (New York, 1978) are two excellent studies. Florette Henri, *Black Migration: Movement North, 1900–1920* (Garden City, N.Y., 1975) traces the movement of southern blacks to northern cities. A recent study of one group of reformers and their relations with immigrants is Rivka Shpak Lissak, *Pluralism and Progressives: Hull House and the New Immigrants, 1890–1919* (Chicago, 1989). Two recent studies concentrate on workers, race, and ethnicity: Kitty Calavita, *U.S. Immigration Law and the Control of Labor, 1820–1924* (London, 1984) and Robert Asher and Charles Stephenson, eds., *Labor Divided: Race and Ethnicity in United States Labor Struggles, 1835–1960* (Albany, N.Y., 1990). Werner Sollors, *Beyond Ethnicity: Consent and Descent in American Culture* (New York, 1986) is the work of a literary scholar who sees both conflict and consensus (and much more) in the American experience.

In recent years the study of both urban and immigration history has moved away from attempts to define an urban or an ethnic consensus in America to efforts to examine the diversity of ethnic experience and the complexity of the city in many times and places. Examples of the new approach can be found in three collections of essays: Stephen Thernstrom and Richard Sennett, eds., *Nineteenth-Century Cities* (New Haven, 1969); Allen F. Davis and Mark Haller, eds., *The Peoples of Philadelphia: A History of Ethnic Groups and Lower-Class Life, 1790–1940* (Philadelphia, 1973); and Richard L. Ehrlich, ed., *Immigrants in Industrial America* (Charlottesville, Va., 1977). One example of many specialized studies is Thomas Kessner, *The Golden Door: Italian and Jewish Immigrant Mobility in New York City, 1880–1915* (New York, 1977). Thomas Sowell, *Ethnic America: A History* (New York, 1981) is a controversial book that examines nine ethnic groups including blacks and argues that all groups can get ahead through hard work, not federal aid. An international perspective on ethnic conflicts is Donald L. Horowitz, *Ethnic Groups in Conflict* (Berkeley, Calif., 1985).

6

The Progressive Movement

rogressivism was a broad and diverse reform movement that had its roots in the 1890s but came to a climax on the national level during the administrations of Theodore Roosevelt and Woodrow Wilson. It affected all areas of American life, including art, literature, religion, and education; but it was also a political movement founded on the idea that the problems arising in an industrialized America could be solved only by expanding democracy and social justice. Reformers in the cities sought to promote clean, honest, efficient government and to end boss rule. Reformers in the states paraded under the banner of "give the government back to the people," seeking the initiative, the referendum, the recall, the direct election of senators, and many other reforms that had been supported by the Populists. Muckrakers sought to expose corruption in the world of business and politics. Social workers and other reformers fought to regulate child labor, to clean up the slums, and to promote better working conditions for both men and women. On the national level, leaders of both political parties, seeking ways to deal with the giant industrial combinations, turned to regulation, control, and "trust busting." Everywhere progressives were concerned with solving the many problems created by industrialism.

Of course, progressives often faced opposition from those who resisted their reform efforts. But gradually the reform impulse gained momentum as leaders in all walks of life proclaimed themselves to be progressives. Both political parties claimed to favor progressive reform, and in 1912, when Theodore Roosevelt bolted the Republican Party to establish a third party, he called it the Progressive Party. A new reform consensus seemed to have arisen, based, as the name the reformers gave to their movement makes clear, on a firm belief in progress. Progressives were convinced that a great many things in America needed to be changed, but, unlike the socialists, they did not want to introduce a new system of government. Problems could be solved, they believed, by reforming, rather than abandoning, the American system.

But behind what appeared to be a new consensus lay differences among the progressives themselves. Reformers disagreed over what kinds of reforms were needed and over the best methods to adopt to achieve reform; indeed, progressives regularly battled over particular policies and over the general objectives of the movement.

The diversity of the movement and the disagreements among reformers is reflected in the work of historians who have sharply disagreed over the meaning and nature of progressivism. Some historians view the progressive era as a time of conflict between reformers on one side and businessmen and political bosses on the other. They stress the Populist origins of progressivism, tending to agree with William Allen White, a leading midwestern progressive, who remarked that the progressives "caught the Populists in swimming and stole all their clothing except the frayed underdrawers of free silver." Such historians see the movement as drawing its chief support from the midwestern farmers and small businessmen engaged in a bitter struggle for survival with the eastern bankers and corporation presidents.

Another group of historians interpret the progressive movement as much more than an extension of populism; indeed, its dominant spirit becomes not "rural and provincial" but "urban, middle-class and nationwide." These historians often explain the movement in terms of what Richard Hofstadter has called "the status revolution." This thesis attempts to show that a group of middle-class, well-educated citizens, including lawyers, doctors, preachers, educators, and small businessmen, who had usually held positions of leadership, were being displaced in the late nineteenth century by the rising power of labor-union leaders, corporation executives, and political bosses. Frustrated by their loss of status and power, driven by a sense of responsibility or guilt when confronted by the problems of urbanism and industrialism, they became reformers in an effort to hold on to a society that they deemed good but rapidly disappearing.

Both these groups find the source of progressivism in opposition to big business. Progressives, they argue, responded to the problems brought by massive industrialization and the rise of giant corporations by looking backward; they suggested reforms that would bring back some of the traditional verities. But other historians insist that the progressives were not looking backward but rather were rejecting the old ways of life and seeking changes that would solve the problems created by the new economic and social order without giving up its benefits. Some see the impetus for progressivism coming from big business itself as it sought reforms that would help to rationalize and to bring order to the new industrial society and economy; others insist that the movement is best understood as an effort to restrain and regulate the power of big business without destroying the advantages that bigness brought in terms of efficiency and increased production.

What many of these varied interpretations have in common is that progressives believed that necessary reforms can and, indeed, must be brought by government action, that is, by local, state, and national laws and regulatory actions. But other historians disagree and insist that progressive reformers tended to be suspicious of government and advocated reform led by experts who would persuade people to change voluntarily. Other sources of disagreement among historians concern their interpretations of the goals of the reformers. Some argue that progressives were undemocratic elitists who claimed to know what was best for the rest of the people and sought to impose their programs on the nation. Others, however, insist that the progressives were intent upon improving life for all through wise and needed reforms.

Some of these disagreements among historians may be seen in the selections that follow.

In the first selection, John C. Burnham describes a progressive "ethos," an "age of positive reform," that swept across the country in the first decade and a half of the twentieth century. He describes the progressive leaders as "primarily one segment of the 'better' people in America" who "possessed unusual confidence in their ability to change the world." Unlike the reformers in the later New Deal era, the progressives looked to science and to experts to solve problems rather than to the government. They were optimists with a "moral fervor" and environmentalists who believed that people would change if conditions changed, and they were convinced that they knew how to make the necessary changes. Although they had diverse and often contradictory goals and did not achieve all they set out to do, the progressives, Burnham maintains, accomplished a great deal, and they prepared the way for other reform movements to follow.

In the second selection, Paul Boyer provides a somewhat different perspective on progressive reform. Like Burnham, he views the progressives as moralists. He sees progressivism as a moral crusade against sin and evil. The progressives, he writes, had "an infinite capacity for moral indignation" in their battle for social justice and against corporate wrongdoing, corruption in government, and immorality of all kinds. They fought for better housing, parks and playgrounds, and improved schools; child labor and urban slums appalled them, as did the immorality of liquor and prostitution. Boyer notes that progressive reformers came increasingly to rely upon experts; the reformers, he notes, supplemented and supported their moral indignation with the findings of social scientists and others with scientific expertise. Boyer, more than Burnham, finds a coercive strain in progressivism. Necessary reforms might have to be imposed; people often had to be forced to give up their improper or evil ways, and the progressive leaders had no doubts about what ways were evil and had to be eradicated.

This attitude has important implications for democratic institutions. Is it not undemocratic to coerce people to behave in a manner deemed to be correct, not by the people themselves but by experts who claim to know what is best? In the third selection, David J. Rothman directly addresses this question. He sees the progressives as liberal reformers who sought to ameliorate wrongs but who in the process often trampled on the rights of those they were helping. Using the power of the state, they sought to impose a middle-class consensus; like parents, they thought they knew what was best for the disadvantaged "children." Rothman argues that the current concern with liberty and the appearance of adversary politics and social relations mark a revolt against the pervasive liberalism that had its origins in the progressive era.

How important were the differences that divided reformers from their opponents during the progressive period? Was there a widespread agreement on fundamentals that led progressives merely to seek minor adjustments in a basically sound society? Or did progressive reformers recognize deep-seated problems and seek major changes?

Were the liberal reformers illiberal in their goals and methods? Did they, in seeking their goals, infringe upon the rights of those they were supposed to be helping? Or does such a view do an injustice to a group of people who spent their time, money, and energy to help people in distress?

Did progressive reform introduce essentially undemocratic features into American life by taking decisions from the people and putting them in the hands of experts? Does democracy require that people who are wrong-headed and might act in a manner that would injure themselves and, perhaps indirectly, others as well, be allowed to continue such behavior? Who should decide?

JOHN C. BURNHAM

The Cultural Interpretation of the Progressive Movement

A whole new perspective on the meaning and significance of Progressivism is . . . long overdue. Recent research suggests two ways of conceptualizing what happened. The first is that a number of streams in American reform coalesced for a few years, reinforcing each other so as to cumulate in what contemporaries recognized as Progressivism. This model has the particular advantage of explaining how many reform efforts, such as those in the cities, existed before and after the critical prewar decade, and how at the same time Progressivism was meaningful in terms of a special ferment that people at the time recognized as important in effecting changes in American life and institutions. Some of the dynamics of this coalescence are discussed below.

The second way to conceptualize Progressivism is to focus on the changes that actually did occur in those years, and on how those changes came about. Clyde Griffen has made a good start in describing a "progressive ethos," an idealism marked by "the juxtaposition of a practical piece-meal approach to reform with a religious or quasi-religious vision of democracy." Even conservatives, Griffen points out, were confused by the moralism and idealism and evangelism that welled up together, affecting and marking a generation. That the coincidence of directions of historical development also coincided with the ethos is what gives substance to the existence of Progressivism.

Because long extant reform movements became a part of Progressivism, various writers tried to set the date of the exact beginnings of Progressivism all the way from the 1880s to several years into the twentieth century. In fact, the movement crystallized sometime around 1907. What happened just then showed up in both public mood and in the pace and quality of change. Maxwell Bloomfield has shown that the popular magazines of the day changed in tone suddenly in

---

1907–1908, from defensive, sometimes muckraking criticisms, to discussions of a positive nature about the promise of American life. The age of the negative exposé gave way to an age of positive reform—Progressivism.

Institutional and organizational developments paralleled the development of the new mood. Dewey W. Grantham, Jr., in tracing the genesis of Progressives' political crusades to the expansion of local activities, cites 1906 as the year when activity boiled up to the state level. In the private sphere, it was about 1908 that philanthropic fund raising was transformed both in organization and in public appeal. Many other signs compel the conclusion that for about a decade before the entry of the United States into World War I, there was a direction of change sufficiently coherent to constitute the Progressive movement—recognizable by the confluence of specific reform streams and by a general ethos. . . .

Numerous studies of the Progressive political leaders and individual biographies of other types of Progressives show that the leadership was almost invariably upper middle or upper class in background. So also, however, were most of the leaders who embodied resistance or opposition to reform. The Progressives differed from the others only in that they were, on the average, substantially younger than the non-Progressives. Progressivism appears therefore to have been reform that was led and supported primarily by one segment of the "better" people in America. What differentiated them besides youth—and started them off to carry out substantial and rapid social changes? These identifiable leaders offer at least a partial answer to the question of the historical origins of the movement.

The actions and the convergence of ideals of the Progressives can be understood in part in terms of negative reactions to earlier events and in part in terms of positive forces that had been building up in the late nineteenth century. On the negative side, David Thelen suggests that in Wisconsin and, presumably, other areas, the depression of the 1890s shocked various elements of the state into an awareness that most members of the community were both consumers and taxpayers, and so attempts to shift power back to "the people" gradually came to replace home-and-morality reform efforts. Other negative reactions to the acute hard times and violence of the 1890s persisted long after hard times had disappeared. In part this negativism metamorphosed itself into the "quest for community," the search for neighbors supportive of traditional values, that was so characteristic of the times. In part negative reactions intensified other aspects of the search for order and righteousness.

The effectiveness of the well-known muckraker movement in the years just after the turn of the century testifies to a widespread discontent that made magazine readers particularly susceptible to believing that the country's businessmen and politicians were causing the most pressing social problems. The negative tone of the muckrakers removes them from the generally constructive spirit of the Progressives, and, in fact, as noted above, the demise of muckraking coincided with the rise of Progressivism proper. In the Progressive years even such a stalwart among the muckrakers as Lincoln Steffens reached a point where he felt the need of positive "solutions" instead of mere criticism. Exposing the corruptions in American life was not a comprehensive part of the reformers' attempts at social reconstruction, but muckraking was nevertheless an important negative preliminary to reform.

Still another type of revulsion that set the stage for a new vision of American life was revulsion against the image of the city. Even within the urban areas themselves large numbers of Americans were still seeking the virtues of rural communities that they had known as children. This contrast of the idyllic with the crowded and diseased city underlined the reaction of most Americans to the evils that festered in the slums, especially as the alien New Immigration increasingly became identified with the large metropolis. A number of Progressive reforms involved attempts to change both the character of the city and its inhabitants. . . .

The uplifters did not reject the city itself, where specialization and cooperation could thrive. The city image engendered negative feelings because of the indolent, indulgent, and degenerate aspect of civilization found there. Beginning with Theodore Roosevelt's advocacy of manliness and the strenuous life right down to the Boy Scout movement and Walter Lippmann's quest for "mastery," the Progressive leaders seemed preoccupied by what James R. McGovern has called the "virility impulse," embodying a positive image of strength, character, personal force, and primitivism exalting the romantic view of the wilderness. This type of thinking could easily be directed against convention or even gentility as well as urban degeneracy and was deeply involved in the upsurge in nationalism that marked the Progressives' visions. During the 1890s, in fact, great changes had taken place in both popular and genteel culture in America. The concern with health, exercise, activity, and vigor that showed up in the virility impulse coincided with the growth of romantic individualism. This new consciousness of self therefore became another element in the Progressive ethos. At first negative, and always subversive of traditional ways and forms, the activism of the new generation provided energy to reform before World War I.

The Progressive ethos, however, could not have developed as a purely negative force. Neither the older moral and community reformers nor the muckrakers were able to galvanize Americans into the activities of Progressivism. Anger about the corruptions of city life, the trusts, the bosses, and "the system" did not suffice to develop post-1907 constructive efforts. The Panic of 1907, the only concrete event connected with the crystallizing of the movement, did move many businessmen to defensive positions as well as inspire others to ally with social workers to reduce the level of discontent in the community. But the real history of Progressivism lies rather in the clearly delineated positive ethos and in the specific accomplishments of that generation.

The ethos has been described by historians already. In the decade before World War I, large numbers of Americans embraced many or all of a number of beliefs that facilitated change: optimism, leadership by an enlightened elite, environmentalism, romantic individualism, and cultural nationalism. That congeries is not equivalent to welfare statism nor what came to be the rationale for the New Deal. What was both real and truly effective was that Progressives, with all of their inconsistencies, were united in a general viewpoint, not in support of particular types of meliorism or agendas of reforms. . . .

The Progressives rightly understood that their sense of their own power to change the world was different from the pessimism of an earlier day, whether represented by thinkers convinced of the futility of disturbing a fragile social order during the 1890s or intellectuals who shared William Graham Sumner's passive belief in automatic progress. As the young Walter Lippmann expressed the new sense of competence in his significant contrasting of *Drift and Mastery* (1914), actuality "is plastic, and ready to be moulded by him who understands it."

The Progressives could be optimists because they were fundamentally environmental determinists. Most of the visions of the future, about which the reformers were so sanguine, depended upon changes in American society that would transform citizens and alter behavior. These leaders argued that human beings are to some extent malleable. Their environmentalism ranged from attacking indirect causes of social problems—housing, recreation, sanitation, and alcohol—to a general advocacy of education, uplifting influences, and fresh air and open spaces. Even inherited defect, many Progressives believed, could be minimized in a society that motivated the practice of eugenics (especially positive eugenics). The many analyses by the social workers, social scientists, educators, and thinkers of the day who talked about achieving social control show that these environmentalists were for the most part sophisticated and hard-headed, however much they shared basic assumptions with enthusiastic reformers of the Enlightenment or pre–Civil War periods. "There is always present the danger of superficiality," wrote Southern reformer Edgar Gardner Murphy, "but the risk of making fools is of smaller import than the chance of making men." And social gospeller Walter Rauschenbusch admitted that "the world can be neither sinless nor painless. . . . If perfection were reached to-day, new adjustments would be demanded tomorrow." Yet he went on to insist on the possibility and urgency of "Christianizing the social order." "We shall demand perfection," he wrote, adding, "and never expect to get it."

About the crucial question of precisely who should manipulate the environment and who should decide which manipulations were desirable, the Progressive leaders had no doubts or hesitations: They would. Deference to experts and technicians was an important theme in Progressive thinking. Intellectuals did talk about the difficulties of reconciling paternalism with "democracy," but usually the goal was an informed, self-reliant citizen who presumably would agree with the controlling elite. In fact, many did, and the reformers often generated widespread public support.

The final ingredients that marked Progressives' outlooks, cultural nationalism and romantic individualism, are difficult to evoke for a cynical later generation. Idealization of the citizen who would be produced by meliorism was one aspect of the individualism. He would be, in the words of Jane Addams, imbued with the "social ethic." Another aspect of individualism was a widespread belief in the power of each person to remake his own life and his own culture (such beliefs often ignoring the social determinism inherent in environmentalism). Charles Brodie Patterson, an inspirationalist writing in 1910, urged Americans to do well but to recall that "individual success must never be considered apart from its effect upon society." Still, such writers urged each man and woman to maximum effort to discover the potentialities within the self:

> The Will is God, the Will is Man
> The Will is power, loosed in thought. . . .
> (Frank Channing Haddock, 1916.)

In so far as these exhortations were directed to the leaders, the individualism was consistent with ideas of social control. The discovery of inner potential in both child and adult gave much of the flavor to both the leadership and the environmentalism that would free those forces.

The fervent nationalism of the Progressives is perhaps even more difficult to re-create sympathetically than romantic self-discovery. Because the rhetoric later was used to justify both participation in World War I, and wartime and postwar suppression of dissent, Americans of another day mistakenly discounted the patriotic fervor that was involved in "the promise of American life." The Progressives' paradoxical attitudes toward imperialism, non-involvement, pacifism, and war dove-tailed well together as versions of "national interest." "The American democracy," wrote Croly, "can . . . safely trust its genuine interests to the keeping of those who represent the national interest. . . . Only by faith in an efficient national organization and by an exclusive and aggressive devotion to the national welfare can the American democratic ideal be made good."

It is entirely possible, as a number of historians have shown, to discover the internal inconsistencies in Progressive thinking and the differences between various leaders or intellectuals. While sometimes suggestive of the sources of tension in the Progressive movement, these studies fail to explain the perceptions of the people of that day that Progressives had a vital commonality that linked their efforts together. "One of the most inspiring movements in human history is now in progress," wrote political scientist Frederick A. Cleveland in 1913. Moreover, the general style that emphasized sometimes conflicting private organizations dedicated to the public interest was symptomatic of a more fundamental agreement that such groups could and should advance the public interest and especially temper the conflict between social demands and individualism.

Just to have thought and felt as they did, and to have expressed themselves, would have made the Progressives significant in American history. But beyond that, they took action on the basis of their beliefs. Many of their endeavors, it is true, resulted in little accomplishment and were essentially bureaucratic exercises in an increasingly bureaucratic society. Other ventures, however, had profound effects upon the lives of many Americans, and on that basis the Progressives, their beliefs, and their accomplishments were and are of major importance.

The Progressives' record shows that those reforming Americans tended to have very broad and inclusive approaches to social problems. The historians' error of emphasizing political events has been particularly misleading by obscuring the diversity and heterogeneity of the Progressives' effective concerns. The Country Life Commission, for instance, was given a comprehensive charge and then went on to investigate homemaking, education, buying and selling, communication, organizations, land (tenancy and rent), farm labor, finance, public health, and social life—an imposingly non-political analysis of the constituents of Americans' existence.

The agency through which the Progressives usually effected change was the traditional American voluntary organization. Just as economic development was based in large part upon private parties operating through private entities, so reformers utilized voluntary groups to mobilize both leadership and monetary support. Each of these organizations existed fundamentally to change the behavior of Americans in a certain limited area, usually by means of persuasion, so that educational programs were common to all of the efforts. Because of the Progressives' increasingly sophisticated views of the causes of particular evils, they often ventured far afield in attempts to overcome those evils. The confluence and cumulation of the programs, both old and new, that constituted the coherence of the movement therefore tended to appear in the form of comprehensive meliorism. The organizations, with their wide range of goals, were the cutting edge of reform, and the achievement of many of those goals the measure of Progressivism.

Typically, the earlier efforts, such as the peace and settlement house movements, all of which coalesced into Progressivism, continued with a vigor derived from social reinforcement. Marginal groups such as the anti-tuberculosis societies found themselves suddenly in the mainstream. And some of the older groups rewrote their history to show that they were "Progressive" in an earlier period. Such were the health officers of New York City who had been collaborating with political bosses interested in patronage matters; when Progressivism became fashionable, the health officials cast off their involvement with compromising politics and pretended that they had always been the purest of reformers, in effect denying the impact of the spirit of the times upon them.

New groups with new hopes flourished. The nationalization of reform, like the nationalization of business, involved a dramatic shift in scale and aspiration. "National," embodying both aspirations to aggrandizement and cultural nationalism, was the first word in the names of many of the most conspicuous reform organizations such as the National Civic Federation. Indeed, the large, private corporation in many ways provided a model for the organizational society that blossomed in the Progressive years.

Progressivism appeared in virtually every aspect of existence—even beyond the list of concerns of the Country Life Commission. Life itself and health were among the most pressing interests of reformers. The safety-in-industry movement grew out of both industrialists' solicitude and a collaboration between social workers and businessmen. Special campaigns against tuberculosis and venereal diseases combined the social workers with physicians. Improvement of diet and "health habits" in general also represented a major task of the uplifters. Special campaigns, such as arranging supplies of pure milk to the cities, were especially effective. Many general alterations of the physical environment, too, were undertaken in part for the sake of health.

Basic social institutions were another focus of the reformers. Both pro- and anti-divorce campaigners wanted to strengthen the family. General purity and anti–venereal disease campaigners came to foster sex education as the best way to make monogamy work. They saw satisfaction in marriage as not only the best preventive of both disease and impurity but the key as well to preservation of the family. Thus wiping out prostitution and preventing disease contributed to both health and marriage. Labor reformers of varying interests, too, invoked the sanctity of the family as an argument for one course of action or another. The churches increasingly became involved in the social gospel in general and in social regeneration in particular. In 1912 the congress of the Men and Religion Forward Movement was told that "religious questions have become so closely related to ethical theories and moral issues that the line of demarcation between the secular and religious, as such, has been erased." The schools, entrusted with a rapidly expanding clientele, served both as objects of reform, as professionalization increased, and as the means through which many of the Progressives hoped to uplift the nation permanently. Through such agencies as settlement houses and the YMCA, adult education, too, expanded dramatically, often in the interest of reforming the way of life of the urban masses, although this generation witnessed also the effective establishment of the county extension agent and other rural education and improvement institutions. Basic charity institutions were organized, reorganized, and invigorated for the purpose of both caring for the unfortunate and, like the churches and schools, uplifting them.

Business was no more immune to reform than other institutions. "The new competition" represented efforts to set up rules of fair play and eliminate extreme competitive practices that benefited no one. Industrial democracy and industrial welfare took root in the United States before World War I. Workmen's compensation schemes and laws came from the efforts of reformers and businessmen together. The gospel of efficiency and scientific management spread from the industrial plant and affected all of society. Nor was the pursuit of efficiency mere rhetoric. The standardization of parts and products that the engineering societies helped implement during World War I had already, a few years earlier, actually reduced production costs. "Rationalization" within business and industry worked out in many ways.

Within the professions the Progressive impulse appeared in multifarious guises. Reformers tried particularly to broaden the nature of professional functioning, most notably in education, social work, and engineering, and to refine the nature of professionalism and professional behavior in American society. The most dramatic example of this trend was the revolution in medical education following the Flexner Report of 1910. The ideal of professional behavior itself was close to the dynamics of Progressivism.

Many of the reforms had to do with the quality of life in general. The conservation movement, for example, based on concern for both efficiency and environment, was one of the most significant legacies of the era. Attempts to adjust children to live rewarding lives in the twentieth century and to become socialized and cooperative were the concern of reformers in education. Housing reformers attempted to make the physical environment more conducive to both personal and social well-being. Each of such reform efforts, so easily listed, affected the lives of millions of Americans, often in most significant ways.

The cumulative impact of all of this activity to upgrade conditions in America and reform American habits was immense. One English student of the American scene suggested in 1911 that the times were ripe for a new prophet to arise in the United States, and people at the time did not entirely discount the idea. In many instances, as noted above, concrete achievements beyond membership lists, meetings, propaganda dissemination, and other formal organizational efforts are hard to demonstrate. But taken as a whole, the programs of the reformers constitute an awesome demonstration of the power of determined private citizens working together to effect social change on a large scale.

Any general textbook in American history lists the federal government policies and enactments that presumably represent Progressivism. Anti-trust efforts and attempts to rationalize competition in interstate commerce appear prominently in these lists, along with pro–labor or pro–labor union actions and incidental items such as the Mann Act and, in the better texts, prohibition. Sometimes imperialism is characterized as Progressive, sometimes not. Most text writers also mention achievements on the state and local levels: workmen's compensation insurance laws; the initiative, referendum, and recall; the city manager and commission systems.

Certainly this list of governmental reforms is impressive. But the fact remains that the Progressives were at best ambivalent about using government action. At times they did have high hopes that a reform executive, legislature, or judiciary, or some specific law, might bring about needed changes. Repeatedly, good government advocates built up their own expectations and those of others. The many attempts to get at the will of the people—presumably wise and public spirited, in contrast to "the interests"—are a tribute to the reformers' good will and optimism. But the overwhelming result of righteous persons' entering politics was an almost unbroken record of ultimate defeat for virtue. It is no doubt symbolic that only after he was defeated for office did Seth Low, mayor of New York, turn to private channels to effect reform.

Events of the late nineteenth century had caused so much distrust of government that few decent people wanted to get involved. One precedent for a private alternative had been set by the purity movement, in which women who could not vote were attempting through the influence of their homes to strengthen basic social institutions. When governments failed even to enforce decency and to protect the family, the private reform groups of the purity crusade, including the Women's Christian Temperance Union and the mothers' movement, attempted to foster in each home and community a social environment that would cause the children to grow up to be pure, public spirited, and strong. Throughout the Progressive years reformers continued to show their mistrust of government by placing primary reliance upon non-political agencies and institutions to make meliorism effective. The reformers did not, for the most part, shy away from organization or bureaucracy in the private sector; indeed, the principal agencies through which they worked, organized groups, were sometimes highly structured. And as Gerd Korman points out, one of the most important and effective agencies through which reformers imposed their ideas on other Americans was the private employer. Industrial firms, by providing a workable, effective alternative for the exercise of power, permitted Progressives to bypass political processes. The Progressives' aversion to government was therefore based on experience, an experience that diminishes dramatically the importance and significance of the political history of that era.

Equating the extension of governmental power for social justice purposes, or what came to be called welfare statism, to the spirit of Progressivism is therefore an error. It is true that many Americans admired German cameralism and socialism. And many Americans did come to think that the neutral state would have to intervene more actively to maintain traditional liberty and freedom in society and so become a service state. But to portray the attitudes of Progressives toward political activity and power as anything beyond ambivalence is to distort the movement beyond recognition. "Our national ideal," wrote David Graham Phillips as early as 1905, "is not a powerful state, famed and feared for bluster and appetite . . . but manhood and womanhood, a citizenship ever wiser and stronger and more civilized—alert, enlightened, self-reliant, free."

Reformers showed their aversion to government in two general strategies. The first was to avoid government involvement entirely, as in endeavors such as the community chest movement, the Boy Scouts, and many aspects of health reform. The reformers' second strategy to keep the private sector dominant was using government in a strictly secondary, derivative way to achieve their ends. A good example is provided by the campaign to wipe out hookworm in the South, the debilitating parasite that became known as "the germ of laziness." Charles Wardell Stiles, a zoologist and public servant, led a persistent campaign that finally resulted in funding by the Rockefeller charities. From 1909 to 1914, using the Rockefeller money and support donated by the railroads, Stiles and his cohorts carried on a campaign to get people to wear shoes and employ sanitary privies. The campaign consisted partly of education, partly of enlisting the administrative powers of sometimes reluctant local health authorities. Stiles and his kind had no commitment to government but only to any means that appeared effective. In terms of economics and health alone, the impact of the hookworm crusade on the lives of millions of people was momentous.

This aversion to government was in part an aversion to party politics, to the selfishness that the reformers saw in partisan loyalty and the working of the party and spoils system. The voluntary associations represented a counterforce to regular parties and sometimes, as in the cases of the purity and temperance movements, to the churches as well. Many of the political changes associated with Progressivism, such as the initiative and referendum, were intentionally subversive of partisan politics (although the innovations were sometimes turned back and used against the reformers themselves). Non-partisan elections and the model law and uniform state law were other tactics symptomatic of a general revulsion against inefficiency and self-serving partisans. It was no coincidence that the rhetoric of the day coupled together selfishness, parties, and inefficiency. Except for the Progressives' commitments to the family, the nation, and morals, they might be considered in effect anti-institutional.

The apolitical or anti-political orientation of the activists was not what distinguished Progressivism from American reforms, whether pre–Civil War or New Deal, however. The Progressive movement differed from other reforms and the era differed from times before and after particularly because of the quality of the moral fervor of the reformers. Clyde Griffen has shown that both within the churches and within many of the individual movements that made up the whole, the ethos involved mass striving for a culture in which small-town virtues such as decency and brotherhood were worked out within a large-scale democratic and melioristic framework.

The evangelistic framework also helps to explain the social basis for the hegemony, for a few years, of a Progressive generation—the young people whose leadership set them apart even in politics. They grew up in the late nineteenth century when there existed a powerful revivalism that separated sentiment and behavior from theological orthodoxy. To a remarkable extent a consensus idealism, worked out in practice in such forms as ne purity and mothers' movements, pervaded the middle classes. Most of the Progressives came of age in the decades of intense religious feeling when the better families devoted themselves to decency, self-improvement, and altruism. Even young Henry Morgenthau, Sr., who was not in the Protestant mainstream, remembered being inspired by "a vision of a life of unselfish devotion to the welfare of others." Benjamin Flower in 1901 recognized "a rapidly growing band of young men and women who are consecrating their lives to the service of man and the making of a higher, juster, and truer civilization." George W. Perkins, later of Progressive political fame, always made social service evangelism a part of his life, even when he was selling insurance. In countless instances, late-nineteenth-century homes in which uplift was stressed can be shown to be the factor that produced a Progressive generation.

Gregory Singleton has suggested that the practical evangelism of late-Victorian Americans was an attempt of the white Anglo-Saxon Protestants and those identified with them to form an ethnic group in response to the development of the Irish ethnic group of the mid-century period. The success of the WASPs in imposing standards upon their own group led them consequently to attempt to impose those standards upon the entire culture. Likewise, numerous commentators have described American imperialism and interventionism as a drive to extend WASP culture to the whole world. Progressivism can be understood, therefore, as the culmination of a general cultural movement that agitated the entire society before World War I.

The moral idealism of the reform generation coincided with other general social developments of the new century. In an increasingly complex and interdependent society, bureaucratic organization and control flourished in all areas of American life at least as much as in uplift groups. As Americans more and more worked out their own specializations of function in society, they tended to view their roles in that society in terms of the function. The ideal functionary could negate self-interest and other interests and view his functioning as a service to society. In innumerable instances appointees who were supposed to represent an interest found themselves playing instead a bureaucratic role and advocating courses of action growing out of role function rather than special interest, courses of action that answered to general rather than selfish needs. The growth of the bureaucratic way of life and of the ideal of unselfish service therefore complemented each other.

Within the constituent reform efforts of Progressivism the professionals were most easily identifiable because of both numbers and contributions. As professionals, they embodied the idea of unselfish service. Physicians, clergymen, educators, and social workers—the men and women of the helping professions—were particularly conspicuous. The Progressive movement in turn accelerated the general trend toward professionalization in all of American life by popularizing the goal of disinterested service and coupling it with social approbation, most dramatically in social work and engineering. The ideal of a vocation as a "profession" found its way into many areas of American existence and carried with it at least some of the service ideal, even, for example, in advertising. Sensitive to moral requirements of the culture, "professionals" were quick to claim moral benefits of their activities. Although affected by Progressivism, the social changes involved in bureaucratization and professionalization in their turn helped to reinforce the idealism and enthusiasm of reformers.

The practical result of all of this moral fervor was that the Progressive movement embodied an immediacy that distinguished the prewar phenomenon from any comparable reform ferment. Contemporary English reformers, for example, although they spoke as fervently as the Americans, were unable to take action effectively on a broad social front. Their reform proved to be merely rhetorical. American reform, by contrast, was marked by not only enthusiasm but also frantic activity. It is easy enough to laugh at the energy of Theodore Roosevelt, recalling the wit who thought him a combination of St. Paul and St. Vitus, but a whole generation of reformers did show their commitment in effort and active organization.

Such immediacy and commitment to reform suggests that the Progressives possessed an unusual confidence in their ability to change the world. And they were confident. Moreover, their optimism was the essential force behind both aspiration and achievement—so much so as to demand explanation.

Despite their sometimes simplistic rhetoric, the Progressives were not naive. Nor was their optimism naive. They did not attempt, for example, so much to get rid of prostitution as to take the profit motive out of it. Likewise they did not attempt so much to do away with the drinking of alcoholic beverages as to get at the profiteers in human misery. Rather than evangelize the lazy Southerners, the Progressives tried to get rid of the physical burdens that disadvantaged so many people. The reformers were as willing to attack hereditary liabilities through the eugenics movement as to try to improve the environment by means of a host of other reforms. The literature as well as the activity of the reformers repeatedly showed that the leaders, at least, were often aware of the complexities of man, of society, and of history. They tried to concentrate on prevention of ills rather than correcting results, and the leaders' conception of causation moved their programs toward the long range—hence their attention to the upbringing and environment of children even more than of misguided adults already set in their ways. It is particularly in the light of the Progressives' sophistication that their optimism demands explanation.

The inspiration for reform was science, broadly understood to embrace also technology and medicine. And the inspiration was not theoretical but very real to those people. The contrast with earlier reform movements underlines the practicality of Progressives. Where the vegetarians of the 1840s, whatever stimulation they may have received from technological innovation, had promised long life and female suffrage, men of 1900 saw both old and young rescued from the grave by new surgical techniques. Where there was in an earlier day promise of governmental reform, in 1903 the Wright brothers' flight had actually taken place. Electricity entered into everyday life, far more eloquent than visions of a republican utopia. What for years had been promise—largely the promise of political institutions—became, in the twentieth century, performance in non-political areas. The performance was not casual or expectable. The ability of physicians suddenly to arrest diphtheria and permit a dying child to breathe once more and recover was a miracle comparable with those described in the Bible. Science had justified both extravagant hopes and men's beliefs in their own power to change the world. Moreover, the changes often involved the details of existence and gave personal meaning to optimism about transforming American life.

Science in the Progressive era had many public aspects. By themselves the material achievements of the generation before 1906 provided concrete evidence of the almost unlimited possibilities of change. But the scientific attitude was abstracted and translated into two strategies that were applied to non-technical areas of endeavor: the cult of efficiency and the use of the expert. In fact the wonders of pure science were not generally a part of the usual conception of science held by the educated public, except when external signs of prestige such as Nobel prizes and research endowments suggested esteem for science on the part of men of affairs.

Efficiency embodied a number of attributes that added up to hardworking, profitable, competent, and socially harmonious individuals and groups. As in the scientific management movement, Progressives conceived of efficiency as the rational maximization of result for effort and organization—and planning and rational control to that end constituted "science." This objective use of intelligence was the nexus between science and the popular conceptions of science, particularly technology and the results of technology.

In so far as the reformers held in common any ideal of technique, the most striking allegiance they showed was to the expert in the service of uplift or democracy (the latter sometimes known as the "Wisconsin idea"). Herbert Croly, in his eloquent verbalization, *The Promise of American Life* (1909), set up the scientists' way of proceeding as the model for citizenship. "No scientist as such has anything to gain by the use of inferior methods or by the production of inferior work. There is only one standard for all scientific investigators—the highest standard." By using experts in all aspects of American life, the Progressives expected to bring the generalized benefits of disinterested science to the entire society. The socialist William English Walling in 1911 looked with approval upon the direction that Progressive reform was tending: "Science is becoming more consciously pragmatic, more consciously concerned with the service of man. . . . And this is the science which now has the unqualified support and respect of the most able and advanced scientists of the time."

The objectivity of the scientist was embodied in the tendency of members of professions, as noted above, to avow their dedication to unselfish service and technical objectivity. As professionals foreswore personal gain, their expertise could serve a democratic society without the self-interest that would otherwise corrupt and discredit such an elite. For this rapidly growing, extremely influential segment of society, the ideals of unselfish service and efficiency served to validate both personal and social goals. And in organizations they tended to reinforce the process of bureaucratization.

Later generations who believed that interest groups and big government constituted the one true model for reform did draw inspiration from the Progressives, but only in some of the rhetoric and some of the tactics and vision of their predecessors. The voluntary organizations could be viewed as pressure groups—but only if each group was turned into a selfish interest group. Voluntary organizations pursuing altruistic ends are decidedly different from interest groups representing the self-serving demands of the New Deal and post–New Deal broker state. Chambers of commerce and trade associations, which also flourished early in the twentieth century, were not of the same category as the Urban League or Mental Hygiene Society. "If by some magic," wrote social gospeller Walter Rauschenbusch in 1914, "business life . . . could be plucked out of our total social life in all its raw selfishness, and isolated on an island, unmitigated by any other factors of our life, that island would immediately become the object of a great foreign mission crusade for all Christendom."

The cultural nationalism of the early twentieth century easily translated into identifying with an enhanced federal government, as was indicated by the common ground often noted between the New Nationalism and the New Deal. Likewise cultural nationalism contributed to the growing eclipse of local and regional nonconformity, another process hastened and blessed by WASP reformers.

Perhaps most intriguing of the Progressive legacies was the vision that for every ill of every person there was or should be a specialist to do away with that ill. Not content with general measures, such as those embodied in laws and public campaigns, the Progressives saw the possibility of reaching every member of society to educate, to uplift, and to care. The anti-tuberculosis and anti–venereal disease campaigns were both based upon treating every infected person, that is, every carrier of disease, regardless of the numbers of persons and the costs involved. This technique of providing special protections and services for each and every citizen was at the heart of the later welfare state strategy and at the same time constituted the major controlling device of the bureaucratic society that came to dominate mid-twentieth-century America. Particularly the health and social work contingents among Progressives pioneered individual care and control. But they worked primarily through voluntary organizations operating for altruistic purposes, as opposed to the welfare state style that came to emphasize personal need and want—that is, selfishness.

The experience of World War I intensified the Progressives' already ambivalent attitudes toward government. The actions of both state and local bodies estranged many, who typically moved into either disillusioned advocacy of purely private endeavor or the American Civil Liberties Union. Still another group saw in the wartime emergency a chance to bypass the usual political barriers to social reconstruction and to use the enhanced powers of the executive for reformist purposes. Such reformers typically lost faith in the power of an intelligent public but did not surrender the idea of leadership by an enlightened elite. These various experiences with government in fact contributed to the disintegration of the reform consensus in the divisiveness and self-centeredness of the 1920s.

After World War I, the parallel reforms that had coalesced into Progressivism once more parted. Many wealthy patrons of uplift associations died. A number of important spokesmen for the movement withdrew into art for art's sake or some similarly pure attempt, often with Progressive roots, to strive for the ideal. Muckrakers of the Jazz Age, as Richard H. Pells observes, aimed their criticism at "stupidity, aimlessness, and vulgarity." Others suffered disillusionments of various kinds, with various consequences. Harold Stearns in 1919 summed up a common reevaluation and reconceptualization of American reform in the years just past:

We are becoming increasingly self-critical and dissatisfied with mere acquisition. Both our intellectuals and our creative literary men were emerging from their Transcendental towers of isolation. But American liberalism had two bad heritages to fight against . . . one the heritage of race-hatred psychology of the unacknowledged negro problem, making for intolerance; the other the heritage of perverted moralism or the attempt to use native idealism for specific prohibitions, making in its turn for coercion. Such, in brief, seems to me the strength and the fragility of American liberalism as it met the challenge of 1914.

This was the "liberal" view that was to become commonplace in another decade, one that ignored the positive achievements of the Progressives.

Yet in the postwar years much of the voluntary associationism of the Progressive era continued, and indeed the "association idea" was of central importance in the 1920s in general and in the career of Herbert Hoover in particular. Industrial welfare and business cooperation represented an enlightened continuation of ideas fostered in an earlier day. When the New Deal came, coercion and centralization grew as an addition onto the core legacy. The tradition of caring and experiment continued, but the essentials of an earlier day, extreme reliance on voluntary groups and aversion to selfishness, diminished significantly.

A number of historians who in later times criticized the Progressives in ahistorical contexts distracted attention from the strengths, accomplishments, and significances of the pre–World War I reformers. The Progressives were not lower class, and they did seek to impose a WASP style of life on other people. The voluntary association is a device that upper classes traditionally used to help control the lower classes. But to suggest that the changes were good or bad simply because of the attitudes of agents who carried them out would be purely ad hominem argument. The intent of the Progressives was, by placing primary reliance on voluntary organizations, to change the living habits of most Americans. The organizations used education and persuasion and sometimes types of coercion to teach people to observe safety regulations and not to spit, and to coerce those who continued anti-social behavior in spite of explanations that would have convinced a prudent, educated WASP. That the Progressives had somewhat less respect for cultural variation than sentimental later generations is hardly relevant to the causes and consequences of a major reform program.

Likewise, later critics, impatient of change in their own times, thought the Progressives worthy of scorn because they were essentially conservative. Perhaps the young intellectuals of the prewar period, who with Randolph Bourne thought of themselves as "radicals," misled later readers. In fact the reformers were interested in morals and in basic institutions, like any conservatives. And the Progressives, whatever their dedication to justice, did not envisage any overturn of the general social hierarchy, although the term uplift involved increased well-being as well as social harmony. No doubt many believed, implicitly as well as explicitly, that reform was necessary for preservation, with emphasis upon the preservation.

Still another line of criticism is advanced by those who argue that the Progressives did not make enough changes, that they failed to achieve completely all of their own goals. The proper historical question is not whether changes matched the avowed aims but, first, how the goals moved people to action, and, second, what actual changes, intended or not, occurred.

And the fact remains that the reformers advocated and carried out many changes in a short time, and, to save some institutions, they attacked others. To save and strengthen the family and traditional morals, the reformers were willing to break taboos and undermine the double standard. To preserve private owner-ship of business and a traditional labor system, the business Progressives were willing to set limits to competition, to organize together, and to begin systems of welfare capitalism. To protect an open society, the Progressives subverted politi-cal parties. These and a myriad of other changes suggest that, in that generation, conservatism may not have been a major force unless defined very flexibly. Prob-ably it is more useful to follow Richard Hofstadter and Samuel P. Hays and char-acterize the reformers as people with guilty consciences who would not stand idly by when they saw social wrongs.

Since the Progressives tried so hard to be unselfish, latter-day critics belittled them by showing that public-spirited actions were really self-serving—that com-fortably well-off people would profit from social stability, that the managers of organizations would benefit from increasing bureaucratization, that businesses would make more money in an efficient society. Progressives have been portrayed as downwardly mobile people who were exalting experts in order to reverse so-cial processes, and also as businessmen bent on greater monopoly. And of course they were damned in particular for not invariably advocating central government and/or cultural pluralistic solutions to all social problems, which fact in itself en-genders suspicion on the part of anti-business "liberal" historians that "inter-ests" were at work.

For all of these doubters and ahistorical critics, two facts are enough answer. First, Progressivism involved many aspects of American life, including every ma-jor social institution—except, in some respects, perhaps, government. And, sec-ond, the Progressives left behind them a substantial number of specific accom-plishments. All of them were products of both human aspiration and complex historical forces.

What is left of Progressivism now is the memory of a moment in time, per-haps ten years, when an altruism that was based on WASP ethnic group values united with hard facts of scientific and technological change. "It is this union of the idealistic and the efficient," wrote intellectual Randolph Bourne in 1913, "that gives the movement its hold on the disinterested and serious youth of to-day." The result of the combination was as pure an unselfishness as has been seen in history, operating through voluntary associations to bring about widespread and significant changes in American life.

Battling the Saloon and the Brothel: The Great Coercive Crusades

On June 25, 1910, President William Howard Taft signed into law a bill introduced by Congressman James Mann of Illinois making it a federal offense to transport a woman across a state line for "immoral purposes." A death blow had been struck, so the framers of the Mann Act claimed, against prostitution, the brothel, and the dread "white-slave traffic."

Seven and a half years later, on December 22, 1917, in the midst of a world war, Congress submitted to the states a constitutional amendment barring the manufacture, sale, or importation of intoxicating liquor within the United States. In January 1919, the necessary thirty-six states having ratified, prohibition became the law of the land. (By the terms of the Eighteenth Amendment, actual enforcement began a year later: a final crumb tossed to the liquor interests by the triumphant prohibitionists.)

These two measures were among the crowning achievements of the great Progressive-era crusades against the "liquor evil" and the "prostitution evil." . . . The brothel and the saloon were widely perceived as the great bastions of urban vice. So long as they stood, the dream of an urban moral awakening would be no more than that; if they could be subdued, the purified, morally homogeneous city might at last become a reality.

Intemperance and prostitution were not, of course, discoveries of the Progressives. Both had been the object of reformist attention since the days of Lyman Beecher and John R. McDowall. In the Gilded Age, the Woman's Christian Temperance Union (1874) had revived the temperance cause, and the antiprostitution banner had been upheld by "social purity" leaders like Abby Hopper Gibbons of New York and the Philadelphia Quaker Aaron Macy Powell, as well as by local civic organizations campaigning against municipal regulation (and hence tacit ac-

Reprinted by permission of the publisher from *Urban Masses and Moral Order in America, 1820–1920,* by Paul Boyer, Cambridge, Mass.: Harvard University Press. Copyright © 1978 by the President and Fellows of Harvard College.

ceptance) of prostitution. The decade of the 1890s saw an intensification of both antialcohol and antiprostitution effort, including state campaigns to raise the legal age of consent, national temperance conventions and "purity" congresses, the formation of the Anti-Saloon League (1895) and the American Purity Alliance, and the organization of rescue work aimed at prostitutes and unwed mothers.

For all this, the dawning century found both vices still deeply entrenched. In 1900 only three states had prohibition laws on the books; saloons, liquor stores, and the infamous "bucket shops" flourished in every major city; and per capita alcohol consumption—augmented by the new national favorite, German lager beer—stood at nearly twice the 1860 figure. As for prostitution, every city had its red-light district, including some now bathed in a nostalgic glow: Gayosa Street in Memphis; the Levee in Chicago; San Francisco's Barbary Coast; New Orleans' Storyville (named for the alderman who drafted the statute establishing its boundaries); "Hooker's Division" in Washington, an appellation immortalizing the Civil War general who had confined prostitutes to that section. In 1900, two Omaha madams, Ada and Minna Everleigh, felt confident enough of their prospects to invest thousands of dollars in a luxurious Chicago brothel, the Everleigh Club, which soon became the showplace of the Levee.

In focusing attention on these evils—indeed, in making them stand symbolically for much that was unsettling about city life—urban moral reformers of the Progressive era succeeded in channeling the urban uplift enthusiasm of the 1890s into highly organized efforts involving specific goals and carefully planned strategies. In the prohibition drive, the Anti-Saloon League—supported by innumerable small contributors and a few very large ones like John D. Rockefeller, Jr., and dime-store baron S. S. Kresge—played the crucial organizational role. From the first, the ASL's single-minded goal was legal prohibition, and its major target, the cities. In countries and townships where prohibitionist sentiment was strong, the league organized local-option campaigns and worked for the election of sympathetic state legislators. The local groundwork laid, it moved to the state level, exhibiting the same skill in legislative lobbying that it displayed in marshaling public opinion. By concentrating on state legislatures (where the cities were underrepresented), the Anti-Saloon League gradually isolated urban America. In the campaign's final stages, thousands of ASL speakers promoted the cause in the nation's Protestant pulpits, and oceans of propaganda (including the League's principal organ, the *American Issue*) poured from ASL presses in Westerville, Ohio. The triumph of 1919 was thus the culmination of more than two decades of grass roots effort, reinforced by wartime fervor, grain-conservation enthusiasm, and anti-German-brewer sentiment.

While the ASL was orchestrating the prohibition campaign, a more complex organizational effort was focusing diffuse sexual-purity impulses on a specific issue: urban prostitution. The issue first surfaced in New York City, where the number of saloons harboring prostitutes had increased sharply after 1896, when a revision of the state licensing code—dubbed the Raines Law after its sponsor—had inadvertently made it advantageous for them to add bedrooms and transform themselves into "hotels." The spread of these "Raines Law hotels" into well-to-do neighborhoods aroused a storm of indignation, and in November

1900 Episcopal Bishop Henry C. Potter penned a stinging protest to Tammany mayor Robert Van Wyck. (Unruffled, Van Wyck declared that New York had "the highest standard of morality in the world"; Tammany boss Richard Croker, taking a rather contradictory tack, argued that in any city there were "bound to be some unusually vile places.")

A few days after Potter's letter, the New York Committee of Fifteen was formed. This organization of businessmen, publishers, academics, and other elite figures—the prototype of antiprostitution commissions that would soon emerge in scores of cities—set out quietly to investigate vice conditions and develop legislative remedies. It soon became involved in more stirring matters, however, through its support for a flamboyant young special-sessions judge, William T. Jerome—the "second Theodore Roosevelt," his admirers claimed—who had won celebrity for his dramatic raids on brothels and other vice dens. In the municipal elections of 1901, thanks in part to the support of the Committee of Fifteen and the Reverend Charles Parkhurst's City Vigilance League, Jerome was elected district attorney while Seth Low, a "fusion" candidate backed by the reformers, defeated Tammany's man in the mayoral race.

Meanwhile, a team of prostitution investigators had been recruited by the Committee of Fifteen, and in 1902 its findings were published as *The Social Evil, with Special Reference to Conditions Existing in the City of New York.* A 1909 *McClure's* exposé, "The Daughters of the Poor: A Plain Story of the Development of New York City as a Leading Center of the White Slave Trade of the World, under Tammany Hall," helped sustain the cause, as did the 1910 investigations of a special grand jury under John D. Rockefeller, Jr.

At the same time, Chicago was emerging as a second major center of the antiprostitution campaign. In a 1907 *McClure's* article, "The City of Chicago: A Study of the Great Immoralities," muckraker George Kibbe Turner accorded prostitution a prominent place in his catalog of evils. ("As in the stock-yards, not one shred of flesh is wasted.") Soon an ambitious assistant state's attorney named Clifford G. Roe was organizing a series of white-slave prosecutions. Thwarted by his superiors, Roe resigned, secretly arranged financial backing from a group of sympathetic Chicagoans, and proceeded with his investigations as a private citizen. In 1911 Roe organized the National Vigilance Society (with himself as director, secretary, and general counsel) and over the next few years published several lurid books on prostitution.

Meanwhile, in January 1910, under pressure from the Chicago church federation, Mayor Fred Busse had appointed a thirty-member vice commission (twenty-eight men, two women), under the chairmanship of Walter T. Sumner, dean of the Cathedral of Saints Peter and Paul (Episcopal), to investigate prostitution in the city. Given a $5,000 appropriation, the Commission in 1911 produced *The Social Evil in Chicago,* a 394-page report ending with a set of recommendations aimed at implementing its motto: "Constant and Persistent Repression of Prostitution the Immediate Method; Absolute Annihilation the Ultimate Ideal." The report was based on data compiled by a research team under George J. Kneeland, a Yale Divinity School dropout who had worked as an editor with several New York magazines before becoming director of investigations for New York's Committee of Fifteen in 1908.

Also involved in the antiprostitution crusade were the American Society of Sanitary and Moral Prophylaxis (founded 1905), a medical group headed by the prominent dermatologist Prince A. Morrow, whose influential *Social Diseases and Marriage* had appeared in 1904, and the Bureau of Social Hygiene (1910), a small, New York-based agency financed with Rockefeller money. Among the latter's publications was *Commercialized Prostitution in New York* (1913), a somewhat popularized version of the various vice reports already in circulation.

Some order emerged in this organizational thicket in 1913 when the Rockefeller and Morrow groups, together with several other societies (including the old American Purity Alliance), merged to form the American Social Hygiene Association. While no single group ever dominated the antiprostitution movement as the Anti-Saloon League did the prohibition crusade, the ASHA and its magazine *Social Hygiene* played a central role.

Sparked by all this organizational activity, the antiprostitution drive had assumed the characteristics of a national crusade. "No movement devoted to the betterment and uplift of humanity has advanced more rapidly within recent years," reported the *New Encyclopedia of Social Reform* in 1909. From 1902 to 1916, 102 cities and 3 states conducted vice investigations modeled on those of New York and Chicago. By 1920 practically every state had outlawed soliciting, and more than 30 had passed Injunction and Abatement laws empowering the courts to close brothels upon the filing of citizens' complaints. At the federal level, the reform found expression not only in the Mann Act but also in President Roosevelt's 1908 announcement of America's adherence to an internal white-slave convention recently adopted in Paris, as well as a series of reports on prostitution—"the most accursed business ever devised by man"—by the United States Immigration Commission.

"White slavery" proved a gold mine to journalists, editors, moviemakers, and publishers. George Kibbe Turner's exposés are merely the best remembered of many in the periodicals of the day. *Traffic in Souls,* a film purporting to document the nationwide prostitution business, appeared in 1913. As for books, the scores of vice commission reports simply added to a torrent of works including such diverse titles as Clifford Roe's *Horrors of the White Slave Trade* (1911), with its 448 pages and thirty-two illustrations; Jane Addams's thoughtful *A New Conscience and an Ancient Evil* (1912); and David Graham Phillips's novel *Susan Lenox; Her Fall and Rise* (1917).

Just as it provided the final impetus for prohibition, the wartime mood of 1917–18 also intensified the antiprostitution crusade. With the support of Secretary of War Newton D. Baker (who as mayor of Cleveland had taken a strong antiprostitution stand), the wartime Commission on Training Camp Activities closed a number of red-light districts hitherto resisting purification—an achievement perhaps praised more heartily in *Social Hygiene* than in the barracks.

Moralism and Expertise: The Links between the Great Coercive Crusades and Progressivism

Historians have engaged in a lively debate over whether prohibition—and, by implication, the antiprostitution crusade—should be included within the canon of legitimate Progressive reforms. Writing in 1955, Richard Hofstadter said no. Prohibition, he contended, was "a ludicrous caricature of the reforming impulse"—a "pinched, parochial substitute" for genuine reform, imposed by spiteful rural folk upon the more tolerant and urbane cities. In the same vein, Egal Feldman in 1967 described the coercive aspects of the antiprostitution crusade as "irrational, evangelical, uncompromising, and completely divorced from the humanitarianism of the early twentieth century." Other historians have challenged this thesis. Demonstrating the close connections—in terms of personnel, mutual affirmations of support, and overlapping organizational commitments—that can be established between the moral-control crusades and other strands of progressivism, they argue that the former must be considered an authentic expression of the broader Progressive impulse.

Interestingly, the Progressives themselves had trouble reaching a consensus on this question. Although some reformers and ideologues welcomed the prohibition and antiprostitution campaigns, others denied any kinship between what *they* stood for and the coercive moral-control crusades. Walter Lippmann, for example, ridiculed the "raucous purity" of some antivice campaigners, and Charles A. Beard in 1912 criticized the "moral enthusiasts" who were "pushing through legislation which they are not willing to uphold by concentrated and persistent action." Herbert Croly in *The Promise of American Life* declared that reformers who functioned merely as "moral protestants and purifiers" were engaged in a fundamentally "misdirected effort." Only "personal self-stultification," he insisted, could result from such an "illiberal puritanism." True reform, Croly characteristically added, involved "an intellectual as well as a moral challenge."

The answer depends in large part, of course, on where one looks on the Progressive spectrum and, indeed, on how one defines progressivism. . . . But one trait common to most reformers of these years—and one which helped establish a bond between the coercive reformers and other Progressives—was an infinite capacity for moral indignation. For Progressives of all stripes, as for their predecessors in the 1890s, questions of social injustice, corporate wrongdoing, governmental corruption, and personal morality were inextricably linked. Almost every Progressive cause had its moral dimension; almost every condition Progressives set out to change was seen as contributing to a debilitating social environment that made it easier for people to go wrong and harder for them to go right. Child labor and the exploitation of women workers were evil not only because they were physically harmful, but also because they stunted the moral and spiritual development of their victims. (Society had the right to limit the hours of women in industry, Louis D. Brandeis argued before the United States Supreme Court in 1908, because the fatigue of long hours was undermining their moral fiber and driving them to "alcoholic stimulants and other excesses.") Urban graft and misgovernment were evil not only because they wasted taxpayers' money but also because they debased the moral climate of the city. ("The influence and example of bad municipal government . . . , of public servants dishonest with impunity and profit," cried an officer of the National Municipal League in 1904, echoing his reform predecessors of the Gilded Age, "constitutes a disease against which we have greater need of a quarantine than we ever had against yellow fever.") As Stanley K. Schultz has written of progressivism's journalistic advance guard the muckrakers, their writings often "assumed the nature of a moral crusade, . . . because ultimately their search was a moral endeavor."

The moral substratum of progressivism is heavily underscored in the autobiography of Frederic C. Howe, in many respects a prototypical Progressive, in which he describes his intensely evangelical upbringing and its shaping influence on his later reform career: "Physical escape from the embraces of evangelical religion did not mean moral escape. From that religion my reason was never emancipated. By it I was conformed to my generation and made to share its moral standards and ideals. . . . Early assumptions as to virtue and vice, goodness and evil remained in my mind long after I had tried to discard them. This is, I think, the most characteristic influence of my generation."

Some historians have drawn sharp distinctions between progressivism's various facets, opposing the economic and political reforms to those that were explicitly moralistic. Such an approach, if too literally applied, does violence to the powerful moral thrust underlying *all* these reforms. For the Progressives, society had the right—indeed the duty!—to intervene at *any* point where the well-being of its members was threatened, since every such threat had its moral aspect. A 1914 article in a reform journal edited by Josiah Strong and W. D. P. Bliss put the matter plainly: "We are no longer frightened by that ancient bogy—'paternalism in government.' We affirm boldly, it is the business of government to be just that—paternal. . . . *Nothing human can be foreign to a true government.*"

Within this intensely moralistic ambience, it was easy to see the coercive social-control crusades as simply one piece in the larger reform mosaic. In *The Shame of the Cities* (1904), for example, muckraker Lincoln Steffens frequently called attention to organized gambling and prostitution as by-products of municipal political corruption. Similarly, a leading San Francisco Progressive, newspaper editor Fremont Older, in fighting boss Abraham Ruef in 1907–1909, revealed many seamy details of Ruef's involvement with organized vice.

Those who were seeking to rid urban America of these vices, for their part, never doubted that they were in the mainstream of the era's broader reform current. "We had tired of poverty, of squalor, of ignorance . . . , of the wretchedness of women and the degradation of men," wrote a prohibition leader in 1908. "Our hearts bleed when we look upon the misery of child life." Convinced that intolerable conditions of work and habitation were driving men into the saloons and women into the streets, they supported such Progressive reforms as wage-and-hour laws, tenement codes, and factory-safety legislation. "Is it any wonder," asked the Chicago Vice Commission rhetorically, "that a tempted girl who receives only six dollars per week working with her hands sells her body for twenty-five dollars per week when she learns there is a demand for it and men are willing to pay the price?"

A second important respect in which the coercive moral reformers were closely attuned to the broader Progressive impulse was in their reliance on statistics, sociological investigation, and "objective" social analysis to buttress their cause—a strategy characteristic of many otherwise quite disparate Progressive reforms. For the antisaloon and antiprostitution forces, this represented a significant shift from earlier approaches. Through much of the Gilded Age, the temperance and social-purity enthusiasts had concentrated on moral appeals to the individual, assuming that they and the objects of their benevolent attention shared, at some level, a common body of values and standards. (There were exceptions to this personalistic approach—the state drives to raise the legal age of consent, the quadrennial electoral campaigns of the Prohibition party—but in general the personal moral appeal was the preferred strategy.)

By the end of the century, as the old assumptions faded, overly moralistic personal appeals were being supplanted by a more generalized emphasis on the reformers' technical expertise and superior factual grasp of urban issues. Moral reform must be rooted in careful investigation and social analysis, insisted Benjamin Flower in *Civilization's Inferno*. "Mere sentimentality will not answer. We must have incontrovertible data upon which to base our arguments." The first step of a prestigious Committee of Fifty for the investigation of the Liquor Problem formed in New York City in 1893 was to "secure a body of facts which may serve as a basis for intelligent public and private actions." Even the WCTU established a Department of Scientific Temperance Instruction that lobbied for alcohol-education programs in the public schools.

In the Progressive years this shift accelerated, and the personalistic approach was largely abandoned. Now, by contrast, intemperance and sexual deviation came to be viewed less as personal failings than as products of an urban environment that needed to be purified—by force of law if necessary. The Chicago Vice Commission expressed the prevailing view when it dismissed as "naive" those who looked for the sources of prostitution in the individual prostitute's flaws of character. The emphasis was now on eliminating from the urban environment those institutions that undermined individual moral resistance—especially the saloon and the brothel.

With this development, the "scientific" aura of urban moral reform intensified. A *Scientific Temperance Journal* was established in Boston in 1906 by Cora Frances Stoddard. Muckraking journalists like George Kibbe Turner marshaled facts, statistics, dates, and names to buttress their indictment of the saloon, and the antiprostitution crusaders similarly strove for a tone of objective expertise as remote as possible from the thundering moral denunciations of earlier years. Indeed, in a number of cities the antiprostitution groups called themselves "Morals Efficiency Commissions." The 1902 report of New York's Committee of Fifteen exuded the scholarly aura appropriate to what its secretary called in the preface "a valuable scientific contribution," and *The Social Evil in Chicago,* a forbiddingly dry compendium of charts, statistics, appendixes, medical data, and analyses of interviews with 2,420 prostitutes, was similarly described by its sponsors as a "scientific study" based on the findings of "experts and trained investigators."

The fetish of scientific objectivity took many forms. One national group concentrated on assigning exact numerical ratings to various cities' success in eradicating prostitution: Chicago, 37 percent; New York, 41 percent; Houston, 86 percent; and so on. In many vice commission reports, the antiseptic aura was heightened by the substitution of numbers and letters for actual names: "One woman, Mollie (X61), lives near Oak Park and solicits in (X62). Her husband is dying in (X62a)." The point of view underlying all this was summed up by the chairman of the Moral Survey Committee of Syracuse, New York. "It is a waste of time and energy to begin dealing with commercialized vice with talk, talk,

talk," he wrote. "What we need is facts, facts, facts." The ASL's *National Issue* and its hefty annual *Yearbook* fairly bristled with charts, tables, and graphs purporting to establish positive or negative correlations between the saloon and death rates, arrest rates, tax rates, divorce rates, wages, insanity, pauperism, bank deposits, industrial efficiency, housing investment, and public-school enrollment. Drawing upon data compiled by Cora Frances Stoddard, the ASL in 1917 reported—with the usual flourish of graphs—that studies undertaken in Germany and Finland had proved conclusively a link between drinking, sloppy typing, and the inability to thread needles.

This obsession with technical expertise and factual data completed the secularization of the urban moral-control movement. To be sure, these reforms ultimately depended on the moral energy of Protestant America, and denominational agencies like the Methodist Board of Temperance and Morals played an important role in rallying support. Yet appeals to the evangelical moral code do not figure strongly in either the prohibition or the antiprostitution movements, and the organizations promoting these reforms were not by any means overweighed with clergymen. The top ASL men were ministers, to be sure, but during the prohibition struggle they functioned almost entirely as secularized managers, lobbyists, and propagandists rather than as latter-day Jeremiahs pronouncing God's judgment on the saloon. The lower echelons of ASL administration were even more completely secular. The organization's general superintendent, Purley A. Baker, set the tone. "The narrow, acrimonious and emotional appeal is giving way," he declared in 1915, "to a rational, determined conviction that the [liquor] traffic . . . has no rightful place in our modern civilization."

The antiprostitution movement, despite the prominence of an occasional cleric like Chicago's Dean Sumner, was even more completely divorced from the Protestant establishment. Indeed, by around 1910, antivice zealots among the clergy had become a distinct embarrassment. The Chicago Vice Commission roundly condemned an evangelist who was conducting prayer meetings in front of the city's leading brothels. An *Arena* writer in 1909 urged that the cause be pursued "sanely and scientifically" and not through " 'moral' rant from the pulpits." The local vice commissions usually had only token ministerial representation, and many delegated the actual investigative work to the team of New York-based researchers originally put together by George Kneeland for the Committee of Fifteen. As an older generation of urban moral reformers passed from the scene, the movement came to exude more of the aura of the laboratory, law library, and university lecture hall than the pulpit.

Indeed, the very shift in terminology in the antiprostitution movement, from "social *purity*" to "social *hygiene*," is significant. The entire urban moral-control effort in these years was suffused with public-health terminology and rhetoric. A writer in *Social Hygiene* in 1917 predicted that New Orleans would soon conquer prostitution just as she had eradicated yellow fever, and in *The Challenge of the City,* Josiah Strong suggested that the polluters of the city's "moral atmosphere" should be considered as deadly as the "vermin of an Egyptian plague." In Boston, the Watch and Ward Society won praise in these years from Harvard professor Francis G. Peabody for "unobtrusively working underground, guarding us from the pestiferous evil which at any time may come up into our faces, into our homes, into our children's lives." Picking up on these cues, the Watch and Ward, like similar moral-control agencies elsewhere, increasingly defined its mission in public-health terms. "The old idea of 'charity' . . . has gradually given way to a larger conception," it declared in 1915, "to prevent . . . the moral diseases which lead to misery and crime."

The fullest elaboration of the public-health analogy in this period was probably that offered by the Massachusetts prohibitionist Newton M. Hall in *Civic Righteousness and Civic Pride* (1914). "The moral evil of the community does not remain in the foul pools in which it is bred," he wrote. "A moral miasma arises from those pools, and . . . enters not the poorest homes of the city alone, but the most carefully guarded, and leaves its trail of sorrow and despair. . . . Why should the community have any more sympathy for the saloon . . . than . . . for a typhoid-breeding pool of filthy water, . . . a swarm of deadly mosquitoes, or . . . a nest of rats infected with the bubonic plague?" For Hall, the logic of the analogy was irresistible: "Cut off the impure water and the typhoid epidemic is conquered"; destroy the saloon and the urban "moral epidemic" would vanish.

The ubiquitous medical terminology in the utterances of these reformers had more than rhetorical significance, because recent advances in venereal disease research had made clear the ravages of the disease's advanced stages, the process of transmission, and the clear link with sexual promiscuity. For the antiprostitution reformers, the moral implications of these findings were no less important than the medical. "In all previous efforts to safeguard the morality of youth," wrote one reformer in *Social Hygiene,* "the ethical barrier was alone available," and "the situation seemed . . . hopeless"; now, happily, the "ethical ideal" could be "grounded upon the most convincing facts." Jane Addams welcomed these findings as a powerful force in the emergence of a "new conscience" on prostitution, and Dr. Prince A. Morrow expressed his pleasure that "punishment for sexual sin" no longer need be "reserved for the hereafter."

Through lectures, tracts, posters, exhibits, and graphic films, the antiprostitution reformers warned of promiscuity's grim consequences—for the wrongdoer and his innocent progeny alike. The Chicago Vice Commission vividly spelled out VD's long-range effects—"the blinded eyes of little babes, the twisted limbs of deformed children, degradation, physical rot and mental decay"—and demanded that every brothel be quarantined forthwith as a "house of contagious disease." The control of sexual expression, in short, was simply another of the social constraints essential to modern urban life. Just as "the storage of gasoline and other combustibles is controlled by the city," argued the Louisville Vice Commission, so dance halls and other "vice combustibles" had to be "carefully watched and controlled."

One significant if inadvertent by-product of this preoccupation with establishing the scientific legitimacy of the urban moral-control effort—particularly through the accumulation of statistical data—was that the researchers often achieved a fragile but authentic intimacy with the objects of their study, and their reports provided glimpses of otherwise obscure facets of turn-of-the-century urban social history. Budding young sociologists danced and talked for hours with prostitutes and girls of the street . . . though always (so far as we know) holding back from the actual sexual encounter. One woman investigator, in particular, was praised by George Kneeland as "extraordinarily successful in winning the confidence of the girls with whom she associated on easy and familiar terms."

In the thousands of pages of vice commission reports lie buried fascinating details illuminating the reality of urban prostitution in this period: the business practices and domestic details of brothel life; the prevalence of oral sex in the "better" houses ("$3.00 straight, $5.00 French"); the slang (in some cities, the police assigned to the red-light district were called "fly cops"); the euphemistic advertising. (One madam who had moved sent out postcards urging her former patrons to renew their "membership in the library." A selection of "new books," she promised, could be found "on file in our new quarters.")

Striving for objectivity, these investigators often evoked the complexity of the urban sexual scene in ways that contradicted the simplistic certitude of the antivice leadership. Even William T. Stead, a first-rate journalist as well as an antivice crusader, offered considerable evidence undermining the stereotyped image of the brothel as a den of wild revels and unbridled sensuality. "The rules and regulations . . . posted in every room," he wrote of one Chicago brothel in *If Christ Came to Chicago,* "enforce decorum and decency with pains and penalties which could hardly be more strict if they were drawn up for the regulation of a Sunday School."

Such observations, with their implication that organized prostitution might sometimes function as a stabilizing and conservative urban social force, appear frequently in the early-twentieth-century vice reports. In *Commercialized Vice in New York,* for example, George Kneeland reported that many of the city's brothels were "cozy and homelike" institutions presided over by madams who possessed not only considerable business acumen but also keen psychological insight and great capacity for human warmth: "It is not uncommon for the girls as well as the customers to call her 'mother.' Strange as it may seem, some men marry these women and find them devoted wives." Describing the various classes of men who patronized brothels, Kneeland wrote:

A numerous but pathetic group is that made up of young clerks who, living alone in unattractive quarters, find in professional prostitutes companions in the company of whom a night's revel offsets the dullness of their lives at other times. There are thousands of these men in New York. No home ties restrain them; no home associations fill their time or thought. Their rooms are fit only to sleep in; close friends they have few or none. You can watch them on the streets any evening. Hour after hour they gaze at the passing throng; at length they fling themselves into the current—no longer silent and alone.

What YMCA leader of the 1850s could have described the plight of the young man in the city more eloquently?

Furthermore, one finds in these vice reports insights into the motivation of the prostitutes that go beyond such stock explanations as alcohol, slum life, early seduction and abandonment, or even the perils of the industrial order. This is particularly true of the often verbatim summaries of interviews with individual prostitutes that are included by the hundred—for no apparent reason except perhaps the investigators' wish that the rich complexities of their findings not be flattened out into a few pat conclusions and recommendations. What emerges most strongly from these interviews with women of the turn-of-the-century city is how many of them, old and young, appear reasonably well satisfied with their lot, insist that they are performing a useful social function for a satisfactory return, and reveal little sense of regret or inclination to reform. "No. 3 is refined looking; no one would take her for a public woman. She is fond of drink. She states, 'I have a lovely boss. He often takes me out in his car. Have made many friends in this town. If a girl is careful she can make good money here.' "

What initially led these women to become prostitutes? The reasons that emerge in these interviews are varied, personal, and unpredictable. Sometimes, to be sure, it was economic, as with twenty-two-year-old Paulette, "interviewed on the corner of Curtis and West Madison" in Chicago, "who 'hustles' to support a two-year-old baby," or nineteen-year-old Tantine who snapped: "It is easier than waiting on table for $1.00 per day." More frequently, however, the impetus was a more complex combination of factors: the lure of the city, the fascination of activity and glitter ("I loved the excitement and a good time"), the drive to achieve a higher living standard, the unwillingness to pass one's life in subservient, deferential roles: "The ladies when they got money to hire servants imagine they have some kind of a dog to kick around, and I didn't want to be kicked around."

Time and again in these interviews one encounters real-life parallels to David Graham Phillips's Susan Lenox—spirited women who have chosen prostitution in preference to boring, demeaning, or otherwise intolerable situations: Bessie, the Indiana farm girl who "prefers city life"; another rural girl who "did not want to live among a lot of 'dead ones' "; the two small-town girls who "ran away from home so they would not have to go to school"; the Hartford young woman just beginning in the street life: "I want nice clothes and a good time . . . I am crazy to get to New York." Many had walked out on husbands they found improvident, inadequate, or simply tiresome:

"I was always fond of life. Married a dead one; he never goes out."

"I married a fellow in Pennsylvania. He is all right but damn slow. He doesn't know he is alive; not the right kind of man for me."

Her husband is employed in the AB164 store as salesman. "Too dumb to be alive. All he knows is work and he makes no money at that."

Her husband is cold; she longs for affection, clothes and pleasure; he never leaves the house. She comes to Hartford two or three times a week from B155. She will go out with a man for a glass of soda.

In the more lurid rhetorical flights of the antivice crusaders, to become a prostitute was to enter a life of "white slavery"; from the perspective of many of the women themselves (as revealed in the very reports generated by the crusade!), the decision represented a liberating escape from bondage.

Thus, buried in the interstices of the vice reports, one comes upon observations, insights, and personal revelations that suddenly illuminate the human reality of urban prostitution two generations ago—a complex reality that resists easy summation or judgment. Seeking to validate their moral-control impulse through sociological investigation, the urban moral reformers of the Progressive era unwittingly sponsored the collection of a wealth of social data that reveals far more about the actual contours of urban "vice" than they perhaps intended.

David J. Rothman

The State as Parent

The Progressive tradition that took hold in the United States during the first two decades of the twentieth century and persisted right through the middle of the 1960s gave a remarkable primacy to the idea of the state as parent. Far more than a rhetorical flourish or convenient metaphor with which to galvanize public support, this concept shaped reformers' definitions of the proper realm for state action and, perhaps even more important, the appropriate methods for the state to adopt in fulfilling its goals. The ideal dictated not only the ends but the means of doing good.

As one would expect from such an orientation, Progressives were far more attentive to the "needs" of disadvantaged groups than to their "rights." Needs were real and obvious—the poor were overworked and underpaid, living in unhealthy tenements and working in miserable sweatshops. Rights, on the other hand, were "so-called"—the right of the poor to sleep under the bridge or the right of the laborer to fix his own contract with an all-powerful corporation. Clearly, a reform platform that looked to needs expanded the boundaries of political intervention, legitimating a wide range of ameliorative action; the state as parent had a lengthy agenda to accomplish. But the concept cut two ways: those in need of help were more or less like children. The disadvantaged were the objects of care, they were to be done for. They did not require protection against the well-meaning parent, rights to be exercised against the paternalistic state.

It is not claiming too much to assert that this perspective was at the core of liberalism in modern America, uniting, for all their minor differences, the first settlement-house workers with later New and Fair Dealers. One can identify a mainstream reform position in the period 1900–1965 that shared a basic agreement on the principles that should guide a benevolent social policy. To be sure, there were critics to either side, socialists and Marxists to the left who defined Progressives as no more than tinkerers with a fundamentally corrupt capitalist organization, and conservatives to the right who saw their interventions as destructive of the essential integrity of the system. Nevertheless, the Progressives enjoyed a centrality and an influence that marked them off in a special way and that enables us to talk meaningfully, if in shorthand terms, of *the reformers.* Then, rather suddenly, beginning in the mid-1960s and continuing to our day, this tradition came under a novel, vigorous, and even bitter attack emanating not from the far left or far right, but—and in more than a metaphorical sense—from the children of Progressivism. We are now, in ways and for reasons that this essay will explore, in a post-Progressive period. A new generation of reformers, drawn to an unprecedented degree from the ranks of lawyers and the dependent groups themselves, are pitting rights against needs, or, to put it more broadly, are challenging the wisdom and propriety of an ideal of the state as parent and the dependent as child. They are highly critical of Progressivism not merely for pragmatic reasons—for what it did or did not manage to accomplish—but for conceptual reasons: for importing a misguided and ultimately mischievous model into the political arena.

Given the centrality of Progressive thinking in this country, it is appropriate to place the contemporary objections to this tradition in still another light. An arrow that the late critic Lionel Trilling once aimed at the far left would now seem to many observers an appropriate barb to hurl against liberalism itself. In 1947 Trilling published an essay, "Manners, Morals and the Novel," in which he elegantly set out his case against Marxist reform. (Indeed, in his novel of the same period, *The Middle of the Journey,* Trilling had Gilbert Maxim, his disillusioned ex-Communist character, voice a variant on this same argument.) Trilling defended the novel for its ability to strip away illusions, to go beyond hyperbolic rhetoric so as to uncover the hidden realities. His praise for such novelists as Balzac, James, and Forster—indeed for the whole genre—reflected a commitment to what he called "moral realism." Moral realism, he explained, taught us "that to act against social injustice is right and noble but that to choose to act so does not settle all moral problems but on the contrary generates new ones of an especially difficult sort." We have so many books, Trilling commented, "that praise us for taking progressive attitudes." We sorely lack those that "ask what might lie behind our good impulses." He fully appreciated that "anything that complicates our moral fervor in dealing with reality . . . must be regarded with some impatience." Yet it was just this impatience that worried him and must worry us. "Moral passions are even more willful and imperious and impatient than the self-seeking passions. All history is at one in telling us that their tendency is to be not only liberating but restrictive." And so he concluded in a sentence that has taken on a new relevance: "Some paradox in our nature leads us, once we have made our fellow men the objects of our enlightened interest, to go on to make them the objects of our pity, then of our wisdom, ultimately of our coercion."

This phrase brings us to the very heart of the current dissatisfactions with Progressivism, for to its critics the movement suffered deeply from an absence of moral realism. Its proponents were so attached to a paternalistic model that they never concerned themselves with the potential of their programs to be as coercive as they were liberating. In their eagerness to play parent to the child, they did not pause to ask whether the dependent had to be protected against their own well-meaning interventions. It was as if the benevolence of their motives together with their clear recognition of the wretchedness of lower-class social conditions guaranteed that ameliorative efforts would unambiguously benefit the poor. The problem, it now appears, is not only that progressives could not accomplish their grand designs but that policies whose legitimacy rested on their promise to do good may actually have produced substantial harms.

Each generation has its own favorite brand of horror stories, its own special set of circumstances that prick its conscience and goad it to action. For Progressives, it was instances of neglect; the state had to intervene to correct inequities. The Jacob Riis and Lewis Hine photographs revealed little waifs selling newspapers on street corners or tending oversized mill looms. The tracts of Jane Addams and Lillian Wald pointed to the desperate need of widows left to their own devices, the horrors of families broken up with the mother entering an almshouse and her children an orphan asylum. Surely men and women of good will ought to be able to halt such practices, and public resources had to be devoted to improving their living conditions. To choose to act against such gross social injustice had to be right and noble, and anything that complicated one's response to these wretched circumstances seemingly had to be treated with impatience.

Now a new kind of horror story has gained popularity. It is aptly represented in the case of Mrs. Lake, a Washington "bag lady," who carried her worldly possessions in two shopping bags. Mrs. Lake went out one day to the Department of Justice to press a claim for a pension; her efforts were unsuccessful, and as she left the Justice building, a police officer, a woman police officer at that, spotted her as someone who might be in need of assistance. Mrs. Lake appeared disoriented in the downtown district. The policewoman asked her for her home address, which Mrs. Lake was unable to supply; and although she had found her way to the Justice Department, the officer believed she could not find her way back home again. In short order, Mrs. Lake was confined to St. Elizabeth's Mental Hospital for "wandering," in mind and body, and despite her persistent efforts to be released from the institution, she remained there, for the rest of her days, ostensibly for her own good. Betty Higden won her battle; Mrs. Lake lost.

That Mrs. Lake's misfortune typifies the prevailing horror stories is another indication of the nature of the attack now being mounted against Progressivism. Put most succinctly, the commitment to paternalistic state intervention in the name of equality is giving way to a commitment to restrict intervention in the name of liberty. If our predecessors were determined to test the maximum limits for the exercise of state power in order to correct imbalances, we are about to test the minimum limits for the exercise of state power in order to enhance autonomy. The dialogue between these two approaches now dominates social policy discussions on dependency, and a close analysis of the assumptions and records of each position may well clarify, and perhaps even advance, the debates.

The Progressives' allegiance to a model of the state as parent rested on a series of propositions all of which seemed to confirm the validity and desirability of their approach. For one, Progressives were convinced that the sum of individual self-interested actions could no longer be counted upon to produce the common good. The nineteenth-century assumption of such a coincidence disappeared with the rise of the cities, business trusts, and immigrant ghettos. As Herbert Croly brilliantly argued, "No preestablished harmony can then exist between the free and abundant satisfactions of private needs and the accomplishment of a morally and socially desirable result." Rather, he insisted, "the American problem is a social problem"; the nation stood in need of "a more highly socialized democracy." To realize the promise of American life, the public sector would have to dominate the private sector. The state, not the individual, would define the common good and see to its fulfillment. In short, the major tenet of Progressive thought was that only the state could make the individual free. Only the enlarged authority of the government could satisfy the particular needs of all the citizens.

Further, Progressives had little doubt of the state's ability to fulfill this charge or, put another way, of the ability of their programs to accomplish their goals. For one, their ranks were composed of the graduates of the new universities, those who had typically spent most of their classroom hours learning the canons of social science. They had been taught to investigate social reality with a clear eye to its improvement. The facts of the case—whether the rates of tuberculosis in the slums or the number of families poverty-stricken because of industrial accidents—would not only locate the source of the problem but at once compel ameliorative action. Progressive tracts and testimony at hearings were filled with statistical tables—as if the data would ensure the success of their legislative efforts.

Progressives, in ways that cannot help but make contemporary analysts nostalgic, also shared a remarkable consensus on the goals for reform. There was no crisis of values that had to be debated, no agonizing consideration of the comparative worth of different life-styles. To Progressives, all Americans were to enter the ranks of the middle class. The melting-pot metaphor implied not only an amalgam of immigrants into a common mold, but an amalgam of classes into a common mold. Everyone was to respect private property, send their children to school, and give up whatever vices—particularly intemperance—that they might have brought with them from the old world, in order to become hardworking and law-abiding. "It is fatal for a democracy to permit the formation of fixed classes," argued that leading Progressive reformer, John Dewey; and one Progressive institution after another, from schools to settlement houses, set out to bridge the gap between the upper classes and the lower classes, between native-born and immigrants. The traffic across this bridge, of course, was to move only in one way, from them to us, from alien to American, from lower class to middle class.

This certain sense of direction among Progressives testified finally, and most significantly, to their keen sense of the essential viability—indeed superiority—of the American system. They stood ready to make immigrants over in their own image because ultimately they did not doubt that this course was in everyone's best interest. No sense of conflict of interests among classes or even among different groups within the same class complicated their analysis. Yes, some greedy businessmen would have to give up excess profits; some greedy speculators would have to be curbed. But no one's "true" or "real" interests (at least as reformers defined them) would be violated. The economic pie was infinitely expandable. The poor need not rise up against the rich to obtain their fair share.

Social mobility promised that all of the deserving would climb the ladder; no one had to remain stuck at the bottom. Thus, that which promoted the stability of the society promoted the welfare of its members. Social cohesion and individual betterment went hand in hand.

Armed with these principles, Progressives enacted a series of novel measures designed to prevent and to relieve dependency and deviancy. Between 1900 and 1920 practically every state passed widow-pension laws, what we know today as Aid to Dependent Children. Heretofore, unless rescued by a private charitable society, the mother and her children had entered institutions; now public funds were to be expended to keep the family together at home. At the same time, practically every major city organized juvenile courts to handle cases of dependency and delinquency. In informal hearings, these special courts would decide, at their own discretion, what was in the best interests of the neglected or delinquent child. Moreover, juvenile courts as well as adult criminal courts began to organize and administer probation departments. Instead of sending youthful or minor offenders to an institution, the court could now sentence them to probation, leaving them in the community under the supervision of an officer.

It is clear that the Progressives were the first American reformers to perceive and to be outraged by the miseries that were endemic to the modern industrial system. The wretchedness of the almshouses—let alone the cruelty of separating the widow from her children, and the injuries inflicted by locking ten-year-olds in a stinking and filthy jail—were terribly real. No one is belittling the good conscience of the Progressives or their effort to go beyond a simple moralism that blamed the poor for their poverty. But what is at issue is how they moved to correct these evils. It is not so much their definitions of what constituted a social problem as the assumptions with which they attempted to ameliorate it that are now controversial.

The design of each of the Progressives' programs assumed a nonadversarial relationship between the state and the client. Since the state, whether in the guise of the juvenile court judge or probation officer or welfare administrator, was to help and not to punish the poor or the criminal, it was unnecessary—in fact it was counterproductive—to limit or to circumscribe officials' discretionary powers. Indeed, since no conflicts of interest divided the welfare of society from that of the dependent or deviant, Progressives were still more determined to endow the state with all necessary authority to fulfill its goals. The great discovery of the juvenile court, noted one reformer, was that "individual welfare coincided with the well-being of the state. Humanitarian and social considerations thus recommended one and the same procedure. . . . Sympathy, justice, and even the self-interest of society were all factors in bringing about the changed attitude." The state could do good without sacrificing anyone's interests, without having to make trade-offs.

In each instance, therefore, enabling legislation and agency practice enhanced the prerogatives of state officials and reduced—and almost eliminated—legal protections and rights for those coming under their authority. To call the acts "widow pensions" was really a misnomer. The widows did not receive their allowance as a matter of right, the way a pensioner received his. Rather, the widow had to apply for her stipend, demonstrate her qualifications, her economic need, and her moral worth, and then trust to the decision of the welfare board. At their pleasure, and by their reckoning, she then obtained or did not obtain help. By the same token the juvenile court proceedings gave no standing to the whole panoply of rights that offenders typically enjoyed, from a trial by jury to assistance from counsel, to protections against self-incrimination. There was nothing atypical about the juvenile court judge who openly admitted that in his Minnesota courtroom "the laws of evidence are sometimes forgotten or overlooked." So too, probation officers were not bound by any of the restrictions that might fetter the work of police officers. They did not need a search warrant to enter a probationer's home, for as another juvenile court judge explained: "With the great right arm and force of the law, the probation officer can go into the home and demand to know the cause of the dependency or the delinquency of a child. . . . He becomes practically a member of the family and teaches them lessons of cleanliness and decency, of truth and integrity." So caught up were reformers with this image of officer as family member that they gave no heed to the coercive character of their programs. To the contrary, they frankly declared that "threats may be necessary in some instances to enforce the learning of the lessons that he teaches, but whether by threats or cajolery, by appealing to their fear of the law or by rousing the ambition that lies latent in each human soul, he teaches the lesson and transforms the entire family into individuals which the state need never again hesitate to own as citizens." With the state eager and able to accomplish so beneficent a goal, there appeared no reason to restrict its action.

The prevalence of such judgments among Progressives practically blinded them to the realities that followed on the enactment of their proposals. Not only did they fail to see the many inadequacies that quickly emerged in day-to-day operations, worse yet, they could not begin to understand that the programs might be administered in the best interests of officials, not clients. In the case of widow pensions, state legislatures appropriated niggardly amounts of funds for relief, so that only a handful of needy cases were served, and the monies that even they received were too limited to allow them to subsist. In effect, the widow had to open her life to the investigatory impulses of her social worker and at the same time still find work to supplement her dole. And those ineligible for even these paltry funds had to bear both the stigma of being labeled unworthy while they too desperately tried to make ends meet. The widow-pension program may have soothed the conscience of reformers—the state was now committed to the care of the worthy widow and her children—but it certainly did not solve the problem that they had originally addressed.

The operation of the juvenile court was no more satisfactory. Judges had unbounded discretion to do as they saw fit, and there was little recourse from their decisions. They still relied upon state reformatories and training schools to discipline the young, only now they justified their sentences, and not cynically either, in the language of rehabilitating the offender instead of punishing him. To incarcerate the young, a Pennsylvania court ruled in upholding the constitutionality of juvenile court sentences, was not to deprive them of their liberty. Commitments to reformatories under the new laws do not contemplate "restraint upon the natural liberty of children." The state was merely assuming the privileges that parents enjoy, exercising the "wholesome restraint which a parent exercises over his child. . . . No constitutional right is violated but one of the most important duties which organized society owes to its helpless members is performed." And the administration of probation was still less successful. Reformers had looked to a group of well-trained officers counseling a small number of clients. In fact, the probation officers were poorly trained, ill-equipped to do very much good at all, and, in any event, there was little that the best-intentioned of them could accomplish when carrying case loads of two to three hundred.

It may well also be that probation, which presented itself as an alternative to incarceration, served more frequently as a supplement to incarceration. The same numbers still went to institutions; the difference was that cases which had once been dismissed or suspended now came under the supervisory network of probation officers. To be sure, the encroachments on the civil liberties of many but certainly not all of the clients were generally not egregious because of the incredible case loads that probation officers carried. But that simply meant that the coerciveness of the state was limited only by the unwillingness of legislators to spend taxpayer money. It is an odd but perhaps accurate conclusion to note that the dependent and deviant may owe what freedom they have more to the fiscal conservatism of elected officials than to the benevolent motives of reformers.

Finally, Progressives' sense of paternalism enabled them to move in harsh and stringent ways against those that they believed to be irreformable and beyond rehabilitation—namely, the recidivist, the defective, the mentally retarded, and the unworthy poor. Since they had designed programs that would keep reformable types out of institutions and in the community, those that they defined as beyond help deserved incarceration, and incarceration for very long periods of time. Accordingly, many Progressives accepted the eugenic arguments of the time and were eager to confine the retarded for life, particularly the borderline retarded who might pass as normal and so go on to propagate a race of defectives. Some Progressives were also ready to sterilize the retarded, to make that operation the prerequisite for release into the community. And in a similar spirit, almost all Progressives were prepared to define broadly the category of PINS, persons in need of supervision, so that the state could move quickly to remove children from parents deemed unworthy, those children, in the language of one reformer, who had been raised in homes "in which they had been accustomed from their earliest infancy to drunkenness, immorality, obscene and vulgar language, filthy and degraded conditions of living."

This sketch of the Progressive tradition has a dual relevance to our understanding of contemporary American attitudes and policies toward the dependent. First, and most obviously, we are today well aware of the record of failure of these programs. We recognize that widow pensions did not reduce or eliminate poverty, that the juvenile court did not eradicate delinquency, that probation was hardly a panacea for crime. But such knowledge is really of minor import. Merely because programs did not work in the past does not mean that they might not work in the future. In no simple sense does history repeat itself. Perhaps less stingy legislatures, perhaps a more munificent federal government, would fund these programs fully and we would then witness their achievements.

Far more important, therefore, to the contemporary sense of dependency is the fact that the underlying assumptions of the Progressive stance no longer seem valid. What is remarkable about current reformist thinking is how far it has moved from these premises, how fundamentally it has rejected every major point in the synthesis.

To characterize this transformation in summary fashion there now exists a widespread and acute suspicion of the very notion of doing good among widely divergent groups on all points of the political spectrum. To claim to act for the purposes of benevolence was once sufficient to legitimate a program; at this moment it is certain to create suspicion. To announce that you are prepared to intervene for the best interests of some other person or party is guaranteed to provoke the quick, even knee-jerk response that you are masking your true, self-interested, motives. Whereas once historians and policy analysts were prone to label some movements reforms, thereby assuming their humanitarian aspects, they are presently far more comfortable with a designation of social control, thereby assuming their coercive quality. Not that one or the other approach is necessarily more intellectually faithful. Rather, fashions have changed. The prevailing perspective looks first to how a measure may regulate the poor, not relieve them.

So too, we share a very acute sense of the failure of institutions to fulfill their caretaker responsibilities. Whereas Progressive reformers did recognize, indeed, by the recurring nature of scandals were compelled to recognize, the inadequacy of institutions—whether reformatories, orphan asylums, or almshouses—invariably they blamed the frugality of legislators, or the incompetence of administrators, or the cupidity of superintendents for the failures. The system was benign; the problem was with its implementation. Now, to the contrary, the system, the very idea of incarceration for the purposes of rehabilitation, is suspect among a surprisingly diverse group of observers, from federal judges to members of state investigatory commissions on nursing homes and juvenile corrections. And not only do a host of more or less well-designed research projects unanimously report on the failure of institutions to be rehabilitative, but a strong and compelling theoretical analysis, such as offered by Erving Goffman in *Asylums*, insists that incarceration by its very nature will inevitably infantilize the inmate and make his future adaptation to society more problematic.

This suspicion of benevolence and antiinstitutionalism has encouraged and is reinforced by an acute distrust of discretionary authority. It no longer seems appropriate to endow public or private officials with a wide latitude for the exercise of their authority. Since neither their motives, which are assumed to be social control, nor their decisions, which might well involve commitment to an institution, now seem acceptable, their prerogatives and powers must be carefully defined, bound in and circumscribed through detailed and precise laws and regulations. The formula is clear: better that a few should suffer from the inflexibility of a code than that the many should suffer through the discretion of an administrator.

Of the fact of this reversal there can be no question. We are in full revolt against the Progressive synthesis. But the more complicated and intriguing question, the answers to which must be more suggestive than definitive, is why this change should have occurred. Why is it that reformers in the 1970s are far more receptive to Trilling's call for moral realism? Why are they so much more comfortable with labels like "social control" and titles like "Regulating the Poor"? Why are they more prepared to rely upon procedural protections than purity of motive? Why is it that while they may grant the accuracy of a biological or psychoanalytic finding of the significance of altruism in many species, they are terribly reluctant to allow such a conclusion to structure social policy? Or, finally, why are they leaving an equality model to test the limits of a liberty model?

To begin to formulate an answer to these questions (or at least to recast them in a still broader context), it is appropriate to note first that these developments are part of a pervasive distrust of all constituted authorities, a general decline in the legitimacy of the authority of a whole series of persons and institutions. The list of those who have suffered this loss is as lengthy as it is revealing: college presidents and deans, high school principals and teachers, husbands and parents, psychiatrists, doctors, research scientists, and, obviously, prison wardens, social workers, hospital superintendents, and mental hospital superintendents. Many of us, either as objects of power or as wielders of power, have experienced this diminution quite directly. To choose but one example, many of us can remember from our own college days the phenomenon of dean's discipline. Having broken some rule or other, a rule which we had probably learned of through an informal student network, we shuffled into the dean's office, sheepishly, head hanging. We told our story, bringing up every exculpatory fact we could imagine, and then sat back hoping for the best. The dean pronounced the punishment, and, mumbling our apologies, we more or less backed out of the office. Such times are over. The student appears not before a dean in the privacy of his office but before a tribunal, whose composition reflects the working of a mathematical formula that brings so many administrators together with so many professors and so many students from the several university divisions. If the charge is of any significance, the student comes with his lawyer. Examination and cross-examination goes on: did the student have a printed, formally distributed listing of the college rules? Was his identity in the incident established beyond a reasonable doubt? And once the hearing is over, the tribunal retires, like a jury, to make its deliberations and reach its verdict. If the student is unhappy with the finding, he will move the case immediately into the courts, where the attention to procedural protections will be only somewhat more rigorous than what was practiced at the original hearing.

So too, the freewheeling exercise of disciplinary authority by high school officials is under challenge. Hearings and legal representation may well become the rule here. And more and more patients are refusing to sign the blanket release form that gives a doctor and his hospital the right to do whatever they think "necessary" to the person's body. Some research scientists are even discovering that their research protocols have to be carefully negotiated not just with the university and government committees on experimentation, but with the community at large. And if the community does not like what is afoot, as was the case, for example, with research into minimal brain dysfunction in Boston's schools, they will exercise political power, often successfully, to terminate the work. Marriage contracts that once vaguely spelled out duties of loving, cherishing, and, yes, obeying, may give way to contracts that detail who will carry out household duties on alternate days. And whereas once it was assumed that parents would invariably act in the best interests of the child, even in the midst of divorce proceedings, now it seems the better part of wisdom to have children represented by their own attorney. Indeed, before parents can commit their child to a mental hospital, it is becoming obligatory that the child be represented separately by an attorney.

In effect, reform policy presupposes a conflict of interests among these parties, conflicts which before were never admitted to or acknowledged. The assumption is that deans will act for the best interest of the university, not the student; that husbands will further their own needs, not their wives'; that parents will satisfy their own desires, not necessarily their children's; that research scientists have their own agenda of priorities that need not fit with the welfare of their subjects; that wardens' first thought is to the prison and not the inmate; and that psychiatrists will be more concerned with the health of the hospital than with the health of the patient. The Progressives' assumption that interests coincided, that the welfare of all parties could be satisfied, has become a thing of the past. Now the game seems to be a zero-sum game: if one party wins, another loses; if you are not one up, you are one down.

To put these changes into still another framework, we are witnessing the dissolution of the Progressive version of community as a viable concept, indeed, the breakdown of normality as a viable concept. To many critics, there no longer seems to be a common weal that can be defined or appealed to as a justification for action. The very notion of a harmony of interests seems deceptive and mischievous. Not only can no one agree on what is good for all of us, no one can agree on what is proper behavior for any one of us. No consensus allows for a clear and uncontroversial division between sane and insane behavior, no unity exists around the once self-evident proposition that it is better to be sane rather than insane. As to any effort to define what constitutes normal sexual behavior— one has only to raise this point to recognize immediately how absurd any such attempt would be.

There is far more agreement on the reality of this state of affairs than on its merits. Some observers describe these developments in terms of loss and corruption, searching, logically enough, for a way to restore a sense of community, to revive the social contract, or, in Daniel Bell's formulation, to rebuild a sense of civitas among citizens. Somehow or other, through the family, or the church, or a new ideology, we will recreate bonds of trust, commonality of goals, a system in which all institutions and individuals will know and take their place. To others, these changes represent something quite different, a coming of wisdom, an ability to see farther than our predecessors, an unmasking of a reality that had been obfuscated for too long by a rhetoric of reform and benevolence.

But in effect, this description has only pushed the question back one stage. Why this loss of civitas? Or, alternately, why this new-found wisdom? We may well be too close to the issues to be able to formulate compelling hypotheses, but nevertheless, some of the elements promoting the change can be sketched. The bridge between the Progressive ideology and this new sense of things may well be the civil rights movement. In its origins, this movement was prototypically Progressive, its leaders confident that the attainment of equality for blacks would in no way conflict with the interest of society as a whole. Throughout the several decades of litigation that led up to the 1954 Supreme Court decision in *Brown* v.

Board of Education, and down until 1966, the civil rights movement assumed that no basic clash of interests existed. Yes, some Southern bigots, the likes of bull-headed sheriffs, would lose out. But apart from the lunatic-fringe racists, there would be no victims.

The finest expression of this optimism came from Martin Luther King. And no speech of his, or perhaps more properly, no sermon of his, better captured this quality than his famous "I have a dream," delivered August 28, 1963. He spoke from the steps of the Lincoln Memorial; the band struck up the "Battle Hymn of the Republic" as he rose; and King opened appropriately enough with the words "Five score years ago." There was no need, King told his rapt audience, "to satisfy our thirst for freedom by drinking from the cup of bitterness and hatred." He went on: "Our white brothers . . . have come to realize that their destiny is tied up with our destiny and their freedom is inextricably bound to our freedom." "My dream," declared King, "is a dream deeply rooted in the American dream. I have a dream that one day on the red hills of Georgia the sons of former slaves and the sons of former slave owners will be able to sit down together at the table of brotherhood. . . . This is our hope. This is our faith. . . . With this faith we will be able to transform the jangling discords of our nation into a beautiful symphony of brotherhood." King ended his speech with the lines: "We will be able to speed up that day when all of God's children, black men and white men, Jews and Gentiles, Protestants and Catholics, will be able to join hands and sing in the words of the old Negro spiritual, Free at Last! Free at Last! Thank God almighty, we are free at last!"

It is almost embarrassing to read King's words today. Not only because we have fallen so far short of living up to his dream, but because his very announcement of his dream seems so very soft, so very tender, so very out of keeping with the realities of the world as we perceive them. Most dramatically, it is his notions of the possibility of brotherhood, or to put it into more mundane terms, the ability to satisfy at once the interests of everyone, that now seems so problematic. The turning point was probably 1966. After a series of impressive legislative victories, the civil rights movement met its first defeat that year—and the issue upon which it met its defeat is still very much with us today, the issue of open housing. 1966 was also the year that the formulations of "black power" first came to the fore. And black power, unlike King's rhetoric, looked first not to brotherhood, but to separatism; it premised itself not upon a mutuality of interests that all members of this society shared, but upon basic conflicts within this society. It announced in no uncertain terms that blacks had better organize themselves, get control of their own economic institutions, their own political institutions, their own community, if they would ever achieve substantial gains. And in all so many ways, the changeover from dreams of brotherhood to black power is paradigmatic of the changes that have transformed our society from 1966 until the present.

The ranks of black power may well have never amounted to more than a fraction of the black community. But far more important, black power became the strategy that every minority group in our society attempted to emulate. One finds this in the organization of welfare rights, with equal clarity, and with direct historical continuities, in the movements for prisoners' rights, mental patients' rights, the rights of the retarded, and the rights of children. The commonalities are clear: organize one's own special-interest group; press one's demands. The perspective is not the perspective of common welfare but the needs of the particular group. The intellectual premises are not unity but conflict. It is "us" versus "them."

In many ways, it was the dissatisfaction among blacks themselves with the advances made by the civil rights movement that helped generate this changed outlook. Rightly or wrongly, they believed that progress was too slow to come, that commonality of interests was not serving their own welfare. And that assumption, based upon the black experience, has fueled the various protest movements of other minority groups. So too, one should not minimize the implications of the changes in the American economy between the pre- and post-1965 period. The slowdown in economic growth that occurred after the mid-1960s, and the recessions that followed, to an extraordinary degree shook people's faith in the idea that an expanding economy would ultimately solve all of America's social problems. Added to this, of course, was a new concern for the allocation of scarce resources. Even before the oil shortages, conservationists and ecologists were warning us that our resources were finite and limited. And finally, every cynical judgment about the nature of American society seemed to be confirmed by the course of the Vietnam war. Here was a moment when a posture of "us" versus "them" seemed to make the best of sense.

One of the leading Progressive social planners, Charles Merriam of the University of Chicago, once wrote: "The most tragic moments in human life are those in which the value systems are unreconciled—when one cries out against another; the family against the state, the state against the church, the neighborhood against the distant capitol, life in the broader sense against nonlife or narrow life—against the end of life." Merriam was ever thankful that his times, he believed, were not so tragic. No final conflict, he insisted, separated "self interest and the public interest." But in Merriam's sense of the term, we do indeed face tragedy. We can no longer entertain the simple hope that interests can be reconciled, that public interest and self-interest will necessarily coincide.

In light of this record and these prevailing assumptions, one can well appreciate how appealing and attractive a host of constituencies find a "liberty" model. Convinced that paternalistic state intervention in the name of the common good has all too typically worked to their disadvantage, they are now determined to rid themselves of the onus of ostensibly protective and benevolent oversight and substitute instead a commitment to their own autonomy. Thus, the emergence of a series of liberation and rights movements, from women's liberation to welfare rights. In all these cases the goal is to reduce state power, to define the groups' aims in terms of rights that should be immune from interference, not needs that ought to be fulfilled. And in many instances this strategy makes fundamental good sense and does further the particular interests of the group. Do not deprive us of our liberty to follow our own life-styles because we are women, or ostensibly in need of treatment, or committed to a different sexual orientation, or because we are young, or because we are poor. A liberty model is most effective and appropriate in removing fetters that have blocked freedom of choice and action.

But the expansion of rights solves only part of the problem, for there do remain, like it or not, needs as well, imbalances in economic and social power, in inherited physical constitutions, that demand redress. It is not the goal of a liberty model to promote neglect, to legitimate cruelty and inattention in the name of rights. Rather, this camp recognizes that state intervention may often be necessary, but must take place with a minimum of discretionary authority, with the objects of protection or improvement having a determinative voice in the shaping of the program itself. To this end, advocates of the liberty model are far more comfortable with an adversarial approach, an open admission of conflict of interest, than with an equality model with its presumption of harmony of interests.

In practice, such a commitment means that liberty-minded groups will advocate a clear delineation of the powers of the state, more prepared to trust to a political process that carefully spells out authority and responsibility than to an open-ended grant of authority to administrators to do as they please. Assuming that the players are competitive, that the game will be won by some and lost by others, it seems best to keep the rules clear, to know in advance how the action will proceed. So, better to list what welfare mothers are entitled to, rather than let the social worker act in her mysterious ways. Import all procedural protections into the juvenile court, rather than trust to the benevolence of its judge. Fix the terms for juvenile delinquents, make them consistent with adult ones, rather than allow the judge to pass indeterminate sentences that could stretch through the years of one's minority.

By the same token, better to trust to the skills of a lawyer in court than to the good intentions of the state or the agency or the institution. Presupposing conflict, let the battle be fought with both sides armed. Hence, the call for lawyers for children so that their wishes can be represented in custody cases, and their needs fully considered before they are institutionalized in the name of treatment. Hence, the call for lawyers inside the mental hospital, so that those diagnosed and committed as mentally ill will be fully informed of their rights and their ability to exercise choice expanded. Hence, the call for lawyers for students, so that their self-interests and not that of the high school or the college will be defended. And hence, the call for lawyers for welfare recipients and prisoners, so that their rights will be promoted, and the authority of social workers, probation officers, wardens, and guards will be reduced.

There is no denying that a liberty model and an adversarial stance may pose as many questions as they solve about the problems of dependency in American society. For one, a focus on rights may well give a new legitimacy to neglect, allowing conservatives to join in the chorus for rights, not for the sake of maximizing choice but for reducing tax-based expenditures. For another, the traits of the lawyers are not those that would necessarily warm anybody's heart, let alone those who stand in need of support. It was Willard Gaylin who commented, with all sarcasm intended, that he finally understood the motive impulse of the adversarial movement: to substitute for the hardnosed, belligerent, and tough-minded psychiatrist the attention of the gentle, understanding, empathetic lawyer! For still another, an adversarial model, setting interest off against interest, does seem to run the clear risk of creating a kind of ultimate shoot-out in which, by definition, the powerless lose and the powerful win. How absurd to push for confrontation when all the advantages are on the other side. Finally, courts are not the most reliable or consistent institutions to trust to in an effort to advance the claims of minorities. The new reformers themselves are fully aware of the grimmer prospects they face as the Warren Court gives way to the Burger Court.

But it is not the point of this essay to predict how a liberty model and adversarial tactics will fare in the future so much as to make clear how far the post-1960s reformers have moved from the Progressive tradition. The optimism and confidence that Progressives shared, both about the wisdom and potential effectiveness of their social policies, their firm sense of having diagnosed the problems of dependency and formulated the right programs to eliminate it, their belief in the superiority of their values and all that meant to their ability to define and to attempt to implement the proper life-styles in all citizens and classes, have disappeared and can hardly be resurrected. To try to recapture their vision of things, to assume as they did that the state should act as parent, is to misread in the most basic way the realities of our own particular social situation and to embark on a futile and probably dangerous endeavor.

Rather than trying to revive an older type of social contract, under which the better sort, the expert and the professional, was to act benevolently toward others and on their behalf, we would do better to address a very different series of issues. Will we as a society be able to recognize and respect rights and yet not ignore needs? Can we do good to others, but on their terms? Rather than wondering how professional expertise and discretionary authority can be exercised in the best interest of the client or the patient, we should ponder how the objects of authority can protect themselves against abuse without depriving themselves of the benefits that experts can deliver—and to turn the matter around in this way represents more than just a stylistic revision. Or to revert to the modern horror stories, is there some way that we can give Mrs. Lake her freedom and yet not breed cruelty? These are the right questions to be confronting, even if the record of American reform gives little reason to be confident that we will answer them well.

SUGGESTIONS FOR FURTHER READING

Eric Goldman, *Rendezvous with Destiny* (New York, 1952) presents a sympathetic view of the progressives that sees them in the tradition of liberal reformers and precursors to the New Deal. Richard Hofstadter, *The Age of Reform* (New York, 1955) finds the progressives responding to a "status revolution" brought by the nation's industrial development; although not completely unsympathetic, Hofstadter sees the progressives as less forward looking and very different from the later New Dealers. David J. Rothman spells out

---

*Available in paperback edition.

his argument that the progressives created a coercive tradition in *Conscience and Convenience: The Asylum and Its Alternatives in Progressive America* (Boston, 1980). George E. Mowry, *The Era of Theodore Roosevelt, 1900–1912* (New York, 1958) and Arthur S. Link, *Woodrow Wilson and the Progressive Era, 1910–1917* (New York, 1954) are balanced studies that fit the two major progressive politicians into the larger progressive movement and in the process reduce some of the conflict that earlier writers emphasized. Samuel P. Hays, *The Response to Industrialism* (Chicago, 1957) and Robert Wiebe, *The Search for Order, 1877–1920* (New York, 1967) see adjustment, consolidation, order, and efficiency, rather than conflict, as the keys to the period. Gabriel Kolko, *The Triumph of Conservatism: A Reinterpretation of American History, 1900–1916* (New York, 1963) sees progressivism as a movement dominated by businessmen who believed that "the general welfare of a community could be best served by satisfying the concrete needs of business." Robert Wiebe, *Businessmen and Reform: A Study of the Progressive Movement* (Cambridge, Mass., 1962) finds business support for progressivism, but, unlike Kolko, describes the business community as divided during the period. James Weinstein, *The Corporate Ideal in the Liberal State, 1900–1918* (Boston, 1968) finds a conservative business consensus, but Allen F. Davis, *Spearheads for Reform* (New York, 1967) still finds the quest for social justice a part of the movement.

Progressive reformers—or at least reformers during the progressive period—seemed to be everywhere, concerning themselves with a wide variety of problems. The following books provide examples of this variety as well as discussions of how reformers viewed the problems and their causes: Aileen S. Kraditor, *The Ideas of the Woman Suffrage Movement, 1890–1929* (New York, 1965); Robert H. Bremner, *From the Depths: The Discovery of Poverty in the United States* (New York, 1956); Lawrence A. Cremin, *The Transformation of the School: Progressivism in American Education, 1876–1957* (New York, 1961); Samuel P. Hays, *Conservation and the Gospel of Efficiency: The Progressive Conservation Movement, 1890–1920* (Cambridge, Mass., 1959); David Thelen, *The New Citizenship: Origins of Progressivism in Wisconsin* (Columbia, Mo., 1972); Peter Conn, *The Divided Mind: Ideology and Imagination in America, 1898–1917* (New York, 1983); and Martin J. Sklar, *The Corporate Reconstruction of American Capitalism, 1898–1916: The Market, the Law, and Politics* (New York, 1988). Eldon J. Eisenach, *The Lost Promise of Progressivism* (Lawrence, Kans., 1994) argues that progressivism was primarily an intellectual movement that lost its promise during the Wilson administration. Three recent works deal with aspects of the role of women in the progressive era: Dorothy Schneider and Carl J. Schneider, *American Women in the Progressive Era, 1900–1920* (New York, 1994); Ellen F. Fitzpatrick, *Endless Crusade: Women Social Scientists and Progressive Reform* (New York, 1990); and Noralee Frankel and Nancy S. Dye, eds., *Gender, Class, Race, and Reform in the Progressive Era* (Lexington, Ky., 1991).

Even the South had its progressive reformers, but as C. Vann Woodward has put it, southern progressivism was "for whites only." See his chapter with that title in *Origins of the New South* (Baton Rouge, La., 1951). A fine recent study of progressivism in the South is Dewey W. Grantham, *Southern Progressivism* (Nashville, 1983). Grantham shows how southern progressives tried to reconcile southern traditions, including race discrimination and agrarianism, with progress. A good study of what this meant for blacks is John Dittmer, *Black Georgia in the Progressive Era, 1900–1920* (Urbana, Ill., 1977). The varying responses of black leaders are brilliantly discussed in August Meier, *Negro Thought in America, 1880–1915* (Ann Arbor, Mich., 1969).

The socialists offered truly radical alternatives to reforms. Varying interpretations of their efforts are David Shannon, *The Socialist Party of America: A History* (New York, 1955); Ira Kipnis, *The American Socialist Movement, 1897–1912* (New York, 1952);

and James Weinstein, *The Decline of Socialism in America, 1912–1925* (New York, 1967).

For convenient selections of writings and good bibliographies see David M. Kennedy, ed., *Progressivism: The Critical Issues* (Boston, 1971) and Arthur Mann, *The Progressive Era: Major Issues of Interpretation,* 2nd ed. (New York, 1975). Interesting and provocative general accounts are David W. Noble, *The Progressive Mind, 1890–1917* (Chicago, 1970); William O'Neill, *The Progressive Years* (New York, 1975); and Robert M. Cruden, *Ministers of Reform: The Progressive Achievement in American Civilization, 1889–1920* (New York, 1982). Arthur S. Link and Richard L. McCormick, *Progressivism* (Arlington Heights, Ill., 1983) is an excellent brief summary and a historiographic overview of the movement.

The 1920s

The Decade between the end of World War I and the stock market crash of 1929 was filled with paradoxes and contradictions. The American people overwhelmingly elected Republicans Warren G. Harding, Calvin Coolidge, and Herbert Hoover president, but chose as their heroes such different figures as Charles A. Lindbergh and Babe Ruth. Americans self-righteously proclaimed prohibition; then, patronizing speak-easies and bootleggers, they increased the amount of social drinking. The 1920s were marked by provincialism, immigration restriction, and fundamentalist rejection of modern science, but this same decade was the occasion for a great burst of literary and artistic activity. It was a period of seeming isolation as the United States pulled back from political involvement with Europe, but it was also a time that saw increasing expansion of American investment overseas. It was a time of unprecedented business prosperity that important groups such as farmers and unorganized workers did not share, and the decade ended with the collapse of the stock market and the onset of a major depression. It was an era during which progressivism and reform all but disappeared on the national level but remained alive in a number of states and cities.

These paradoxes and contradictions were the source of much conflict during the 1920s. A group of intellectuals and writers, alienated from the mainstream of American life, rejected the materialism and the social and political values that they associated with the small-town Midwest. For some, such as Ernest Hemingway and F. Scott Fitzgerald, this "revolt against the village" led them to leave the country to become expatriates in France or Spain. Others, such as H. L. Mencken and Sinclair Lewis, stayed at home, leading an attack on the "booboisie" and the Babbitts. Out of the disillusionment of this "lost generation" came some of the most searching critiques of American life and some of the most creative and enduring of American art and literature.

Other manifestations of conflict were also evident in the 1920s. The Scopes trial in Dayton, Tennessee, in 1925, trying and convicting a high school biology teacher for teaching Darwinian ideas, symbolized the conflict between fundamentalists and modernists, between the small town and the city. The trial, conviction, and eventual execution of two Italian immigrants, Nicola Sacco and Bartolomeo Vanzetti, for a robbery-murder in Massachusetts elicited widespread protest among many who believed that they were convicted on inadequate evidence because of prejudice against immigrants and radicals. A resurgent Ku Klux Klan, boasting some five million members, North and South, carried on an intensive campaign directed against blacks, Catholics, Jews, and immigrants. Organized labor lost many of its wartime gains and suffered a decline in membership in the face of a renewed employer offensive often supported by the courts and local law-enforcement agencies.

If class, religious, racial, and ethnic conflict seemed close to the surface in the 1920s, when viewed another way, the decade seemed to represent a time of unprecedented national unity and consensus based on prosperity, smug isolation from the evils of Europe, and the enjoyment of an expanding consumer society that made available the radio, the refrigerator, the automobile, and other material symbols of the jazz age. Americans enjoyed more telephones, automobiles, good roads, and electrical appliances than any other people in the world, and they never tired of informing the rest of the world of this fact. Indeed, it was against this self-satisfied complacency that the critics often railed.

Booming prosperity bred widespread optimism among those who enjoyed its benefits; they found it easy to ignore those who did not share in the prosperity and to dismiss critics as sour, alien, and un-American. But the stock market crash in 1929 and the depression that followed quickly destroyed the decade-long optimism. Americans who no longer enjoyed prosperity could see more clearly the problems of those who never participated in the boom and appreciate more fully the words of the critics.

The paradoxes and contradictions that marked the decade of the 1920s, along with the sobering experience of the crash and onset of depression, have profoundly affected the ways in which historians have viewed the period, as may be seen in the following selections.

John Higham, in the first selection, describes the 1920s as a time of racial and ethnic conflict, a period of hate and distrust of radicals, immigrants, Catholics, Jews, and blacks by an ethnocentric majority, at once complacent about its own superiority and fearful that its privileged position was endangered. Higham notes that the hatred and distrust was not new but became especially virulent during the 1920s because of a resurgence of nativism— "100 percent Americanism," as Higham calls it—stimulated, paradoxically, by a combination of wartime nationalism and postwar disillusionment. For Higham, therefore, the 1920s were marked by sharp conflicts between conservative, 100 percent Americans and the minority groups who seemed different and un-American.

In the second selection, Eric F. Goldman describes a popular conservative consensus that rejected the reforms of the progressives, imposed conformity, and supported big business. Catholics, Jews, blacks, and other minorities organized in an attempt to protect themselves, and a few progressives sought to maintain the reformist spirit, but the most they could achieve in the face of the aggressive conservatism of the era were delaying actions "staving off the complete triumph of the Babbitts."

Robert S. McElvaine, in the final selection, looks at the 1920s from the perspective of the depression that began with the stock market crash in the decade's final year. Although McElvaine rejects simple, monocausal explanations for the onset of depression, he concludes his analysis of economic developments during the decade that produced an unsound economy in the midst of prosperity by arguing that in assessing the causes of the depression "the greatest weight must be assigned to the effects of an income distribution that was bad and getting worse."

In trying to understand this fascinating time, should we emphasize a national consensus based on prosperity, isolation, and the luxuries of the jazz age? Or should we stress the racial, ethnic, and class conflicts that were also present during the 1920s?

Why were critics so unhappy with conditions in the 1920s? Interestingly enough, some of the critics were very popular during the decade. Many Americans read and delighted in the criticisms of writers such as H. L. Mencken and Sinclair Lewis, even as they continued to act in ways that these writers ridiculed. Did these popular critics fail to recognize the real problems facing the country, making it possible to listen to them while ignoring more important, but less popular, criticisms? Why did those who pointed to economic problems—to the suffering of farmers, to segregation and jim crow, to widespread unemployment in the midst of prosperity, and to the grossly unequal distribution of wealth—receive a sympathetic hearing from so few Americans? Were these problems, which seem so evident in retrospect, difficult to discern in the midst of prosperity? Or did a majority of Americans become so smug, so self-satisfied, that they simply ignored the plight of those who were not enjoying the benefits of prosperity?

JOHN HIGHAM

The Tribal Twenties

*The old Americans are getting a little panicky, and no wonder. . . .
America, Americans and Americanism are being crowded out of
America. It is inevitable that there should be silly forms of protest
and rebellion. But the Ku Klux Klan and the hundred percenters
are fundamentally right from the standpoint of an American unity
and destiny.*

—Ltr. to ed., *New Republic,* 1924

*. . . not nostrums but normalcy . . . not experiment but equipoise,
not submergence in internationality but sustainment in triumphant
nationality.*

—Warren G. Harding, 1920

During the night of August 5, 1920, and all through the following day hundreds of people laden with clothing and household goods filled the roads leading out of West Frankfort, a mining town in southern Illinois. Back in town their homes were burning. Mobs bent on driving every foreigner from the area surged through the streets. Foreigners of all descriptions were beaten on sight, although the Italian population was the chief objective. Time and again the crowds burst into the Italian district, dragged cowering residents from their homes, clubbed and stoned them, and set fire to their dwellings. The havoc went on for three days, although five hundred state troops were rushed to the scene.

The immediate background of the affair was trivial enough. Thousands of workers were idle and restless owing to a strike in the coal mines where the Italians and a large part of the native population were employed. A series of bank robberies, popularly attributed to a Black Hand Society, had lately occurred; this was followed by the kidnapping of two boys. The discovery of their bodies touched off the civic explosion. The region, to be sure, had a bloody history. Violent anti-foreign incidents had occurred there during and before the war. But never on this scale.

About the same time, an exuberance not wholly unrelated to the miners' frenzy sprang up elsewhere on the national scene in sundry ways. In California anti-Japanese hysteria, quiescent during the war, broke out again in the latter part of 1919 and rose to unprecedented heights during the election of 1920. A new law forbidding Japanese ownership of land passed by popular initiative; a fearful clamor against Japanese "picture brides" went up; and for the first time

---

the agitation was beginning to have a real effect on eastern opinion. In Georgia the 1920 primaries brought the old warrior, Tom Watson, back to the hustings to end his career with a successful campaign for a seat in the United States Senate. The issue was popery. Silenced by the federal government during the war because of his anti-war attitudes, Watson now heaped ridicule on the authors of the discredited Red Scare while crying up the peril of Catholic domination. Not to be outdone, the adjoining state of Alabama had recently set up a convent-inspecting commission to ensure that no Protestant maidens were held under durance vile. Out of the Midwest in May 1920 came the opening blast of a propaganda campaign against Jews launched by Henry Ford, America's leading industrialist and a man idolized by millions. Almost simultaneously the most widely read magazine in the United States, the *Saturday Evening Post,* began to quote and urgently commend the doctrines of Madison Grant. At another intellectual level one of the country's foremost literary arbiters instigated a general critical assault on writers of alien blood and spirit for corrupting American literature. And during that same summer, quite outside the public eye, an insignificant little society named the Ku Klux Klan was feeling a sudden flutter of life. The upheaval in West Frankfort was only the gaudiest of the portents signaling another great nativist wave that was boiling up in the wake of the Red Scare.

Blighted New World

In its basic patterns, the new ferment of 1920–1924 was far from new. The nativisms that came to the fore in 1920 essentially continued prewar trends. They consisted largely of hatreds—toward Catholics, Jews, and southeastern Europeans—that had gathered strength in the late Progressive era, reaching a minor crescendo in 1914. The war had simply suspended these animosities while American nationalism vented itself in other directions. Once the war and immediate postwar period passed, the two leading nativist traditions of the early twentieth century, Anglo-Saxonism and anti-Catholicism, reoccupied the field. Anti-radicalism, their historic partner, had grown hugely under the conditions which temporarily blocked the other two, but its collapse cleared the way for their revival.

As they passed into the 1920's, the Anglo-Saxon and anti-Catholic traditions retained the distinctive character that the prewar decade had stamped upon them. Racial nativism remained fixed on the new immigration (together with the Japanese), rooted in primitive race-feelings, and rationalized by a scientific determinism. It owed to the early twentieth century its prophet, Madison Grant, its southern and western political leadership, and its nationwide appeal. Anti-Catholic nativism similarly exhibited the characteristics it had developed just before the war. Whereas racism knew no limits of section or class and preserved an air of respectability, anti-Romanism throve outside of the big cities and the cultivated classes. Reborn after 1910 in the small towns of the South and West, religious nativism resumed its prewar pattern of growth, feeding on the continuing surge of rural fundamentalism and the deepening frustration of progressive hopes. Despite the incongruities between religious and racial xenophobias, they had begun to intersect before the World War in the demagoguery of Tom Watson and, less melodramatically, in the program of the Junior Order United American

Mechanics. After the war, the two traditions flowed together in the comprehensive nativism of the Ku Klux Klan, an organization which itself dated from 1915.

Yet the tempestuous climate of the early twenties is not to be accounted for simply as a resumption of storms after a temporary lull. The very fact that the lull did prove temporary, that old hatreds came to life after the war instead of being consumed by it, needs explanation. In some degree the causes lay in the objective circumstances of 1920. That year, as part of a general adjustment to peacetime conditions, two factors which time and again in American history encouraged anti-foreign outbreaks vividly reappeared. One was economic depression, the other a fresh wave of immigration. During the latter months of the year the war and postwar boom collapsed. For a year and a half businessmen, farmers, and workers felt the pinch of hard times, with all the consequences of unemployment, credit stringencies, and tobogganing prices. Unfortunately for the immigrants, the economic downswing synchronized with a sudden revival of immigration. Virtually halted by the war, immigration had remained at low ebb through 1919 and into the early months of 1920. In the second half of 1919 so many aliens, flushed with wartime savings and embittered toward America, had returned home to Europe that immigration figures showed a net loss. But the tide turned decisively around the end of May 1920. By early September an average five thousand arrivals per day were pouring into Ellis Island. Before the year was out newspapers teemed with hostile comment on the relation between this torrential influx and the worsening unemployment problem. Some thought that immigration was undermining the whole economic system.

A third well-known irritant to ethnic relations intruded into the postwar era, assuming somewhat more importance that it had hitherto displayed. Whereas the scale of immigration and the state of the economy had often contributed significantly to nativist movements, the association of foreigners with crime had not affected their reception to a comparable degree. Crime had helped to make anti-foreign stereotypes rather than anti-foreign hatreds. Prohibition, however, created a much more highly charged situation, for it precipitated a head-on collision between mounting lawlessness and a new drive for social conformity.

On the one hand, the Eighteenth Amendment attempted an unprecedented regimentation of morality by law. Although a tradition of reform originally sired the prohibition movement, its national triumph awaited the strenuous spirit of conformity which the war unleashed. Riding the wave of 100 percent Americanism, the Drys identified their crusade to regulate behavior with preservation of the American way of life. On the other hand, constraint bred revolt. Prohibition aggravated the normal lawlessness of a postwar era by opening a vast illicit traffic in alcohol. The immigrants, whose own cultures imposed no alcoholic taboos, were Wets by habit and conviction. The dazzling opportunities that prohibition created for organized gangsterism thrust immigrant children into a special notoriety, for city gangs had long recruited a high proportion of their members in the disorganizing environment of foreign slum quarters. Thus the ban on alcohol hit the immigrants two ways: it increased their conspicuousness as lawbreakers and brought down upon their heads the wrath of a 100 percent American morality.

By the end of 1919 the press was commenting on a rising "crime wave" and speculating on its alien origins, but it remained for the eruption at West

Frankfort to demonstrate the intensity of the hatred of foreign lawlessness. In the years ahead similar feelings would find a powerful outlet through the hooded legions of the Ku Klux Klan; in the Midwest the Klan delivered more real assaults on the bootleggers than on any other target. At the same time, one state after another tackled the specter of the foreign criminal with legislation to disarm all aliens. Wyoming took particular care to forbid the possession by aliens of "any dirk, pistol, shot gun, rifle, or other fire arm, bowie knife, dagger, or any other dangerous or deadly weapon."

The resumption of immigration, the onset of depression, a wave of crime—each of these formed part of a social pattern shaped by a return to peace, and all three had precedents in the circumstances of earlier peacetime eras in which nativism flourished. But if these events help to account for the regeneration of historic xenophobias in 1920, in themselves they can hardly explain the peculiar force and magnitude that the reawakened hatreds now displayed. Indeed, the alien lawbreaker owed his new significance as an anti-foreign symbol more largely to a state of mind that had crystallized during the war than to the objective circumstances of the postwar period. In many respects the level of hysteria in the early twenties was a heritage of mind and spirit from the World War. Pre-1914 traditions supplied the massive roots of that hysteria; post-1919 conditions provided fertile soil for a new season of growth; but 100 percent Americanism was the vital force that gave it abundant life.

On first thought one may wonder how the new nationalism survived so vigorously the transition from war to peace, when many other wartime ideals were shipwrecked. It is important to realize that during the years from 1915 to 1919, 100 percent Americanism shared in the heady optimism that flourished during the war and collapsed soon after. If the guardians of an exclusive loyalty had nothing else in common with the cosmopolitan, democratic nationalists, at least they felt a common exaltation. Despite the obsessive fears that tortured the 100 percenters, they too looked forward to a brave new world once the nation had passed through its ordeal. To be sure, their assurance was a grimmer and narrower thing than that of their liberal opponents; real victory would require iron resolution and heroic measures. But a crusading idealism formed a fundamental part of the 100 percent American outlook. The millennial expectations dominant in public opinion since 1898 had reached a culmination during the war period, deeply affecting almost the whole spectrum of American thought, and 100 percenters acquired much of their evangelical zeal from the general hope that the war's turmoil would usher in a purified, regenerate society. So Americanizers set about with a will to transform the immigrants; patriotic clergymen testified to the spiritually ennobling results of warfare; prohibitionists carried the point that outlawing alcohol would accomplish a general moral improvement and call for little enforcement at that; few seriously challenged President Wilson's vision of a new reign of peace founded on a league of nations.

Perhaps this utopian spirit could not long have survived unsullied under any circumstances. Certainly the harsh facts of the postwar world produced, during 1919 and 1920, a general disillusion. The quarreling at Versailles and the class strife that broke out at home and abroad began the process of deflation and embitterment. It went forward under the influence of partisan wrangling in Congress, economic depression, the manifest failure of Americanization, and the scandalous consequences of prohibition. The letdown seriously undermined democratic, cosmopolitan values, for many who held them abandoned a crusading stance, repudiating their ideals as delusive, nationalism as nasty, and society as unsalvageable. One hundred percent Americanism, on the other hand, had a built-in shock-absorber which not only saved it from disintegrating but converted every disappointment into rebounding aggressiveness. Believing implicitly that the great source of evil lay outside of their own society, super-nationalists could not hold their own principles at fault when failure mocked them. The trouble must come instead from the tenacity and secret cunning of alien influences, together with a lack of sufficient solidarity on the part of true Americans in resisting them. The nation must gird anew against protean forces working in ever grander and more mysterious ways. Thus, instead of crippling the force of 100 percent Americanism, the discouragements of 1919–1920 broadened the fears which it expressed and turned it against enemies vaguer and more elusive than either the German or the Bolshevik.

The persistence, then, of the fundamental premises of wartime nationalism was crucial to the nativist climate of the early twenties, but equally important was the loss of the spirit of confidence characteristic of the war years. In their own fashion, 100 percenters reflected the general psychological letdown. They ceased on the whole to look forward to a total defeat of the forces of darkness. The evil was too great, the world too deeply infected. Americans must concentrate their efforts on holding their present ground. In short, 100 percent Americanism passed entirely to the defensive. Its aggressions took the form not of conquest but of a holding operation to save "the last best hope of earth." The result was an intense isolation that worked hand in hand with nativism. By mid-1920 a general revulsion against European entanglements was crystallizing. In the debate over the Versailles Treaty an afterglow of Wilsonian ideals had lingered through 1919, and the League of Nations commanded immense support in public opinion (though with increasing qualifications) until the early months of 1920. By autumn not 10 percent of the daily press, and hardly a single national magazine, still backed the league. America now seemed vulnerable to European influences of every kind. Policies of diplomatic withdrawal, higher tariffs, and more stringent immigration restriction were all in order.

Flowering of Racism

Logically, a nationalism so committed to isolation, so distrustful of entanglements with Europe, should find expression in a general revulsion against all foreigners. Indeed, an indiscriminate anti-foreignism did extend far and wide in the early twenties. It echoed through the debate on the League of Nations; it swayed the policies of the American Legion and rumbled in the "konklaves" of the Ku Klux Klan; it unloosed a new torrent of state legislation excluding aliens from a great many occupations. Nevertheless the most intense and significant anti-foreign feelings still focused on symbols of hatred more specific than the whole foreign population. One hundred percent Americanism had greatest impact through interaction with older cultural traditions.

As the Red Scare subsided, the Anglo-Saxon tradition displayed more than ever the special magnetism it acquired in the prewar period. No other nativism spoke with equal authority or affected so much of American society. This was the flowering time of the semi-scientific racism that had burgeoned in the decade before the war. Although this ideology had the limitation (from a 100 percent point of view) of not rejecting all Europeans, it was peculiarly well suited as a channel for the defensive nationalism of an age undergoing disillusion. In the nineteenth and early twentieth centuries racial nativism had developed in minds of a gloomy cast; it registered a failure of nerve on the part of an exhausted elite. Explicitly, racism denied the regnant optimism of the Progressive era; a pessimistic determinism imprisoned ideals within iron laws of heredity. Thus, when the utopian hopes of the war years dissolved, the harsh racial doctrines fitted a prevailing mood. Those doctrines not only explained the apparent imperviousness of the immigrant to Americanization. They also accounted for the failure of all efforts at universal uplift. And they showed that the United States could trust in no ideals save those that rested upon and served to protect the nation's racial foundations. . . .

The International Jew

Of all the European groups that lay outside of the charmed Nordic circle none was subjected to quite so much hatred as the Jews. They had always played a special role in the American imagination, but until the postwar period anti-Jewish sentiment, though unique in kind, probably did not exceed in degree the general level of feeling against other European nationalities. The fear of a Jewish money-power during the 1890s and Georgia's emotional debauch at the height of the Frank Case in 1914 were merely preludes to the much more widespread and tenacious anti-Semitism that developed after the World War. No pogrom has ever stained American soil, nor did any single anti-Jewish incident in the 1920s match the violence of the anti-Italian riot in southern Illinois. Nevertheless the Jews faced a sustained agitation that singled them out from the other new immigrant groups blanketed by racial nativism—an agitation that reckoned them the most dangerous force undermining the nation.

During a period of a general weakening in democratic values social discrimination against Jews would undoubtedly have spread even if no new ideological attack on them had occurred. After the war a flood of Jewish students into private eastern colleges resulted in restrictions on admission similar to those earlier adopted by preparatory schools and college fraternities. Beginning in 1919, New York University instituted stringent restrictions. Columbia soon cut the number of Jews in her incoming classes from 40 to 22 percent. At Harvard, where Brahmin students feared that the university was becoming a new Jerusalem, President Lowell in 1922 moved, with unseemly frankness, to raise the bars. At the same time job opportunities were continuing to shrink. By the end of the twenties one informed estimate indicated that Jews were excluded from 90 percent of the jobs available in New York City in general office work.

What was startling, however, was not so much the steady growth of discrimination as the rise of a new anti-Semitic nationalism. On the whole the wartime spirit of fraternity had repressed and inhibited anti-Semitic ideas. Nevertheless, the seeds of a new movement against Jews were to be found in 100 percent Americanism of the war years. The more wealthy and prominent Jews in the United States were of German background. Certain 100 percenters, therefore, applied to the Jews the suspicion of all things German. Among some of the bitter, overwrought men who believed that the Wilson administration was dealing laxly, perhaps treasonably, with traitors within and enemies without, dark rumors circulated concerning German-Jewish influence in high places. Henry Cabot Lodge and others whispered about secret ties between Wilson and Germany through Paul Warburg, a recent Jewish immigrant who sat on the Federal Reserve Board. "The government," a Texas businessman exploded, "seems to be permeated with the atmosphere of different kinds of Jews."

The growth of anti-radical nativism during the war opened another channel for anti-Semitic feelings—one that broadened enormously after the armistice. Morris Hillquit's remarkably strong showing as the Socialist, anti-war candidate for mayor of New York City in 1917 gave a good many people a glimpse of the radical ferment at work in Lower East Side tenements. Leon Trotsky's departure for Russia in 1917, after a brief stay in New York, and the sympathy with which other Russian Jews in the United States greeted the Bolshevik revolution sharpened an emerging image of the Jew as a subversive radical. In September 1918, Brooklyn witnessed a debut of a periodical "Devoted to the Defense of American Institutions Against the Jewish Bolshevist Doctrines of Morris Hillquit and Leon Trotsky."

The Big Red Scare turned these surreptitious by-products of the war into a thriving anti-Jewish agitation. Most commonly, of course, the nativists of 1919 identified radicalism with foreigners generally, so that anti-Semitism remained a subordinate aspect of an attack upon the larger immigrant community. Nevertheless, the Jew offered the most concrete symbol of foreign radicalism, and his significance as such increased very greatly when 100 percent Americanism burst through the confining dikes of wartime unity. Stories circulated about the streets of New York to the effect that every Jewish immigrant would become a soldier in the revolutionary army assembling in America. A Methodist clergyman testified before a Senate committee that Bolshevism in Russia was drawing much of its inspiration and support from the Yiddish sections of New York. The same doctrine that Bolshevism was a Jewish movement echoed from public meetings and from the pulpits of many churches. A powerful propaganda organization of conservative businessmen in the Midwest, the Greater Iowa Association, spread word throughout the state that Russian Jewish peddlers were disseminating Bolshevik literature. . . .

The new anti-Semitism secured its standard-bearer and its prophet in one of the commanding figures of the day, Henry Ford. In the *Dearborn Independent,* a general magazine which he published and distributed through his thousands of dealerships, Ford, in May 1920, launched an offensive against the International Jew which continued off and on for several years. Then and after, the "Flivver

King" was enormously popular (and not a little feared) as America's greatest industrialist, as a folk philosopher, and as a potential politician. In 1923 he was one of the most popular and widely discussed candidates for the next Presidential nomination. That he was a food faddist, a suspicious factory-master, a man of mercurial mood swings and dogmatic opinions, and a quixotic crusader who once sent a boatload of pacifists to Europe to stop the World War, counted for little in the public eye. To millions he embodied the old pioneer virtues: a farm-bred simplicity contemptuous of elegance or intellect, a rugged individualism, a genius for practical achievement.

Ford carried over into the industrial field not only the personal traits but also the social ideas typical of his rustic background. The son of Michigan tenant farmers, he looked upon big cities as cesspools of iniquity, soulless and artificial. He hated monopoly and special privilege. He jealously guarded his enterprises from banker influence and was regarded, in the words of the Detroit *News,* as "the recognized crusader against the money changers of Wall Street." In short, Ford, for all of his wealth, typified some of the key attitudes for which Watson had stood. It is hardly surprising that in Ford and in many others with an agrarian background, nativism took a violently anti-Semitic turn at a time of depression, isolation, and disillusion.

Each of the factors that apparently impelled the extension of anti-Semitism after the Red Scare affected Henry Ford in an acute and special way. The economic slump of 1920 hit him hard and early. Swallowing his scruples, he had borrowed $75,000,000 in 1919 from eastern bankers in order to buy out his partners. The decline of sales in 1920 left him loaded with debts and unsold cars. His anti-Jewish campaign began in the midst of this crisis, and at first his propaganda presented the International Jew solely in the role of financier. Jewish bankers, according to the *Dearborn Independent,* operating through a vast international network, dominate the American economy. The great struggle of the hour lies between the contending forces of "international Finance" and "creative Industry," and apparently the latter cannot triumph until control of the world is wrested from the Jewish money-kings. . . .

Another index of the locus and relative importance of the anti-Semitic theme may be found in the chief organization that fostered it, the Ku Klux Klan. Since all of the xenophobias of the 1920's flowed into this central apotheosis of a tribal spirit, the Klan furnishes a kind of litmus-paper test of rural nativism. Significantly, the Klan's home was not in the great cities. Its strength came chiefly from the towns, from the villages, and from the ordinarily tranquil countryside. Through the theory and practice of a "noble Klannishness," anti-Semitism achieved, for the first time in American history, substantial organizational expression.

Klan propaganda echoed the Ford attack on the Jewish banker-Bolshevik, adding a special emphasis on vice that reflected the powerful strain of evangelical morality in the organization. To the Klan the Jew stood for an international plot to control America and also for the whole spectrum of urban sin—for pollution of the Sabbath, bootlegging, gambling, and carnal indulgence. Thus Klan publications described the Jew as a subversive radical, a Shylock seeking power through money, and a "Christ-killing" monster of moral corruption. All of these destructive forces radiated from the centers of population, and Klansmen had the assurance—in the words of one Oregon spellbinder—that in some cities "the Kikes are so thick that a white man can hardly find room to walk on the sidewalk."

Still, later generations of Americans, remembering the Hitlerite groups of the 1930s, can easily exaggerate the part that anti-Semitism played in the organized nativism of the postwar decade. The Jew occupied, on the whole, a distinctly secondary rank in the Klan's demonology. On the level of ideas, other passions outweighed, other hatreds outreached the attack on the Jew. As for direct action, he suffered largely from sporadic economic proscriptions. In southern as well as western towns boycotts harassed long-established Jewish merchants; sometimes enterprising Klansmen launched their own proudly labeled "100 per cent American" clothing stores. But personal violence was quite rare. Klan energies found larger outlet in the older, more massive traditions of American nativism. It is time to turn to the whole range of the Klan's operations, and to its central meaning. . . .

The Klan Rides

The first acknowledged public appearances of the Klan in the postwar period reflected its underlying racial spirit. On the eve of the election of 1920, Klansmen paraded in many southern towns as a silent warning against Negro voting. A large number of anti-Negro outrages were committed in the next few months under Klan auspices, provoked partly by fear that a "New Negro" had emerged from the war. (In point of fact, Negro veterans returning from France in 1919 and 1920 were often determined to stand militant and upright.) The men in white bludgeoned employers into downgrading or discharging Negro employees, intimidated Negro cotton-pickers into working for wages they would not otherwise accept, forced Negro residents out of a part of South Jacksonville coveted by whites, and branded the letters "KKK" on the forehead of a Negro bellboy. In these early months of expansion the organization presented itself very largely as a means for keeping "the nigger in his place."

White supremacy remained an important theme even when the Klan spread into the North, but it would be a mistake to regard the Negro issue as the mainspring of its career. Fear of the "New Negro" rapidly declined as he either accepted his old place or moved to northern cities. By mid-1921 the Klan was specializing in attacking white people, and thereafter the great bulk of its disciplinary activities in all parts of the country had to do with whites. This shift of emphasis by no means indicated a slackening of the racial imperative. To a considerable degree, however, it suggested that race-thinking was more and more taking a nativistic and nationalistic direction. The Klan's snowballing advance in the early twenties paralleled the upthrust of racial nativism in public opinion generally. And within the order an insistence on preserving the superiority of the old Anglo-Saxon stock over foreigners of every description became pronounced. Edward Y. Clarke exemplified this trend in 1922 by defining the Klan's mission as one of creating national solidarity by protecting "the interest of those whose forefathers established the nation." Other Klan leaders, in particularizing on the old stock's interest, called immigration restriction the most momentous legislative issue of the day, asserted that only Anglo-Saxons or Nordics had an inherent capacity for American citizenship, dammed "the cross-breeding hordes" of the new immigration, and trembled lest the "real whites" fail to keep the nation "free from all mongrelizing taints." The emphatic Anglo-Saxonism did not, of course, prevent the same men from ranting loudly at foreigners as such, on the plea that America must be made safe for Americans.

If the Ku Klux Klan had mobilized only this much of the emotional ferment of the period, if it had functioned only through an Anglo-Saxon version of 100 percent Americanism and through related fears of Jews and of foreigners generally, it would have incarnated a very large part of the current tribal spirit. Yet the Klan had another big side. By embracing the anti-Catholic tradition along with the racial tradition and the new anti-Semitism, it comprehended the whole range of post-1919 nativism. Anti-Catholicism did not prevail as widely in American public opinion as did the Anglo-Saxon ideas reflected in the organization; an urban, materialistic culture had stifled in too many Americans the religious feelings on which Protestant xenophobia fed. Due, however, to the semirural base of the Klan, within its ranks anti-Catholicism actually grew to surpass every other nativistic attitude. In fact, a religious impulse, perverted but not devoid of idealistic implications, accounts for much of the Klan's distinctive energy, both as a nativist organization and as an agent of other kinds of repressions too.

Although the Klan was Protestant from the day its first cross burned on Stone Mountain, an anti-Catholic emphasis came into the order only in the course of its expansion in 1920 and 1921. Simmons, Clarke, and Tyler had not at first expected to sell the organization as a bulwark against Rome. The Klan's stress on religious nativism, even more than the parallel expansion of its Anglo-Saxon agitation, reflected the passions of the people who joined it. By 1920 the anti-Catholic crusade that had appeared in the South and West after 1910 was reasserting itself more powerfully than ever. Under a prohibitionist governor, Alabama pointed the way as early as 1919. While laying plans for inspecting convents, the state also challenged Catholic (and secular) sentiment by requiring daily Bible reading in the public schools, thus reviving a trend begun in Pennsylvania in 1913. The following year the tide came in strongly. Tom Watson's Senatorial campaign spread about Georgia an impression that President Wilson had become a tool of the Pope; Governor Sidney J. Catts stomped up and down Florida warning that the Pope planned to invade the state and transfer the Vatican there; an able journalist reported that anti-Catholicism had become "second only to the hatred of the Negro as the moving passion of entire Southern communities"; Michigan and Nebraska debated constitutional amendments banning parochial schools; and in Missouri the once-mighty anti-Catholic weekly, *The Menace,* revived under a new name, *The Torch.*

Sentiment of this kind amounted to a standing invitation to secret societies. The first to respond prominently was not the Klan but rather the True Americans, a local southern organization. The T. A.'s acquired such influence in Birmingham in 1920 that they dominated the city administration and secured a purge of Catholic municipal employees. Before long Ku Kluxers eclipsed and very likely absorbed the True Americans. Klan propaganda, reviving all of the old stories about arms stored in Catholic church basements, began to lay special stress on the menace of Rome to the nation. Instead of relying entirely on professional organizers, the Klan engaged itinerant preachers as heralds of its message. Increasingly its arrival in the new area was signaled by public lectures on popish conspiracies to destroy *"the only truly Christian nation . . . where prophecy is being fulfilled."* As if to demonstrate that the hatred transcended rhetoric, in the summer of 1921 a Methodist minister who belonged to the Klan shot to death a Catholic priest on his own doorstep, and incendiaries destroyed a Catholic church in Illinois two hours after a monster Klan initiation.

The storm of anti-Catholic feeling, for which the Klan proved a wonderfully sensitive barometer, was closely related to the growth of fundamentalism. This militant repudiation of a liberalized gospel and a secularized culture was making itself felt in the closing years of the Progressive era, but only after the World War did it become a major force in American Protestantism. In truth, fundamentalism owed so much to the emotional aftermath of the war that one may almost define it as the characteristic response of rural Protestantism to the disillusion following America's international crusade. The wartime hope for a new and beatific world had produced nothing but crime, moral chaos, and organized selfishness on a grander scale than before. Surely here was proof that the nation had misplaced its faith, that the only true salvation for a sinful society lay in blotting out the whole spirit of innovation and returning to the theological and moral absolutism of an earlier day. Insistence on a Biblical Christianity naturally sharpened the historic lines of Protestant-Catholic cleavage, but the vigor of anti-Catholicism in the twenties could only result from the affiliations between fundamentalism and 100 percent Americanism. The fundamentalist determination to fix and purify a Protestant orthodoxy followed the same channels and obeyed the same laws that governed the course of 100 percent Americanism. Both epitomized a kind of crusading conformity, reacted to a common disillusion, and represented an urge for isolation from an evil world. Who can wonder that the two movements intermingled in rural areas, or that fundamentalism energized a religious version of postwar nationalism? . . .

The Klan torrent rolled onward through 1923, reaching a high point late in the year. By that time the organization had enrolled an aggregate membership probably close to three million. Arkansas and Oklahoma fell vassal to it, and a spectacular expansion in the Midwest made Indiana and Ohio the leading Klan states in the nation. Except for Colorado, the order touched the Rocky Mountain states only negligibly; it left no considerable impression on the Atlantic seaboard outside of Pennsylvania and upstate New York. In Indiana and Texas, however, it could organize vast public gatherings attended by seventy-five thousand people. . . .

At the same time, anti-Klan mobs were beginning to lash back at the organization in areas where the immigrants were strongly entrenched. A bomb wrecked the offices of the Klan newspaper in Chicago. In a suburb of Pittsburgh an angry throng pelted a white-robed parade with stones and bottles, killing one Klansman and injuring many others. In the small industrial city of Steubenville, Ohio, a mob of three thousand attacked a meeting of one hundred Klansmen. In Perth Amboy, New Jersey, a mob six-thousand-strong, led by Jews and Catholics, closed in on a Klan meeting place, overwhelmed the entire police and fire departments, and fell upon some five hundred Ku Kluxers, kicking, stoning, and beating them as they fled.

Such, from the West Frankfort riots of 1920 to the collapse of civil government in Oklahoma three years later, from the triumphant demonstrations of racist scholarship to the nightmares of Henry Ford, were some of the fruits of nativism in a postwar world neither brave nor new.

ERIC F. GOLDMAN

The Shame of the Babbitts

It was shortly before Christmas 1920, and William Allen White was writing to his old friend Ray Stannard Baker, but the best the genial White could manage in the way of season's cheer was: "What a God-damned world this is! . . . If anyone had told me ten years ago that our country would be what it is today . . . I should have questioned his reason."

Something or somebody had certainly damned the world of reformer William Allen White. In the White House a bitter, broken Wilson awaited death and Harding. Too ill to know much of what was going on, too changed to care very deeply, the one-time progressive hero headed a country that was racing to the right. Congress whooped through pro-corporation legislation, the courts interpreted New Freedom laws in a way that harassed unions and encouraged trusts, official and unofficial Red-hunts hounded reformers even more relentlessly than the wartime inquisition. In the midst of it all, the crowning symbol of the drive for conformity, the nation decreed that anyone who drank a liquid containing as much as one two-hundredth part of alcohol was a criminal. From the sickroom in the White House came a weakly worded veto of the Prohibition enforcement act. It was the last gasp of Wilsonian progressivism.

A few months later Warren Harding's amiable smile broke over the inaugural crowd. The new President's father once spoke a three-sentence biography of his son. "Warren, it's a good thing you wasn't born a gal," the old man said. ". . . You'd be in the family way all the time. You can't say No." Harding couldn't say no to politicians wheedling privilleges for corporations. He couldn't say no to job-seekers like the Reverend Heber H. Votaw, whose qualifications to be Superintendent of Federal Prisons consisted of having been a missionary in Burma and a Republican in Ohio. He couldn't say no to a gang of thieves that swept into

Washington with him, including jolly Jesse Smith, who used to hum "My God, how the money rolls in" while he sold federal favors from the notorious little green house at 1625 K Street. Jesse Smith's friend in the White House did manage three positive achievements. The President, according to his mistress, left behind an illegitimate daughter, conceived in the Senate Office Building shortly before his nomination. He added "back to normalcy" to the American language because he misread the correct phase that a professor had written for him. And he took a firm stand on the tariff. "We should," the President of the United States told a reporter, "adopt a protective tariff of such a character as will help the struggling industries of Europe to get on their feet." The reporter rose and left the room, speechless.

After Harding there was Coolidge and after Coolidge there was Hoover. As President, Coolidge permitted no flagrant boodling, made no additions to the language or to the population. Hoover was not only virtuous and grammatical; he was intelligent. He had, besides, entered the White House something of a darling among reformers. He wore the garland of a humanitarian for his war relief work, and had shown his interest in new thinking by offering to purchase stock in the *New Republic*. Hoover's Presidential candidacy was first pushed by progressive journalists, against the strong opposition of old-guard Republicans (even Mary Ellen Lease, in the early Twenties, was hailing Hoover as "one sent by God"). But reformers soon discovered that intelligence, or respectability, or even feeding the Belgians was not quite the point. Under Hoover and Coolidge, no less than under Harding, government proved increasingly responsive to the will of corporations.

Economists have long since made plain the real nature of the prosperity of the Twenties. The national income was fabulously high, unemployment was relatively low, but the control of the country's industries was steadily concentrating and the returns from the increased national wealth were not proportionately distributed. The Twenties were another intensive period of trust-building, new combines constantly forming, old combines gaining new power through the holding-company device or through establishing links with international cartels. By their ability to control prices, these giants brought unprecedented wealth to a few and substantial gain to thousands of skilled workers and white-collar employees, while small business was also generally prosperous. For the rest of the nation the glow of prosperity was largely reflected heat. Statisticians with no strong ideological bent have agreed that about $2,000 was the minimum necessary to provide a family with the decencies during the Twenties, and almost one third of the breadwinners received less than $2,000—one fifth, less than $1,000. Child labor was increasing; all industrial laborers had to face new dangers to their health from the speed-up of mass production and new risks of unemployment from the onrushing technology.

To the farmers the Twenties brought another disaster. In the years immediately after the Armistice farm prices took the sharpest drop in American history. In 1919 a bushel of corn bought five gallons of gasoline; a year later it bought one gallon; one year more and it bought half a gallon. Throughout the Twenties, farm prices never went up enough to stop an ominous increase of tenant farming in the South and in the Midwest. The distress of the farmers was so great and their political power so concentrated that a number of governmental moves were made to aid them. But even the farmers never got the legislation they wanted most, the McNary-Haugen bill, and the general reaction of government to the maldistribution of prosperity was to aid in distributing it still more unequally.

Business triumphant, of course, included a reconquest of the American mind by conservatism. With no widespread protest, an official United States Government publication defined democracy as "a government of the masses. . . . Results in mobracy. Attitude toward property is communistic—negating property rights. Attitude toward law is that the will of the majority shall regulate, whether it be based upon deliberation or governed by passion, prejudice, and impulse, without restraint or regard to consequences. Results in demagogism, license, agitation, discontent, anarchy." Conservative Darwinism reasserted itself in a thousand sleek apostrophes to the economic jungle. Walter Rauschenbusch's Jesus of low food prices had become Bruce Barton's Jesus as the prototype of the go-getting businessman. Magazines that only a few years before were deploring the unbridled competitiveness of the marketplace now featured articles on "It Is Up to You," "What a Whale of a Difference an Incentive Makes," and "The Bookkeeper Who Refused to Stay Put."

If any one man was the American folk hero of the Twenties, unquestionably the man was the winner in the race for automobile millions, Henry Ford. The peevish, erratic manufacturer did his best to fray the halo. He conducted his business with a coarse tyranny. He succumbed to a whole menagerie of fads, announcing that crime could be cured by changes in diet, and that cows, which were lazy besides being crime-breeding, "must go." He proved himself an ignoramus by financing assaults on a supposed Jewish conspiracy to rule the world, and a coward by wriggling for weeks to avoid appearing in the libel trial that ensued. The halo simply would not fray. The American people played mah jong, devoured five million telegraphed words on the murder of the Reverend Mr. Hall and his choir-singer mistress, repeated with M. Coué: "Day by day in every way I am getting better and better," and made Henry Ford a major threat for the Presidency of the United States.

For progressives, here was certainly a post-Civil War all over again, only worse. Reform in the Seventies and Eighties had the buoyancy of a movement that was just taking the offensive. Progressivism of the Twenties was a beaten army, muscles aching, its ranks seriously depleted. As the new era opened, so the story goes, Herbert Croly went home and refused to see anyone for three days. On the fourth day he summoned his editors to his office and told them that progressivism was finished. "From now on we must work for the redemption of the individual." Then Croly began bringing to *New Republic* luncheons a bearded Englishman named Orage, who explained that what the world needed was the self-discipline of yoga. Croly's death in 1930, some of his friends believed, was hastened by forcing his frail body through the rigors of the cult.

Others found a less strenuous escape. Thousands were like the progressive the authors of *Middletown* talked to in Muncie, Indiana. With witch-hunters thrashing through the state, this man was no longer signing petitions or making speeches at the town meeting. "I just run away from it all to my books," he explained resignedly. Still other progressives turned to the cushion of cynicism, or to expatriation, which offered the delights of disillusionment on a devaluated franc, or to the exhilaration of Socialism or Communism. The varieties of Marxism that were winning American converts before 1917 were certainly not made less attractive by the progressive debacle at Paris and at home. Besides, as Robert Morss Lovett has remarked in his autobiographical account of the Twenties, only from Russia did there seem to be any light breaking on the world.

In the middle of the Twenties, the remaining progressive aspirations, ignored by the leaders of both the Republican and the Democratic organizations, found their natural outlet in the third-party effort headed by Robert La Follette. The election of 1924 was La Follette's last campaign, and pathos surrounded the exit of the gallant old battler. Two generations of reformers swung to his support; the famous pompadour, now totally gray, bristled as belligerently as ever, flame still leaped from his words. But when the votes were counted, the ticket had polled only seventeen percent of the total—about ten percent less than Roosevelt's third-party vote in 1912. In seven months La Follette was dead, finally exhausted by his thirty-year crusade, scarcely concealing his bitterness that progressivism had become a nagging aunt unwanted in the cozy rendezvous of business and America.

Why the failure of progressivism in the Twenties, reformers asked themselves then and have continued to ask. The most common explanation boiled down to two points: the effects of the war and of an atmosphere of general prosperity. Unquestionably these factors were important. In the modern history of many countries war has frequently exalted the large-scale businessman and smothered discontent; hard times certainly have increased the appeal of programs for change. But it is possible to make these explanations carry too heavy a load, as Professor Arthur M. Schlesinger has suggested in an essay on "The Tides of National Politics." From the beginnings of political parties in the United States to the anti-Fair Deal Congressional landslide in 1946, Professor Schlesinger maintained, the country has shifted eleven times from "conservative" governments to those which represented an inclination for change. Analysis of the eleven instances indicates that "the worsening of material conditions invariably disturbs the political waves, but, unless reinforced by other factors, does not affect the deeper waters." Foreign wars, he continued, offer no more satisfying an explanation. "These conflicts have taken place about equally in conservative and liberal periods, sometimes coming at the start, sometimes at the end and sometimes midway."

What's more, explaining progressive weakness in the Twenties by prosperity and war suggests the same type of incomplete analysis as explaining the progressive debacle at the peace conference by blaming Woodrow Wilson. Both explanations were the natural kind for progressives to make—they assigned the whole fault, or almost the whole fault, to factors external to progressivism. But placing Jeffersonian, New Freedom progressivism alongside Crolyite, New Nationalist progressivism has revealed important deficiencies in both varieties of reform. Going at the problem in this way suggests that war and prosperity, in addition to being causes of the progressive decline in the Twenties, provided the circumstances that brought out progressivism's own inner difficulties. These difficulties lost followers for reform, rendered less effective certain factors on which the progressives had depended heavily, and made the rule of conservatives more disastrous to progressive purposes.

II

At the heart of traditional, Jeffersonian progressivism had been a faith in the people, or, more specifically, in the majority. The trouble with America was that the people did not really rule, most reformers had argued; democratize government, and government would really serve the whole community. The years immediately surrounding the war brought climactic successes in the drive for more democracy. By the time of the Armistice, the direct election of United States senators had been made mandatory by a Constitutional amendment. Direct primaries were in operation in all but four of the states; the initiative and referendum, in almost a half; the recall, in scores of state and municipal governments. Within a year after the Armistice, and partly as a result of the war, the woman-suffrage amendment was ratified. With that, a far larger percentage of American citizens could participate in the processes of government than ever before in the history of the country. And the results that appeared during the twenties in no way justified the hopes and the claims of the progressives.

The most conspicuous result was the lack of any result. The initiative, referendum, and recall were invoked sparingly, and to a lessening extent. When the techniques were used, they produced no significant change in the political and economic situation. The experience of California, probably the most active direct-democracy state during the twenties, was revealing. The initiative was employed in attempts to license "naturopaths," to close barbershops on Sunday, and to create the Klamath Fish and Game District; referendums were staged in efforts to get rid of laws enforcing the Volstead Act, to increase the registration fee on trucks, and to prohibit shingle roofs in incorporated places. A wide variety of groups, practical-minded and crackpot, turned to the new devices. But when the decade was over, two political scientists reviewed the California experience and emerged with this "indubitable fact": direct democracy had changed California very little.

No more perceptible effect came from the direct elections of senators, unless it was in increasing the chances of a candidate with a talent for demagogy. As early as 1912 the reform-minded political scientist Charles Merriam had sighed: "Some bosses are wondering why they feared the law; and some reformers why they favored it." The primary did seem to make political bosses interested in picking a candidate who could appeal to the general public more than the rival faction's candidate. But one of the shrewdest and most intensive students of democratic processes, Professor V. O. Key, Jr., has concluded that in general the direct primary left elections where they had always been, in the hands of party managers. If reform forces were strong enough to make the bosses recognize them within the primary, Professor Key pointed out, they were also strong enough to force approximately the same degree of recognition under any nominating system.

Women suffrage made the most spectacular lack of difference. Elections became no cleaner, no glow of motherly kindness spread over the industrial scene.

In election after election large numbers of women failed to use their hard-won ballots. (In 1924 the estimated percentages of males and females voting were sixty-five and thirty-five, respectively.) When women did vote, the fact that they were women did not seem to matter particularly. Using the data available after a decade of woman suffrage, observers concluded that sex had less to do with determining a vote than place of residence, wealth, occupation, race, nationality, or religion. . . .

III

A few years before La Follette was defeated, Bagdasar K. Baghdigian walked up to the registration desk of a Kansas City school and struggled through an application for courses. The teacher glanced at the Armenian name and snapped: "Oh, give that up and change your name to Smith, Jones or a name like that and become Americanized. Give up everything you brought with you from the Old Country. You did not bring anything worth while anyway."

Baghdigian froze into group consciousness. "The Turkish sword," he told himself, "did not succeed in making me become a Turk, and now this harebrained woman is trying to make an American out of me. I defy her to do it." After that, Baghdigian recalled later, "I was more of an Armenian patriot than I had ever thought of being." And after that he was a perfect symbol of the rapid accentuation of another type of special interest in the United States.

The trend had been spurred on by two quite different developments. Wilson's appeal to nationalism during the war had an electric effect within the United States. Czech, Slovak, and Polish immigrants, pouring funds into movements for the creation of an independent Czechoslovakia and Poland, became a good deal more nationality-conscious in all their attitudes, and every other American group felt the surge of nationality feeling. This positive effect of Wilsonianism, important as it was, proved less significant than the kickback from another wartime phenomenon.

Until 1917, most Americans, progressive or conservative, had glided along in the happy illusion that the melting-pot was working with great efficiency. But as soon as the foreign-policy issue became acute, the country split into a babble of groups, many of them obviously influenced by Old World ties. Suddenly it was plain that the melting-pot had failed in important respects, and this revelation provoked the campaign that made sure the melting-pot would fail still more. After the Armistice a call for "Americanization" sounded across the country. To informed and humane people, Americanization might still mean the old progressive policy, the two-way procedure of bringing all the American people into a common community. But for an overwhelming percentage of the Americanizers, the campaign quickly turned into the process that Baghdigian met; the whole population was to be insulted and browbeaten into "one-hundred-percent Americanism," which meant what the local guardians of Americanism defined as the ways of white, Protestant Americans who were not recent immigrants. Such Americanization stimulated all racial, religious, and nationality prejudices, and the resulting discrimination hurried all minorities along the way to minority chauvinism.

The Twenties saw the reaction of Bagdasar Baghdigian repeated time and again. Scores of organizations sprang up to assert that their members, no matter how much the Americanizers shrilled, were still Armenian patriots, Irish patriots, or Scandinavian patriots. In the previous generation it was not difficult to find prominent Catholics who were so leery of marking out Catholics from the general population that they opposed parochial schools; by the mid-Twenties the newly created National Catholic Welfare Conference was busily coordinating the segregation of Catholics, hurrying them toward parochial schools, a Catholic Boy Scouts, a Catholic Daughters of America, and a Catholic Total Abstinence Union, not to speak of the election of a Catholic Mother of the Year. Among the Jews and Negroes, the groups hit hardest by the intolerance of the Twenties, the long-running trends toward inward-looking minority feeling speeded up two- or three-fold. "Until the Twenties," one Zionist leader, Stephen Wise, has recalled, "we were a movement. Then we became an avalanche, and we tumbled along with us many a boulder of Jewish respectability."

Negro nationalism leaped ahead to its own full-blown Zionism. The leader was a chubby, elegantly mustached immigrant from the West Indies, Marcus Aurelius Garvey, who had organizational abilities worthy of a Gompers and a flair for publicity which no muckraker had excelled. Establishing himself in Harlem in 1916, Garvey summoned his fellow Negroes to have done with "boot-licking" organizations like the National Association for the Advancement of Colored People, and mulattoes like William Du Bois, who could not possibly understand the national glories of the black man. "As much as the white man may boast of his glorious deeds to-day," Garvey blustered, "the fact remains that what he now knows was inherited from the original mind of the black man who made Egypt, Carthage and Babylon, the centres of civilization, that were not known to the unskilled and savage men of Europe." So glorious a race deserved its own home. The immediate necessity for the Negroes was a "Back to Africa" movement, which would give all the black men of the world their "motherland." When "the Jew said, 'We shall have Palestine,'" Garvey added, "we said, 'We shall have Africa.'"

Soon Garvey had churned black America into a chauvinistic froth by his inflammatory speeches, wild receptions for Negro dignitaries, and resplendent parades in which uniformed troops and "Black Cross" nurses chanted:

> Oh, glorious race of mighty men
> The homeland calls to you.

An estimated one hundred thousand Negroes were buying subscriptions to Garvey's journal, and according to Garvey's wife, ten million dollars poured in to pay for the "Black Star" ships that were to carry the American Negroes "home." At the height of Garvey's influence, about 1921, his organization boasted the largest membership of any Negro society in American history: four million dues-paying enthusiasts. In Europe, nervous chancelleries pondered the possible effects of the "Back to Africa" movement on their delicate colonial arrangements.

The leader never quite got around to mundane details. He was too busy making his ornate offices still more ornate, supporting a bevy of very nationalistic and very good-looking women, equipping, gazetting, and knighting the aristocracy of the coming black empire. The United States Government, skeptical about Garvey's use of the mails, sent him to Atlanta Penitentiary in 1925, but even this did not entirely quash him. Negro political pressure secured Garvey's release in return for his deportation, and he went on agitating in the freedom of Jamaica. When Garvey died, in 1940, the decorous *Journal of Negro History,* which lived conspicuously above sex and parades, chose to point out that if Garvey was a criminal, "he was no more a criminal . . . than thousands of other persons in the business world." Besides, he was the only well-known American Negro who did not owe his prominence "mainly to white men."

Few educated Negroes were captured by the rococo Garvey, but many went on sympathetically reading W. E. B. Du Bois, who, in one important sense, was an honest and a sophisticated Marcus Garvey. Though the brilliant official of the NAACP showed no sympathy for "repatriating" Negroes to Africa, he was increasing his emphasis on the point that Negroes were a separate people and should act as one. For all of Garvey's scurrilous attacks on him, Du Bois could never quite get himself to repudiate the Negro Zionist completely. Garvey's methods were "bombastic, wasteful, illogical," but he was also a "sincere" leader, speaking for "one of the most interesting spiritual movements of the modern world." Du Bois's intense racialism became most clear in 1919, when he began organizing "Pan-African Congresses," where representatives of Negroes from all nations were to plan "concerted thought and action." The trouble with progressivism among white Americans, Du Bois declared, was that it "did not envisage Africa and the colored peoples of the world. They [the progressives] were interested in America and securing American citizens of all and any color, their rights." Most Negroes made the same mistake. "They felt themselves Americans, not Africans. They resented and feared any coupling with Africa."

Pan-Africanism easily blended into the more general movement that is often called the "Black Renaissance." On the surface, this Renaissance was simply an exciting and long overdue recognition of Negro talent. Publishers suddenly found that Negroes could write highly salable books, Negro musicals became the vogue, night-rounders discovered that many ebony clubs offered a better show than the monotonous gyrations of white thighs on Broadway. But in the mind of the Negro, the Renaissance increasingly became an expression of the chauvinism that was marking all minority life. Negroes complained about the white invasion of "our" night clubs, campaigned to have Negroes deal only in Negro stores and read only Negro newspapers, and started a drive to substitute the term "Afro-American" for "American Negro." An Association for the Study of Negro Life, headed by a man who announced that he hated "interracialists," made rapid progress among Negro intellectuals.

The psychology of many of the Negro writers was expressed by James Weldon Johnson, a major literary figure in the Renaissance as well as the executive secretary of the NAACP. The writing of which Johnson was most proud was his "Negro National Hymn," which he wrote in a "feverish ecstasy" and could never hear performed without reliving the ecstasy. Editing a group of Negro poems in 1922, Johnson asserted that the Negro was "the creator of the only things artistic that have yet sprung from American soil and been universally acknowledged as distinctive American products." When some readers were aghast at the statement, Johnson compounded his racialism by adding a footnote in the second edition which conceded, perhaps, that skyscrapers were of some importance and not an invention of Negroes. Nor did Johnson fail to get around to the argument that always seems to creep into embittered chauvinisms—our women are better-looking than your women anyhow. Writing his autobiography at the end of the Black Renaissance, Johnson paused to emphasize that Negroes too often accepted white ideals of beauty. He had once actually compared the types, said Johnson, and it was clear that "the Negro woman, with her rich coloring, her gayety, her laughter and song, her alluring, undulating movements—a heritage from the African jungle—is a more beautiful creature than her sallow, songless, lipless, hipless, tired-looking, tired-moving white sister."

And the progressive in the midst of all this? By the Twenties, urban influences had marked reform so deeply that the progressive who spoke Anglo-Saxonism was rare and was promptly denied the label "progressive" by most reformers. Edward Ross, still alive, was already history, and was bluntly told so every time he bemoaned "race suicide." The progressive of the Twenties was outraged by the blatant bigotry of the period, and out of outrage, his sympathies, his admiration, went to the Negro or Jew or Armenian immigrant who reared back and tried to declare his self-respect. Since declaring self-respect so often took the form of minority chauvinism, the progressive's emotions easily swept him toward acceptance of, or at least failure to attack, the mounting glorification of group.

The effect of this acquiescence on progressivism during the Twenties was mixed. To the extent that minorities identified the interests of their group with a reform cause, the reform received the additional impetus of powerful clan feelings. Al Smith, a much more progressive candidate than Herbert Hoover, was aided in the Presidential election of 1928 by thousands of conservative Catholic votes, which went to him only or primarily because he was a Catholic. La Guardia was ardently backed in his campaigns for Congress by many slum-dwelling Italians and Jews, whose fervor for him was compounded of an approval for his program and an enthusiasm for his descent.

But the available evidence on the point suggests that progressivism was hurt rather than helped by the rising group consciousness. The more employees felt identified with the homeland or a particular race or religion, the easier it was for employers to divide and conquer them. "We want you," the United States Steel Corporation displayed the pattern in sending out instructions during a strike, "to stir up as much bad feeling as you possibly can between the Serbians and the Italians. . . . Call up every question you can in reference to racial hatred between these two nationalities." In the political field, closer identification with a nationality group, the Negro community, or the Catholic Church—the minority attachments that were, numerically, the most important in the Twenties—brought the citizen more under conservative influences. The popular picture of the immigrant community as more inclined to radicalism than the older settlers was incorrect, and came from a few conspicuous exceptions. Both Negro and Catholic leadership were markedly conservative. (Clarence Darrow, with pardonable hyperbole, called the hierarchy "the right wing of the right wing," and when the depression struck, it was not surprising that the only Negro Congressman, De Priest, of

Chicago, fought federal relief funds.) Most important from the long-range view, the increased tendency toward religious, racial, and nationality feeling was a tendency toward thinking which asked not the progressive question: what is good for "the people" as a whole? but rather: what is good for us special few? The question could, by coincidence, aid reform, but movements do not keep their power by coincidence. . . .

IV

The progressive practice of not seeing progressivism's inherent difficulties reached a high point in the La Follette campaign of 1924. A few leaders in the third party effort, like the attorney, Donald Richberg, worked hard to have the campaign based on something beyond the traditional reform cries, but their efforts were wasted. The La Follette campaign song, Richberg remarked as he looked back at the election, should have been "Tenting Tonight on the Old Camp Ground."

Simultaneously, many urban progressives of the better-educated group were giving their enthusiasm to a cause that involved no nagging difficulties. Even before the campaign of 1924 was over, they were neglecting La Follette's speeches for the invective that came once a month in a newly founded journal, the *American Mercury*. The magazine's editor, Henry L. Mencken, was hardly in the usual progressive tradition. He looked like a German burgher out of the eighteenth century and, in many ways, he thought like one. Suspicious of anything new, even New York, Mencken valued Pilsner, Beethoven, a sharp sally, or a workmanlike job of brick-laying far more than any plans to change society. Violently contemptuous of ordinary men, he pronounced democracy "the worship of jackals by jackasses," and the American people, "the most timorous, sniveling, poltroonish, ignominious mob of serfs and goose-steppers ever gathered under one flag in Christendom." He flayed all reformers and their "bilge of idealism," lauded "free competition . . . to the utmost limit," advocated wars, aristocracy, and a frank recognition that it made no difference whether the union or the employer won a strike. The *Nation*, Mencken merely "deplored"; the *New Republic*, because it was subsidized by the Straights, had coined for it the famous sneer "kept idealists." As for the *American Mercury*, the first issue made emphatically plain that "the Editors have heard no Voice from the burning bush. . . . The world, as they see it, is down with at least a score of painful diseases, all of them chronic and incurable."

Of course, Mencken, who was at least half Puck, loved to hear the rumble of his own hyperboles, and at bottom he was as much of a reformer as any cornfield Populist. No one outside an insane asylum ever stayed so vitriolic for so long out of sheer cussedness, and Mencken was anything but crazy. He simply had no use for much of the program that had become associated with American progressivism. He was devoted, and passionately so, to the essence of the 1872 liberalism which had been assumed with little discussion by succeeding generations of reformers until the ruthless standardization of the Twenties placed it in real jeopardy—the freedom of the individual to think and act as an individual. Simeon Strunsky was quite right when he suggested that the Mencken approach was really a kind of latter-day muckraking, exposing and assailing The Shame of Prohibition, The Shame of Comstockery, The Shame of the Babbitts.

With powers of scorn unexcelled in American letters, Mencken flailed away at Prohibitionists, Fundamentalists, book-censors, Rotarians, Ku-Kluxers, farm-bloc leaders—anyone who wanted to cajole or force anyone into a pattern. The existence of Prohibition gave Mencken's bastinado a daily workout. The Scopes trial in Tennessee brought his campaign to a rollicking climax. Here was a state forbidding by law the teaching of a doctrine that more than two generations of scientists had accepted. Here was William Jennings Bryan, a three-time nominee for the Presidency of the United States, defending the law to the cheers of thousands. Mencken hurried down to Tennessee, agonized through the insistence that all schoolchildren should accept as literal truth every word in the Bible, and wired back descriptions of rule by "gaping primates" which brought him an avalanche of invitations to leave the United States on the next boat.

Mencken's china-blue eyes took on their most ingenuous softness. Why did he continue to live in America, he catechized himself. "Why do men go to zoos?"

After a few years of the *American Mercury,* Walter Lippmann could call Mencken "the most powerful influence on this whole generation of educated people," and not a few of these educated people were men and women who in 1914 had been busy pushing the political and economic program of progressivism. Reform in the Twenties, as always, included an enormous variety of dissidents, but unquestionably the group that was most articulate and most effective were those who adopted the Mencken-type emphasis. Unlike Mencken, the typical reformer of the Twenties did not actually oppose the political and economic program of progressivism; he simply gave less stress to these problems and more stress to the battle against conformity. Appropriately enough, with the change in emphasis came a change in title, and the group that had called itself "progressive" was now more and more using the old term "liberal." In part, this shift was attributable to a desire to shake free from the clammy aftermath of Wilsonianism. In part, it reflected concern over getting rid of any connection that could play into the hands of the witch-hunters. (Vernon Louis Parrington, coming to appreciate the well-aged respectability of the term "liberal," went through his manuscript substituting it for "radical.") But most significantly, the revival of the term "liberal" corresponded to the revival of the major concern of dissidence in the late Sixties and early Seventies. Whatever the squeezings of opportunity in the days of Ulysses Grant and of Calvin Coolidge, lack of opportunity was not the problem that protruded most conspicuously. In both periods individual liberty was in danger, and plainly so.

Prewar and entirely new reform figures now engaged in a brilliantly varied campaign for personal and intellectual freedom. The effort was most noticeable in the literary field. Harold Stearns, restless in "the shadows . . . of intolerance," delayed his European exile long enough to edit *Civilization in the United States,* which made each aspect of American life a self-convicting pursuit of sameness. Sherwood Anderson, a puzzled manager of a paint factory before the war, emerged in the Twenties a mordant analyst of the village twisting under respectability. The cherubic W. E. Woodward, a frolicsome socialist in 1912, a restless employee of the Morris Plan Bank in 1920, invented a word and a profession by gaily "debunking" all the icons of the Rotaries and the ladies' clubs. Theodore Dreiser, grimly portraying Sister Carrie in the early 1900's, was grimmer still in his 1928 *American Tragedy* of a boy, a girl, and an illegitimate baby in Lycurgus, New York. Most widely read of all, as savage as Mencken, as wistful as Fitzgerald, as impish as Woodward, Sinclair Lewis came out of a socialist past to assail the Twenties in terms of the pathetic conformity of George F. Babbitt.

"I really didn't have any answers to it all," Lewis once said of his thinking in the Twenties. "I only knew that the answers could come only from free men." The dominant liberalism of the Twenties offered few answers, except from those who found an answer in despair, but at that it served a vital function in the history of American reform. It fought a magnificent delaying action, staving off the complete triumph of the Babbitts, trading positive thinking for sorely needed time.

ROBERT S. MCELVAINE

Who Was Roaring in the Twenties?— Origins of the Great Depression

Tariff policies were not at the root of the Great Depression, but international forces did play a role in causing the collapse. The trouble began with the World War and the drastic changes it made in the relative economic positions of the world's leading nations. Throughout the nineteenth century, Great Britain had been the world's dominant economic power. By the beginning of the present century, that position was being severely challenged by both the United States and Germany. The war temporarily eliminated Germany as a competitor, but it also weakened the British position and strengthened that of the Americans. Most significantly, the war converted the United States from a net debtor to a creditor nation. This change obligated the country to take more responsibility for the smooth operation of the international economy and to make adjustments in its other policies, including exports and tariffs.

As the leader of the world economy in the century prior to 1914, Great Britain had used its lending policies as a means of stabilizing the international situation. It had also clung to free trade for more than a half century. Doing so caused short-term disadvantages for some British manufacturers during economic slumps, but it helped prevent the sort of self-defeating tariff war that worsened the world depression in the 1930s. In the 1920s the British were no longer able to act as the stabilizer of the world economy. That position should have gone to the United States, but American leaders did not want it, or rather, they wanted only part of it. Much of the historical debate over whether the United States was isolationist in the 1920s misses the point. The nation wanted all the advantages (and profits) of participation in world affairs, while minimizing the responsibilities that went with world leadership. American leaders sought to make their country an isolated participant in world affairs. They wanted to be in the world, but not of it. It did not work.

The World War also made for instability in the international economy because of the reparations and war debts problems. The Dawes Plan of 1924, the first of several international attempts to ease the reparations-debts problem, set in motion an arrangement whereby Americans lent money to Germany to pay reparations to France and others, who in turn made debt payments to the United States. Although American financiers had already made some large foreign loans before this, the Dawes loan started American foreign lending on a massive scale. Americans in the mid-twenties were new to the role of international financier and approached the market like "a sales department with a new article." The volume of American foreign lending soared to $900 million in 1924 and $1.25 billion in both 1927 and 1928. This large-scale lending accomplished several things: it provided an outlet for the excess incomes of wealthy Americans, it allowed reparations and war debts to be paid for a time, it offset tariff barriers, and it helped American producers secure overseas markets. This last function was similar to that of domestic credit; it helped an unbalanced economy avoid collapse for a few years, but ultimately made the Crash worse when it came.

American lending abroad slowed in 1928 and 1929, as the opportunities for money-making on Wall Street became more attractive than the interest rates of foreign loans. British lending in the 1800s had generally been countercyclical. When times were good, investment opportunities at home attracted British capital away from international loans, but during slumps the British expanded foreign lending. This policy had had an obvious stabilizing influence. American foreign lending in the twenties and early thirties, though, followed an opposite pattern: lending expanded during the early part of the boom and contracted drastically with the Depression.

By the late twenties, each country was seeking to advance its own interests, even if in the process it worsened the positions of others. In a delicate, interdependent world economy, these "beggar thy neighbor" tactics were suicidal. Nowhere should this have been more clear than in the United States. This country was trying nothing less in the 1920s than to be the world's banker, food producer, and manufacturer, but to buy as little as possible from the world in return. This attempt to eat the world and have it, too, was the epitome of a self-defeating policy. This is one of the two points on which the popular blaming of Herbert Hoover for the Depression has some validity. As secretary of Commerce, Hoover was a dynamo in promoting both foreign sales and foreign investment, yet he consistently favored high tariffs for the United States. Such attempts to assure a very "favorable" balance of trade cannot succeed for long. It is impossible, in fact, for a country to maintain a "favorable" balance of trade over a prolonged period. What all nations should strive for is a balance that is neither favorable nor unfavorable. If the United States would not buy from other countries, there was no way for others to buy from Americans, or to meet interest payments on American loans.

The weakness of the international economy and contradictory American foreign economic policy unquestionably contributed to the coming of the Great Depression. If the origins of the calamity are to be kept in perspective, though, it must be realized that while the world collapse was cutting $1.5 billion from American exports between 1929 and 1933, domestic contraction was slicing

$12 billion from the American gross national product. Statistically, internal problems appear to have had an effect on the American Depression some eight times greater than did foreign ones. This is not to underestimate the significance of the nearly 10 percent of American GNP that went into exports in 1929. That $5 billion was of great importance, and the loss of a large portion of it undoubtedly affected domestic parts of the economy. But if we are to find the most telling causes of the Depression, we must look within the borders of the United States.

In some respects, the agricultural problems of the 1920s were closely tied to the international difficulties just recounted. The fundamental problem facing the American farmer in the twenties was chronic overproduction of agricultural commodities around the world. ("Overproduction" in the economic sense, of course, does not necessarily mean that there was more food and fiber than the world's ill-fed and ill-clad multitudes could use. It refers only to more than there was a paying market for.) For some reason this excess agricultural supply did not create its own demand. This is especially extraordinary from the perspective of classical economics, because farm products were in as close to a genuine free market as existed. This was a big part of the farmers' problem. They still sold on a largely unregulated world market and had no control over the prices they received, but the companies from which they bought and the banks from which they borrowed were often in a position to dictate terms.

The more immediate cause of the farmers' troubles in the 1920s was World War I. Here is Herbert Hoover's other small contribution to the origins of the Depression. During the war the American government, particularly in the person of Food Administrator Hoover, encouraged a vast increase in agricultural production. This was fine during the war, when European production was way down and demand was very high. But after the war the success of the wartime stimulation of increased production came back to haunt the nation's farmers. Added to this were increased mechanization and more specialization and intensive methods. Another little-noted but quite significant cause of overproduction of farm products in the twenties was the coming of the automobile and tractor on a large scale. Some 25 million acres previously used to grow feed for horses and mules was turned to other agricultural uses as the demand for beasts of burden declined. The result of all these factors was, as I noted earlier, that farmers struggled with a depression throughout the prosperity decade.

Although the farmer was declining in American society in the 1920s, his continuing importance to the economy must be recognized. In 1929 fully one-quarter of all employment in the United States was in farming. A solidly based prosperity could not leave out this segment of the population. If the whole economy was dependent upon agriculture, agriculture was particularly dependent upon the export market. More than one-quarter of American farm income in 1929 came from exports. The economy as a whole could be harmed by a sharp reduction in exports, but farming could be devastated by such an export drop. That is precisely what happened in 1929 and subsequent years.

The weak position of American farmers was exacerbated by their heavy burden of debt. The expansion of the war years had helped to double farm mortgages from $3.3 billion to $6.7 billion between 1910 and 1920. In the first five years of the twenties, another $2.7 billion was added to the total. When the debt burden is added to chronic overproduction and the perennial farmers' problems, such as uncertain weather, it is clear that the structural weaknesses in this quarter of the American economy were sufficiently grave as to pose a threat to the whole economy.

Until the middle of 1928 the abundance of credit, both at home for the farmers and abroad for those who bought their products, helped to keep the decidedly leaky craft that was American agriculture afloat. Beginning in 1928, though, the already overloaded ship had new weights dumped upon it. It began to sink. As American international lending declined, the ability of consuming countries to pay for imports of American foodstuffs dropped sharply. At the same time, the world market was becoming further glutted. The Soviet Union decided to begin large exports of wheat in 1928. The full impact of this decision on the world market was not felt until 1930, but it did not help the worldwide surplus.

Agriculture in the 1920s was more than a blemish on the face of Coolidge Prosperity; it was a vital segment of the economy that was falling further behind and increasingly unable to keep its consumption up to the level the rest of the economy required of it. Plainly this was not the trigger of the Depression, but it was an unsound feature of the fundamental business of the country.

The structure of American business and industry itself—the crown jewel of Coolidge Prosperity—was another contributing factor in bringing on the collapse of that prosperity. The idealized American economy of small, freely competing units upon which much of the nation's economic thought and social philosophy was based was largely a thing of the past by the 1920s. In the preface to the classic study of corporate concentration in the twenties that he undertook with Gardiner C. Means, *The Modern Corporation and Private Property,* Adolf A. Berle put his finger on the crux of the phenomenon: "American industrial property, through the corporate device, was being thrown into a collective hopper wherein the individual owner was steadily being lost in the creation of a series of huge industrial oligarchies." By the end of the twenties, roughly two-thirds of the industrial wealth of the United States had passed "from individual ownership to ownership by the large, publicly financed corporations," Berle said. It was enough to make a red-blooded American uneasy, even in the midst of unprecedented prosperity.

In 1929, 200 corporations controlled nearly half of all American industry. The $81 billion in assets held by these corporations represented 49 percent of all corporate wealth in the nation and 22 percent of all national wealth. Moreover, the trend was rapidly in the direction of even more concentration. The estimates for three years earlier were that the same corporations held 45 percent of corporate and less than 20 percent of all national wealth. And by 1932, Berle calculated that 600 American corporations owned 65 percent of the nation's industry. The rest was "spread among millions of little family businesses." Some 2000 men, the active directors of the giant corporations, were in a position to dominate the life of the United States.

What the degree of concentration exposed by these figures meant, Berle and Means said, was that the political economy of Adam Smith, which had dominated American thinking for a century and a half, no longer applied. The competitive model drawn by Smith as the "great regulator of industry" was based upon the assumption of numerous small units whose prices were determined by market forces. This was not the case in the United States of the late 1920s, and so the market had lost its inherent tendency toward equilibrium.

The booming decade of the twenties saw a new headlong rush into corporate mergers. President Hoover's Committee on Social Trends reported that between 1919 and 1928 some 1200 mergers "involving the disappearance of over 6000 independent enterprises" had been registered.

Clearly a major cause of the unstable foundation beneath the prosperity decade was the dichotomy between the reality of massive concentration in American business and the classical economic model upon which policy was still being based. Coolidge and Mellon were playing by the rules of Adam Smith's pin factory at a time when Henry Ford's River Rouge plant was more indicative of the true nature of the economy. It would have been remarkable if disaster had not resulted from this discrepancy.

One result of the use of eighteenth-century theories to deal with twentieth-century reality was a growing maldistribution of income in twenties America. No cause of the Great Depression was of larger importance.

According to the famous Brookings Institution study, *America's Capacity to Consume,* the top 0.1 percent of American families in 1929 had an aggregate income equal to that of the bottom 42 percent. Stated in absolute numbers, approximately 24,000 families had a combined income as large as that shared by more than 11.5 million poor and lower-middle-class families. Fully 71 percent of all American families (a term that includes unattached individuals) in what was generally regarded as the most prosperous year the country and the world had ever known had incomes under $2500. At the other extreme, the 24,000 richest families enjoyed annual incomes in excess $100,000 and 513 American families that year reported incomes above $1 million. Nor was the prosperity of the twenties narrowing the gap. On the contrary, the authors of the Brookings study concluded, it appeared that "income was being distributed with increasing inequality, particularly in the later years of the period." The income of those at the very top was increasing more rapidly than that of any other group. Late in the twenties, "a larger percentage of the total income was received by the portion of the population having very high incomes than had been the case a decade earlier." Between 1920 and 1929, per capita disposable income for all Americans rose by 9 percent, but the top 1 percent of income recipients enjoyed a whopping 75 *percent* increase in disposable income. The share of disposable income going to the top 1 percent jumped from 12 percent in 1920 to 19 percent in 1929. Here in stark statistics was one of the principal causes of the Great Depression.

Maldistribution of wealth in 1929 was even greater than that of income. Nearly 80 percent of the nation's families—some 21.5 million households—had no savings whatsoever. The 24,000 families at the top—0.1 percent—held 34 percent of all savings. The 2.3 percent of families with incomes of more than $10,000 controlled two-thirds of America's savings. Stock ownership, as we shall see shortly, was even more concentrated. The top 0.5 percent of Americans in

1929 owned 32.4 percent of *all* the net wealth of individuals. This represented the highest concentration of wealth at any time in American history. The Depression and World War II cut into this concentration somewhat, and the amount held by the top 0.5 percent has hovered around 20 percent throughout the postwar years.

A large part of the reason for the growing gap between rich and poor was that productivity was increasing at a far faster rate than wages. In the decade ending in 1929 output per worker in manufacturing leaped upward by a remarkable 43 percent. In only six years between 1923 and 1929 manufacturing output per person-hour increased by almost 32 percent. During the same period, wages increased also, but only by 8 percent—a rate one-fourth as fast as the rise in productivity. With production costs falling rapidly, prices remaining nearly stable, and wages rising only slowly, the bulk of the benefits from increased productivity went into profits. In that same six-year period ending in 1929, corporate profits soared upward by 62 percent and dividends rose by 65 percent.

This, in cold figures, was the essence of the New Era. Prosperity was shared by fairly large segments—although certainly not all—of the populace, but in very unequal portions. The rich were getting richer at a much more rapid rate than the poor were becoming less poor. Government policies during the twenties were designed to achieve just this end. The unfavorable climate for labor unions made it more difficult for workers to obtain their share of the benefits of rising productivity. And Mellon's tax cuts for the wealthy helped to aggravate the gross disparity in income levels.

The maldistribution of income, although growing worse, was already marked in the mid-twenties, while prosperity reigned. Any interpretation of the origins of the Depression that places significant emphasis on maldistribution must account for the peaceful coexistence of prosperity with maldistribution in the years preceding the Crash. This is not as much of a problem as it may appear.

For the economy to remain on an even keel, it is of course necessary for total demand to equal total supply. Say's Law to the contrary notwithstanding, there was no automatic assurance that this would happen, especially in a mass production economy with a poor distribution of income. The balance could be achieved in a number of ways. The largest part of the demand side was made up of domestic consumption of nondurable and durable consumer goods. These categories range from food and clothing in the former to automobiles and houses in the latter. Almost all the income of more than three-fourths (the lower three-fourths, of course) of the American people went for these purposes. These people were doing their part to maintain prosperity. They could do no more for the demand side of the balance unless they were paid more.

But what of the huge incomes of those at the top of the scale, most conspicuously the 24,000 families with annual incomes above $100,000? They bought consumer goods, too, and in far larger quantities than their less affluent neighbors. They could, however, be expected to eat only so much and buy only so many cars and houses. The income of the $100,000 per year man, we find by simple arithmetic, was 40 times greater than that of the above-average $2500 man. It was not reasonable to ask the former to eat 40 times as much or buy 40 Model A's (or 15 Cadillacs). The wealthy and nearly-so had to find other ways to use their money. Up to a point, this was beneficial. Saving and investment, as well as consumption, are necessary for the well-being of the economy. This, along with luxury spending, was the principal use to which excess profits were put in the twenties. Maverick economist William Trufant Foster may have gone too far when he said of the decade, "Far from having been profligate, the nation wasted its substance in riotous saving," but there was a serious point beneath the exaggeration. Investment remained at a high level throughout the years 1925–29, dipping below 15 percent of GNP only in 1928 (a threshold that investment did not break again until 1948). This high level of investment helped keep the economy in temporary balance during the boom years, but it was intensifying the long-term problem. That is, greater investment usually meant further increases in productivity. All other things being equal, this would be to the good. But when are all other things equal? Surely they were not in the twenties. Since the gains in productivity were not being fairly distributed, the heavy investment was making the problem of income distribution worse.

Other means existed for disposing of the supply for which there was insufficient domestic demand. Two of these came to be heavily relied upon in the twenties: exports and credit sales. We have already discussed the former. The purpose and effects of the latter were similar. The basic macroeconomic problem growing out of maldistribution was that those with the means to buy more of the products of mass production industry could satiate their needs and desires by spending only a small fraction of their incomes, while those whose needs and desires were not satisfied had no money. One obvious temporary solution was to let those who wanted goods to buy them without the money. Thus the installment plan arose for the first time on a massive scale. By the second half of the decade, it was possible to purchase cars, appliances, radios, furniture, and other expensive items on "easy monthly (or weekly) payments."

Convincing Americans to buy now and pay later required a reversal of many traditional American values. People brought up on the aphorisms of Poor Richard had to be weaned. Advertising was the medium through which this message was transmitted to American consumers. First, people had been convinced to consume rather than save. Now they must go further. The idea that a penny saved is a penny earned was passé. It was now to be: Spend the penny before you earn it. It was no longer necessary to save for a rainy day, since in the New Era of eternal prosperity the sun would always shine.

By the last years of the decade, three of every five cars and 80 percent of all radios sold were purchased with installment credit. Between 1925 and 1929 the amount of installment credit outstanding in the United States more than doubled, from $1.38 billion to $3 billion. In keeping with the live-for-today attitude of many Americans in the 1920s, as the President's Committee on Social Trends pointed out, time payment schemes allowed people "to telescope the future into the present." The device helped to put off the day of reckoning by unnaturally keeping up demand, but it made the collapse worse when it came. When the supply of consumers who could be persuaded to make time purchases and the credit of those customers were exhausted, the installment stopgap could no longer perform its service. What made matters worse, though, was the fact that all those carrying installment debt could no longer even use all of their regular wages or salaries for new buying; part of their current income was taken up paying off past purchases.

There were at least two other ways in which demand might have been brought into balance with supply. One possibility was for the government to buy the surplus through deficit spending. Suicide would have been a more welcome suggestion to most politicians, businessmen, and economists in the pre-Depression decade. The remaining solution was, if anything, more repulsive to the powers-that-be than were peacetime deficits: higher taxes on the rich. Again it was William T. Foster who brazenly spoke the truth. In the interests of the rich (as well as of everyone else), he said, "we should take from them a sufficient amount of their surplus to enable consumers to consume and business to operate at a profit. This," Foster neatly added, "is not 'soaking the rich'; it is saving the rich." The rich, on the whole, chose to remain unregenerate.

Under these circumstances, the New Era economy was peculiarly dependent on a continued high level of luxury spending and investment by those receiving a disproportionately large share of the national income. If something caused a sudden loss of confidence by these affluent Americans, the whole economic structure might collapse, particularly if the decline in investment and luxury spending coincided with a loss of foreign markets and a saturation of the credit-purchase market at home. Just such a confluence occurred in the fall of 1929.

American values, it should be plain by now, were undergoing important changes during the 1920s. Some were long-term and more or less permanent. Others were part of recurring shifts in attitude. Among the latter, the most notable of the twenties was an unusually high degree of self-centeredness and emphasis on financial gain.

American society—or rather, a large portion of it—came in the twenties to be preoccupied with the single-minded pursuit of riches. A growing number of people accepted the proposition that "God intended the American middle class to be rich." (Had He not so intended, why had He made middle-class Americans with wallets and savings accounts?) The mood of the times was evident in the title of a 1929 article Democratic national chairman John J. Raskob wrote for the *Ladies' Home Journal,* "Everybody Ought to be Rich." The new convert to the Democracy had a plan whereby a company would be established to help the little fellow pool his meager resources with those of others like him, so they could enjoy the benefits of stock ownership and speculation. It was, doubtless, one of the more altruistic thoughts of the age. Cynics might point out that if more people could be gotten into the market, demand for stocks would keep rising and hence the boom and profits would be bigger and better for large speculators, of whose number Raskob was one. But who are we to question the motives of a man who would make everyone rich?

The values of the society were shown, albeit in a somewhat exaggerated form, in a 1929 *New York Times* ad offering the securities of the National Waterworks Corporation: "Picture this scene today, if by some cataclysm only one small well should remain for the great city of New York [how much could be charged for water?]—$1.00 a bucket, $100, $1,000, $1,000,000. The man who owned the well would own the wealth of the city." The thought of so many parched lips was surely enough to wet those of an investor.

As more and more Americans came to believe that "they were predestined . . . to become rich without work" and excess income accumulated in the accounts of many, the likelihood of the rise of large speculative bubbles increased. The medium of speculation was of little importance. As it happened, the first one to present itself in the mid-twenties was Florida real estate. Sunshine had already done wonders for southern California; the automobile and growing wealth put Florida within reach as a winter haven for the well-to-do of the Northeast. That much of the 1924–26 boom in Florida property was based on reality. The rest was largely fantasy, but a financial fantasy in which one could get rich quickly.

Some of the land sold in Florida at rapidly appreciating prices was genuinely attractive; much of it was not. But that was of no concern to most buyers once the bubble had begun to inflate. Roughly 90 percent of those who made purchases in the Florida land boom had no intention of ever occupying the property—or even of owning it for long. Its actual value (or the fact that it turned out to be in a swamp forty miles from the nearest beach) was immaterial. One bought the land not for its use value, but in the expectation that it could be sold shortly to someone else at a handsome profit. The new purchaser was not a fool, either. He bought for exactly the same reason. Anyone who stopped to consider the situation had to realize that this game had limits and the bubble was bound to burst. The trick was, though, to ride with the expansion as long as possible and get out before the collapse. Some did. But greed was what it was all about, and many investors were tempted into staying too long. Indeed, it could not have been otherwise, because as soon as any significant number decided the time had come to get out, it inevitably became that time.

It was grand while it lasted. In 1925 the *Miami Herald* carried more advertising than any paper anywhere in the history of the world ever had before. Soon it was over, though. In 1926 deflation of values set in, and it is extremely difficult for a speculative boom to start up again after it has begun to subside. Nature provided the mandatory exclamation point at the end of the Florida boom. Two vicious hurricanes ripped through the state in the summer of 1926 and destroyed any hope for a quick revival. For the remainder of the decade, while much of America boomed, Florida sat in the doldrums. Its land boom proved to be only the dress rehearsal for the decade's biggest speculative mania: the stock market. It was a tribute to the extent of confidence Americans had in their destiny to get rich that the popping of the Florida bubble was not sufficient to make people wary of another round of speculation.

Before we delve into the mysteries of the Great Bull Market, it must be made clear that while "speculation" and "boom" are often used in close proximity one to the other, there was nothing speculative about the economic boom of the Coolidge years. It was real. The boom was built on the foundation of new technology, especially upon the automobile. Numerous other industries surged forward in the twenties, holding on to the rear bumper of the automobile. Rubber, steel, oil, road construction, suburban housing, service stations, and many others were dependent upon automotive sales. When those sales tapered off, the boom slowed; when they dropped sharply, the boom turned bust. The automobile was so central to the economy, in fact, that most authorities identify Henry Ford's decision to shut down production for six months while he shifted from the Model T to the Model A as the chief cause of the recession of 1927. The genuine industrial boom helped to fuel optimism and the belief that anyone could get rich. As the Florida bubble deflated, excess profits were already moving on a large scale into the stock market.

It was not true, as was often heard in the late twenties, that "everyone's in the market." Roughly 4 million Americans owned stock in 1929, out of a population of approximately 120 million. Only 1.5 million of those stockholders had a sufficiently large interest to have an account with a broker. The bulk of the "stockholders" owned only a few shares. The distribution of dividends tells the story of concentration of stock ownership. Almost 74 percent of all 1929 dividends went to the fewer than 600,000 individual stockholders with taxable incomes in excess of $5000. Just under 25 percent went to the 24,000 taking in over $100,000 for the year, and nearly 6 percent of all dividends went to 513 individuals whose families reported an income of more than $1 million for the year.

The reasons for the great speculative boom of the late twenties have long been debated. One culprit often pointed to is the Federal Reserve Board's decision early in 1927 to lower the rediscount rate one-half point to 3.5 percent. The decision was based on the need to save international liquidity in the wake of Britain's overvaluation of the pound. Of course it also meant easier money at home. Surely this made stock speculation easier, but it did not cause it. The source of the Great Bull Market was the same as that of the Florida land boom that preceded it: the notion that it was easy to get rich quickly. Stocks, once bought principally on the basis of their earning power, came to be purchased only for resale after their price had risen. As with a swamp lot in Florida, the quality of a stock was largely immaterial, as long as prices continued to rise. That earnings were of little interest can be seen in the case of one of the "glamour" stocks of the age: Radio Corporation of America, which leaped from 85 to 420 during 1928, even though it had never paid a dividend. When the Fed reversed its easy-money policy in the spring of 1928, it had no effect on the market. By this time the lure of fantastic easy profits had become sufficiently bright that higher interest rates were no deterrent.

The Dow Jones industrial average rose from 191 early in 1928 to 381 in September 1929, a 100 percent increase in less than two years. By most standards, this represented more than reasonable returns, but it was no measure of the possibilities for gamblers during the period. The magic words of the fantasy land in lower Manhattan in those years were "margin" and "leverage." Buying stocks on margin was similar to buying an automobile on credit. The purchaser paid a part of the price—say 10 percent—and used the stock as collateral for a loan of the remainder. Just as installment credit stimulated industry, margin buying aroused the market. Such borrowing gave the customer leverage. An illustration will show how this worked. Suppose a buyer purchased on margin a share of the aforementioned RCA stock at the beginning of 1928, putting up $10 and borrowing the remaining $75 from his broker. At the end of the year he could have sold it for $420. The stock itself had appreciated by 394 percent, which wasn't bad; but Mr. X saw his $10 investment bring him $341.25 ($420 less $75 and 5 percent interest owed to the broker). His profit for the year was over 3400 percent!

It seemed too good to be true. The miracle of leverage when prices were rising would operate in reverse if prices fell. The host of margin buyers could be wiped out quickly. What was more, the whole market in 1929 compounded the leverage idea as "investment trusts" proliferated and pyramids were erected from one end of Wall Street to the other. The investment trust existed for the sole purpose of owning stocks. It had no assets other than the securities of other companies. It, in turn, sold stock of its own. By the summer of 1929, such businesses were being piled one on top of another. More and more speculators saw them as centers of intelligence—or at least inside information—that could do a better job with a person's investments than he could do for himself. It seems that the investment trusts had become a kind of electoral college for Wanniski's "global electorate." The individual investor would buy—on margin—stock in Investment Trust A, which would buy—on margin—stock in Investment Trust B, which would buy—on margin—stock in "genuine" corporations. Here was "leverage" on a grand scale. The principal building material used on Wall Street in 1929 was credit. The economic equivalent of the 1926 Florida hurricanes could easily blow down such ill-built structures.

In the uncalm before the storm, Wall Street was attracting much of the available capital in the world. As the demand for call money (for brokers' loans to allow margin buying) rose, so did the interest rate. Eventually call money rates reached 10 and 12 percent, finally even touching 20 percent. Such returns on what seemed like utterly safe investments (the loans were secured by the stocks) were irresistible. The amount banks provided for brokers' loans actually declined in 1929, but that was more than made up for by the funds being made available by corporations. In particular, corporations with surplus capital (of which there was a great deal in the wake of the Mellon tax cuts and refunds) often found lending money on Wall Street a more attractive option than expanding their own production.

Foreign investors came to the same conclusion. Some observers charged that the New York Stock Exchange was sucking up all the money in the world. Of course funds used to purchase stocks did not vanish. For every buyer, a seller received money. This obvious fact did not mean, though, that Wall Street was not absorbing funds normally available for productive purposes. Most of the money used for speculation was held for that purpose on a continuing basis and was not offered for productive investment. Moreover, as the call money rate rose, credit for other purposes became very tight. Speculators might be willing to pay 12 percent interest, since they expected a far higher return; but companies considering expansion could not afford to borrow at such rates.

Brokers' loans—probably the best measure of the extent of speculation—sped upward from less than $5 billion in the middle of 1928 to nearly $6.5 billion at year's end. Six months later the total of outstanding brokers' loans was just over $7 billion. In the next three months—July through September 1929—they shot up by another $1.5 billion. Such massive speculation was obviously unhealthy. In his *Memoirs*, Herbert Hoover passed his judgment on speculators:

"There are crimes far worse than murder for which men should be reviled and punished." But who would have done so in 1928 or 1929? It was not the speculators who were reviled in that fantastic time, but those who dared to criticize speculation. *The Wall Street Journal* reacted to one criticism in September 1929 by asking: "Why is it that any ignoramus can talk about Wall Street?"

Under the circumstances, government action to deflate the bubble was virtually impossible. Ending the boom would not only have been unpopular, it almost certainly would also have caused a bust. Bubbles are hard to deflate without popping them. If the choice is between a collapse now or later, politicians and regulators normally prefer to put off until tomorrow what they could do today. Thus in his last days as president, Calvin Coolidge issued a statement declaring that prosperity was "absolutely sound" and stocks were "cheap at current prices."

One observer pointed out that by the late twenties the broker's office had replaced the saloon; it had "the same swinging doors, the same half-darkened windows." The offices of one New York investment service even had a speak-easy-style peephole. It was a telling analogy. Stock speculation provided a legal spirit of intoxication in a time when intoxicating spirits were prohibited by the Eighteenth Amendment. By the fall of 1929, those who were guiding the market were driving under the influence. A terrible crash, to be followed by unpleasant sobering experiences and an awful hangover were the likely results.

Contrary to popular impression, the Wall Street Crash of 1929 was not a single collapse of one or two days (Black Thursday and Black Tuesday, October 24 and 29, are usually identified), but a long, rolling downward slide that went on for weeks, from September 3 through November 13. There were brief upsurges after some of the worst days.

The speculative boom was, of course, dependent upon confidence. Confidence was a commodity, however, that was available in abundance in 1929. The bull market had suffered two sharp breaks, in December 1928 and March 1929, only to come back stronger than ever. Accordingly, it took a prolonged, devastating collapse to convince speculators that it was really over. Even after the collapse had started in the fall of 1929, the demand for confident statements kept bringing forth a plentiful supply. Noted economist Irving Fisher of Yale, for example, declared on October 15: "Stock prices have reached what looks like a permanently high plateau." As the decline degenerated into the Crash, a wide array of leaders repeated phrases containing the words "fundamentally sound."

Not everyone was so sure, though. Since taking office in March, President Hoover had tried on several occasions to warn against speculation. In April the President ordered his financial agent to sell some of Hoover's stocks, "as possible hard times coming." When the President issued his famous October 25 statement about "the fundamental business of the country" being "on a sound and prosperous basis," he reportedly declined a request from a group of bankers to say something specifically about the stock market.

The story of the Crash itself is summarized easily. The peak of the bull market was reached on September 3. Two days later there was a break. It was not too serious, and the general assumption was that it was just another "adjustment." Thereafter the market drifted generally downward, but unevenly. Optimism remained the official watchword, and speculators continued to flock into the market. Brokers' loans rose by more in September than ever before. Prices continued downward in early October. Then on Monday, October 21, the real rout began. Although far worse days were to come, the style of the next few weeks was set on this day. The volume was huge, causing the ticker to fall far behind. This added a terrible ingredient of uncertainty to the gathering panic. Knowing that prices were falling, but not knowing by how much, produced great fear and led many to sell quickly, before prices dipped further. Such sales, of course, added to the price declines.

Wednesday, October 23, although not as often noted as the 24th or the 29th, may have been the key day of the Crash. An hour before the closing bell, a slide began which saw the Dow Jones industrials lose 21 points in 60 minutes, wiping out all the fantastic advances of July and August. Greater losses and higher volumes would be registered on subsequent days, but October 23 was the trigger. After trading closed amid the hour-long scramble to sell, many investors concluded that this time the boom was really over. They would sell the next day, before it was too late. Once a sizable number of important investors decided the boom had ended, it had ended. It had all been built on expectations of rising prices. As soon as those expectations were reversed, the market had to fall. Adding to the deflationary pressures were a large number of margin calls, which forced many to sell who did not want to. (Since the stocks provided the security for the loans, when their value fell more money had to be put up to cover the loans.)

The voluntary and involuntary decisions to sell that evening took their toll when the market opened the following morning, October 24. If the image of a downward slide had been appropriate for earlier days, the metaphor for Black Thursday was that of the bottom falling out. A vast supply of shares for sale hit the market that morning, but they failed to create their own demand until prices had plummeted. Partial recovery was achieved in the afternoon when a group of leading bankers headed by Thomas W. Lamont of J. P. Morgan moved in to support prices. This calmed the situation and restored some confidence. In the afternoon most of the terrible losses were reversed. By the end of the day, *The New York Times* industrial average had climbed back to within 12 points of where it opened.

On Friday and Saturday prices stabilized. Then on Monday the 28th, everything fell apart. The Dow lost more than 38 points, nearly 13 percent of its value at the start of the day. The bankers' group threw in the towel that afternoon, admitting that it could not stem the collapse. The next day was the infamous Black Tuesday, October 29, 1929, usually cited as *the* day of the Crash. An unprecedented 16.4 million shares changed hands. At many points during the day, no buyers were available at any price. Even after a closing rally, the *Times* index was down another 45 points at the close.

The day after Black Tuesday saw a remarkable recovery in which two-thirds of Tuesday's losses were regained. But the Crash was far from over. After a short session on Thursday, the market closed for the rest of the week. When trading reopened on Monday, November 4, a startling new collapse set in. The *Times* industrials lost 22 points that day, 37 on Wednesday (the Exchange was closed on

Tuesday for election day), and a total of 50 more points during the first three days of the following week. When the Crash bottomed out (for 1929—prices would go much lower in subsequent years of the Depression), the *Times* index had lost 228 points since the high point of September 3. Fifty percent of the value of stocks in the index had been lost in ten weeks. The New Era was over.

As J. K. Galbraith has pointed out, nothing was lost in the Crash "but money." Given the values of the day, though, many losers might have responded: "What else is there?" Americans soon found out what else there was. Industrial production fell by more than 9 percent from October to December 1929. American imports dropped by 20 percent from September to December. The Great Depression was under way.

The unavoidable question must be asked again: Did the Crash cause the Depression? There are two correct answers. If it is meant as a "why" question, the answer is: "Of course not!" If it is a "how" or a "when" question, the response must be: "Yes, in part." "Whatever happens in a stock market," Milton Friedman has declared, "it cannot lead to a great depression unless it produces or is accompanied by a monetary collapse." Although I disagree with Friedman's exclusive emphasis upon monetary factors, his statement is a useful one. He is absolutely right in contending that a stock market collapse is unlikely to produce a large depression by itself. But the stock market, fantasy land though it had become in 1929, was not operating in a vacuum. Wall Street's connections with other parts of the economy meant that the Crash would do more than merely reflect the weaknesses in the economic structure. Among other things, the fragile economy was heavily dependent upon confidence and the spending and investment of the well-to-do. These were precisely the things that the Crash most effectively undercut.

The fact is that, despite all the statements about fundamental soundness, both the domestic and international economies were fundamentally unsound by the late 1920s. When someone becomes ill after "catching a chill," it is not the cold itself that causes the sickness. Rather the cold reduces the body's resistance to micro-organisms already present in it, which then are able to cause the illness. Some such role is the proper one to assign to the Crash. The cold wind that swept through lower Manhattan in October and November 1929 lowered the economy's resistance to the point where already existing defects could multiply rapidly and bring down the whole organism. The Crash is important in explaining how and when the Depression happened.

As for the question of where the Depression began, it clearly started in the United States. The American collapse need not have set off a worldwide depression had the United States not been the leader of the world economy. But it was. This placed certain responsibilities on the United States—responsibilities that, in the main, the nation shunned. When the United States cut lending and erected higher tariff walls, the world economy faltered further. Doubtless the world situation—sparked by American actions—in turn made the Depression worse in this country. Cause and effect should not be reversed. Geographically, the origin and spread of the Depression went in just the opposite direction from that traced by Herbert Hoover.

By far the most important question about the origins of the Depression is why? Unicausal explanations simply cannot stand up. When an American today develops cancer, it is usually impossible to say precisely what caused it. Such environmental factors as diet, chemicals, radiation, and tobacco, to name a few, may be among the possible causes. The "typical" American's environment is filled with carcinogens. The same was true of the nation's economy in the 1920s. Yet it is often possible in studying the cancer patient's life to identify things that were more likely than others to have done the most damage. Exposure to some carcinogens is more apt to be sufficient cause of the disease than others. This seems to have been the case with the Great Depression as well.

The causes of the Great Depression were many, sufficiently so that they have required a long chapter to explore. In the end, though, the greatest weight must be assigned to the effects of an income distribution that was bad and getting worse. Michael Harrington has succinctly stated the problem: "The capitalist genius for production was on a collision course with the capitalist limits on consumption." A recent statistical analysis of the origins of the Depression has concluded that, although the data are not sufficient to answer many questions, they do point toward the belief that "the Depression was the result of a drop in autonomous expenditures, particularly consumption." The most persuasive reasons for that drop have to do with poor distribution of income. It seems more than coincidental that the shares of income going to the upper reaches of American society have been appreciably smaller in the years of postwar prosperity than they were in 1929. . . .

Maldistribution was only one among many roots of the Great Depression, but it was the taproot. It led to both underconsumption and oversaving, and it helped fuel stock speculation. Maldistribution was the most important factor in the greatest paradox of the Depression. As eloquently stated in a 1932 article in *Current History*:

We still pray to be given each day our daily bread. Yet there is too much bread, too much wheat and corn, meat and oil and almost every other commodity required by man for his subsistence and material happiness. We are not able to purchase the abundance that modern methods of agriculture, mining and manufacture make available in such bountiful quantities. Why is mankind being asked to go hungry and cold and poverty stricken in the midst of plenty?

Here was the central question of the Depression.

SUGGESTIONS FOR FURTHER READING

Frederick Lewis Allen, *Only Yesterday: An Informal History of the Nineteen Twenties* (New York, 1931) is an entertaining popular account that is out-of-date in many respects, but is still worth reading. Other, more recent studies that recognize more conflict and

---

*Available in paperback edition.

diversity are William E. Leuchtenburg, *The Perils of Prosperity, 1914–1932* (Chicago, 1958); Ellis W. Hawley, *The Great War and the Search for a Modern Order: A History of the American People and Their Institutions, 1917–1933* (New York, 1979); Geoffrey Perrett, *America in the Twenties: A History* (New York, 1982); Page Smith, *Redeeming the Time: A People's History of the 1920s and the New Deal* (New York, 1987); and Michael E. Parrish, *Anxious Decades: America in Prosperity and Depression, 1920–1941* (New York, 1992).

Frederick Hoffman, *The Twenties: American Writing in the Postwar Decade* (New York, 1955) is the best account of the rebellion of writers and intellectuals. In addition to books about the literature of the twenties, much can be learned by sampling the literature itself. The works of F. Scott Fitzgerald, Ernest Hemingway, H. L. Mencken, Sinclair Lewis, and other writers are readily available in paperback. The important black literary and artistic achievement known as the Harlem Renaissance is discussed in Nathan Irvin Huggins, *Harlem Renaissance* (New York, 1971); the same author's *Voices from the Harlem Renaissance* (New York, 1976) gives the reader a more direct taste of the work of the black writers. On the culture of the 1920s, see the two fascinating essays by Warren I. Susman in his *Culture as History* (New York, 1984). Studies of popular music and art are Arnold Shaw, *The Jazz Age: Popular Music in the 1920s* (New York, 1987) and Susan Noyes Platt, *Modernism in the 1920s: Interpretations of Modern Art in New York from Expressionism to Constructivism* (Ann Arbor, Mich., 1985). Ann Douglas, *Terrible Honesty: Mongrel Manhattan in the 1920s* (New York, 1995) and Lynn Dumenil, *Modern Temper: American Culture and Society in the 1920s* (New York, 1995) find diversity and conflict, but both describe an overriding consensus that makes it possible to describe an "American culture" in the 1920s.

Two accounts that find a survival of progressivism during the decade are Arthur M. Schlesinger, Jr., *The Crisis of the Old Order* (Boston, 1957) and Clarke A. Chambers, *Seedtime of Reform: American Social Service and Social Action, 1918–1933* (Minneapolis, 1963). Nancy F. Cott, *The Grounding of Modern Feminism* (New Haven, Conn., 1987) finds the origins of the modern feminist movement in the 1920s.

Some of the issues raised by John Higham in the selection above are discussed in Paul A. Carter, *Another Part of the Twenties* (New York, 1977) and Paul Murphy, "Sources and Nature of Intolerance in the 1920s," *Journal of American History*, 51 (June 1964), 60–76. Aspects of intolerance are considered in David M. Chalmers, *Hooded Americanism* (Garden City, N.Y., 1965) on the Ku Klux Klan and Norman F. Furniss, *The Fundamentalist Controversy, 1918–1931* (New Haven, Conn., 1954).

For various interpretations of the economic aspects of the decade, including explanations for the stock market crash and the onset of depression, see John Kenneth Galbraith, *The Great Crash, 1929* (Boston, 1954); Robert Sobel, *The Great Bull Market: Wall Street in the 1920s* (New York, 1968); and Peter Temin, *Did Monetary Forces Cause the Great Depression?* (New York, 1976).

Two collections of essays will take the interested reader further into the historians' debate: Milton Plesur, *The 1920s: Problems and Paradoxes* (Boston, 1969) and John Braeman, Robert H. Bremner, and David Brody, *Change and Continuity in Twentieth Century America: 1920s* (Columbus, Ohio, 1968). A useful analysis of the historical writing on the period is Burl Noggle, "The Twenties: A New Historiographical Frontier," *Journal of American History* 53 (September 1966), 299–314.

8

The New Deal

The Depression following the stock market crash in the fall of 1929 was the longest and most devastating the nation had ever faced. Millions lost their jobs and their savings; many, unable to meet mortgage payments or to pay rent, found themselves homeless. Hungry men and women stood in bread lines awaiting meager meals from charity organizations and churches. Farmers burned their corn for fuel because it did not pay to haul it to market, and they watched sullenly as their creditors came to evict them from their farms. Many of the homeless, hungry, and unemployed listened to radicals who urged massive social and economic change, even revolution. When a group of unemployed army veterans marched on Washington in the summer of 1932 to demand a bonus payment, a panicky President Hoover ordered troops and tanks to drive them out of town.

As the depression deepened, the two political parties prepared for the 1932 election. The results were inevitable. The voters rejected President Herbert Hoover and the Republican party and turned to the Democrats and their candidate, Franklin Delano Roosevelt. "Only a foolish optimist can deny the dark realities of the moment," declared the newly elected president in his inaugural address. Roosevelt went on to announce that he interpreted his victory in the elections of the previous November as a "mandate" for "direct, vigorous action" under active leadership. This leadership he promised to give.

The result was the New Deal, a period of intensive legislative activity lasting roughly from 1933 to 1938. Virtually no part of the economy failed to feel the effects of the New Deal legislation. Newly formed government agencies provided relief and work for the unemployed; farmers were paid to cut production in order to raise crop prices; workers organized trade unions under the protection of federal law. The banks and the stock exchange came under strict government supervision. Federal funds paid for flood control and other forms of natural-resource conservation, provided rural electrification, and supported the building of urban parks and public buildings. Federal legislation established the Social Security program, the minimum wage, and unemployment insurance.

New Deal legislation won Franklin D. Roosevelt and the Democratic party a great deal of support among the American people. But at the same time, the New Deal program elicited sharp opposition. When New Dealers noted that their goals were the Three R's—Relief, Recovery, and Reform—many opponents bitterly insisted that a fourth "R," Revolution, be added, arguing that the New Deal had turned the country toward socialism.

Few historians accept the view that the New Deal was socialistic either in its goals or its results, but some do argue that it was revolutionary in that it marked a radical break with the traditions and methods of the past. They maintain that the reforms so altered the nature of the relationship between government and society that they marked a fundamental change to which the term *revolutionary* may be aptly applied. Others, however, argue that the New Deal was not radical either in intent or in method, having borrowed its techniques and its goals from a long tradition of American reform. In this sense, the New Deal reforms were really conservative; they were designed to conserve the basic features of the American system in the midst of crisis. Some find this conservatism of the New Deal to be wise and beneficial because it resulted in needed reforms that preserved the strength of the nation's economic and social system while opening the way to solve some of its most serious problems. But others disagree, insisting that the reforms were tentative and incomplete and, therefore, left unsolved a myriad of problems that continued to plague the nation. Examples of these conflicting views may be seen in the selections that follow.

In the first selection, Carl N. Degler argues that the New Deal represents a cataclysmic and revolutionary development. He finds a fundamental political reorientation in the New Deal reforms and argues that the New Deal constituted a sharp break and a real conflict with the political values of the 1920s. The New Deal, he insists, ended the old and created a new consensus, a change that he views sympathetically.

Ronald Radosh, in the second selection, disagrees. Far from being revolutionary, the New Deal, he argues, made only minor changes in the American system, changes that did not represent a fundamental break with the past. Although many people benefited from the social reforms, the major accomplishment of the New Deal, he argues, was a successful effort by leading big businessmen to modernize corporate capitalism. Businessmen recognized that conditions had changed and the system had to be altered to adjust to those changes. Radosh concludes that only socialism would mark a truly radical change, and only socialism would really solve the problems faced by the people.

In the third selection, Anthony J. Badger notes some of the limitations of the New Deal, but he also lists many of its considerable achievements, including some that were accidental and unanticipated. For Badger, the New Deal was neither revolutionary nor reactionary; rather it was "essentially a holding operation for American society because in the democratic, capitalist United States that was what most Americans wanted it to be." Thus, according to Badger, the New Deal revealed a consensus among Americans in the midst of depression.

Without question, the legislation of the New Deal years had a great impact on American life, producing changes that persist to this day. But how significant were those changes? Do they justify calling the New Deal a revolutionary break with the past? Or would it be more accurate to say that the New Deal was essentially conservative, seeking to make only those innovations that would prevent revolutionary change?

One possible way to answer these questions is to consider the degree to which New Deal legislation met the needs of various groups in American society. Did the New Deal solve—or at least provide the means to solve—the major problems of workers or farmers? If not, how can we account for the support these groups gave to the New Dealers? If the New Deal was basically conservative, why did large sections of the business community oppose it?

Another way to assess the New Deal is to consider its long-term effects. What are the consequences of the New Deal reforms for the 1990s? Have we moved beyond New Deal solutions to social, economic, and political problems, or are we still dominated by the framework of the reforms of the 1930s?

The Third American Revolution

Twice since the founding of the Republic, cataclysmic events have sliced through the fabric of American life, snapping many of the threads which ordinarily bind the past to the future. The War for the Union was one such event, the Great Depression of the 1930's the other. And, as the Civil War was precipitated from the political and moral tensions of the preceding era, so the Great Depression was a culmination of the social and economic forces of industrialization and urbanization which had been transforming America since 1865. A depression of such pervasiveness as that of the thirties could happen only to a people already tightly interlaced by the multitudinous cords of a machine civilization and embedded in the matrix of an urban society.

In all our history no other economic collapse brought so many Americans to near starvation, endured so long, or came so close to overturning the basic institutions of American life. It is understandable, therefore, that from the experience should issue a new conception of the good society.

"Hunger Is Not Debatable"

The economic dimensions of the Great Depression are quickly sketched—too quickly perhaps to permit a full appreciation of the abyss into which the economy slid between 1929 and 1933. The value of stocks on the New York Exchange, for example, slumped from a high of $87 billion in 1929 to a mere $19 billion in 1933. Wholesale prices dropped 38 percent by 1933 and farm prices seemed almost to have ceased to exist: they were 60 percent below the low level of 1929. Within less than three years, realized national income plummeted to almost half of what it had been in the last boom year; and the same was true of industrial production. The human cost of this catastrophic breakdown in the complicated industrial machine, *Fortune* magazine estimated in September, 1932, was 10 million totally unemployed or 25 million people without any source of income.

To worsen matters, the industrial stagnation was accompanied by a spreading fever of bank failures. First here and there, then all over the country, the banks began to close their doors in the faces of their depositors. By the beginning of 1933, the financial self-confidence of the nation reached a dangerously low level, requiring the new administration of Franklin Roosevelt, as its first official act, to order the closing of all banks. In all, more than 10,000 deposit banks failed in the five years after 1929. If the banks, the custodians of the measure of value, proved to be unsound, men might well wonder what was left to cling to as the winds of disaster gained in fury.

Unnerving as the failure of the banks undoubtedly was, for most people the Great Depression became starkly real only when unemployment struck. No one knew whom it would hit next; the jobless were everywhere—in the cities, in the towns, on the farms. Their helplessness, their bewilderment, were often written in their faces, reflected in their discouraged gaits, and mirrored in their run-down dwellings. John Dos Passos reported seeing the unemployed of Detroit in 1932 living in caves scooped out of giant abandoned sand piles. Though it was said that no one would be allowed to starve, *Fortune,* in September, 1932, suggested that some had already. The magazine counted the millions of the unemployed and told of families subsisting on a single loaf of bread for over a week or of going without food for two or three days on end. Discarded and spoiled vegetables or wild dandelions were the substance of meals for some families. Other reports in 1933 told of at least twenty-nine persons who died of starvation in New York City. Moreover, thousands must have died from diseases which gained an easy foothold in weakened and underfed bodies; but these unfortunates were never counted. Food, casually consumed in good times, suddenly became the focus of existence for thousands. In their desperation some urban folk actually tried to wring their food from the barren soil of the city. In Gary, Indiana, for example, 20,000 families were raising food on lots lent by the city; Robert and Helen Lynd reported that in Middletown in 1933, 2,500 of the town's 48,000 people eked out their food budgets with relief gardens.

The spreading unemployment generated new and deep-seated fears. When the unkempt veterans of the First World War camped in Washington in 1932, demanding a bonus to tide them over their joblessness, a fearful and unsure President had them dispersed by troops armed with tear gas. And when Congress in that same year voted a 10 percent cut in government salaries, President Hoover sent a secret message urging that the enlisted men of the Army and the Navy be excluded from such decreases so that in case of domestic troubles the federal government would not be compelled to rely upon disgruntled troops.

Nor was it only the federal government that felt uneasy in the presence of the specter which was stalking the land. Malcolm Cowley, in an eyewitness account, described how the trucks bearing the disillusioned veterans out of Washington were quickly sped through town after town, the local authorities fearing that some of the unemployed veterans would jump off and become burdens on already overtaxed communities. Cowley tells of one citizen in Washington, not a marcher at all, who was hurriedly bundled into a truck by mistake and could not get off until he reached Indianapolis!

Driven by their desperation, some Americans began to talk of violence. Mutterings of revolution and threats to return with rifles were heard among the bonus marchers as they left Washington. Out on the farms, the dissatisfaction of the veterans was matched by sullen farmers who closed the courts and disrupted mortgage auctions to save their homes. The ugly turn which the discontent could take was revealed by the arrest of a man in Wisconsin in 1932 on suspicion of having removed a spike from the railroad track over which President Hoover's train was to pass. In that bleak year it was not uncommon for the President of the United States to be booed and hooted as he doggedly pursued his ill-starred campaign for re-election. To Theodore Dreiser, as the cold night of the depression settled over the land, it seemed that Karl Marx's prediction "that Capitalism would eventually evolve into failure . . . has come true."

Even for the Lords of Creation, as Frederick Lewis Allen was to call them, the Great Depression was an unsettling and confusing experience. "I'm afraid, every man is afraid," confessed Charles M. Schwab of United States Steel. "I don't know, we don't know, whether the values we have are going to be real next month or not." And in the very early months of the Roosevelt administration, Harold Ickes, attending a dinner of the Chamber of Commerce of the United States, could sense the pitiable impotence to which the nation's industrial leaders had sunk. "The great and the mighty in the business world were there in force," he rather gleefully noted in his diary, "and I couldn't help thinking how so many of these great and mighty were crawling to Washington on their hands and knees these days to beg the Government to run their businesses for them."

But it was the unspectacular, the everyday dreariness of unemployment that must have cut the deepest and endured the longest as far as the ordinary American was concerned. The simplest things of life, once taken for granted, now became points of irritation. "I forget how to cook good since I have nothing to cook with," remarked one housewife. Children lost their appetites upon seeing the milk and mush "that they have seen so often." Even the rare treat of fresh meat could not awaken an appetite long accustomed to disappointment and pallid food.

The routine entertainments of the poor were casualties to unemployment. "Suppose you go to a friend's house and she gives you a cup of tea and something," the wife of an unemployed worker told a social worker. "You feel ashamed. You think, now I got to do the same when she comes to my house. You know you can't so you stay home." Shifts in entertainment patterns among the unemployed were revealed in a study made of some 200 families in New Haven. Before the breadwinner lost his job, some 55 percent went to the movies; once unemployment hit, however, only 16 percent did. In the days when work was to be had, only 13 percent found recreation in "sitting around the house," but now 25 percent did so. With the loss of their jobs, 12 percent of the men admitted they "chatted and gossiped" for recreation, although none of them did when they had work.

Unemployment's effect upon the family was often more profound and far-reaching. In recounting the case history of the Raparka family, one sociologist wrote that when Mr. Raparka "lost his job in the fall of 1933, he dominated the family. Two years later it was Mrs. Raparka who was the center of authority." Again and again social workers chronicled the alteration in the father's position in the family during a period of unemployment. Humiliation settled over many a father no longer able to fulfill his accustomed role in the family. "I would rather turn on the gas and put an end to the whole family than let my wife support me," was the way one unemployed father put it. One investigator found that one-fifth of her sample of fifty-nine families exhibited a breakdown in the father's authority, particularly in the eyes of the wife. For example, one wife said, "When your husband cannot provide for the family and makes you worry so, you lose your love for him."

Fathers discovered that without the usual financial power to buy bikes or bestow nickels, their control and authority over children were seriously weakened and sometimes completely undermined. In one family where the father was unemployed for a long time, his role was almost completely taken over by the eldest son. The father himself admitted: "The son of twenty-two is just like a father around the house. He tries to settle any little brother-and-sister fights and even encourages me and my wife." In the same family, a younger son who was working summed up his relationship to his parents in a few words. "I remind them," he said, "who makes the money. They don't say much. They just take it, that's all. *I'm* not the one on relief." In such circumstances, it is no exaggeration to say that the massive weight of the depression was grinding away at the bedrock of American institutions.

The ties of a home struck by unemployment were weak and the opportunities for fruitful and satisfying work were almost totally absent in 1932–33. *Fortune* reported in February, 1933, that something like 200,000 young men and boys were traveling around the country on railroad trains for lack of anything better to do. Tolerated by the railroads because of their obvious poverty and lack of jobs, the boys were often suffering from disease and malnutrition. The authorities in Los Angeles asserted, for example, that 25 percent of those coming into the city needed clinical attention and 5 percent required hospitalization. During a single season, one railroad announced, fifty such footloose boys were killed and one hundred injured. From Kansas City it was reported that girl wanderers, dressed in boy's clothing, were on the increase. To many such young people, now grown, the Great Depression must still seem the most purposeless, the most enervating period of their lives.

What Robert and Helen Lynd concluded for their study of Middletown in 1935 can be applied to America as a whole: ". . . the great knife of the depression had cut down impartially through the entire population cleaving open lives and hopes of rich as well as poor. The experience has been more nearly universal than any prolonged recent emotional experience in the city's history; it has approached in its elemental shock the primary experiences of birth and death."

The End of Laissez Faire

Perhaps the most striking alteration in American thought which the depression fostered concerned the role of the government in the economy. Buffeted and bewildered by the economic debacle, the American people in the course of the

1930's abandoned, once and for all, the doctrine of laissez faire. This beau ideal of the nineteenth-century economists had become, ever since the days of Jackson, an increasingly cherished shibboleth of Americans. But now it was almost casually discarded. It is true, of course, that the rejection of laissez faire had a long history; certainly the Populists worked to undermine it. But with the depression the nation at large accepted the government as a permanent influence in the economy.[1]

Almost every one of the best-known measures of the federal government during the depression era made inroads into the hitherto private preserves of business and the individual. Furthermore, most of these new measures survived the period, taking their places as fundamental elements in the structure of American life. For modern Americans living under a federal government of transcendent influence and control in the economy, this is the historic meaning of the great depression.

Much of what is taken for granted today as the legitimate function of government and the social responsibility of business began only with the legislation of these turbulent years. Out of the investigation of banking and bankers in 1933, for example, issued legislation which separated commercial banking from the stock and bond markets, and insured the bank deposits of ordinary citizens. The stock market, like the banks, was placed under new controls and a higher sense of responsibility to the public imposed upon it by the new Securities and Exchange Commission. The lesson of Black Tuesday in 1929 had not been forgotten; the classic free market itself—the Exchange—was hereafter to be under continuous government scrutiny.

The three Agricultural Adjustment Acts of 1933, 1936, and 1938, while somewhat diverse in detail, laid down the basic lines of what is still today the American approach to the agricultural problem. Ever since the collapse of the boom after the First World War, American agriculture had suffered from the low prices born of the tremendous surpluses. Unable to devise a method for expanding markets to absorb the excess, the government turned to restriction of output as the only feasible alternative. But because restriction of output meant curtailment of income for the farmer, it became necessary, if farm income was to be sustained, that farmers be compensated for their cut in production. Thus was inaugurated the singular phenomenon, which is still a part of the American answer to the agricultural surplus, of paying farmers for *not* growing crops. The other device introduced for raising farm prices, and still the mainstay of our farm policy, came with the 1938 act, which provided that the government would purchase

---

[1]A complementary and highly suggestive way of viewing this trend away from laissez faire, of which the events of the 1930's are a culmination, is that taken in K. William Kapp, *The Social Costs of Private Enterprise* (Cambridge, Mass., 1950). Kapp observes that for a long time private enterprise had shifted the social costs of production—like industrially polluted water, industrial injuries, smoke nuisances and hazards, unemployment, and the like—onto society. The decline of laissez faire has, in this view, actually been a movement to compel industry to pay for those social costs of production which it has hitherto shirked.

and store excess farm goods, thus supporting the price level by withdrawing the surplus from the competitive market. Both methods constitute a subsidy for the farmer from society at large.[2]

Though the Eisenhower administration in the 1950's called for a return to a free market in farm products—that is, the removal of government supports from prices—very few steps have been taken in that direction, and probably very few ever will.[3] A free market was actually in operation during the twenties, but it succeeded only in making farmers the stepchildren of the golden prosperity of that decade. Today the farm bloc is too powerful politically to be treated so cavalierly. Moreover, the depression has taught most Americans that a free market is not only a rarity in the modern world but sometimes inimical to a stable and lasting prosperity.

Perhaps the most imaginative and fruitful of these innnovations was the Tennessee Valley Authority, which transformed the heart of the South. "It was and is literally a down to earth experiment," native Tennesseean Broadus Mitchell has written, "with all that we know from test tube and logarithm tables called on to help. It was a union of heart and mind to restore what had been wasted. It was a social resurrection." For the TVA was much more than flood and erosion control or even hydroelectric power—though its gleaming white dams are perhaps its most striking and best-known monuments. It was a social planning of the most humane sort, where even the dead were carefully removed from cemeteries before the waters backed up behind the dams. It brought new ideas, new wealth, new skills, new hope into a wasted, tired, and discouraged region.

At the time of the inception of the TVA, it was scarcely believable that the "backward" South would ever utilize all the power the great dams would create. But in its report of 1956, the Authority declared that the Valley's consumption of electricity far exceeded that produced from water sites: almost three-quarters of TVA's power is now generated from steam power, not from waterfall. In large part it was the TVA which taught the Valley how to use more power to expand its industries and to lighten the people's burdens. Back in 1935, Drew and Leon Pearson saw this creation of consumer demand in action. "Uncle Sam is a drummer with a commercial line to sell," they wrote in *Harper's Magazine*. "He sold liberty bonds before, but never refrigerators."

Measured against textbook definitions, the TVA is unquestionably socialism. The government owns the means of production and, moreover, it competes with

---

[2]On the day that the first AAA was declared unconstitutional, a Gallup poll revealed that, although the nation as a whole did not like the AAA, the farmers of the South and Midwest did. As a result, invalidation of the act by the Court did not mean the end of such a policy, but only the beginning of a search to find a new way of accomplishing the same end. Hence there were successive AAA's, whereas, when NRA was declared unconstitutional in 1935, it was dropped, primarily because neither business nor labor, for whose interests it had been organized, found much merit in its approach to their problems.

[3]As reported in the *New York Times,* July 2, 1958, forecasts for the fiscal year 1958–59 see government subsidies to agriculture reaching $6 billion—an all-time high.

private producers of electricity.[4] But pragmatic Americans—and particularly those living in the Valley—have had few sleepless nights as a consequence of this fact. The TVA does its appointed job and, as the recent fight over the Dixon and Yates contract seemed to show, it is here to stay. It, too, with all the talk of "creeping socialism," has been absorbed into that new American Way fashioned by the experimentalism of the American people from the wreckage of the Great Depression.

Undoubtedly social security deserves the appellation "revolutionary" quite as much as the TVA; it brought government into the lives of people as nothing had since the draft and the income tax. Social security legislation actually comprises two systems: insurance against old age and insurance in the event of loss of work. The first system was completely organized and operated by the federal government; the second was shared with the states—but the national government set the standards; both were clear acknowledgment of the changes which had taken place in the family and in the business of making a living in America. No longer in urban America could the old folks, whose proportion in the society was steadily increasing, count on being taken in by their offspring as had been customary in a more agrarian world. Besides, such a makeshift arrangement was scarcely satisfying to the self-respect of the oldsters. With the transformation of the economy by industrialization, most Americans had become helpless before the vagaries of the business cycle. As a consequence of the social forces which were steadily augmenting social insecurity, only collective action by the government could arrest the drift.

To have the government concerned about the security of the individual was a new thing. Keenly aware of the novelty of this aim in individualistic America,[5] Roosevelt was careful to deny any serious departure from traditional paths. "These three great objectives—the security of the home, the security of livelihood, and the security of social insurance," he said in 1934, constitute "a minimum of the promise that we can offer to the American people." But this, he quickly added, "does not indicate a change in values."

Whether the American people thought their values had changed is not nearly as important as the fact that they accepted social security. And the proof that they did is shown in the steady increase in the proportion of the population cov-

---

[4]The extent of the intellectual changes which the depression measures introduced can be appreciated by a quotation from President Hoover's veto in 1931 of a bill to develop a public power project in what was later to be the TVA area. "I am firmly opposed to the Government entering into any business the major purpose of which is competition with our citizens." Emergency measures of such a character might be tolerated, he said. "But for the Federal government deliberately to go out to build up and expand such an occasion to the major purpose of a power and manufacturing business is to break down the initiative and enterprise of the American people; it is destruction of equality of opportunity amongst our people; it is the negation of the ideals upon which our civilization has been based."

[5]Characteristically enough, as his memoirs show, President Hoover had long been interested in both old-age and unemployment insurance, but always such schemes were to be worked out through private insurance companies, or at best with the states—never under the auspices of the federal government. "It required a great depression," he has written somewhat ruefully, "to awaken interest in the idea" of unemployment insurance.

ered by the old-age benefit program since 1935; today about 80 percent of non-farm workers are included in the system. Apart from being a minimum protection for the individual and society against the dry rot of industrial idleness, unemployment insurance is now recognized as one of the major devices for warding off another depression.

It is true, as proponents of the agrarian life have been quick to point out, that an industrialized people, stripped as they are of their economic self-reliance, have felt the need for social insurance more than people in other types of society. But it is perhaps just as important to recognize that it is only in such a highly productive society that people can even dare to dream of social security. Men in other ages have felt the biting pains of economic crisis, but few pre-industrial people have ever enjoyed that surfeit of goods which permits the fat years to fill out the lean ones. But like so much else concerning industrialism, it is not always easy to calculate whether the boons it offers exceed in value the burdens which it imposes.

For the average man, the scourge of unemployment was the essence of the depression. Widespread unemployment, permeating all ranks and stations in society, drove the American people and their government into some of their most determined and deliberate departures from the hallowed policy of "hands off." But despite the determination, as late as 1938 the workless still numbered almost ten million—two thirds as great as in 1932 under President Hoover. The governmental policies of the 1930's never appreciably diminished the horde of unemployed—only the war prosperity of 1940 and after did that—but the providing of jobs by the federal government was a reflection of the people's new conviction that the government had a responsibility to alleviate economic disaster. Such bold action on the part of government, after the inconclusive, bewildered approach of the Hoover administration, was a tonic for the dragging spirits of the people.[6]

A whole range of agencies, from the Civil Works Administration (CWA) to the Works Progress Administration (WPA), were created to carry the attack against unemployment. It is true that the vast program of relief which was organized was not "permanent" in the sense that it is still in being, but for two reasons it deserves to be discussed here. First, since these agencies constituted America's principal weapon against unemployment, some form of them will surely be

---

[6]It was the misfortune of Herbert Hoover to have been President at a time when his considerable administrative and intellectual gifts were hamstrung by his basic political philosophy, which, instead of being a guide to action, served as an obstacle. Much more of an old-fashioned liberal than a reactionary, and deeply attached to the Jeffersonian dogma of the limited powers of the federal government, Hoover was psychologically and philosophically unable to use the immense powers and resources of his office in attacking the urgent threat of unemployment. Back in 1860–61, another President—James Buchanan—had been paralyzed in the midst of a national crisis by his limited conception of the federal power, but in that instance his inaction was palliated by the fact that his successor was to take office within less than three months. Hoover, however, wrestled with the depression for three years, and all during that trying period he stoutly held to his rigid intellectual position that federally supplied and administered relief would destroy the foundations of the nation. Never has an American President, including the two Adamses, defied overwhelming popular opinion for so long for the sake of his own ideals as Herbert Hoover did then; and never has a President since Buchanan fallen so quickly into obscurity as Hoover did after March 4, 1933.

utilized if a depression should occur again. Second, the various relief agencies of the period afford the best examples of the new welfare outlook, which was then in the process of formation.

Though in the beginning relief programs were premised on little more than Harry Hopkins' celebrated dictum, "Hunger is not debatable," much more complex solutions to unemployment were soon worked out. The relief program of the WPA, which after 1935 was the major relief agency, was a case in point. In 1937, *Fortune* magazine commented on "the evolution of unemployment relief from tool to institution"—a recognition of the importance and duration of relief in America. "In 1936, the federal government was so deeply involved in the relief of the unemployed," *Fortune* contended, "that it was not only keeping them alive, but it was also giving them an opportunity to work; and not only giving them an opportunity to work but giving them an opportunity to work at jobs for which they were peculiarly fitted; and not only giving them an opportunity to work at jobs for which they were peculiarly fitted, but creating for them jobs of an interest and usefulness which they could not have expected to find in private employment." The statement somewhat distorts the work of the WPA, but it sums up the main outlines of the evolution of the relief program.

The various artistic and cultural employment programs of the WPA are excellent examples of how relief provided more than employment, though any of the youth agencies like the Civilian Conservation Corps or the National Youth Administration (it subsidized student work) would serve equally well. At its peak, the Federal Writers' Project employed some 6,000 journalists, poets, novelists, and Ph.D.'s of one sort or another; unknowns worked on the same payroll, if not side by side, with John Steinbeck, Vardis Fisher, and Conrad Aiken. The $46 million expended on art—that is, painting and sculpture—by the WPA in 1936–37 exceeded the artistic budget of any country outside the totalitarian orbit—and there art was frankly propagandistic. *Fortune,* in May, 1937, found the American government's sponsorship of art singularly free of censorship or propaganda. The magazine concluded that "by and large the Arts Projects have been given a freedom no one would have thought possible in a government run undertaking. And by and large that freedom has not been abused." During the first fifteen months of the Federal Music Project, some fifty million people heard live concerts; in the first year of the WPA Theater, sixty million people in thirty states saw performances, with weekly attendance running to half a million. T. S. Eliot's *Murder in the Cathedral,* too risky for a commercial producer, was presented in New York by the Federal Theater to 40,000 people at a top price of 55 cents.

"What the government's experiments in music, painting, and the theater actually did," concluded *Fortune* in May, 1937, "even in their first year, was to work a sort of cultural revolution in America." For the first time the American audience and the American artist were brought face to face for their mutual benefit. "Art in America is being given its chance," said the British writer Ford Madox Ford, "and there has been nothing like it since before the Reformation. . . ."

Instead of being ignored on the superficially plausible grounds of the exigencies of the depression, the precious skills of thousands of painters, writers, and musicians were utilized. By this timely rescue of skills, tastes, and talents from the deadening hand of unemployment, the American people, through their government, showed their humanity and social imagination. Important for the future was the foresight displayed in the conserving of artistic talents and creations for the enrichment of generations to come.

The entrance of the federal government into a vast program of relief work was an abrupt departure from all previous practice, but it proved enduring. "When President Roosevelt laid it down that government had a social responsibility to care for the victims of the business cycle," *Fortune* remarked prophetically in 1937, "he set in motion an irreversible process." The burden of unemployment relief was too heavy to be carried by local government or private charities in an industrialized society; from now on, the national government would be expected to shoulder the responsibility. "Those who are on relief and in close contact otherwise with public matters realize that what has happened to the country is a bloodless revolution," wrote an anonymous relief recipient in *Harper's* in 1936. The government, he said, has assumed a new role in depressions, and only the rich might still be oblivious to it. But they too "will know it by 1940. And in time," they will "come to approve the idea of everyone having enough to eat."[7] Few people escaped the wide net of the depression: "Anybody sinks after a while," the anonymous reliefer pointed out. "Even you would have if God hadn't preserved, without apparent rhyme or reason, your job and your income." That the depression was a threat to all was perhaps the first lesson gained from the 1930's.

The second was that only through collective defense could such a threat be met. By virtue of the vigorous attack made upon the economic problems of the thirties by the government, the age-old conviction that dips in the business cycle were either the will of God or the consequence of unalterable economic laws was effectively demolished. As recently as 1931, President Hoover had told an audience that some people "have indomitable confidence that by some legerdemain we can legislate ourselves out of a world-wide depression. Such views are as accurate as the belief that we can exorcise a Caribbean hurricane." From the experience of the depression era, the American people learned that something could and ought to be done when economic disaster strikes. No party and no politician with a future will ever again dare to take the fatalistic and defeatist course of Herbert Hoover in 1929–33.

As the enactment of the Employment Act of 1946 showed, the prevention of depression now occupies top listing among the social anxieties of the American people. The act created a permanent Council of Economic Advisers to the President, to keep him continuously informed on the state of the economy and to advise him on the measures necessary to avoid an economic decline. And the Joint Committee on the Economic Report does the same for Congress.

Today political figures who indignantly repudiate any "left-wing" philosophy of any sort readily accept this inheritance from the depression. "Never again

---

[7]The providing of work relief instead of the dole did more than fill hungry stomachs; it re-established faith in America and in one's fellow man. "I'm proud of our United States," said one relief recipient. "There ain't no other nation in the world that would have sense enough to think of WPA and all the other A's." The wife of one WPA worker was quoted as saying, "We aren't on relief any more—my man is working for the government."

shall we allow a depression in the United States," vowed Republican candidate Eisenhower in 1952. As soon as we "foresee the signs of any recession and depression," he promised, ". . . the full power of private industry, of municipal government, of state government, of the Federal Government will be mobilized to see that that does not happen." Ignoring the fact that as a prospective federal official he had promised more than he could deliver, he innocently and accurately added, "I cannot pledge you more than that." Sensing the tremendous importance of the matter to the American people, Eisenhower made substantially the same statement three other times—at Yonkers, Peoria, and Pittsburgh. At Yonkers he said that he had "repeated this particular pledge over and over again in the United States" and that he and his associates were "dedicated to this proposition. . . ."

In the White House, Eisenhower continued to reflect this underlying and persistent fear that a depression would once again stride though the land. According to the account in Robert Donovan's semiofficial *Eisenhower: The Inside Story,* at session after session of the Cabinet during the recession of 1953–54, it was the President who stressed the urgency of the economic situation. It was he who constantly prodded Arthur F. Burns of the Council of Economic Advisers to prepare plans with which to forestall a serious drop in the economic indicators. Indeed as late as June, 1954, just after Burns had delivered an optimistic report on the condition and future of the economy, as Donovan tells it, "The President . . . was still concerned about whether the administration was doing enough. Even though it jarred the logic of some members of the Cabinet, he insisted, everything possible must be done to restore vigor to the economy. It was important, the President said, to produce results and to err on the side of doing too much rather than too little."

In the midst of the recession of 1957–58, Vice-President Nixon, speaking on April 24, 1958, specifically repudiated the Hoover approach of permitting the economy to right itself without government intervention. "Let us recognize once and for all," he told his audience, "that the time is past in the United States when the Federal Government can stand by and allow a recession to be prolonged or to deepen into depression without decisive Government action." Though Eisenhower was obviously worried that hasty measures might bring on further inflation, on May 20, in a public address, he agreed with the Vice-President that the government has "a continuing responsibility . . . to help counteract recession." In the same speech the President enumerated concrete measures already taken, such as extension of unemployment benefits, speeding up of defense and civilian procurement, acceleration of government construction projects, and the easing of credit by the Federal Reserve.

The Republican administration's evident acceptance of the new obligations of government in the economy is strikingly suggestive of the shock which the depression dealt conventional economic thought in America. . . .

Was It a New or Old Deal?

One of the most enduring monuments to the Great Depression was that congeries of contradictions, naïveté, humanitarianism, realistic politics, and economic horse sense called the New Deal of Franklin D. Roosevelt. As the governmental agent which recast American thinking on the responsibilities of government, the New Deal was clearly the offspring of the depression. As we have seen, it was also more than that: it was a revitalization of the Democratic party; it was the political manifestation of that new spirit of reform which was stirring among the ranks of labor and the Negro people.

In their own time and since, the New Deal and Franklin Roosevelt have had a polarizing effect upon Americans. Probably at no time before Roosevelt has the leader of a great democratic nation come to symbolize as he did the hopes and the fears of so many people.[8] Not even Jackson, in whom Roosevelt himself recognized a President of his own popularity- and hatred-producing caliber, could rival him. Over a decade after Roosevelt's death, the mention of his name still evokes emotions, betrayed by the wistful look in the eye or in the hard set of the jaw. The election of 1956, moreover, demonstrated once again that the Old Guard of the Republican party still fights the dead Roosevelt while the Democratic party wanders leaderless in his absence. This too is a measure of the political revolution he led.

For the Democratic party, Roosevelt was like a lightning rod, drawing to himself all the venom and hatred of the opposition, only to discharge it harmlessly; nothing, it seemed, could weaken his personal hold on the affections of the majority of Americans. That something more was involved than sheer popularity is shown by the example of Dwight Eisenhower. Though held in even greater popular esteem, Eisenhower has been unable to invest his party with his own vote-getting power; Republicans lose though Eisenhower wins. The difference between F.D.R. and Ike is that one stood for a program, a hope, and a future, while the other stands for himself as a good, well-intentioned man whom all instinctively trust and perhaps even admire. The one is a leader of a nation, the other a popular hero. Roosevelt is already a member of that tiny pantheon of great leaders of Americans in which Washington, Jackson, Lincoln, and Wilson are included; it is difficult to believe that Eisenhower will be included. His monument is more likely to be inscribed: "The best-liked man ever to be President."

In the thirties, as now, the place of the New Deal in the broad stream of American development has been a matter of controversy. Historians and commentators on the American scene have not yet reached a firm agreement—if they ever will—as to whether the New Deal was conservative or radical in character, though it does appear that the consensus now seems to lean toward calling it conservative and traditional.[9] Certainly if one searches the writings and utterances of

---

[8]According to Harold Ickes, Roosevelt was profoundly struck by the adoration which was bestowed upon him by his admirers. During the 1936 campaign, the President told Ickes "that there was something terrible about the crowds that lined the streets along which he passed. He went on to explain what he meant, which was exclamations from individuals in the crowd, such as 'He saved my home,' 'He gave me a job,' 'God bless you, Mr. President,' etc." In May, 1936, Marquis Childs published an article in *Harper's*, entitled "They Hate Roosevelt," in which he described and tried to account for the unreasoning hatred for the President on the part of what Childs called the upper 2 percent of the population.

[9]For example, one of the most recent short evaluations of the New Deal, by a most knowledgeable historian, Arthur Link, concludes as follows: "The chief significance of the reform legislation of the 1930's was its essentially conservative character and the fact that it stemmed from a half century or more of discussion and practical experience and from ideas proposed as well by Republicans as by Democrats." *American Epoch* (New York, 1955), p. 425.

Franklin Roosevelt, his own consciousness of conservative aims is quickly apparent. "The New Deal is an old deal—as old as the earliest aspirations of humanity for liberty and justice and the good life," he declared in 1934. "It was this administration," he told a Chicago audience in 1936, "which saved the system of private profit and free enterprise after it had been dragged to the brink of ruin. . . ."

But men making a revolution among a profoundly conservative people do not advertise their activity, and above all Franklin Roosevelt understood the temper of his people.[10] Nor should such a statement be interpreted as an insinuation of high conspiracy—far from it. Roosevelt was at heart a conservative, as his lifelong interest in history, among other things, suggests. But he was without dogma in his conservatism, which was heavily interlaced with genuine concern for people.[11] He did not shy away from new means and new approaches to problems when circumstances demanded it. His willingness to experiment, to listen to his university-bred Brains Trust, to accept a measure like the TVA, reveal the flexibility in his thought. Both his lack of theoretical presuppositions and his flexibility are to be seen in the way he came to support novel measures like social security and the Wagner Act. Response to popular demand was the major reason. "The Congress can't stand the pressure of the Townsend Plan unless we have a real old-age insurance system," he complained to Frances Perkins, "nor can I face the country without having . . . a solid plan which will give some assurance to old people of systematic assistance upon retirement." In like manner, the revolutionary NLRA was adopted as a part of his otherwise sketchy and rule-of-thumb philosophy of society. Though ultimately Roosevelt championed the Wagner bill in the House, it was a belated conversion dictated by the foreshadowed success of the measure and the recent invalidation of the NRA. In his pragmatic and common-sense reactions to the exigencies of the depression, Roosevelt, the easygoing conservative, ironically enough became the embodiment of a new era and a new social philosophy for the American people.

"This election," Herbert Hoover presciently said in 1932, "is not a mere shift from the ins to the outs. It means deciding the direction our nation will take over a century to come." The election of Franklin Roosevelt, he predicted, would result in "a radical departure from the foundations of 150 years which have made this the greatest nation in the world." Though Hoover may be charged with nothing more than campaign flourishing, it is nevertheless a fact that his speech was made just after Roosevelt's revealing Commonwealth Club address of September. Only in this single utterance, it should be remembered, did Roosevelt disclose in clear outline the philosophy and program which was later to be the New Deal. "Every man has a right to life," he had said, "and this means that he has also a right to make a comfortable living. . . . Our government, formal and

---

[10]It is significant that only once during the 1932 campaign, according to Ernest K. Lindley, did Roosevelt call for "a revolution"; and then he promptly qualified it to "the right kind, the only kind of revolution this nation can stand for—a revolution at the ballot box."

[11]When an economist suggested to F.D.R. that the depression be permitted to run its course and that then the economic system would soon right itself—as Frances Perkins tells the story—the President's face took on a "gray look of horror" as he told the economist: "People aren't cattle you know!"

informal, political and economic," he went on, "owes to everyone an avenue to possess himself of a portion of that plenty [from our industrial society] sufficient for his needs, through his own work." Here were the intimations of those new goals which the New Deal set for America.

Accent as heavily as one wishes the continuity between the reforms of the Progressive era and the New Deal, yet the wide difference between the goals of the two periods still remains. The Progressive impulse was narrowly reformist: it limited business, it assisted agriculture, it freed labor from some of the shackles imposed by the courts, but it continued to conceive of the state as policeman or judge and nothing more. The New Deal, on the other hand, was more than a regulator—though it was that too, as shown by the SEC and the reinvigoration of the antitrust division of the Justice Department. To the old goals for America set forth and fought for by the Jeffersonians and the Progressives the New Deal appended new ones. Its primary and general innovation was the guaranteeing of a minimum standard of welfare for the people of the nation. WPA and the whole series of relief agencies which were a part of it, wages and hours legislation, AAA, bank deposit insurance, and social security,[12] each illustrates this new conception of the federal government. A resolution offered by New Deal Senator Walsh in 1935 clearly enunciated the new obligations of government. The resolution took notice of the disastrous effects of the depression "upon the lives of young men and women . . ." and then went on to say that "it is the duty of the Federal Government to use every possible means of opening up opportunities" for the youth of the nation "so that they may be rehabilitated and restored to a *decent standard of living* and ensured proper development of their talents. . . ."

But the guarantor state as it developed under the New Deal was more active and positive than this. It was a vigorous and dynamic force in the society, energizing and, if necessary, supplanting private enterprise when the general welfare required it. With the Wagner Act, for example, the government served notice that it would actively participate in securing the unionization of the American worker; the state was no longer to be an impartial policeman merely keeping order; it now declared for the side of labor. When social and economic problems like the rehabilitation of the Valley of the Tennessee were ignored or shirked by private enterprise, then the federal government undertook to do the job. Did private enterprise fail to provide adequate and sufficient housing for a minimum standard of welfare for the people, then the government would build houses. As a result, boasted Nathan Straus, head of the U.S. Housing Authority, "for the first time in a hundred years the slums of America ceased growing and began to shrink."

Few areas of American life were beyond the touch of the experimenting fingers of the New Deal; even the once sacrosanct domain of prices and the

---

[12]Social security is an excellent example of how, under the New Deal, reform measures, when they conflicted with recovery, were given priority. In siphoning millions of dollars of social security taxes from the purchasing power of the workers, social security was a deflationary measure, which must have seriously threatened the precariously based new economic recovery. For this reason and others, Abraham Epstein, the foremost authority in America on social security, denounced the act as a "sharing of poverty."

valuation of money felt the tinkering. The devaluation of the dollar, the gold-purchase program, the departure from the gold standard—in short, the whole monetary policy undertaken by F.D.R. as a means to stimulate recovery through a price rise—constituted an unprecedented repudiation of orthodox public finance. To achieve that minimum standard of well-being which the depression had taught the American people to expect of their government, nothing was out of bounds.

But it is not the variety of change which stamps the New Deal as the creator of a new America; its significance lies in the permanence of its program. For, novel as the New Deal program was, it has, significantly, not been repudiated by the Eisenhower administration, the first Republican government since the reforms were instituted. Verbally, it is true, the Republican administration has had to minimize its actual commitments to the New Deal philosophy, and it tends to trust private business more than the New Dealers did—witness, for example, its elimination of the minor governmental manufacturing enterprises which competed with private firms. But despite this, the administration's firm commitment to the guaranteeing of prosperity and averting depression at all costs is an accurate reflection of the American people's agreement with the New Deal's diagnosis of the depression. Nor has the Republican party dared to repeal or even emasculate the legislation which made up the vitals of the New Deal: TVA, banking and currency, SEC, social security, the Wagner Act, and fair treatment of the Negro. The New Deal Revolution has become so much a part of the American Way that no political party which aspires to high office dares now to repudiate it.

It may or may not be significant in this regard (for apothegms are more slippery than precise) but it is nonetheless interesting that Roosevelt and Eisenhower have both been impressed with the same single sentence from Lincoln regarding the role of government. "The legitimate object of Government," wrote Lincoln, "is to do for a community of people whatever they need to have done but cannot do at all or cannot do so well for themselves in their separate or individual capacities." Twice, in 1934 and again in 1936, F.D.R. in public addresses used this expression to epitomize his own New Deal, and Robert Donovan in his officially inspired book on the Eisenhower administration writes that this same "fragment of Lincoln's writing . . . Eisenhower uses time and again in describing his own philosophy of government." Between Lincoln and Eisenhower there was no Republican President, except perhaps Theodore Roosevelt, who would have been willing to subscribe to such a free-wheeling description of the federal power; in this can be measured the impact of the New Deal and the depression.

The conclusion seems inescapable that, traditional as the words may have been in which the New Deal expressed itself, in actuality it was a revolutionary response to a revolutionary situation. In its long history America has passed through two revolutions since the first one in 1776, but only the last two, the Civil War and the depression, were of such force as to change the direction of the relatively smooth flow of its progress. The Civil War rendered a final and irrevocable decision in the long debate over the nature of the Union and the position of the Negro in American society. From that revolutionary experience, America emerged a strong national state and dedicated by the words of its most hallowed document to the inclusion of the black man in a democratic culture. The searing ordeal of the Great Depression purged the American people of their belief in the limited powers of the federal government and convinced them of the necessity of the guarantor state. And as the Civil War constituted a watershed in American thought, so the depression and its New Deal marked the crossing of a divide from which, it would seem, there could be no turning back.

The Myth of the New Deal

Great Depression, labor unrest, massive unemployment, growing consciousness among the working classes, bitter hostility toward the multimillion-
dollar corporations, failure of the reigning Republican Administration to quiet
the brewing explosion—and then the New Deal. The social revolution, which
many expected and others feared, failed to materialize. Why? Was it because the
New Deal, in its own special way, was indeed a third American Revolution?

From the perspective of the 1970s, with the stark realization that the United
States had failed to deal with the race question, or to eradicate poverty, or even to
begin to deal with the urban crisis, or to handle the general malaise and cultural
poverty, or to adapt itself to the growing realization that revolutions abroad
would have to be accepted and dealt with on their own terms—all of these events
of the past ten years seemingly provided living evidence that a revolution had not
occurred.

The new generation of New Left historians has asserted cogently that the
New Deal instituted changes that only buttressed the corporate-capitalist order;
that the vaunted Welfare State reforms hardly addressed themselves to the existing social needs of the 1930s, not to speak of working to end poverty, racism,
and war. Historians Howard Zinn and Barton J. Bernstein have already written
critical essays seeking to evaluate the New Deal from a radical perspective, and
this essay shall not seek to repeat the critique advanced therein. The essence of
their critical view has been best expressed by Bernstein:

*The liberal reforms of the New Deal did not transform the American system;
they conserved and protected American corporate capitalism, occasionally by absorbing parts of threatening programs. There was no significant redistribution*

of power in American society, only limited recognition of other organized groups. . . . The New Deal failed to solve the problem of depression, it failed to raise the impoverished, it failed to redistribute income, it failed to extend equality and generally countenanced racial discrimination and segregation.

Once having presented this argument, however, the radical critic has in effect merely chastised the New Deal for what it failed to achieve. This does not work to answer the counterargument that Franklin D. Roosevelt and the New Dealers wanted more, but were stopped short because of the power of the congressional conservative block and other impenetrable obstacles.

It is undeniable that to many of the over-forty generation, Franklin D. Roosevelt was and remains the unassailable hero—the man who used all the powers at his command to ease the plight of the dispossessed, and who introduced dramatic reforms that would soon be accepted by the most staunch Old Guard Republican. That generation remembers the animosity with which many in the business community greeted Roosevelt, and the way in which Roosevelt condemned the forces of organized wealth that were out to destroy him. They did not have the tools of historical perspective to evaluate F.D.R.'s actual performance, or to understand what historian Paul Conkin has noted: that the New Deal policies actually functioned in a probusiness manner. . . .

What Conkin was suggesting is that the anger of some businessmen was misdirected; another example of how members of the governing class can be so shortsighted that they will oppose their own best long-range interests. The confusion of the businessmen had its mirror image in the high regard in which so many members of the underclass held F.D.R. and the New Deal. Roosevelt was able, for a while, to build and maintain the famous New Deal coalition that swept him into office in 1936. White workers from the North, blacks from the urban ghettos, and farmers from the Midwest all responded to the New Deal and claimed it as their own. Explaining this success as a result of the "powers of rhetoric," as did Bernstein, evades the real question. How could rhetoric alone convince so many that their lives had changed, if indeed, life was the same as it had always been? Perhaps reality did change just enough so that the failure of the New Deal to make substantive structural changes remained hidden.

Before we can begin to deal with these questions, it may be wise to start by citing the answer presented to the New Left historians by the dean of American corporate liberalism, Arthur M. Schlesinger, Jr., author in 1948 of the theory of a crucial "vital center" in American politics. Schlesinger has carefully presented his generation's answer to the New Left, and has defended the traditional view that the New Deal was a major watershed in American history.

A young radical told him, Schlesinger wrote, that all F.D.R. did was

"abort the revolution by incremental gestures." At the same time, he dangerously cultivated a mood for charismatic mass policies, dangerously strengthened the Presidency, dangerously concentrated power in the national government. In foreign affairs, he was an imperialist who went to war against Germany and Japan because they were invading markets required by American capitalism.

Claiming that Roosevelt "will survive this assault from the left as he has survived the earlier assault from the right," Schlesinger ended with his own brief estimate of F.D.R.'s policies and times. Roosevelt

led our nation through a crisis of confidence by convincing the American people that they had unsuspected reserves of decency, steadfastness and concern. He defeated the grand ideologists of his age by showing how experiment could overcome dogma, in peace and in war.

Schlesinger's writings help us to understand how those who only mildly benefited from the New Deal praised it, defended it, and allowed their experience during the 1930s to shape their social and political attitudes for more than a decade. Undoubtedly, many Americans have the same analysis of Social Security as does Schlesinger.

No government bureau ever directly touched the lives of so many millions of Americans—the old, the jobless, the sick, the needy, the blind, the mothers, the children—with so little confusion or complaint. . . . For all the defects of the Act, it still meant a tremendous break with the inhibitions of the past. The federal government was at last charged with the obligation to provide its citizens a measure of protection from the hazards and vicissitudes of life. . . . With the Social Security Act, the constitutional dedication of federal power to the general welfare began a new phase of national history.

The assumptions behind Schlesinger's evaluation of Social Security are those he revealed years earlier. Writing in his classic *The Age of Jackson*, Schlesinger noted that "Liberalism in America has been ordinarily the movement of the part of the other sections of society to restrain the power of the business community." This statement assumes that a popular movement, opposed by business, continually arises in America to challenge the one-sided power of large corporate business. But new historical research by a generation of revisionists has all but wiped out this assumption. William Appleman Williams, Gabriel Kolko, James Weinstein, and Murray N. Rothbard have argued that liberalism has actually been the ideology of dominant business groups, and that they have in reality favored state intervention to supervise corporate activity. Liberalism changed from the individualism of laissez-faire to the social control of twentieth-century corporate liberalism. Unrestrained ruthless competition from the age of primitive capital accumulation became an anachronism, and the new social and political regulatory measures emanating from the Progressive Era were not so much victories for the people over the interests, as examples of movement for state intervention to supervise corporate activity on behalf of the large corporate interests themselves.

Just as all historians used to look at the accomplishments of the Progressive Era as antibusiness, equating state regulation with regulation over business, and with the assumption that corporate business opposed the new regulatory acts, so do many historians of the New Deal view the achievements of F.D.R.'s first two terms as a continuation of the Progressive tradition. The New Deal thus becomes the culmination of a "progressive" process that began with the age of Jackson.

Once again, it is assumed that the "money changers" whom Roosevelt supposedly drove out of the temple were the New Deal's major opposition, and that government programs were per se progressive and part of a new phase of our history.

This analysis was stated most strongly by Carl N. Degler, when he referred to the New Deal as the "Third American Revolution." Seeing in the various New Deal measures "a new conception of the good society," Degler claimed path-breaking significance once the "nation at large accepted the government as a permanent influence in the economy." Is such an influence sufficient to describe the New Deal as revolutionary?

To Degler it was. Like Schlesinger, historian Degler saw the Social Security Act as revolutionary because "it brought government into the lives of people as nothing had since the draft and the income tax." Yet another proof of revolutionary effect, even more important, was the "alteration in the position and power of labor." Noting that the decline in union growth had come to an end, and that the new spurt in unionism was that of the industrial unionism of the CIO, Degler argued that it was Robert F. Wagner's National Labor Relations Act that "threw the enormous prestige and power of the government behind the drive for organizing workers." The "placing of the government on the side of unionization," Degler wrote, "was of central importance in the success of many an organizational drive of the CIO, notably those against Ford and Little Steel."

In summation, the Wagner Act was depicted as revolutionary because, prior to the Act, no federal law prevented employers from discharging workers for exercising their rights or from refusing to bargain with a labor union, whereas after the Act was passed, workers had new rights against their employers. The result, according to Degler, was a truly pluralistic structure to American society. "Big Labor now took its place beside Big Business and Big Government to complete a triumvirate of economic power." The Wagner Act particularly revealed that:

the government served notice that it would actively participate in securing the unionization of the American workers; the state was no longer to be a impartial policeman merely keeping order; it now declared for the side of labor.

Although the New Deal used traditional rhetoric, Degler asserted, "in actuality it was a revolutionary response to a revolutionary situation."

This estimate was upheld by even such a critical historian as William E. Leuchtenburg. Although he modified Degler's analysis a degree, by noting that the Wagner Act was partially motivated by a desire to "contain 'unbalanced and radical' labor groups," Leuchtenburg agreed that the New Deal was a "radically new departure." But to Leuchtenburg, the New Deal had major shortcomings. It failed to demonstrate "that it could achieve prosperity in peacetime," perhaps its greatest failure. The fact that the unemployed disappeared only with war production meant to Leuchtenburg that the New Deal was only "a halfway revolution; it swelled the ranks of the bourgeoisie but left many Americans—sharecroppers, slum dwellers, most Negroes—outside of the new equilibrium." But, argued Leuchtenburg, it was a revolution anyway. Here, we might raise the question of what type of "revolution" is it that fails to deal with the most basic problems produced by the old order, especially when an end to unemployment was the key task confronting the first New Deal, and while there were still by Leuchtenburg's count six million unemployed "as late as 1941."

The myth of a New Deal revolution, or a new departure, or a basic watershed, call it what you will, dies hard. New Left critics have correctly emphasized the New Deal's failures to destroy some part of the myth. But their critique, valuable as it has been, has failed to take up a more essential question. How does one confront the truth that the New Deal obviously did move in new directions, in some ways quite dramatically, and still keep the old order intact? And how is it that, although the old order remained basically untouched and even preserved, Roosevelt and the New Dealers were able to win the everlasting gratitude of the dispossessed and the white working class?

Rather than discuss all of the policies of the New Deal, we can begin to cope with this question by a more thorough look at a few key areas, particularly the National Recovery Administration (NRA), the birth of the Congress of Industrial Organizations (CIO) and the origins of the Wagner or National Labor Relations Act, and the passage of the Social Security Act. These three areas have been pointed to as evidence for the pathbreaking if not revolutionary character of the New Deal. Close attention to them should therefore prove most helpful in arriving at a more historically accurate assessment of what the New Deal wrought.

Most historians have discussed the Social Security Act in terms of what it offered American citizens for the first time, not in terms of how and why it was passed. Fortunately, sociologist G. William Domhoff has enabled us to take a new look at what lay behind some of the major New Deal reforms. Domhoff, following the lead supplied by the New Left revisionist historians, put his emphasis on the sponsorship of major reforms by leading moderate big businessmen and liberal-minded lawyers from large corporate enterprises. Working through reform bodies such as the American Association for Labor Legislation (AALL) and the Fraternal Order of Eagles, model bills for social insurance had been proposed and discussed in the United States as early as 1910–15.

These proposals had come to naught. But when the Great Depression hit, the need for reform was clear to all. The first unemployment bill in the United States passed the Wisconsin State Legislature in 1932, and it had evolved from a bill drafted by John R. Commons for the AALL in 1921. In the discussions in Washington, which eventually led to the Social Security Act, AALL members taking part included Paul A. Raushenbush and his wife Elizabeth Brandeis, Henry Dennison, and three New Dealers trained in corporate law, Charles W. Wyzanski, Jr., Thomas H. Eliot, and Thomas G. Corcoran. Wyzanski was graduated from Harvard and Exeter and was with the Boston law firm Ropes, Grey, Boyden and Perkins. Eliot was graduated from Brown, Nichols preparatory school, and Harvard College, and was a grandson of a former president of Harvard. Corcoran was graduated from Harvard Law School and was with the New York corporate law firm Cotton and Franklin.

In June 1934, Roosevelt appointed a Committee on Economic Security, headed by Secretary of Labor Frances Perkins. It included Treasury Secretary Henry Morgenthau, Jr., Secretary of Agriculture Henry A. Wallace, Attorney General Homer Cummings, and F.D.R.'s chief aide, Harry Hopkins. They met for the purpose of working on a comprehensive social security and old-age pensions bill. Like any other committee, they depended on advisors, and among their chief aides were men identified closely with the work of the AALL. But the basic outlines of the plan were put forth by F.D.R. himself in his June 6, 1934, message to Congress. The President called for federal-state cooperation, a contributory plan rather than a government subsidy through a tax increase, and he stressed the need for employment stabilization.

The Committee on Economic Security got to work after F.D.R.'s speech, and met eleven times. On January 15, 1935, they presented the President with their report. Two days later, Roosevelt sent his own report to Congress. Roosevelt's proposal was essentially the one prepared by corporate lawyers like Thomas Eliot, who played the major role in drafting the "bill to carry out the committee's recommendations." Yet large-scale opposition to the proposed bill came immediately from other business circles, especially from the National Association of Manufacturers.

What is important is that liberal historians have traditionally equated the NAM and small-business opposition to social reform legislation as business-community opposition. They have depicted an all-out fight between the forces of big business versus the people; the former opposing and the latter supporting reform. In his book Schlesinger wrote as follows:

While the friends of social security were arguing out the details of the program, other Americans were regarding the whole idea with consternation, if not with horror. Organized business had long warned against such pernicious notions. "Unemployment insurance cannot be placed on a sound financial basis," said the National Industrial Conference Board; it will facilitate "ultimate socialist control of life and industry," said the National Association of Manufacturers. . . . One after another, business leaders appeared before House and Senate Committees to invest such dismal prophecies with what remained of their authority.
Republicans in the House faithfully reflected the business position.

Of significance are Schlesinger's last words, "the business position." This telling phrase reveals the ideological mask on reality that helps to hide the manner in which the corporate state maintains its hegemony over the country. Schlesinger not only overstated big-business opposition; he did not account for the *support* given Social Security by moderate yet powerful representatives of the large-corporation community. Particularly important is the backing given the Act by the Business Advisory Council, which formed a committee on Social Security headed by Gerard Swope, president of General Electric, Walter Teagle of Standard Oil, Morris Leeds of the AALL, and Robert Elbert. These men were major corporate leaders, or as Domhoff put it, "some of the most powerful bankers and industrialists in the country." . . .

Despite the support given the Act by these key corporate figures, the original bill was to be watered down by the Congress. This was because many congressmen and senators reflected their local constituencies, which included local antilabor and small-town mentality NAM business-types. Congress, in other words, did not have the political sophistication of the corporate liberals. Once the bill got to Congress, the setting of minimum state standards in old-age assistance was discarded, as was the concept that states had to select administering personnel on a merit basis. Workers were to contribute half of the old-age pension funds, while employers paid unemployment compensation. But the large corporations would still be able to pass the costs of their contribution to the consumer. Finally, the rich were not to be taxed to help pay for the program.

As Domhoff showed, the Social Security Act was the measured response of the moderate members of the power elite to the discontent of the thirties. These moderates took their program, based on models introduced by various corporate policy-making bodies during the previous twenty years, to the Congress. Congress, however, listened more to the NAM-type businessmen. The result was a legislative compromise between the original moderate and conservative position on the Act. Radicals among labor who wanted a comprehensive social-insurance program remained unsatisfied. It was their pressure, however, that induced the moderates to present their plan to Congress. The demands of the poor and the working class provided the steam that finally brought the modified Act to fruition.

The result, as Domhoff wrote:

from the point of view of the power elite was a restabilization of the system. It put a floor under consumer demand, raised people's expectations for the future and directed political energies back into conventional channels. The difference between what could be and what is remained very, very large for the poor, the sick, and the aged. The wealth distribution did not change, decision-making power remained in the hands of upper-class leaders, and the basic principles that encased the conflict were set forth by moderate members of the power elite.

Social Security may have been a symbolic measure of the new Welfare State. But, to the corporate liberals in the governing class, it served as the type of legislation that eased tension, created stability, and prevented or broke any movements for radical structural change. Hence, it served an essentially conservative purpose because it helped maintain the existing system of production and distribution.

The pattern of corporate support to New Deal programs is even more vivid when we consider the first great program initiated by the New Deal to produce recovery, the National Recovery Administration. NRA arose from a background of collectivist plans such as the one proposed in 1931 by Gerard Swope, president of General Electric. Presented to a conference of the National Electrical Manufacturers Association, the plan, as Murray N. Rothbard has described it, "amounted to a call for compulsory cartelization of American business—an imitation of fascism and an anticipation of the NRA." . . .

It is no accident that the early New Deal was characterized by the introduction of planning techniques that had antecedents in trade associations developed within industry during the Hoover years. Bernard Baruch's War Industries Board and the Hoover trade associations reached fruition with F.D.R.'s NRA. Men who had been involved with wartime planning were brought back to government service. "In quest of a precedent for government-business cooperation," Leuchtenburg wrote, *the draftsmen of the recovery bill turned to the experience with industrial mobilization in World War I. Swope himself had served in a war agency, and his plan was one of many . . . which drew on recollections of government coordination of the economy during the war. Since they rejected laissez-faire, yet shrank from embracing socialism, the planners drew on the experience of the War Industries Board because it offered an analogue which provided a maximum of government direction with a minimum of challenge to the institutions of a profit economy. . . .*

As Leuchtenburg went on to state, the New Dealers also rejected class struggle, as well as "mass action and socialist planning, and assumed a community of interest of the managers of business corporations and the directors of government agencies." They feared not discredited conservatives, but the "antiplutocratic movements," or we might put it, the forces of the radical left. Hence the New Deal cartelization efforts, which culminated in NRA.

One of NRA's major architects was Donald Richberg, who had been chosen for his position because of his prolabor background. But again, Richberg's commitment to labor lay within the framework of the corporate state. As a young Chicago Lawyer, Richberg had written both the Railway Labor Act of 1926 and later the Norris-LaGuardia Act of 1932. He was chosen to help frame the NRA, Schlesinger pointed out, because Hugh Johnson wanted Richberg because "he assumed that Richberg had the confidence of labor and liberals." No other early appointment of F.D.R.'s, Schlesinger concluded, gave "more satisfaction to labor and liberals than that of Richberg."

As a prolabor formulator of the NRA, Richberg revealed his private vision of a new corporate state, but one in which industrial unions would have to become the prerequisite for an American corporatism. "If industrial workers were adequately organized," he explained, "it would be entirely practical to create industrial councils composed of representatives of managers, investors and workers and then to create a national council composed of similar representatives of all essential industries." In this council, "all producing and consuming interests would be so represented that one group could hardly obtain sanction for a policy clearly contrary to the general welfare." Richberg was critical of craft-union leaders. He wished they had "seized" labor's great "opportunity to organize the unemployed," and simply ignored "the hampering tradition of craft unionism" by organizing men and women "denied their inherent right to work." Labor should have demanded that "their government should no longer be controlled by rulers of commerce and finance who have utterly failed to meet their obligations." If such a movement had been built, if labor had created one "mighty arm and voice" of the "unemployed millions," Congress would have listened to the dispossessed.

Richberg also forecast the conservative role that industrial unions would play. "Let me warn those who desire to preserve the existing order," he cautioned, "but intend to do nothing to reform it, that if this depression continues much longer the unemployed will be organized and action of a revolutionary character will be demanded." To avoid that, people had to be put back to work and mass purchasing power had to be increased. The solution was to mobilize the nation "through the immediate creation of a national planning council, composed of representatives of major economic interests who recognize the necessity of a planned economy." The need: to avoid radicalism. The means: a formal American corporate state, or the NRA.

The NRA, which became law on June 16, 1933, was the agency meant to evolve into a corporate state. The NRA, John T. Flynn perceptively noted in 1934, was based on the need of businessmen to have the government control prices, production, and trade practices. "Industry wanted not freedom from regulation," he wrote, "but the right to enjoy regulation." Modification of antitrust laws was desired "so that employers might unite to fabricate and enforce regimentation of industry though trade associations." The NRA also developed plans for shorter working hours and payment of minimum wages; but Flynn noted that it was "pure fiction" that such legislation was forced on big business against its will. Actually, the corporations wanted the opportunity to force the NRA on the "unwilling ten percent" of smaller operators who competed unfairly by cutting costs through wage reductions. The NRA, Flynn remarked, represented almost "entirely the influence and ideal of big businessmen." . . .

The NRA reformers, unlike our contemporary liberal historians, understood that their program was meant to be a conservative prop to the existing order. They also realized the dire need to include social reform as an essential component of the corporate state. They understood that many liberals and even political radicals would overlook the conservative origin and effect of the NRA if reform, especially public works, was offered as part of a package deal. Hence Title I of the NRA promoted the organization of industry to achieve cooperative action among trade associations, and it included the codes of fair competition and exemption of industry from prosecution under the antitrust laws. Title II set up a Public Works Association with a federal appropriation of three billion dollars. It should be understandable why Henry I. Harriman, president of the United States Chamber of Commerce, argued that there was "ample justification for a reasonable public works program" in conjunction with a corporate plan that would free industry from antitrust restrictions. If there was any doubt that the large corporations would support a program that would result in wage increases along with a fair return on dividends, Harriman assured reluctant congressmen that the "big ones will rush to it."

But the problem was to win the allegiance not of the big ones, but of the "liberals." The means to this end was the technique of public works. Of all the New Deal reforms, public works seemed to most people to have the aura of "socialism" or at least of an attack on private interests. To the hungry and unemployed, it symbolized a direct concern by the government for their plight. That public works, as Murray N. Rothbard has shown, was introduced effectively by the Hoover Administration was unrecognized. That the New Deal's public works was of a limited nature and did not interfere with private business prerogatives went unnoticed. In the area in which public-works development was most needed, housing, the New Deal program was hardly successful and in many ways a total failure. All this was ignored. The name *public works* and the PWA itself produced a sympathetic response from the populace, the "liberal" political groups, and the organized political left. . . .

In the words of William Appleman Williams, our leading radical historian:

the New Deal saved the system. It did not change it. Later developments and characteristics of American society which suggest an opposite conclusion are no more than the full extension and maturation of much earlier ideas and policies that were brought together in what a high New Dealer called a shotgun approach to dealing with the depression.

Unlike . . . Williams, most of our contemporary historians do not seem to realize that institution of "a new set of plans" is conservative, not to speak of not being radical or revolutionary. But what happens when an area emerges where the "old methods" are entirely done away with? Can one rightly call such an area of innovation revolutionary? As Degler has argued, this is indeed the case with organized labor, and the passage of the Wagner or National Labor Relations Act. More than any other piece of New Deal legislation, the policy toward labor seemed to suggest a new revolutionary stance toward the worker on the part of government.

In reality, the role played by the Wagner Act was the same as that of the NRA and the other conservative New Deal programs. It was the Wagner Act that allowed the Administration to obtain the final integration of organized labor into the existing political economy of corporation capitalism. Unions, which had a sudden revival under the NRA, even before the Wagner Act period, were industrial in nature—the United Mine Workers and the Amalgamated Clothing Workers showing exceptional growth. Craft unions grew only 13 percent between 1933 and 1935, as against 132 percent by the AF of L's four industrial unions and 125 percent for their semi-industrial unions. The NRA provided the original impetus to organization. Between July and August, 1933, the AF of L issued 340 new charters to affiliated local trade and federal labor unions, and Green estimated that in two months AF of L membership increased by about 1,500,000 members.

With the NRA, the federal government took over the traditional organizing function that had previously been an exclusive union domain. The old AF of L craft unions had refused to initiate a widespread program of unionization in unorganized basic industries. But now the New Deal was seeking a labor movement that would gain working-class support and provide the necessary structural parallel to industry that would allow integration of the labor force into the new system. The New Deal, contemporary reporter Benjamin Stolberg observed, "needed organized labor to save big business." While the NRA was a "price fixing mechanism to enable big industry to regain the control of scarcity," it needed big labor to police "the 'social planning' of stabilizing prices in an economic system" that was "partly irresponsibly competitive and partly dictatorially monopolistic." Thus the NRA turned the labor movement "into a semipublic unionism whose organization was part of a government program." . . .

The leading figure among the moderates was Gerard Swope, president of General Electric. As chieftain of one of the key multimillion-dollar corporations, Swope was quite an important figure in the corporate community. Herbert Hoover had stood fast against introduction of his plan, viewing it as a stepping stone toward a business fascism. But during F.D.R.'s Administration, Swope began to get results. . . .

Swope understood what many contemporary historians do not. Industrial unionism was not inherently radical, and its recognition by government was not revolutionary. Rather, industrial unions functioned in the era of corporate capitalism to exert discipline on the work force so that labor productivity would be improved and cooperative relations with employers would emerge. The existence of such an industrial unionism benefited the long-range interests of the corporations. It was precisely for this reason that so many employers ignored section 7-a of the NRA, and continued to build their own company unions. They simply preferred to deal with their own unions organized industrially rather than with "legitimate" trade unions organized on a craft basis. . . .

The New Dealers devised, in this case, a means to integrate big labor into the corporate state. But only unions that were industrially organized, and which paralleled in their structure the organization of industry itself, could play the appropriate role. A successful corporate state required a safe industrial-union movement to work. It also required a union leadership that shared the desire to operate the economy from the top in formal conferences with the leaders of the other functional economic groups, particularly the corporate leaders. The CIO unions, led by Sidney Hillman of the Amalgamated Clothing Workers, provided such a union leadership.

It was for this reason that the moderates in the governing class pushed for passage of the Wagner Act. As Domhoff noted, the antiunion diehards did have leverage for one major reason.

From the point of view of the employers, it had to be an all or nobody proposition, for any holdouts would supposedly have the competitive advantage brought about by lower wage costs. Thus, the diehards held great power over the majority, making it ultimately necessary to legislate against them. Perhaps there is something to the claim that most employers would go along with union recognition if all their compatriots would. But not every employer would go along, which set the stage for the battle over the Wagner Act, a battle which precipitated a serious split in the power elite.

As Domhoff showed, the moderate members of the power elite played shrewd politics. After a vast amount of strikes occurred, they refused to heed the many calls for sending in troops. The result was that the diehards were forced into negotiation and compromise. Roosevelt even accused the NAM forces of trying to precipitate a general strike. But in refusing to stand with the antilabor groups, Roosevelt was not the master broker, a man who favored "a balance between business and labor"; rather, he was an

integral member of the upper class and its power elite. However, he was a member of that part of the power elite that had chosen a more moderate course in attempting to deal with the relationship of labor and capital. . . . While he did not encourage unionism, his record during the thirties makes very clear, he was nonetheless unwilling to smash it in the way the NAM had hoped to do since 1902.

Referring back to Roosevelt's prolabor ideology formed during World War I, when he was a member of the Executive Board of the National Civic Federation, Domhoff noted that when the "time came for choosing, he and the moderate members of the power elite chose bargaining rather than repression." . . .

Even if a majority of businessmen opposed the Wagner Act, the moderate group within the elite was able to use political power to its own advantage. Once the Supreme Court voted in favor of the Act, the NLRB [National Labor Relations Board], an administrative body, became the final arbitrator of all labor disputes. This was, as Domhoff wrote, the "favorite solution of the moderate members of the power elite, the 'nonpolitical' administrative body or regulatory agency." Thus Biddle noted that

the feature of the act attacked as the most radical was in fact the least novel—the provisions authorizing the Board to request a court to enforce its order, which derived from the Federal Trade Commission Act of 1914.

Even before the Court decision favorable to the Act, F.D.R. had moved to conciliate diehards among the elite. Working through Thomas Lamont, Roosevelt made overtures toward United States Steel. Lamont brought F.D.R. and U.S. Steel president Myron Taylor together, and a contract with the Steelworkers was signed on March 3, 1937, one month before the Court decision. Only Little Steel held out on its antiunion course. Roosevelt similarly worked with Bill Knudsen, head of General Motors, and with Walter P. Chrysler, who backed him in the 1936 election. According to Perkins, F.D.R. was able to gain help from Averell Harriman and Carl Grey of the Union Pacific Railroad, Daniel Willard of the Baltimore & Ohio, Walter Teagle of Standard Oil, Thomas Lamont of J.P. Morgan, Myron Taylor of U.S. Steel, Gerard Swope of General Electric, and textile manufacturer Robert Amory. "It may be surprising to some people," Perkins wrote:

to realize that men looked upon as the conservative branch of the Roosevelt Administration were cooperative in bringing about a new, more modern, and more reasonable attitude on the part of employers toward collective bargaining agreements.

But the final goal for which these conservative industrialists worked was the creation of an American corporate state. This was made clear in the 1960s by Leon Keyserling, who had been legislative assistant to Robert F. Wagner during the 1930s and who helped the group that formulated the Wagner Act's principles. In 1960, economist Keyserling called for a "new national agency to embody top level discussions among those who hoped that such a body would move the country away from fruitless wrangles between competing groups." He hoped that a new agency would bring the "organized powers in our enterprise system," unions and trade associations, into a "relationship of participation and concert with the efforts of government." He then noted that this was the goal fought for by Wagner during the 1930s.

This detailed examination of the roots of the Wagner Act, as well as the NRA and the Social Security Act, should help us to assess the meaning of the New Deal. We now should be able to answer some of the questions raised earlier. First, it is clear that nonelite groups—the unemployed, workers, farmers—were the beneficiaries of many of the new social reforms. Social Security did produce benefits despite its limitations, NRA did eliminate sweatshops, and organized labor was able to strengthen its position in society. Reform, after all, would be a meaningless word if it did not have any partial effect. That is, indeed, the very meaning of reform.

But reform is not revolution. Revolution means a substantive fundamental change in the existing social structure, a massive dislocation and revamping of the existing system of production and distribution. Schlesinger's "New Left" student, if he is quoted correctly, has emphasized the wrong issue. The New Deal reforms were not mere "incremental gestures." They were solidly based, carefully worked out pieces of legislation. They were of such a character that they would be able to create a long-lasting mythology about the existence of a pluralistic American democracy, in which big labor supposedly exerts its countering influence to the domination that otherwise would be undertaken by big industry.

One cannot explain the success of the New Deal by pointing to its rhetoric. The populace responded to F.D.R.'s radical rhetoric only because it mirrored their own deeply held illusions. They could not comprehend how the reforms that changed their lives only worked to bolster the existing political economy, and they did not realize that many sponsors of the reforms came from the corporation community themselves. The integration of seemingly disparate elements into the system was successful. Labor did get its share and it did benefit from the development of a permanent war economy and the military-industrial complex. Many of those who lived through and benefited from the New Deal most likely view its accomplishments in much the same way as Schlesinger or Carl Degler. One can never be sure whether they reflect the explanations offered by the "vital center" historians, or whether these historians merely reflect the false consciousness of their own epoch.

The New Deal policies, as that conservative Chicago lawyer so aptly put it, were only a change in the way of doing things. They were a means of working out new arrangements to bolster the existing order. That so many businessmen were shortsighted and rejected acting in terms of the system's long-term interests does not change that truth. One cannot judge the meaning of an era's policies by pointing to the opposition these policies generated. The NAM and small-business types, with their own conservative mentality, responded to the epoch in terms of the consciousness of a previous era. The moderates in the governing class had to put up a stubborn, prolonged fight until the law would be able to reflect the realities of the new epoch of corporation capitalism.

That many on the political left viewed the New Deal as "progressive" or "neosocialist" is also no clue to the meaning of New Deal policies. Like the small businessmen, the left was a victim of its own particular myths, and its support of F.D.R. cannot tell us anything about New Deal policies either. It may reveal the essential liberalism of the 1930s left, but this is another story. The failure of contemporaries properly to evaluate the epoch in which they live is traditional. One can never, as Karl Marx warned, evaluate an era by concentrating on the consciousness of an era's major protagonists. The New Deal was conservative. Its special form of conservatism was the development of reforms that modernized corporate capitalism and brought corporate law to reflect the system's changed nature. To many, these New Deal reforms seemingly proved that the system had changed its basic essentials. As we move into the era of a fully matured corporate capitalism, whose contradictions are just beginning to emerge, it has become easier to see what the New Deal accomplished. Only in an epoch where consciousness begins to soar beyond the capitalist marketplace can a critique of the major reform era that marketplace had to offer emerge. This is such an epoch. Understanding how the New Deal worked will enable us to resist policies based on further extensions of the Welfare State, and to commit ourselves instead to the collective effort to forge a socialist community in America.

Unanticipated Consequences

The deficiencies of the New Deal were glaring. As the 9,000,000 unemployed in 1939 testified, the policies for industrial recovery did not work. The NRA failed to inject additional purchasing power into the economy. The commitment to deficit spending was belated and half-hearted. Neither through taxation nor through anti-trust prosecution was the Roosevelt administration able to break up the economic power of large corporations or to redistribute wealth. The New Deal's support for the countervailing power of trades unions was ambivalent. Roosevelt was a late convert to the Wagner Act and the Act itself was less responsible for the great organisational breakthrough in the mass-production industries than was the militancy of the rank-and-file workers.

In agriculture, crop reduction and price-support loans could not eliminate surplus production. The New Deal was unable to stimulate urban demand and absorb farm overproduction, nor did it solve the problem of too many people living on the land. Recovery programmes offered little to marginal farmers, sharecroppers, and farm labourers. The ambitious plans to solve the problems of rural poverty were largely still-born.

Spending on direct relief was always inadequate both under the FERA and later by the states. Too often relief perpetuated traditional and degrading attitudes towards welfare recipients. Work relief never reached more than 40 per cent of the unemployed. Spending constraints meant that WPA jobs were never invested with the legitimacy and dignity that New Dealers had hoped to impart. The social security system excluded many who needed help most, paid for benefits from the earnings of the beneficiaries, penalised the old and dependent in poorer states, and made no provision for health insurance. For the urban poor, the failure to develop a significant low-cost government housing programme left the worst problems of the inner city untouched. For the poor who were black, the New Deal did little. It enacted no civil rights measures and sanctioned continued discrimination and segregation in its programmes.

It is equally easy to replace this bleak catalogue of New Deal failure with a positive assessment of its success—the more so when New Deal activism is contrasted to the inaction of the federal government under Hoover.

In contrast to Hoover's vain exhortations to keep wages up, the NRA put a statutory floor under wages, checked the downwards deflationary spiral, and halted the relentless erosion of labour standards. Together with direct federal public works expenditure, the NRA seemed to prevent matters from getting worse and, through 1936, government intervention in the economy paralleled, if it did not cause, modest but definite recovery. A stabilised banking and securities system, eventual deficit spending, and protected labour standards gave hope for ultimate orderly recovery. The New Deal's acceptance of organised labour may have been halting, but the attitude of the state to labour was effectively reversed. No longer were the forces of government automatically arraigned against trades unions. Rank-and-file militancy could not succeed without government protection. The Wagner Act and the change in government stance disciplined the most anti-union employers and protected the great gains of 1936–37 against economic downturn and employer backlash.

In contrast to Hoover's vain exhortations to reduce acreage, the voluntary domestic allotment plan gave farmers positive incentives to cut production. The benefit payments, farm credit, and debt adjustment all provided farmers with the tangible assistance that the Federal Farm Board had failed to give. The votes of farmers both in crop control and the 1936 elections were striking testimony to their perception that the New Deal had rescued commercial farmers both large and small, and almost all farmers were commercial farmers. In the 1980s, as American farmers once more face[d] drought and foreclosure, the New Deal's achievement for agriculture recapture[d] some of its lustre. While the resettlement projects and tenant purchase loans of the Farm Security Administration may have 'skimmed the cream' of the rural poor, rehabilitation loans and grants did reach many of the 'submerged third' of the rural population. For all its defects, the FSA nevertheless was effective enough to arouse the fear of conservative politicians in the South.

The Depression had exhausted private, local, and state resources for relief before 1933. Hoover had bitterly resisted the remedy of direct federal grants. New Deal welfare programmes gave the unemployed money and jobs. The lasting loyalty of lower-income voters to Roosevelt expressed their appreciation of the very real and essential benefits they received. The Social Security Act created insurance for the old and unemployed which had existed nowhere in the public sector before and only minimally in the private sector. The Act initiated a quantum leap in the provision of assistance to the old, the blind, and dependent children. The Act might not have been rounded out in the way New Dealers hoped, but the interlocking and contributory system launched in 1935 did ensure that Congress would not lightly abolish it. The New Deal welfare programmes provided direct assistance to perhaps as many as 35 per cent of the population. It bequeathed a commitment to a minimum level of social welfare from which successive governments have never been entirely able to escape.

The political realignment that these welfare measures helped shape ensured that the measures needed to tackle urban poverty would in the future be a part of the liberal Democratic agenda. Similarly, the demands of blacks would now be pushed on the national Democratic Party by the developing civil rights coalition which included New Deal liberals. The shift in political allegiance by blacks in the 1930s bore witness to the genuine assistance they had received in the northern cities from relief and WPA programmes. Despite continued discrimination and segregation, southern blacks received assistance on a scale that surpassed anything they had been granted by any state or private sources. Farm programmes lessened the bonds of dependency of tenants and sharecroppers on white landlords, and the ferment of activity in Washington gave southern black leaders new hope that the federal government might eventually be the source of their salvation.

To lament the New Deal's deficiencies or to celebrate its achievements has only limited utility. Instead, what is needed is an examination of the relationship between reforms instituted by the New Deal and the longer-term developments of American society.

What needs to be explained therefore is why New Deal reforms had such unanticipated consequences. The business-warfare-welfare state that America eventually became was not the intentional construct of New Dealers. Much New Deal policy had been designed to curb the power of the key corporations that became so firmly entrenched after 1945. The advocates of social security had envisaged the withering away of assistance programmes not the mushrooming of welfare rolls. Those advocates expected to enact national health insurance in the future: they live instead to see the explosion of private medical insurance plans.

In the 1940s and 1950s Americans fled from the land. Yet in the 1930s rural planners had aimed to keep people on the land. New Dealers aimed to eradicate slums, regenerate the inner cities, and revitalise small towns. Yet their housing policies fostered suburban sprawl.

These unexpected developments were not the result of a plot in the 1930s by a corporate capitalist élite. New Deal reforms were not corporate liberal reforms designed to extend the hegemony of large-scale business over the economy and to defuse the threat of radical protest.

Banking and securities reforms may have stabilised credit and the stock exchange but they were opposed by the very businessmen who ultimately benefited from them. The NRA may have been the brain-child of trade association spokesmen, but few members of the corporate élite positively supported it: most regarded the NRA as a reform to be endured. When the NRA did not bring recovery, a few businessmen saw the virtue of working with it to limit the damage it could do but most fervently hoped for its demise.

Nor did corporate élites support New Deal labour reforms. These reforms did not represent a sophisticated strategy of containment of trades unions by the business community. The Wagner Act may have led to conservative and responsible unionism, but businessmen in the 1930s did not foresee the benefits of such a stabilised industrial relations system. On the contrary, many went to great lengths to try to forestall independent unions. At best, some grudgingly accepted the inevitable, but even they were determined to make no substantive concessions.

Nor does the evidence support the argument that the New Deal welfare measures were designed to ward off the threat of disorder by the unemployed and the poor. Perceived need identified by welfare workers and the political opportunity to act, not the threat of violence, explains the genesis and development of welfare policies. New Dealers did predict increased radicalism in due course if no steps were taken to improve the lot of the poor. The threat of disorder was also a useful spectre to raise before the eyes of conservative politicians. But, if anything, the New Deal stimulated rather than defused disorder. Demonstrations by the unemployed were mostly unavailing efforts to prevent cuts in New Deal benefits.

Some limitations of the New Deal were nevertheless self-imposed; some of its wounds self-inflicted. Roosevelt never pretended that his aim was anything other than to save and preserve capitalism. The consequences of banking and securities reform were conservative precisely because Roosevelt wanted to restore conservative investment practices. His anger at the business community sprang not from an anti-business philosophy, but from his irritation at the ingratitude of the group for whom the New Deal had done so much. This commitment to basic capitalist values made it all the more damaging that he failed to embrace early enough a compensatory fiscal policy. Such a policy might have brought the recovery he sought without disturbing the basic structure and value system of capitalism. The policy was intellectually available and the spending alternative was clearly presented to the president, particularly at the end of 1936. Instead, Roosevelt opted for policies that, first, starved many of his agencies of the funds needed to attain their social justice goals and, then, hastened recession in 1937–38, thereby immensely strengthening the conservative opposition that thwarted so many of the wider-ranging purposes of New Deal reform.

Roosevelt and the New Dealers were also handicapped by the contradictory or ambiguous vision of the America that they were seeking to create. Ultimately most of them believed that economic recovery would come from the revival of private enterprise, yet their convictions and political sensitivities inhibited them from wooing the business community wholeheartedly. There was no unanimity on the future industrial structure of the country. Some New Dealers continued to regard large corporations as efficient and inevitable businesses which should accordingly be regulated; others believed they should be broken up.

The New Deal consolidated an urban liberalism that frankly recognised the desirability of an increasingly urbanised America. Yet Roosevelt himself was reluctant fully to accept that vision, and his lack of sympathy for urban dilemmas in part accounts for the inadequacy of the 1937 Housing Act. Roosevelt and others yearned to move people back on to the land yet the Department of Agriculture knew that there were actually too many people on the land. Planners in Agriculture were never entirely certain of their goals: were they to hasten the modernisation and rationalisation of farming, or were they to try to increase the numbers of small owners and enable them to stay on the land?

The fear of social security administrators that generous assistance programmes might undermine social insurance prevented the development of an adequate and comprehensive welfare programme.

Many New Dealers were fully conscious of these inconsistencies and acknowledged their reform limitations. Frances Perkins was once described by a friend as 'a half-loaf girl: take what you can get now and try for more later'. New Dealers were not blind to the failures of their own programmes: they had a practical appreciation of political constraints and hoped to refine and improve programmes in due course. Perkins herself was under no illusions about the weaknesses and gaps in the social security system. The Bureau of Agricultural Economics was fully aware of the long-term limitations of planned scarcity and of the need to stimulate urban consumption. No one had a shrewder perception of the damage spending constraints imposed on work relief than Harry Hopkins.

They were remarkably accessible to their critics. In part, accessibility reflected the still manageable size of the federal government. Sharecroppers from Arkansas could travel through the night to Washington, sit down in the early morning outside the Secretary of Agriculture's office, and actually talk to Henry Wallace when he came in to work. In part, accessibility reflected the lack of dogmatic certainty amongst New Dealers. Even the arbitrary Hugh Johnson responded to a shouting match with Leon Henderson by inviting him in to head the Research and Planning Division. When Will Alexander and Frank Tannenbaum exposed the consequences of the collapse of cotton tenancy, they were brought in to draft the Bankhead-Jones bill and to work in the Resettlement Administration. Even when the experience of critics was less happy—when for example Jerome Frank and the liberal reformers were purged from the AAA after the reinterpretation of the cotton contract—they were not cast aside. They went on to work in more congenial parts of the New Deal experiment—in Justice, the Labor Department, at the NLRB, or at the SEC.

Many of the problems that the New Deal found intractable were problems first uncovered by the New Dealers themselves. The existence of a permanently poor rural population in the South was not a problem much recognised by agricultural economists or farm policy-makers in 1933. It was a problem exposed by FERA workers who found an unexpected demand for relief in rural as well as urban areas. Their initiatives led to the assault on rural poverty through rehabilitation loans and resettlement communities. The full dimensions of the needs of the cities and the possibilities of federal action were first laid out by the National Resources Committee in their 1937 report *Our Cities: Their Role in the National Economy*. The TNEC identified in 1938 the needs of the South. The Great Plains Committee partially mapped the problems of the West in *The Future of the Great Plains*. Field studies for the relief agencies first highlighted the health and educational deficiencies of both rural and urban America and the particular plight of the young and women.

The New Deal was not static, it improved over time as deficiencies in existing programmes were exposed and new problems identified. Nowhere was this clearer than in its treatment of blacks. The ignorance of even sympathetic liberals like Eleanor Roosevelt mirrored at first the indifference with which the NRA and the AAA regarded blacks. Slowly she and others became aware that black problems could not be eradicated by generally targeting poverty. As a result of their perception of the special needs of blacks, agencies like the PWA, the WPA, and the Farm Security Administration pursued racial policies that had changed significantly from the white preoccupations of 1933.

Nevertheless, the first steps the reformers took too often turned out to be last steps. Their hopes of a more suitable distribution of wealth, of permanent emergency employment agencies, of a comprehensive welfare state, of coordinated planning and control of the nation's physical resources, and of a full-scale assault on rural poverty were dashed. Sometimes this failure was the result of missed opportunities. The New Dealers' pragmatism may have been self-limiting. As R. Alan Lawson noted, 'Practicality can be treacherous. It urges compromise but may be used against compromise by deeming some evils too firmly rooted for practical reform to touch.' It was undoubtedly prudent not to challenge the American Medical Association, for example, over national health insurance in 1935 in order to safeguard the Social Security Act itself. But in the future, the times were even less opportune to take on the AMA. For so many New Deal reforms, if the opportunity was not grasped in 1935, it would never present itself again.

Liberals were impatient with Roosevelt's lack of a thoroughgoing vision of reform and the administration's lack of valour, but the New Deal was more often restricted by external constraints imposed by the political and economic environment: the lack of a sufficient state apparatus, the strong forces of localism, the great difficulty of policy-making in an economic emergency, and entrenched conservative leadership in Congress.

The structure of the federal government of the early 1930s was inappropriate to centrally-directed radical reform. There was simply not the 'state capacity' in Washington to manage central planning of the economy. Even if the political mandate for coercive overhead planning had existed in 1933, the government had neither the information with which to devise planning policies nor the bureaucracy with which to implement them. By the time the government had acquired the necessary information, the political opportunity to impose such plans had long gone, if it had ever existed. Nor was there a disinterested welfare bureaucracy capable of administering a national relief scheme or launching a purely federal social security system. The Department of Agriculture possessed a federal bureaucracy which had acquired considerable information about American farms. But even there neither crop control nor long-term planning could have been implemented without vesting crucial power in local committees of the farmers themselves.

The political constraints on centralised planning or purely federal programmes were formidable. Hostility to big government was not the preserve simply of conservative reactionary opponents of the New Deal. Suspicion of centralised federal authority governed the attitude of midwestern progressives, dissident demagogues, decentralist intellectuals like the Southern Agrarians, and many New Dealers themselves.

The forces of localism were in themselves a powerful check on New Deal aspirations. Not only were many New Deal programmes operated by state government agencies, but everywhere New Deal programmes were run by local officials who might defer more to local community sentiment than to directives emanating from Washington. Local administration of the farm program put power in the hands of the local rural power structure and discriminated against the rural poor. Even the FSA found it difficult to overcome the tendency of its local officials to defer to local custom. Local administration of relief often allowed free play to the miserly and conservative prejudices and self-interest of local businessmen and farmers. Everywhere, local administration tended to countenance and perpetuate racial discrimination. The local role in the social security system gave rise to vast discrepancies in coverage and benefits. The intentions of the 1937 Housing Act were often defeated by local real estate interests that prevented the creation of local housing authorities. The formation of local REA cooperatives was thwarted by the ability of power companies to build 'spite lines' to cream off the best business. Everywhere the pressure in Congress was to increase, not decrease, local involvement in the administration of New Deal programmes and to assert wherever possible state, not federal, control in order to safeguard entrenched local interests.

In any case some New Dealers saw positive virtues in such localism. They wanted to resurrect grass-roots democracy, to foster citizen participation. Local committees of farmers ran the AAA programmes, guided the TVA, advised on farm debt adjustment, land-use planning, and farm credit loans. The inhabitants were meant to govern Subsistence Homestead projects and Greenbelt towns. The REA operated through local cooperatives, the Soil Conservation programme through self-governing soil conservation districts. The aim of Indian reorganisation was to give self-government to the tribal councils. But this democratic vision was only partially successful. In the first place New Deal experiments in community building and participatory democracy were almost entirely rural in orientation. New Deal relief and welfare programmes made no attempt to draw on the tradition of urban community organisation that came from the settlement houses or the social unit experiment in Cincinnati. This social unit experiment in 1917 was an urban variant of the rural land-use planning committees—local community residents formed representative committees that met with a parallel committee of representatives from social service agencies. This was not a route taken in the 1930s. It would be the 1960s before urban welfare policy with Community Action Programs took up that approach again.

Post-war social scientists were quick to point to the drawbacks of participatory democracy in the rural areas. Sometimes grass-roots democracy meant capitulation to local interest groups. At other times, interest groups destroyed democratic institutions that threatened them. Time and again it was also clear that the grass roots did not want to participate in the way New Deal planners wanted them to. Grass-roots democracy gave local sectional interests a veto over policy designed for the national interest. It is not surprising, given the constraints of localism, that many liberal New Dealers in the 1930s put their faith in enlightened national bureaucracy. Only in the 1960s and 1970s did this faith in federal bureaucracy seem misplaced.

The constraints of localism were compounded by the circumstances of policy-making and implementation in 1933. The economic emergency gave the New Deal vast opportunities to exercise powers that had not been used since World War I. Yet the spectacular exercise of that power for coherent planning required special circumstances, like the power vacuum in the Tennessee Valley in 1933.

For the most part in 1933 the emergency, by contrast, severely restricted New deal options. First, the emphasis was of necessity on recovery, rather than reform. Second, action had to be taken quickly. The banks had to be reopened in a week. NRA codes had to be drafted very quickly to provide an immediate boost to purchasing power. Relief money had to be distributed and spent at once. Millions of farmers had to be signed to contracts in weeks, not months.

Given both the lack of existing 'state capacity' in Washington and the constitutional doubts on coercive government regulation, the New Deal had to rely on the consent of those being regulated to put recovery programmes into operation quickly. To reopen the banks required the cooperation of local bank officials and reliance on their information and good faith. The cooperation of businessmen who possessed a monopoly on information about their industries was essential if codes were to be drafted and administered. There was no alternative to the administration of the AAA by the Extension Service and local committees of farmers. Relief programmes had to be run by state government agencies. So it was that the New Deal fostered interest groups that in the long run obstructed its reforming designs. Thus, businessmen distorted the intent of the NRA and severely limited its ability to raise mass-purchasing power. Grass-roots democracy in agriculture facilitated the creation of commodity interest groups that pressed for ever more generous price supports in their own particular interest. The AAA also promoted the revival of a farm pressure group like the Farm Bureau Federation which ultimately turned against the New Deal's efforts to help the rural and the urban poor.

The circumstances of 1933 contributed to another major constraint on the New Deal: the power of the conservative opposition in Congress. The New Deal had to work with the existing congressional Democratic leadership in 1933 to secure the speedy passage of its essential recovery legislation. The recognition that the New Deal gave and the patronage it distributed undoubtedly bolstered the position of southern congressional leaders. Loyal congressional support for the New Deal was replaced by scepticism and mounting hostility about the direction of the nonemergency New Deal. As Roosevelt moved to complete the unfinished business of the New Deal in attacking urban and rural poverty, so he found it increasingly difficult to take Congress with him.

It is difficult to see how Roosevelt could have avoided this opposition from southern conservative Democrats and Republicans. He had achieved a partial political realignment. But the elimination of the southern conservative wing of his party would have required a much more systematic commitment that would have to have started in 1933 when his first priority was on immediate recovery. Even a more systematic commitment to realignment would probably have foundered on the unreliability of progressive non-Democrats, the refusal of conservatives to allow themselves to be portrayed as opponents of the New Deal, the difficulty of identifying from Washington genuine liberals with local political strength, and the difficulty of fighting local elections on national issues.

Congressional conservatives had effectively checked the expansion of the New Deal by 1940. What created, however, the political economy of modern America was the impact of the dramatic social changes unleashed by World War II on the 'broker state' unwittingly created by the New Deal.

World War II was the juggernaut that ran over American society. The war opened up for the first time for the majority of Americans the possibility of affluence rather than subsistence. For city dwellers, full employment and high wages offered the chance that, once private construction resumed after the war, they might be able to own their own homes and move to the suburbs. For farmers, war-time prosperity suggested that at the end of the war they might be able to enjoy the consumer goods—refrigerators, radios, and air conditioning—that rural electrification was making available to them. During the war 75 per cent of the population paid federal income tax: testimony to their affluence, not to legislative intent.

For businessmen, the war opened up undreamt-of profitability, restored leaders of large corporations to public esteem and respectability, and removed most threats of government regulation. For trades unions, the war forced management for the first time to sit down with them and bargain meaningfully. It established the parameters of post-war industrial relations. The war, not the New Deal, transformed rural America. High prices made possible mechanisation, investments in fertiliser and scientific farming, and consolidation into larger farms. Full employment gave the excess agricultural labour force the chance to dash gratefully to the new industrial jobs.

For blacks, the labour shortages in the defence industries and the armed services eventually broke down some discriminatory barriers and had some belated impact on the levels of their unemployment. As they flocked to the southern and northern cities, their political leverage increased. Urban migration in the South was an essential precondition for the development of the modern civil rights movement. The war similarly created new jobs for women, although it took longer for women than for blacks to translate new economic opportunity into increased consciousness and political gains. For the South, military spending during the war and Cold War, first on defence then later on space also, was the catalyst that sparked the region's takeoff into self-sustaining economic growth. This growth would eventually draw most of the remaining rural population away from the cotton fields, reverse the traditional migration out of the region, and help facilitate the breakdown of traditional patterns of race relations. In the West, the defence industries on the coast once again attracted the migration that had been such a feature of the 1920s. The Depression, despite the extensive migration of the Arkies and Okies, had curtailed that population shift. From 1940 that expansion westwards would never again be slowed.

Seen through the lens of the war, the New Deal's overall function appears as a holding operation for American society: a series of measures that enabled the people to survive the Depression and to hold on until World War II opened up new opportunities. Industrial recovery programmes checked the deflationary spiral and yielded modest recovery that enabled businessmen to survive to enjoy dramatic war-time profits. Relief and welfare measures allowed the unemployed to struggle through until the war brought them jobs. Farm programmes enabled an underemployed labour force to stay on the land until the war created the urban demand which would absorb the surplus farm production and the industrial jobs which would absorb the surplus population. The plight of the poorest one third of the nation largely remained the New Deal's unfinished business.

The Office of War Information told Roosevelt that the American people's post-war aspirations were 'compounded largely of 1929 values and the economics of the 1920s, leavened with a hangover from the makeshift controls of the war'. This survey highlighted the ultimate constraint that circumscribed the New Deal's achievement: the underlying conservative response of the people themselves to the Depression. Middle-income Americans may have had more sympathy with the poor and the jobless in the 1930s than before or after. Workers may have exhibited greater class solidarity in those years. But more striking is the pervasive and persistent commitment to self-help, individual liberty, localism, and business-oriented individualism.

Businessmen, who had extracted many concessions from government, worked to end government regulation. Farmers, who had been rescued by massive government subsidies and price supports, argued that they wanted a fair price in the market place. Dust Bowl farmers, whose plight had been caused in part by their passion to plant wheat, wanted to grow more wheat. Submarginal farmers and tenant farmers wanted to own their own land, despite chronic rural overpopulation. The unemployed, having suffered from the collapse of the economic system, wanted another job, not a change in the system. Industrial workers, despite the unprecedented economic disaster, wanted a union contract and some rights on the shop floor, not control of the means of production. Mississippians, who had been rescued by unprecedented federal aid, stressed their steadfast commitment to states' rights. Westerners, who received more largesse than anyone else, proceeded again to elect conservative Republicans. Traditional values survived the Depression and the New Deal with great resilience. In the end, the New Deal was essentially a holding operation for American society because in the democratic, capitalist United States that was what most Americans wanted it to be.

SUGGESTIONS FOR FURTHER READING

A number of general studies will take the interested reader more deeply into the debate over the meaning and significance of the New Deal reforms. A balanced, general account, tightly packed and entertainingly written, is William E. Leuchtenburg, *Franklin Roosevelt and the New Deal* (New York, 1963). Leuchtenburg emphasizes the change in American life brought about by the New Deal, but not to the extent that Carl Degler does in the selection here or that Mario Einaudi does in *The Roosevelt Revolution* (New York, 1959). In his three volumes on *The Age of Roosevelt* (*The Crisis of the Old Order, *The Coming of the New Deal,* and *The Politics of Upheaval* [Boston, 1957, 1959, 1960]), Arthur Schlesinger, Jr., shows Roosevelt, the pragmatic idealist, moving from cooperation with the business community early in his first term to a more critical attitude after 1935. James MacGregor Burns, *Roosevelt: The Lion and the Fox* (New York, 1956) views Roosevelt as essentially conservative on political and economic issues. Richard S. Kirkendall, *The United States, 1929–1945: Years of Crisis and Change* (New York, 1974) denies that the New Deal was either conservative or revolutionary, but he argues that it brought significant changes. Anthony J. Badger's more recent study, *The New Deal: The Depression*

---

*Available in paperback edition.

Years, 1933–1940 (New York, 1989), a portion of which is reprinted here, comes to similar conclusions, as does Frank Freidel, *Franklin D. Roosevelt: A Rendezvous with Destiny* (Boston, 1990). Robert S. McElvaine, **The Great Depression* (New York, 1984) argues that the New Deal's creation of the welfare state marked a significant break with the past.

Other historians find much more conflict during the New Deal era and are more critical of FDR and the New Deal. Edgar Robinson, *The Roosevelt Leadership, 1933–45* (Philadelphia, 1955) is an evaluation from the right that stresses conservative opposition to the New Deal. Critical assessments that find that the New Deal did not go far enough in its reforms are Paul K. Conkin, **The New Deal* (New York, 1967) and Barton Bernstein, "The New Deal: The Conservative Achievement of Liberal Reform," in Bernstein, ed., **Towards a New Past: Dissenting Essays in American History* (New York, 1968).

Two books by economists stress the economic significance of the depression and the New Deal. Lester V. Chandler, **America's Greatest Depression, 1929–1941* (New York, 1970) discusses the economic impact of the depression and the response of the government to it and concludes that the experience brought a "revolutionary change in our state of economic understanding," creating a "popular consensus that government can and must promote economic stability." Charles P. Kindleberger, **The World in Depression, 1929–1939* (Berkeley, Calif., 1973) discusses the depression and its effects in a world context, concluding that the depression took hold and spread throughout most of the world because significant changes had taken place in the Western economic community. Britain was unable and the United States was unwilling to take economic leadership, and the resulting economic instability allowed the depression to spread and become prolonged. Other, more specialized studies also emphasize economic matters: Rhonda F. Levine, *Class Struggle and the New Deal: Industrial Labor, Industrial Capital, and the State* (Lawrence, Kans., 1988); James S. Olson, *Saving Capitalism: The Reconstruction Finance Corporation and the New Deal, 1933–1940* (Princeton, N.J., 1988); William R. Brock, *Welfare, Democracy, and the New Deal* (New York, 1988); Stanley Vittoz, *New Deal Labor Policy and the American Industrial Economy* (Chapel Hill, N.C., 1987); and Lizabeth Cohen, *Making a New Deal: Industrial Workers in Chicago, 1919–1939* (New York, 1990).

Jordan A. Schwarz, *The New Dealers: Power Politics in the Age of Roosevelt* (New York, 1993) discusses a number of men associated with the New Deal who promoted state capitalism. Alan Brinkley, *The End of Reform: New Deal Liberalism in Recession and War* (New York, 1995) describes the decline of certain liberal ideas after 1937.

On the New Deal in the South, see Roger Biles, *The South and the New Deal* (Lexington, Ky., 1994) and Chester M. Morgan, *Redneck Liberal: Theodore G. Bilbo and the New Deal* (Baton Rouge, La., 1985). Bilbo was a racist, a segregationist, and a supporter of the New Deal. FDR was also able to gain support from blacks. Harvard Sitkoff, **A New Deal for Blacks: The Emergence of Civil Rights as a National Issue—The Depression Decade* (New York, 1978) describes the gradual emergence of blacks as part of the New Deal political coalition. But, as Sitkoff notes, Roosevelt was reluctant to advocate any really significant reforms on civil rights for fear of alienating his southern white support. On these matters see also Nancy J. Weiss, **Farewell to the Party of Lincoln: Black Politics in the Age of FDR* (Princeton, N.J., 1983) and John B. Kirby, *Black Americans in the Roosevelt Era: Liberalism and Race* (Knoxville, Tenn., 1980).

Richard H. Pells, **Radical Visions and American Dreams* (New York, 1973) discusses the radical critique of the New Deal, including the influence of the Communists among the critics. A recent balanced study of the Communist party during the depression is Harvey Klehr, **The Heyday of American Communism: The Depression Decade* (New York, 1984). An earlier partisan anti-Communist polemic is Eugene Lyons, *The Red Decade: The Stalinist Penetration of America* (Indianapolis, 1941). Irving Howe and Lewis Coser, *The American Communist Party: A Critical History, 1919–1957* (Boston,

1957) is a more general history. Alan Brinkley, *Voices of Protest: Huey Long, Father Coughlin and the Great Depression* (New York, 1982) examines two influential critics of the New Deal.

Those who wish to investigate further the debate over the meaning of the New Deal should consult the essays collected in Otis L. Graham, Jr., ed., *The New Deal: The Critical Issues* (New York, 1971) and Alonzo L. Hamby, ed., *The New Deal: Analysis and Interpretation,* 2nd ed. (New York, 1981). Richard S. Kirkendall's guide to the literature, "The New Deal as a Watershed: The Recent Literature," *Journal of American History,* 14 (March 1968), 839–52, may be supplemented by the annotated bibliography in Hamby's book. Howard Zinn, ed., *New Deal Thought* (Indianapolis, 1966) is a good collection of contemporary documents.

Several recent volumes contain essays assessing and evaluating the effects of the New Deal over the past fifty years: Wilbur J. Cohen, ed., *The Roosevelt New Deal: A Program Assessment Fifty Years After* (Austin, Tex., 1986); Harvard Sitkoff, ed., *Fifty Years Later: The New Deal Evaluated* (Philadelphia, 1985); and Steve Fraser and Gary Gerstle, eds., *The Rise and Fall of the New Deal Order, 1930–1980* (Princeton, N.J., 1989).

9

The Conservative 1950s

World War II ended the economic depression of the 1930s and united the nation in enthusiastic support of the fight against fascism. Victory on the battlefield and the prospect of international cooperation through the United Nations generated widespread optimism.

But this unity and optimism quickly faded, giving way to a combination of frustration, fear, and anger as the nation faced the uncertainties of the immediate postwar years. The end of wartime price controls and the slowness of conversion from wartime to peacetime production produced skyrocketing prices and continued shortages of goods. Although the war had produced prosperity, those who had lived through the hardships of the Great Depression feared that the prosperity could not be sustained once war production came to an end. Even more frightening was the prospect of another world war. The alliance with the Soviet Union collapsed into a crisis-ridden cold war. Winston Churchill, invited to the United States by President Harry Truman, announced in a speech in Fulton, Missouri, in March 1946, that "from Stettin in the Baltic to Trieste in the Adriatic, an Iron Curtain has descended across the Continent." Nations in eastern Europe and then China became Communist states, and Communist parties in western Europe enjoyed strong support from the voters. The United States continued to expand its atomic arsenal, but soon lost its monopoly on the powerful new weapon. In the fall of 1949, President Truman announced that the Soviet Union had exploded a nuclear device. Then, in 1950, just five years after the end of World War II, the United States entered a hot war in Korea.

Uncertainties and fears led to a polarization in politics. Disturbed by growing communist strength throughout the world, by a cold war that threatened to become a devastating third world war, and by a war in Korea that could not be won, some Americans concluded that the nation's problems stemmed from subversive agents who were undermining American democracy. New Deal liberalism was put on the defensive when rightist organizations linked it to communism and labeled any criticism or dissent as subversion. Harry Truman, who had become president after the death of Franklin D. Roosevelt in 1945, promised to extend the New Deal reforms while at the same time blocking communist advances in the world and ferreting out any subversives in government. Conservatives in Congress blocked most of his domestic reforms, and rightist and leftist elements of his own Democratic Party bolted to form the States' Rights (Dixiecrats) and the Progressive parties. Liberals who remained within the Democratic party took heart when Truman won an upset victory over Thomas Dewey in 1948, but his victory did not increase his ability to get Congress to extend the social legislation of the New Deal.

Nor did Truman's victory in 1948 still the charge that the nation's problems stemmed from subversion within. In a 1950 speech in Wheeling, West Virginia, the junior Republican senator from Wisconsin, Joseph R. McCarthy, declared that he had a list of State Department employees who were members of the Communist party. Thus began a campaign ostensibly designed to rid the government and the nation of communists and communist sympathizers, but it quickly became a campaign to support conservatism and to discredit the Democrats. McCarthy and his supporters insisted that during their twenty-year domination of the presidency the Democrats had been "soft on communism" and therefore guilty, in McCarthy's words, of "twenty years of treason."

Although some applauded McCarthy's investigations as necessary to purge the nation of subversion, others attacked McCarthy as a witch-hunter who threatened the basic American rights of free speech and free association. Liberals sought to protect themselves by differentiating their views from those of the Communists, insisting that one could be an ardent anticommunist and still advocate liberal social reforms. McCarthy's supporters sometimes admitted that the Wisconsin Senator at times cast too wide a net in his efforts to find subversives, but they argued that his goals, if not always his particular methods, were admirable.

But when McCarthy questioned the loyalty of such leaders as General George C. Marshall and Adlai Stevenson, when he extended his investigations to the army, when he maligned even his conservative Republican opponents in the Senate, and when he continued his attacks on subversives in the government after the election of Republican Dwight D. Eisenhower in 1952, opposition began to grow. Republican conservatives in the Senate, supported by the Democrats and the Republican White House, succeeded in getting a formal resolution of condemnation passed by the Senate. By the end of 1954, McCarthy's influence, once so formidable, had disappeared.

The election of Eisenhower, the repudiation of McCarthy, the agreement ending the Korean war, and the death of Josef Stalin, which lessened East-West tensions, allayed conflict and ushered in a period of calm. Both the left and the right collapsed, and there was a noticeable absence of any meaningful ideological conflict in American politics. Prosperity continued and seemed to be the answer to all of the nation's problems. American stability and prosperity stood in marked contrast to the situation in the rest of the world and appeared to signal the beginning of an era of American supremacy, the beginning of what was termed an "American Century."

Beneath the calm, however, was a growing restiveness. A few critics complained about the conservatism, which they claimed was a legacy of McCarthyism; they bemoaned the complacency of the "silent generation" of American youth and the conformity of the "organization men" in their grey flannel suits. By the late 1950s the disenchanted increased their criticism, and they gained a wider audience as new problems arose and older, unsolved problems became more apparent. American economic growth was slowing; the Russians launched a space vehicle before the United States was capable of doing so; prosperity turned out to have been primarily for middle-, upper-, and certain favored working-class whites; and democracy seemed to be reserved for white conformists. Hipsters and beats challenged traditional culture; blacks, soon to be joined by increasing numbers of white supporters, increased their challenge to Jim Crow laws. Even conservatives and businessmen began to challenge the complacency and inaction of the government, especially in foreign policy. John F. Kennedy, running against Richard Nixon in 1960, promised to get the country moving again and to open a "New Frontier." But what this meant and how Kennedy's policies would differ from those of Nixon, whom he narrowly defeated in the election, remained unclear.

Writing the history of the decade and a half following World War II is a formidable task. Historians must describe and explain what seems to be bewilderingly erratic behavior marked by rapid shifts in political outlook and sharply contradictory attitudes. Some historians find the period to be a time of sharp conflict. They see McCarthyism as a blatant and crude attack on the New Deal and its reforms and conclude that although McCarthy himself suffered defeat, the conservatism and reaction he represented ended liberal reform. Others, however, see the period as one of a growing conservative consensus, finding McCarthyism a temporary and extreme aberration. Still others, while noting the lack of ideological conflict in the 1950s, stress that the decade only *appeared* to be complacent, and that sharp political, economic, and social dissent existed behind the apparent agreement. Variations of this debate among historians may be seen in the following selections.

In the first selection, Earl Latham begins by reviewing the many interpretations of McCarthyism by liberals and conservatives, by opponents and supporters, and finds them all inadequate. McCarthy was not the advance agent of totalitarianism or a midwestern demagogue playing upon the status anxieties of the people, as liberals claimed; nor was he the ardent defender of the nation against subversion and communist totalitarianism, as the conservatives claimed. Rather, Latham argues, McCarthyism represented the reassertion of a long-term "fundamentalist conservatism" in America, a conservatism that sometimes reluctantly gave way to short periods of reform in order to quiet discontent, but then again became dominant because Americans traditionally accepted and favored the conservative consensus. Just as the conservative consensus reasserted itself after the reformist years of the progressive era, so too did the consensus reassert itself after the reformist years of the New Deal. McCarthyism, in this view, was merely a means to that reassertion, and the conservative consensus remained after McCarthy himself had been repudiated.

Godfrey Hodgson, in the second selection, comes to a similar conclusion but by a very different route. He calls the 1950s "an age of consensus," a time when "few . . . doubted the essential goodness and strength of American society." Politicians, popular writers, intellectuals, and labor leaders all shared a basic confidence in the American political and economic system. Differences among them were minor, well within what Hodgson calls "a strange hybrid, liberal conservatism," a view that rested upon prosperity and confidence that major domestic problems had been solved or could easily be solved. But this consensus, Hodgson argues, although it seemed to be pervasive, was really unstable because it was based upon fiction, not fact, and because the left, divided by ethnic, sectional, and ideological differences, remained silent. For a while, Hodgson concludes, the celebrations of American exceptionalism made it possible to ignore those who did not share in the benefits of prosperity, but by the early sixties, disagreements resurfaced and destroyed the consensus that once seemed so formidable.

Elaine Tyler May, in the third selection, also points to consensus and relates it to the suburban ideal of the 1950s. Fear and uncertainty, fed by the danger of annihilation if the cold war turned into a new world war, by the fear of internal subversion, and by the feeling that traditional American values had somehow decayed, "prompted Americans to create a family-centered culture" in the years following World War II. "The self-contained home held out the promise of security in an insecure world" and symbolized "abundance and fulfillment," she writes. Surveys indicated that men and women alike were willing to make personal sacrifices to secure the love and security that home and family seemed to offer. This consensus, May concludes, lasted for only one generation; the children who grew up in the comfort of postwar domesticity rebelled in the 1960s against the values their parents held so dear. But those values have not disappeared, May insists; they continue to inform current political debates.

How can we explain what appears to be a seesaw in American attitudes? Within a few years wartime unity seemed to disintegrate into the bitter conflicts of the McCarthy years, only to change again into the complacent consensus of the later 1950s. Were changes in popular attitudes simply the result of sharp and rapid changes in social and economic conditions?

Perhaps Americans, even when they seemed to be locked in bitter conflict, never fundamentally disagreed. If so, how can we evaluate McCarthyism? Was it merely a momentary aberration from traditional values? Or was it a somewhat crude and extreme manifestation of widely held traditional conservative values reasserting themselves after a period of reform? Or were McCarthyism and the conservative consensus that followed the results of the failure of reformers to maintain the unity necessary to make their voices heard?

Did the traditional family values that seemed so pervasive in the 1950s reflect a general consensus? Or did they merely reflect the views of middle-class whites and have little reality for most Americans who did not enjoy the suburban, prosperous ideal? Why did the children of those who seemed to enjoy the benefits of prosperity and the haven of home and family seem to repudiate these very benefits?

EARL LATHAM

The Meaning of McCarthyism

Explanations of McCarthyism

McCarthyism was regarded by thousands as a disturbance of domestic tranquility of oppressive weight and pain, especially by workers and officials in government, politics, and the professions; and, indeed, rather generally throughout the articulate and better-educated circles of the society. The evidence of a substantial study of communism, conformity, and civil liberty by Samuel Stouffer, however, was that the vast masses were largely unconcerned with the turmoil. In 1954 the number of people who said that they were worried either about the threat of Communists in the United States or about civil liberties was less than one per cent. Nearly one-third of the population could not name a single Senator or Congressman who had taken a leading part in the investigation of communism, not even the name of Senator McCarthy. Among those categorized in the sample as "less interested" a total of 50 per cent failed to name a single Congressman or Senator. The same survey showed that 68 per cent of a national cross-section favored forbidding a Communist the right to make a speech in their communities.

But depressing though it is to be reminded in numerous polls of the relatively small part that liberal values, or any kind of political concern, plays in the lives of most Americans, the real wonder in McCarthyism is the nature of the phenomenon itself. Political scientists have been especially remiss in failing to treat it as a political problem of high consequence, and most of the writing on the subject has been contributed by sociologists, historians, and literary people. The basic political question is whether McCarthyism was a flash of stunning but temporary impact, associated with a demagogue of great force and fire; or the surface appearance of more serious strains in the social and political system which must find ease, or threaten ruin. Opinions have differed. There are at least five kinds of explanations in the literature contributed by liberal and neutral commentators, and a common theme presented by conservative writers in varying degrees of sophistication.

The first explanation by writers of liberal or neutral perspective is that McCarthy was a demagogue, one of many who have appeared in American history to stir discontents, most of whom have been of only passing significance and who have disappeared from the public scene without regret or lasting effect. Viewed so, McCarthyism is simply the behavior of Senator McCarthy, and with the departure of McCarthy the "problem" of McCarthyism disappears. A twist to this explanation was provided by Will Herberg who argued that McCarthyism was the logical fulfillment of a political style made popular by Franklin Roosevelt—direct appeals to the people against their elected representatives—a species of government by rabble-rousing in which the rabble was urged to take instant action against their duly chosen officers. Any good result accomplished by the committees was only incidental to "their primary *political* function" which was to rouse the masses and keep them in turmoil. The difference between Roosevelt and McCarthy was that Roosevelt, like Pericles, was a gentleman, and McCarthy, like Cleon, was a clod.

Second, there is the view that McCarthyism was incipient totalitarianism. One should exclude from this category those who merely used such words as "totalitarian" and "authoritarian" as terms of abuse in the rhetoric of dissent. These apart, there were writers who thought that there were strong resemblances in philosophy and program between McCarthy and the twentieth-century totalitarian leaders of Europe. For example, Marya Mannes, in a report on the Army-McCarthy hearings, described the pattern of McCarthy's behavior as totalitarian in structure and psychology. Said she,

When you come down to it, slowly, reluctantly, but inevitably, the real horror of these hearings has been in this: that the pattern of the protagonist was totalitarian. Senator Potter got closer to it when he said, "We have all been through a brainwashing here." For here were all the dread familiar methods: the relentless, interminable breaking down of the witness; the repeated statements of unverified fact; the assumption of guilt without proof; the deliberate evasion of the basic issues; the constant diversionary moves to obscure them. Here were the totalitarian clichés, the inversions of Communist labels: "Pentagon Politicians," "Fifth Amendment Communist," "Leftist Press." Here, most appalling of all, was the open admission and condonement of a spy-and-informer system within our government—the "Loyal American Underground." Here, finally, was the radical attempt to wreck the Executive Branch of the United States Government.

Miss Mannes thought that the hearings symbolized a grave and desperate division among Americans, sharpened into an antagonism not far from civil war.

Two others, arguing from different grounds, also represent the view that McCarthyism was considerably more than the eccentricity of a politician on the make. Richard Hofstadter in "The Pseudo-Conservative Revolt" suggested that authoritarianism was the key to many of the most zealous followers of

McCarthy, although this goes little beyond a literary appreciation of the psychology of authoritarianism (the essay depends strongly on Adorno and others on the authoritarian personality) without empirical demonstration of the supposed authoritarianism of some of the most zealous of McCarthy's followers. For Hofstadter, the "pseudo-conservative" was impossible to identify by class "for the pseudo-conservative impulse can be found in practically all classes in society." Carey McWilliams tended to write of McCarthyism as a form of American reactionism fostered by the classical Right of progressive prophecy. When Senator Flanders of Vermont introduced the resolution in the United States Senate to condemn McCarthy, McWilliams wrote that "McCarthy is only a symbol; the movement he represents would not vanish if his power were utterly destroyed." And what was this movement? It was the reaction of the right, and although it might have seemed as strange to progressives as it had to Senator Goldwater that the champion of the right should be under attack by a conservative New England Senator, there was an explanation. For "McCarthy is now being attacked from the right in an effort to preserve the movement which he helped to bring to maturity." Goldwater was sure it was Communist cunning.

Third, there is the thought that McCarthyism was a kind of mid-century Populism, and several writers have accepted this view in whole or in part. Hofstadter, Lipset, and Parsons work with this notion, for example. Another statement of it is that of Leslie Fiedler in an essay titled "McCarthy and the Intellectuals." For Fiedler

... McCarthyism is, generally speaking, an extension of the ambiguous American impulse toward "direct democracy" with its distrust of authority, institutions, and expert knowledge; and, more precisely, it is the form that populist conviction takes when forced to define itself against a competing "European" radicalism.

And elsewhere,

The emergence of McCarthy out of the wreckage of the La Follette Progressive movement in Wisconsin is a clue to what he represents. He inherits the bitterest and most provincial aspects of a populism to which smooth talking has always meant the Big City, and the Big City has meant the Enemy.

Statements of this kind, however, help more to explain than to understand, for even if it is conceded that a provincial populistic distaste for smooth-talkers, mincing accents, Harvard degrees, wealth, effete culture, and New York lent vigor to McCarthy's attacks, it does not explain the abnormal tensions of McCarthyism.

It is true that the small-town rural outlook is the one that has tended to dominate the committees. It is Southerners who have come to the chairmanships when the Democrats have a majority, and it is rural or small-town mid-Westerners who have come to dominate the committees when the Republicans have a majority in the houses of Congress. The committees then tend to reflect the small-town rural skepticism of the cities and other urban areas. The attitude is likely to be anticosmopolitan as well as antimetropolitan but this does not establish the proposition that the tension over subversion and security was basically a revolt of the American interior against eastern seaboard intellectuals and the polyglot cities with their enthusiasm for social security, modern art, communism, coffeehouses, poetry, high taxes, Zionism, and education. It may only be that these hostilities gave zest and a self-consciousness of doing good in a context of opportunity created by other influences.

During the New Deal era, the Roosevelt programs seemed to many to have more in common with Populism than with the later Progressivism, although Populism lost its seal of literary approval and became a word of opprobrium as a result of the "shock of the encounter with McCarthyism." C. Vann Woodward has shown that there is a considerable difference between the contemporary conception of the Populism of the nineteenth century and the historical reality. The assumption has been widespread that Populism was historically a Western affair, that Wisconsin was the "seed-bed of the movement," and that the elder La Follette was its principal champion. None of these assumptions is true. In fact Populism had "negligible appeal in the Middle Western states," and was most attractive in the South where the Populists were more often the victims than the authors of thought control, racism, and the lynch spirit. Populism was neither class politics nor "status politics" (to be discussed presently) but more like interest politics in the familiar manner. As to racialism, the anti-Semitism of the historical Populists was (although not innocent) largely rhetorical, and Professor Woodward is of the opinion that perhaps the most remarkable aspect of the whole Populist movement was the resistance its leaders put up in the South against racism and racialist propaganda. As to the supposed element of isolationist feeling, the South was perhaps the least isolationist section of the country in the foreign policy crisis before the Second World War.

Fourth, a set of attitudes and behaviors called status politics is thought by some to be the key to McCarthyism, and Daniel Bell (building on certain theses stated by Lipset and Hofstadter) has explained McCarthy as a catalyst of these tensions in "Status Politics and New Anxieties." Sectional politics, class politics, and interest group politics are all incapable of helping us to "understand the Communist issue, the forces behind the new nationalism of, say, Senators Bricker and Knowland, and the momentary range of support and the intense emotional heat generated by Senator McCarthy." Even after one allows for the Korean war and the emotional reaction against Chinese and Russian Communists that carried over to domestic Communists, the discovery of Communists in high places in the Federal government and the existence of espionage rings in Washington, and the Canadian spy investigations—even "after the natural effects of all these are taken into account, it is difficult to explain the unchallenged position so long held by Senator McCarthy."

McCarthy's targets, however, are presumed to provide important clues to a "radical right" that backed him and to the reason for that support. The groups in support were "soured patricians," the "new rich," the rising middle class strata of various ethnic groups especially Irish and German, and a small group of intellectuals "some of them cankered ex-Communists, who, pivoting on McCarthy, opened up an attack on liberalism in general." What do these groups have in common? They have status anxieties in common. The central notion is that groups that are on their way up in wealth and social position are "often as anxious and politically feverish as groups that have become *declasse.*" Groups on their way up and groups on their way down seek to impose upon all groups the basic values of the society. Status issues characterized the politics of prosperity; economic class and interest group issues characterize the politics of depression periods.

It is possible, however, that this explanation accounts for a single instance and then only imperfectly. If it explains McCarthyism before December 1954, what about the immediate loss of vogue he suffered after the condemnation? Did the groups on their way up stop climbing or, still climbing, did they stop being anxious? One would have thought they should be even more anxious with the political decapitation of their totem. Did the groups becoming *declasse* stop worrying about their loss of status? If neither of these changes occurred, it is possible that the collapse of McCarthyism after 1954 is connected with the disappearance of some other kind of tension that in fact generated it in the first place, and the sweats of the old rich and the new rich are irrelevant—and, at most, collateral— to the phenomenon of McCarthyism.

The suggestion is also dubious that McCarthyism is one of the diseases of affluence—that status anxieties and the issues they create occur in prosperous times and that economic class and interest group issues characterize the politics of hard times. There were two occasions before the McCarthy era when subversion was a pressing question of real or imaginary importance—in the time of the Palmer raids directly after the First World War, and in the time of the Alien and Sedition Acts. These were not times of prosperity but of economic decline, temporary in each case, but marked in each case. Now it may be said that although there was an excitement about subversion and an insistence upon conformity in these two periods, this was not status politics as defined, but something else. It might be said in answer that the phenomenon of McCarthyism was not status politics either, but something else. In both periods there was social mobility, up and down—in the earlier one the Federalists were on the decline and the Jeffersonians were on the rise, each of them roughly representative of different class concentrations; and in the later period, lower class immigration was on the point of being stopped, and the rise to middle class status of those already here was about to begin. But the whole history of the United States has been one of movement of social classes, so there may be nothing especially peculiar about such changes in the late forties and early fifties. The status politics interpretation of McCarthyism, then, fails to fit the McCarthy period because tensions both preceded and followed the McCarthy era without producing McCarthyism; because notable tensions over subversion in the past appeared in the absence of the necessary conditions (prosperity) which are supposed to supply the reason for status anxiety; and because the issue of subversion did appear under conditions that are supposed to beget economic class and interest group activities, not status anxiety.

Fifth, there is the suggestion that McCarthy's strength was really Republican strength, that he had a vogue where the Republicans were strong and had no vogue where the Republicans were not strong, that he had no substantial personal following at the polls independent of the party and unique to him, and that he was not responsible for beating Benton and Tydings in Connecticut and Maryland. Such a statement usefully supports the notion that McCarthyism is to be explained primarily in political terms, but while explaining what McCarthyism was not, it does not get far into an explanation of what it was.

The theory of McCarthyism that has been presented by writers with a conservative identification has appeared in three versions of increasing sophistication. First, there is the simplistic notion that "McCarthyism" was an invention of those who did not want to see communism exposed, attacked, and uprooted—that it was merely an organized slander. The reasons for anti-anti-communist rejection of McCarthy and his works were various—fear of discovery, toleration of communism as a philosophy, refusal to regard communism seriously as a moral threat to American institutions, pro-Communist bias, an amiable and ignorant relativism which refuses the priority that right can claim over wrong, and a soft compassion for the brutal defendant which forgets the crime. As John T. Flynn said in an article titled "What Is Joe McCarthy Trying to Do?" there was no mystery about Joe McCarthy, who was actually "the most obvious person in Washington." He "just doesn't like Communists."

One variation of this theme was that of William F. Buckley, Jr. in "The New Conformity," a chapter in his defense of McCarthy against his enemies. The argument is that there are basic value preferences in every society, an orthodoxy of outlook on fundamentals, that anti-communism is the American orthodoxy, and that McCarthyism is simply the hardening of that orthodoxy. The tension between liberals and conservatives is a dispute about the fundamentals of the society and the debate over McCarthyism is a skirmish in a conflict that covers a much broader front.

The most thoroughly developed of the conservative statements about McCarthyism is that of Willmoore Kendall in "McCarthyism: The Pons Asinorum of American Conservatism." There it is said that the American people, like other free peoples in the late 1930's, had to make a decision of fateful consequence: to choose whether or not it would allow totalitarian movements to emerge in its midst. The American consensus rejected totalitarian movements of both right and left: the leader of the Nazi Bund went to jail, the Smith Act of 1940 outlawed subversive activity and the advocacy of subversive activity, and there were later prosecutions of a parcel of fringe radicals of the right, such as the Silver Shirts, and to the left, such as the Trotskyites of Minneapolis. The central cases against the Communists were the prosecutions against Eugene Dennis and ten other defendants for violation of the Smith Act.

Consensus is incomprehensible unless it is taken to exclude ideas that are contrary to itself. The rejection of totalitarianism is incomprehensible if totalitarianism is to be condoned and tolerated. The thought that even in an "open society" some questions are closed and that not every first principle is forever arguable counters much supposition to the contrary. It is said to be a characteristic of the liberal view of politics to suppose that nothing is settled, that all is flux, that every idea has a license to compete for custom in the market places of thought and discourse, and that this is the basic American political theory. But what is this notion but an "orthodoxy" of its own? It thus appears that liberals like conservatives have "first principles" that are not arguable and that the statement of this "first principle" falsifies its very purport, namely, that there are no closed questions. The dispute between conservatives and liberals is, then, at bottom, a struggle of orthodoxies. Anti-McCarthyites "got mad" at McCarthyites over opposing claims about the basic nature of the American society. Disputation over the "methods" of McCarthy is a trifle over procedure when one compares it with the more profound rift over the fundamentals of politics.

This is a very free rendition of the rationale of the division between the two camps—the liberal and the conservative—as seen in conservative expositions, but it is intended to be close and not just remotely approximate. It is a casuistical argument in the literal meaning of the adjective—a set of inferences about conduct drawn from moral principles. The conflict is thus viewed as one of heresy, in which each side thinks the other heretical. The logic of this position is to support both prosecution and persecution, and regret was expressed that McCarthyism was no longer an issue, and that it was put to an end in the middle fifties.

McCarthyism and the Politics of Social Change

What are we to make of the numerous speculations about the meaning of McCarthyism, some of which are contradictory? We certainly touch hands with history to be told that McCarthyism has something in common with the rise of the middle class out of the feudal system; or paradoxically, that McCarthy was really a leftist looking right, the same kind of fellow as Robespierre except that Robespierre looked left and acted left; or that McCarthyism is really latter-day Populism or would be if latter-day Populism were like McCarthyism; or that he is to be explained by anxieties about status in a country of fluid social change which has never had a rigid class system and in which everybody is an immigrant or the descendant of one.

Apart from certain shortcomings in each of the principal explanations, none gives much weight to the existence of political elements in the problem. Despite the paradox that McCarthy may have been a "leftist," he was a member of and a spokesman for a position that came to be identified with the Republicans. Although his position had adherents in the Democratic party also, it was as a Republican that McCarthy came into office, stayed in office, made his first attacks upon the Administration, acquired the full authority of a chairmanship, and lost his influence when he attacked the leadership of his own party. It is true that he started his political career as a Democrat, and that he was thought by many to be the stereotype American Catholic—a man with only surface commitments to democratic values. But this socio-religious aspect of the McCarthy experience is collateral to the main fact that he was a Republican spokesman in a time when the Republicans were, most of the time, out of office.

Most of the conservative explanations of McCarthy are as difficult to accept as those of the liberal commentators but for different reasons. If the liberal commentators are sometimes short on the history they invoke, many of the conservative commentators tend to confuse religious truth with political conviction. It is a confusion of religion and politics to import into political discourse such constructs as the freedom of the Western will, the "gargoyles of Anti-Christ," absolute choices between good and evil, and the like. The antiliberal orthodoxy that proceeds to purge the liberal heresy in the name of democracy makes democracy—which is a procedure—the vessel of substantive religious truth which, in its way, is as reprehensible as the familiar Communist tactic which would use the procedure of democracy to end democracy. There can be no such thing as a political heresy in a democracy because there can be no such thing as a political orthodoxy. Heresy and orthodoxy are the concerns of theologians.

McCarthyism may have been more than a political phenomenon—but it was at least a political phenomenon. McCarthy acquired his vogue and most of his meaning from the immediate political circumstance which begot him, and for which he was the temporary instrument. But the political roots of McCarthyism are to be found in the past, and the branches stretch into the future.

The industrial revolution after the Civil War created an economic system of marvelous productivity, a true wonder of the world, and brought to dominance new elites of economic enterprise whose very success made them the cultural idols of the society, to whom deference was expected and was accorded, who left the imprint of their taste and interest on every aspect of the society. They constituted a new system of power over the wealth and the material resources of the land. There were critics of the new order but they were not destined to prevail any more than did the machine-smashers and barn-burners of England when the industrial revolution took hold there. In the years after the Civil War, what may be called the "conservative consensus" became fixed in the structure of American social values, and there was to be, thereafter, no major challenge to the domination of the economy by private business enterprise.

The new business oligarchy came to wield presiding influence in the affairs of the Republican party. As Malcolm Moos, a biographer of the Republican party, has said,

For Grant, a man who could never make a success in business, those who had become so fabulously successful seemed to have almost a fatal fascination. But it was more than merely appointments and special favors that went to business—it was the Republican party. And as the party became the champion of capital, it did so with the hearty approval of a great mass of American people. . . . Nor was it an unnatural alliance, this new combine of politician and capitalist. As business looked to Washington for support, aid and comfort, the businessman looked to the politician as a broker—albeit a broker who sometimes had a little bet on the side.

The party of Grant was not the party of Lincoln, for the principal energy was no longer provided by moral concern for the human condition but by concern for the gospel of free enterprise, for the protection and advancement of an economic philosophy which tended to equate the public interest with the well-being of the managers of the economy.

The President of the United States, in this conception of the public policy, was merely the minister of the desire of the Congress, the agent charged by the Constitution to see that the laws (of Congress) were faithfully executed, a conception that has characterized the conservative perspective throughout American history, as Wilfred Binkley has observed. The weak-President model of the Executive office is congenial to an economic philosophy in which the major decisions are to be left in private hands. In practical effect the fracture and decentralization of the public power that this model entails works to the advantage of the business community in two ways: it makes governmental regulation of the business community more difficult; and it favors the enactment of promotions, subsidies, tariffs, and other tangible benefits that may be negotiated through bargain and compromise among legislators who are responsive to the separated constituencies that Congressmen represent. In short, it tends to favor Congress over the Executive as the center of Federal authority.

There seems to operate in democratic politics something like a presumption of continuous office. In the absence of strong doctrinary alternatives, the case has to be made *against* incumbents. As Eugene Burdick has his protagonist instructor say in *The Ninth Wave,* people tend to vote often for negative reasons, that is, out of dislike, hatred even, and fear. The sum total of the statements made in a political campaign is likely to be a minus. Political campaigns take on some of the aspects of a public litigation, with all the narrowness and distortion that special pleading involves. By contrast, the sum total of statements made in business competition is a plus. By the common law and by many statutes, there are certain forms of destructive statement and action against business competitors that will not be tolerated in the courts. The business competitor is required to confine himself to superlatives about himself. When all political campaigners plead the venality of each other and all businessmen argue which of them is the more virtuous, it may be supposed that stereotypes become fixed in the public consciousness (or unconsciousness) of the politician as a suspicious character and that of the businessman as a praiseworthy fellow, although some might be more praiseworthy than others. Working in favor of incumbents, then, is their tenure—if only because a case must be made for throwing them out. But the presumption of continuous office can be rebutted. It will generally be rebutted when there is a sufficiently large and onerous accumulation of grievances to impel the people at the polls to act.

With the domination of the economy and of the commonwealth by business influence after the Civil War, the presumption of continuous office favored unlimited tenure. But the regimes of Grant and his successors could and did forfeit their right to rule in the gradual accumulation of grievances that a narrow and sectarian view of the public interest and public policy produced. Resistance, in the first instance, took such forms of political self-help as the Granger movement in the states, when farmers lobbied and pressured state legislatures for political relief from economic disadvantage, and even ruin. The depression of 1873, which the manipulations of Jay Cooke and others in the stock market helped to create, produced widespread social unrest. Among the railroad workers, this led to blind and leaderless protest as in the spontaneous strike actions of 1877. Among other workers, it led first to the development of the Knights of Labor and then to the American Federation of Labor when the principle of organization of the Knights proved to be so vulnerable in the 1880's.

The experience of the farmers in Illinois and other states of the Middle West in the 1870's and 1880's showed that political relief could be had through coalitions of the disaffected. As the potency of the symbol of the "bloody shirt" faded with the advent of a new generation to whom the tensions of the Civil War were relatively less strainful than the painful economic urgencies of the present, the Democratic party began to win seats in Congress. Although the capture of the White House by the Democrats had been frustrated in 1876, the portent of the election of 1882 for the presidential election of 1884 was unmistakable. The businessman-Republican party alliance had become like a corporate management that the creditors can force into bankruptcy. They continue to own the enterprise but the referees in bankruptcy liquidate some of their assets to pay claims that have been defaulted.

It was the historic function of the Democratic party in the 1880's to serve as the people's referee to redistribute some of the assets. The Grange, the Alliance, the Wheel, the 700,000 members of the Knights of Labor, the railroad strikes, the Haymarket riots, the rise of the American Federation of Labor, the organization of the Pinkerton Detective Agency to conduct industrial espionage—many elements in this great social ferment of the ninth decade of the nineteenth century were material to be organized into a coalition of the disaffected, capable of obtaining political compensation for economic disadvantage through welfarist and social benefit programs. This was the historic role of the Democratic party in 1912 and 1932 and it might have been realized in 1884.

But in 1884, Cleveland misconceived the role of the party. It is true that he had to contend with a Republican Senate, but he had trouble with the Democratic House also. The root difficulty was his conception of what he was doing. So firmly stuck was the notion that free enterprise had some of the organic authority of the Constitution of the United States (a view that the Supreme Court in the 1880's was busy promoting) that he acted as though the chief function of government was to apply "business principles to public affairs." With respect to the farmer, Cleveland took the narrow view of Federal authority favored by the Republicans and their business constituency, and he vetoed a measure to supply free seed. Even when he returned to the White House in 1892, after losing the election of 1888, he refused inflationary formulas for the relief of agriculture, supported the gold standard, and thereby alienated the West. His view of the powers of the Federal government was not so narrow, however, that he could not send his Attorney General into the Pullman strike of 1894, to break it, which he did with the injunction. It took almost forty years to undo the effects of this unhappy intervention, in the Norris-La Guardia Act of 1932.

Since the grievances of farmers and workers and other casualties of the new industrialism of the eighties and the nineties were evidently not on the agenda of the two major parties, disaffected groups sought political compensation for their economic disadvantage in the formation of separate political movements like the Alliance and the Populists, which scored great successes. Although the protest parties never won the presidency, they had victories in the Congress, both in the capture of seats and in influencing the enactment of measures like the Sherman Antitrust Act of 1890, the income tax law of 1890, the Silver Purchase Act of 1890, and other progressive measures. Populist sentiment was counteracted and frustrated by the courts which voided the income tax law, made a nullity of the Interstate Commerce Commission Act of 1887, and reduced the scope of the Sherman Antitrust Act; while the business world helped itself to substantial portions of benefit through the tariff. But the force of the Populist crusade had far-reaching effects. It won electoral votes, captured state governments, frightened southern whites into programs of racial restriction, and provided lessons for all to learn of the value of political organization. It spent its force in the nineties, and the grievances that set it in motion were assuaged with returning prosperity. Although class tensions were rife in the election of 1896, the Republican party succeeded in putting together support from city workers and western farmers that was strong enough to prevail.

By 1912, however, the Democrats under the leadership of Woodrow Wilson understood their historic role. As V. O. Key has said, "If a party is to govern, it must bring into mutually advantageous alliance an aggregate of interest powerful enough to win a presidential election. If it is to govern for long, it must see that the loaves and fishes are divided in a manner to command popular approbation." The alliance contrived by McKinley and Hanna and continued by Theodore Roosevelt got power to govern for a considerable period. It could not solve the problem of the loaves and the fishes, however, because important sectors of the society were not content to wait until the benefits of the new enterprise trickled slowly down to the multitude, with the government confined to the role of auxiliary to the businessman as strike-breaker, policeman, and customs collector. Theodore Roosevelt's gestures towards reform were often verbalisms with a political function rather than an operational effect. Wilson seized the leadership of the disaffected and made it clear that the business community was finally to be challenged, for the first time, effectively, since the days of Andrew Jackson. The election was a split among three candidates and Wilson won largely because the Republicans were divided between Roosevelt and Taft, but the total votes for progressive reform were greater than the total votes for the *status quo*.

By 1920, the country had had enough of reform (the discontents of the disaffected had been appeased for that matter after the first Wilson election and he almost lost the second), and the country was returned to the control of the business managers who succeeded, after a decade, in producing a real bankruptcy. The persistence of the Cleveland myth—that the national Democratic party was really just like the Republican, only a little less so—was revived in 1924, and it offered a conservative candidate with remarkably good credentials in the world of business affairs, and little appeal to the groups concerned with liberal action. John W. Davis was the 1920's counterpart of Alton B. Parker who had also failed to move multitudes with his promises to be like the Republicans. As in 1892, when Cleveland was so strongly promoted by business groups, there appeared in 1924 a third party, the Progressives of La Follette, but it failed to run again in 1928. The Democrats perpetrated a political debacle in 1928 with Alfred E. Smith who, although more liberal than Davis, was not much more so, as his subsequent attacks upon the New Deal and his membership in the American Liberty League were to attest; and who, moreover, was, for most of the country, a caricature of the East Side with whom it was difficult to make any kind of personal identification.

The party of General Grant, Rutherford B. Hayes, Chester Alan Arthur, William McKinley, William Howard Taft, Warren Gamaliel Harding, Calvin Coolidge, and Herbert Hoover found it difficult not only to get into the White House after 1932 but to get its candidates nominated for the presidency. Herbert

Hoover was shunted to one side in 1936, Vandenberg (before his conversion to internationalist causes) was defeated by Wendell Willkie, John Bricker of Ohio lost it to Dewey in 1944, Taft lost it to Dewey in 1948 and to Eisenhower in 1952. Like the Democratic party of Cleveland, Parker, and Davis which imitated the Republicans, the Republicans between 1936 and 1964 made no frontal assault upon the programs of the New Deal but only a collateral harassment, promising to keep the social gains (although not to add to them) while administering programs more economically and efficiently. There was no restoration in 1940, as there had been in 1920, following the political adjustment of credit claims, and the prevailing leadership in successive Republican national conventions did not seem capable of obtaining it.

The decline of the New Deal after 1936 as measured by the gradual loss of Democratic seats in the House and Senate and the shrinkage of the popular margins in the presidential elections of 1940 and 1944, presaged the expected change in 1948 which did not take place. Eager for office, disappointed by frustration, the Republican party with the help of conservative Democrats took control of the Congress in 1950, found a storm leader in McCarthy, developed the technique of prescriptive publicity as a formidable weapon of political harassment, and with an assist from the timorous and defensive leadership of the Administration managed to achieve in 1952 the victory they had been denied for two decades, which the politics of eighty years promised and, according to which, was overdue.

McCarthyism in this view of the party movements of almost a century was the agent of fundamentalist conservatism that was prepared to yield public policy to the reformers for the relatively short periods required to satisfy grievances but which expected to recover predominance when these intervals were over. McCarthy had no social program of his own and in this respect was the perfect instrument for the realization of the social aims of those who were to benefit from his attacks, for the restoration which a third term and a war had denied. The Communist issue was the cutting edge for the attack. The Communist problem lent itself to quiet and nonsensational solutions before the late forties and after 1954. When McCarthy and the Communist issue had served their purposes, they both disappeared.

The fundamentalist conservatism that McCarthy served has been an enduring aspect of the American system since the Civil War and has not been dissipated. It believes with profound faith in free enterprise, reacts to symbols that seem to threaten it, is suspicious of welfare and other social reform, tends to stand pat, and is moved only by exigency. The stronghold of this faith in the Republican party has been centered in the Middle and Rocky Mountain West and it has not been satisfied with the moderate conservatism of the eastern states. It regards itself as the heart and soul of the Republican party, uncorrupted by the liberalism that has softened the eastern wing, and is determined to recover the conservative spirit of the 1920's and earlier times. It is pre–New Deal in its mentality. It came to office if not to power with the help of McCarthy in the three years after 1950, and may some time surge again in an effort to hold time still, and perhaps even turn it back a little.

It has been said that the tyrant with the sword is followed by the historian with the sponge, but no erasure has softened the image of former Senator Joseph R. McCarthy of Wisconsin since his condemnation by the United States Senate on December 2, 1954, for unsenatorial behavior. Although he was to serve a short-run goal in a short span of years, he has achieved permanent prominence of a sort. The clamors of that anxious time have guaranteed that McCarthy's name, like that of Pope's Cromwell, will be "dam'd to everlasting fame."

GODFREY HODGSON

The Ideology of
the Liberal Consensus

It is always risky to draw the portrait of the ideas and beliefs of a society at any point in its evolution. Contradictions and crosscurrents defy generalization. Too much survives from the past, and too much anticipates the future. Usually, perhaps, the attempt is doomed to end either in superficiality or in intellectual dishonesty. But the period from the middle of the 1950s in the United States up to the impact of the crisis of the 1960s was not usual in this respect. It was an age of consensus. Whether you look at the writings of intellectuals or at the positions taken by practicing politicians or at the data on public opinion, it is impossible not to be struck by the degree to which the majority of Americans in those years accepted the same system of assumptions. Official and semiofficial attempts were even made to codify these assumptions in such works as the report of President Eisenhower's Commission on National Goals or in the Rockefeller Brothers Fund panel reports. The crisis of the late 1960s was caused partly by the mistakes and shortcomings of this system of assumptions and partly by a series of attacks upon it.

In the late 1950s Professor Hadley Cantril of Princeton, one of the pioneers of the statistical study of public opinion, conducted a survey of thousands of individuals in ten countries. The results were published in 1965 in a book called *The Pattern of Human Concerns*. Cantril showed that the subject, and the intensity, of human concerns varied widely from one society to another. People in poorer countries, he found, worried more, and about a wider range of possible personal catastrophes, than did people in richer countries.

The American pattern, Cantril discovered on the basis of survey work done in 1959, was the most distinctive of all. Americans were the most confident people in the world:

The total volume of concerns of the American people was relatively low, especially those related to their hopes and fears for the nation, except for the single overriding concern that war be avoided. On the personal side there was an unusual emphasis on good health. . . . Americans appeared to be chiefly concerned with the two major threats they felt were most beyond their control, war and illness.

Professor Cantril attributed this mood of confidence not to any peculiarity of American culture but to prosperity. As other countries became similarly prosperous, he expected their people also to feel "a general satisfaction with a way of life which promises continued development." And he made an interesting prediction: Confidence and satisfaction would remain the prevailing mood in a prosperous, developed country

until some major event or crisis transpires which creates major and widespread frustrations. Only then are people likely to become awakened to the inadequacy of the assumptions they have come to take for granted.

All cross bearings confirm the essential accuracy of this picture. At the end of the 1950s, Americans worried about their own personal lives—about health and status. At the other end of the scale of immediacy, they worried about the danger of nuclear war. But few of them doubted the essential goodness and strength of American society.

Four times between 1959 and 1961, the Gallup poll asked its sample what they regarded as the "most important problem" facing the nation. Each time, the most frequent answer (given in each case by at least close to half of the respondents and sometimes by far more than half) was "keeping the peace," sometimes glossed as "dealing with Russia." No domestic issue came anywhere close to challenging that outstanding concern.

In the presidential campaign of 1960, only two types of domestic issues were rated as critical by either candidate or by his advisers: on the one hand, atavistic ethnic issues—the Catholic vote, or Martin Luther King's arrest—and on the other hand, the behavior of the economy. And the latter, to Kennedy, at least, seemed important mainly as a prerequisite of foreign policy.

Kennedy built his appeal around the call to get the country moving again. He left a strong impression that his main reason for doing so was in order to recover lost prestige in the competition with the Soviet Union. Summing up his campaign, in Hartford, Connecticut, on the eve of polling, Senator Kennedy listed three major differences between his opponent and himself:

first a different view of the present state of the American economy; secondly a different view of our prestige in the world, and therefore, our ability to lead the free world; and thirdly, whether the balance of power in the world is shifting in our direction or that of our adversaries.

Nixon, too, had three themes. First, that Kennedy was running America down; second, that the Democrats would cause inflation; and third, that he,

Richard Nixon, could speak better for America in confrontation with the Soviet leader.

When it came to sensing the issues that had a gut appeal to the electorate as a whole, that is, each candidate chose to stress foreign dangers (and glories) over domestic problems, in the proportion of two to one.

The various American elites took more complicated views. A good deal of concern was expressed by intellectuals in the late 1950s about the lack of excellence in American education (especially in the context of an alleged inferiority to Soviet achievements in space science and missile technology), about the (temporarily) lagging growth rate of the economy, and in diffuse and cloudy jeremiads about the materialism of mass culture. But in the most ambitious contemporary analyses, the same dualism was the recurrent major theme: never so much hope in America, never so much danger abroad. . . .

In political terms, the beginnings of consensus date back to 1954. That was the pudding time when moderation came back into fashion after the acerbities of the Korean War and the McCarthy era.

Stalin died in 1953. The Korean War ended four months later, at Panmunjom.

The Cold War was far from over. One historian considers it reached its zenith with John Foster Dulles's speech, in January 1954, in which he called for "the deterrent of massive retaliatory power . . . by means and at times of our own choosing." Still, the Geneva conference and the Indochina settlement in the summer of 1954 did bring a warmer international climate. The successors of Stalin had problems enough on their hands. They proclaimed coexistence as their goal, and if they never gave up on the attempt to turn the new atmosphere to their advantage, they did show genuine signs of tractability. In the spring of 1955 they unexpectedly agreed to sign an Austrian peace treaty, and that summer Bulganin and Khrushchev met the American President at the summit. Peace was still a long way off, but war seemed farther away.

It was in June 1954 that a soft-spoken New England lawyer named Joseph Welch destroyed Senator McCarthy by asking him the question no one had dared ask him before: "Have you no sense of decency, sir, at last?" In December, the Senate voted aye to a motion of censure. Intolerance and anti-communist hysteria were not dead, but at least exploiting them was no longer fashionable.

There was a sharp recession over the winter of 1953–54. Industrial production actually declined by 10 per cent. The President had the good sense to turn to the chairman of his Council of Economic Advisers, Dr. Arthur Burns, who prescribed a modest course of Keynesian spending. "It is no longer a matter of serious controversy," Burns was soon saying, "whether the government shall play a positive role in helping to maintain a high level of economic activity." After 1954, traditional Republican orthodoxy as represented by Secretary of the Treasury George M. Humphrey was in retreat.

For some seven years after 1955, few fundamental disagreements, foreign or domestic, were aired in either presidential or Congressional politics. That the United States should in principle seek better relations with the Soviet Union while keeping its guard up and seeking to contain communism—this was common ground. Disagreement was relegated to issues of the second order of importance: the extent to which the United States should support the United Nations, the level of foreign aid, the speed of space development. The main lines of domestic policy were equally beyond controversy. The Eisenhower administration accepted that the federal government must continue social security and such other New Deal programs as had stood the test of public popularity. It was ready to enforce due compliance with the law in civil rights, though reluctantly and with caution. And it was prepared to use fiscal and monetary measures to maintain full employment and economic growth. Not much more, and no less, could be said of the Kennedy administration in its first two years.

The political process, it was taken for granted throughout that period, was a matter of emphasizing one nuance or another of this generally agreed program. A "liberal" congressman, as the word was then used, was one who might be expected to speak up for the particular interests of organized labor; a "conservative" would voice the reservations of corporate business or of the armed services.

Not only in Washington but in the press, on television, and—with few exceptions—in the academic community, to dissent from the broad axioms of consensus was to proclaim oneself irresponsible or ignorant. That would risk disqualifying the dissenter from being taken seriously, and indeed often from being heard at all.

A strange hybrid, liberal conservatism, blanketed the scene and muffled debate. It stretched from Americans for Democratic Action—which lay at the leftward frontiers of respectability and yet remained safely committed to anticommunism and free enterprise—as far into the board rooms of Wall Street and manufacturing industry as there could be found a realistic willingness to accept the existence of labor unions, the rights of minorities, and some role in economic life for the federal government. Since the consensus had made converts on the Right as well as on the Left, only a handful of dissidents were excluded from the Big Tent: southern diehards, rural reactionaries, the more *farouche* and paranoid fringes of the radical Right, and the divided remnants of the old, Marxist, Left. Together, they hardly added up to a corporal's guard. And they were of course never together. . . .

In September 1955, at precisely the moment when consensus was settling like snow over U.S. politics, something very similar was happening in American intellectual life. That month, some one hundred fifty intellectuals from many countries foregathered at a conference in Milan to debate "The Future of Freedom." They had been invited there at the initiative of an organization called the Congress for Cultural Freedom, and their proceedings were later reported in the Congress's London monthly review, *Encounter,* by the sociologist Edward Shils. (Both the congress and *Encounter* were later found to have been in receipt of secret funds from the Central Intelligence Agency.) The title the editor put on Shils's article was *The End of Ideology?*

The idea was not new. "Liberal civilization begins when the age of ideology is over," Lewis Feuer had written in an article called "Beyond Ideology," published earlier that same year. Seymour Martin Lipset called one of the chapters in his *Political Man,* published in 1960, "The End of Ideology." But the person with whom the phrase came to be most closely associated was Lipset's close friend the sociologist and journalist Daniel Bell. Originally a product of one of the many fragments of the New York socialist Left, Bell became the labor editor of *Fortune* magazine and was also for a time the director of international seminars for the Congress for Cultural Freedom. His career epitomized, in fact, the intellectual consensus that underpinned its political equivalent during the 1950s. He saw clearly its double foundation: on the fear of communism abroad and on the assumption that American society could solve its problems without irresoluble conflict.

"Politics today," he wrote in 1960, "is not a reflex of any internal class divisions but is shaped by international events. And foreign policy, the expression of politics, is a response to many factors, the most important of which has been the estimate of Russian intentions . . . the need for containment.

What sort of domestic politics did this acceptance of the primacy of anti-Communist foreign policy imply?

In the West, therefore, there is today a rough consensus among intellectuals on political issues: the acceptance of a Welfare State; the desirability of decentralized power; a system of mixed economy and of political pluralism. In that sense, too, the ideological age has ended.

Both those two highly explicit formulations are taken from the book, published in 1960, which Bell, too, called *The End of Ideology.*

What Bell meant by that was, above all, the end of the ideology of the Left. "By 'the end of ideology,' " even his friend Irving Kristol, the editor who had originally published Shils's article of the same title, was constrained to comment, "Mr. Bell appears to mean, above all, the collapse of the socialist ideal."

Bell and his group, in fact, announced the death of ideology somewhat in the way in which the death of royalty used to be announced. "The King is dead," said the courtiers. "Long live the King!"

At one point in his book, he defines what he called "a total ideology":

. . . an all-inclusive system of comprehensive reality, it is a set of beliefs, infused with passion, and seeks to transform the whole of a way of life. This commitment to ideology—the yearning for a "cause," or the satisfaction of deep moral feelings—is not necessarily the reflection of interests in the shape of ideas. Ideology, in this sense . . . is a secular religion.

Consciously or not, Daniel Bell was describing the American ideology of the age of consensus. Cause, commitment, system of beliefs and way of life, it was indeed a secular religion.

Confident to the verge of complacency about the perfectibility of American society, anxious to the point of paranoia about the threat of communism—those were the two faces of the consensus mood. Each grew from one aspect of the experience of the 1940s: confidence from economic success, anxiety from the fear of Stalin and the frustrations of power.

Historical logic made some form of consensus likely. It was natural that the new prosperity should calm the class antipathies of the depression years. It was normal that the sense of an enemy at the gate should strengthen national unity. And a reaction was predictable after the lacerating politics of the McCarthy period. But the basis for the consensus was something more than a vague mood or a reaction to passing events. The assumptions on which it was built had an intellectual life and coherence of their own. In barest outline, they can be summarized in the following set of interrelated maxims:

1. The American free-enterprise system is different from the old capitalism. It is democratic. It creates abundance. It has a revolutionary potential for social justice.

2. The key to this potential is production: specifically, increased production, or economic growth. This makes it possible to meet people's needs out of incremental resources. Social conflict over resources between classes (which Marx called "the locomotive of history") therefore becomes obsolete and unnecessary.

3. Thus there is a natural harmony of interests in society. American society is getting more equal. It is in process of abolishing, may even have abolished, social class. Capitalists are being superseded by managers. The workers are becoming members of the middle class.

4. Social problems can be solved like industrial problems: The problem is first identified; programs are designed to solve it, by government enlightened by social science; money and other resources—such as trained people—are then applied to the problem as "inputs"; the outputs are predictable: the problems will be solved.

5. The main threat to this beneficent system comes from the deluded adherents of Marxism. The United States and its allies, the Free World, must therefore expect a prolonged struggle against communism.

6. Quite apart from the threat of communism, it is the duty and destiny of the United States to bring the good tidings of the free-enterprise system to the rest of the world.

The germ of this intellectual system, which by about 1960 had emerged as the dominant American ideology, was a simple yet startling empirical discovery. Capitalism, after all, seemed to work. . . .

As late as the war years, most American economists, led by Alvin Hansen, predicted that capitalism was entering a phase of chronic stagnation. Most other intellectuals took the economists at their word and assumed that the task was to replace capitalism with some more promising system.

Suddenly, in the late 1940s, the moribund system was declared not *only* alive but healthy. The economic *ancien régime* was acclaimed as the revolutionary harbinger of a brave new world.

In 1949 Daniel Bell wrote an article called "America's Un-Marxist Revolution."

"Keynes, not Marx," wrote Arthur Schlesinger in the same year, "is the prophet of the new radicalism."

"The world revolution of our time is 'made in U.S.A.,'" wrote Peter Drucker, the champion of management, also in 1949. "The true revolutionary principle is the idea of mass production."

And in 1951 the editors of *Fortune* magazine gave to an ambitious, much noticed synthesis of the American Way of Life a title borrowed from Marx and given currency by Trotsky. They called it *U.S.A., the Permanent Revolution:*

There has occurred a great transformation, of which the world as a whole is yet unaware. . . . No important progress whatever can be made in the understanding of America unless the nature of this transformation is grasped. . . . There has been a vast dispersal of ownership and initiative, so that the capitalist system has become intimately bound in with the political system and takes nourishment from its democratic roots. . . . U.S. capitalism is popular capitalism.

At the root of this optimistic new political philosophy, there lay an appropriately optimistic new economic doctrine. It came to be known as the New Economics, though by the time of its triumph, in the 1960s, when its licensed practitioners monopolized the President's Council of Economic Advisers, many of its leading ideas were going on thirty years old.

There were many strands to the New Economics. But the essence of it was the acceptance in the United States of the ideas of John Maynard Keynes, *not* as first received in the 1930s but as modified by American economists in the light of the success of the American economy in the 1940s.

The nub of Keynes's teaching was that, contrary to the tenets of classical economics, savings did not necessarily become investment. This was the cause of cyclical depression and of unemployment: left to itself, the capitalist system contained forces that would tend to produce stagnation. To that extent his position was pessimistic. But Keynes was a political economist. He did not think that things should be left to themselves. He believed that government could cure the kind of deflation that had caused the Great Depression by spending, and if necessary by deficit spending. He actually wrote a long letter to FDR, in early 1938, pleading with him to spend his way out of the recession. The letter was ignored. But after 1945 the university economists succeeded in persuading the more enlightened businessmen, and some politicians, that Keynes was right. Capitalism could be *made* to work. Depression and unemployment were avoidable, and it was up to the government to avoid them. . . .

In practical terms, the gospel of the New Economics could be translated into exciting propositions. Government can manage the economy by using fiscal and monetary policy. The tyranny of the business cycle, which had brought economic catastrophe and the specter of political upheaval, need no longer be tolerated. Depressions could be a thing of the past.

By changing interest rates and by increasing or decreasing the money supply—technical matters that had the added advantage of being remote from the scrutiny of everyday politics—government could flatten out fluctuations in economic activity.

The economists were emboldened to maintain that these fiscal and monetary controls could be manipulated with such precision—"fine tuning" was the phrase used—that in effect they would be able to fly the economy like an airplane, trimming its speed, course and altitude with tiny movements of the flaps and rudder. That was a later claim. The essential promise of the Keynesian system was that it would allow government to guarantee low and diminishing unemployment without inflation. It could thus banish at a stroke the worst terrors of both liberals and conservatives. At the same time, thus managed, the economy would also be able to deliver growth. . . .

In theory, there could be little arguing with that proposition. Its truth in practice would depend on a number of questions: one's definition of social progress, the extent to which social progress could be guaranteed to follow from the application of resources, and the propensity of government to devote incremental resources to other purposes, such as fighting wars. But the relevant point here is that it was a proposition ideally suited to be one of the main props of an ideology of liberal conservatism. It offered to the liberals the hope of progress and a feeling of benevolence, and to the conservatives a vista of business prosperity and an unthreatened *status quo*. . . .

No tenet of the consensus was more widely held than the idea that revolutionary American capitalism had abolished the working class, or—as approximately the same thought was sometimes expressed—that everybody in America was middle class now or that American society was rapidly approaching economic equality.

A small encyclopedia of statements to this effect can be garnered from the historians, the social scientists and the journalists of the time.

"The organizing concept of American society," wrote Peter Drucker, "has been that of social mobility . . . which denies the existence of classes."

"The union," said the editors of *Fortune,* "has made the worker, to an amazing degree, a middle class member of a middle class society."

"New Dealism," said historian Eric Goldman, ". . . found that it had created a nation of the middle class."

Yet another historian, Samuel Eliot Morison, boldly dated the abolition of the proletariat rather earlier than some would say the proletariat came into existence. He cited the observations of a Polish Communist visitor to confirm "a fact that has puzzled socialists and communists for a century: the American workman is an expectant capitalist, not a class-conscious proletarian."

Frederick L. Allen, on the other hand, wrote a best seller to prove that "the big change" in American life between 1900 and 1950 was the "democratization of our economic system."

One's first reaction is to yield to the cumulative weight of so many impassioned opinions and to conclude . . . what? For even the most cursory reading of such a miscellany raises questions. Had class stratification never existed in the United States, as Drucker seemed to think? But, then, can one imagine social mobility without class? Mobility between what? Had there never been an American proletariat, as Professor Morison seemed to believe? Or had there been a "big change"? Perhaps the proletariat had ceased to exist. But, then, which agency had earned the credit for this transformation? "Industrial enterprise," as some claimed? *Fortune*'s unions? Or Goldman's "New Dealism"? Corporate business, labor and government may work in harmony. But they are hardly synonyms.

A second reading of this miscellany of texts and of the other evidence suggests two more-modest conclusions:

1. A great many Americans, moved by the ideal of equality but perhaps also by reluctance to admit what was seen as a Marxist analysis of their own society, passionately wanted to believe that the concept of class was alien to the United States.

   It suited business to believe this. It suited labor. It suited intellectuals, and it suited the press. It suited liberals, and it suited conservatives. Who was left to argue otherwise?

2. Nevertheless, something *had* happened. In the profound transformations of the 1940s the class structure of American society and its implications for politics had changed in complex and confusing ways—though not to the point of making "everybody middle class," still less of invalidating class analysis.

The abolition of the working class, in fact, was a myth. Like most myths, it did have a certain basis in fact. But it oversimplified and distorted what had really happened. It transformed a modest and temporary decline in inequality into a social revolution. At the same time, it confused the idea that many Americans were far better off than they had been, which was true, with the claim that poorer Americans had made dramatic gains at the expense of the better off, which was at best dubious.

Two developments probably explain the strength of this myth. The real performance of the economy during and after World War II made it possible to believe it. And the triumph of the liberals over the Left made a lot of people want to believe it.

The prosperity of the 1940s really was widespread. Mass unemployment ended, after twelve years. Dollar wages, especially for workers in such strongly unionized (and highly visible) industries as steel, automobiles, and rubber, rose dramatically. But real wages for most workers rose too.

There was also a highly obvious equalization of *consumption,* which looked like an equalization of wealth, all the more so because it was concentrated in the most visible forms of consumption: clothes, for example, and cars. Nylon stockings were a favorite example with economists and journalists alike. They were introduced in September 1939, the month Europe went to war. Ten years later, they were still a luxury in Europe. But in the United States, production in 1949 was 543 million pairs; every typist could afford to be dressed like a film star from ankle to thigh. The parking lots full of shiny, late-model automobiles outside factories were much commented upon; and "everybody" could afford the new electrical household gadgets.

In other ways, too, it really did look as though the rich were getting poorer and the poor richer. The rich complained bitterly about the income tax, and in fact the maximum rate rose from 54 per cent in 1932 to 91 per cent in the 1950s. Meanwhile, the after-taxes income of families in the lower income brackets was rising faster than that of the better-off families, and the income of the wealthiest 5 per cent actually dropped. . . .

The best way to measure the distribution of income is to measure what proportion of the total national income has gone at different times to different fractions of the population, ranged in order from the richest to the poorest.

When the historian Gabriel Kolko did this, he came up with a result that shattered the liberal assumption that income had been redistributed to the poor. Here is how he summarized his findings in his book *Wealth and Power in America*:

Despite the obvious increase in prosperity since the abysmal years of the Great Depression, the basic distribution of income and wealth is essentially the same now as it was in 1939, or even 1910. Most low-income groups live substantially better today, but even though their real wages have mounted, their percentage of the national income has not changed.

Kolko computed the percentage of national personal income received, before taxes, by each tenth of the population by income, over the whole period from 1910 to 1959. He found that while the share of the highest tenth had dropped, it had dropped only from 33.9 per cent in 1910 to 28.9 per cent in 1959. And over the same period, the share of the national income that went to the whole lower half of the population dropped from 27 per cent to 23 per cent. It is certainly hard to talk about the abolition of the proletariat, or even of economic democratization, in reference to a society in which the whole poorer half of the population has been getting relatively poorer.

The same distribution tables also suggest what has actually occurred to give the illusion of social progress. The pattern is best described by comparing the proportions of the national income that went at five different dates to three fractions of the population: the rich, represented by the top tenth of all incomes; the middle class, represented by the next four tenths, taken together; the poor, represented by the lower half. (I should perhaps say that I am not suggesting that the terms "the rich," "the poor" and the "middle class" correspond to those fractions; I am merely using a convenient shorthand for three groups.)

In 1929, before the Depression and the New Deal, the top tenth received 39 percent of the national income. The middle class got exactly the same share. And the poor got the rest: 22 per cent.

In 1941, after twelve years of massive unemployment, the poor's share had fallen still further, to 19 per cent. The share of the rich had also fallen, by five percentage points, to 34 per cent. The whole gain, at the expense of both rich and poor, had gone to the "middle class."

In 1945, after four decisive years of war, boom and full employment, the poor had . . . recovered to exactly the point where they stood before the Depression: 22 per cent. The rich had lost another five percentage points, to 29 per cent. The middle class took just short of half the national income: 49 per cent.

And in 1949 and 1959, the years of the Permanent Revolution and the Affluent Society? Nothing had changed. That was the remarkable thing. To be precise, the top tenth gained one percentage point in 1949 and had lost it again by 1959. The middle four tenths together dropped a point in 1949, and stayed on 48 percent in 1959. The poor gained one point, moving to 23 per cent by 1959. That was all.

The fact that the distribution of income in America is not equal, and is not noticeably getting any more equal, is not generally accepted. In a study for the Joint Economic Committee of Congress published in 1972, Lester C. Thurow and Robert E. B. Lucas of M.I.T. showed that the distribution of income from 1947 to 1969 had remained approximately constant: "Everybody's income (male, female, majority, minority, rich and poor) had been rising at approximately the same rate, leaving their ratios unaffected." An analysis of the 1970 census data by Peter Henle, a Library of Congress statistician, reported what he called "a continuing slow trend towards inequality." The common-sense conclusion would seem to be that there has been essentially no change in the distribution of income in the United States since World War II.

There has been only one rather sharp change in the twentieth century. This was the gain made between 1929 and 1945 by the second and third tenths of the population at the expense of the first. Their combined share went up from 22.1 per cent in 1929 to 29 per cent in 1945 and has since remained roughly constant. The redistribution of wealth, then, such as it was, seems to have been over by 1945. And it was a redistribution not from the rich to the poor, but from the very best off to the next best off. The second and third tenths of the income scale at that time would have included some executives, managers, professionals, some higher-paid clerical workers, and the very best-paid craft and industrial workers in the strongest unions. A shift of 10 per cent of the national income in their direction scarcely constituted either the abolition of the proletariat or the coming of the universal middle class. Yet, by a kind of intellectual parallax error, that was how it was seen.

The mood of the country may have been relatively complacent in the late fifties and the early sixties. But this was not, as the liberal analysis assumed, because the condition of the American people left so little to be desired. It was because a number of historical factors had weakened the political unity and consciousness of the working class and deprived it of the means to perceive its own interests and to defend them.

One of these factors was the way the idea of equality had evolved in the United States. Historically, the actual condition of American society—with the two major exceptions of black and red Americans—had probably always more closely approached a condition of equality than European society. The availability of land, the unexploited resources of a "new" country of continental extent, the absence—or near absence—of an established feudal upper class with a vested interest in maintaining inequality, all tended to minimize inequality in practice. Yet in theory Americans had always been less concerned than Europeans with equality of condition. The paradox is only apparent. Because of the relative abundance of their environment, Americans could afford to think equality of condition less important than equality of opportunity. In most other cultures, people knew all too well that there would never be enough opportunities to go round.

The historian David Potter argued powerfully in his 1954 essay *People of Plenty* that almost every distinctive aspect of American life, from child rearing to political institutions, could be traced to the pervasive influence of economic abundance:

> *The very meaning of the term "equality" reflects this influence. . . . A European, advocating equality, might very well mean that all men should occupy positions that are roughly on the same level in wealth, power or enviability. But the American, with his emphasis on equality of opportunity, has never conceived of it in this sense. He has traditionally expected to find a gamut ranging from rags to riches, from tramps to millionaires. . . . In America, "liberty," meaning "freedom to grasp opportunity," and "equality," also meaning "freedom to grasp opportunity," have become almost synonymous.*

To a European mind, to equate equality with a freedom to grasp opportunity which guarantees an abundance of tramps and millionaires . . . comes close to equating equality with inequality. It is in any case a habit of mind whose tendency is to inculcate conservative social attitudes. It has tended to make working-class Americans suspicious of appeals to class solidarity. It has enhanced the appeal of the free-enterprise system, which has certainly been a lot more successful at creating opportunities than at creating equality of condition. It explains why people should not be particularly concerned about the failure to redistribute income so long as everyone was getting richer. And it does partially account for the fact that domestic discontent played so small a part in the politics of the fifties.

There was a second group of reasons why American politics failed to reflect class interests or class consciousness. It is true, as Arthur Schlesinger has written, that "in spite of the current myth that class conflicts in America were a fiendish invention of Franklin Roosevelt, classes have, in fact, played a basic part in American political life from the beginning." But the horizontal class lines in American society have always been crosshatched by deep-cut vertical divisions: ethnic, sectional, and racial. Ultimately, these can be traced back to two of the great facts that set American history apart from that of all the other developed Western nations: slavery and immigration. But there were also reasons why their combined impact blurred the reality of class conflict at this particular moment in American history.

One reason was obvious.

The American working class was divided, because the feeling of belonging to a particular ethnic group often took priority over an individual's economic interests or over any sense of class solidarity. In political terms, this frequently meant that the votes of ethnically conscious low-income voters could be recruited to support politicians who, once in office, only fitfully defended the social and economic interests of their constituency. This was notoriously true of the big-city machines, which, in a decadent form, were still one of the typical forms of political organization in the fifties and, for example, played a part in the election of President Kennedy in 1960. But by the fifties the machine no longer fought for the bread-and-butter interests of its immigrant supporters as it had in its classic phase. Instead, traditional ethnic loyalties were played upon at election time to enlist the support of ethnic blocks on behalf of policies that frequently countered the real interests of lower-class voters. Ethnic antics at election time only briefly interrupted the politicians' eager co-operation with the dominant business interests.

The historical fact of immigration had another, less obvious effect. To the extent that Americans are a self-chosen people, their patriotism has always been a more self-conscious emotion than the more visceral tribal feelings of other nations. The immigrant's patriotism has tended to be compounded in roughly equal proportions of status anxiety—the desire to be assimilated as a good American—and of gratitude for his share in the abundance of American life.

Both the abundance and the anxiety were far more visible in the fifties than they had been in the thirties. In the immigrant, this desire to prove oneself a good American had often been in conflict with the impulse to protect the social and economic interests of the lower class. By the fifties, a full generation after the end of mass immigration, the drive for full assimilation was as strong as ever in second- and third-generation Americans; economic needs, as a result of the postwar prosperity, seemed far less urgent. Again, the effect was to increase the conservatism of that considerable proportion of the working class that came of relatively "new" immigrant descent. For this large group, the free-enterprise system was seen as Americanism; social criticism, class solidarity and radical politics were rejected as "un-American."

If ethnic factors dating back to the days of mass immigration, and the preoccupation with equality of opportunity, both helped to obscure the working class's interests from its own members, the sectional and racial basis of the political system derived from the struggle over slavery was responsible for the fact that no great party of the Left was available to represent those interests. In so far as working-class interests were to be effectively represented within the two-party system, they must be represented by the Democrats. But the Democratic Party under Harry Truman and Adlai Stevenson was no party of the Left: It was not only the party of the immigrant, the Negro, the Roman Catholic, the Jew, the city dweller, and the industrial worker; it was also the party of the rural, conservative, nativist South, an element that not only accounted for a third and more of its strength in Congress but held the balance of power in presidential elections.

During the Depression, the New Deal had come closer to being a party of the Left, because the contradiction at the heart of the Democracy was partially concealed by the sheer economic need of the South. Southern Democrats could vote for and work with Roosevelt because they knew the South desperately needed the federal government's economic help. Southerners in Congress might be racial and therefore constitutional conservatives, willing to fight the national Democratic leadership if they must in defense of the South's peculiar social system; but in the New Deal period, that system was not under direct attack. The immediate issues for the South were economic. So long as that remained true, southern "economic liberals"—which often meant men who were not liberals at all except when it came to accepting federal largess—could work happily enough with northern Democrats.

The prosperity of the years after 1941, and in particular the improvement in the economic situation of the southern white working class as a result of industrialization, diminished this incentive for southern Democrats to co-operate with the national party. In spite of much picturesque mythology about their populist fervor and the wool-hats and galluses of their disciples, most of the leading Southerners in Congress in the fifties were essentially responsive to the business elites of the South. While they continued to support some liberal programs, they were not about to allow the Democratic Party to evolve into a national party of the Left. The more racial issues supplanted economic ones in the forefront of their constituents' concern, as they did increasingly after the *Brown* decision in 1954, the more the sectional dilemma made any such evolution of the Democratic Party unlikely.

The Left, in short, had by the late 1950s virtually ceased to count in American political life. But this fateful eclipse was masked by the triumph of the liberals.

To draw a distinction between the Left and the liberals may sound sectarian or obscure. It is not. It is vital to understanding American politics in the age of the consensus, and therefore to understanding what happened after it.

When I say that the Left had almost ceased to exist, I am not thinking of the socialist Left, though that had indeed withered into insignificance long before the collapse of Henry Wallace's Progressive Party, in 1948.

What I mean by the "Left" is any broad, organized political force holding as a principle the need for far-reaching social and institutional change and consistently upholding the interests of the disadvantaged against the most powerful groups in the society. The liberals were never such a force.

What I mean by the liberals is those who subscribed to the ideology I have described: the ideology that held that American capitalism was a revolutionary force for social change, that economic growth was supremely good because it obviated the need for redistribution and social conflict, that class had no place in American politics. Not only are those not the ideas of the Left; at the theoretical level, they provide a sophisticated rationale for avoiding fundamental change. In practice, the liberals were almost always more concerned about distinguishing themselves from the Left than about distinguishing themselves from conservatives.

The confusion between the liberals and the Left arose partly, perhaps, because, in the 1950s, "liberal" was often used as a euphemism for "Left." In the McCarthy era, to call someone a man of the Left carried a whiff of treason with it; to call him a liberal was a graceful alternative.

A deeper reason for the confusion lay in the fact that in the very parts of American society that might have been expected to hold out as the bastions of the Left, the liberals had triumphed. Organized labor, the intelligentsia, and the universities had become the citadels of what was in effect a conservative liberalism.

There were three important developments in the American labor movement in the 1940s, said the editors of *Fortune:* First was the renaissance of the craft-based, politically conservative American Federation of Labor. Fighting back after a period in which it had seemed destined to be swamped by the industrial unions, the AFL doubled its membership in the 1940s and almost recovered parity with the CIO. The second was the "anti-ideological" trend in the CIO, as *Fortune* put it, in the Daniel Bell sense, meaning the trend toward the liberal ideology. And the third was the decline of the left wing in the labor movement generally.

In the forties, the big industrial unions deliberately concentrated on collective bargaining, as opposed to either political activity or drives to increase their membership. They succeeded in winning high wages and fringe packages of social benefits—for their members. But the proportion of union members to the total work force, which had increased sharply in the thirties and the early forties, began a long decline after 1950. By the 1970s, no more than 15 million out of more than 80 million American workers were organized by unions affiliated to the AFL/CIO. Most low-paid workers remain unorganized.

Just as industrial unionism really got going only after the Supreme Court upheld the Wagner Act, in 1937, so two legislative defeats seriously impeded labor's power to organize the unorganized and increased the temptation for the leadership to sit back and enjoy the power and emoluments of its existing strongholds, not to mention the Florida sunshine. Each followed a successful campaign by labor's enemies to capitalize politically on unfavorable news exposure.

The first defeat was the enactment of the Taft-Hartley Law, in 1947, and in particular of its notorious Section 14b, which gave the states the power to pass labor laws that in effect nullified federal law. Taft-Hartley would probably not have passed had the press not given unsympathetic prominence to the series of major postwar strikes symbolized in the UAW's 113-day strike against General Motors over New Year's 1946. The Republicans recaptured the House of Representatives that fall with the slogan: "Had enough?" Enough had.

"Labor"—that unreal collectivity—had itself more to blame for the second setback: the Landrum-Griffin Act of 1959, which might with equal justice have been called the Kennedy-Griffin Act, since so much of its preparation was done by Senator John F. Kennedy on the Senate Labor Committee.

The background to Landrum-Griffin was the series of exposures of union racketeering that began with the 1952 New York State Crime Commission report on Joe Ryan of the Longshoremen. In 1957, the McClellan Committee, with Robert Kennedy as a young tiger on the staff, began its hearings on the Teamsters. By 1959, George Meany was saying ruefully: "We thought we knew a few things about trade union corruption, but we didn't know the half of it. . . ." Gallup findings show that public approval of labor unions had never subsequently recovered the level (76 per cent) it stood at before the McClellan Committee hearings began. By late 1959, under the influence of this barrage of evidence that some unions were little better than organized crime, Gallup recorded another result that would have been truly astonishing to any European, or to any American in the thirties: almost three times as many Americans (41 per cent) thought Big Labor carried the greatest threat to the economy as thought Big Business did (15 per cent).

When the American Federation of Labor and the Congress of Industrial Organizations finally bit the bullet and merged, in 1955, one of the formal articles of the merger declared:

the merged federation shall constitutionally affirm its determination to protect the American trade union movement from any and all corrupt influence and from

*the undermining efforts of Communist agencies and all others who are opposed
to the basic principles of our democracy. . . .*

It was understandable that the new organization to represent American labor should put itself on record as determined to oppose communism. After all,
the vast majority of American workers had always been devoutly anti-Communist. Yet is was unfortunate that in the very years when the American labor
movement was losing the battle to organize the general mass of American workers, and so ultimately condemning itself to be no more than a pressure group for
one particular fraction of the population, it should have thrown itself so very en-
thusiastically into the diversion of anti-communism. . . .

Whatever the exact causes, the intellectual ballast shifted. In 1932 those who
endorsed the Communist Party's candidate for President of the United States included Ernest Hemingway, John Dos Passos, James T. Farrell, Langston Hughes,
Theodore Dreiser, Erskine Caldwell, Lincoln Steffens, Richard Wright, Katherine
Anne Porter, Edmund Wilson, Nathanael West and Malcolm Cowley. Twenty
years later, scarcely an intellectual with a shred of reputation could be found even
to raise a voice against the outlawing of that same party. The change is measured,
too, by the trajectory, in hardly more than a decade, of *Partisan Review,* the most
admired highbrow periodical of the time, from dutiful Stalinism through Trotskyite heresy to the bleakest Cold War anti-communist orthodoxy.

Yet it is striking, in retrospect, how central to that supposedly apolitical culture anti-communism became. The formation of Americans for Democratic Action, excluding Communists, Arthur Schlesinger thought, marked "the watershed at which American liberalism began to base itself once again on a solid
conception of man and of history." Of American history? No: for Schlesinger, liberalism had virtually been created by anti-communism, apparently. "The growing necessity of checking Communism," he wrote, "by developing some constructive alternative speeded the clarification of liberal ideas in 1947 and 1948." . . .

After World War II, in almost every department of intellectual life, the doctrine of "American exceptionalism" revived. At the same time, utilitarian doctrines, stressing that morality in politics was an illusion, undercut the moralistic
basis of left-wing politics. Sociology, history, economics, political science, even
theology in the hands of Reinhold Niebuhr, for example, followed parallel paths,
rejecting those who argued for radical change and emphasizing the virtues of
"the American way." . . .

In the great American universities, the twenty years after World War II are
beginning to be remembered with nostalgia as a Golden Age. Enrollments were
multiplying. Endowments were accumulating. Funds from the federal and state
governments and from private foundations were becoming available on a scale
undreamed of. The salaries and the social status of professors were rising. They
were certainly higher, both absolutely and in relation to those of the business
world, than they had been since before World War I, and perhaps higher than
they had ever been, at least for men sensible enough to have specialized in some
useful subject that would earn them consultancy fees from large corporations,

from government, or from the armed services. At a time when the U.S. Air Force was paying (through the RAND Corporation) for a sociological study of the toilet training of the French, even that qualification need not stand in the way of a man of imagination. . . .

By the fifties, the academic profession was drawing talent from a wider catchment area. At one end of the income scale, able men of prosperous families who would earlier have gone into business were attracted to the universities in the Depression; at the other, a growing proportion of the population was now graduating from college. Finally, tens of thousands of gifted refugees from Europe leavened American academic life. But the essential reason for the intellectual excitement that blossomed in the best American universities in the late fifties was neither academic influence nor increased competition. It came from the feeling that, for the first time, the academic world seemed thoroughly integrated into the life and purposes of the nation.

To begin with, this may have owed something to the achievement of the atomic scientists. When the mightiest arm of American power was the product of research science, it was hard to dismiss any research as impractical dreaming. Physicists, mathematicians, engineers, were among the first to be accepted by government. But the social scientists were not far behind. (Indeed, one branch of social science, economics, had long moved with assurance in the world of business as well as in Washington.) The earliest big government research contracts dealt with such "nuts-and-bolts" questions as the design of unmanned satellites or the nose cones of missiles. But as early as 1948 Nathan Leites was calling on the academic techniques of textual and literary criticism to describe "The Operational Code of Politburo." It was not long before sociologists, political scientists, even historians, were being called into service by the government—all of the social sciences received from the relationship an injection of adrenalin, as well as of money.

This was the broader context in which the system of thought I have called the liberal ideology was fitted together and came to predominate not only in the universities but in government and to some extent in politics. The interaction, however, was reciprocal. The intellectuals tended to be influential only in proportion as their ideas fitted in with the needs, fears or preconceptions of their new patrons. They tended to be forced into the role of technicians. The "hot" topics of specialization were those most immediately related to the government's most urgent perplexity, or at best to the tactics of its political opponents. Either way, that generally recommended those studies which assumed the permanence and the paramountcy of the Cold War. . . .

The liberal ideology equipped the United States with an elaborately interrelated structure of coherent and plausible working assumptions, all poised like an inverted pyramid on two fundamental assumptions, both of which happened to be diametrically wrong.

American capitalism had not, it turned out, eliminated the possibility of serious social conflict at home. Nor was the most urgent danger to the nation from communism abroad. On the contrary, the United States stood on the eve of exceptional social turmoil. Abroad, unified Communist power was breaking up, confronting the world with all the dangers of a period of fragmentation and "*détente.*"

This error was to be pitilessly exposed, and that soon enough. Yet the effect of the liberal consensus was to be even more disastrous than the particular mistaken assumptions on which it was based. It condemned the United States to face the real dangers for too long without any fundamental debate. Thanks to the liberal triumph, the powerful emotions and interests that always work for conservative policies were not balanced by equally powerful forces and principles of the Left. Instead, they were opposed by a liberalism that was in effect hardly to be distinguished from a more sophisticated and less resolute conservatism.

ELAINE TYLER MAY

Cold War—Warm Hearth: Politics and the Family in Postwar America

In the summer of 1959, a young couple married and spent their honeymoon in a bomb shelter. *Life* magazine featured the "sheltered honeymoon," with photographs of the duo smiling on their lawn, surrounded by canned goods and supplies. Another photo showed them descending twelve feet underground into the twenty-two-ton, eight-by-eleven-foot shelter of steel and concrete where they would spend the next two weeks. The article quipped that "fallout can be fun," and described the newlyweds' adventure—with obviously erotic undertones—as fourteen days of "unbroken togetherness." As the couple embarked on family life, all they had to enhance their honeymoon were some consumer goods, their sexuality, and total privacy. This is a powerful image of the nuclear family in the nuclear age: isolated, sexually charged, cushioned by abundance, and protected against impending doom by the wonders of modern technology.

The stunt itself was little more than a publicity device; yet seen in retrospect it takes on symbolic significance. For in the early years of the cold war, amid a world of uncertainties brought about by World War II and its aftermath, the home seemed to offer a secure, private nest removed from the dangers of the outside world. The message was ambivalent, however, for the family also seemed particularly vulnerable. It needed heavy protection against the intrusions of forces outside itself. The image of family togetherness within the safety of the thick-walled shelter may have been a reassuring one to Americans at the time, for along with prosperity, World War II left new unsettling realities in its wake. The self-contained home held out the promise of security in an insecure world. At the same time, it also offered a vision of abundance and fulfillment. As the cold war began, young postwar Americans were homeward bound.

Demographic indicators show that Americans were more eager than ever to establish families. The bomb-shelter honeymooners were part of a cohort of

From Fraser, Steve and Gerstle, Gary (eds.), *The Rise and Fall of the New Deal Order, 1930–1980.* Copyright © 1989 by Princeton University Press. Reprinted by permission of Princeton University Press.

Americans who brought down the age at marriage for both men and women, and quickly brought the birth rate to a twentieth-century high after more than a hundred years of steady decline, producing the "baby boom." These young adults established a trend of early marriage and relatively large families that lasted for more than two decades and caused a major but temporary reversal of long-term demographic patterns. From the 1940s through the early 1960s, Americans married at a higher rate and at a younger age than their European counterparts. Less noted but equally significant, the men and women who formed families between 1940 and 1960 also reduced the divorce rate after a postwar peak; their marriages remained intact to a greater extent than did those of couples who married in earlier as well as later decades. Although the United States maintained its dubious distinction of having the highest divorce rate in the world, the temporary decline in divorce did not occur to the same extent in Europe. Contrary to fears of the experts, the roles of breadwinner and homemaker were not abandoned; they were embraced.

Why did postwar Americans turn to marriage and parenthood with such enthusiasm and commitment? Scholars and observers frequently point to the postwar family boom as the inevitable result of a return to peace and prosperity. They argue that depression-weary Americans were eager to "return to normalcy" by turning the fruits of abundance toward home and hearth. There is, of course, some truth to this point; Americans were indeed eager to put the disruptions of hardship and war behind them. But prosperity followed other wars in our history, notably World War I, with no similar rush into marriage and childbearing. Peace and affluence alone are inadequate to explain the many complexities of the postwar domestic explosion. The demographic trends went far beyond what was expected from a return to peace. Indeed, nothing on the surface of postwar America explains the rush of young Americans into marriage, parenthood, and traditional gender roles.

It might have been otherwise. The depression had brought about widespread challenges to traditional gender roles that could have led to a restructured home. The war intensified these challenges, and pointed the way toward radical alterations in the institutions of work and family life. Wartime brought thousands of women into the paid labor force as men left to enter the armed forces. After the war, expanding job and educational opportunities, as well as the increasing availability of birth control, might well have led to delayed marriages, fewer children, or individuals opting out of family life altogether. Indeed, many moralists, social scientists, educators, and other professionals at the time feared that these changes would pose serious threats to the continuation of the American family. Yet the evidence overwhelmingly indicates that postwar American society experienced a surge in family life and a reaffirmation of domesticity resting on distinct roles for women and men in the home.

The rush began in the early 1940s and continued for two decades. But then it stopped. The family explosion represented a temporary disruption of long-term trends. It lasted only until the baby-boom children came of age, challenged their inherited gender roles, and began to reverse the demographic patterns. Their parents, having grown up during the depression and the war, had begun their families during years of prosperity. These children, however, grew up amid affluence during the cold war; they reached adulthood during the sixties and seventies, creating the counterculture and a new women's liberation movement. In vast numbers, they rejected the political assumptions of the cold war, along with the family and sexual codes of their parents. The baby-boom generation, in fact, brought the American birth rate to an all-time low and the divorce rate to an unprecedented high—both trends in excess of what demographers would have predicted based on twentieth-century patterns.

Observers often point to the 1950s as the last gasp of time-honored family life before the sixties generation made a major break from the past. But the comparison is shortsighted. In many ways, the youth of the sixties resembled their grandparents more than they did their parents. Their grandparents had come of age in the first decades of the twentieth century; like many of their baby-boom grandchildren, they challenged the sexual norms of their day, pushed the divorce rate up and the birth rate down, and created a unique youth culture, complete with music, dancing, movies, and other new forms of urban amusements. They also behaved in similar ways politically, developing a powerful feminist movement, strong grass-roots activism on behalf of social justice, and a proliferation of radical movements to challenge the status quo. Against the backdrop of their grandparents, then, the baby boomers provide some historical continuity. The generation in between—with its strong domestic ideology, pervasive consensus politics, and peculiar demographic behavior—stands out as different.

It is important to note that observers normally explain the political activism and the demographic behavior of the baby-boom generation as the effects of affluence and the result of expanding opportunities for women in education and employment. Yet precisely those conditions obtained twenty years earlier, at the peak of the domestic revival. The circumstances are similar, yet the responses are quite different. What accounts for this time lag? How can we explain the endorsement of "traditional" family roles by young adults in the postwar years and the widespread challenge to those roles when their children, the baby boomers, came of age? Answering these questions requires entering the minds of the women and men who married and raised children during these years. The families they formed were shaped by the historical and political circumstances that framed their lives.

The context of the cold war points to previously unrecognized connections between political and familial values. Diplomatic historians paint one portrait of a world torn by strife, and a standoff between two superpowers who seem to hold the fate of the globe in their hands. Sociologists and demographers provide a different picture of a private world of affluence, suburban sprawl, and the baby boom. These visions rarely connect, and we are left with a peculiar notion of domestic tranquility in the midst of the cold war that has not been fully explained or fully challenged. In this exploration, public policy and political ideology are brought to bear on the study of private life, allowing us to see the family as existing within the larger political culture, not outside of it. The approach enables us to see the cold war ideology *and* the domestic revival as two sides of the same coin: postwar Americans' intense need to feel liberated from the past as well as secure in the future.

The power of this ideological duality, as well as its fundamental irony, are most apparent in the anti-Communist hysteria that swept the nation in the postwar years. It is well to recall that McCarthyism was directed against perceived internal dangers, not external enemies. The Soviet Union loomed in the distance as an abstract symbol of what we might become if we became "soft." Anti-Communist crusaders called upon Americans to strengthen their moral fiber in order to preserve both freedom and security. The paradox of anticommunism, however, was precisely in that double-edged goal, for the freedom of modern life itself seemed to undermine security. McCarthyism was fueled in large measure by suspicion of the new secularism, materialism, bureaucratic collectivism, and consumerism that represented not only the achievement but also potential "decadence" of New Deal liberalism.

Cosmopolitan urban culture represented a threat to national security akin to the danger of communism itself; indeed, the two were often conflated in anti-Communist rhetoric. If American democracy resided in adherence to a deeply rooted work ethic tied to a belief in upward mobility as the reward for the frugal and virtuous, then the appeal of mass purchasing, sexual temptations in the world of amusements, and even the "cushion" of the welfare state could serve to unravel that essential virtue. Many feared that the restraints imposed by the watchful eyes of small-town neighbors would dissolve in the anonymous cities. The domestic ideology emerged as a buffer against those disturbing tendencies. Rootless Americans struggled against what they perceived as internal decay; the family seemed to offer a psychological fortress that would, presumably, protect them against themselves. Family life, bolstered by scientific expertise and wholesome abundance, might ward off the hazards of the age.

This challenge prompted Americans to create a family-centered culture that took shape in the early years of the cold war. This "cold war culture" was more than the internal reverberations of foreign policy, and it went beyond the explicit manifestations of anti-Communist hysteria such as McCarthyism and the Red Scare. It took shape amid the legacy of depression and war and the anxieties surrounding the development of atomic weapons. It reflected the aspirations as well as the fears of the era, as Americans faced the promises as well as the perils of postwar life. Prosperity had returned, but would there be a postwar slump that would lead to another depression, as there had been after World War I? Would men returning from war be able to find secure positions in the postwar economy? Women such as the proverbial "Rosie the Riveter" had proved themselves competent in previously all-male blue-collar jobs, but what would happen to their families if they continued to work? Science had brought us atomic energy, but would it ultimately serve humanity or destroy it? The family was at the center of these concerns, and the domestic ideology taking shape at the time provided a major response to them. The legendary fifties family, complete with appliances, a station wagon, a backyard bar-b-que, and tricycles scattered along the sidewalk, represented something new. It was not, as common wisdom tells us, the last gasp of "traditional" family life with roots deep in the past. Rather, it was the first wholehearted effort to create a home that would fulfill virtually all of its members' personal needs through an energized and expressive personal life.

One of the most explicit descriptions of this modern domestic ideal was articulated, significantly, by a major politician in an international forum at the peak of the cold war. In 1959, Vice-President Richard M. Nixon traveled to the Soviet Union to engage in what would become one of the most noted verbal sparring matches of the century. In a lengthy and often heated debate with Soviet premier Nikita Khrushchev at the opening of the American National Exhibition in Moscow, Nixon extolled the virtues of the American way of life, as his opponent promoted the Communist system. What is remarkable about this exchange is its focus. The two leaders did not discuss missiles, bombs, or even modes of government. Rather, they argued over the relative merits of American and Soviet washing machines, televisions, and electric ranges. According to the American vice-president, the essence of the good life provided by democracy was contained within the walls of the suburban home.

For Nixon, American superiority rested on a utopian ideal of the home, complete with modern appliances and distinct gender roles. He proclaimed that the "model home," with a male breadwinner and a full-time female homemaker, and adorned with a wide array of consumer goods, represented the essence of American freedom. Nixon insisted that American superiority in the cold war rested not on weapons but on the secure, abundant family life available in modern suburban homes, "within the price range of the average U.S. worker." Houses became almost sacred structures, adorned and worshiped by their inhabitants. Here women would achieve their glory, and men would display their success. Consumerism was not an end in itself, but rather the means for achieving a classless ideal of individuality, leisure, and upward mobility.

With such sentiments about gender and politics widely shared, Nixon's remarks in Moscow struck a responsive chord among Americans at the time. He returned from Moscow a national hero. The visit was hailed as a major political triumph; popular journals extolled his diplomatic skills in this face-to-face confrontation with the Russian leader. Many observers credit this trip with establishing Nixon's political future. Clearly, Americans did not find the kitchen debate trivial. The appliance-laden ranch-style home epitomized the expansive, secure life-style postwar Americans wanted. Within the protective walls of the modern home, worrisome developments like sexual liberalism, women's emancipation, and affluence would lead not to decadence but to wholesome family life. Sex would enhance marriage; emancipated women would professionalize homemaking; affluence would put an end to material deprivation. Suburbia would serve as a bulwark against communism and class conflict, for, according to the widely shared belief articulated by Nixon, it offered a piece of the American dream for everyone. Although Nixon vastly exaggerated the availability of the suburban home, one cannot deny the fact that he described a particular type of domestic life that had become a reality for many Americans, and a viable aspiration for many more.

What gave rise to the widespread endorsement of this familial consensus in the cold war era? The depression and war laid the foundations for a commitment to a stable home life, but they also opened the way for what might have become a radical restructuring of the family. The yearning for family stability gained momentum and reached fruition after the war; but the potential for restructuring did not. Instead, that potential withered, as a powerful ideology of domesticity became imprinted on the fabric of everyday life. Traditional gender roles revived just when they might have died a natural death, and became, ironically, a central feature of the "modern" middle-class home.

Since the 1960s, much attention has focused on the plight of women in the fifties. But at the time, critical observers of middle-class life considered homemakers to be emancipated and men to be oppressed. Much of the most insightful writing examined the dehumanizing situation that forced middle-class men, at least in their public roles, to be "other-directed" "organization men," caught in a mass, impersonal white-collar world. The loss of autonomy was real. As large corporations grew, swallowing smaller enterprises, the numbers of self-employed men in small businesses shrank dramatically. David Riesman recognized that the corporate structure forced middle-class men into deadening, highly structured peer interactions; he argued that only in the intimate aspects of life could a man truly be free. Industrial laborers were even less likely to derive intrinsic satisfactions from the job itself; blue-collar and white-collar employees shared a sense of alienation and subordination in the postwar corporate work force. Both Riesman and William Whyte saw the suburbs as extensions of the corporate world, with their emphasis on conformity. Yet at the same time, suburban home ownership and consumerism offered compensations for organized work life.

For women, who held jobs in greater numbers than ever before, employment was likely to be even more menial and subordinate. Surveys of full-time homemakers indicated that they appreciated their independence from supervision and control over their work, and had no desire to give up their autonomy in the home for wage labor. Educated middle-class women whose career opportunities were severely limited hoped that the home would become not a confining place of drudgery, but a liberating arena of fulfillment through professionalized homemaking, meaningful childrearing, and satisfying sexuality.

While the home seemed to offer the best hope for freedom, it also appeared to be a fragile institution, in many ways subject to forces beyond its control. Economic hardship had torn families asunder, and war had scattered men far from home and thrust women into the public world of work. The postwar years did little to alleviate fears that similar disruptions might occur again. In spite of widespread affluence, many believed that reconversion to a peacetime economy would lead to another depression. Peace itself was also problematic, since international tension was a palpable reality. The explosion of the first atomic bombs over Hiroshima and Nagasaki marked not only the end of World War II but also the beginning of the cold war. At any moment, the cold war could turn hot. The policy of containment abroad faced its first major challenge in 1949 with the Chinese revolution. That same year, the Russians exploded their first atomic bomb. The nation was again jolted out of its sense of fragile security when the Korean War broke out in 1950, sending American men abroad to fight once again. Many shared President Truman's belief that World War III was at hand. . . .

Americans were well poised to embrace domesticity in the midst of the terrors of the atomic age. A home filled with children would provide a feeling of warmth and security against the cold forces of disruption and alienation.

Children would also provide a connection to the future, and a means to replenish a world depleted by war deaths. Although baby-boom parents were not likely to express conscious desires to repopulate the country, the deaths of hundreds of thousands of GIs in World War II could not have been far below the surface of postwar consciousness. The view of childbearing as a duty was painfully true for Jewish parents, after six million of their kin were snuffed out in Europe. But they were not alone. As one Jewish woman recalled of her conscious decision to bear four children, "After the Holocaust, we felt obligated to have lots of babies. But it was easy because everyone was doing it—non-Jews, too." In secure postwar homes with plenty of children, American women and men might be able to ward off their nightmares and live out their dreams.

In the face of prevailing fears, Americans moved toward the promise of the good life with an awareness of its vulnerability. The family seemed to be one place left where people could control their own destinies, and maybe even shape the future. Of course, nobody actually argued that stable family life could prevent nuclear annihilation. But the home did represent a source of meaning and security in a world run amok. If atomic bombs threatened life, marriage and reproduction affirmed life. Young marriage and lots of babies offered one way for Americans to thumb their noses at doomsday predictions. Commenting on the trend toward young marriages, *Parents Magazine* noted in 1958, "Youngsters want to grasp what little security they can in a world gone frighteningly insecure. The youngsters feel they will cultivate the one security that's possible—their own gardens, their own . . . home and families."

Thoughts of the family rooted in time-honored traditions may have allayed fears of vulnerability. Nevertheless, the "traditional" family was quickly becoming a relic of the past. Much of what had previously provided family security became unhinged. For many Americans, the postwar years brought rootlessness. Those who moved from farms to cities lost a way of life familiar to them and rooted in the land itself. Children of immigrants moved from familiar ethnic neighborhoods with extended kin and community ties in order to form nuclear families in the homogeneous suburbs, and invested them with extremely high hopes. Suburban homes offered freedom from kinship obligations, along with material comforts that had not been available on the farm or in the ethnic urban ghetto. As William Whyte noted about the promoters of the Illinois suburb he studied, "At first they had advertised Park Forest as housing. Now they began advertising happiness." But consumer goods would not replace community, and young mobile nuclear families could easily find themselves adrift. Whyte noted the "rootlessness" of the new suburban residents. Newcomers devoted themselves to creating communities out of neighborhoods comprised largely of transients: "In suburbia, organization man is trying, quite consciously, to develop a new kind of roots to replace what he left behind."

Young adults aged twenty-five to thirty-five were among the most mobile members of the society, comprising 12.4 percent of all migrants but only 7.5 percent of the population. Higher education also prompted mobility; fully 45.5 percent of those who had one year of college or more lived outside their home states, compared with 27.3 percent of high school graduates. Overwhelmingly, these young, educated migrants worked for large organizations: three-fourths of all clients of long-distance movers—those affluent enough to afford the service—worked for corporations, the government, or the armed services, with corporate employees the most numerous. In their new communities, they immediately forged ties with other young transients. As Whyte noted, "The fact that they all left home can be more important in bonding them than the kind of home they left is in separating them." In the new community, they endeavored to forge ties that would be as rewarding and secure as the ones left behind, without the restraints of the old neighborhood.

Postwar Americans struggled with this transition. The popular culture was filled with stories about young adults shifting their allegiances from the old ethnic ties to the new nuclear family ideal. When working-class situation comedies shifted from radio to television, ethnic kin networks and multigenerational households faded as the stories increasingly revolved around the nuclear family. One of the most successful films of the 1950s was *Marty,* winner of the Academy Award for Best Motion Picture. In this enormously popular film, the main character, a young man living with his mother, sustains a deep commitment to the ethnic family in which he was reared. The sympathy of the audience stays with Marty as he first demonstrates tremendous family loyalty, allowing his mother to bring her cranky aging sister to live with them and doing his filial duty as the good son. As the story unfolds, Marty falls in love, and to the horror of his mother and his aunt, decides to marry his sweetheart and move away from the old neighborhood. Far from his family and their obligations, the young couple can embark upon a new life freed from the constraints of the older generation. By the film's end, the audience has made the transition, along with the main character, from loyalty to the community of ethnic kinship to the suburban ideal of the emancipated nuclear family.

The film ends there, providing no clues as to what would replace the loving kinship network portrayed so favorably at the beginning of the story. New suburbanites would need to figure that out for themselves. One way this could be achieved was through conformity to a new, modern, consumer-oriented way of life. William Whyte called the suburbs the "new melting pot" where migrants from ethnic neighborhoods in the cities moved up into the middle class. Kin and ethnic ties were often forsaken as suburban residents formed new communities grounded in shared experiences of home ownership and childrearing.

Young suburbanites were great joiners, forging new ties and creating new institutions to replace the old. Park Forest, Illinois, had sixty-six adult organizations, making it a "hotbed of Participation." Church and synagogue membership reached new heights in the postwar years, expanding its functions from prayer and charity to include recreation, youth programs, and social events. Church membership rose from 64.5 million in 1940 to 114.5 million in 1960—from 50 percent to 63 percent of the entire population (a hundred years earlier only 20 percent of all Americans belonged to churches). In 1958, 97 percent of all those polled said they believed in God. Religious affiliation became associated with the "American way of life." Although many observers have commented upon the superficiality and lack of spiritual depth in much of this religious activity, there is no question that churches and synagogues provided social arenas for suburban-ites, replacing to some extent the communal life previously supplied by kin or neighborhood.

Still, these were tenuous alliances among uprooted people. As William Whyte observed, suburbs offered shallow roots rather than deep ones. With so much mobility in and out of neighborhoods, and with success associated with moving on to something better, middle-class nuclear families could not depend upon the stability of their communities. Much as they endeavored to form ties with their neighbors and conform to each other's life-styles, they were still largely on their own. So the nuclear family, ultimately, relied upon itself. As promising as the new vision of home life appeared, it depended heavily on the staunch com-mitment of its members to sustain it. The world could not be trusted to provide security, nor could the newly forged suburban community. What mattered was that family members remained bound to each other, and to the modern, emanci-pated home they intended to create.

To help them in this effort, increasing numbers of women and men turned to scientific expertise. Inherited folkways would be of little help to young people looking toward a radically new vision of family life. The wisdom of earlier generations seemed to be increasingly irrelevant for young adults trying self-consciously to avoid the paths of their parents. As they turned away from "old-fashioned" ways, they embraced the advice of experts in the rapidly expanding fields of social science, medicine, and psychology. After all, science was changing the world. Was it not reasonable to expect it to change the home as well?

Postwar America was the era of the expert. Armed with scientific techniques and presumably inhabiting a world above popular passions, the experts had brought the country into the atomic age. Physicists developed the bomb; strate-gists created the cold war; scientific managers built the military-industrial com-plex. It was now up to the experts to make the unmanageable manageable. As the readers of *Look* magazine were assured, there was no reason to worry about ra-dioactivity, for if ever it became necessary to understand its dangers, "the experts will be ready to tell you." Science and technology seemed to have invaded virtu-ally every aspect of life, from the most public to the most private. Americans were looking to professionals to tell them how to manage their lives. The tremen-dous popularity of treatises such as Dr. Benjamin Spock's *Baby and Child Care* reflects a reluctance to trust the shared wisdom of kin and community. Norman Vincent Peale's *The Power of Positive Thinking* provided readers with religiously inspired scientific formulas for success. Both of these best-selling authors stressed the centrality of the family in their prescriptions for a better future. . . .

Testimonies drawn from a survey of six hundred husbands and wives during the 1950s reveal the rewards as well as the disappointments resulting from these fervent efforts to create the ideal home. The respondents were among the cohort of Americans who began their families during the early 1940s, establishing the patterns and setting the trends that were to take hold of the nation for the next two decades. Their hopes for happy and stable marriages took shape during the depression, while many couples among their parents' peers struggled with dis-ruption and hardship. They entered marriage as World War II thrust the nation into another major crisis, wreaking further havoc upon families. They raised children as the cold war took shape, with its cloud of international tension and impending doom. Yet at the same time, they were fiercely committed to the families they formed, determined to weather the storms of crises.

These women and men were hopeful that family life in the postwar era would be secure and liberated from the hardships of the past. They believed that affluence, consumer goods, satisfying sex, and children would enhance and strengthen their families, enabling them to steer clear of potential disruptions. As they pursued their quest for the good life at home, they adhered to traditional gender roles and prized marital stability highly. Very few of them divorced. They represented a segment of the predominantly Protestant white population that was relatively well-educated and generally lived a comfortable middle-class life. In other words, they were among those Americans who would be most likely to fit the normative patterns. If any Americans had the ability to achieve the dream of a secure, affluent, and happy domestic life, it would have been these prosperous young adults.

These women and men were among the first to establish families according to the domestic ideology taking shape at the time. Their children would be among the oldest of the baby-boom generation. By the time their families were well established in the 1950s, they easily could have been the models for the American way of life Nixon extolled in Moscow. Relatively affluent, more highly educated than the average, they were among those Americans who were best able to take advantage of postwar prosperity. They looked toward the home, rather than the public world, for personal fulfillment. No wonder that when they were asked what they felt they sacrificed in life as a result of their decision to marry and raise a family, a decision that required an enormous investment of time, energy, and resources, an overwhelming majority of both men and women replied "nothing." Their priorities were clear.

One of the most striking characteristics of these respondents was their apparent willingness to give up autonomy and independence for the sake of marriage and family. Although the 1950s marked the beginning of the glamorization of bachelorhood, most of the men expressed a remarkable lack of nostalgia for the unencumbered freedom of a single life. Typical were the comments of one husband who said he gave up "nothing but bad habits" when he married, or another who said he relinquished "the empty, aimless, lonely life of a bachelor. I cannot think of anything I really wanted to do or have that have been sacrificed because of marriage." Many of these men had been married for over a decade, and had seen their share of troubles. Particularly poignant was the comment of a man with an alcoholic wife whom he described as sexually "frigid." Brushing aside these obvious difficulties, he wrote, "Aside from the natural adjustment, I have given up only some of my personal independence. But I have gained so much more: children, home, etc. that I ought to answer . . . 'nothing at all.' "

Women were equally quick to dismiss any sacrifices they may have made when they married. Few expressed any regret at having devoted themselves to the homemaker role—a choice that effectively ruled out other lifelong occupational avenues. Although 13 percent mentioned a "career" as something sacrificed, most claimed that they gained rather than lost in the bargain. One wife indicated the way in which early marriage affected the development of her adult identity.

Stating that she sacrificed "nothing" when she married, she continued, "Marriage has opened up far more avenues of interest than I ever would have had without it . . . I was a very young and formative age when we were married and I think I have changed greatly over the years. . . . I cannot conceive of life without him."

Many of the wives who said they abandoned a career were quick to minimize its importance. One said she gave up a "career—but much preferred marriage," suggesting that pursuing both at the same time was not a viable option. Many defined their domestic role as a career in itself. As one woman wrote of her choice to relinquish an outside profession: "I think I have probably contributed more to the world in the life I have lived." Another mentioned her sacrifices of "financial independence. Freedom to choose a career. However, these have been replaced by the experience of being a mother and a help to other parents and children. Therefore the new career is equally as good or better than the old." Both men and women stressed the responsibilities of married life as a source of personal fulfillment rather than sacrifice. One man remarked that "a few fishing trips and hunting trips are about all I have given up. These not to keep peace in the family, but because the time was better (and more profitably) spent at home."

Further evidence of the enormous commitment to family life appears in response to the question, "What has marriage brought you that you could not have gained without your marriage?" While the most common responses of both men and women included family, children, love, and companionship, other typical answers included a sense of purpose, success, and security. It is interesting to note that respondents claimed that these elements of life would not have been possible without marriage. Women indicated that marriage gave them "a sense of responsibility I wouldn't have had had I remained single," or a feeling of "usefulness I have had for others dear to me." One said marriage gave her a "happy, full, complete life; children, feeling of serving some purpose in life other than making money." Another remarked, "I'm not the 'career girl' type. I like being home and having a family. . . . Working with my husband for our home and family brings a satisfaction that working alone could not."

Men were equally emphatic about the satisfactions brought about by family responsibility. Responding in their own words to an open-ended question, nearly one-fourth of all the men in the sample claimed that their marriages gave them a sense of purpose in life and a reason for striving. Aside from love and children, no other single reward of marriage was mentioned by so many of the husbands. Numerous comments pointed to marriage as the source of "the incentive to succeed and save for the future of my family," "above all, a purpose in the scheme of life," or "a motivation for intensive effort that would otherwise have been lacking." One confessed, "Being somewhat lazy to begin with the family and my wife's ambition have made me more eager to succeed businesswise and financially." A contented husband wrote of the "million treasures" contained in his family; another said that marriage offered "freedom from the boredom and futility of bachelorhood."

Others linked family life to civic virtues by claiming that marriage strengthened their patriotism and morals, instilling in them "responsibility, community spirit, respect for children and family life, reverence for a Supreme Being, humility, love of country." Summing up the feelings of many in his generation, one husband said that marriage "increased my horizons, defined my goals and purposes in life, strengthened my convictions, raised my intellectual standards and stimulated my incentive to provide moral, spiritual, and material support; it has rewarded me with a realistic sense of family and security I never experienced during the first 24 years of my life."

The modern home would provide not only virtue and security, but also liberation and expressiveness. Most of the survey respondents agreed with the widely expressed belief that "wholesome sex relations are the cornerstone of marriage." Sexual expertise was one of several skills required of modern marital partners; as one historian has noted, by the 1940s experts had fully articulated the "cult of mutual orgasm." The respondents repeatedly noted that sexual attraction was a major reason they married their particular partners, while sexual compatibility and satisfaction were deemed essential elements in a marriage. One man wrote about his future wife, "I like particularly her size and form. . . . She attracts me strongly, physically." Others wrote about the centrality of "sex desire" in their relationships, and how important it was that they were "passionately attracted to each other." Women as well as men were likely to mention the "great appeal physically" of their partners. In essence, sexual liberation was expected to occur *within* marriage, along with shared leisure, affluence, and recreation. The modern home was a place to feel good. . . .

The cold war consensus, politically as well as domestically, did not sustain itself beyond this single generation. The politics of the 1930s, 1940s, and 1950s had helped to shape the postwar home. In turn, the postwar home had a direct bearing on the politics of the 1960s. Much of what sparked the social and political movements forged by the baby-boom children as they came of age stemmed from a rejection of the values of postwar domesticity and the cold war itself. The children were keenly aware of the disappointments of their parents—that the domestic ideal had not fully lived up to its promise. Unlike their depression- and war-bred parents, they were less security-minded and less willing to tolerate the restraints and dissatisfactions experienced by their elders. Yet they did not wholly give up on the dream of a more liberated and expressive life; they simply looked for the fulfillment of that promise elsewhere. This new quest took more overtly political forms, since much of their energy poured out of the family into public life. In many ways, then, the children's effort to gain what their parents had failed to achieve in the way of the true liberation gave rise to the New Left, the antiwar movement, the counterculture, and the new feminism. As a result, by the late 1960s they had shattered the political and familial consensus that had prevailed since the 1940s.

In the years since the 1960s, politics and personal life have remained intertwined. The lines remain drawn around the same sets of values. Militant cold warriors still call for the virtues of "traditional domesticity"; critics on the Left challenge the assumptions of the cold war and champion gender equality inside and outside the home. Issues of personal life, such as abortion and day care, have landed squarely in the center of hot political debates. Although it is unclear which side will ultimately prevail, there can be no doubt that public and private life continue to exert a powerful influence on each other.

SUGGESTIONS FOR FURTHER READING

David Halberstam, *The Fifties* (New York, 1993) is a lively portrait of the decade; Halberstam's comprehensive discussion ranges from politics to popular culture. Athan Theoharis, *Seeds of Repression: Harry S Truman and the Origins of McCarthyism* (Chicago, 1971) argues that McCarthyism was a conservative, anti–New Deal movement. Although McCarthy often directed his fire at the Democrats, Theoharis has little sympathy for Truman, who, he insists, differed from McCarthy "not so much over ends as over means and emphasis." Also critical of Truman and the Democrats is Robert Griffith, *The Politics of Fear; Joseph R. McCarthy and the Senate* (Lexington, Ky., 1970). Earl Latham has collected a useful sampling of the varied analyses he discusses in the selection here in his book *The Meaning of McCarthyism*, 2nd ed. (Boston, 1973). Richard M. Freeland, **The Truman Doctrine and the Origins of McCarthyism: Foreign Policy, Domestic Politics, and Internal Security, 1946–1948* (New York, 1985) traces the connections between Truman's foreign policy and the rise of McCarthyism. Stephen J. Whitfield, *The Culture of the Cold War* (Baltimore, 1991) is a general account that traces the impact of the cold war consensus on all aspects of American life.

For many liberals, McCarthyism was one manifestation of what they called the "radical right." The essays attempting to analyze this group in Daniel Bell, ed., **The Radical Right* (Garden City, N.Y., 1964) find in McCarthyism, the John Birch Society, religious fundamentalists, and others a fear of "modernity," leading, in Bell's words, to a "challenge to the American democratic consensus." As the title of Richard Hofstadter's **The Paranoid Style in American Politics* (New York, 1965) suggests, these rightists were irrational. Sharply critical of this view is Michael Rogin, *The Intellectuals and McCarthy* (Cambridge, Mass., 1967). Rogin argues that the consensus approach of writers such as Bell and Hofstadter led them to consider the conservative opponents of liberalism as psychological misfits, which made it impossible for them to see the real conflicts that divide liberals from conservatives. Ellen Schrecker, *No Ivory Tower: McCarthyism and the Universities* (New York, 1986) is critical of the response of intellectuals in the nation's universities to McCarthyism. Alonzo L. Hamby, **Liberalism and Its Challengers: FDR to Reagan* (New York, 1985) takes a longer view of the evolution of American liberalism, as does Steven M. Gillon in his study of the liberal organization Americans for Democratic Action in *Politics and Vision: The ADA and American Liberalism, 1947–1985* (New York, 1987).

Conservatives, of course, deny that they are maladjusted opponents of modernity. But they, like the liberals, are divided. A good analysis of the conservative intellectuals and the differences among them is George H. Nash, *The Conservative Intellectual Movement in America Since 1945* (New York, 1976). Jerome J. Himmelstein, *To the Right: The Transformation of American Conservatism* (Berkeley, Calif., 1990) finds a combination of religious, economic, and political factors responsible for the growing influence of the right in the post-depression years. The notes and bibliographies in Nash and Himmelstein will lead the interested reader deeply into the writings of the conservatives, but all students should sample the works of William F. Buckley, Jr., and the articles in his *National Review*. Buckley's sympathetic view of McCarthy may be found in William F. Buckley, Jr., and

---

*Available in paperback edition.

L. Brent Bozell, *McCarthy and His Enemies: The Record and Its Meaning* (Chicago, 1954). A paperback edition of this book, published in the early 1960s, contains a new introduction by Buckley that responds to some of the critics of the first edition. A recent, critical analysis of Buckley and his influence is John B. Judis, *William F. Buckley, Jr., Patron Saint of the Conservatives* (New York, 1988). McCarthy's own views may be found in his *McCarthyism: The Fight for America* (New York, 1952; reprinted, Salem, N.H., 1988). Richard Gid Powers, *Not Without Honor: The History of American Anticommunism* (New York, 1995), taking a long view of the history of anticommunism, finds some anticommunists to be undemocratic fanatics, but he argues that most were responsible and sensible opponents of communism.

Useful discussions of Communists and their supporters in the post-depression years may be found in Maurice Isserman, *Which Side Were You On?: The American Communist Party During the Second World War* (Middletown, Conn., 1982); Joseph Starobin, *American Communism in Crisis, 1943–1957* (Cambridge Mass., 1972; paperback, Berkeley, Calif., 1975); and David A. Shannon, *The Decline of American Communism: A History of the Communist Party of the United States Since 1945* (New York, 1959). These studies stress policies and leadership. A view from the bottom is Vivian Gornick, *The Romance of American Communism* (New York, 1977); sympathetic and nostalgic, Gornick's interviews with ordinary CP members give a personal view of motivations and attitudes.

Two good studies of the politics of the Truman era that trace the efforts to build a new liberal consensus that could maintain and extend the New Deal in the face of attacks from the left and right are Eric Goldman, *The Crucial Decade and After* (New York, 1960) and Alonzo L. Hamby, *Beyond the New Deal: Harry S Truman and American Liberalism* (New York, 1973). Both credit Truman with success in creating what Arthur M. Schlesinger, Jr., called "the vital center," a revitalized, tough-minded, anti-Communist liberalism. In his book (*The Vital Center* [Boston, 1949]), Schlesinger, writing as both a historian and an advocate, called for a middle position between communism and conservatism, which he termed a "new radicalism," emphasizing continued reliance on liberal solutions to problems—the support of individualism and individual welfare through a more active role for government in domestic affairs even as it pursued the cold war abroad. Richard Pells, *The Liberal Mind in a Conservative Age: American Intellectuals in the 1940s and 1950s* (New York, 1985) is a perceptive and sympathetic but critical discussion of the liberals as they attempted to create the vital liberal center—an effort, Pells argues, that divided liberals. Many moved into the conservative camp, while others became more critical of the McCarthyite challenge and the growing conservatism and conformism of the fifties. William L. O'Neill, *A Better World: The Great Schism: Stalinism and the American Intellectuals* (New York, 1982) considers the same matters but is broader in its coverage and is more critical of the leftist intellectuals.

Elaine Tyler May's views in the selection here are spelled out in more detail in her *Homeward Bound: American Families in the Cold War Era* (New York, 1988). See also the chapter "Family Culture" in James Gilbert, *Another Chance: Postwar America, 1945–1985* (New York, 1986) and Bruce W. Brown, *Images of Family Life in Magazine Advertising 1920–1978* (New York, 1981).

A good example of the complacency and confidence, even smugness, that prevailed in the United States following World War II may be found in a volume by the editors of *Fortune, *USA, the Permanent Revolution* (1951). More sophisticated contemporary analyses that are mildly critical of conformity are Daniel Bell, *The End of Ideology: On the Exhaustion of Political Ideas in the Fifties* (New York, 1959); David Riesman, et al., *The Lonely Crowd* (New York, 1959); William H. Whyte, Jr., *The Organization Man* (New York, 1956); and Samuel Lubell, *Revolt of the Moderates* (New York, 1956).

Some contemporary writers were sharply critical of the conformity, and their analyses helped to stimulate the opposition among young people in the sixties. Especially significant examples are Paul Goodman, *Growing Up Absurd* (New York, 1960); Michael Harrington, *The Other America: Poverty in the United States* (New York, 1962); C. Wright Mills, *The Power Elite* (New York, 1956); and Herbert Marcuse, *One Dimensional Man: Studies in the Ideology of Advanced Industrial Society* (Boston, 1964). The beats and hipsters provided another form of opposition during the period. See Lawrence Lipton, *The Holy Barbarians* (New York, 1959). A selection from the writing of the beat generation, along with a number of critical essays, both favorable and antagonistic, and a bibliography of writings by and about the beats may be found in Thomas Parkinson, ed., *A Casebook on the Beat* (New York, 1971).

Two valuable recent analyses of the relationship between culture and politics and the tension and conflict this relationship sometimes produced are John Patrick Diggins, *The Proud Decades: America in War and in Peace, 1941–1960* (New York, 1988) and Lary May, ed., *Recasting America: Culture and Politics in the Age of the Cold War* (Chicago, 1989).

The Turbulent 1960s

I n the presidential campaign of 1960 the platforms of the two major parties were very similar, but the election was hotly contested, bringing a record 68.8 million to the polls. The voters provided John F. Kennedy with a tiny majority over Richard M. Nixon; only about 100,000 votes separated the two candidates. Kennedy promised a "new frontier" that would get the nation moving again and called for renewed idealism. "Ask not what your country can do for you—ask what you can do for your country," he urged in his inaugural address. But he also promised government action and leadership to bring needed changes, comparing his efforts to the vigorous first "hundred days" of the New Deal.

Kennedy's actual legislative accomplishments were meager, but outside of government, changes were under way that would polarize politics. Blacks, with some white supporters, continued to organize massive civil rights demonstrations—

boycotts, protest marches, sit-ins, and other direct actions—and others began to adopt these militant tactics in their efforts to bring other reforms. At the same time, the right, fearing a growing communist conspiracy at work in the country, also organized and gained in strength.

The assassination of Kennedy in 1963 put Lyndon B. Johnson in the White House. Less personally popular than Kennedy but a more effective politician, Johnson, taking advantage of widespread support in the wake of the assassination and using his considerable talent in dealing with Congress, succeeded in beginning a new round of social legislation designed to end poverty, ensure civil rights, and improve urban conditions. Strong opposition quickly appeared. During the presidential campaign of 1964, Barry M. Goldwater of Arizona mobilized the conservative and rightist discontent and, to the surprise of many, won the Republican nomination. He promised to move the country in a new direction, offering the voters "a choice not an echo." But despite the enthusiasm he generated among his supporters, the voters rejected the choice he offered and chose Lyndon Johnson in the century's largest presidential landslide. A new liberal consensus seemed to prevail. Provided with a cooperative Congress and a powerful coalition that included not only labor, the farmers, the blacks, and the intellectuals but a large portion of the business community as well, Johnson pushed through Congress his "Great Society," a program of social legislation that in many ways continued the reforms begun by the New Deal.

But the Johnson consensus faded as rapidly as it had grown as critics from both the left and the right became more vociferous and more active. Opposition to the war in Vietnam and increasing militancy among blacks and students elicited a "backlash" response from the conservatives. Politics again became polarized, and Johnson's withdrawal from the 1968 presidential race did not stem the growing bitterness and violence. The country seemed hopelessly divided; and when assassins gunned down civil rights leader Martin Luther King and presidential hopeful Robert F. Kennedy, many concluded that the country was sick with hate and violence. During the Democratic National Convention meeting in Chicago, television viewers alternately watched the delegates nominate Hubert H. Humphrey and the police battle young people outside the convention hotels.

Richard M. Nixon was elected president by a narrow margin in 1968; but, with George Wallace running on an independent ticket and taking 13 percent of the vote, Nixon, with his 43 percent, was a minority president. Although the new president promised to "strive to listen in new ways" to the people in order to bring the divided country back together, the war went on and the country remained sharply divided. When in the spring of 1970 American forces invaded Cambodia, thousands of students protested. Violence broke out on hundreds of campuses; on two of them—Kent State in Ohio and Jackson State in Mississippi—several students were killed in clashes with the National Guard. Urban strife also continued, as a portion of the black militants and new left resorted to planned violence. The police responded in kind; indeed, many charged that the police sometimes initiated the violence against militant students and blacks. "There is in the American psyche today an alienation from the central government that is new in our experience," concluded Richard Rovere. And George Reedy, a former aide to President Johnson, saw in the conflict a fundamental danger to the system: "The question is raised: Can our political system cope with the strains? The answer is probably not."

In the election of 1972 politics remained polarized. The Democrats nominated George McGovern and adopted a platform calling for immediate withdrawal from Vietnam, an end to the draft, and amnesty for draft resisters, while the Republicans nominated Nixon for a second term on a platform supporting his foreign policy. Nixon's landslide victory—he received almost 61 percent of the vote and won 49 states—seemed to indicate that the balance of power had shifted sharply to the conservatives. Some analysts viewed the shift as the beginning of a new Republican majority and the end of the dominant Democratic coalition that had been forged during the New Deal.

Some historians see the turbulent 1960s and early 1970s as a time of fundamental conflict when militant radicals called basic American institutions into question. But others, noting how quickly the militancy abated in the mid-1970s when the Vietnam war and the draft ended, insist that the militant rhetoric and the violence were radical mainly in tactics and words but not in intent. Some in the first group reply that the relative calm beginning in the 1970s signaled the defeat of the militants and the failure of their radical demands, which resulted in apathy born of discouragement, frustration, and fear of repression; but others insist that the militancy did in fact bring significant reforms, although not everything that the militants demanded. A portion of this debate may be seen in the selections that follow.

Milton Cantor, in the first selection, describes the "New Left" that began as a kind of amorphous opposition movement—romantic, intuitive, and personal in its opposition and all-inclusive in the people it accepted and the issues it supported. Civil rights, opposition to the war in southeast Asia, women's rights, and a myriad of other issues—some political, some personal, some cultural—became a part of the movement. Its very variety gave it strength and influence beyond its largely middle-class white student constituency, but it also created divisions within the movement itself. Never able to develop a radical theory that would unite the disparate elements within it and unable to broaden its base of support, it divided into ineffective small sects and factions and, as a movement, disappeared. Some of the movement's constituent parts, Cantor concludes, remained viable, but neither the movement itself nor its parts created a real radical opposition in the nation.

One difficulty in assessing the results of the activities of the New Left is the great variety of its demands as well as the methods it employed. William H. Chafe, in the second selection, concentrates on one part of the movement, the fight for civil rights, tracing its development from court challenges of segregation to direct-action, nonviolent confrontations in the streets. The struggle against second-class citizenship had a long tradition among blacks, Chafe argues, but he insists that the young blacks who led the sit-ins and other demonstrations adopted a "new method" that "represented a new stage of black insurgency," which, in turn, often elicited sharp and usually violent reaction among the whites.

Jane Sherron De Hart, in the third selection, considers what she calls the "feminist revolution of the 1960s." She identifies two wings of the movement—"women's rights advocates," whose demands continued the long struggle women had waged for equal rights; and "women's liberationists," whose experiences in the civil rights and New Left movements led them to adopt more radical goals as well as more militant tactics. The two groups remained intact during the sixties, but the interaction between them blurred the distinctions as women from both groups sought both equal opportunities for women and an end to sexism and oppression—the latter goals requiring, in the views of many, a fundamental restructuring of American society.

Readers will notice in all the selections how the various groups within the New Left movement tended to push traditional reformers into making more radical demands and adopting more radical methods. But if some sought an answer to the problems they identified in a socialist transformation of society, others did not go that far. Does it follow, therefore, that the agitation of the 1960s was not radical and did not question the fundamentals of American society? Should one argue that equal rights for blacks and women and an end to racism and sexism were hardly radical in a nation that claimed to favor equality and justice for all? But if these rights were merely proclaimed but never put into effect and if inequality and injustice were the practice and, in many places, the law, then efforts to change the practice and the law might indeed be considered radical.

Did the tactics adopted by the various groups within the New Left movement signal a significant change in American politics? Did the mass movements and demonstrations alter traditional two-party politics by providing a new and potent vehicle by which the people, or at least an organized group of people, could influence politicians and political parties?

It is obvious that there was a great deal of conflict in this turbulent era. At few times in American history have presidential candidates been so ideologically divided as they were during the Johnson-Goldwater election campaign of 1964 and the Nixon-McGovern battle in 1972. The struggle of blacks, women, and students for greater rights and opportunities certainly represented conflict with established institutions and the larger society. Yet how significant was all this conflict? Did it represent fundamental differences with American values? Did it lead to a permanent change in American society? Or did the conflict pose no real challenge to basic American values? Did the conflict lead to a new consensus that attached more value to the rights of blacks, women, and students?

The New Left

Only in the early 1960s did the "silent generation" of the 1950s, those who grew up in the Eisenhower years, begin to find its voice. It was drawn to a new radicalism out of the shaping events of childhood and adolescence. Its members had been born toward the end of possibly the most savage and destructive war in our history. Their earliest consciousness of outside life was associated with Auschwitz and with genocide. They began their "maturity with Hiroshima." These "children of the bomb" lived through violence, atrocities, atomic bombs, the possibility of global cataclysm, and a growing sense of powerlessness. Their adolescence was played out against a background of nuclear terror, involvement in Korea, America's military presence around the planet, the Cuban Revolution, followed by those which swept Algeria and Vietnam; against a setting of swollen governmental bureaucracies and special interests, the rigidities of a homogenized two-party system; against public unresponsiveness to social needs and priorities, and the violation of civil liberties on an unprecedented scale. They became sensitive to the paradox of a national creed of social equality and the grim facts of bigotry; the myth of affluence and the realities of poverty; the pronouncements of peaceful goals and the preparations for nuclear conflict. Government misstatement and deception became ever more visible to them; the circle of awareness widened, penetrating ever more into an adolescence of relative ease. Bomb testing, Caryl Chessman's execution, the discovery of poverty, the threat of urban violence—still only on the perimeter of America's consciousness—began to touch impressionable youth. Their came, as Robert Lifton describes it, "the sense of being betrayed by a nation, a government, by specific political leaders, or by the older generation in general." And their instinctive conclusion was Yeats's—that innocence had been drowned in the blood-dimmed tide.

Thus innumerable national and international crises formed their lives. And all of it made vividly real by, among the bewildering actualities, air-raid drills in small communities and the requirement to huddle under schoolroom desks. Commenting on these realities of childhood, David Horowitz recalled: "We have been made to live as no other generation has, on the edge of the world's doom." They received an early awakening with the 1960 San Francisco demonstration against the House Un-American Activities Committee—and students remote from Berkeley were left troubled by the police response to undergraduate demonstrators. For most, too young to be aware of McCarthyism, it was the first conscious instance of repression and official lies in their own country. For this small sector of students, itself a minor segment of America's youth, a crisis of legitimacy had begun to unfold.

It would take time. These future radicals, after all, were shaped by the facts of economic opportunity as well as by domestic turbulence. They were not brutalized peasants or products of the ghetto; they were not social and economic failures; they were, as the 1962 Port Huron statement (the founding document of SDS) affirmed, the children of an affluent generation, "bred in at least modest comfort." They were mostly white, well-educated, suburban youth of similar backgrounds. Their parents had frequently been left-of-center, usually liberal Democrats, and often politically aware in their own student days. Their offspring, however, would not be radicalized in the home, but by society at large and specifically on the campus. In college, they were customarily enrolled in the humanities and the social sciences—which transmitted the strong Western traditions of skepticism and dissent—and they usually did impressive academic work. They grew unhappy with their classes because they were too large and impersonal; and they became scornful of fraternity and sorority life and even of athletic competition.

By the late 1950s, these students were numerous enough to form a genuine subculture. And their political liberalism was rooted in cultural changes which had begun to take shape, with such harbingers as folk music and the Beats, those alienated and apolitical poets of the Eisenhower years. This embryonic "counterculture," as it would be called, was a tocsin—for those who groped for ways to question society's fundamental assumptions. At first pointedly anti-middle-class, this counterculture would become pervasive and nationwide within a decade. It would turn into a highly commercial enterprise, filter down to working-class and non-college youth, and be absorbed into the middle class. That such a counterculture should spring up first on college campuses is understandable. Students, as Daniel Cohn-Bendit has pointed out, were under less pressure to conform. The campus permitted an unusual degree of social latitude. It offered hothouse conditions for germinating culture radicalism.

One segment of the counterculture never turned overtly political. Its tastes ran to D. H. Lawrence, who wanted the revolution "for fun," not for the proletariat. Becoming known as "hippies," this minority never made the great leap forward into the political activism of the Movement, sharing only its sense of alienation, the belief that impersonal powers controlled their lives. They engaged in love-ins and rock festivals rather than sit-ins and antiwar protests. But whether the counterculture was political or not, one thing is certain: there was a rising hostility to the dominant ethos of consumerism, materialism, and personal success—a repudiation of money, work, career, marriage.

The counterculture first appeared on selected campuses. Berkeley became a shrine for student pilgrims from across the country. But even here, it should be cautioned, the radicalized students were only a minority of undergraduates—and even when bitterly anti-militarist, antiwar sentiment neared its peak, some 63 percent of students polled thought that "the ROTC belongs on campus." In the late 1960s, to jump ahead momentarily, three fifths of the nation's students were "getting tired of all the campus unrest." They were at best reform-oriented and non-alienated, with only 8 percent seeking to replace the existing social system. Still, as New Left leader Al Haber prophesied, "if any really radical liberal force is going to develop in America, it is going to come from the colleges and the young." Moreover, it became an unspoken assumption that such a force would be concentrated in the liberal arts programs.

New Left students were the product of a class society and enjoyed its best advantages. They could never really cross over to white working-class youth, whom they charged—as they did all of America's labor force—with having "a false consciousness of their role and status." Their sentiments were reciprocated, for their values and long hair were offensive to labor. Behind the workers' pique was a powerful class hostility which AFL-CIO head George Meany and others effectively exploited.

The New Left's attitude toward labor bureaucrats was much like its reaction to government or to the Communist Party. It was hostile to virtually all discipline and all authoritarian forms—whether that of parent, teacher, lawgiver, or priest; it was deeply distrustful of the state, opposed to the bigness and remoteness of both government and trade union. Appalled by the quality of American life and its institutions, New Leftists would shift to localism, community organizing, decentralized controls, and, a favored term, "participatory democracy."

What occurred, then, was a moral rebellion, a protest by the middle class against the middle class, a kind of anguished children's crusade against "the careful young men" (as *The Nation* described the class of '58) who never expressed any political discontents. As such, it was unlike the leftist student movements of earlier days, which were umbilically linked to adult political groups. The New Left was a genuine youth movement, mostly of white undergraduates. Their youthfulness was perhaps their outstanding feature. Except for the middle-aged Christian pacifists and some aging gurus like philosopher Herbert Marcuse, most New Leftists were born after 1940. No wonder the admonition of Berkeley's Free Speech Movement (FSM), "Don't trust anyone over thirty," seemed appropriate.

Unlike the Old Left in many respects, the New Left also differed from countless other groups in our history who felt pushed out, left behind by change, unable to transmit their legacy; they rejected the legacy offered to them. They were different, too, in that they rose spontaneously and lacked the hopefulness of interwar radicals, with their concrete model of an alternative economic order. Having no faith in the great October Revolution, they combined instead an insouciant disregard for revered radical systems with antagonism toward the existing order and with vague utopian longings. They were in a way even more romantic than the older radicals and bore virtually all the stigmata of romanticism, though some of its features matured only in the late 1960s. They were more inclined toward the intuitive and emotional, unlike their Depression liberal-radical parents, who had trusted in reason. They displayed an intense subjectivity, a preoccupation with private problems, a propensity for physical violence, a revulsion against theory, an attraction to mysticism, a cultish worship of youth as the repository of wisdom and beauty. . . .

For this New Left, the values of the Port Huron statement—anti-elitism, anti-bureaucracy, participation, community—were crystallized by the civil rights movement then germinating in the South. Indeed, the blacks would virtually replace the working class as central to radical social change—as student radicals identified emotionally with southern civil rights workers and transferred student discontent and humanistic values onto the civil rights movement. Of the eventual black reaction, more will be said later. For the moment it should be noted that the civil rights movement preceded the New Left. First came the monumental desegregation decision of 1954, *Brown v. Board of Education.* Then, in 1955, the Montgomery bus boycott led by Martin Luther King, which induced Irving Howe to hope "that the mute should find their voices." The boycott involved the entire black community in a sustained confrontation with the white power structure, something unprecedented in our history. Five years later came the real catalyst for blacks and for college students: four neatly dressed black undergraduates deliberately challenged state racial segregation by sitting down at the "whites only" lunch counters of Greensboro, North Carolina stores; they asked for coffee and refused to leave until the stores closed. Thus new tactics were developed. These needed an organization not "subject to the authority of anyone but themselves"; consequently, southern blacks founded the Student Nonviolent Coordinating Committee (SNCC) in October 1960. Its goal was the elimination of segregation—and not simply at lunch counters, "but in every aspect of life." Its focus was on the immediate situation—not one involving a socialist future.

In 1961 came a first climax, the "freedom rides" organized by the Congress of Racial Equality (CORE)—in which northern "riders," many of them white, flooded southern cities and refused to accept segregated accommodations at bus terminals, lunch counters, and rest rooms. SNCC's greatest achievement would be the voter registration drives across the South, in which it was joined by CORE and staffed by 500 organizers, many of them northern white undergraduates. Always living in the shadow of the noose, these organizers would work alongside rural blacks from 1961 to 1965. Their efforts were shaped by non-resistant black leaders, such as Martin Luther King, and by those radical pacifists who founded *Liberation* in 1956 and who immediately endorsed nonviolent protest.

The Greensboro tactics quickly caught on. By the end of 1960, an estimated 50,000 had participated in some civil rights protest across the South, and over 3,600 had spent some time in jail for violation of local ordinances. Many were Northerners, galvanized into action by the notes of high idealism which John Kennedy had early struck. Southern treatment of the black and the poor seemed like a blot on the promise of American life and, for the first time in their comfortable existence, suburban white youth saw how the other half lived; for the first time dogs attacked them and hoses were turned on them; for the first time they were witness to the poverty and illiteracy of rural black labor and exposed to the brutality of American life—to arrests, beatings, occasionally to murder. These experiences were traumatizing. They would return to college with a new awareness of the national ills and with a new sense of camaraderie and purpose.

Thus a new breed of civil rights activists gathered in SNCC, CORE, and the Southern Christian Leadership Conference (SCLC). Primarily middle-class in origins, they were now "trying to heighten consciousness," as SNCC leader James Foreman declared, to reduce black powerlessness. They sought at first legal and formal equality with whites in such matters as public education and the right to vote, but their goal would shift somewhat to a political struggle for socioeconomic parity; it would also evolve into a racially exclusive movement, as blacks increasingly took over. They fought for those rights already possessed by the white middle class. Hardly revolutionary goals, but essential to integrating the rural black work force into the capitalist system. To find their demands governed by a social-democratic, not revolutionary, perspective, does not suggest that they were any less worthwhile; they were in response to immediate need and they were a cry for justice. That student liberals and leftists should equate the aims and objectives of the civil rights movement with their own, that SDS in the early 1960s sought to deepen its ties with militant southern blacks, that the Port Huron statement expressed hope that a new movement for social change could be enfolded within a broadened civil rights campaign, was natural and inevitable.

Thus a new radical mood began to percolate in the early 1960s. It would become immensely complicated, striking out in many directions and including many groupings, with a few, the offspring of the Old Left—YPSL, the Young Socialist Alliance (YSA), Progressive Labor, the Du Bois Clubs—invoking the theorists of the past. But the Movement, as the new radicalism came to be called, was far more inclusive. Lacking a long-range perspective, it was able to create and maintain a powerful student crusade. It came to believe that such a crusade could be a potent agency for change. Massive protest demonstrations confirmed this belief. Students could indeed make history. . . .

The very uncoordinated and non-programmatic nature of the New Left facilitated cooperation with pacifists. New Leftists cared more for informal and improvised forms of social action, as Kenneth Keniston has observed, than for explicit programs that would restructure society. And being a mood, a mode of life, an élan rather than a prospectus, the Movement was thus thrown open to a variety of tactical as well as philosophical perspectives, some of which were readily shared by peace workers—whether these be social-democratic efforts to elect peace candidates on the Democratic Party ticket or confrontation politics against nuclear testing. Since even such confrontations were non-violent before 1965, a working alliance was all the easier. So pacifists joined student radicals in collecting signatures for petitions and in fasting against nuclear tests in the autumn of 1961. The New Left rekindled pacifist energies, eventually communicated a sense of crisis, and turned peace workers into militant critics of society.

Reflecting an ex officio collaboration between Christian pacifists and the New Left, *Liberation* opened its columns to those who held deep ethical convictions about war, specifically the war in Vietnam—with appeals by Bertrand Russell, the doyen of pacifism, and by Staughton Lynd, a major New Left spokesman. Both writers, indeed all who called themselves "radical," affirmed, as *Liberation* stated, that "our role in Indochina has always been immoral." "Stop shooting and get out!" it exhorted. . . . To the New Left, its radicalism grounded in genuine moral conviction, such sentiments had a powerful appeal.

Radical activism was equally appealing. It was necessarily so in a society that historically reflected a tension between the athletic and the contemplative—and that invariably chose the former. Thus even those most committed to the life of the mind frequently found action superior to theory. Hence activism, and activism of a violent sort, would become increasingly fashionable. In more recent times, it lost its remedial purpose and became a means without any coherent end.

In any case, a mounting number of peace workers would soon reject democratic processes and gradualism. Pacifist David McReynolds soberly noted their departure—with Dellinger endorsing the Cuban Revolution and Lynd "disengaging from his pacifism as it applies to Vietnam." And, McReynolds concluded, the real dilemma confronting the peace movement was its wavering between peaceful change and violence, with one bloc adhering to traditional pacific modes of action and the other, growing powerful, seeking peace through violent means. So it would fall out. Suffice to note that pacifist non-resistance mingled with the pure streams of antiwar radicalism from the outset.

The inclusiveness of the New Left is one of its most striking characteristics. It would comprise anarchists, antiwar students, draft resisters, GI dissidents, radically inclined intellectuals, liberals, libertarians, socialists, young professionals, apostate Catholics, syndicalists, followers of R. D. Laing, who sought personalism, the first generation of liberated women, high school dropouts, brilliant graduate students, and a growing number of black nationalists. It would embrace SDS, SNCC, ad hoc groups such as the Free Speech Movement (FSM) and the successor Vietnam Day Committee (VDC), the Mississippi Freedom Democratic Party (MFDP), as well as social idealists from Vista and the Peace Corps. It would attract nihilists off the Columbia University campus, single-issue antiwar religious or radical organizations like the National Mobilization, Vietnam Summer (1967), the Moratorium (1969), Clergymen Concerned, Women's Strike for Peace. This left-liberal coalition welcomed college faculty, high school and college students, doctoral candidates. Some were unsophisticated, unable to distinguish between a Maoist and a liberal; others were refreshingly trenchant voices like Mills and Paul Goodman, writing in *Studies on the Left*. Still others, including Adlai Stevenson's followers and Young Democrats, sought only campus reform; while more rejected Stevenson, owing to his defense of the Bay of Pigs, and rejected that misadventure as well, and they found New Deal liberalism and Stalinism, capitalism and socialism, equally flawed.

The Movement transcended any single individual or organization. Its massive reunions in the streets of New York, Washington, and San Francisco were conducted by ad hoc coalitions—in which SDS, so often synonymous with the New Left in the popular mind, was only one among many sponsoring or participating organizations. The April 1965 demonstration, for instance, brought together former Peace Corps volunteers, SANE members out of white suburbs, urban black teen-agers, Berkeley activists, members of MFDP, short-haired freshmen out of Catholic colleges, liberals drawn from the ADA, Communists who belonged to the Du Bois Clubs. A "new generation of American radicals," Jack Newfield has written, they were not nourished "by the alien cob-webbed dogmas of Marx, Lenin, and Trotsky. . . . They were there not to protest anything so simple as war or capitalism."

The New Left, then, was a most capacious vessel of change. It was much like the Popular Front, the product of a symbiotic relation between liberals and radicals, between those who sought reform and those who were indifferent to politics, those who were dogmatic radicals and those who were bohemians. Thus one sector of the Movement would turn its back on society, its sexual morality, technology, rationalism, militarism, social regimentation. These rebels against the culture were themselves not an undifferentiated whole. Some, for instance, copied the "life style" of the now widespread counterculture, superficially identifying with its appearances—its scatological speech, eccentric dress and behavior, use of drugs, wearing of flowers and bells—and they were the "love, peace, groovy" flower children of the mid-1960s.

Others, more profoundly troubled by the prevailing work ethic and social norms, questioned the conventional pieties and authority of any kind. They exalted the spontaneous and unexplored, the individual and personal relationships, existential experience for its own sake. They proposed a pastoral ethos and a romantic celebration of nature and of the senses. They wanted to feel and be, not to know. They were convinced that sex, rock, drugs, and meditation were avenues to a new culture, and these values, not changes in doctrines and institutions, were fundamental and would reshape the world.

Though largely indifferent to politics, at times they did make common cause with the political rebels and with the civil rights movement. After all, they shared some of the same grievances and sources of inspiration: they had a common enemy in the vaguely defined "establishment"; they also searched for communal involvement, displayed contempt for the authorities of the past, sought a decisive break with the nation's bureaucratic systems.

It is a mistake, then, to separate entirely political and cultural rebels in these early years. Indeed, the Movement's partisans deliberately linked antiwar and counterculture politics. There is, furthermore, a linkage that is political in a less obvious way. Those converted to the counterculture, including the hippy-acid-head sector, gradually created an underculture, involving dress, drugs, community, and rejection of democratic processes. Largely unaware of it, this non-doctrinal segment inadvertently undermined the politics of legitimacy. No Movement component, at least not until the late 1960s, would elect to mount the barricades. Rather, they all joined in a campaign that, as Keniston has observed, was not "a movement in the traditional sense," but a cluster of customarily uncoordinated groups which attacked poverty, racism, discrimination against women—a nearly inexhaustible list of domestic ills—and, turning overseas, condemned the traditional "liberal" orientation in foreign affairs.

The discrete, often ephemeral nature of the constituent parts would be debilitating for the whole. Different political styles and social emphases made it unlikely that a single guideline could be maintained. Moreover, each group, rather than combining and then mediating among the needs of the diverse elements, locked into one stratum—blacks, youth, labor—as the catalyst for change. Some groups rejected the hereditary left and its objectives; others secretly lionized it. And there was still another sector which, being pacifist, was not ideological, though rejecting America's "imperialism" and her role as global policeman.

The Movement surely had no clear political program, no viable organization, and, early on, no substantial constituency. All of which made it relatively easy for many of its votaries, over the objections of the doctrinally pure, to join the McCarthy and Robert Kennedy primary campaigns and thereby work their way back into the system. It is useful to note that the "new politics"—of the McCarthy and then the McGovern presidential drive—was entirely conventional. It involved precinct organizing and endless canvassing, among other activities, to fight for reform-radical goals within the existing party structure. And, ironically, seeking such goals meant cooperating with politicians who were themselves implicated in the Vietnam War or unable to break from it, unable to repudiate its growing horrors even after Richard Nixon made those horrors his own.

The relative ease with which many in the Movement crossed over into Democratic Party work further confirms the flexibility of most of its components. At the outset more open to ideas than most, the New Leftists stressed, as Keniston tells us, immediate tactics, limited goals, short-range activities. They refused to deify theoretical schema or to develop a revolutionary strategy. To the contrary, they scorned those trapped in the theoretical dustbins of Europe, neglecting the saints and renegades who so preoccupied the radical imagination for nearly a century. Their governing tone was proclaimed at the December 1965 SDS conference: "We have slogans which take the place of thought: 'There's a change gonna come' is our substitute for social theory. . . . What sociology, what psychology, what history do we need to know the answers?" The question itself discloses an implicit skepticism and cognitive sterility. New Leftists attacked not so much "the world of ideas," as Irving Louis Horowitz shrewdly concludes, as "the idea that reason is the only mode of knowing." Or, as a contemporary found, contemptuous of theory, they "rarely read anything unless it came from the underground press." In this manner they abandoned the Old Left's certainties and reductivism, its doctrinal rigidity and historical inevitability. . . .

Lacking the massive certainties of the hereditary left, the new radicals were pluralistic and amorphous. They willingly accepted recruits with divergent social and political views—anarchist, Trotskyite, socialist, pacifist, Communist. Because of their refusal to exclude Communists, or even express anxiety about them, they were viewed with growing alarm by old-time social-democratic trade unionists and groups like SANE, LID, and ADA, by over-thirty liberals as well as by socialists. After all, for those scarred by Depression-decade struggle with the Communist *apparatchiki,* such indifference and lack of selectivity seemed naïve and hopeless. Hence the response of Robert Gilmore, executive director of Turn Toward Peace (TTP), when SDS failed to exclude Du Bois Club members from its April 1965 antiwar demonstration. He quietly sought to convince several peace leaders to withdraw from the march and, whether or not he influenced them, some prominent socialists as well as liberals and pacifists (including Thomas, Rustin, and Muste) signed a statement which obliquely slapped at SDS. "We welcome the cooperation of all those groups and individuals who, like ourselves, believe in the need for an independent peace movement," they declared, but not those "committed to any form of totalitarianism nor drawing inspiration or direction from the foreign policy of any government." Their language seemed un-exceptionable; however, for those touched by McCarthyism it was clear warning that even the most courageous of over-thirty pacifists were not inured to red-baiting. . . .

The New Left did endorse some classic liberal goals as well as an issues-oriented perspective. But it had contempt for what was thought to be the cant of liberalism, was estranged from civil rights and trade-union moderates when they endorsed Lyndon Johnson's candidacy in 1964 and asked, to the vast discomfort of Democratic liberals, "How can we continue to sack the ports of Asia and still dream of Jesus?" New Leftists were ready to condemn American actions in Viet-nam without voicing comparable imprecations against repression by Hanoi, a prerequisite for holding unimpeachable liberal and anti-Communist credentials in these years. Both powers were equally culpable, Movement leaders thought, a conclusion violating historic guidelines for both Communists and anti-Commu-nists. The Port Huron statement, for example, was typically evenhanded in as-sessing the failure to promulgate a nuclear test-ban treaty: "Our paranoia about the Soviet Union has made us incapable of achieving agreements absolutely nec-essary for disarmament and the preservation of peace. We are hardly able to see the possibility that the Soviet Union, though not 'peace loving,' may be seriously interested in disarmament."

Subsequent New Left tracts made much of the sins of "corporate liberal-ism," and it became a major theoretical construct of SDS'ers. It was responsible for such reprehensible facts as segregation in the South, for social welfare pro-grams which were at best palliatives, for the effort to subvert Cuba's revolution, for the slow escalation of war in Vietnam. SDS arraigned Adlai Stevenson, a lib-eral darling, for his bald lies at the time of the Bay of Pigs. *Studies on the Left,* perhaps the earliest theoretical journal of the Movement, first appeared in 1959 and three years later was assailing the Kennedy liberals and the CIA in the same breath: one failed to "recognize the nature of anticolonial revolutions," and the other sought to subvert them. Liberals and New Leftists, of course, appealed largely to the same constituency, and they went some way down the same road together; witness the civil rights and antiwar movements. Perhaps that is why lib-erals were the "chief enemy." Because, as Michael Walzer has wisely speculated, SDS was searching for an independent identity. . . .

That the Movement died was inevitable. The reasons for its end are less ap-parent and highly complex, a mix that is generic to radical failures after 1900. And we may claim continuities even while recognizing that specific historical fac-tors are partly responsible—the antiwar movement, after all, was a function of a specific and unique event in our history.

The war brought prominence and power to the Movement. It was the pri-mary passion, providing the glue which bound abrasive elements. Moreover, Vietnam provided the common denominator, even a set of common grievances against society, and, with its end, each element—e.g., women and blacks—lapsed into the usual pluralistic pattern of pressure-group action on behalf of its own limited constituency. Paradoxically, then, the war which cemented discrete seg-ments was the Movement's undoing. The changed historical situation contributed to radical loss and disintegration. For when Nixon, under enormous pressure, ended the draft and began withdrawing American forces from Vietnam, he defused public concern and irreparably damaged the Movement.

The Movement's inability to develop a new radical theory beyond liberalism left it deeply flawed. For it meant that the United States produced no Gramsci, Lukács, Lenin, Luxemburg, no theoreticians who might go beyond the contributions of Marx over a century ago, no school of social analysis comparable to the Frankfurt group of Marxists today. It meant, too, that gesture and rhetoric would replace good, tough theoretical system building. It virtually guaranteed that radicals would end up reinforcing the business civilization they proposed to change. It also assured that when the overseas conflict ground to a halt, the New Left would lose its *raison d'être*.

The war heightened domestic social tensions but could not be the basis for a viable revolutionary movement. For that a sustained theoretical overview was needed. None developed—which partly explains the New Left's abrupt departure from the scene. It also helps us understand why a decade of militancy and social turbulence has left virtually no institutional remnants, no ongoing parties, no nationally recognized radical cadres or leadership, no established formulas, as Walzer concludes, by which one can keep on being radical.

Political protest of the early 1960s, which had been directed by the blacks or the New Left, shifted after 1966, when important black groups and sectors excluded whites from participation and adopted disciplined organizational forms incompatible with the spontaneous protest that had brought them numbers and visibility. Then, too, the antiwar movement was gradually taken over by the Old Left, which had different goals and more rigid practices than earlier activists.

In sum, the New Left never possessed what George Vickers has called "historical self-consciousness" which would provide theoretical coherence. It failed to supply the normative framework which would encourage workers to understand their society and provide a durable mass base. Spawned by the most highly educated and most privileged sectors of society, New Leftists distinguished themselves both from capitalists and from the proletariat. They confused their own protest and interests with those of the blacks and the unskilled; and they confused their desire "to rationalize social relationships *within* a system of structured social inequality," as Vickers shrewdly observes, with the truly radical desire to abolish social inequality—which would mean abolition of the very structures which shaped their desire.

There are other factors to consider in explaining this latest failure of the left. First, the very encounter with American politics was a bruising if not fatal one. For the political system again demonstrated its immense flexibility. Assimilative in function, adapted to gradualism, it easily reincorporated groups which had moved out of it. For such disaffected, a non-ideological *Realpolitik* governed, which meant devising tactics that would preserve their ideals and yet respect fixed political and cultural guidelines. Specifically, it meant boring from within trade unions and the Democratic Party. Thus radicals, as in the interwar years, could not be insensitive to immediate human needs. They permitted narrowly reformist activity to take priority over any doctrinal perspective, thereby serving the purposes of liberal capitalism. Explicitly socialist groups, not serving their socialist integrity, became left-liberal and populist, pragmatic and non-ideological—which is itself an ideology and not simply an automatic response to structural constraints. . . .

Still another fact merits a final mention: working-class indifference or hostility to the New Left, indeed to radicalism generally. In explaining the reasons for the Movement's disappearance, it bears repeating that radicals were deprived of what was always thought the essential revolutionary base. America's union bureaucrats enjoyed the sun at Miami Beach, and making capitalism work more efficiently governed their strategic vision. Much like Gompers then and George Meany today, they believed in a fundamental identity of interests between business and labor, and endorsed goals of liberal capitalism: anti-Communism, social welfare, democratic practices; and both worried over workplace insurgency. Nor did it cease in the 1960s. Rather, labor's resistance to management practices intensified. Usually it took the form of controlling the pace of work, combating unsafe labor conditions, establishing production-output quotas, organizing slow-downs, evading speedups, sabotaging machinery, and comparable forms of resistance, rather than direct confrontation with corporate power. But such tactics, such fitful working-class dissidence, should not suggest revolutionary restlessness. Labor was not even nominally socialist. It lacked the insurrectionary voice which, given the opportunity, would—like E. P. Thompson's yeomanry or Richard Cobb's artisans of prerevolutionary Paris—prompt rebellion. True enough, its most depressed elements, such as farm workers and coal miners, did have a real sense of class identity, but class antagonisms were only infrequently expressed and they were articulated, as Gramsci noted, "within the existing fundamental structure." Hence even those elements within the labor movement which had a sense of their identity were contained. Their goals were mediated and formulated—to some extent reformulated, adapted to their situation—by the dominant class ideology and its complex network of values and institutions.

Labor's tactics, to be sure, indicated a declining respect for the work ethic, which reflected a comparable decline in society at large. But this did not produce class solidarity or a challenge to the dominant social ethic. It failed to threaten a value system which measured class divisions primarily in terms of income and material possessions. By the 1960s, there were obvious changes in the occupational structure of American capitalism—with the sharp growth of white-collar and service workers as well as the rise of a "new middle class" of salaried wage earners—unlike an "old middle class" of self-employed small entrepreneurs. But the changes in class structure reflected the growth, not the breakdown, of capitalist economic organization. These changes possibly rendered some dominant cultural forms obsolete, but the interaction between structure and consciousness was uninterrupted. Consequently, middle-class ideology, while undergoing adjustments, remained relatively stable. It still transmuted labor's values, consciousness, and institutions. The result: the self-legitimizing capacity of industrial capitalism went on apace and radicals over the last decade became more isolated from the work force than at any other time in our history.

Thus the Movement came to an end, though in some ways its consequences have never wholly disappeared. Marxism, for instance, experienced a modest revival after being dormant for at least a generation. It reappeared in the social sciences, as Warren Susman has noted, but it took on a new form. No longer a test of political orthodoxy, Marxism is studied for its relevance to American society or as a legitimate academic exercise. And in one of the twists of history, those who study it are frequently the very New Leftists who had once eschewed theory.

This is not to suggest that all former New Leftists turned to a serious study of Marxist thought. Most settled for liberalism—which meant the old drift toward the left, the party of humanity and generosity, the durable enemy of ignorance and injustice. They remained obstinately, if quietly, reformist. Many simply settled for the retention of private doubts about the government, internalizing their cynicism and dissent. They continued to be repelled by its manipulative and repressive character, and to find it less credible and "obeyable" than ever. No less than 79 percent believed that American foreign policy was governed by economic interests, and 94 percent charged that business was too concerned with profits and too indifferent to public responsibility. In this sense the Movement also left its mark. It contributed a legacy of cultural opposition. It created a substantial body of young men and women who could no longer clearly identify our "enemies" abroad, who had their doubts about capitalism, and who, when Watergate became part of the amalgam, helped produce a crisis in legitimacy shared by many non-radicals as well.

The veterans of the early radical campaigns are not terribly interested in renewing the political contests, in undertaking the hard work necessary to build institutional bases. They now seek careers and assured incomes, but they have also retained the earlier premises about money, competition, sexual openness. As novitiates in the law, medicine, social work, education, they are caught between personal ambitions and the social implications of these ambitions. They take on jobs, join institutions, begin families, assume positions of authority, but still have reservations about these matters and remain stubbornly loyal to the new departures in family structure, child rearing, the meaning of work, sexual relations, which the 1960s generated.

So this earlier decade transmitted a wide-ranging spirit of inquiry, nourished a tradition of cultural insurgency that did not suddenly expire. There were the religious cults devoted to personal salvation or charismatic expression. There were the continuing articulation of black identity, the Indians' growing sense of their history, the effort to build women's consciousness, the new journals focusing on drugs, music, sexual behavior—in lieu of political interests. And gradually these cultural features became for many transmuted substitutes for the old political enthusiasms.

But the drugs, music, and sexual openness of the 1970s were no longer part of the highly visible counterculture of the Movement. Rather than being "counter"—part of Raymond Williams' "oppositional culture"—they were absorbed into the residual culture. The government provided token support for women and blacks in the national political and economic life, gave verbal fealty to ecology, closed its eyes to homosexuality and marijuana—and hence made for a more smoothly functioning and better integrated society.

The new populism is a case in point. Evolving out of the social turbulence of the 1960s, it had an anti-corporate bias but was far more concerned with "bread and butter" issues than with explicit ideology. It would not, unlike Marxism, seek a social transformation or depend upon the working class as the agent of change. Rather, it would defend the democratic system against corporate depredations, expose bureaucratic muddles, and appeal to the "citizenry" at large, much as populists have always done. It displayed little more than an unfocused suspicion of great power—whether in public or private hands—and would balance private interests against countervailing public power, thereby demonstrating a hostility to privilege that has been deeply engrained in the nation's past. It had no other options. It is, at this time, engaged in only a piecemeal attack on the business-government alliance, one that is largely localist in orientation.

Some of these observations apply to the minority groups which emerged in the late 1960s and found their voice in the early 1970s. The black movement, for instance, took a separatist cultural form and pre-capitalist emphasis—with its Afro hairstyles and "black is beautiful" slogans—but simply sought its share of the capitalist pie. The claims of the blacks, like those of the new populists and the feminists, like those of virtually all marginal and excluded groups, have been easily accommodated by the system.

The women's movement had its beginnings in the late 1960s, given impetus in part by the women's caucuses in SDS, but it rapidly developed into an autonomous crusade to end the systematic oppression of all women. Recognizing that all women were oppressed, the feminist movement mushroomed out of its radical matrix and developed separate issues and organizations. That it split off from traditional radicalism, Weinstein notes, was due to a number of factors: the socially conservative character of most segments of the left, which would do no more than imitate Old Left views of revolution and insist upon the primacy of the working class. But the social base of the feminist movement remained among college-educated and professional women, without deep roots among blacks or working-class women. Like the New Left from which it issued, women's lib had an anti-intellectual animus and has thus far failed to develop a political theory adequate to bona fide radicalism. Hence it became easy for feminists to target men as the primary enemy, to focus upon entry into the male world, rather than consider transforming the social relations and political economy of that world, rather than analyze women's oppression within the context of advanced capitalism. The women's movement has also suffered from as much divisiveness as the Old Left, the New Left, and the black movement. Its one stable national movement—the National Organization of Women (NOW)—is no more than a lobbying group within the existing political institutions, state and federal legislatures as well as the Democratic Party. It would work for liberal reforms—like equal pay, equal opportunity, elimination of job discrimination and of inequitable representation for women in politics and business. Another feminist sector is outside of politics altogether. Deriving from the consciousness-raising and support groups of the first years, it seeks alternative styles in family life and child rearing and, as Weinstein notes, is "largely anti-male, and radical Lesbianism in its ultimate form of expression." A small segment, lacking an organizational voice, has a socialist-feminist viewpoint. It is concerned with "private" relations but understands them to be determined by the prevailing cultural values and class structure.

In effect, minority groups sought legitimacy within the residual culture. By their tendency to separatism, they would unintentionally divide socio-cultural opposition to the existing attitudes and institutions. They are all, like the New Left, lacking in a coherent theory, and they have a taste for patient and pedestrian strategies unknown to the radicalism of the late 1960s. Certainly, however socialism is defined, none of these new movements and trends may be subsumed under its rubric, though they are suggestive of the continuity of American radicalism, as well as the variables in its expression. All of these post-1960s groups and movements were also manifestations of a changing capitalism and its cultural values. Virtually all would merely mitigate one or another evil existing under capitalism. Such was frequently the way of a failed American radicalism.

What has been said at the outset of this study bears repeating: one must be careful about the assumption hidden in these observations, for it cannot be concluded that, had organized radicals acted differently in the 1960s and 1970s, or in the interwar years for that matter, their story or America's future would have been qualitatively altered. It is a mistake to assume that had factionalism not existed—that had Los Angeles Communists not formed the all-black Che-Lumumba Club, which deeply divided a Party membership, that had Berkeley's YSA (the SWP student affiliate) not formally recognized the right of dissident opinion, thereby evoking SWP cries of heresy—socialism would have succeeded. Whether or not radical organizations became sterile sects, descended into irrelevance, engaged in "Mecca watching," deteriorated into bureaucratic rigidity—whether or not they became basically reformist or still voiced the opinions of Lenin and looked forward to the Götterdämmerung—it is doubtful that a durable socialist consciousness could have developed.

Radicals have ever been caught in the dilemma created by concrete historical conditions and by the nature of capitalism—by the facts of a vaunted occupational mobility; by the celebrated, if partly mythic, fluidity of class structure; by the absence of a feudal tradition; by the flexibility of the political process, the capacity of the two-party system to accommodate and absorb radicals and radical issues; by the popularly held conviction of a democratic and egalitarian ethos, which, as Hillquit observed, was "another check to the progress of the socialist movement in America." These factors suggested, for Gramsci, an "Americanism" which was a distinct ideological alternative to socialism. Laslett, agreeing with him and elaborating, concludes that in the United States "the ideals of bourgeois civilization—individualism, the sanctity of private property, antipathy toward state interference in the economy, as well as a whole host of other factors—have become diffused throughout society in all its institutional and private manifestations, informing with its spirit all taste, morality, customs, religions and political principles." Marcuse would add the media, growing leisure, relative affluence as more recent phenomena that produced the "spontaneous" consent of the masses in capitalism. Then, too, there were two world wars and the spoils of imperialism which benefited favored sectors of the labor force. Thus a large mix of economic, political, social and ideological factors shaped a non-revolutionary society and militated against a sustained socialist tradition in the United States. There is every reason to believe that these factors, which have always presented a critical problem for America's socialists and for an effective radical movement, are still operative.

The Civil Rights Movement

Nothing about May 17, 1954 seemed particularly different as court reporters gathered for the weekly pronouncement of decisions by the court. There had been no advance notice of any significant rulings. Then, suddenly, one hour after proceeding with the decisions in other cases, the Chief Justice announced that he would begin reading the court's opinion in *Brown*. Scrambling, reporters dashed to the court. Forcefully, the Chief Justice read his first major opinion. Education, he declared, represented a central experience in life. Those things that children learned in school remained with them for the rest of their time on earth. The critical question, then, was: "Does segregation of children in public schools solely on the basis of race . . . deprive the children of the minority group of equal education opportunities?" Answering, the Chief Justice declared: "We believe that it does."

To separate [those children] from others of similar age and qualifications solely because of their race generates a feeling of inferiority as to their status in the community that may affect their hearts and minds in a way unlikely ever to be undone. . . . We conclude that in the field of public education the doctrine of "separate but equal" has no place. Separate educational facilities are inherently unequal. . . . Any language in Plessy v. Ferguson *contrary to these findings is rejected.*

Fifteen years after the *Gaines* decision in Missouri, seven years after J. A. DeLaine agreed to challenge the Clarendon County School Board, and sixty years after Jim Crow was legally born, segregated schools were acknowledged to be an abomination. Unanimously, the Supreme Court had ruled that the Fourteenth Amendment required equal admission of all students to public schools. The decision, the *Chicago Defender* proclaimed, was "a second emancipation proclamation . . . more important to our democracy than the atom bomb or the hydrogen bomb." Within five years, Thurgood Marshall predicted, all segregated schools would be abolished. "We have won," blacks exulted. It appeared that the Supreme Court had done what politicians had refused to do.

The Response to *Brown*

Initially, response to the *Brown* decision offered reason for optimism. Black newspapers hailed the court's action, confident that the structure of segregation would now quickly be dismantled. Even the white South reacted more with resignation than with rebellion. Only James Byrnes of South Carolina, Herman Talmadge in Georgia, and Hugh White in Mississippi engaged in the rhetoric of outraged resistance. More representative were comments that regretted the *Brown* decision, but called for calm acceptance of its consequences. Thus, Governor Frances Cherry of Arkansas declared: "Arkansas will obey the law. It always has." And "Big" Jim Folsom of Alabama stated: "When the Supreme Court speaks, that's the law." "The end of the world has not come for the South or for the nation," the *Louisville Courier Journal* editorialized. "The Supreme Court's ruling is not itself a revolution. It is rather an acceptance of a process that has been going on for a long time." Cities like Louisville, Kentucky, Little Rock, Arkansas, and Greensboro, North Carolina, indicated that they were ready to begin the process of compliance.

Yet the *Brown* decision by itself existed in a vacuum. It required commitment, leadership, and tangible action if it were to become more than empty rhetoric. As one legal scholar said at the time:

The law is a landing force [of change]. It makes the beachhead. But the breakthrough, if it is to be significant, is broadened by forces from behind which take advantage of the opening to go the rest of the way. Where these forces are present, significant alteration of social practices is the result. Where they do not exist, the law has been unable to hold its beachhead and the legal action becomes a kind of military monument on which is only recorded "we were here."

Despite initial positive signs, it quickly became clear that "the forces from behind" were unwilling to act. The Supreme Court itself, as one price for securing unanimity, delayed for a year its own decision on how to implement desegregation. When the second *Brown* ruling was handed down in May 1955, it called for remanding cases to the district courts. Implementation procedures were to begin "with all deliberate speed," but no deadline was set. In the South itself, meanwhile, those willing to act decisively in support of integration suddenly found themselves alone, without reinforcement from either economic or political leaders, or from the courts. In city after city, education leaders who were ready to begin desegregation, and who had even postponed building plans because the new ruling would require integrated schools, looked in vain for pressure from above to support their initiatives. With no tangible encouragement to proceed, they decided to withdraw from the battle, forsaking the beachhead that had been won to defenders of the old order.

No one deserved more censure for the failure to follow through than the president himself. In 1954 Dwight Eisenhower enjoyed more moral authority and political strength than any president since Franklin Roosevelt at the beginning of the New Deal. His position, in some ways, was analogous to that of Andrew Johnson at the end of the Civil War. At that time, the South had been defeated, overwhelmingly. White Southerners felt helpless, resigned, waiting for cues as to how to respond. Decisive, immediate leadership in such a situation held the promise of transforming the social and political landscape. . . .

White Southern Resistance

Just as Andrew Johnson had given cues to former confederates that they could reassert control over the South without interference from the White House, so President Eisenhower, through his reticence and ambiguity, encouraged segregationists to believe that they had free rein to resist the Supreme Court. Within a year, the resignation that had prevailed after the first *Brown* decision had gradually changed into optimism about the possibility of preserving the status quo and, finally, into outright and systematic resistance to desegregation. Those who might have supported compliance if the president had given them no other option now found themselves competing against the rabid right for control of the political spectrum, attempting to become more racist than even the worst segregationist just to stay in office. In states like Alabama the NAACP was outlawed; elsewhere, supporters of civil rights were pilloried as agents of a communist conspiracy to take over the South. "In this atmosphere," the historian C. Vann Woodward has observed, "words began to change their meanings so that a moderate became a man who dared to open his mouth, and an extremist someone who favored eventual compliance with the law."

Resistance mushroomed in direct correlation to the growing evidence that the federal government would do nothing to counteract it. After the Supreme Court indicated in the second *Brown* decision that immediate compliance would not be necessary, state governments shifted their attention from how to comply to how to circumvent. As Eisenhower offered tacit sanction to segregationists in Texas and at the University of Alabama, state legislatures began to pass resolutions calling for massive resistance, with Virginia, Alabama, Mississippi, and Georgia claiming the right, à la John Calhoun's nullification movement of 1828, to "interpose" themselves between the people and the federal government, declaring the Supreme Court's decision "null, void, and of no effect." Nearly every state passed a pupil assignment law that transferred authority over schools to local school boards to avoid statewide suits by the NAACP. Under such legislation, criteria such as "the general welfare" were substituted for race as a basis for assigning pupils to schools. In this way segregation could be maintained in practice without mentioning the word in law, and anyone challenging the results would be forced on an individual basis to fight layers of bureaucratic control before being able to secure a court hearing. Even then, the U.S. Fourth Circuit Court ruled in 1959, parents must prove beyond a doubt that race was the basis for exclusion. Within such a structure of judicial interpretation the total burden rested with the individual plaintiff, making a mockery of any notion of far-reaching desegregation. So widespread did the atmosphere of resistance become that, in the spring of 1956, 101 of 128 congressmen from the former confederate states signed the "Southern Manifesto" promising resistance to the federal government.

The crisis at Central High School in Little Rock, Arkansas, dramatized the political forces at work. Under court order to desegregate, Little Rock school officials were prepared to comply and, in an atmosphere of relative peace and stability, had carefully mobilized community support for the desegregation process. But Orville Faubus, the governor, decided to intervene. Caught in a tight re-election battle, he chose the strategy of "out-niggering" his opponents, using the black school children of Little Rock as his foil. After creating a crisis by announcing that it would not be possible to maintain order in the face of integration (a bald-faced lie), he instructed National Guard troops to block the entry of black children into Central High. Rallied by Faubus's words, angry whites now began to act out the scenario that Faubus had predicted. Eisenhower refused to intervene, instead agreeing to meet with Faubus in an effort to find a compromise. Faubus gave his word that he would create no further problems. Then, unashamedly breaking his promise, the governor withdrew National Guard troops from the high school and left the capital. When, on Monday morning September 23, 1957, black children attempted to attend their first day of school at Central High, a shrieking crowd surrounded them chanting "two, four, six, eight, we ain't going to integrate," and "niggers, keep away from our school. Go back to the jungle."

Stunned and embarrassed, Eisenhower denounced the "disgraceful occurrence," federalized the Arkansas National Guard, and dispatched a thousand paratroopers to Little Rock. To have done otherwise, he recognized, would have been to "acquiesce in anarchy and the dissolution of the union." Yet his action was too little and too late. The time for the use of moral authority to prevent resistance had passed. Indeed, when Eisenhower was finally moved to act, it was primarily because his own sense of the military code had been breached: a lieutenant (the governor) had been guilty of insubordination. The principle of integration was quite secondary.

Nor was it possible, in the long run, to call the Little Rock episode a victory for desegregation. Despite a Supreme Court order, Governor Faubus closed the schools in Little Rock for the entire next year. Virginia cities did the same to prevent integration in that state. Indeed, during the last three years of the Eisenhower administration the number of school districts engaged even in token desegregation fell to 49—a stark contrast to the total of 712 that had desegregated during the first three years after *Brown*. As one Civil Rights Commission official observed, during the last years of the 1950s, the rights of black Americans had become a "White House orphan." . . .

No people, however brave and resilient, could accept such subterfuge without frustration. All the victories that had been secured seemed hollow. National policy was ignored or contradicted by politicians given the responsibility for enforcing it. Court decisions were vitiated by legalistic manipulation. "Nothing could be worse," Justice Felix Frankfurter had said before the *Brown* decision, "than for this court to make an abstract declaration that segregation is bad and then have it evaded by tricks." Yet that is precisely what happened. Through callous disregard and distortion, black civil rights had been defined out of existence, with basic guarantees of citizenship made playthings for shrewd politicians. As much as any other group of American citizens, blacks believed in the political process, the sanctity of the judiciary, and the rule of law. Yet all of these had been turned against them. If they were victimized by the very processes they believed in, then it would be necessary for blacks to take action on their own terms and to express their convictions in ways that could no longer be ignored or misunderstood. Whatever else the history of the 1950s had shown, it was now obvious that, if America was to change its ways, blacks would have to start the process.

The Montgomery Movement

The decision to act sprung from the impatience and anger of average black Americans no longer willing to accept second-class citizenship. On a cold fall afternoon in Montgomery in 1955, Rosa Parks, a black seamstress, boarded a city bus after a long day at the sewing machine. She sat in the first row of the "colored" section of the bus, but Montgomery's Jim Crow rules provided that whenever enough white people boarded a public carrier to take up all the "white" seats, blacks must move back and give up their positions until the whites had places. As more and more whites boarded the bus that day, Mrs. Parks stared out the window. The atmosphere around her filled with tension. One black got up to give his seat, but she remained. Finally, the bus driver demanded that she move as well. No, she said, I will stay. "I felt it was just something I had to do," she later recalled. At that moment, Eldridge Cleaver subsequently noted, "somewhere in the universe a gear in the machinery shifted." Word of her arrest quickly spread through the community, and within hours, black leaders had decided that the time was right to strike a blow for freedom: they would boycott the city bus system the next Monday in protest.

The city's black leaders were ready. E. D. Nixon, president of the Alabama NAACP and head of the local chapter of the Brotherhood of Sleeping Car Porters, had long been looking for a cause around which to build a mass protest. Jo Ann Robinson, leader of the local Women's Political Council (parallel in purpose to the segregated League of Women Voters), was ready too. She had worked hard for the desegregation of drinking fountains and the hiring of black police in the city. Now, through their telephone network, she and her associates spread the word that the time had come to act; it was time to move the struggle to a new level.

The idea of a bus boycott was not unheard of. Earlier, when other arrests had happened under similar circumstances, there had been talk of similar action. But the occasion had not been right. In one instance, the arrest victim had been an unwed mother; in another, a person from a family one of whose members was in jail. Everyone knew that in order to carry out a mass action successfully, all the circumstances had to be right. Now, they were. Rosa Parks was one of the most revered women in Montgomery. A churchgoer, secretary of the NAACP, beloved by everyone, she was a person who would unify the community. As E. D. Nixon later recalled:

She was decent. And she was committed. First off, nobody could point no dirt at her. You had to respect her as a lady. And second, if she said she would be a certain place at a certain time, that's when she got there. . . . So when she stood up to talk, people'd shut up and listen. And when she did something people just figured it was the right thing to do.

Because she was who she was and did what she did, Rosa Parks became the rallying point for mobilizing the collective anger of Montgomery's black citizens.

That night and all the next day, E. D. Nixon set in motion the groundwork for protest. More than fifty community representatives gathered at the Dexter Avenue Baptist Church to plan the bus boycott, to rally church congregations on Sunday, and to create a transportation network among Negro taxi companies to take the place of the buses. By Monday, every black in Montgomery had received a message not to ride the city buses that day. Fearful that the boycott might not succeed, yet committed as never before to action, Montgomery's black leaders rose early to watch the buses go by. As dawn turned into morning and midday, the verdict was clear: virtually no black person in Montgomery rode the bus that day.

The bus boycott in Montgomery would last for 381 days. It provided the organizing basis for the mass movement that fought back against every legal, economic, and psychological effort to destroy it. When city leaders threatened to arrest taxi drivers for violating their chauffeur licenses, blacks created car pools instead. When whites attempted to sow seeds of dissension among leaders of the movement, the black community came together to affirm its solidarity in support of mass protest. And when white violence threatened to provoke black counterviolence and provide a basis for police action, the Negro community responded with discipline and devotion to the philosophy of nonviolence. No incident encapsulated the story of Montgomery more than the occasion when a white reporter, driving a car, stopped beside an elderly black woman walking to work. Asked if she wished a ride, the woman replied: "No, my feets is tired, but my soul is rested."

Like the first movement in a symphony, the Montgomery movement highlighted themes that would dominate the civil rights struggle for years to come. First, it demonstrated dramatically and conclusively that black Americans would sacrifice their comfort and risk their jobs to stand up for their dignity. For years, whites interested in appeasing their own conscience had insisted that "*our* black people are happy," and that any trouble of a racial nature must reflect the work of outside agitators. For 381 days, more than 90 percent of the black citizens of Montgomery demonstrated with their feet, everyday, their vivid rejections of the white illusion.

Second, the boycott exhibited how a movement, once begun, generates its own momentum, expanding the horizons of its participants and creating the basis for an ever-widening belief in, and ability to achieve, social change. Ironically, the boycott did not begin with the demand that the buses be integrated. Instead, community leaders advanced only a modest three-point agenda: (1) greater courtesy toward black passengers; (2) the hiring of Negro drivers for routes that were predominantly black; and (3) the creation of a flexible line, separating the black and white sections of the bus so that, where blacks comprised the majority of passengers, they would not be forced to move when additional whites boarded the bus. Yet Montgomery's white leadership consistently refused to respond to those demands, and as the daily sacrifice of energy generated a mass sense of self-confidence and determination, the movement decided that nothing short of complete integration would satisfy its demands. Over and over again, through the next fifteen years, the same experience of working together for a common cause would create a similar heightening of consciousness and the refusal to accept anything less than full equality.

Third, the boycott produced an articulate and persuasive leader. Martin Luther King, Jr., had been in Montgomery only six months when the boycott started. Still in his mid-twenties, he was neither a radical nor an activist. Reared in the relative prosperity of Atlanta's black middle class, King had been sheltered from many of the worst aspects of white racism. Bright, reflective, and academically successful, he seemed destined to achieve the success and comfort available to some black leaders—particularly ministers—within a Jim Crow society. There was little, on the surface at least, to suggest that he would become a protest leader. Indeed, he had turned down an invitation to become head of the local NAACP because he wished to build his congregation, to finish his doctorate, and to work his way slowly into the community.

But now a challenge came before him that he could not refuse. King's very newness made him the ideal leader to mediate between competing factions and to speak for the forces of change. As a student of existentialism, he understood how one moment of crisis could galvanize and direct an entire lifetime. Faced with that crisis, he rose mightily to the challenge, in the process forging for himself and his people a new message to America of the transforming power of Christian love. "There comes a time," King told more than 5,000 blacks on the first night of the boycott,

> when people get tired. We are here this evening to say to those who have mistreated us so long that we are tired—tired of being segregated and humiliated, tired of being kicked about by the brutal feet of oppression. . . . For many years we have shown amazing patience. . . . But we've come here tonight to be saved from that patience that makes us patient with anything less than freedom and justice. . . . If you will protest courageously and yet with dignity and Christian love, in the history books that are written in future generations, historians will have to pause and say "there lived a great people—a black people—who injected a new meaning and dignity into the veins of civilization." This is our challenge and our overwhelming responsibility.

As thousands listened, they found the meaning that would justify the sacrifices that were to come—that here in Montgomery and elsewhere throughout the South, black Americans, embodying the redemptive love of the Christian Savior, would set out to restore the wholeness of their society and redeem the sins of their oppressor.

Finally, the Montgomery bus boycott laid the foundation for the civil rights movement of the 1960s. Thousands of people had come together, and by the time the Supreme Court ruled that Montgomery's buses must integrate, they had demonstrated beyond a doubt the power of a collective body to shape a new world and a new self-confidence. On the very night the boycott ended, the white-robed Ku Klux Klan drove through black Montgomery in one more effort to splinter and intimidate. But no one ran away. Instead, blacks jeered and laughed at the invaders, highlighting their new strength and determination. Out of the bus boycott also would come the Southern Christian Leadership Conference (SCLC), headed by Dr. King, uniting black ministers throughout the South in a common determination to struggle for civil rights. The church would be the gathering place and central institution of the movement, its ministers primary spokesmen for the people.

Yet with all these accomplishments, the bus boycott itself was not enough. To a large extent, it remained a reactive strategy, depending on the right person being arrested, under the right circumstances, with the right leadership structure in place. The very genius of the boycott was also its major weakness. People could refuse to ride the bus without directly or individually placing themselves at risk. The boycott was a passive act; it was important—above all psychologically important—but not adequate to the struggle ahead. Ideal as a way of collective expression, it nevertheless was not a vehicle for individual assault against the racist status quo. It did not, for example, lend itself to the goal of seeking black admittance to previously all-white schools, hotels, lunch counters, theatres, churches, or government buildings. Boycotting a restaurant from which one was already excluded was not a viable option. For this, a new form of expression would be necessary—a form that would provide the vehicle for black Americans to topple the entire structure of Jim Crow racism.

The Sit-in Movement

On February 1, 1960, four young black freshmen at North Carolina A&T College in Greensboro set forth on a historic journey that would ignite a decade of civil rights protests. Walking into downtown Greensboro, they entered the local Woolworth's, purchased toothpaste and other small items, and then sat at the lunch counter and demanded equal service with white persons. "We do not serve Negroes," they were told. But instead of leaving, the students remained. The next day they returned, with twenty-three of their classmates. The day after that it was sixty-six. The next day, more than one hundred. By the end of the week a thousand students joined them in downtown Greensboro. The student phase of the civil rights revolution had begun.

The story of the Greensboro sit-in movement represents a microcosm of the frustration, anger, and determination that surged through black America in the years after the *Brown* decision. Three of the four young men who journeyed to Woolworth's that day had been raised in Greensboro, a city that prided itself on its progressivism, its enlightenment, its "good race relations." Thirteen or fourteen years old in 1954, these young people had come of age, intellectually and politically, in the years since the *Brown* decision. Their parents were activists, some of them belonged to the NAACP, others to churches in the forefront of efforts to build a better political and educational life for blacks. The young men attended Dudley High School, the pride of the black community, a place where teachers taught you to aspire to be the best that was in you. "We were always talking about the issues," Nell Coley, an English teacher recalled. "We might read [a poem or a novel] as a kind of pivot," but the words of a Langston Hughes or Thomas Hardy were always related to the inalienable rights of human beings to respect, freedom, and dignity. "I had to tell youngsters," Coley said, "that the way you find things need not happen . . . I don't care if they push and shove you, you must not accept [discrimination]. . . . You are who you are."

The message the young men heard at school was reinforced at home and in the church. Some went to Shiloh Baptist, whose minister had led civil rights protests at Shaw University in Raleigh, and who always provided support and encouragement to activists. Under his leadership, the local NAACP had almost doubled its membership in 1959, and it was to him that the students came for assistance with supplies and mimeographing materials after the demonstrations began. Two of the students had also belonged to the NAACP Youth Group started in 1943 after Ella Baker had visited town. At the weekly meetings, the youth chapter would discuss local and national protest activities. Students from Little Rock came to share their desegregation experience. The Montgomery bus boycott also provided a focus for discussion. "It was like a catalyst," one of the four original sit-in demonstrators recalled. "It started a whole lot of things rolling." When Martin Luther King, Jr., came to Greensboro to deliver his sermon about Christ's message for America, things began to fall into place. Dr. King's sermon was "so strong," one demonstrator recalled, "that I could feel my heart palpitating. It brought tears to my eyes."

The situation in Greensboro provided the classic example of sophisticated American racism. Although the school board had said it would desegregate schools after the *Brown* decision, its resolve dissipated when state political and economic leaders failed to offer support. Although black parents appeared at all but two school board meetings in the eighteen months after *Brown* to demand either better black facilities or substantive action on desegregation, the board did nothing. Then, in 1957, it admitted six blacks to previously all-white schools. But the action was taken, not to promote integration, but—as the school board leader later recalled—to "hold an umbrella" over the rest of the state and preserve segregation. As long as one or two school districts had token desegregation, it would be impossible for the NAACP to launch a class action suit against the entire state.

Thereafter, no matter how many black parents applied for transfer of their children to previously all-white schools, the board stood pat. Typical of its approach was its response to a 1959 court suit by black parents. Shrewdly, the NAACP had organized four parents to press for admission of their children to nearby schools rather than have them bused a mile or two away. Faced with the prospect of losing what the school board attorney called "as important a suit of litigation as has arisen in North Carolina in the whole history of the state," the board finally gave the appearance of admitting the four black applicants to the previously all-white school to which they had applied. Then, with school board initiative and encouragement, PTA leaders in that school contacted every white parent in the community to explain how they might transfer their children out of the theoretically integrated school into an all-white institution. Two months later, it officially moved every white child and every white faculty member out of the school, replacing all of them with blacks. It could then argue in court that the legal action of the black parents was "moot," because the students were in fact assigned to the schools they had initially applied to attend. One white observer called it "one of the cleverest legal maneuvers yet used in the desegregation field." More to the point was a black minister's comment: "These folks were primarily interested in evading, and they weren't even embarrassed."

Elsewhere in Greensboro, the same kind of duplicity prevailed. When blacks attempted to integrate the local golf course, they were arrested. Then mysteriously, the clubhouse burned down and the golf course was closed. Black college graduates from A&T and Bennett College were told by employers that they could apply for jobs as janitors and maids, but not as salesclerks or receptionists. In all of this, good manners and "civility" prevailed. (As one black leader said, "no one ever called me nigger here.") Greensboro's whites took pride in their paternalism, the way in which they looked out for "their" Negroes. Yet the underlying structure of racism remained. Greensboro, another black leader observed, was "a nice-nasty town."

As they discussed these conditions in their dormitory room at night, the four black students resolved to act. "We challenged each other, really," one of them later recalled. "We constantly heard about all the evils that are occurring and how blacks are mistreated and nobody was doing anything about it. . . . We used to question, 'Why is it that you have to sit in the balcony? Why do you have to ride in the back of the bus?'" Now, about to become voting-age citizens, with none of the rights of citizenship, they determined to do something. No longer were they willing to tolerate the perpetuation of the injustices that they saw all around them, particularly when the highest court in the land had condemned such practices as fundamentally unacceptable. "In 1959, 1960," one student remembered, "I don't know how many black babies had been born eighteen years ago, but I guess everybody was pretty well fed up at the same time." If whites had not been able to hear the peaceful protests and petitions offered by the older generation, perhaps they would listen to the voice of a new generation as it recorded its dissent by sitting silently at a lunch counter.

The four young men drew from each other the resolve to act. "The thing that precipitated the sit-ins," Franklin McCain declared, "was that little bit of incentive and that little bit of courage that each of us instilled in each other." On a Sunday night at the end of January, Ezell Blair, Jr., came home and asked his parents if they would be embarrassed if he got into trouble. "Why?" his parents wondered. "Because," he said, "tomorrow we're going to do something that will shake up this town." Nervous and fearful, afraid that someone might get "chicken," the four friends shored up each other's confidence until the next afternoon. "All of us were afraid," another demonstrator recalled. "But we went and did it." The result became history. "We had the confidence . . . of a Mack truck," Franklin McCain noted. "I felt better that day than I had ever felt in my life. I felt as though I had gained my manhood."

Within days it had become clear that a spontaneous action by a few had mobilized the entire community. When hundreds of students, including the A&T

football team, gathered downtown on Saturday, they were met by white gangs carrying Confederate flags. Carrying their own small American flags purchased in advance by student leaders, the football players provided a wedge so that sit-in demonstrators could reach the counters. "Who do you think you are," the whites asked. "We the union army," the football players responded. Nell Coley, the teacher who had done so much to inspire black students in Greensboro, excitedly looked on. "You are never going to see this kind of thing [again]," she said,

and I'm always happy that I [was there] because here were these black kids lined around this counter with books in their hands . . . and the white kids had confederate flags in their hands . . . and you could hardly get through [until] finally they had to close the store . . . and I was right there when the store was closed and when those black youngsters formed lines and yelled "we won."

In one town, at one moment, in a manner not planned by anyone, four people had decided to "express something that had been in their mind for a long time." In doing so, they helped the Greensboro "coffee party" take its place alongside the Boston Tea Party as an event symbolizing a new revolutionary era.

The Movement Spreads

By the time Greensboro's students had finished the first week of demonstrating, the new tactic they had discovered had already begun to transform student consciousness elsewhere. Within two months demonstrations had broken out in fifty-four cities in nine states. It was as if an entire generation was ready to act, waiting for a catalyst. Greensboro provided the spark, but young blacks throughout the South provided the tinder for the response that followed. Although representatives of CORE, the NAACP, and SCLC traveled from flash point to flash point, there was no conspiracy or collective planning involved. Instead, each group—hearing about the actions of its comrades elsewhere—drew on the example and decided to do something. Julian Bond in Atlanta, John Lewis in Nashville, Bernard Lee in Montgomery, Cleveland Sellers in Denmark, South Carolina—all heard the news and set out to join the crusade. "My identification with the demonstrating students was so thorough," Cleveland Sellers noted, "that I would flinch every time one of the whites taunted them . . . I had a burning desire to get involved." With an electricity and speed that no one could contain, the word spread that the time had come to act.

Ella Baker understood. Sitting in her office in Atlanta where she was executive secretary of SCLC, Baker sensed the new voice and new spirit of a younger generation. With $800 of SCLC money, she sent out a call for the student protestors to meet at her alma mater, Shaw University in Raleigh, North Carolina, on Easter weekend. There they came, from the sixty cities where sit-ins were going on, from fifty-eight southern communities in twelve states, and from colleges and universities in the North as well. In her opening remarks, Baker set forth an agenda as long as her experience in the South and as broad as her vision into the future. It was "more than a hamburger" they were after, Baker told the young people, more than a seat in a restaurant, more than a place in a pew. It was freedom—from economic squalor, from educational deprivation, from inhuman treatment. Martin Luther King addressed the crowd as well, affirming the importance of "revolt against the apathy and complacency of adults" and urging an army of volunteers "who will willingly go to jail." But it was James Lawson who galvanized the group. Recently expelled from Vanderbilt Theological Seminary because he had urged nonviolent resistance and civil disobedience, Lawson conveyed the spirit of democracy, of sacrifice, of love, and of faith that the students had experienced and helped to create. Giving voice to the credo of a generation, Lawson declared:

We affirm the philosophical . . . ideal of non-violence as a foundation of our purpose, the presupposition of our faith, and the manner of our action. . . . Love is the central motif of non-violence. . . . Such love goes to the extreme; it remains loving and forgiving even in the midst of hostility. It matches the capacity of evil to inflict suffering with an even more enduring capacity to absorb evil, all the while persisting in love.

With Baker as its shepherd and Lawson as its moral voice, the conference declared its independence and organized itself as the vanguard of the nonviolent civil rights struggle. While King, Ralph Abernathy, and Wyatt Tee Walker assumed that the students would form themselves as an arm of the SCLC, Baker supported the students' drive for self-determination and independence. In fact, the students were deeply suspicious of their elders, fearful that King and others might try to "capture" the movement, manipulate it for their own purposes, place it in service of someone else's cause. By contrast, they sought a minimum of structure, a maximum of group participation, and the social space to create their own program of action. With Robert Moses who would become one of their spiritual leaders, they believed they should "go where the spirit" moved them, confident that with initiative and faith on their side they could topple the walls of oppression and eliminate every vestige of segregation from the earth.

The spirit of the movement was best expressed in its music. Like a circle without a break, the spirituals of slavery-time joined the freedom songs of the movement to affirm the solidarity of black people. Chanting and clapping, marchers would confront the police with the song: "Ain't Gonna Let That Sheriff Turn Me Around." In jail at night the freedom songs provided warmth and solidarity between cold cells. And in the churches, when the people gathered to restore their spirit and revitalize their strength, it was the music that imparted courage. "We'll walk hand in hand . . . we're not afraid . . . black and white together . . . we shall overcome." As Charles Sherrod recalled one such meeting:

When the last speaker among the students, Bertha Gober, had finished, there was nothing left to say. Tears filled the eyes of hard, grown men who had seen with their own eyes merciless atrocities committed. . . . Bertha told of spending Thanksgiving in jail . . . and when we rose to sing "We Shall Overcome," nobody could imagine what kept the church on four corners . . . I threw my head back and closed my eyes as I sang with my whole body.

The spirit and faith of "We Shall Overcome" infused those who joined SNCC. The young people were not ideological, not captive to any programmatic dream. They believed in people. As Jane Stembridge said, "Finally it all boils down to human relationships . . . the question of whether we . . . whether *I* shall go on living in isolation or whether there shall be a we. . . . Love alone is radical. Political statements are not." Living on $10 a week subsistence pay, SNCC workers found their sustenance in the people with whom they worked—and the adults they stayed with who placed their own lives and property in jeopardy by offering their homes and their food to the young civil rights workers. SNCC workers were revolutionaries for whom the word revolution meant the creation of a beloved community where people would care for each other. And they were held together by a strength that transcended any single issue—a strength evoked in one civil rights worker's description of a friend taking part in the sit-ins:

The manager said something obscene, and grabbed her by the shoulder. "Get the hell out of here nigger." Lana was not going. I don't know whether she should have collapsed in a non-violent manner. She probably did not know. She put her hands under the counter and held. He was rough and strong. She just held and I looked down at her hands, . . . strained . . . every muscle holding. . . . All of a sudden he let go and left. I thought he knew he could not move that girl—ever.

That strength would be sorely tested in the years ahead. During the year after the Greensboro sit-ins, more than 3,600 demonstrators spent some time in jail. In Nashville, where students went to sit-in just two weeks after the Greensboro demonstrations, protestors were pelted with garbage, lighted cigarettes were ground out on their backs, and ketchup was poured over their heads. "The devil has got to come out of these people," James Bevel remarked. In Orangeburg, South Carolina, police knocked protestors off their feet with high-pressure fire hoses in subfreezing weather and then arrested 500 young people, jamming 350 of them into a chicken coop that had no shelter from the cold. Although several hundred lunch counters were desegregated as a consequence of these and other demonstrations, the price was heavy—and it could only increase as the movement traveled south to the hardcore racist areas of Georgia, Alabama, and Mississippi.

The first sign of things to come occurred during the Freedom Rides of May 1961. Determined to test the freedom of interstate bus facilities for people of both races, James Farmer of CORE and others set out from Washington on a Greyhound bus and a Trailways bus, both bound for New Orleans. The journey through Virginia and North Carolina proceeded peacefully enough, but in Rock Hill, South Carolina, twenty whites slugged and beat John Lewis, a young veteran of the Nashville sit-ins. Then came the Mother's Day Crisis in Anniston, Alabama. A mob surrounded the Greyhound bus, cut its tires, and threw a fire bomb into a window, driving the passengers out into the assembled throng where they were beaten. An hour later, the Trailways bus—following the Greyhound— arrived. Immediately, these Freedom Riders too were assaulted, as many as six or ten men beating on a single demonstrator, pummeling them with fists and pipes.

As the Southern Regional Council later observed, all the while, "police were either inactive, not present, or strangely late in arrival," even though they knew well in advance when the bus would arrive.

The Anniston beatings were sufficiently brutal to persuade most of the Freedom Riders to complete the trip to New Orleans by air. But when SNCC students in Nashville heard the news, they insisted that the rides must continue. Only in that way could the purpose of nonviolence be tested, the goal achieved. Diane Nash, Ruby Doris Smith, John Lewis—people whose names would become legendary in the movement because of all the years of struggle they would endure—journeyed to Birmingham to continue the ride for freedom. "Bull" Connor met them and transported them back to the Tennessee border—back 120 miles—and let them out. But they returned again, intent on reaching Montgomery, then Jackson, then New Orleans. When they arrived in Montgomery, the same scenario occurred, with a totally uncontrolled mob pummeling the demonstrators, even inflicting a concussion on John Siegenthaler, an assistant attorney general from the Justice Department. Still they would not stop their journey. Gathering that night at Ralph Abernathy's church, 1,200 blacks shouted "Freedom!" and refused to be intimidated when the sanctuary was surrounded by a white mob.

The next day they rode to Jackson, knowing that here—if nowhere else—rested the "heart of darkness" in the Southern white soul. After all, Governor Ross Barnett had declared that "the Negro is different because God made him different to punish him." It was not surprising, then, that as soon as the demonstrators stepped from the buses they were immediately arrested. By August, 300 more had joined them in jail, all committed to staying there without accepting bail. At the infamous Parchman Prison the demonstrators were stripped of all personal goods and belongings and prohibited from singing or speaking in more than a whisper. When the prisoners persisted—because that was what affirmed the meaning of their suffering—their mattresses were taken away, then their sheets, then their toothbrushes, then their towels, and they slept on steel.

Mississippi was like that. Blacks earned one-third the family income of whites, feudal-style landlords kept them in poverty, and the provision of even a tar-paper shack to live in was used as an instrument for keeping "their Negroes" under control. If anyone dared to protest, food, lodging, even life, would be snuffed out. In Amite County, Herbert Lee, a black farmer who was willing to work for voter registration, had driven into town in his truck, followed by a white farmer named E. H. Hurst who lived nearby. Hurst approached Lee and started to argue with him, pulling a gun. After Lee refused to talk to the white man unless he put the gun away, Hurst slipped it inside his coat. When Lee got out of the truck, Hurst pulled the gun and shot him in the head. As Bob Moses recalled,

Lee's body lay on the ground that morning for two hours, uncovered, until they finally got a funeral home in McComb to take it in. No one in Liberty would touch it. They had a coroner's jury that very same afternoon. Hurst was acquitted. He never spent a moment in jail. . . . I remember reading very bitterly in the papers the next morning, a little item on the front page of the McComb Enterprise Journal [that] said that a Negro had been shot as he was trying to attack

E. H. Hurst. And that was it. Might have thought he was a bum. There was no mention that Lee was a farmer, that he had a family, nine kids, beautiful kids, and he had farmed all his life in Amite County.

Nor was it over. Three years later Lewis Allen, a black man who had told a grand jury what had actually transpired that summer day, was shot dead in his front yard, felled by three shotgun blasts.

But SNCC and the people it served would not be stopped. If they were beaten in a town like McComb, they would go back the next day in greater strength, hold a mass meeting, show that they were not intimidated. Robert Moses charged a white man who had beaten him with assault and battery—the first time such a charge had ever been brought, and even though the white man was acquitted, it was clear that there was a new determination in the air. Living in the homes of the people they worked with, going to church with them, talking to their children about the history of freedom and the struggle to achieve it, SNCC staff people shaped, and were shaped by, the movement they were building. When a black high school principal in McComb insisted that the students promise not to demonstrate, they stayed home, and when he insisted that they return or be expelled, 103 young people went to the school, deposited their books, and walked out. A revolution was happening, forged through the combined courage of the young civil rights workers and the people whose lives they touched. As Bob Moses wrote,

You combat your own fears about beatings, shootings, and possible mob violence; you stymie by your mere physical presence the anxious fear of the Negro community . . . you create a small striking force capable of moving out when the time comes. . . . After more than six hundred lined up to receive food in Greenwood on Wednesday, 20 February, and Sam's subsequent arrest and weekend in prison on Thursday, 21 February, over one hundred people overflowed City Hall to protest at his trial, over two hundred and fifty gathered at a mass meeting that same night, and on Tuesday by 10:30 A.M. I had counted over fifty people standing in silent line in the County Court House; they say over two hundred had stood in line that day. This is a new dimension. . . . Negroes have never stood en masse in protest at the seat of power in the iceberg of Mississippi politics.

No words could describe fully the experience shared by those who put their lives on the line in Mississippi, Alabama, Georgia, and elsewhere. But the historian Howard Zinn has given us some sense of those moments in his description of his own participation in the movement. One night in Hattiesburg, Mississippi, Zinn and his fellow civil rights workers arrived in the middle of the night at a black family's house where they were to stay prior to a massive Freedom Day demonstration the next morning. Dragging a mattress into the living room, the man and his wife made their guests comfortable, and then went back to bed. Zinn woke at dawn, hearing a sound.

At first I had thought it part of a dream, but I heard it now still, a woman's voice, pure and poignant. She was chanting softly. At first I thought it came from

outside, then I realized . . . and it was his wife, praying, intoning . . . "oh, Lord, Jesus, oh, let things go well today, Jesus . . . oh, make them see, Jesus . . . show your love today, Jesus . . . oh, it's been a long, long time, oh, Jesus . . . oh, Lord, oh, Jesus."

As the lights came on, one of the civil rights workers declared: "Wake up fellows, it's Freedom Day," and Zinn, through an open doorway, could see that there was no mattress on the bed of the black couple, because they had given it to the civil rights workers.

By 1963, there were thousands of such stories of suffering, sacrifice, courage, and triumph. The nation had begun to listen. Each day, papers like the *New York Times* printed three or four pages of stories from the South, documenting the war for America's soul that was taking place there. Each night, on the network news, at least five minutes would be devoted to the latest outrages, the newest demonstrations, the most recent manifestations of nonviolent protest. As civil rights became part of the daily agenda of life for all Americans, and as more and more white students joined their black brethren in the Southern struggle, civil rights and racial equality became a focal point for the entire nation. More than any other issue, it focused on the heart of the contradiction in the American creed—equality of opportunity versus slavery and caste oppression. More than any other issue, also, it provided the ethical focus that would galvanize the discontent and contradictions of America's postwar history. Something massive and new had entered the American experience. And it came, not from above, not from the nation's political leadership, but from below, from the people themselves, who had been victims and who now said, "No more."

Conclusion

Although many Americans believe that the demonstrations of the 1960s represented a radical break with the past, in fact there existed remarkable continuity within the black protest movement between 1945 and 1960. The veterans who came back from World War II to demand their citizenship rights helped to provide the inspiration for those who carried forward the struggle during the 1950s, who refused to ride the buses in Montgomery, and who helped to make the sit-in movement possible in 1960. Events like World War II and the *Brown* decision were clearly important. They created new contexts, new possibilities. But the thread that linked these moments to each other was the willingness of blacks to seek change, to struggle for freedom, to act for justice.

In 1943, Ella Baker had sparked the NAACP Youth Group in Greensboro that would give birth to the sit-in movement. Seventeen years later, Ella Baker convened the conference of student demonstrators in Raleigh that more than anything else helped to give rise to the Student Non-Violent Coordinating Committee—perhaps the most important civil rights organization of the 1960s. It was E. D. Nixon who started the NAACP in Montgomery during the 1940s, and it was E. D. Nixon who organized the bus boycott of the 1950s. Medgar Evers had first challenged the tyranny of Mississippi's white racism when he went to cast his vote as a returning veteran in 1946; it was also Medgar Evers who led the struggle for voting rights and racial justice in Mississippi until his assassination in 1963. Such continuity was not incidental. It was inherent in the protest struggle.

The movement also grew out of, and depended on, the strength of black institutions. The foundation of E. D. Nixon's activism was the all-black Brotherhood of Sleeping Car Porters. The NAACP meeting that inspired J. A. DeLaine to attack segregation in Clarendon County, South Carolina, took place at Allen University, a black college. Ella Baker went to Shaw, an all-black school founded during Reconstruction, and it was at Shaw that the first meeting of SNCC took place. Black high schoolers generated the pride and aspirations that motivated the original sit-in demonstrators in Greensboro; and black colleges provided the primary base of recruitment for the movement. Ironically, many of these all-black institutions, which did so much to make possible the fight against segregation, would themselves suffer as a consequence. Yet their centrality testifies to the absolute necessity in the struggle for social change of retaining a strong home base, even as one seeks integration in the wider society.

Throughout these years, it would be difficult to overstate the failure of white political and economic leaders. With only a few exceptions, whites in positions of power refused to support the cause of civil rights unless it was directly in their self-interest to do so. Even then, the response was more often verbal than substantive. For the most part, Southern white politicians refused even to recognize the existence of blacks, or to acknowledge the extent to which the black experience created a totally different perspective on American society and politics than the white experience. All too often, the best that could be anticipated from white leaders, either in the North or the South, was paternalism. Yet from a black perspective, such an approach simply compounded the age-old problem. The time for accommodation to gestures and symbols from all-powerful white people had passed. The moment for freedom had come.

Precisely because whites refused to act on the black agenda, it became necessary for black Americans to seize the initiative, take control of their own lives, and create new vehicles for protest. As the events of the 1950s and early 1960s proved, simply to demand one's rights was not enough. The courts proved inadequate, and most politicians gave little more than lip service to racial justice. The law itself—even when clearly and simply stated—proved as much an invitation to subtle circumvention as an instrument of securing change. It seemed that only by taking new initiatives, striking at the white man's pocketbook, creating discomfort in his life, would any change occur.

In this sense, the direct-action protests manifested in the sit-in movement provided an effective new vehicle through which traditional patterns of white domination could be attacked. Direct-action protests were both a consequence and a cause of black activism. The sit-ins grew out of a tradition of protest; but they also helped to reinforce and extend that tradition, and to change the forms through which old as well as young would now express their demands for dignity and equality. Building on the lessons of the older generation, the young were forging a new method for carrying on the struggle. Thus, the student movement represented a new stage of black insurgency, reflecting the lessons as well as the frustrations of past experiences with protest. If the courts and politicians would not listen to traditional forms of expression, then new ones would have to be found. The sit-ins had created a new language, one which would have to be heard, one which could not be ignored. After 1960, the forms of communication between white and black would never again be the same. The question was whether white America would respond to the message, and how.

Jane Sherron De Hart

The New Feminism and the Dynamics of Social Change

Fifty years after gaining the right to vote, women who had been suffragists and women young enough to be their great-granddaughters embarked on a new feminist movement. Referred to as feminism's second wave to distinguish it from an earlier surge occurring around 1910, this new movement was vigorous, diffuse, and highly controversial. It was, in fact, many movements. Some were predominantly white and acquired the labels liberal, radical, socialist, and cultural feminism. Others consisted largely of women of color who identified themselves variously as Black, Chicana, Asian American, Native American, or U.S. Third World Feminists. One cannot make simplistic assumptions about which variant an individual woman might embrace. (For example, Pauli Murray, an African American lawyer and writer, would have been more likely to describe herself as a liberal feminist rather than a Black feminist.) Nor can one assume that only women embraced this new feminism or that all women did so. "As an *ism* (an ideology), feminism presupposed a set of principles not necessarily belonging to every woman—nor limited to women," wrote historian Nancy Cott of first wave feminism. Her observation also applies to second wave feminism. Some men, but not all women, embraced those principles and joined this renewed struggle to dismantle gender hierarchy. For those who did so, the goal became not mere formal equality, but genuine liberation. Their objective: to change not only laws and institutions, but values, patterns of behavior, personal relationships, and ultimately themselves.

The feminism explored in this essay is sometimes referred to as mainstream feminism. Emerging out of liberal and radical feminism, it has been a predominantly white phenomenon. In order to understand its origins and agendas, its opponents, and most important, its potential for changing society, it is necessary to

From Jane Sherron De Hart, "The New Feminism and the Dynamics of Social Change," in Linda K. Kerber and Jane Sherron De Hart (eds.), *Women's America: Refocusing the Past*, 4/e. Copyright © 1995. Reprinted by permission of Jane Sherron De Hart.

examine the long-term economic and social changes that created an environment within which this strand of the movement could emerge. It is important also to appreciate the ferment of the 1960s, much of it initiated by African Americans, that provided white mainstream feminism with its ideological core, vitality, and impetus. To explore such origins is also to explore the extent to which these feminists confronted issues that their ideological foremothers had left unresolved. . . .

The Creation of a Feminist Consciousness

Revolutions are seldom started by the powerless. The revolution of mainstream feminists was no exception. It was begun largely by educated, middle-class women whose diverse experiences had sharpened their sensitivity to the fundamental inequality between the sexes at a time when America had been thrust into the throes of self-examination by a movement for racial equality. Some were young veterans of the civil rights movement and the New Left, steeped in a commitment to equality and the techniques of protest. Others were young professionals increasingly aware of their secondary status. Still others were older women who in their long careers as professionals or as activists had used organizations such as the American Civil Liberties Union (ACLU), the Young Women's Christian Association (YWCA) and the United Auto Workers (UAW) to fight sex-based discrimination. Included, too, were those whose outwardly conformist lives belied an intense awareness of the malaise of domesticity and the untenably narrow boundaries of their prescribed roles. To explore how they came self-consciously to appraise women's condition as one demanding collective action is to explore the process of radicalization that helped to create a new feminist movement.

In its early state, a major component of that movement consisted of two different groups—women's rights advocates and women's liberationists. Although the differences between the two groups began to blur as the movement matured, initial distinctions were sharp. Women's rights advocates were likely to have been older, to have had professional training or work experience, to have been more inclined to form or join organized feminist groups. Reform oriented, these organizations used traditional pressure group tactics to achieve changes in laws and public policy that would guarantee women equal rights. Emphasis on "rights" meant extending to women in life outside the home the same "rights" men had, granting them the same options, privileges, and responsibilities that men enjoyed. There was little suggestion initially of personal or cultural transformation.

Women's liberationists were younger women, less highly educated, whose ideology and political style, shaped in the dissent and violence of the 1960s, led them to look at women's predicament differently. Instead of relying upon traditional organizational structure and lobbying techniques, they developed a new style of politics. Instead of limiting their goals to changes in public policy, they embraced a transformation in private, domestic life as well. They sought liberation from ways of thinking and behaving that they believed stunted or distorted women's growth and kept them subordinate to men. Through the extension of their own personal liberation they hoped to remake the male world, changing it as they had changed themselves. For women's liberationists as for women's rights advocates, however, the first step toward becoming feminists demanded a clear statement of women's position in society, one that called attention to the gap between the egalitarian ideal and the actual position of women in American culture. There also had to be a call to action from women themselves, *for* women, *with* women, *through* women. Redefining themselves, they had to make being a woman a political fact; and, as they did so, they had to live with the radical implications of what could only be called a rebirth.

The Making of Liberal Feminists: Women's Rights Advocates

For some women, the process of radicalization began with the appointment of a Presidential Commission on the Status of Women in 1961. Presidents, Democrat and Republican, customarily discharged their political debt to female members of the electorate, especially to those who had loyally served the party, by appointing a few token women, usually party stalwarts, to highly visible posts. John Kennedy was no exception. He was, however, convinced by Esther Peterson, the highest-ranking woman in his administration, that the vast majority of women would be better served if he also appointed a commission charged with investigating obstacles to the full participation of women in society. Peterson, who was assistant secretary of labor and head of the Women's Bureau, believed that the report of such a commission could sensitize the public to barriers to equality just as her own experience as a labor organizer had sensitized her to the particular problems confronting women workers. Citizens thus informed could then be mobilized on behalf of governmental efforts at reform. Accordingly, the commission was appointed with Eleanor Roosevelt serving as chair until her death a year later. Its report, *American Women* (1963), was conservative in tone, acknowledging the importance of women's traditional roles within the home and the progress they had made in a "free democratic society." Acknowledging also that women were an underutilized resource that the nation could ill afford to ignore, the report provided extensive documentation of discriminatory practices in government, education, and employment, along with substantial recommendations for change. Governors, replicating Kennedy's move, appointed state commissions on the status of women. In these commissions hundreds of men and women encountered further evidence of the economic, social, and legal disabilities that encumbered the nation's "second sex." For some, the statistics were old news; for others, they were a revelation.

Although there were variations from state to state, the pattern documented by the North Carolina Commission soon became increasingly familiar to a small but growing number of women throughout the nation. According to that commission's report, women workers, who made up over one-third of the state's labor force, suffered economically from job segregation and pay inequities. Of the 600,000 women employed outside the home in 1960, most (68 percent) were concentrated in blue-collar jobs or in traditionally low-paying "female" professions such as teaching and nursing. Whatever their occupational level, women earned significantly less than their male counterparts with comparable skills, experience, and responsibilities. They also had fewer opportunities for advancement.

(Female mill operatives, for example, earned nearly 30 percent less than male operatives.)

Educational experience, seemingly more equitable, actually foreshadowed economic inequities. At the graduate level, women constituted only a tiny fraction of those enrolled in schools training future members of high-paying professions such as medicine. At the undergraduate level, female students clustered in the humanities, avoiding the math and science courses necessary for providing greater career choice. Whatever their educational level, most women lacked access to diversified vocational training, enlightened career guidance, and the kind of role models provided by women, especially minority women, holding important nontraditional jobs. Worse still, they lacked expert, readily available child care. (Licensed day care facilities had only one space available for every seventeen preschool children of working mothers.)

Legally, women in North Carolina, as elsewhere, were handicapped not only by hundreds of discriminatory federal statutes but also by state laws denying them equal treatment under the law. For example, married women still lacked complete control over their own property; state law required the written assent of the husband before a wife could convey her real property to someone else. Nor did women function as political equals. In North Carolina, as in other states, women were less likely to vote than men and far less likely to hold elective office or significant policy-making jobs. Especially disturbing to the commission was the failure of most women to understand "the direct connection between their own active and informed participation in politics . . . and the solution to many of their most pressing problems."

Some women, however, could make that connection. Aroused by growing evidence of "the enormity of our problem," members of state commissions gathered in Washington in 1966 for the Third National Conference of the Commissions on the Status of Women. Individuals who were coming to know and rely on one another as they pooled their growing knowledge of widespread inequities, they were a network in the making. They were also women who wanted something done. This time they encountered a situation that transformed at least some of those present into activists in a new movement for women's equality. The catalyst proved to be a struggle involving Representative Martha Griffiths and the Equal Employment Opportunity Commission (EEOC), the federal agency in charge of implementing the Civil Rights Act of 1964.

Despite the fact that the law proscribed discrimination on the basis of sex as well as race, the commission refused to take seriously the problem of sexual discrimination. The first executive director of EEOC, believing that "sex" had been injected into the bill by opponents seeking to block its passage, regarded the sex provision as a "fluke" best ignored. Representative Griffiths from Michigan thought otherwise. While the bill was still in Congress she encouraged a small group of women in the House to become part of an unlikely alliance with legislative opponents of a federal civil rights act in order to keep the sex provision in the bill. Liberals objected, fearing that so encumbering a bill would prevent passage of much-needed legislation on behalf of racial equality. But despite such objections—and the ridicule of many of her male colleagues—Griffiths persisted. She urged her fellow representatives not to give black women and men advantages which white women were denied. A racist appeal, it revealed the exclusivity of Griffiths's vision of sisterhood. Her commitment to the sex provision, however, was unqualified. Once the bill passed she was determined to see the new law enforced in its entirety. When EEOC failed to do so, she lambasted the agency for its inaction in a biting speech delivered on the House floor only days before the Conference of the Commissions on the Status of Women met.

Griffiths's concern was shared by a group of women working within EEOC. Echoing an argument made the year before by a black trade unionist in the Women's Bureau, they insisted that the agency could be made to take gender-related discrimination more seriously if women had a civil rights organization as adept at applying pressure on their behalf as was the National Association for the Advancement of Colored People (NAACP) on behalf of blacks. Initially the idea was rejected. Conference participants most upset by EEOC's inaction decided instead to propose a resolution urging the agency to treat sexual discrimination with the same seriousness it applied to racial discrimination. When the resolution was ruled inappropriate by conference leaders, they were forced to reconsider. After a whispered conversation over lunch they concluded the time for discussion of the status of women was over. It was time for action. Before the day was out twenty-eight women had paid five dollars each to join the National Organization for Women (NOW), including author Betty Friedan, who happened to be in Washington at the time of the conference.

Friedan's presence in Washington was auspicious; her involvement in NOW, virtually inevitable. The author of a brilliant polemic published in 1963, she not only labeled the resurgent domestic ideology of recent decades but exposed the groups perpetuating it. Editors of women's magazines, advertising experts, Freudian psychologists, social scientists, and educators—all, according to Friedan, contributed to a romanticization of domesticity she termed "the feminine mystique." The result, she charged, was the infantilization of intelligent women and the transformation of the suburban home into a "comfortable concentration camp." Harsh words, they rang true to those who found the creativity of homemaking and the joys of motherhood vastly exaggerated. Sales of the book ultimately zoomed past the million mark.

By articulating heretofore inarticulated grievances, *The Feminine Mystique* had advanced a process initiated by more dispassionate investigations of women's status and the discriminatory practices which made that status inferior. That process was the collective expression of discontent. It is not surprising that the voices initially heard were those of women who were overwhelmingly white, educated, and middle or upper middle class. College women who regarded themselves the equals of male classmates by virtue of intellect and training were, as Jo Freeman points out, more likely to develop expectations they saw realized by their male peers but not, in most cases, by themselves. The frustrations were even greater for women with professional training. The very fact that many had sought advanced training in fields not traditionally "female" meant that they were less likely to find in traditional gender roles the identity and self-esteem such roles provided other women. Moreover, when measuring themselves against fellow professionals who happened to be men, the greater rewards enjoyed by their white male counterparts seemed especially galling. Privileged though they were, such women *felt* more deprived in many cases than did those women who were in reality less privileged. By 1966 this sense of deprivation had been sufficiently articulated and shared and the networks of like-minded women sufficiently developed so that collective discontent could be translated into collective action. The formation of NOW signaled a feminist resurgence.

The three hundred men and women who gathered in October for the organizational meeting of NOW included mainly professionals, some of them veterans of commissions on the status of women as well as a few feminist union activists, notably Dorothy Haener. Adopting bylaws and a statement of purpose, they elected officers, naming Friedan president. Her conviction that intelligent women needed purposeful, generative work of their own was reflected in NOW's statement of purpose, which attacked "the traditional assumption that a woman has to choose between marriage and motherhood on the one hand and serious participation in industry or the professions on the other." Determined that women should be allowed to develop their full potential as human beings, the organization's goal was to bring them into "full participation in the mainstream of American society NOW, exercising all the privileges and responsibilities thereof in truly equal partnership with men." To that end NOW developed a Bill of Rights, adopted at its 1967 meeting, that exhorted Congress to pass an equal rights amendment to the Constitution, called on EEOC to enforce antidiscrimination legislation, and urged federal and state legislators to guarantee equal and unsegregated education. To ensure women control over their reproductive lives, these new feminists called for removal of penal codes denying women contraceptive information and devices as well as safe, legal abortions. To ease the double burden of working mothers, they urged legislation that would ensure maternity leaves without jeopardizing job security or seniority, permit tax deductions for child care expenses, and create public, inexpensive day care centers. To improve the lot of poor women, they urged reform of the welfare system and equality with respect to benefits, including job-training programs.

Not content simply to call for change, NOW leaders, following the lead of equality advocates within the labor movement, worked to make it happen. Using persuasion, pressure, and even litigation, they, with other newly formed women's rights groups such as the Women's Equity Action League (WEAL), launched a massive attack on sex discrimination. By the end of the 1960s NOW members had filed legal suits against newspapers listing jobs under the headings "Help Wanted: Male" and "Help Wanted: Female," successfully arguing that such headings discouraged women from applying for jobs they were perfectly capable of doing. Building on efforts begun in the Kennedy administration such as the passage of the Equal Pay Act, they pressured the federal government to intensify its commitment to equal opportunity. They urged congressmen and labor leaders to persuade the Department of Labor to include women in its guidelines designed to encourage the hiring and promotion of blacks in firms holding contracts with the federal government. They persuaded the Federal Communications Commission to open up new opportunities for women in broadcasting. Tackling the campus as well as the marketplace, WEAL filed suit against more than three hundred colleges and universities, ultimately securing millions of dollars in salary raises for women faculty members who had been victims of discrimination. To ensure that women receive the same pay men received for doing the same work, these new feminists lobbied for passage of a new Equal Employment Opportunity Act that would enable EEOC to fight discrimination more effectively.

NOW also scrutinized the discriminatory practices of financial institutions, persuading them to issue credit to single women and to married women in their own—not their husband's—name. WEAL, in turn, filed charges against banks and other lending institutions that refused to grant mortgages to single women, or in the case of married couples, refused to take into account the wife's earnings in evaluating the couple's eligibility for a mortgage. Colleges and universities that discriminated against female students in their sports programs came under fire, as did fellowship programs that failed to give adequate consideration to female applicants.

While NOW and WEAL attacked barriers in industry and education, the National Women's Political Caucus (NWPC) focused on government and politics. Formed in 1971, the caucus was initiated by Friedan, New York congresswomen Bella Abzug and Shirley Chisholm—both outspoken champions of women's rights—and Gloria Steinem, soon to become founding editor of the new mass-circulation feminist magazine *Ms.* Abzug, a lawyer and veteran activist for peace and civil rights, and Chisholm, the first black woman elected to Congress, were especially concerned about the small numbers of women in government. Accordingly the caucus concentrated on getting women elected and appointed to public office while also rallying support for issues such as the Equal Rights Amendment. Meanwhile women in the professions, aware of their small numbers and inferior status, began to organize as well. Physicians, lawyers, and university professors fought for equal opportunity in the meetings of such overwhelmingly male groups as the American Medical Association, the American Association of University Professors, and the American Historical Association. Union women also mobilized. In 1974, three thousand women from fifty-eight unions attended the founding convention of the Coalition of Labor Union Women (CLUW), resolving to fight for equality in the workplace and within organized labor.

Collectively such protests served notice that more women were becoming radicalized. The particular combination of events that transformed these women into feminists varied with the individual. A southern legislator, describing the process that brought home the reality of her own second-class citizenship, wrote:

As a State Senator, I succeeded in getting Mississippi women the right to sit on juries (1968); the opposition's arguments were appalling. When women began hiring me in order to get credit, I became upset at the discrimination I saw. After I was divorced in 1970, I was initially denied a home loan. The effect was one of the worst traumas I've suffered. Denial of a home loan to one who was both a professional and a member of the legislature brought things to a head.

Although the number of women who understood what it meant to be the "second sex" were still only a tiny minority, they were nonetheless a minority whose energy, talents, and experience enabled them to work for changes necessary to ensure equal rights.

The Making of Radical Feminists: Women's Liberationists

The process of radicalization that transformed some individuals into liberal feminists occurred simultaneously—but in different fashion and with somewhat different results—among a younger generation of women who were also predominantly white and middle class. Many of them veterans of either the civil rights movement or of the New Left, these were the activists who would initially become identified as women's liberationists. Differing in perspective as well as style, they would ultimately push many of their older counterparts beyond the demand for equal rights to recognition that true emancipation would require a far-reaching transformation of society and culture.

The experiences awakening in this 1960s generation a feminist consciousness have been superbly described by Sara Evans in her book, *Personal Politics*. "Freedom, equality, love and hope," the possibility of new human relationships, the importance of participatory democracy—letting the people decide—were, as Evans points out, part of an egalitarian ideology shared by both the southern-based Student Nonviolent Coordinating Committee (SNCC) in its struggle for racial equality and the Students for Democratic Society (SDS) in its efforts to mobilize an interracial organization of the urban poor in northern ghettos. Membership in both organizations—"the movement"—thus reinforced commitment to these ideals among the women who joined. In order to translate ideals into reality, however, young, college-age women who had left the shelter of middle-class families for the hard and dangerous work of transforming society found themselves doing things that they would never have thought possible. Amidst the racial strife of the South, they joined picket lines, created freedom schools, and canvassed for voter registration among blacks, often enduring arrest and jailing. SDS women from affluent suburbs entered decaying tenements and were surrounded by the grim realities of the ghetto. They trudged door-to-door in an effort to reach women whose struggle to survive made many understandably suspicious of intruding strangers. In the process, not only did these young activists achieve a heightened sense of self-worth and autonomy, they also learned the skills of movement building and the nuts and bolts of organizing.

Particularly important was the problem of getting people, long passive, to act on their own behalf. SDS women began by encouraging ghetto women to come together to talk about their problems. This sharing of experiences, they believed, would lead these women to recognize not only that their problems were common but that solutions required changes in the system. In the process of organizing, the organizers also learned. They began to understand the meaning of oppression and the valor required of those who fought it. They found new role models, Evans suggests, in extraordinary southern black women whose courage seemed never to waiver in the face of violence and in those welfare mothers of the North who confronted welfare bureaucrat and slum lord after years of passivity.

But if being in the movement brought a new understanding of equality, it also brought new problems. Men who were committed to equality for one group were not necessarily committed to equality for another group. Women in SNCC, as in SDS, found themselves frequently relegated to domestic chores and treated as sex objects, denied most leadership positions, and refused a key voice in the formulation of policy. Moreover, the sexual freedom that had been theirs as part of the cultural revolution taking place in the 1960s soon began to feel more like sexual exploitation as they saw their role in the movement spelled out in the draft resister's slogan: "Girls Say Yes to Guys Who Say No." Efforts to change the situation were firmly rebuffed. When SNCC leader Stokely Carmichael joked that the only "position for women in SNCC is prone," he encapsulated views which, while not his own, reflected all too accurately the feelings of males in the New Left as well as many in SNCC.

By 1967 the tensions had become so intense that white women left the movement to organize on behalf of their own "liberation." Black women stayed, resolving to work for change from within and give voice to their own priorities.

The women who left did not leave empty-handed. As radicals, they were impatient with liberalism, critical of capitalism, and profoundly suspicious of authority. Accustomed to challenging prevailing ideas and practices, they had acquired a language of protest, an organizing tactic, and a deep-seated conviction that the personal was political. How that legacy would shape this burgeoning new feminist movement became evident as small women's liberation groups began springing up spontaneously in major cities and university communities across the nation.

Structure, Leadership, and Consciousness-Raising

Initially, at least, the two branches of mainstream feminism seemed almost to be two different movements, so unlike were they in structure and style. Linked only by newsletters, notices in underground newspapers, and networks of friends, women's liberation groups rejected both traditional organizational structure and leadership. Unlike NOW and the other women's rights groups associated with liberal feminism, they had no central headquarters, no elected officers, no by-laws. There was no legislative agenda and little of the activism that transformed the more politically astute women's rights leaders into skilled lobbyists and tacticians. Instead this younger generation of feminists, organizing new groups wherever they found themselves, concentrated on a kind of personal politics rooted in movement days. Looking back on male-dominated meetings in which, however informal the gathering, a few highly verbal, aggressive men invariably controlled debate and dictated strategy and left less articulate and assertive women effectively excluded, they recalled the technique they had used in organizing the poor. They remembered how they had encouraged those women to talk among themselves until the personal became political, that is, until problems which, at first glance, seemed to be personal were finally understood to be social in cause—rooted in society rather than in the individual—and political in solution. Applying this same process in their own informal "rap groups," women's liberationists developed the technique of "consciousness-raising." Adopted by women's rights groups such as local chapters of NOW, consciousness-raising sessions became one of the most important innovations of mainstream feminism.

The immediate task of the consciousness-raising session was to bring together in a caring, supportive, noncompetitive setting women accustomed to relating most intimately not with other women but with men—husbands, lovers, "friends." As these women talked among themselves, exchanging confidences, reassessing old options, and mentally exploring new ones, a sense of shared problems began to emerge. The women themselves gradually gained greater understanding of how profoundly their lives had been shaped by the constraints of culture. Personal experience with those constraints merged with intellectual awareness of women's inferior status and the factors that made it so. By the same token, new understanding of problems generated new determination to resolve them. Anger, aggression, and frustration formerly turned inward in unconscious self-hatred began to be directed outward, becoming transformed into new energy directed toward constructive goals. If society and culture had defined who women were through their unconscious internalization of tradition, they could reverse the process, and, by redefining themselves, redefine society and culture. Or, to put it another way, if woman was a *social construct*—the product not so much of biology, but of what people in a particular society and culture believed to be the implications of biology—then women themselves would re-create the construct. At work was a process of discovery so radicalizing that the individuals undergoing it ultimately emerged in a very real sense as different people. Now feminists, these were women with a different understanding of reality—a new "consciousness," a new sense of "sisterhood," and a new commitment to change.

Consciousness-raising was an invigorating and sometimes frightening experience. As one young woman wrote, "This whole movement is the most exhilarating thing of my life. The last eight months have been a personal revolution. Nonetheless, I recognize there is dynamite in this and I'm scared shitless." "Scared" or not, such women could no longer be contained. Veterans of one rap group fanned out, creating others, often with arresting names such as Cell 16, the Furies, Redstockings, or simply Radical Women. For the feminist movement, this mushrooming of groups meant increased numbers and added momentum. For some of the women involved, it meant confronting and articulating theoretically as well as personally what "oppression," "sexism," and "liberation" really meant: in short, developing a feminist ideology.

Toward a Feminist Ideology: Oppression, Sexism, and Change

To explain the significance of the discovery that woman is a *social construct* and that subordination was built into that construct was no simple process. The concept itself was complex. Moreover, women's rights advocates who were essentially pragmatic were more interested in practical results than in theoretical explanations. Even among women's liberationists who were far more theoretically oriented and ideologically fractious, intellectual perspectives reflected differences in experience, temperament, style, and politics. Manifestos, position papers, and books began to pile up as liberationists searched for the historical origins of female oppression. Those whose primary loyalty was still to the New Left—soon dubbed "politicos"—attributed women's oppression to capitalism. Others, who would come to be known as socialist-feminists, insisted that both male supremacy and capitalism were responsible for women's subordination and that feminists must be allied with, but apart from, the left. Still other liberationists argued that male supremacy, not class or race, was the more fundamental and universal form of oppression and that women as a group constituted an oppressed class. Known as radical feminists, their emphasis on the primacy of gender would prevail, although it would be ultimately challenged by feminists of color. In the meantime, however, radical feminists' identification of the family as the basic unit in the system of oppression led to new debates among radical feminists themselves. If marriage as an intersexual alliance divided women, leading them to identify with the oppressor from whom they derived economic advantages rather than each other, ought marriage to be abolished? If so, what new structure should take its place? Pushing the logic of this position, lesbian feminists argued that the ultimate rejection of male domination required not just the rejection of marriage, but the rejection of sexual intimacy with men. Other radical feminists, seeking to desexualize lesbianism, argued that sexual behavior—who one slept with—was less important than being "woman identified." Still others insisted that heterosexual relationships were essential: men should be reformed, not abandoned. Feminists familiar with role theory pointed to sex-based role differentiation as a source of oppression, arguing that work and family roles should be restructured in ways that would encourage greater mutuality and fulfillment for both sexes. Other feminists argued that personality—men and women's psychic identity—were also overly differentiated by sex. Only by merging role and personality characteristics of both sexes within each individual could androgynous men and women be developed and real liberation achieved.

Given the great variety of perspectives and positions even among women's liberationists alone, it is impossible to talk about *a* feminist ideology to which all those who identified with the women's movement subscribed. The ascendancy of radical feminism among women's liberationists in the early 1970s and the eventual embrace of many of their insights by liberal feminists, however, does make it possible to talk about a common conceptual framework shared by mainstream feminists. Most believed that *gender hierarchy* is a primary factor essential to any understanding of why women *as a group* suffer from an unequal distribution of power and resources in a society. They agreed that men have been the dominant sex and that women as a group are subordinate. While not all mainstream feminists were comfortable talking about a *system* of oppression or even using the word "oppression," they were quick to list the many areas where inequities were—and still are—evident.

At the top of the list was the economy. Men, they agreed, are more likely to be economically independent than women because the latter work within the home where their labor has no monetary value and/or outside the home in sex-segregated jobs for wages too meager to ensure economic self-sufficiency. Society and culture also provided numerous examples of the higher status, greater options, and greater power conferred upon men by virtue of their sex. Just as traditional male roles provide access to power and independence, whereas female roles do not, so, feminists pointed out, masculine values define what attributes are admired and rewarded. The very fact that strength, competence, independence, and rationality are considered masculine values, that they are more highly regarded by both sexes, *and* that they constitute the standard by which mental health is judged these new feminists found revealing indeed. The problem, they insisted, is not simply that the qualities themselves, intrinsically neither "male" or "female," are the product of gender socialization. It is the preference, conscious and unconscious, for whatever society regards as "masculine" that is so persistent and so objectionable—a preference feminists termed *sexism*.

Sexism, they believed, is persistent, pervasive, and powerful. It is internalized by women as well as men. It is most dramatically evident in the programmed-to-please women who search for happiness through submissiveness to men and in the men who use their power to limit women's options and keep them dependent. It is also evident in a more subtle fashion among women who emulate male models and values, refusing to see those aspects of women's lives that are positive and life-affirming, and among men who are unaware of the unconscious sexism permeating their attitudes and actions. Internalized in individuals, sexism is also embedded in institutions—the family, the education system, the media, the economy, politics, law, organized religion, language, and sexual morality.

Given the pervasiveness of sexism, many feminists saw no possibility for real equality short of transformation not only of individuals but also of social institutions and cultural values. Even what was once seen as the relatively simple demand of women's rights advocates for equal pay for equal work no longer looked so simple. What seemed to be a matter of obtaining equal rights *within* the existing system in reality demanded changes that *transform* the system. Involved was:

a reevaluation of women as workers, of women as mothers, of mothers as workers, of work as suitable for one gender and not for the other. The demand implies equal opportunity and thus equal responsibilities. It implies a childhood in which girls are rewarded for competence, risk taking, achievement, competitiveness and independence—just like boys. Equal pay for equal work means a revision in our expectations about women as equal workers and it involves the institutional arrangements to make them so.

"There is nothing small here," a feminist scholar observed. And indeed there was not.

Feminism in Action

While mainstream feminism contains under its broad umbrella women who differ significantly in the degree of their radicalism, the changes implied in achieving sexual equality are of such scope as to make radical by definition those who genuinely understand what is involved in equality and, beyond that, emancipation. To change self and society so that all women can achieve legal, economic, and social parity requires courage, energy, and commitment—commitment that has to be sustained over time and through defeat. To fundamentally restructure private and public life so as to benefit both sexes constitutes an even greater challenge. Yet despite the obstacles, millions of women during the past decades have participated in the process.

For some the changes have consisted largely of private actions—relationships renegotiated, careers resumed. Others, preferring to make public statements of new commitments, used flamboyant methods to dramatize the subtle ways in which society so defined woman's place as to deny not only her full participation but also her full humanity. As part of the confrontational politics of the 1960s, radical feminists picketed the 1968 Miss America contest, protesting the commercialization of beauty and our national preoccupation with bust size and "congeniality" rather than brain power and character. (In the process they were dubbed "bra burners," despite the fact that no bras were burned.) Activists pushed their way into all-male bars and restaurants as a way of forcing recognition of how these bastions of male exclusivity were themselves statements about "man's world/woman's place." They sat in at the offices of *Ladies' Home Journal* and *Newsweek* protesting the ways in which the media's depiction of women perpetuated old stereotypes at the expense of new realities. They demonstrated on behalf of legalized abortion, arguing that the right to terminate unwanted pregnancy is essential if women are to control the direction of their lives.

Still other feminists chose to work for social change in a different fashion. They created nonsexist day care centers, wrote and published nonsexist children's books, monitored sex stereotyping in textbooks, lobbied for women's studies programs in high schools and colleges, and founded women's health clinics. They formed rape crisis centers so that rape victims could be treated by caring females; they agitated for more informed, sympathetic treatment on the part of hospital staffs, the police, and the courts. They created shelters for battered women, insisting that physical abuse was not a private family matter but a social problem requiring a public response. Feminists also lobbied for programs to retrain displaced homemakers so that such women could move from economic dependency to self-support. Feminist scholars used their talents to recover and interpret women's experience, opening new areas for research and in the process furthering change. Feminist legislators, especially black Congresswoman Shirley Chisholm, sponsored legislation to extended minimum wage coverage to domestic workers. Other lawmakers sponsored bills, not always successful, to help housewives to secure some form of economic recognition for work performed, to enable women workers to obtain insurance that would give them the same degree of economic security afforded male coworkers, and to secure for battered women protection from the physical violence that is the most blatant form of male oppression. Black feminists, speaking out on the "double jeopardy" of being black and female—"the most pressed down of us all"—lent their support to feminist measures of especial importance to minority women. Trade union feminists, concerned about their dual oppression as wage workers and as women, struggled to keep the needs of working women in the forefront. Actions, like voices, differed. Such diversity, however, was basic to the movement.

Feminism: The Public Impact

In a society in which the media create instant awareness of social change, feminism burst upon the public consciousness with all the understated visibility of a fireworks display on the Fourth of July. The more radical elements of the movement, with their talk of test tube conception, the slavery of marriage, and the downfall of capitalism, might be dismissed out of hand. But it was hard to ignore 50,000 women parading down New York's Fifth Avenue, the presence of *Ms.*

magazine on newsstands, feminist books on the best-seller lists, women in hard hats on construction jobs, or the government-mandated affirmative action programs that put them there. It was harder still to ignore the publicity that accompanied the appointment of women to the Carter cabinet, the enrollment of coeds in the nation's military academies, and the ordination of women to the ministry. A Harris poll of December 1975 reported that 63 percent of the women interviewed favored most changes designed to improve the status of women, although some were quick to insist that they were not "women's libbers."

Evidence of changing views was everywhere. The list of organizations lined up in support of ratification of the Equal Rights Amendment included not only such avowedly feminist groups as NOW, WEAL, and NWPC as well as longtime supporters such as the National Woman's Party and the National Federation of Business and Professional Women's Clubs, but also well-established women's organizations such as the General Federation of Women's Clubs, the American Association of University Women, the League of Women Voters, the National Council of Jewish Women, the National Council of Negro Women, and the YWCA.

Even more potent evidence that feminism had "arrived" was the 1977 International Women's Year Conference in Houston. Before more than two thousand delegates from every state and territory in the United States and twenty thousand guests, three First Ladies—Lady Bird Johnson, Betty Ford, and Rosalynn Carter—endorsed the Equal Rights Amendment and the goals of the Houston Conference, their hands holding a lighted torch carried by women runners from Seneca Falls where, in 1848, the famous Declaration of Sentiments had been adopted. Confessing that she once thought the women's movement belonged more to her daughters than to herself, Lady Bird Johnson added, "I have come to know that it belongs to women of all ages." Such an admission, like the presence of these three women on the platform, proclaimed a message about feminists that was boldly printed on balloons throughout the convention hall: "We Are Everywhere!"

Opposition to Feminism

For some women the slogan was not a sign of achievement but of threat. Gathered at a counter-convention in Houston were women who shared neither the critique nor the goals of the movement. They were an impressive reminder that social change generates opposition and that opposition to feminism had crystallized in the struggle for ratification of the Equal Rights Amendment. ERA—as the amendment is called—simply stated: "Equality of rights under the law shall not be denied or abridged by the United States or by any State on account of sex." First suggested in 1923 as the logical extension of suffrage, the amendment had long been opposed by those who feared it would be used to strike down laws intended to protect women in the workplace. By the 1960s, those concerns no longer applied. Prodded by NOW, Congress once again turned its attention to a constitutional amendment removing sexual bias from common, statutory, and constitutional law. After a massive lobbying effort by women's rights advocates and their allies, the Senate finally joined the House and sent ERA to the states for

ratification by a lopsided vote of eighty-four to eight in 1972. Almost immediately twenty-one states rushed to ratify. Within a year, however, opponents of ratification had begun a counterattack that ultimately stalled the number of ratified
states at thirty-five, three short of the needed three-fourths majority when the
deadline for ratification expired on June 30, 1982. Opponents even induced
some ratifying states to rescind their approval. Early successes indicated a majority of Americans favored ERA—but not a large enough majority.

   Opposition to ERA is starkly paradoxical. A constitutional amendment proposed especially to benefit women was opposed by women. The paradox is resolved in part by remembering that many Americans who claim to believe in
equality become profoundly apprehensive when the principle is identified with
specific governmental policies they consider to be intrusive and unreasonable.
When supporters of ERA said that implementation of a constitutional ban on sex
discrimination would be left to the Supreme Court, conservatives of both sexes
were reminded that this was the same Supreme Court that had not only mandated racial integration, but prohibited prayer in the public schools and struck
down bans on birth control, abortion, and pornography. Court-enforced sexual
equality, like racial equality, many people believed, would further diminish the
power of state and local governments and the right of individuals to live as they
choose. As one woman wrote her U.S. senator: "*Forced* busing, *forced* mixing,
forced housing. Now *forced* women! No thank you!"

   Such logic also illuminates antiratificationist charges, mystifying to ratifica-
tionists, that ERA would destroy the family. Although ERA supporters correctly
pointed out that the amendment had nothing to do with private relationships, social conservatives were not convinced; they had seen what a federal agenda in
feminist hands looked like at the International Women's Year Conference in
Houston. A meeting subsidized by the U.S. government had endorsed not only
women's rights and ERA, but government-sponsored child care, federal funding
of abortions for poor women, contraception for minors without parental consent, and gay rights. If Big Brother or, more appropriately, Big Sister, had her way
in Washington, women might well be forced to live in the kind of post-ERA
world invoked by anti-ERA spokeswoman Phyllis Schlafly—a world in which
mothers, no longer financially able to remain at home, would be forced to surrender their children to government-sponsored day-care centers. There child-care
personnel would supplant parental authority and family identification with loyalty to the state.

   The danger, as anti-ERA women saw it, was not just to family, but to women
themselves. Feminists believed that theirs was a struggle for justice and liberation—liberation from economic inequities, social roles, and cultural values that
denied rights and limited autonomy. To require *all* women to endure constraints
dictated not by biology (sex) but by culture (gender) was, from the standpoint of
feminists, to deny freedom and self-determination to half the population simply
because they were born female. To women who did not believe they were oppressed, feminists' efforts at liberation, especially the rhetoric of radical feminists, appeared *not* as an attack on traditional gender categories, but rather an
assault on familiar patterns that provided security, identity, and meaning. Fusing

feminism and ERA, an antiratificationist begged her senator not to vote for the amendment, insisting that she did not want to be liberated. "My husband," she wrote, "works for me and takes care of me and our three children, doesn't make me do things that are hard for me (drive in town), loves me and doesn't smoke, drink, gamble, run around or do anything that would upset me. I do what he tells me to do. I like this arrangement. *It's the only way I know how to live.*" Insisted another: "I am a widow, have three children, and work to make ends meet. I am still against ERA. I am a woman—and want to be treated as a woman."

When ERA supporters responded that treating women as individuals legally rather than classifying them by sex had nothing to do with the division of labor between husbands and wives, social etiquette, or the masculinization of women, their reassurances fell on deaf ears. The free-floating anxiety aroused by the enormity of the social change inherent in feminism had acquired concrete focus in ERA. Opponents' predictions of the terrible consequences that would result from ratification of the amendment were not so important as the function such statements served—an indictment of what Schlafly called the "unisex" society and an affirmation of traditional gender categories. For women living in a world in which personal identity, social legitimacy, economic viability, and moral order were rooted in traditional gender categories, calling those categories into question in the name of gender-neutral law meant that feminists must want men and women to be "the same." Finding it difficult to separate gender from sex—to see gender as a social construction—ERA opponents could only conclude that this latest drive for equality was not only absurd ("you can't fool Mother Nature") but dangerous. By rallying women to this danger, Schlafly revealed that the issue was not whether women should stay at home minding the children and cooking the food—Schlafly herself did not do that. The issue was the *meaning* of sexual differences between men and women.

In the early years of the movement, both radical and liberal feminists minimized those differences, believing reproductive control and work in the public sector have made women's lives more like men's. Antifeminists inflated those differences. Their response is a measure both of their belief that women are "eternal in their attributes and unchanged by events" and their anger and distress at changes that had already occurred. It is a reminder, too, of how far the feminist movement has still to go to achieve the reforms sought by women's rights advocates, much less its more far-reaching goals.

New Progress and Old Problems

There were gains to be sure. New reproductive freedom came in 1973 with the Supreme Court's liberalization of abortion laws that removed the danger of the illegal, back-alley abortions so long the recourse of desperate women. Sexual preference and practice became less an occasion for denial of civil rights and more a matter of individual choice. Evidence of expanding educational and employment opportunities seemed to be everywhere. Women assumed high-level posts in government, the judiciary, the military, business, and labor. In a new batch of female "firsts," Sandra Day O'Connor assumed a seat on the Supreme Court, NASA's Sally Ride zoomed into space, and Geraldine Ferraro won the vice-presidential slot on the 1984 Democratic ticket. From an expanding population of female college graduates, younger women moved in record numbers into professional schools, dramatically changing enrollment patterns in such fields as law, medicine, and business. Their blue-collar counterparts, completing job training programs, trickled into the construction industry and other trades, finding in those jobs the decent wage that had eluded them as waitresses, hairdressers, salesclerks, or domestics. Political participation also increased. Women emerged from years of lobbying for ERA with a new understanding of the political process. (So, too, did their opponents.) More female candidates filed for office and more female politicians worked themselves into positions of power. Revision of discriminatory statutes, while by no means completed, brought a greater measure of legal equality. A heightened public consciousness of sexism ushered in other changes. School officials began admitting boys to home economics classes, girls to shop. Some employers transformed maternity leaves into child-care leaves, making them available to fathers as well as mothers. Liberal religious leaders talked of removing gender-related references from prayer books.

Such gains, while in some cases smacking of tokenism, are not to be minimized. Most required persistent pressure from feminists, from government officials, and often from both. They were by no means comprehensive, however. As in the case of the civil rights movement, the initial beneficiaries of the feminist movement were predominantly middle-class, often highly educated, and relatively young. The increase in the number of single women, the older age at which women married for the first time, the declining birth rate—changes characteristic of the entire female population during the 1970s—were especially characteristic of a younger generation of career-oriented women. But even for these women and their partners, financial as well as personal costs were sometimes high: couples living apart for some portion of the week or year in order to take advantage of career opportunities; married women devoting virtually all of their salaries to domestic and child-care costs, especially during their children's preschool years. Perhaps the personal recognition, independence, and sense of fulfillment associated with career success made the costs "affordable"—especially given the alternatives.

The women who stood to gain most from the implementation of feminists' efforts to change the nation's economic and social structure were not those who were young, talented, and educated but those who were less advantaged. Yet by the 1990s the latter could with good reason argue that two decades of feminist activity had left their lives little changed in ways that really count. While the number of women in the work force continued to rise from less than 20 percent in 1920 to 59 percent by June 1991, with a projected 87 percent by 2000, working women in the 1970s and 1980s saw the gap between male and female income remain virtually unchanged. By 1990 female workers earned 70 cents for every dollar earned by males. College graduates were no exception. Their earnings averaged $21,362 compared to $19,241 earned by men *without* even a high school diploma, although the gap has substantially narrowed among younger women. Part of the explanation for this persistent gap lies in pay inequities. More fundamental, however, is the continuation of occupational segregation and the undervaluation of work done by women. Around 80 percent of all working women still cluster in gender-segregated occupations in which wages are artificially low. That women made up two-thirds of all minimum-wage workers in the United States is, therefore, hardly surprising.

With the dramatic rise in the number of female-headed households—33 percent of all working mothers are their family's breadwinners—the continuation of this occupational ghetto has disturbing implications not only for women workers but also for their children. Female heads of households, often lacking both child-care facilities and skills that would equip them for better-paying jobs if such jobs were available, earn enough to enable less than two-thirds to stay above the poverty level. Their struggle for economic survival is shared by other women, especially older women—widows or divorcées whose years of housework have left them without employment skills. Indeed divorce often contributes to the problem, for with the breaking up of a marriage, the standard of living for most women falls dramatically. The fact that child support, if awarded, is frequently inadequate, unpaid, and uncollectible further exacerbates the economic plight of those women who have custody of their children. Thus, ironic as it may seem, the decade that witnessed the revival of the feminist movement also saw the feminization of poverty. By the end of the 1970s, two out of every three poor persons in the United States were female. If this trend continues at the present rate, it is estimated that by the year 2000 the poverty population will be composed entirely of women and their children.

Ironic, too, given the feminist insistence that child-care and household responsibilities should be shared by working spouses, is the persistence of the double burden borne by women working outside the home. Working women continue to do 80 to 90 percent of the chores related to running a household, with husbands and children "helping out." For all the talk about the changing structure of family roles, major shifts have occurred slowly, even in households in which women were informed and engaged enough to be familiar with current feminist views. Although some fathers, especially among the middle class, have become more involved in parenting, the primary responsibility for children still remains the mother's. And working mothers still receive little institutional help despite the fact that by 1990 over half of all mothers with children under six worked outside the home. Without a fundamental rethinking of both work and family, women will continue to participate in the labor force in increasing numbers. Many, however, will remain in its lower echelons as marginal members.

In sum, economic and demographic change has been the basis of important changes in attitudes and behavior. As a result, life is more challenging for many women, but the feminization of poverty reminds the nation of its failures. We have yet to see the new social policies necessary to create the egalitarian and humane society envisioned by feminists.

Indeed, in the climate of political conservatism of the 1980s feminists had to fight hard to maintain gains already won. The reproductive freedom of poor women had already been eroded by limitations on federal funding of abortions, and the reproductive freedom of all women had been threatened by congressional advocates of the Human Life Bill. Although that bill never received the votes necessary to become law, an increasingly conservative Supreme Court dealt reproductive rights a further blow. The 1989 *Webster* and the 1992 *Planned Parent-*

hood decisions, while not overturning the right to an abortion, upheld the right of states to limit access. With reproductive rights now a contested issue in state legislatures, the struggle to keep abortion legal and unrestricted has escalated dramatically.

During the 1980s legislation mandating equal opportunity in education and employment was also weakened by the courts and assaulted by the Reagan and Bush administrations, whose budget cuts further hampered EEOC's antidiscrimination efforts. There were also cuts in funds for Title IX, which seeks to ensure sex equality on campus; cuts in grants for traditionally female programs such as nursing; cuts in Small Business Administration funding for programs benefiting women. Also under attack was comparable worth, a policy designed to reduce pay inequities by evaluating skills, effort, and responsibilities associated with jobs traditionally held by men and those traditionally held by women so that pay can be equalized for jobs that are indeed comparable.

Setbacks occurred in other areas as well. Day care centers, battered women's shelters, and legal aid centers have had their work curtailed by budget cuts. Legal equality has also suffered. Without an equal rights amendment requiring legislators to revise the discriminatory statutes that remain, the impetus will have to come not from the governments—state and local—but from individual women and men genuinely committed to equality before the law. Although the election of 1992 brought a pro-choice president to the White House and new feminist legislators to Capitol Hill, the need for collective action on the part of feminists is as great in the 1990s as it was in the 1970s and 1980s.

Social change is complex and results from the interplay of many factors. Nowhere is this truer than in the women's movement. The swiftness with which a resurgent feminism captured the imagination of millions of American women dramatized the need for change. The inability of feminists to win ratification of ERA dramatized the limits of change. The irony of the polarization, however, was that the failure of ERA did not and could not stop feminism in its tracks and that antifeminist women, in mobilizing to fight the amendment, were themselves assuming a new role whether they acknowledged that fact or not. They organized lobbies, political action committees, and conventions; they also ran for and won public office. Where feminists have led, antifeminists would not be too far behind, defining themselves within the context of change they could not stop. But the rhetoric of liberation that had been so important to the awakening and maturation of women in the 1970s seemed by the 1980s to be less appealing. Women could happily benefit from the achievements of feminism without understanding or embracing its critique of style. Transformational politics seemed to have given way to a bevy of career women armed with a copy of *Savvy* or *Working Woman,* "dressed for success," and busily playing "games their mothers never taught them" with scant realization, as one observer noted, that "only a decade ago they would never have been allowed to play." Commentators, speculating that feminism had become careerism, pronounced the movement dead.

Although press speculation was off the mark, feminism had changed. By the mid-seventies, radical feminism had given way to cultural feminism. The appeal that alternative institution-building held for cultural feminists in the conservative eighties was understandable. But the kind of valorization of the female reflected in the search for lost matriarchies and goddess worship seemed to radical and liberal feminists to represent not only female separatism but a retreat from political struggle. Both seemed alien to women whose aim had been to transcend gender, not reaffirm it. Valorization of female difference was also at the heart of still newer varieties of feminism such as eco-feminism: women as natural nurturers were presumed to be uniquely concerned with ecological ruin. If eco-feminism focused on issues that radical and liberal feminists of the 1960s would have regarded as broad human issues rather than distinctively feminist ones, the groups themselves functioned as a sharp reminder that second wave feminism had always been an ideologically pluralistic, decentralized, and structurally amorphous movement. Indeed diversity is a source of strength—a point made with renewed intensity in the 1980s by women of color. Their insistence that racism, classism, and sexism are multiple and interlocking forms of oppression has served to remind mainstream feminists that women speak in different voices from multiple historical, cultural, racial, economic, and sexual locations. The need to move beyond totalizing notions of "sisterhood," recognizing the extent to which women have themselves been oppressors of other women, requires of mainstream feminism further transformation. There can be no mistaking black poet and feminist Audre Lorde's meaning when she asked, "What woman here is so enamored of her own oppression that she cannot see her heelprint upon another woman's face?" If feminism is to become genuinely egalitarian and multicultural, mainstream feminists who bear the greater responsibility for that transformation will have much to do.

Meanwhile the movement continues to expand even in the midst of antifeminist backlash as women continue to make the connection between the personal and political as they confront in their own lives or the lives of others the trauma of sexual harassment, job discrimination, inequitable divorce settlements, as well as rape and other forms of sexual violence. Moreover, the challenge of the New Right has made abundantly clear that old patterns of gender-based discrimination have not lost their force. Those patterns had hindered efforts of women to establish a public role in the nineteenth century; they had restricted that public role once it was won. The same patterns, so indelible even under attack, continue to obstruct contemporary efforts to dismantle gender hierarchy in the drive for equality. The tension between past position and future possibility, however, demands of all women—not merely feminists—a definition of self that extends beyond the definitions of the past.

SUGGESTIONS FOR FURTHER READING

A good general survey of the domestic politics of the sixties is Allen J. Matusow, *The Unraveling of America: A History of Liberalism in the 1960s* (New York, 1984). Matusow argues that the election of John F. Kennedy marked the beginning of a liberal consensus. But despite the efforts of Kennedy and Johnson, opposition from the left and the right destroyed that consensus, leaving the nation sharply divided and opening the way to the defeat of the liberals in the 1968 election. William H. Chafe, *The Unfinished Journey: America Since World War II,* 2nd ed. (New York, 1991), a portion of which is reprinted here, is another general account, but Chafe is more sympathetic to many of the sixties movements than is Matusow.

The development of the counterculture, the New Left, and the student radicals elicited an outpouring of books and articles, some sympathetic and some sharply antagonistic. Irwin Unger, *The Movement: A History of the American New Left 1959–1972* (Lanham, Md., 1988) credits the student radicals with forcing the U.S. withdrawal from Vietnam but finds little more of lasting significance. Lewis Feuer, *Conflict of Generations* (New York, 1969) and Daniel J. Boorstin, *The Decline of Radicalism* (New York, 1969) are conservative critics. Irving Howe, ed., *Beyond the New Left* (New York, 1970) contains a group of essays that are sympathetically critical from a leftist perspective. Kenneth Kenniston, *Young Radicals: Notes on Committed Youth* (New York, 1968); Paul Jacobs and Saul Landau, *The New Radicals: A Report with Documents* (New York, 1966); and Theodore Roszak, *The Making of a Counter Culture* (New York, 1970) are generally sympathetic. Peter Clecak, *America's Quest for the Ideal Self* (New York, 1983) sees both the radical sixties and the more conservative seventies as united by a search for fulfillment that was both personal and social. Kirkpatrick Sale, *SDS* (New York, 1973) is a sympathetic study of the rise and decline of the Students for a Democratic Society, concluding that the organization left a long-lasting legacy in the form of "a pool of people . . . who have forever lost their allegiance to the myths and institutions of capitalist America." Edward J. Bacciocco, Jr., *The New Left in America* (Stanford, Calif., 1974) argues that the movement lost its opportunity to achieve lasting changes when it abandoned its reformist stance in favor of radicalism. Nigel Young, *An Infantile Disorder? The Crisis and Decline of the New Left* (Boulder, Colo., 1977) finds much of the New Left to be a romantic, utopian, "infantile disorder" although he argues that some parts of the movement, such as the women's-liberation movement, made a lasting and important contribution. Godfrey Hodgson, *America in Our Time* (New York, 1976) is a sympathetic and lively account that discusses the various parts of the movement. Matthew Stolz, ed., *Politics of the New Left* (Beverly Hills, Calif., 1971) is a collection of contemporary essays by New Left leaders and sympathizers. A more general survey of the left, both old and new, is John P. Diggins, *The American Left in the Twentieth Century* (New York, 1973). Public-opinion pollster Louis Harris traces changes in public attitudes, as revealed in opinion polls in *The Anguish of Change* (New York, 1973). Maurice Isserman compares the old and the new left in his *If I Had a Hammer: The Death of the Old Left and the Birth of the New Left* (New York, 1987).

Todd Gitlin, *The Sixties: Years of Hope, Days of Rage* (New York, 1987) is a fascinating account, part autobiography, part analysis, written by a former president of SDS. Gitlin's account may be compared to Peter Collier and David Horowitz, *Destructive Generation: Second Thoughts About the Sixties* (New York, 1989), which details the views of participants whose "second thoughts" lead them to repudiate their actions in the sixties. David Faber, *The Sixties: From Memory to History* (Chapel Hill, N.C., 1994) is a collection of ten original essays that cover a wide range of issues, including civil rights, the youth culture, the Vietnam War, and women's liberation.

Numerous books deal with the civil rights movement and its leaders, its varied goals and the results it achieved, and its opponents. Clayborne Carson, *In Struggle: SNCC and the Black Awakening of the 1960s* (Cambridge, Mass., 1981) traces the efforts of the Student Nonviolent Coordinating Committee to end segregation and discrimination in the South, showing how the organization became increasingly radical but by the end of the

---

*Available in paperback edition.

decade became divided internally and isolated from the masses of the black people it presumed to be leading. August Meier and Elliott Rudwick find a similar story in their study of the Congress on Racial Equality: *CORE: A Study in the Civil Rights Movement 1942–1968* (New York, 1973; paperback, Urbana, Ill., 1975). Two books by David J. Garrow critically but sympathetically appraise the SCLC and the leadership of Martin Luther King, Jr.: *Bearing the Cross: Martin Luther King, Jr. and the Southern Christian Leadership Conference, 1955–1968* (New York, 1986) and *We Shall Overcome: The Civil Rights Movement in the United States in the 1950s and 1960s* (Brooklyn, N.Y., 1989). J. Harvie Wilkinson III, *From Brown to Bakke: The Supreme Court and School Integration, 1954–1978* (New York, 1979) discusses the school desegregation decision, the opposition it generated, the complexities, problems, and debates arising from efforts to enforce the decision and extend it through affirmative action, busing, and similar policies. Raymond Wolters, *The Burden of Brown: Thirty Years of School Desegregation* (Knoxville, Tenn., 1984) attacks court-ordered integration (as distinct from desegregation) on constitutional and practical grounds. Herbert H. Haines, *Black Radicals and the Civil Rights Mainstream, 1954–1970* (Knoxville, Tenn., 1988) considers the views of the more radical black leaders and organizations. Some scholars have argued that it is more important to emphasize class differences rather than race and racism in order to understand the problems faced by blacks. See Thomas Sowell, *Race and Economics* (New York, 1975) and William J. Wilson, *The Declining Significance of Race: Blacks and Changing American Institutions* (New York, 1978). But Robert Huckfeldt and Carol Weitzel, *Race and the Decline of Class in American Politics* (Urbana, Ill., 1989) argue that since the mid-1960s electoral politics in the United States have centered on race rather than class differences.

Collections of contemporary essays debating the policies and actions of the various civil rights organizations are Sondra Silverman, ed., *The Black Revolt and Democratic Politics* (Lexington, Mass., 1970) and August Meier and Elliott Rudwick, *Black Protest in the Sixties* (Chicago, 1970). Works by leaders of various groups within the civil rights movement are invaluable for understanding motivations and behavior. See in particular Martin Luther King, Jr., *Stride Toward Freedom* (New York, 1958); King, *Where Do We Go From Here: Chaos or Community?* (New York, 1967); Whitney M. Young, Jr., *To Be Equal* (New York, 1964); James Farmer, *Freedom–When?* (New York, 1965); Robert Williams, *Negroes with Guns* (New York, 1962); and *The Autobiography of Malcolm X* (New York, 1964).

Betty Friedan's critique, *The Feminine Mystique* (New York, 1963), which had an enormous influence on the rebirth of the feminist movement, deserves to be read by any serious student. Mary Ryan, *Womanhood in America* (New York, 1983) and Carl N. Degler, *At Odds: Women and the Family in America from the Revolution to the Present* (New York, 1980) are two excellent surveys that place the contemporary movement in historical context. Two books by William H. Chafe, *The American Woman* (New York, 1972) and *Women and Equality* (New York, 1978), provide information for judging the progress of the women's movement in America, as does the more narrowly focused study by Susan M. Hartmann, *From Margin to Mainstream: American Women and Politics Since 1960* (New York, 1989). Sara Evans, *Personal Politics* (New York, 1979) discusses the connection between the New Left and the feminist movement. Robin Morgan, ed., *Sisterhood Is Powerful* (New York, 1970) is a good collection of articles and documents from the militant wings of the feminist movement. For a powerful opposing view see Midge Decter, *The New Chastity and Other Arguments Against Women's Liberation* (New York, 1974).

An important part of the 1960s is the conservative opposition to the various radical and liberal movements. David Farber, *The Age of Great Dreams: America in the 1960s* (New York, 1994) and William C. Berman, *America's Right Turn: From Nixon to Bush*

(Baltimore, 1994) describe the clash of ideologies in the 1960s. Robert Alan Goldberg, *Barry Goldwater* (New Haven, Conn., 1995); Joan-Hoff Wilson, *Nixon Reconsidered* (New York, 1994); and Roger Morris, *Richard Milhous Nixon: The Rise of an American Politician* (New York, 1990) are recent biographic studies of conservative Republican leaders. Dan T. Carter, *The Politics of Rage: George Wallace, the Origins of the New Conservatism and the Transformation of American Politics* (New York, 1995) discusses the career of a leading opponent of desegregation and a leader of conservative opposition from the South who gathered a significant following from other parts of the nation. John Ehrman, *The Rise of Neoconservatism: Intellectuals and Foreign Affairs, 1945–1994* (New Haven, Conn., 1995) emphasizes foreign policy but also considers the influence of neoconservative intellectuals on domestic issues. On the development of the new conservatism by one of its founders, see Irving Kristol, *Neoconservatism: The Autobiography of an Idea* (New York, 1995).

11

Vietnam: Crisis in United States Foreign Policy

American politicians often insist that partisan politics ends at the nation's borders, but in fact, foreign policy has often divided Americans, causing massive disagreements over the proper role to take in international affairs. From the beginning, most Americans felt that the United States was unique and special, giving the nation a responsibility and a mission to help other less fortunate people. But how this American sense of mission translated into foreign policy often stirred controversy. The idealistic American desire to help frequently became mixed with a realistic search for economic and strategic gain.

In the early days of the Republic, Jeffersonians and Federalists argued over whether to support France or England in the European struggle or to stay out of the conflict completely; both sides mixed idealism and realism when they argued about such matters as trade advantages and honoring treaty obligations. When the country entered the conflict in the War of 1812, massive dissent and disagreement continued, even provoking talk of secession. The Mexican War similarly stimulated strong opposition that usually linked the war to sectional interests. Many Americans opposed even the brief and generally popular Spanish-American War, a growing group of "anti-imperialists" vigorously opposing the acquisition of an overseas American empire. The path that led the United States into World War I was also strewn with controversy and disagreement. But if many pacifists and others continued their opposition even after 1917, when the nation entered the war most opposition faded, bringing a widespread consensus in support of Woodrow Wilson's promise to make the world safe for democracy.

Disillusionment followed when Wilson's promises proved unattainable, and throughout the 1930s as war clouds again gathered in Europe, Americans divided, some arguing that the United States should remain aloof and isolated while others insisted that the nation's interests required its becoming involved. The attack on Pearl Harbor and the growing appreciation of the dangers of fascism ended most of the disagreement. World War II, which Studs Terkel has called "The Good War," was the last time that the American people were united in a common foreign-policy consensus.

The euphoria following victory in World War II was short-lived as the wartime coalition between the western powers and the Soviet Union collapsed. Within two years the United States was helping to rebuild its former enemies, Germany and Japan, and negotiating international agreements to oppose its former friend, the Soviet Union. Sharp opposition to this new policy quickly arose— even leading to a split in the Democratic party with the creation of the Progressive party, led by Henry Wallace—but it just as quickly faded. The fear of communism brought a new consensus in support of the policy of "containment," developed during the Truman administration and continued by both Republican and Democratic administrations that followed.

The basic idea of the containment policy was to draw a ring around the Soviet empire and to prevent further expansion of that empire through pressure and persuasion if possible and by military action if necessary. Containment led to the Marshall Plan and other programs for strengthening Western Europe, to military aid to Greece, to the airlift to Berlin, and to the negotiation of a series of mutual-aid treaties among the noncommunist nations surrounding the Soviet Union and its allies. The policy also led to the Korean War as the United States came to the defense of South Korea after the North Koreans crossed the 38th parallel in June 1950. The Korean War dragged on for three years and eventually resulted in a stalemate; but in the end it strengthened the American resolve to oppose communism around the world.

One crucial danger spot was Vietnam, a country few Americans had heard of in the 1950s. Vietnam, which had been captured by the Japanese during World War II, had been part of French Indochina before the war. In 1945, after the expulsion of the Japanese, a strong and popular nationalist movement led by Ho Chi Minh seemed destined to rule the country, but the French were determined to reassert their control over their former colony. The United States, believing that any Marxist was a Soviet puppet, supported the French. Between 1950 and 1954 the United States spent $2.6 billion to help the French "save" Vietnam, but to no avail. In 1954, the forces of Ho Chi Minh surrounded 12,000 French troops at Dien Bien Phu, and when that garrison fell, the French withdrew. An international conference in Geneva produced agreements to divide Vietnam along the 17th parallel and to hold a national election in two years to bring reunification— agreements that the United States did not accept. The United States was determined not to let South Vietnam "fall" to the communists because, as President Eisenhower announced in 1954, the fall of Vietnam would have a "domino" effect. "You have a row of dominoes set up," he explained. "You knock over the first one, and what will happen to the last one is a certainty that it will go over very quickly." This view would dominate American thinking about Vietnam for the next twenty years.

Vietnam became America's war after 1955. Determined to prevent reunification under Ho Chi Minh and to support South Vietnam's struggle against its internal, pro–North Vietnam opposition, the Viet Cong, the United States sent military advisors, economic aid, and increasing amounts of military equipment to prop up the Saigon regime of Ngo Dinh Diem. Diem, with U.S. backing, had rejected the Geneva agreements and had proclaimed himself president of the Republic of South Vietnam. But the shaky Diem regime lacked popular support and was unable to mount an effective fight against the Viet Cong. John F. Kennedy, sharing the determination of Eisenhower to prevent the fall of South Vietnam, sent additional American forces and military aid and also authorized covert actions within South Vietnam. In the fall of 1963, with the approval of the United States, a military coup overthrew the Diem government and murdered the president.

Lyndon B. Johnson, who became president after Kennedy's assassination, decided early in his presidency that "I am not going to lose Vietnam. I am not going to be the President who saw Southeast Asia go the way China went." American involvement increased sharply. When Johnson became president there were 16,000 American troops in Vietnam; when he left, brought down by the unpopular war he could not win, there were more than 500,000 Americans fighting in Vietnam.

Johnson had a sense of honor and patriotism and was convinced that the war was a good cause. We are in Vietnam, he once remarked, because "we remain fixed on the pursuit of freedom, a deep and moral obligation that will not let us go." But the war would not end. The more troops he sent, the more were needed. The more bombs that were dropped, the more the military commanders wanted to drop. American troops seldom faced an opposing army, but instead encountered guerrillas. The enemy was everywhere—and nowhere. Soldiers, in frustration or desperation, often killed women and children and destroyed villages and crops while bombers and helicopters systematically destroyed the country. The frustration of the war was perhaps best expressed by an Army major after a battle in 1968: "It became necessary to destroy the town to save it," he announced quite seriously.

The mounting casualties in a war that seemed impossible to win, along with growing doubts about the wisdom of any American involvement in a tiny country 9,000 miles from the United States and evidence of atrocities by American troops, produced bitter opposition to the war at home. Opposition began among students but increasingly spread to other sections of the population, and politicians, sensing the changing views of the people, joined in the attack on the policies of the Johnson administration. The attacks on the war policies of the government intensified when Johnson's successor, Richard M. Nixon, ordered the bombing and invasion of Cambodia and Laos, the resumption of the bombing of Hanoi, and the mining of North Vietnamese harbors; when newspapers revealed that American troops had shot some 450 South Vietnamese civilians at My Lai; and when the press published the "Pentagon Papers," which revealed secret government policy decisions concerning the war.

At the same time that he stepped up the war, Nixon began the process of ending American involvement. Secret peace negotiations, the withdrawal of some American troops, and the disintegration of the South Vietnamese military and government in the face of increased attacks by North Vietnam and the Viet Cong finally brought an end to the war. On April 29, 1975, American helicopters evacuated the last Americans from Saigon, and on the following day the South Vietnamese government surrendered to the Viet Cong.

The bitter divisions caused by the war had a lasting impact on an entire generation, creating a crisis in American foreign policy and undermining confidence in the government at home. More than fifty thousand Americans were killed; many more were wounded, some permanently maimed physically and psychologically. Opponents of the war charged that the United States acted as an imperialist power intervening in ruthless and brutal ways in a civil war that was none of its affair, while supporters insisted that the war to defend freedom and democracy against an evil communist empire was hobbled by domestic opposition.

The Vietnam experience influenced American attitudes toward foreign policy in the years that followed, but different groups learned quite different lessons from the disaster. When the United States went to war against Iraq in 1991, President George Bush announced, "It won't be another Vietnam," and Vice President J. Danforth Quayle maintained that in this war the "United States forces will not be asked to fight with one arm tied behind their backs." The Bush administration and the military commanders apparently accepted the idea that the United States could have won the war in Vietnam if only the military had not been restrained from using more force by restrictions imposed by politicians in Washington who were influenced by public opposition to the war. This same idea influenced American policy in the war in the Persian Gulf in another way. The Bush administration put extremely tight controls on press coverage of the war, apparently believing that the pessimistic stories written during the Vietnam War helped turn the public against the war and ultimately prevented an American victory. But, while the Bush administration learned one lesson from Vietnam, those who opposed the war in the Persian Gulf and the use of massive military force there dusted off their old banners and took to the street to "Stop the War Now," perhaps under the assumption that protest marches had influenced government policy during the Vietnam War.

At the end of the twentieth century the lessons learned in Vietnam, and the haunting specter of a war lost and mistakes made, continue to have an impact on American foreign policy in the Middle East, the Balkans, and in Central and South America. Thus, long after the Vietnam War ended, Americans remained divided about the meaning of the war and the lessons to be learned from the experience. These differences are clearly revealed in the selections that follow.

In the first selection, Loren Baritz argues that an American myth of superiority based on nationalism, technological know-how, and moral fervor brought the country into a war against a people it never understood and never sought to understand. Blind to the real issues involved and confident that its material and moral prowess would prevail, the nation turned against itself, divided by frustration and failure. In brief, Baritz argues that Americans entered the war united by a consensus that misled them and resulted in their defeat. When evaluating Baritz's argument, readers should consider whether the conflict that eventually brought an end to the war also destroyed the underlying consensus that got the country involved in the first place.

Guenter Lewy, in the second selection, addresses that question in his discussion of the "legacy" of the war. American policymakers, he writes, "considered Vietnam and indeed all of Southeast Asia, to be of important strategic and economic value to the noncommunist world." But Lewy insists that this assessment was incorrect, making American involvement a mistake. Nevertheless, once the United States had committed itself, it could not simply pull out, as critics demanded, without losing its credibility. When the United States finally did withdraw, the result was "an overall weakening of faith in the worth of American commitments" in Southeast Asia and elsewhere in the world as well. Moreover, Lewy argues, the insistence that the United States never again become involved in an overseas war, an insistence summarized in the slogan, "No More Vietnams," currently hobbles American foreign policy, as do the moralistic preachings that underlay the opposition to the war. Had American actions, both political and military, been different, Lewy concludes, the tragedy of defeat might have been averted.

In the third selection, Chester J. Pach, Jr., discusses the depiction of the war on television news. Although some historians as well as politicians and generals charge that television coverage of the war helped to undermine the military effort, Pach argues that anchorpersons as well as reporters in the field were not critics of American involvement; on the contrary, the content and tone of the reporting were patriotic and supportive of the American effort. But the actual effect of television coverage was quite different: "Because of the nature of the medium rather than any conscious effort, television nightly news exposed the irrationalities of a war that lacked coherent strategy or clear purpose."

Neither Baritz nor Lewy defends the American intervention in Vietnam, but they differ sharply in their assessments of the causes of the war and the lessons it taught. Has Lewy presented a convincing argument that Americans must base their foreign policy on a hard-headed and realistic appraisal of national interests and that Americans must be prepared to make the sacrifices necessary to carry through that policy even if it involves war? To answer this question requires an answer to others: How are true national interests to be defined? And by whom shall they be defined? Lewy insists that sentimental moralism is an inappropriate guide to foreign policy making. Does Baritz's description of American attitudes support this argument? Or should one conclude from Baritz's analysis that American efforts to make the world conform to its expectations are arrogant and dangerous?

Pach concludes his discussion of the coverage of the Vietnam War on network television by asking two important questions that readers should consider in the light of his discussion: "Did it matter that the Vietnam War was covered on television? How did TV reporting affect public attitudes toward the war?" Is Pach correct in arguing that the problem was not the nature of the television coverage but rather the kind of war being fought in Vietnam? If so, then, the lesson to be learned would be quite different from that which would conclude that unrestricted television (and, by extension, other media) coverage of the war hurt the nation's war effort. Obviously, limitations on providing information concerning troop movements and similar matters are justified when they would give an enemy information that would reveal military plans and endanger the lives of soldiers. But are similar limitations on the press in its reporting of the behavior and activities of the military also justified on the grounds of protecting the nation's war effort even when some doubt the wisdom of participating in the war?

At issue in the answers to all of these questions are popular participation in policy making and freedom of the press as well as the protection of American interests in the world. The answers are neither simple nor unimportant.

LOREN BARITZ

God's Country and American Know-How

America was involved in Vietnam for thirty years, but never understood the Vietnamese. We were frustrated by the incomprehensible behavior of our Vietnamese enemies and bewildered by the inexplicable behavior of our Vietnamese friends. For us, this corner of Asia was inscrutable. These Asians successfully masked their intentions in smiles, formal courtesies, and exotic rituals. The organic nature of Vietnamese society, the significance of village life, the meaning of ancestors, the relationship of the family to the state, the subordinate role of the individual, and the eternal quest for universal agreement, not consensus or majorities, were easily lost on the Americans.

Most of the Vietnamese were so poor, American GIs said that they lived like animals. Some said they were animals. They did not bathe, had no toilets, and ate food whose smell made some young Americans vomit. There was something about the very great age of Vietnamese culture that seemed to resist our best efforts to understand. There was something about the exhausting heat, the depressing rainy seasons, and the red dust that made even the geography of the place seem out of reach. Most of all, the peasant in his rice paddy, his young son in a pointed hat sitting on a water buffalo, represented what peasants had done forever. They seemed eternal, immune to change. They were not part of our century and not part of our world.

When we did try to impose changes for the better of course, the resistance of the people could seem like ingratitude or stupidity, as it did to a young GI, Steve Harper. The Vietnamese enraged him. "We were there to help but Vietnamese are so stupid they can't understand that a great people want to help a weak people." He said that "somebody had to show poor people better ways of livin', like sewer disposal and sanitation and things like that." He once watched an American team enter a village to teach the peasants sanitation while members of South

---

Vietnam's army stood around laughing because they thought it was a pointless waste of energy. His worst experience was his R&R tour in Tokyo, "the greatest sin city":

I would walk down the Ginza, their main street, and look at all the slant eyes and I swear I'd start to get sick. I was even tempted by some of the prostitutes but one look at their faces and I'd walk away in disgust. . . . I began to get angry at Asians and at my own country. Why couldn't they take care of their own problems?

Americans who were most responsible for our Vietnam policies often complained about how little they knew about the Vietnamese. They mistakenly thought they were especially uninformed about the northerners. For example, General Maxwell Taylor, America's ambassador to Saigon, admitted that "we knew very little about the Hanoi leaders . . . and virtually nothing about their individual or collective intentions."

General Taylor sent a cable to President Johnson that included the western cliché that the Vietnamese were "well aware we place higher value on human life than they do." General Westmoreland also believed that "life is cheap in the Orient." This bigotry was a result of the Americans' ability to use technology to protect our own troops while the North Vietnamese, too poor to match our equipment, were forced to rely on people, their only resource. This did not mean that a Vietnamese parent did not grieve the loss of a child. It meant two other things: Nations fight with whatever they have; and, what we had was not enough to compensate for our cultural ignorance.

Beyond the usual American preference for European culture, manners, and languages, the Far East was, as the cliché has it, "mysterious" to American policymakers. The fact is that Americans were monumentally ignorant of that part of the world where they were attempting to build a nation in our own image. A young man then in the Defense Department, Daniel Ellsberg, admitted this ignorance: "It is fair to say that Americans in office read very few books, and none in French; and that there has never been an official of Deputy Assistant Secretary rank or higher (including myself) who could have passed in office a midterm freshman exam in modern Vietnamese history, if such a course existed in this country." Such a course did not exist.

In the summer of 1970, after twenty-five years of American involvement, Henry Kissinger, then Mr. Nixon's security adviser, met with Dr. Ellsberg in San Clemente. Dr. Kissinger asked for the name of someone who knew "anything" about North Vietnam because "as you know, no one in this government understands North Vietnam." Nine years later, Dr. Kissinger wrote about the opaque strangeness of all of Vietnam. He believed that the land and people of that faraway place were mysterious, beyond the reach of strategic planners and geopolitical policymakers, even beyond the reach of reason:

Psychologists or sociologists may explain some day what it is about that distant monochromatic land, of green mountains and fields merging with an azure sea, that for millennia has acted as a magnet for foreigners who sought glory there

and found frustration, who believed that in its rice fields and jungles some princi-
ple was to be established and entered them only to recede in disillusion. What has
inspired its people to such flights of heroism and monomania that a succession of
outsiders have looked there for a key to some riddle and then to be expelled by a
ferocious persistence that not only thwarted the foreigner's exertions but haz-
arded his own internal balance?

Our difficulties were not with the strangeness of the land or the inscrutabil-
ity of its people. Modern, secular, well-educated people, such as we are, such as
General Taylor and Dr. Kissinger were, can learn about exotic people in distant
places. Our difficulty was not the peculiarities of the Vietnamese. The problem
was us, not them. Our difficulty was that the foot soldier slogging through a rice
paddy, the general in his Saigon office planning great troop movements, the official in the Pentagon, and the Presidents who made the war were all Americans.
Peer de Silva, a CIA chief of station in Saigon, said, "The American official
posted in Asia very often finds himself, whether he realizes it or not, standing
solemnly before the Asians, his finger pointed skyward and the word 'repent' on
his lips." We wanted the Vietnamese to repent for being Vietnamese. There was
something about the condition of being an American that prevented us from understanding the "little people in black pajamas" who beat the strongest military
force in the world.

In common with most Asians, the Vietnamese had one custom that American
soldiers could not tolerate. The people of Vietnam hold hands with their friends.
Two Vietnamese soldiers would walk down the street holding hands. An American marine from south Boston noticed this custom: "They all hold hands, see. I
fucking hated that." The intensity of this marine's reaction was characteristic of
America's fighting men. The custom proved to the GIs that South Vietnamese
men were homosexuals, and this diagnosis explained why the Vietnamese were
incompetent warriors, raising the question about why Americans had to die in
defense of perverts.

A traditional technique for turning American teenagers into soldiers at boot
camp was for the drill sergeants to accuse slackers of being queer. The formula
was that only "real men" could become soldiers, and the military's first job was
to teach youngsters manhood, not soldiering. Relying on deep cultural shame,
the drill instructors shouted, "Ladies attention." The novelist Tim O'Brien described what happened to him during basic training at Fort Lewis. He and a
friend were sitting alone polishing their boots. Their sergeant screamed at them:
"A couple of college pussies . . . Out behind them barracks hiding from everyone
and making some love, huh?" The sergeant stared at them: "You afraid to be in
the war, a goddamn pussy, a goddamn lezzie?" They were given guard duty for
that night, and the sergeant thought he had the perfect punishment: "You two are
gonna walk 'round and 'round the company area, holdin' hands, and you can
talk about politics and nooky all the goddamn night." But "the bastard didn't
have the guts to order us to hold hands."

For American teenagers struggling "to measure up" to the military's definition of manhood, or not struggling because the standard had been earlier ab-

sorbed on the street corners, football fields, or in local bars, the handholding Vietnamese were repulsive and dangerous. If a Vietnamese took the hand or touched the leg of an American grunt, as the foot soldiers were called, the gesture, if unchallenged, would call into question the American's "manhood." In an attempt to deal with this, the marines gave lectures to the men about this custom, saying that all Vietnamese do it. The lecture made things worse because its implicit message was that all Vietnamese were homosexuals. General Westmoreland observed that the hand-holding struck the GIs as "odd and effeminate. . . ."

Americans were ignorant about the Vietnamese not because we were stupid, but because we believe certain things about ourselves. Those things necessarily distorted our vision and confused our minds in ways that made learning extraordinarily difficult. To understand our failure we must think about what it means to be an American.

The necessary text for understanding the condition of being an American is a single sentence written by Herman Melville in his novel *White Jacket:* "And we Americans are the peculiar, chosen people—the Israel of our time; we bear the ark of the liberties of the world." This was not the last time this idea was expressed by Americans. It was at the center of thought of the men who brought us the Vietnam War. It was at the center of the most characteristic American myth.

This oldest and most important myth about America has an unusually specific origin. More than 350 years ago, while in mid-passage between England and the American wilderness, John Winthrop told the band of Puritans he was leading to a new and dangerous life that they were engaged in a voyage that God Himself not only approved, but in which He participated. The precise way that Brother Winthrop expressed himself echoes throughout the history of American life. He explained to his fellow travelers, "We shall find that the God of Israel is among us, when ten of us shall be able to resist a thousand of our enemies, when he shall make us a praise and glory, that men shall say of succeeding plantations [settlements]: the Lord make it like that of New England: for we must Consider that we shall be as a City upon a Hill, the eyes of all people are upon us." The myth of America as a city on a hill implies that America is a moral example to the rest of the world, a world that will presumably keep its attention riveted on us. It means that we are a Chosen People, each of whom, because of God's favor and presence, can smite one hundred of our heathen enemies hip and thigh.

The society Winthrop meant to establish in New England would do God's work, insofar as sinners could. America would become God's country. The Puritans would have understood this to mean that they were creating a nation of, by, and for the Lord. About two centuries later, the pioneers and the farmers who followed the Puritans translated God's country from civilization to the grandeur and nobility of nature, to virgin land, to the purple mountains' majesty. Relocating the country of God from civilization to nature was significant in many ways, but the conclusion that this New World is specially favored by the Lord not only endured but spread.

In countless ways Americans know in their gut—the only place myths can live—that we have been Chosen to lead the world in public morality and to instruct it in political virtue. We believe that our own domestic goodness results in strength adequate to destroy our opponents who, by definition, are enemies of virtue, freedom, and God. Over and over, the founding Puritans described their new settlement as a beacon in the darkness, a light whose radiance could keep Christian voyagers from crashing on the rocks, a light that could brighten the world. In his inaugural address John Kennedy said, "The energy, the faith, the devotion which we bring to this endeavor [defending freedom] will light our country and all who serve it—and the glow from that fire can truly light the world." The city on a hill grew from its first tiny society to encompass the entire nation. As we will see, that is one of the reasons why we compelled ourselves to intervene in Vietnam. . . .

The myth of a city on a hill became the foundation for the ritualistic thinking of later generations of Americans. This myth helped to establish nationalistic orthodoxy in America. It began to set an American dogma, to fix the limits of thought for Americans about themselves and about the rest of the world, and offered a choice about the appropriate relationship between us and them.

The benevolence of our national motives, the absence of material gain in what we seek, the dedication to principle, and our impenetrable ignorance were all related to the original myth of America. It is temptingly easy to dismiss this as some quaint idea that perhaps once had some significance, but lost it in this more sophisticated, tough-minded, modern America. Arthur Schlesinger, Jr., a close aide to President Kennedy, thought otherwise. He was concerned about President Johnson's vastly ambitious plans to create a "Great Society for Asia." Whatever the President meant, according to Professor Schlesinger, such an idea

. . . demands the confrontation of an issue deep in the historical consciousness of the United States: whether this country is a chosen people, uniquely righteous and wise, with a moral mission to all mankind . . . The ultimate choice is between messianism and maturity.

The city myth should have collapsed during the war. The war should have taught us we could not continue to play the role of moral adviser and moral enforcer to the world. After the shock of the assassinations, after the shock of Tet, after President Johnson gave up the presidency, after the riots, demonstrations, burned neighborhoods, and the rebellion of the young, it should have been difficult to sustain John Winthrop's optimism. It was not difficult for Robert Kennedy who, after Senator Eugene McCarthy had demonstrated LBJ's vulnerability in New Hampshire, finally announced that he would run for the presidency himself. The language he used in his announcement speech proved that the myth was as alive and as virulent as it had ever been: "At stake," Senator Kennedy said, "is not simply the leadership of our party, and even our own country, it is our right to the moral leadership of this planet." Members of his staff were horrified that he could use such language because they correctly believed that it reflected just the mind-set that had propelled us into Vietnam in the first place. He ignored their protests. This myth could survive in even the toughest of the contemporary, sophisticated, hard-driving politicians. Of course, he may have used this language only to persuade his listeners, to convince the gullible. But, even so, it showed that he believed that the myth was what they wanted to hear. In either case, the city on a hill continued to work its way.

In some ways American nationalism resembles that of other countries. Between God's Country and Holy Russia there is not much of a choice. Between ideas of moral superiority and racial superiority there is even less of a choice, since one invariably leads to the other. The Middle Kingdom of China, the Sacred Islands of Japan, the Holy Islamic Republic of Iran, all rest in some sense on being Chosen. Israel also knows about this. More secular bases for self-congratulation are nearly ubiquitous: the glory of France, dominion of Britain, power and racial purity of the Third Reich, the satisfaction of thinking of oneself as the "cradle of civilization," as claimed by Egypt, Syria, Greece, and virtually every other ancient country on the face of the earth, along with the *Pax Romana, Pro patria mori,* the willingness to die for one's uniquely favored country, has no national boundary. The longer such a list grows the more trivial it is. National myths become important to the rest of the world only when they are coupled to national power sufficient to impose one nation's will on another. The old Puritans were only interesting, not important, because they were so weak.

A whisper runs throughout our history that the people of the world really want to be like us, regardless of what they or their political leaders say. The evidence that this is true is very powerful. Immigration to this country was the largest movement of people ever. Our entire history is the history of a magnet. However, the slave runners were obliged to use a whip instead of a lure, and so the record is far from consistent. But, since the Civil War, the overwhelming majority of new immigrants came voluntarily. Many were forced to leave their old countries, but almost all chose to come here rather than to go elsewhere. We refused to admit additional millions who wanted to become Americans. For most of this century our standard of living was the world's highest, and Americans ate better, had more leisure, and suffered less political or religious oppression. The Statue of Liberty meant what it said. Its torch lights the way to a better life. Who could deny it?

In fact, almost anyone could. For all the accomplishments of the American nation, its promises so far outstrip its reality as to leave its many victims gasping in disbelief at the betrayal of their dreams. This culture detests poverty and fears the poor. The ladder of economic mobility is a conceit of the many who have climbed it and a reproach to the many who cannot get on it. To defend themselves against their new country, many of the immigrants maintained their own cultures, their own ways of speaking and of doing things, instead of integrating into what Americans in the mainstream of American life call the mainstream of American life.

Everyone naturally prefers their own language, diet, and funeral customs. The ancient Greeks defined a barbarian as one who did not speak Greek. The classical Chinese defined the civilized man as one who spoke Chinese and used chopsticks. Much of the rest of the world would surely like to be richer and more powerful. But an unknown number would not exchange the familiarity of their local horizon, ritual comforts of the family graveyard, or their daily competence for greater material strength. We all prefer who we are and what we know, sometimes at the expense of the chance to make it big. It is an old story to almost everyone, except that American nationalism in its purest form thinks of the world as populated by frustrated or potential Americans. This is unique among the world's nationalisms. Thus, we believe that we can know others reasonably easily because of our assumption that they want to become us.

The great ocean that defended us throughout our history also kept us from knowing others. The less one knows of the world, the more appalling the local customs of others may seem. The other side of that is also true: The less one knows of the world, the more one's own little daily rituals seem to have been decreed either by God or nature. People in other countries have different domestic customs. This may make them seem colorful, and for the most strident nationalists, even stupid or disgusting. For some of us it is hard to imagine that there are people for whom the day of rest, the day when the stores and banks are closed, is Friday, and for others it is Saturday. For some people, belching during a meal is a compliment to the chef. Some people wear white to funerals.

The cultural arrogance that comes from cultural isolation is not, of course, an American monopoly. Many South Vietnamese considered Americans as barbarians. For example, Bruce Lawlor, a CIA case officer in Vietnam during the war, said,

they thought we were animals. A lot of little things that we took for granted offended them fiercely, such as putting your hand on a head. Sitting with your feet crossed, with your foot facing another person, is a high insult.

We seem to think that people who have such strange ideas do not really mean them. We seem to believe that they do such things out of ignorance or poverty. They cannot help it. If they could, they would become more like us. It is apparently beyond reason to believe that anyone would follow these exotic customs for deep cultural reasons, as deep as the reasons that compel us to shake hands instead of bowing.

This way of thinking about the world has a name—solipsism—and means that someone believes that he is the world. In the foreign affairs of the nation, solipsistic thinking—they are us—has been dangerous. The advantage of imposing the imperial American self on the rest of humanity is that it serves as a justification of ignorance.

Solipsism supports American optimism. Because they are thought really to be us, we think that we know what we are doing, know what makes them tick, and know what we can do that will work. In Southeast Asia this optimism proved to be brutal in the sense that American power was believed sufficient to compensate for our ignorance, to make the detailed particularities of Vietnam's otherness beside the point. This combination of solipsism and optimism finally revealed its enabling ignorance. Because we were ignorant, we could proceed. It is a reasonably good guess that had we somehow repressed our solipsism; had we as a result learned something of both North and South Vietnam, we would not have intervened quite so smugly. Our ignorance, in short, permitted us to trust our guns in the first place and to fail in our stated national objectives in the last place.

The myth of the city on a hill combined with solipsism in the assumptions about Vietnam made by the American war planners. In other words, we assumed that we had a superior moral claim to be in Vietnam, and because, despite their quite queer ways of doing things, the Vietnamese shared our values, they would applaud our intentions and embrace our physical presence. Thus, Vice-President Humphrey later acknowledged that all along we had been ignorant of Vietnam. He said that "to LBJ, the Mekong and the Pedernales were not that far apart." Our claim to virtue was based on the often announced purity of our intentions. It was said, perhaps thousands of times, that all we wanted was freedom for other people, not land, not resources, and not domination.

Because we believed that our intentions were virtuous, we could learn nothing from the French experience in Vietnam. After all, they had fought only to maintain their Southeast Asian colonies and as imperialists deserved to lose. We assumed that this was why so mighty a European power lost the important battle of Dien Bien Phu to General Giap's ragged army. America's moral authority was so clear to us that we assumed that it also had to be clear to the Vietnamese. This self-righteousness was the clincher in the debate to intensify the conflict in Vietnam, according to George W. Ball, an undersecretary of state for Presidents Kennedy and Johnson. Washington's war planners, Mr. Ball said in 1973, had been captives of their own myths. Another State Department official also hoped, after the fact, that Americans "will be knocked out of our grandiosity . . . [and] will see the self-righteous, illusory quality of that vision of ourselves offered by the high Washington official who said that while other nations have 'interests' the United States has 'a sense of responsibility.' " Our power, according to this mentality, gives us responsibility, even though we may be reluctant to bear the burden. Other peoples' greed or selfishness gives them interests, even though they may not be strong enough to grab all they want.

Our grandiosity will, however, not be diminished so easily. At least since World War II, America's foreign affairs have been the affairs of Pygmalion. We fall in love with what we create. We create a vision of the world made in what we think is our own image. We are proud of what we create because we are certain that our intentions are pure, our motives good, and our behavior virtuous. We know these things to be true because we believe that we are unique among the nations of the world in our collective idealism. . . .

How was it possible for the Vietnamese to fail to realize that the ideas of Democracy and God are more important than life? American nationalism, especially when its fist clenched, went forward not to pillage, but to instruct. That is what missionaries do. And, therefore, we did not need to bother about learning who it was we were saving. We know, as both JFK and LBJ told us, that the South Vietnamese were uneducated and poor. We believed that this made them susceptible to bad ideas. To stiffen their resistance we undertook a program of "nation-building" that would provide a "stable" government in the South, provide more and better education for the children, and improve the economy. To protect them from their lunatic northern brothers, we would make them a new country. We would invent South Vietnam. They would be delighted, we assumed, because we believed their old country was a mess and was responsible for the ignorance, disease, and illiteracy. They must have hated it all along.

Tangled up in old myths, fearful of speaking plain English on the subject, the political conscience of many Americans must be troubled. There is bad faith in accepting the city myth of American uniqueness as if the myth can be freed from its integral Protestantism, almost always of a fundamentalist flavor. Conservatives have less need to launder the myth of its religion. Because liberals require a secular version of nationalism, and if they need or want to retain some sense of the unique republic, they are required to rest their case on a secular basis. Wilsonian idealism was the answer in the 1960s, as liberals argued that America was the only society capable of creating social justice and genuine democracy at home and abroad. These ideals merged with the cold war and persuaded the best of American liberals to bring us Vietnam.

In America, as elsewhere, elected officials are especially susceptible to the fundamental myths of nationalism because they must embody them to get elected and act on them to govern. The vision of the world that suffused Mr. Wilson's Fourteen Points and League of Nations was also the vision of John Kennedy and his circle. They were pained by the knowledge that a people anywhere in the world struggled toward freedom but was frustrated by the imposition of force. So it was that John F. Kennedy's inspired inaugural address carried the burden of Woodrow Wilson's idealism, and also carried the deadly implication that America was again ready for war in the name of goodness.

President Kennedy's language must be understood in the light of what was just around the corner in Vietnam. He announced to the world, "We shall pay any price, bear any burden, meet any hardship, support any friend, oppose any foe to assure the survival and the success of liberty." He said that it was the rare destiny of his generation to defend freedom when it was at its greatest risk. "I do not shrink from this responsibility—I welcome it."

The difference between the two sons of the Commonwealth of Massachusetts, John Quincy Adams and John Fitzgerald Kennedy, was the difference between good wishes and war, but also the difference between a tiny and isolated America and the world's most powerful nation. Presidents Wilson and Kennedy both fairly represented American liberalism at its most restless and energetic. This was a liberalism that wanted, as President Wilson put it, to make the world safe for democracy, or as President Kennedy said, to defend "those human rights to which this nation has always been committed, and to which we are committed today at home and around the world." JFK described this as "God's work."

An important part of the reason we marched into Vietnam with our eyes fixed was liberalism's irrepressible need to be helpful to those less fortunate. But the decency of the impulse, as was the case with President Wilson, cannot hide the bloody eagerness to kill in the name of virtue. In 1981, James C. Thomson, an aide in the State Department and a member of the National Security Council under President Johnson, finally concluded that our Vietnamese intervention had been motivated by a national missionary impulse, a "need to do good to others." In a phrase that cannot be improved, he and others called this "sentimental imperialism." The purity of intention and the horror of result is unfortunately the liberal's continuing burden.

American conservatives had it easier, largely because they believed in the actuality of evil. In his first public statement, President Eisenhower informed the American public, "The forces of good and evil are massed and armed and opposed as rarely before in history." For him the world struggle was not merely between conflicting ideologies. "Freedom is pitted against slavery; lightness against the dark."

Conservatives in America are closer than liberals to the myth of the city on a hill because they are not embarrassed by public professions of religion. They are therefore somewhat less likely to ascribe American values and behavior to other cultures. This is so because of the conservatives' conviction that America is so much better—more moral, godly, wise, and especially rich—than other nations that they could not possibly resemble us. Thus, President Eisenhower announced that one of America's fixed principles was the refusal to "use our strength to try to impress upon another people our own cherished political and economic institutions." The idea of uniqueness means, after all, that we are alone in the world.

Conservatives shared with liberals the conviction that America could act, and in Vietnam did act, with absolute altruism, as they believed only America could. Thinking of this war, President Nixon, another restless descendent of Mr. Wilson, declared that "never in history have men fought for less selfish motives—not for conquest, not for glory, but only for the right of a people far away to choose the kind of government they want." This was especially attractive because in this case the kind of government presumably sought by this faraway people was opposed to Communism, our own enemy. It was therefore an integral part of the universal struggle between freedom and slavery, lightness and dark. As a result it was relatively easy for conservatives to think of Vietnam as a laboratory to test ways to block the spreading stain of political atheism.

Power is sometimes a problem for liberals and a solution for conservatives. When Senator Goldwater rattled America's many sabers in his presidential campaign of 1964, and when General Curtis LeMay wanted to bomb North Vietnam "back to the stone age," they both made liberals cringe, partly from embarrassment, and partly because the liberals were appalled at the apparent cruelty. In the 1950s, Dr. Kissinger cleverly argued that the liberal embarrassment over power made its use, when necessary, even worse than it had to be. "Our feeling of guilt with respect to power," he wrote, "has caused us to transform all wars into crusades, and then to apply our power in the most absolute ways." Later, when he ran America's foreign policy, his own unambivalent endorsement of the use in Vietnam of enormous power inevitably raised the question of whether bloody crusades are caused only by the squeamishness of liberals or also by the callousness of conservatives.

Implicit in John Winthrop's formulation of the city myth was the idea that the new Americans could, because of their godliness, vanquish their numerically superior enemies. The idea that warriors, because of their virtue, could beat stronger opponents, is very ancient. Pericles spoke of it in his funeral oration to the Athenians. The Christian crusaders counted on it. *Jihad,* Islam's conception of a holy war, is based on it. The Samurai believed it. So did the Nazis.

In time, the history of America proved to Americans that we were militarily invincible. The Vietnam War Presidents naturally cringed at the thought that they could be the first to lose a war. After all, we had already beaten Indians, French, British (twice), Mexicans, Spaniards, Germans (twice), Italians, Japanese, Koreans, and Chinese. Until World War II, the nation necessarily had to rely on the presumed virtue, not the power, of American soldiers to carry the day, and the war. This was also the case in the South during our Civil War.

Starting in the eighteenth century, the nation of farmers began to industrialize. As the outcome of war increasingly came to depend on the ability to inject various forms of flying hardware into the enemy's body, victory increasingly depended on technology. The acceleration of industrialization in the late nineteenth century inevitably quickened the pace of technological evolution. By then no other power could match the American's ability to get organized, to commit resources to development, and to invent the gadgets that efficiently produced money in the marketplace, and, when necessary, death on the battlefield. The idea of Yankee ingenuity, American know-how, stretches back beyond the nineteenth century. Our admiration for the tinkerer whose new widget forms the basis of new industry is nowhere better shown than in our national reverence of Thomas Edison.

Joining the American sense of its moral superiority with its technological superiority was a marriage made in heaven, at least for American nationalists. We told ourselves that each advantage explained the other, that the success of our standard of living was a result of our virtue, and our virtue was a result of our wealth. Our riches, our technology, provided the strength that had earlier been missing, that once had forced us to rely only on our virtue. Now, as Hiroshima demonstrated conclusively, we could think of ourselves not only as morally superior, but as the most powerful nation in history. The inevitable offspring of this marriage of an idea with a weapon was the conviction that the United States could not be beaten in war—not by any nation, and not by any combination of nations. For that moment we thought that we could fight where, when, and how we wished, without risking failure. For that moment we thought that we could impose our will on the recalcitrant of the earth.

A great many Americans, in the period just before the war in Vietnam got hot, shared a circular belief that for most was probably not very well formed: America's technological supremacy was a symptom of its uniqueness, and technology made the nation militarily invincible. In 1983, the playwright Arthur Miller said, "I'm an American. I believe in technology. Until the mid-60s I never believed we could lose because we had technology."

The memory of World War II concluding in a mushroom cloud was relatively fresh throughout the 1950s. It was unthinkable that America's military could ever fail to establish its supremacy on the battlefield, that the industrial, scientific, and technological strength of the nation would ever be insufficient for the purposes of war. It was almost as if Americans were technology. The American love affair with the automobile was at its most passionate in the 1950s, our well-equipped armies stopped the Chinese in Korea, for a moment our nuclear supremacy was taken for granted, and affluence for many white Americans seemed to be settling in as a way of life.

It is, of course, unfortunate that the forces of evil may be as strong as the forces of virtue. The Soviet Union exploded its first atomic bomb way ahead of what Americans thought was a likely schedule. This technology is not like others because even a weak bomb is devastating. Even if our bombs are better than theirs, they can still do us in. America's freedom of action after 1949 was not complete. President Eisenhower and John Foster Dulles, the Secretary of State, threatened "massive retaliation" against the Soviet Union if it stepped over the line. They knew, and we knew, that this threat was not entirely real, and that it freed the Soviets to engage in peripheral adventures because they correctly believed that we would not destroy the world over Korea, Berlin, Hungary, or Czechoslovakia.

Our policy had to become more flexible. We had to invent a theory that would allow us to fight on the edges without nuclear technology. This theory is called "limited war." Its premise is that we and the Soviets can wage little wars, and that each side will refrain from provoking the other to unlock the nuclear armory.

Ike threatened the Chinese, who at the time did not have the bomb, with nuclear war in Korea. JFK similarly threatened the Soviets, who had nuclear capability, over Cuba. But, although some military men thought about using nuclear weapons in Vietnam, the fundamental assumption of that war was to keep it limited, not to force either the Soviets or the Chinese, who now had their own sloppy bombs, to enter the war. Thus, we could impose our will on the recalcitrant of the earth if they did not have their own nuclear weapons, and if they could not compel the Soviets or the Chinese to force us to quit.

In Vietnam we had to find a technology to win without broadening the war. The nuclear stalemate reemphasized our need to find a more limited ground, to find, so to speak, a way to fight a domesticated war. We had to find a technology that would prevail locally, but not explode internationally. No assignment is too tough for the technological mentality. In fact, it was made to order for the technicians who were coming into their own throughout all of American life. This war gave them the opportunity to show what they could do. This was to be history's most technologically sophisticated war, most carefully analyzed and managed, using all of the latest wonders of managerial procedures and systems. It was made to order for bureaucracy.

James C. Thomson, who served both JFK and LBJ as an East Asia specialist, understood how the myths converged. He wrote of *"the rise of a new breed of American ideologues who see Vietnam as the ultimate test of their doctrine."* These new men were the new missionaries and had a trinitarian faith: in military power, technological superiority, and our altruistic idealism. They believed that the reality of American culture "provides us with the opportunity and obligation to ease the nations of the earth toward modernization and stability: toward a full-fledged *Pax Americana Technocratica*." For these parishioners in the church of the machine, Vietnam was the ideal laboratory.

One major by-product of technology is faith in technology. For example, after an enormously bright group of computer-science graduate students recently tried to explain their research to me, I asked them to tell me about the limits of computers. Several responded at the same time: "What limits?" Their excitement and certainty are almost contagious. They are obviously participating in a great intellectual adventure that they believe will have beneficial results. They can develop appropriate algorithms to "disaggregate" sloppy questions, produce probabilities for various "options," and create endless "scenarios" for assorted tactical contingencies. It is easy to understand the imperial technological optimism of the young initiates who are being introduced to the new mysteries.

The technological view of the world is broader than the application of science to industrial and informational procedures. At its root it is an attitude about the nature of reality. At a dinner with a group of sophisticated engineers I was told that "if it doesn't have a solution it isn't a problem." According to my dinner partners, if there is no solution to what is needed or wanted, the problem was either badly stated or was not a "real" problem in the first place. One computer engineer explained that unreal problems are usually invented by woolly-minded politicians or out-of-focus humanists. Another explained that technology now rules the entire world, and he said it with the quiet certainty of a fact so firmly established that it was not worth discussing.

These attitudes focus many of the tendencies within technology that have been there all along. The technological mentality designs standardized means to achieve predetermined results. It does this when it designs machinery, but the process is also applied to finding out what products the public will buy, to advertising and other forms of propaganda, to the organization of business and governmental agencies, and to the tactics appropriate to a particular war. This way of thinking has, in short, become characteristic of all advanced industrial societies. What distinguishes these societies from others is their acceptance of standardized procedures. In a technological society authority is located in the process itself. In a more traditional society, such as Vietnam, authority is always vested in a person who may grant a favor, bend a rule, and get something done.

Spontaneity and eccentricity are the enemies of technology. It demands methods that are foolproof, that even a fool cannot disrupt. It has no praise to give to folly. It is impatient with intuition, experience, and judgment. It has an irresistible tilt toward mathematical conclusions. Technology demands rationality in place of individuality. It is immune to charm. It is sober, tireless, and irresistible. It can be slowed but not stopped by external forces.

When the technological mind is turned to the problems of organizing human activity, the result is bureaucracy. This means that an office is created with a predefined function and then a person is sought who meets the specifications of the office. Standardization, technology, never rely on the talents or inspiration of officeholders for solutions. The result, again in its purest form, is impersonality, procedures rather than on-the-spot intelligence, authoritative regulations, not people with authority. Legitimacy resides in the office, not the officer.

Bureaucracy is democratic. It is a way to stifle autocracy by the imposition of a previously accepted and impersonal system. The goal is to achieve the predefined objectives of the organization with the least amount of energy and money. The offices were designed with that goal in mind. It never works that way.

Although efficiency is a means, not an end, there is an overwhelming likelihood that bureaucracies will sooner or later, usually sooner, confuse means and ends, or will simply lose sight of the organization's objectives in the continuous search for higher levels of efficiency. A French sociologist explained: "Our civilization is first and foremost a civilization of means: in the reality of modern life, the means, it would seem, are more important than the ends. Any other assessment of the situation is mere idealism." This is the case whether the technological mind has produced a machine—a tool, a means—or an organization—another tool or means. Both a helicopter gunship and the Department of Defense are means to an end. America's enormous technology is marvelously adept at making the tool, and is incompetent at providing the purpose.

The national purpose is supplied by the myth of the city on a hill, technology provides the tools, and bureaucracy provides the procedures. The city myth is, however, soft-minded, while technology is hard-headed. The first is mushy while the second is tough, "realistic," and more often than not can actually deliver on its tactical assignments. It is more difficult to be specific and concrete about the "city" than about the technological means for either its defense or expansion. But it therefore follows that it is much more difficult to attack the city myth. It lies beneath the surface, more in the bloodstream than in the mind, in the national atmosphere rather than in specific policies. The city myth is unassailable while the technological mentality is irresistible. . . .

American culture values performance. Performance means the ability to "deliver the goods." Technology always delivers, and functions as it was designed to do. When it creates problems the fault is with the operators, what the airlines call pilot error and computer specialists call user error. Of course the military understands that technology performs. It has the time and facilities to train its people in the care and use of new machines, as well as new technological systems of organization and communication. In its dependence on technology the military is reflecting wider cultural values.

The traditional American male, as John Wayne personified him in scores of movies, performs, delivers the goods, is a loner, has the equipment, usually a six-shooter or a superior rifle, to beat the bad guys, and he knows what he is doing. He does not need to depend on others because he can perform, can deliver, and can bring home the bacon. He is also very good.

It is astonishing how often American GIs in Vietnam approvingly referred to John Wayne, not as a movie star, but as a model and a standard. Everyone in Vietnam called dangerous areas Indian country. Paraphrasing a bit of Americana, some GIs painted on their flak jackets THE ONLY GOOD GOOK IS A DEAD ONE. They called their Vietnamese scouts who defected from the Communists Kit Carsons. These nineteen-year-old Americans, brought up on World War II movies and westerns, walking through the jungle, armed to the teeth, searching for an invisible enemy who knew the wilderness better than they did, could hardly miss these connections. One after another said, at some point, something like, "Hey, this is just like a movie." What they lacked in cartoon bravery, they made up in technology. Their deadly machines transformed at least some of them from boys into warriors, into dominating men, not "fags" like the South Vietnamese. . . .

We had to find a technology to win in Vietnam because of our delusion that machinery allows us to fight a clean war, using tools instead of men, and the more complex and sophisticated the better. We thought we could bomb them into their senses with only limited human costs to ourselves. We seemed to believe that the mammoth federal hardware store would always stock just the right gadget to kill them and save us. It also permitted us not to get our hands too dirty. The B-52 crew never saw the results of pushing that button. The artillery squad's job was to get the numbers of the coordinates right and push the button. Only the grunts, the walking warriors, had to look death in the face. And they, despite the American faith in our mighty machinery, determined the outcome. Everyone knew this except the air force, the navy, and the men who plan our wars.

In summary, our national myth showed us that we were good, our technology made us strong, and our bureaucracy gave us standard operating procedures. It was not a winning combination.

The Legacy of Vietnam

The American Stake in Vietnam

There can be little doubt that the four presidents dealing with the increasingly intractable Vietnam problem would have acted differently had they been able to foresee what the eventual costs of U.S. intervention would be—in terms of American lives, financial costs and domestic and foreign political repercussions. But what about the original assessment of the importance of Vietnam? Did Vietnam and Southeast Asia represent a vital interest to the United States?

"History is lived forward," the English author C. V. Wedgewood has written, "but it is written in retrospect. We know the end before we consider the beginning and we can never wholly recapture what it was like to know the beginning only." Living in today's world with its bitter conflict between the Soviet Union and China, it is difficult to understand the political atmosphere of the time when the communist bloc was indeed a monolith. During the years following the end of World War II the fear of communism was not an irrational obsession, for the Soviet Union, having absorbed Eastern Europe and even Czechoslovakia in the very center of the continent, did constitute an expansionist force in a highly unstable world. A communist victory anywhere therefore appeared to threaten the U.S. because it represented a further extension of Soviet power. Communist Russia at that time cast a menacing shadow over Western Europe, the American army in Korea had been fought to a standstill and Mao's cry after the launching of the Russian Sputnik in 1957 that "The East Wind is prevailing over the West Wind" reflected the conviction of many that communism represented the wave of the future. The commitment of the U.S. to the independence of South Vietnam was part of the attempt to halt these reserves. Together with American promises to defend Berlin in the grip of a Russian blockade and the show of force in response to the placement of Russian missiles in Cuba in 1962, the decision of the

---

Kennedy administration to prevent the loss of Indochina was meant to demonstrate U.S. resolve and thus discourage Soviet pressures in other areas.

The American endeavor during those years to contain Communist China was similarly not the result of an ideological crusade against communism but was primarily a response to China's attempt to change the status quo in Asia by force. The signing of the Sino-Soviet alliance in 1950 provided a boost to communist revolutionaries throughout Asia, and China appeared to be the cutting edge of Soviet influence in that continent. "China was big, an advocate of revolutionary violence, bellicose and anti-American in its propaganda," recalls the former director of the State Department's Office of Chinese Affairs at the time. "True, after Korea the Chinese were cautious about using their forces outside Chinese territory, but they flexed their military muscles often enough—against the offshore islands in 1954 and 1958, on the Indian border in 1962, and with nuclear explosions from 1964 on—to remind the United States of their latent military power." During World War II the U.S. had fought to prevent the control of continental Asia and the islands of the Pacific by Japan. The Moscow-Peking axis now once again threatened the domination of Asia by a single power. Preventing the balance of power in Asia from being upset in this manner, it was believed, required the maintenance of independent states in South and Southeast Asia.

The Sino-Indian clash of 1962, argued Sen. Mike Mansfield in February 1963 after his return from the area, "makes clear that it is now necessary for the southeast Asian nations to reckon with the enlargement of the Chinese role at any time to include the use of military power in a full modern revival of the classic pattern of Chinese imperial techniques in southeast Asia." Any sudden U.S. withdrawal from this area, therefore, "would open the region to upheaval and chaos." A communist victory in Vietnam, achieved with Chinese help, would enhance Chinese power and prestige in Asia and vindicate the Chinese revolutionary strategy. When Hans J. Morgenthau argued in 1965 that the U.S. should abandon the military containment of China and that "we must learn to accommodate ourselves to the predominance of China on the Asian mainland," he was answered by Arthur M. Schlesinger, Jr., that such an alleged geopolitical necessity was no more persuasive in Asia than it had been with regard to the German domination of Europe in the 1930s. "Asia is a very large continent. It has a diversity of cultures, traditions, states, and so on. Nations like their independence in Asia just as much as they do in other parts of the world. To assume that some mystic inevitability has decreed that they are all to be swallowed up in the Chinese empire is not convincing."

Australia and New Zealand, and especially the leaders of Southeast Asia, encouraged the U.S. in the view that a loss of Vietnam would quickly lead to the unraveling of the entire region and that the U.S. stand in Vietnam therefore was crucial to their survival as independent states. The removal of the presence of the U.S. from the region, maintained the Cambodian head of state, Prince Sihanouk, in June 1965, would lead to the victory of communism. Malaysia fully supported U.S. actions in Vietnam, declared Prime Minister Abdul Rahman in the summer of 1965: "In our view it is imperative that the United States does not retire from the scene." The leaders of Singapore and Thailand concurred in this appraisal of the situation. As a result of the broadened American commitment in Vietnam and China's failure to respond to the bombing of North Vietnam, reported Seymour Topping of the *New York Times* in January 1966, the Chinese dragon was considerably deflated. And Tom Wicker, writing from Bangkok in February 1967, noted that the actions of the Johnson administration in Vietnam had provided new confidence in an American umbrella of protection over Asia and enhanced the stability of Southeast Asia. Even Asian leaders publicly critical of U.S. policy in Southeast Asia privately encouraged America to remain in Vietnam; their ranks included Prime Minister Indira Gandhi of India, who told Vice President Humphrey in February 1966 that the continued U.S. presence in Vietnam was important to India.

The fears of the leaders of Southeast Asia that a communist victory in Vietnam would have grave consequences for their own security did not, however, constitute adequate evidence that these repercussions would indeed occur and thus establish the correctness of the domino theory. Still less did it prove that the loss of Southeast Asia would jeopardize essential American interests. Policy-makers often find it convenient to justify important decisions in foreign policy in terms of vital interests affecting the security of their country, yet neither national security nor the national interest represents a fixed point of reference or provides a ready guide for action. Decision-makers see the national interest through the fallible spectacles of their subjective judgment; in making determinations of threats, dangers and interests they are liable to make mistakes such as being unduly influenced by "worst case" calculations or ideological preconceptions. The assessment of the geopolitical importance of Vietnam and Southeast Asia by American leaders from 1950 on was an example of such misjudgment.

American policy-makers were probably justified in fearing the domination of Asia by a single power. Yet only Japan, with its immense physical and industrial resources, was of sufficient economic importance to upset the balance of power in Asia. The facilities and skills of the Japanese added to the economy of Communist China could have constituted a direct threat to U.S. security. However, the assumption that a communist domination of Southeast Asia would force Japan into an accommodation with China was one of the arguments made by American policy-makers that was far from self-evident. Failure of the U.S. to react to a military conquest of Southeast Asia by the Soviet Union or China was bound to damage Japan's confidence in the worth of American commitments to its defense. But the triumph of Chinese-backed insurgencies was not necessarily going to endanger the U.S.-Japan alliance. The importance of Southeast Asia for Japan's trade was also less than vital. In 1969, for example, Japan's imports from the area were about 9 percent of all Japanese imports; exports to Southeast Asia were 15 percent of all exports. Moreover, a communist Southeast Asia was not necessarily going to stop trading with Japan.

The crucial strategic and economic importance of Indochina and Southeast Asia to the noncommunist world was similarly more an endlessly repeated article of faith than a proven fact. The military occupation of Indochina by Japan in World War II was held to have demonstrated the strategic significance of the region, sitting astride the passageway between the Indian and Pacific oceans. The Strait of Malacca, it was pointed out, was Japan's lifeline for its oil imports from the Middle East. But Japan lost in World War II even though it controlled all of Southeast Asia; a closing of the Malacca strait, forcing the use of detours further east, was bound to create an economic burden but would not cripple the Japanese economy. The commodities produced by the area, such as rubber, tin and coconut oil, though important, similarly were not irreplaceable.

Some members of the New Left shared the belief in the economic importance of Vietnam. Private investment opportunities, both immediate and projected, stated one such writer in 1973, "positively affected the U.S. government's continued military commitment to a succession of Saigon regimes from 1954 to the present." But the evidence for this thesis is hardly convincing. U.S. investments in Vietnam have always been a tiny and insignificant fraction of total American investments overseas. By 1969 South Vietnam accounted for less than one percent of American exports. The stock market showed itself to be an accurate barometer of the drain which the Vietnam war caused the American economy; after 1967 the market reflected the desire of the American financial community to see the conflict brought to a speedy conclusion. Each time either side engaged in some conciliatory step the stocks responded with rising prices. By 1970 the war, with all its ramifications, had turned into a near-disaster for the American economy, a disaster for which even the discovery of potential oil off the shores of South Vietnam that same year could not compensate. Needless to say, this discovery in 1970 can hardly explain decisions taken in the previous 20 years.

American policy-makers not only exaggerated the geopolitical importance of Vietnam and Southeast Asia, thus making the consequences of failure far more critical than the facts warranted, but, more importantly, their decisions were overtaken by important changes in the character of world communism, which gradually undermined the premises on which U.S. policy in Southeast Asia was based. By the mid-1960s, Russia and China were no longer close allies but open enemies. The world communist movement no longer represented a monolith, and the addition of a new communist state did not necessarily contribute to the power of America's adversaries. The Sino-Soviet split created a new balance of power in Asia in which China, constrained by Russian pressure on its northern borders, no longer was an aggressive force exporting revolution. In 1971 China entered the United Nations and an accommodation took place with the United States: Chinese foreign policy now was oriented toward finding allies and creating counterbalances to the Soviet Union. This shift in big-power relationships coincided with the cultural revolution in China, which meant a further turning inward. The model for rapid economic growth in Asia was no longer communism but Japan's capitalist economy. Communism had ceased to be the wave of the future.

But before these changes in the Asian balance of power had fully manifested themselves, American commitment in Vietnam had become solidified with the introduction of ground combat forces in 1965. Both the Communists and the U.S. made the outcome of the struggle in Vietnam a test of strength and prestige. North Vietnam's Defense Minister Giap declared in July 1964 that "South Vietnam is the vanguard fighter of the national liberation movement in the present era . . . and the failure of the special war unleashed by the U.S. imperialists in South Vietnam would mean that this war can be defeated anywhere in the world." China's Marshal Lin Piao, in a much-publicized article in September 1965, called revolutionary warfare the method of encircling the developed capitalist countries; he predicted that the defeat of U.S. imperialism in Vietnam would show the people of the world "that what the Vietnamese people can do, they can do too."

Not surprisingly these bellicose claims stiffened the back of the U.S. and strengthened the argument that America could not afford to lose in Vietnam. A communist success in South Vietnam, declared McNamara in August 1965,

would be taken as positive proof that the Chinese Communists' position is correct and they will have made a giant step forward in their efforts to seize control of the world Communist movement. . . . In that event we would then have to be prepared to cope with the same kind of aggression in other parts of the world wherever the existing governments are weak and the social structure fragmented. If Communist armed aggression is not stopped in Viet-Nam as it was in Korea, the confidence of small nations in America's pledge of support will be weakened, and many of them, in widely separated areas of the world, will feel unsafe. Thus the stakes in South Viet-Nam are far greater than the loss of one small country to communism.

After three American presidents had declared that the independence of South Vietnam represented a vital interest of the U.S., it could with much justice be said that the American commitment had in fact created a vital interest, for the prestige and credibility of a major world power cannot be dismissed as unimportant. By early 1966 the U.S. had over 200,000 military personnel in Vietnam; American involvement in the war was a fact that could not be wished away. Vietnam was not a region of major military and industrial importance, the veteran diplomat George F. Kennan explained to the Senate Foreign Relations Committee in February 1966, but American prestige was now irrevocably engaged. "A precipitate and disorderly withdrawal could represent in present circumstances a disservice to our own interests, and even to world peace, greater than any that might have been involved by our failure to engage ourselves there in the first place." Protecting the nation's prestige in such a situation meant not the enhancement of national glory or grandeur but the preservation of the nation's ability to influence events and pursue American interests without the use of force.

A smaller nation like France could withdraw from Indochina and North Africa without a serious loss of prestige, argued George W. Ball, a critic of U.S. policy in Vietnam, in 1968. "But the authority of the United States in world affairs depends, in considerable part, on the confidence of other nations that we can accomplish whatever we undertake." There had been a failure to analyze adequately the importance of Vietnam to America's national interests, Henry Kissinger suggested in early 1969. "But the commitment of five hundred thousand Americans has settled the issue of the importance of Vietnam. For what is involved now is confidence in American promises. However fashionable it is to ridicule the terms 'credibility' or 'prestige' they are not empty phrases; other nations can gear their actions to ours only if they can count on our steadiness." In agreement with Kissinger's position, the orderly disengagement of America from the defense of South Vietnam became the cornerstone of U.S. policy in Southeast Asia under the Nixon administration.

The validity of the belief of both the Johnson and Nixon administrations that the loss of Vietnam would have worldwide repercussions and that, at the very least, it was important to liquidate the American commitment in Vietnam without a humiliating defeat was put to the test in 1975. The full consequences of the collapse of South Vietnam will not be apparent for some time to come, but enough is known to show that this outcome represents not only a tragedy for millions of South Vietnamese but also an important defeat for the United States. Hanoi's victory inevitably came to be seen as a victory for Hanoi's major allies and supporters. Moreover, the long-drawn-out conflict, culminating in failure to achieve American objectives, has had bruising and traumatic effects on American attitudes toward world affairs in general.

The Impact of the Vietnam Debacle

While the Vietnam war was still in progress it was part of the conventional wisdom to ridicule the domino theory, though some of those who today talk about the foolishness of this metaphor and the dire consequences of American belief in the theory at the time saw in it considerable validity. The domino theory, wrote Tom Wicker in February 1967, had much truth, and a communist victory in Vietnam through internal subversion assisted by a neighboring nation "would greatly encourage the use of the same technique for attempted conquest elsewhere in the world." The real and deeper meaning of the domino theory has always been the idea that a communist victory in Vietnam and a demonstration of American failure to prevent such a triumph would have repercussions elsewhere, especially in Southeast Asia, and events since 1975 bear out this prediction. We find an overall weakening of faith in the worth of American commitments and, on the part of the nations of Southeast Asia, attempts to appease the victorious communist powers. The American intervention in Vietnam probably bought time for these countries to improve their own political and social institutions and thus left them in a stronger position to resist external or internal communist pressures. They have also benefited from the competition of Russia and China for influence in the area and from the re-emergence of the historic animosities between the former allies Vietnam and Cambodia. Still, spirits in the region today are reported to be low.

The consequences of the communist victories in Southeast Asia manifested themselves quickly. The fall of the Cambodian capital of Phnom Penh on 17 April 1975 further demoralized the South Vietnamese army, already fighting a losing battle, and the communist victory in Vietnam was soon followed by a communist takeover in Laos. Communist leadership in Laos was always dominated by ethnic Vietnamese, and the country today appears to be under complete Vietnamese control. The Thais, as was to be expected, asked U.S. troops to leave their country, and they now seek their security in a position of neutrality. The government of the Philippines asked for a review of the future status of U.S. bases in that country, and President Ferdinand E. Marcos declared shortly after the fall of Saigon: "The United States must understand we cannot wait until events overtake us. We reserve the right to make our accommodations with the emerging realities in Asia." Even before the guns had fallen silent in South Vietnam, Foreign Minister Adam Malik of Indonesia, a rigidly anticommunist country ever since the bloody suppression of its own communist movement in 1965, predicted that Indonesia would be able to cooperate with the communist regimes in Indochina. The Saigon government, Malik told a *New York Times* correspondent on 26 March 1975, expected too much of the Americans, but others would not make that mistake. "You always tell us, 'My Seventh Fleet is here,' but if there's trouble, nothing happens."

Back in 1964, Assistant Secretary of Defense John T. McNaughton expressed the hope that if South Vietnam ever disintegrated it would be possible to leave the image of "a patient who died despite the extraordinary efforts of a good doctor." But many of America's allies, in and outside Southeast Asia, are not convinced that the U.S. made "extraordinary efforts" on behalf of its "patient." To the contrary, South Korea and Israel in particular are now concerned about the reliability of the American commitment to their defense. Congressional inaction on Indochina in the face of the North Vietnamese onslaught in the spring of 1975 has raised for them disturbing questions about a similar future congressional reaction on aid to their beleaguered countries and about the value of an American guarantee.

In the wake of the trauma of Vietnam, America is in the grip of a "No more Vietnams" psychology which stands in sharp contrast to the spirit of active involvement in global affairs prevailing in the years following World War II; this fear of becoming entangled has led to a decline in the political influence of the United States. There is no reason to assume that the weakening of America's will to act will make for a better and more peaceful world. Discussing the dangers created by the spread of nuclear weapons, a State Department official pointed out on 30 June 1977 that American "security guarantees, where we are able to make them credible in this post-Vietnam era of public attitudes, are some of the most important instruments of our nonproliferation policy." One of the consequences of the current mood of isolationism appears to be diminished confidence abroad in the security provided by the American defense umbrella, which in turn may encourage nuclear proliferation. The greater the number of states possessing nuclear weapons, the greater, of course, the chances of a nuclear conflict.

The tragic and unsuccessful involvement in Vietnam should teach America lessons on how to prevent a repetition of such a disaster, but overreaction is probably as bad as a refusal to understand and learn the correct lessons. Mark Twain told the story of the cat who, after burning herself on a hot stove lid, never again sat on any stove—hot or cold—and he warned against getting out of an experience more wisdom than was in it. An acceptance of the simplistic slogan "No more Vietnams" not only may encourage international disorder, but could mean abandoning basic American values. As John Stuart Mill pointed out more than 100 years ago, "The doctrine of non-intervention, to be a legitimate principle of morality, must be accepted by all governments. The despots must consent to be bound by it as well as the free States. Unless they do, the profession of it by free countries comes but to this miserable issue, that the wrong side may help the wrong, but the right must not help the right." It is well to remember that the non-intervention of the Western democracies in the Spanish Civil War of 1936–39 represented a crucial factor intervening in favor of Franco's victory and helped prepare the way for World War II. America cannot and should not be the world's policeman, but, it can be argued, the U.S. has a moral obligation to support nations in their endeavor to remain independent when we, and we alone, possess the means to do so. "A wealthy man who watches a poor neighbor starve to death cannot disclaim responsibility for the event; a powerful man who watches a weak neighbor being beaten to death cannot avoid being accused (if only through self-accusation) of culpability." As the case of Spain in the 1930s demonstrates, the fulfillment of the moral obligation to intervene in defense of freedom and independence at times may also coincide with prudential long-term national interests.

The original decision to intervene in South Vietnam probably was based on a misreading of the national interest, but it was not wrong because the government of South Vietnam was not truly democratic. To insist that we support or ally ourselves with only governments whose conduct we approve is another fallacious lesson of the Vietnam tragedy. The shortcomings of the Diem and Thieu regimes—and they were many—did not prove that the U.S. should not help South Vietnam and that communist North Vietnam deserved to win. The Western democracies were right in regarding Mussolini's attack on Ethiopia in 1935 as an act of flagrant aggression even though Ethiopia was ruled by an autocratic emperor and was a backward and dismal country—with slavery to boot. America was right to ally itself in World War II with the Soviet Union even though Russia's paranoid dictator had murdered millions of innocent citizens and kept other millions in slave-labor camps. Our own self-respect and regard for the principles for which this country stands should dictate caution in the support of nondemocratic, let alone truly oppressive regimes, but moral considerations alone should not and cannot be the decisive standard for our foreign alliances.

The current moralizing about covert operations represents another overreaction to Vietnam. There are times when for various reasons a nation must undertake actions that cannot be publicly divulged, and it may even be necessary in some cases to violate norms of international law. It is curious, the theologian Paul Ramsey correctly notes, that many of those favoring civil disobedience and even direct action in the internal life of the nation "can see no warrant for ever going beyond the law in international affairs where the legalities are far more imperfect and where the social due process for significantly changing the legal system is even more wanting."

The preservation of the country, the national interest, and national security are standards of conduct which an unprincipled leader can abuse and distort, but their pre-eminence in the conduct of foreign policy should not on that account be questioned or rejected. National leaders who habitually practice concealment and evasion will erode the trust of their people. President Nixon, in particular, at times carried secrecy to excess and therefore eventually laid himself open to the charge of having created an "imperial presidency." Indeed, even in international politics a reputation for probity carries its own pragmatic rewards. But in the final analysis the statesman cannot be a saint, and the requirements of power and national survival in a world without government will dictate moral compromises.

Could the United States Have Won in Vietnam?

One can begin to answer this difficult question by pointing to certain mistakes made by American leaders in holding together the home front, though this task for reasons to be discussed below, would probably have presented almost insuperable difficulties even to the most adroit leadership. There was the failure, especially on the part of the Johnson administration, to provide a convincing explanation and justification of the American involvement. Simplistic rhetoric like, "fighting for democracy in Vietnam" or halting "communist aggression," though not without some element of truth, was inappropriate to the complex situation faced in Southeast Asia; it also was highly vulnerable to the retort of the critics who pointed to the undemocratic character of the Saigon government and to the extensive involvement of Southerners in the conflict.

The government in its pronouncements spoke of success and light at the end of the tunnel, but continued to dispatch additional troops while casualties mounted steadily. As the director of the *Pentagon Papers* task force, Leslie H. Gelb, has observed, optimism without results could only work so long; after that, it had to produce a credibility gap. To be sure, the Johnson administration had never expected to become engaged in a protracted ground war on such a scale, and even when the involvement deepened it attempted to keep the war limited, a war without full mobilization of the home front and without a hated enemy. President Johnson is said to have rejected the view of some of his advisers that in order to hold the support of the country he would have to engage in some outright chauvinistic rabble-rousing and provide the American people with a vivid foe. Such a mobilization of patriotic sentiments, he apparently concluded, could force him into unduly risky actions such as unrestricted bombing, and even an invasion of North Vietnam—which, in turn, could lead to a confrontation with Communist China or Russia. At the very least, a widening of the war would prevent the achievement of his domestic "Great Society" programs.

For the same reasons, Johnson refrained from asking Congress for a declaration of war, which until 1967 he probably could have gotten without much difficulty. It is well to remember that at the time even critics of the president's Vietnam policy did not want to press for a formal declaration of war by Congress on the grounds that it would have undesirable consequences—it might trigger secret treaties between North Vietnam and Russia and China, thus risking a dangerous expansion of the conflict, and it could lead to the enactment of wartime curbs on free speech and press. Only years later did charges of an abuse of the Gulf of Tonkin resolution arise. Even though this resolution, considered by most legal authorities a functional equivalent of a declaration of war, was repealed by Congress in January 1971, the Nixon administration did not rely on it for its policy of withdrawal, and Congress did not end military appropriations for Vietnam until the last U.S. serviceman had left Vietnam and the prisoners of war had returned in 1973. Citing these appropriations, the courts consistently rejected charges of an unconstitutionally conducted war. And yet in retrospect it is apparent that Presidents Johnson and Nixon would have been spared much opposition and grief if Johnson had asked Congress for a declaration of war.

As a result of many different considerations, then, the nation fought a limited war, with the full employment of its military power restricted through elaborate rules of engagement and limitations on operations beyond the borders of South Vietnam, while for its determined opponent the war was total. The U.S. fought a limited war whose rationale was never convincingly explained and which, in any event, even an able leader would have had a most difficult time justifying. How does one tell a young conscript that he should be prepared to die in order to create a balance of power in Asia or in order to improve the American bargaining position at the upcoming negotiations that would lead to a compromise settlement?

If the Vietnam war had occurred in a different age some of these difficulties might have been surmountable. There was a time when the mass of the people were deferential to any official definition of the national interest and of the objectives of the nation's foreign policy. For good or for bad, this situation no longer holds in a modern democracy. Moreover, the war was fought at a time when major social evils had come to light in America and when a social transformation at home, the achievement of the "Great Society," was widely and urgently expected. Attacks on the mounting cost of the war in Asia were given special pertinence by the rioting in the urban black ghettos in 1967 and 1968 and by the deterioration of American cities which these racial explosions held up for all to see.

But the most important reason for the steadily spreading acceptance of the view that the American involvement in Vietnam had been a mistake was probably neither the implausibility of the rationale given for the war nor the preoccupation of both the educated classes and the poor with social reform. The decisive reason for the growing disaffection of the American people was the conviction that the war was not being won and apparently showed little prospect of coming to a successful conclusion. There was a clear correlation between declining support and a mounting casualty toll; the increasing cost in lives, occurring in a war without decisive battles or conquered territory, was the most visible symbol of failure. Hanoi's expectation that the American democracy would not be able to sustain a long and bloody conflict in a faraway land turned out to be more correct than Westmoreland's strategy of attrition, which was supposed to inflict such heavy casualties on the Communists as to force them to cease their aggression.

Had the intervention succeeded, say, by 1967, the public's disaffection probably would not have arisen and President Johnson would have emerged as a highly popular figure. As John F. Kennedy is supposed to have said of the reaction to the Bay of Pigs invasion: Success has a thousand fathers, but failure is an orphan. The capacity of people in a modern democracy to support a limited war is precarious at best. The mixture of propaganda and compulsion which a totalitarian regime can muster in order to extract such support is not available to the leaders of a democratic state. Hence when such a war for limited objectives drags on for a long time it is bound to lose the backing essential for its successful pursuit. It may well be, as an American political scientist has concluded, that "unless it is severely provoked or unless the war succeeds fast, a democracy cannot choose war as an instrument of policy."

That American public opinion, as Leslie Gelb has put it, was "the essential domino" was, of course, recognized by both American policymakers and the Vietnamese Communists. Each geared his "strategy—both the rhetoric and the conduct of the war—to this fact." And yet, given the limited leverage which the leaders of a democracy have on public opinion, and in view of the various liabilities to which the American war effort was subject, the ability of American decision-makers to control this "essential domino" was always precarious. For the Vietnamese Communists, on the other hand, ideological mobilization at home and carrying the propaganda effort to the enemy was relatively easy, and they worked at both objectives relentlessly and with great success. Enormous amounts of effort, manpower and money were devoted to creating the image of the Viet Cong as a highly motivated, honest and noble human being, who was engaged in a just war against an imperialist aggressor and his corrupt puppets. This concerted activity, Douglas Pike stresses, was not just pretense and sham. "The communists worked hard to create their image. They altered policy in its name. They shot looters, purged cadres, refused alliances, ordered military offensives, all for the sake of perception abroad." The outcome of this uneven contest was predictable. The Western observer, essentially unable to check out the claims of the communist camp, was left with the image of a tough and highly effective enemy while at the same time he was daily exposed to the human and bureaucratic errors and shortcomings of his own side. Image was bound to triumph over reality.

The coverage of the war by television was a crucial factor in this one-sided publicity. The VC were notoriously uncooperative in allowing Western cameramen to shoot pictures of the disemboweling of village chiefs or other acts of terror, while scenes of South Vietnamese brutality, such as the mistreatment of prisoners, were often seen on American TV screens. Television stresses the dramatic and contentious, and the Vietnam war offered plenty of both. The result was a one-dimensional coverage of the conflict—apparently meaningless destruction of lives and property in operations which rarely led to visible success. War has always been beastly, but the Vietnam war was the first war exposed to television cameras and seen in practically every home, often in living color. Not surprisingly this close-up view of devastation and suffering, repeated daily, strengthened the growing desire for peace. The events of Tet and the siege of Khe Sanh in 1968, in particular, shook the American public. The nightly portrayal of violence and gore and of American soldiers seemingly on the brink of disaster contributed significantly to disillusionment with the war. Gallup poll data suggest that between early February and the middle of March 1968 nearly one person in five switched from the "hawk" to the "dove" position.

Despite the small percentage of individuals actively involved in organized opposition to the war, the antiwar movement had a significant impact on both the Johnson and Nixon administrations. Not only does a small percentage of a country of 200 million constitute a sizable number of people, but the active and articulate few, often strategically placed, can have an importance well beyond their proportion of the population. The tactics of the antiwar movement were often unpopular, and the association of the drive for peace with other causes and groups regarded as radical by most Americans further contributed to its political isolation. Some of the leaders were old-time or New leftists, others were admirers of the Viet Cong, whose struggle and tactics they romanticized. To politically seasoned Americans it was obvious that many of these men and the organizations and committees they spawned were not so much for peace and against the war as they were partisans of Hanoi, whose victory they sought to hasten through achieving an American withdrawal from Vietnam. But the great majority of those who joined peace demonstrations were ordinary Americans—Democrats, Republicans and independents—simply fed up with the seemingly endless bloodletting.

The impact of the antiwar movement was enhanced by the widely publicized charges of American atrocities and lawlessness. The inability of Washington officials to demonstrate that the Vietnam war was not in fact an indiscriminate bloodbath and did not actually kill more civilians than combatants was a significant factor in the erosion of support for the war, especially among the media and the intellectual community generally. The view held by many of these critics that the war did not involve any important national stakes further contributed to their unwillingness to accept a level of violence that was probably less extreme than in many previous wars fought by this country. To attempt such an effort at explanation without appearing to have a callous disregard for human life would, of course, have been extremely difficult. Moreover, there can be little doubt that while the casualties inflicted on the civilian population of Vietnam were not out of line in comparison with World War II and Korea, they did have a highly detrimental effect in a counterinsurgency setting like Vietnam. The realization on the part of many civilian policy-makers that this was so, combined with the unwillingness of the military to forego the highly destructive tools of heavy weaponry, may be one of the reasons why no meaningful effort at explanation was ever undertaken.

In the absence of a frank and convincing official justification of the high level of violence in Vietnam, speculation and unsupported allegations of wrongdoing held sway. Given respectability by the support of well-known public figures, this agitation eventually had an effect upon the larger educated public. Self-flagellation for the alleged gross immorality of America's conduct in the war and its moral decline as a nation became rampant, and calls for the trial of "Amerika's" leaders for crimes against peace and humanity fell on sympathetic ears. Unable to end the war on their terms, many intellectuals vented their frustration in verbal overkill which probably will not be remembered as their finest hour. Shrill rhetoric created a world of unreality in which the North Vietnamese Communists were the defenders of national self-determination, while U.S. actions designed to prevent the forceful takeover of South Vietnam stood branded as imperialism and aggression. Many of those who complained of the repressive character of the Thieu regime were uncritical of or found nothing but praise for the totalitarian regime in Hanoi. Politically innocent citizens paid hundreds of thousands of dollars for newspaper advertisements which recorded their support of charges concerning American actions and motives which they could not possibly have confirmed by any kind of evidence. Academics lent these ads an aura of authority by signing them with their titles and university affiliations. Everyone—from clergyman and biologist to movie actor and pediatrician—could become an instant expert on international law, Southeast Asia, and foreign policy generally. Professors who would never have dared treat their own disciplines in such a cavalier fashion proclaimed with assurance solutions to the Vietnam problem at "teach-ins," complete with folk singers, mime troupes and other forms of entertainment.

The disaffection of large segments of the country's intellectual leadership—in the media, the professions, on the college campuses, and increasingly in Congress—reinforced the growing war-weariness and disillusionment in the country, often quite unrelated to wider political or humanitarian concerns. The Vietnam war ended up as the longest and most unpopular war in the nation's history.

As was to be expected, North Vietnam sought to make the most of the antiwar movement in America. North Vietnamese officials, at meetings with radical antiwar activists held in Cuba, Hungary, Czechoslovakia and North Vietnam, provided tactical advice and helped coordinate worldwide antiwar demonstrations. Communist propaganda regularly reported peace demonstrations as proof that the American people were weakening in their resolve. The North Vietnamese were convinced that just as the Viet Minh had defeated France not only, or primarily, on the battlefield but rather by outlasting the patience of the French people for the war in Indochina, so North Vietnam and the Viet Cong would eventually triumph over the United States on account of their own determination and the failure of the American people to last the course. As Assistant Secretary of Defense John T. McNaughton put it with considerable understatement in a memorandum in May 1967: "The state of mind in the US generates impatience in the political structure of the United States. It unfortunately also generates patience in Hanoi." Well-meaning as most participants in the peace movement were, James Reston wrote in October 1965, "the truth is that . . . they are not promoting peace but postponing it. They are not persuading the President and the Congress to end the war, but deceiving Ho Chi Minh and General Giap into prolonging it."

The opponents of the war had a constitutional right to express their views, but it was folly to ignore the consequences of this protest. American public opinion indeed turned out to be a crucial "domino"; it influenced military morale in the field, the long-drawn-out negotiations in Paris, the settlement of 1973, and the cuts in aid to South Vietnam in 1974, a prelude to the final abandonment in 1975. A more supportive public opinion in America would probably have led to a slower pace of disengagement, but whether this additional time would have materially changed the fighting ability of the South Vietnamese armed forces and thus could have prevented an ultimate collapse remains, of course, an open question.

Opposition to the war in Vietnam benefited from America's moralistic approach to world affairs which, as the political scientist Lucian Pye has suggested, makes Americans uneasy about being identified with governments striving to suppress rebellions. "We tend to suspect that any government confronted with a violent challenge to its authority is probably basically at fault and that a significant number of rebels can be mobilized only if a people has been grossly mistreated. Often we are inclined to see insurgency and juvenile delinquency in the same light, and we suspect that, as 'there is no such thing as bad boys, only bad parents,' so there are no bad people, only evil and corrupt governments." In point of fact, while the communist insurgency in Vietnam undoubtedly for a long time drew strength from the failure of the government of South Vietnam to address and remedy the social and economic problems of its rural population, the GVN eventually carried out a far-reaching land reform and undertook other successful measures to better relations with its people. Just as the internal strength and cohesion of the Republic of Korea did not save it from attack in 1950 and would not have staved off a communist victory without American military intervention, so the strengthening of the GVN did not prevent the North Vietnamese invasions in 1972 and 1975 which finally led to the collapse of South Vietnam. Indeed, at least in part, it was this very improvement of the GVN and the greatly weakened posture of the VC which led to the decision of Hanoi to abandon the tactic of revolutionary war and to resort to conventional warfare with tanks and heavy artillery.

And yet it is also true that the way in which both the Americans and South Vietnamese carried out the effort to suppress the communist insurgency often alienated the population of the countryside. The record . . . does not bear out charges of genocide or indiscriminate killings of civilians and wholesale violations of the law of war. However, the strategy and tactics of the allied counterinsurgency, especially the lavish use of firepower, did undermine the efforts of the GVN to win the allegiance of its people. There is reason to believe that the suffering inflicted upon large segments of South Vietnam's rural population during long years of high-technology warfare contributed to the spread of a feeling of resignation, war-weariness and an unwillingness to go on fighting against the resolute opponent from the North. It is also well to remember that revulsion at the fate of thousands of hapless civilians killed and maimed by the deadly arsenal of a modern army may undercut the willingness of a democratic nation to fight communist insurgents and that reliance upon high-technology weapons in an insurgency setting therefore may be counterproductive on still another level.

Despite much talk about "winning hearts and minds," the U.S. failed to understand the real stakes in a revolutionary war and for all too long ignored the conflicts in Vietnamese society which the VC exploited and used to motivate their forces. The U.S. also never really learned to fight a counterinsurgency war and used force in largely traditional ways, and the South Vietnamese copied our mistakes. The military, like all bureaucracies encountering a new situation for which they are not prepared and in which they do not know what to do, did what they knew to do. That happened to be the inappropriate thing. "The Vietnamese Communist generals," Edward G. Lansdale has written, "saw their armed forces as instruments primarily to gain political goals. The American generals saw their forces primarily as instruments to defeat enemy military forces. One fought battles to influence opinions in Vietnam and in the world, the other fought battles to finish the enemy keeping tabs by body count." As it turned out, the enemy's endurance and supply of manpower proved stronger than American persistence in keeping up the struggle. More importantly, the strategy of attrition downgraded the crucial importance of pacification and ignored the fact that the enemy whom it was essential to defeat was in the hamlets and not in the jungles. American forces, applying classic Army doctrines of aggressively seeking out the enemy and destroying his main-force units, won most of the battles but lost the war.

Many of America's military leaders argue to this day that their ability to conduct a winning strategy was hamstrung not only by overly restrictive rules of engagement, designed to protect civilian life and property, but also by geographical constraints imposed on them for fear of a collision with Communist China and the Soviet Union. This argument is less than persuasive, for the war, in the final analysis, had to be won in South Vietnam. Military action in Laos and Cambodia at an early stage of the war, seeking permanently to block the Ho Chi Minh Trail, would have made the North Vietnamese supply effort far more difficult, but basically an expansion of the conflict would not have achieved the American task. Certainly, an invasion of North Vietnam would only have magnified the difficulties faced.

The war not only had to be won in South Vietnam, but it had to be won by the South Vietnamese. Unfortunately, to the end South Vietnamese performance remained the Achilles' heel of the allied effort. A totalitarian state like Communist North Vietnam, possessing a monopoly of indoctrination and social control, was bound to display greater military morale and unity than a fragmented and barely authoritarian country like South Vietnam. Also, the Republic of Vietnam, under American prodding, gradually did improve its stability and cohesion. But progress in building a viable political community was painfully slow, and it was not far-reaching enough to create the sense of purpose necessary for a successful defense against the communist enemy. The ignominious collapse of ARVN in 1975, as I have tried to show, was due not only to ARVN's inferiority in heavy weapons and the shortage of ammunition but in considerable measure was also the result of lack of will and morale.

All this does not mean that the U.S. could not have succeeded in achieving its objectives in Vietnam. It may well be, as Barbara Tuchman has argued, that the American goal of saving Nationalist China after World War II from communist domination was unachievable. "China was a problem for which there was no American solution." But South Vietnam in the early 1970s was not China in the 1940s, and the U.S. position, too, was incomparably stronger.

The U.S. in the years from 1954 to 1975 could have pursued policies different from those actually followed. What if, instead of making a piece-meal commitment of military resources and adopting a policy of gradualism in their use, America had pursued a strategy of surprise and massed strength at decisive points? What if the mining of North Vietnamese harbors had taken place in 1965 instead of 1972? What if the U.S. from the beginning had implemented a strategy of population security instead of fighting Westmoreland's war of attrition, perhaps utilizing the Marines' CAP concept or the village defense program developed by the Special Forces-trained Civilian Irregular Defense Group? What if Vietnamization had begun in 1965 rather than 1968? While one cannot be sure that these different strategies, singly or in combination, would necessarily have brought about a different outcome, neither can one take their failure for granted.

Relations with the South Vietnamese and Vietnamization, too, could have followed a different course. As a result of anticolonialist inhibitions and for other reasons, the U.S. refrained from pressing for a decisive reorganization of the South Vietnamese armed forces and for a combined command, as America had done in Korea under the mantle of a UN mandate. Similarly, in regard to pacification and matters of social policy generally, America sought to shore up a sovereign South Vietnamese government and therefore, for the most part, limited itself to an advisory and supporting role, always mindful of the saying of Lawrence of Arabia: "Better they do it imperfectly than you do it perfectly, for it is their country, their war, and your time is limited." Western aggressiveness and impatience for results, it was said, ran counter to oriental ways of thinking and doing things and merely created increased resistance to change and reform. But if internal weaknesses in South Vietnamese society and the high level of corruption were as important a factor in the final collapse as the evidence . . . seems to suggest, might a radically different approach perhaps have been indicated?

Should the U.S. initially have accepted full responsibility for both military and political affairs, as suggested by experienced Vietnam hands like John Paul Vann, and only gradually have yielded control over the conduct of the war to a newly created corps of capable military leaders and administrators? Should America have played the role of the "good colonialist" who in this way slowly prepares a new country for viable independence? At the very least, should the U.S. have exerted more systematic leverage on its Vietnamese ally? The long record of American failure to move the GVN in directions which in retrospect would clearly have been desirable—for both the people of South Vietnam and America—writes Robert Komer, suggests "that we would have had little to lose and much to gain by using more vigorously the power over the GVN that our contributions gave us. We became their prisoners rather than they ours—the classic trap into which great powers have so often fallen in their relationships with weak allies."

We will never know, of course, whether any of these different approaches would have yielded better results. However, these alternative policy options must be mentioned in order to challenge facile and unhistorical assumptions of an inevitable collapse of South Vietnam. Just as the success of a policy does not prove that it was the only possible successful course of action, a policy can be correct even if for a variety of reasons it fails. The commitment to aid South Vietnam was made by intelligent and reasonable men who tackled an intractable problem in the face of great uncertainties, including the future performance of an ally and the actions and reactions of an enemy. The fact that some of their judgments in retrospect can be shown to have been flawed and that the outcome has been a fiasco does not make them villains or fools. If Hitler in 1940 had succeeded in conquering Britain, this would not have proven wrong Churchill's belief in the possibility and moral worth of resistance to the Nazis. Policy-makers always have to act on uncertain assumptions and inadequate information, and some of the noblest decisions in history have involved great risks. As long as there exists a reasonable expectation of success, the statesman who fails can perhaps be pitied, but he should not be condemned.

Both critics and defenders of American policy in Vietnam can agree that, as Kissinger put it in June 1975, "outside effort can only supplement, but not create, local efforts and local will to resist. . . . And there is no question that popular will and social justice are, in the last analysis, the essential underpinning of resistance to subversion and external challenge." To bolster local ability, effort and will to resist was, of course, the basic purpose of the American policy of Vietnamization. The fact that South Vietnam, abandoned by its ally, finally succumbed to a powerful and ruthless antagonist does not prove that this policy could not have had a less tragic ending. Neither does it vitiate the moral impulse which played a significant part in the original decision to help protect the independence of South Vietnam. Indeed, the sad fate of the people of Indochina since 1975 lends strength to the view that the American attempt to prevent a communist domination of the area was not without moral justification.

CHESTER J. PACH, JR.

And That's the Way It Was
The Vietnam War on
the Network Nightly News

"A s I sat in my office last evening, waiting to speak," Lyndon B. Johnson told the National Association of Broadcasters on 1 April 1968, the day after he announced he would not seek another term as president, "I thought of the many times each week when television brings the [Vietnam] war into the American home." What Americans saw each night in their living room, Johnson believed, was a distorted picture of the war, one dominated by "dramatic" events, such as the spectacular but temporary enemy successes during the recent Tet Offensive. Johnson conceded that it was impossible to determine exactly how "those vivid scenes" had shaped popular attitudes. He also acknowledged that "historians must only guess at the effect that television would have had . . . during the Korean war, . . . when our forces were pushed back there to Pusan" or during World War II when the Germans counterattacked at the Battle of the Bulge. Still, Johnson suggested that it was no accident that previous administrations had weathered these military reverses, but his had suffered a debilitating loss of popular support during the Tet Offensive. The reason for the "very deep and very emotional divisions" in public opinion was that Vietnam was America's first televised war.

Johnson was one of many who have criticized, albeit for different reasons, TV coverage of the Vietnam War. Like Johnson, some observers have faulted television for oversimplifying the complexities of Vietnam or for emphasizing spectacular, but horrifying scenes of combat that shocked viewers into opposing the war. In contrast, other commentators have denounced TV journalists for all too easily accepting official pronouncements of progress, at least until Tet, or for making the war's brutality seem so stylized, trivialized, or routine that the result was acceptance or ennui rather than revulsion. Many scholars have argued that television news came of age during Vietnam, although one influential critic has insisted that fundamental weaknesses in American journalism produced a distorted assessment of the Tet Offensive as an American failure. The most extreme critics blame television for reporting so ignorant, biased, or deceptive that it turned the victory American soldiers had won on the battlefields of Vietnam into defeat by producing irresistible political pressures for withdrawal.

Television, however, did better at covering the war than many of these critics allow. To be sure, television's view of the war was limited, usually to what the camera could illustrate with vivid images. Too many film reports on the network newscasts dealt with American military operations, and too often they concentrated on immediate events—a firefight or an airstrike—with little, if any, analysis of how those incidents fit into larger patterns of the war. Yet television also showed the war as it was—a confused, fragmented, and questionable endeavor. Brief reports, usually no more than three minutes long, of isolated, disconnected military engagements, broadcast night after night, week after week, magnified the confusing features of a war that, at best, was hard to fathom—one usually without fronts, clearly identifiable enemies, reliable progress toward victory, or solid connections to American security. Because of the nature of the medium rather than any conscious effort, television nightly news exposed the irrationalities of a war that lacked coherent strategy or clear purpose.

When Johnson decided in 1965 to send American combat troops to Vietnam, TV journalists faced a unique challenge. Vietnam was television's first war. The three major networks rapidly enlarged their operations in Vietnam and by 1967 were each spending over $1 million annually on covering the war. The expansion of the nightly newscasts on CBS and NBC from fifteen to thirty minutes in September 1963—ABC did not follow suit until January 1967—provided more time for Vietnam news. The state of broadcast technology, however, made for substantial delays in airing stories from Vietnam. Not until February 1967 was it possible to relay film by satellite from Tokyo to New York, but then only at a cost of as much as $5,000 for a five-minute transmission. Thus all but the most urgent stories continued to be flown from Saigon to New York for broadcasting. Television viewers usually learned about the most recent developments in Vietnam from the anchor's summary of wire service copy. They commonly had to wait another two days to see film reports of those events.

Unlike those who covered World War II or Korea, Vietnam correspondents did not have military censors review their reports, but they did face informal restrictions and pressures. Johnson was obsessed with the news—"television and radio were his constant companions," wrote one biographer—and he was determined to get reporters to promote his version of the national interest. "I'm the only president you've got, and . . . I need your help," he told members of the White House press corps. But if they did not cooperate, Johnson warned them, "I know how to play it both ways, too." Like Johnson, public information officers for the U.S. command in Vietnam tried to use informal pressures to shape reporting on Vietnam. They rejected censorship because they doubted its effectiveness and feared that it would anger correspondents. Instead, they outlined a series of guidelines that restricted identification of specific units or disclosure of the exact number of casualties in individual battles. They relied on daily news briefings, derisively known as the "Five O'Clock Follies," to influence the coverage of military operations. And they hoped that a vast array of incentives—transportation on military aircraft, interviews with commanders, lodging at bases—would secure or maintain a good working relationship with correspondents and thus favorable coverage of the war effort.

The war that these reporters covered had a superficial, but ultimately specious logic. In South Vietnam, U.S. ground forces tried to win the war with a strategy of attrition. Their primary mission was to search out and destroy the main units of the Vietcong and the North Vietnamese army. The U.S. commander, General William C. Westmoreland, insisted that wearing down these conventional forces had to take precedence over rooting out guerrillas from populated areas. "It was, after all, the enemy's big units—not the guerrillas—that eventually did the South Vietnamese in," he later explained. Although he would have preferred an invasion of North Vietnam—an option that Johnson refused to sanction—Westmoreland still believed that enormous advantages in mobility and firepower would enable American forces to win the big-unit war. Helicopters would allow American troops to bring the North Vietnamese or Vietcong to battle even in remote jungles or mountains, artillery and airpower would inflict enormous losses on enemy manpower and equipment, and seemingly inexhaustible stores of supplies would let American forces maintain the offensive. The combination of aggressive ground operations and the bombing of North Vietnam and the Ho Chi Minh Trail would push the enemy's main units beyond the crossover point, a level of casualties and equipment losses so great that they could not be replaced. This was war American-style—a high-tech, conventional way of fighting that accorded with U.S. army experience, training, and doctrine that the surest way to win was to pound the enemy into submission. Westmoreland's strategy of attrition, according to Earle Wheeler, the chairman of the Joint Chiefs of Staff, provided "the best assurance of military victory in South Vietnam."

Despite Wheeler's assertion, the strategy of attrition utterly failed. The big battles that Westmoreland sought occurred only infrequently. Instead, by 1967 Vietnam had become a small-unit war in which 96 percent of the engagements involved an enemy force no larger than a company (150 soldiers). These battles usually took place only when the enemy chose to fight. By seizing the initiative, the North Vietnamese and the Vietcong were able to control their casualties and frustrate the strategy of attrition. Even though the body count always added up to an American victory, the more telling figures were in intelligence reports that showed that despite American bombing, Hanoi had increased the flow of reinforcements into South Vietnam and mobilized sufficient resources to carry on the war indefinitely. Equally dismal were the results of the "other war," the effort to win the hearts and minds of the South Vietnamese. While American combat units engaged in search-and-destroy missions, the Vietcong stepped up guerrilla attacks on population centers. When U.S. forces mounted counterinsurgency operations, their heavy reliance on artillery, napalm, herbicides, and defoliants produced countless civilian casualties, hordes of refugees, environmental devastation, and untold resentment against the South Vietnamese government and its profligate patron.

Attrition proved to be, at best, an incoherent strategy, at worst, no strategy at all. A study ordered by the army's chief of staff found that there was "no unified effective pattern" to U.S. military operations. Troops in the field reached the same conclusion through hard experience. The lack of front lines or territorial objectives made them frustrated and cynical. "Without a front, flanks, or rear, we fought a formless war against a formless enemy who evaporated like the morning jungle mists, only to materialize in some unexpected place," recalled Philip Caputo, a marine officer who saw action in 1965–66. "It was a haphazard, episodic sort of combat." Attrition produced a war of disconnected military operations, whose surest result was a relentless demand for more American soldiers and supplies. From 184,000 at the end of 1965, U.S. troop strength rose to 385,000 a year later and to 486,000 at the close of 1967. "Boiled down to its essence," as one official army historian has observed, "American 'strategy' was simply to put more U.S. troops into South Vietnam and see what happened."

On television, the most important story about Vietnam was the fighting that involved U.S. forces. About half of the film reports on network newscasts concerned U.S. troops on foot or in helicopters searching out the enemy, exchanging fire with snipers, calling in air strikes on base camps and supply depots, or clearing guerrillas from hostile villages. This "bang, bang" coverage crowded out stories about pacification or the inefficiencies of the South Vietnamese government, reports that would have provided viewers a deeper understanding of the complexities of counterinsurgency warfare. Yet TV journalists thought that they were giving their audience the news it wanted. "There are approximately 500,000 American men there," one reporter explained. "When this is multiplied by parents, friends and other relatives, there is no doubt what is of most importance to Americans." TV journalists also believed that they were using their visual medium to best advantage. "The sensationalism in Vietnam is obviously in the combat," remarked one network reporter. "Editors want combat footage. They will give it good play." If forced to choose, declared ABC news executive Nick Archer, "a good fire fight is going to get on over a good pacification story." Indeed, the executive producer of the "CBS Evening News" considered "a really great piece of war film . . . irresistible."

Such footage, however, was rare. Despite its potential to "describe in excruciating, harrowing detail what war is all about," the television camera only infrequently did so. Obtaining combat film was difficult; the television crew had to get out to the field, be lucky enough to accompany a unit that made contact with the enemy, and make sure that its equipment worked properly. "Then, if the battle is fierce," noted NBC's John Paxton, "the cameraman does not get the film because he usually has his face in the dirt."

If the camera operator did film the action, though, it might not be aired. In Saigon and Washington, military authorities cautioned television journalists that networks that showed objectionable scenes of American casualties might have their reporters barred from combat zones. Because of these warnings or their own scruples, editors hardly ever allowed ghastly pictures of the dead or dying into American homes during the dinner hour. Indeed, just 3 percent of news reports from Vietnam showed heavy fighting. Those who remember graphic scenes of death and suffering simply recall a war that television did not show.

Instead, television provided only suggestive glimpses of the war. Typical was a report by Morley Safer on 17 November 1965 from the attack troop ship *Paul Revere*, which was carrying marines to beaches south of Danang to begin a search-and-destroy mission. Safer's film captured the anticipation of combat, but none of the fighting. Network correspondents covered the Battle of the Ia Drang Valley, the first engagement between North Vietnamese regulars and U.S. soldiers in October–November 1965, mainly from rear areas. Viewers who watched ABC, for example, heard correspondent Ray Maloney describe the "very hard" fighting from the American base at Pleiku and listened to Lieutenant Colonel Hal Moore recount the action. But the only combat footage showed strikes against North Vietnamese positions by B-52s, which for the first time flew missions to support ground troops. In a similar way, television provided only a flavor of other big American operations during 1966–67. During Operation Attleboro, a sweep through Tay Ninh province in November 1966 involving some 22,000 U.S. troops, ABC's Kenneth Gale and his crew filmed the defoliation of hedgerows with flamethrowers and the interrogation of a Vietcong prisoner. CBS reporter Ike Pappas opted for much lighter fare—the "seeming unreality" of performances by the First Infantry Division's band during pacification of a Vietcong village—while NBC's George Page took a familiar approach—an interview with General John Deane that summarized the accomplishments of the operation. When U.S. forces returned to the same area in February 1967 during Operation Junction City, some became the first Americans to make a combat jump in Vietnam, as Safer reported on the "CBS Evening News." His film showed the soldiers parachuting from the plane, but not their landing, which, as Safer mentioned, was "virtually unopposed." One of the great frustrations of Vietnam for Americans in the field was the elusiveness of the enemy. "Reporters," as Erik Barnouw has noted, "seldom saw 'the war' or 'the enemy.' "

Often television focused not on battles but on the Americans who fought them. Human interest features reflected television's tendency to entertain as well as inform. A personalized story, TV journalists believed, appealed to their mass audience, perhaps because it often simplified—or avoided—complex or controversial issues. A staple of network newscasts was the combat interview, either with a commander or a hero. NBC's George Page, for example, reported in May 1967 from the Mekong Delta, where he talked to soldiers in the Ninth Infantry Division whose bravery had saved the lives of their comrades. Several days later, the "CBS Evening News" carried an interview that correspondent Mike Wallace had conducted with Lieutenant Colonel Robert Schweitzer, who had been wounded eight times and decorated on eleven occasions. Roger Staubach was no war hero, but he had been a college football star at Annapolis, and so his routine duties at a naval supply depot merited a film report by CBS's Ike Pappas in October 1966. Occasionally newsworthy were the lives of ordinary soldiers away from battle, as when Safer interviewed a group on rest and recreation traveling to Hong Kong to catch up, they said, on sleeping, letter writing, and drinking "good homogenized milk." Stories about the air war frequently concentrated on the pilots rather than the bombing, since correspondents could not fly on the B-52 missions over North Vietnam. Typical was a report by CBS's Peter Kalischer in November 1965 from Andersen Air Base on Guam, which showed the preflight routines of the pilots and lauded each mission as a "minor masterpiece" of planning and execution. Television viewers, then, often saw the war from the perspective of the Americans in Vietnam who were experiencing it.

Interpreting the war news was difficult, and television reporters often failed to provide analysis or commentary. The anchors of the nightly newscasts—Walter Cronkite on CBS, Chet Huntley and David Brinkley on NBC, and, successively, Peter Jennings, Bob Young, Frank Reynolds, and Howard K. Smith on ABC—offered no interpretation in more than half of the stories that they read. Their reticence was a result of their role in the program, which was to read short news items or introduce correspondents' reports. Less than one-fifth of their stories exceeded seventy-five words, which left little room for analytical comments. The canons of objective journalism—accuracy, balance, fairness, impartiality—also encouraged anchors to limit interpretive remarks. So too did the importance of inspiring confidence and loyalty among viewers, who often chose which network newscast to watch on the basis of their reaction to the personal qualities of the anchor. Walter Cronkite did not earn his reputation as the most trusted man in America by making partisan, gratuitous, or controversial comments about the news, but by reporting it "the way it was."

Network correspondents also did not supply much analysis in many of their stories about the war. Again, time limitations affected the content of their reports. With just twenty-two minutes each weekday night to present the news—commercials took up the rest of the half-hour program—television functioned as an electronic front page, covering little more than the day's most important occurrences, often in spare summaries. Correspondents' reports almost never ran more than three minutes and often considerably less. Television's preoccupation with the immediate—today's news—severely limited analytical reports intended to provide perspective. One of the infrequent attempts to do so, Morley Safer's wrap-up of the Battle of the Ia Drang Valley, failed to examine the effectiveness of search and destroy or the significance of new tactics of carrying troops to battle in helicopters. Instead, the only perspective came from the soldier in the field, as Safer interviewed members of a company of the Seventh Cavalry who had survived some of the deadliest combat with the North Vietnamese. Viewers of the nightly news, then, often got information about the Vietnam War without much analysis or interpretation.

Yet television journalists did try to make sense of the war, frequently by comparing current military operations with previous ones. Measuring the size, scope, or cost of a military action was a convenient, albeit simplistic, way of assessing its importance. Network correspondents and anchors, for example, described the Battle of the Ia Drang Valley as the "biggest engagement yet," the "bloodiest, longest" battle since Korea, "classic infantry warfare," and "the biggest American victory yet in Vietnam." Viewers learned that Operations Attleboro and Junction City were, successively, the largest of the war and that Operation Cedar Falls (January 1967) yielded the "biggest prize" so far, when U.S. troops captured the base camp of a Vietcong regiment. Television journalists also imputed significance to military operations in Vietnam by comparing them with those in

World War II. Reporting in November 1965 on marines preparing for an amphibious landing near Danang, Morley Safer thought that the scenes he witnessed resembled the Pacific war. CBS correspondent John Laurence suggested that the bloody, prolonged Battle of Hue in early 1968 looked like World War II action, a comparison endorsed by a marine battalion commander. On 4 July 1966 Dean Brelis closed his report from "the First Infantry Division, the Big Red 1 of North Africa, Omaha Beach, Normandy, Germany, and now the Cambodian border." Comparisons such as Brelis's, of course, associated intervention in Vietnam with a heroic and victorious tradition of American warfare.

Television reporters also tried to understand current military events by speculating about their relationship with future developments in the war. Reasoning by extrapolation—projecting what happened today into next week or next month—was an easy, if risky, way of simplifying the complexities of Vietnam. Cronkite, for example, declared that the Battle of the Ia Drang Valley was a portent of "dramatic change" in the Vietnam War, while Dean Brelis considered it a harbinger of more big battles. Yet staggering losses encouraged the North Vietnamese to avoid major engagements after Ia Drang and utilize guerrilla tactics instead. One year later, Cronkite predicted that a series of North Vietnamese and Vietcong military initiatives "could set the pattern of the war for months to come." But the anticipated major offensive did not occur. ABC's Bill Brannigan reported in February 1967 about the forced removal of villagers near Danang to a relocation center and speculated that such evacuations would become the preferred method of depriving the Vietcong of civilian support. Yet the American command began to modify its policy of mandatory relocation only two months later and abandoned it at the end of the year. However logical or appealing to television journalists, extrapolation clearly was a dubious method of discerning the future in Vietnam.

Much of the information and many of the interpretive comments in television newscasts prior to the Tet Offensive suggested that the United States was winning the war. When TV journalists assessed the results of battles during 1965–67, they concluded that about two-thirds were American victories. A key to this success, network correspondents frequently emphasized, was American firepower. In November 1965, for example, Ray Maloney informed viewers of the "ABC Evening News" that the Vietcong were defenseless against B-52 strikes and that airpower was "turning the tide in Vietnam." A year later, Bruce Morton covered the air attacks supporting Operation Attleboro and declared that firepower was a "principle" that had proved its worth. Reporting in January 1967 from the Iron Triangle northwest of Saigon during Operation Cedar Falls, NBC's George Page assured those who tuned into the "Huntley-Brinkley Report" that high-tech weaponry would destroy the region's elaborate tunnel system and so deprive the Vietcong of an important base area. The same night, CBS's John Hart explained how airstrikes with napalm had silenced Vietcong snipers that had pinned down American troops. Another major advantage, according to television reporters, was the high quality of American troops. During the Ia Drang fighting, for example, Brelis interviewed Lieutenant Colonel Hal Moore, who asserted that "we have the best soldiers that the world has ever seen." From time to time military officials appeared in news reports to assure the public that American troops were achieving their goals, as when General John Deane told Page in November 1966 that the war was going "very well."

Television journalists also frequently reported that the air war was producing favorable results. Interviews with pilots always generated assurances that the bombing of North Vietnam was effective. That was what CBS's Bruce Morton heard, for example, when he talked to fliers in February 1967. Despite their objections to political restrictions on targets, the pilots were still making sure that the air campaign achieved its goals, Morton concluded, largely because of their professionalism in carrying out their missions. During the first year of the air war, television newscasts carried several stories that lauded the sophistication or superiority of American aircraft. Typical was Chet Huntley's narration in September 1965 of a Defense Department film of the A-4 Skyhawk, a fighter that eventually made more bombing raids in Vietnam than any other navy plane. The A-4 had produced "spectacular" results, Huntley exclaimed, and "should have even better shooting in the days ahead" because of improving weather.

John Hart's report on the "CBS Evening News" in February 1967 on a lesser-known part of the air war, aerial defoliation and crop destruction, was so one-sidedly favorable that it bordered on propaganda. Hart asserted that the herbicides that the air force sprayed on jungles and forests were no stronger than dandelion killer and caused no damage to the soil. Air Force Major Charlie Hubbs added that Operation Ranch Hand, as the defoliation campaign was known, was not a form of chemical warfare, but a "humane" way of fighting. Although the toxic effects of Agent Orange, the principal herbicide, on the environment and humans were not yet fully known, many scientists had urged the Johnson administration to halt this form of warfare, something Hart did not mention. He simply noted that Ranch Hand pilots were "sensitive to criticism that came regularly from conservationists in the United States" but even more concerned about hostile fire from enemy guns. Yet the air force had not altered its Ranch Hand operations at all because of the objections of civilian scientists. Defoliation operations actually reached a peak in 1967.

The favorable treatment of the war effort reflected television's acceptance of the cold war outlook that was responsible for U.S. intervention in Vietnam. TV journalists did not challenge President Johnson's conviction that the national interest required the containment of communism or the president's decision to commit U.S. combat troops to Vietnam. Those policies had such strong, mainstream support in 1965 that the network newscasts did not present them as matters of legitimate controversy. Instead, TV journalists responded to Johnson's decision to go to war in Vietnam less as objective journalists than as patriotic citizens. They reported the war effort in language that revealed a lack of detachment. Commonly in 1965–66, they referred to "our" troops, planes, and losses in Vietnam. The North Vietnamese or Vietcong were usually the "enemy," frequently the "Communists," and occasionally the "Reds." On one occasion Huntley mocked the term *National Liberation Front* as "Hanoi's name for its own forces." Editorial comments on television newscasts about the North Vietnamese or the Vietcong were overwhelmingly negative. Indeed, in one remarkable instance, the name of the Vietnamese revolutionaries became a synonym for deception and mendacity, when NBC correspondent Garrick Utley dismissed a National Liberation Front film as "unadulterated Vietcong."

There were several reasons why the network newscasts seemed "to express a massive political consensus" at the beginning of the Vietnam War. Dependent on advertising revenues, subject to federal regulation, and vulnerable to pressure from affiliates, television networks were wary of controversial programming or discordant opinion. When J. William Fulbright (D-Ark.), the chair of the Senate Foreign Relations Committee, held hearings in February 1966 that disputed the Johnson administration's Vietnam policies, CBS broke off its coverage in favor of reruns of "I Love Lucy," "The Real McCoys," and "The Andy Griffith Show." Network executives cited neither commercial nor ideological reasons for their decision, but—fantastically—the danger that extended telecasting of the hearings would "obfuscate" or "confuse" the issues about the war. Yet it is hard to believe that political considerations had no role in the network's action, since CBS president Frank Stanton considered a previous interview with Fulbright "a dirty trick . . . to play on the President of the United States."

Such episodes have persuaded many observers that television in the mid-1960s was "the most timid" of the news media, the most willing to accept official statements at face value, the most reluctant to air dissenting opinions, the most likely to knuckle under to government pressure. Yet recent studies have cast doubt on the independence of newspaper reporting of the Vietnam War. One analysis of six newspapers of different sizes and political orientations revealed that reporters and editors relied heavily on government sources for information about military operations and tended not to doubt their credibility. Another concluded that print journalists generally accepted "the assumption and consensus of the foreign policy establishment" and hoped for the success of "foreign policies designed to meet the nation's problems," at least when those policies were first carried out. Television newscasts may have expressed this consensual outlook in unique or distinctive ways—by focusing, for example, on "our boys" in Vietnam or stigmatizing the Vietcong as representatives of alien, evil ways. But the news media in general seems to have shared dominant core values that made it inclined in 1965–66 to support—or, at least, not to question—the fundamental reasons for American intervention in Vietnam.

Television may have expressed those consensual values in unique or distinctive ways because network newscasts were not simply a source of information but also of entertainment. As media analyst Peter Braestrup has argued, the job of the network correspondent in Vietnam "was not to produce news in the sense of 'fact-finding' . . . , but to obtain and produce film vignettes" that were "presented as 'typical' or a 'microcosm' " of the entire war. The correspondents who submitted these film reports often had only the most rudimentary knowledge of Vietnamese politics and culture, since their overseas assignments usually lasted between six months and one year. Their expertise was not in Southeast Asian affairs or even in international relations, but in producing vivid, engaging, and dramatic stories. Even more than the correspondents, the editors and producers in New York who assembled the nightly newscasts were masters not of interpreting the news but of packaging it. Their concern was good television—reports from

Vietnam that provided spectacular images that would attract large audiences and somehow encapsulate the entire war effort in one three-minute segment. This was neither adversarial nor even deeply analytical journalism. Instead, it was theatrical reporting, a reflection of the nature of the expertise of television journalists.

Yet television journalists did question the implementation of American policy in Vietnam, and their stories occasionally caused controversy, as when CBS correspondent Morley Safer and his crew filmed a report in Cam Ne about a search-and-destroy operation. The mission was one of the first of its kind for U.S. marines, who had been previously concentrated on protecting air bases and other important military installations. On 3 August 1965 a marine company swept into Cam Ne, a village complex southeast of Danang that was supposed to be an enemy stronghold. "If there were Viet Cong in the hamlets," Safer asserted in his film report, "they were long gone" by the time the U.S. forces arrived. The only certain Vietnamese casualties were a ten-year-old boy, who was killed, and four villagers, who were wounded, by the marine fire. The apparent lack of enemy resistance made all the more sensational the image of a marine using a cigarette lighter to set afire a thatched hut. The U.S. forces had orders to "level" Cam Ne, Safer explained just before the camera showed another marine incinerating a hut with a flamethrower. "There is little doubt that American fire power can win a military victory here. But to a Vietnamese peasant whose home means a lifetime of backbreaking labor, it will take more than presidential promises to convince him that we are on his side."

Enraged military authorities immediately accused Safer of inaccuracy and distortion. U.S. forces, they said, had faced not just the "burst of gunfire" that Safer had reported, but snipers that had wounded four Americans and forced the marines to withdraw under the cover of an artillery barrage. Cam Ne was no ordinary village, but an "extensively entrenched and fortified hamlet" with hundreds of booby traps and an elaborate network of tunnels. Although the marines may have burned the huts of innocent civilians, they did so incidentally, according to the battalion commander, while trying "to neutralize bunkers, trenches, and firing positions actually in use by the VC." The hut ignited by the cigarette lighter appeared to be "a tactical installation rather than a peaceful dwelling," according to a military spokesperson in Saigon. The marines, another information officer added, had not wantonly or callously used force but, like all American troops in South Vietnam, followed Westmoreland's orders to exercise "the utmost discretion, judgment and restraint" in applying firepower.

Safer stood by his story. In reply to the nervous inquiries of CBS news president Fred W. Friendly, he confirmed the accuracy of his film report before it aired on 5 August. Despite the barrage of official criticism, he also maintained that friendly fire, not Vietcong resistance, was responsible for the American casualties at Cam Ne. In a follow-up story several days later, Safer provided additional evidence that the marines entered Cam Ne determined to "teach [the villagers] a lesson." Was it necessary to burn "all the houses . . . to fulfill the mission?" he asked a marine who had seen action at Cam Ne. It was, the marine replied, in order "to show these people over a period of time that we're done playing with them." Another marine declared, "You can't have a feeling of remorse for these people. I mean, like I say, they are an enemy until proven innocent." A third disclosed that he entered villages such as Cam Ne, where marines had previously faced hostile fire or suffered casualties, with a desire for revenge. Such statements belied official assurances that U.S. policy was "to bend over backward" to avoid harming civilians or their property, "even at possible cost of U.S. lives."

Even more vehement than the official criticism of Safer's reporting was the attack on his integrity. Leading the assault was Lyndon B. Johnson. "Are you trying to fuck me?" Johnson asked caustically in a telephone conversation with CBS president Frank Stanton. "Your boys shat on the American flag." The president was convinced that Safer was a communist, but an investigation proved only that he was a Canadian. "Well, I knew he wasn't an American," Johnson sneered. "Why do you have to use foreigners to cover that war?" inquired Bill Moyers, an aide to Johnson, of another CBS correspondent. Canadian birth was reason enough for Arthur Sylvester, the assistant secretary of defense for public affairs, to demand Safer's relief. "I think that an American reporter," Sylvester wrote Friendly, "would be more sensitive" to the need for "balance" in reporting U.S. actions in Vietnam. Friendly dismissed Sylvester's letter as "character assassination," but Stanton repeatedly expressed doubts about Safer. A friend of Johnson, Stanton did not like having CBS accused of undercutting the president's war policies, especially since the source of trouble was a reporter who had been working for the network only a year and whose background he considered "sketchy." CBS news executives, however, kept Safer from learning about Stanton's reservations and Johnson's accusations while he remained in Vietnam.

Nevertheless, Safer was terribly aware of the hostility he faced in Vietnam, and that pressure may have affected his reporting. Safer feared for his life and began carrying a gun after hearing a rumor that he might become the victim of "an accident" and after watching a drunk marine officer fire his pistol in front of the press center while yelling "Communist Broadcasting System." Despite these threats, Safer insisted that he did not temper his reporting. Yet although he continued to cover the war's nasty side, he began describing it as part of the timeless brutality of warfare. Thus he explained the casualties that resulted from a mistaken U.S. bombing strike on the South Vietnamese village of Bong Son in October 1965 as an "inevitable" error. He also portrayed the Vietnamese hustlers and prostitutes who swarmed around the American installations at Danang as an "age-old misfortune of war." And in a report that must have pleased the American high command, he concluded that the South Vietnamese army regular, if led well, fought as effectively "as any other soldier."

The upshot of Safer's Cam Ne story, then, was an intense debate, not over the effectiveness of search-and-destroy tactics but the legitimacy of critical television reporting of the war. Morley Safer raised all the right issues—the difficulty of identifying the enemy, the adverse effects of heavy firepower, and the problem of innocent victims of military action in populated areas. Yet an official expression of regret about civilian casualties and assurances of restraint in future missions effectively ended any discussion of whether operations such as Cam Ne could help win the war. Instead, government officials thought more about whether reports such as Safer's might help lose it. Pentagon officials began recording the network newscasts in order to monitor more effectively television's coverage of the war. Once more military authorities studied the feasibility of censoring war stories, but these reconsiderations only confirmed previous conclusions that such severe restriction of the news would be ineffective and counterproductive. Still, the inflamed reaction to Safer's story revealed the narrow limits of acceptable war reporting on television.

Despite the furor over Cam Ne, television newscasts did occasionally examine problems with the war effort in 1965–66. Some of the most perceptive stories came from NBC correspondent Ron Nessen. After the first engagements in the Ia Drang Valley, Nessen was the only TV journalist who recognized that the North Vietnamese were dictating the terms of battle. Their attack had come as a surprise, he explained, and they had succeeded with the same tactics that had worked against the French. Even though they had retreated in the face of American and South Vietnamese reinforcements, the fighting "could break out again," Nessen correctly predicted, whenever the North Vietnamese wanted to resume it. One year later, Nessen probed the difficulties of "the other war," when he reported from Voila, a village that had been "pacified" four times. The real problem at Voila was the ineffectiveness of South Vietnamese government efforts to win the loyalty of the villagers. For example, the revolutionary development cadre that was supposed to provide security, improve public services, and rally support for the government once had all but two of its fifty-nine members desert. Each night, Nessen declared, the Vietcong proved that government forces could not protect the village. Pacification would succeed, he concluded, only when Voila was secure.

Another problem that attracted the attention of television journalists in 1965–66 was the sordid conditions of life in South Vietnam. On the "CBS Evening News" on 14 September 1965, Walter Cronkite introduced a film report about "one of the ugliest and saddest aspects of the Vietnam War." What followed was correspondent John Laurence narrating footage of South Vietnamese civilians who swarmed like "flies" and fought like "animals" in a U.S. marine garbage dump. Laurence explained that these "scavengers of war" risked crippling injury as well as infection, since the dump contained live ammunition. Seconds later, a grenade exploded, wounding a youth. The following month, Morley Safer described the degradation of the "once charming" city of Danang, the victim of con men and call girls who hustled for American dollars. A year later, he reported about an impending crackdown on the Saigon black market. Safer noted wryly, though, that business as usual would resume "next week at the latest."

During 1967 network newscasts contained stronger and more frequent criticisms of American methods of warfare. New sources of information cast doubt on official evaluations of the war effort. At the end of 1966, Harrison Salisbury of the *New York Times* had become the first American correspondent to visit North Vietnam since the beginning of the air war. Salisbury said in interviews on the three networks in mid-January 1967 what he had written in articles for the *Times*—that the bombing had caused extensive civilian casualties but had not diminished the North's capacity to move war materiel to the South. By exposing the North Vietnamese to a common danger, Salisbury added, the bombing had actually raised civilian morale and united the country. One week later, Harry

Ashmore, a Pulitzer Prize–winning former newspaper correspondent who had also traveled to Hanoi, endorsed Salisbury's conclusions in an interview with CBS's Charles Kuralt.

Network correspondents made more interpretive comments in 1967 that cast doubt on the effectiveness of American military operations. Typical were David Burrington's stories in February about U.S. efforts to clear the Vietcong from their tunnel complexes. Experience showed, Burrington said, that the guerrillas would be back in a few days or weeks. During Operation Cedar Falls, NBC and ABC aired reports that pointed out the persistent problems in relocation camps and refugee resettlement programs. Adam Raphael informed CBS viewers in February about a failed search-and-destroy mission after which American troops took out their frustration on a suspected Vietcong prisoner. When the cameras were off, Raphael revealed, the suspect's treatment may not have been "exactly according to the Geneva Convention." Though common, such critical comments did not dominate the network newscasts in 1967. Indeed, favorable remarks about the American war effort were still far more numerous. But television journalists were more inclined to question American methods of warfare, perhaps because of their growing familiarity with the difficulties of achieving victory in Vietnam.

There were far more profound doubts about American strategy in the White House and the Pentagon, and television newscasts revealed those reservations in sensational stories in May 1967. Several weeks earlier General Westmoreland had asked for an additional 200,000 troops, a request that added to the fears of Secretary of Defense Robert S. McNamara that the strategy of attrition would continue to produce a larger war, higher casualties, but no clear progress toward victory. "When we add divisions, can't the enemy add divisions? If so, where does it all end?" Johnson asked Westmoreland. With his own military advisers divided, Johnson denied Westmoreland the desired reinforcements. The administration's deliberations leaked out in a story on the "Huntley-Brinkley Report" on 8 May, and correspondent George Page concluded that Westmoreland's request showed that there was no limit to the number of troops that might be needed to protect South Vietnam. Two weeks later, ABC's Frank Reynolds reported on Johnson's Memorial Day proclamation, in which the president described the war as a "bloody impasse." This dramatic phrase, though, was misleading, since the president still clung to the hope that Westmoreland could make slow but steady progress toward victory without additional troops. Reynolds then added his own note of pessimism. The "isolated victories on the battlefield," he declared, "do not add up to any sort of overall victory against the North Vietnamese or Vietcong." Since enemy resolve had not lessened, the United States faced a "predicament from which there is no obvious escape."

What kind of war, then, did a television viewer watch on the network nightly news during the American buildup in Vietnam from 1965 through 1967? He or she saw, as critic Michael Arlen has remarked, a "generally distanced overview of a disjointed conflict which was composed mainly of scenes of helicopters landing, tall grasses blowing in the helicopter wind, American soldiers fanning out across a hillside on foot, rifles at the ready, with now and then (on the soundtrack) a far-off ping or two, and now and then (as the visual grand finale) a column of dark, billowing smoke a half mile away, invariably described as a burning Vietcong ammo dump." Night after night the American people peered at these scenes of battle from a war that had been domesticated by TV cameras. The war was always there on the screen, close enough to fascinate or repel but not so close as to spoil dinner. Most television battles ended in American victories, although increasingly they revealed problems that suggested that all might not be well. Rarely, though, could the viewer see beyond the battlefield. Television's war was a series of disconnected episodes of combat. Television reporters usually did not look for the connections, but when they did, they had trouble finding them. That was because the strategy of attrition had produced a war of isolated engagements. The fragmented war on television was precisely the war fought in Vietnam.

TV journalists reported the war this way not because of their perceptual acuity or analytical power, but because of the routines of their medium. Television consists of bits and pieces—segments, in the vocabulary of scholars who use semiotics to analyze communications. Each channel broadcasts a flow of programs, commercials, and announcements, and each program, in turn, consists of smaller segments. On a network newscast, those segments include reports, either by the anchor or correspondents, that together total only twenty-two minutes. Because of the shortness of time, these reports condense and simplify the news. And because of journalists' preoccupation with immediacy, the reports usually focus only on today's news, with little, if any, analysis of how recent events fit into larger patterns. Anchors may try to provide some context for the reports, but they usually must do so in a few sentences. Some studies have shown, however, that viewers often fail to make the intended connection between an anchor's introduction or conclusion and a correspondent's story. Brevity and segmentation thus made television likely to cover large events, such as the Vietnam War, through a series of largely self-contained reports. Television's fragmented reporting just happened to coincide with a disjointed war.

Television suddenly had a different war to cover once the Tet Offensive began. On 30 January 1968 the North Vietnamese and Vietcong launched a coordinated series of attacks that seemed to turn almost all of South Vietnam into a battlefield. They struck with 100,000 troops in practically all major cities, most provincial and many district capitals, and quite a few hamlets—altogether more than 150 places. Vietcong sapper teams assaulted the most visible symbols of American and South Vietnamese authority—the embassy in Saigon and the presidential palace, respectively. At the last two locations, U.S. and South Vietnamese forces repelled the attacks within a few hours; almost everywhere else, they regained the advantage in a matter of days. Yet the breadth and fury of the Tet Offensive surprised American intelligence authorities and stunned public opinion. No one had imagined that the North Vietnamese and Vietcong were capable of such extraordinary action, especially since the Johnson administration had recently mounted a "progress campaign," a major public relations effort to show, as Westmoreland proclaimed, that the war had advanced into a new stage "when the end begins to come into view." Upon learning of the Tet attacks, Walter Cronkite expressed the bewilderment and betrayal felt by many Americans when he snapped, "What the hell is going on? I thought we were winning the war."

Tet was high drama on television. No longer was the war in the background; instead, the fighting intruded into film reports in frightening and uncontrollable ways. Within a week, viewers saw two members of television crews suffer wounds while covering battle. During the fighting near the presidential palace, ABC's Piers Anderton and his camera operator recorded the anguish of an injured South Vietnamese soldier moaning in the street, while NBC's Douglas Kiker described the agony of Ban Me Thuot, as the film showed a city of rubble and refugees. "The nastiest kind of street fighting" occurred in Hue, CBS's Robert Schakne observed, and it exacted a heavy toll on U.S. marines, who had to clear out the enemy house by house, and on the city, which had ceased to function. From Danang, Saigon, Khe Sanh, and elsewhere correspondents reported that the fighting was hard and unpredictable. Not merely spectators at these engagements, yet not fully participants, they captured in words and images the surprise, horror, and confusion that engulfed South Vietnam during Tet.

The most sensational story during Tet was the cold-blooded execution of a Vietcong officer in the streets of Saigon. The shooting followed a street battle between the Vietcong and South Vietnamese marines. An NBC crew recorded the fighting and the assassination in its entirety; an ABC camera operator stopped filming at the moment of death. Both reports aired on the nightly newscasts on 2 February; both contained commentary that was extraordinarily restrained. As the victim was led to his death, NBC's Howard Tuckner explained, "Government troops had captured the commander of the Viet Cong commando unit. He was roughed up badly but refused to talk. A South Vietnamese officer held the pistol taken from the enemy officer. The chief of South Vietnam's national police, Brigadier General Nguyen Ngoc Loan, was waiting for him." Neither Tuckner nor Roger Peterson, who narrated the ABC film, suggested that the shooting was an atrocity or a measure of the authoritarianism of the South Vietnamese regime. For Robert Northshield, the executive producer of the "Huntley-Brinkley Report," the film was newsworthy not because of its political implications but on account of its stunning images of death. Northshield, though, considered some of the scenes too "rough" for the television audience, and so he trimmed footage of blood spurting from the shattered skull of the victim. Perhaps as many as 20 million people watched the execution film on NBC; many more saw a photograph of the moment of death, published in almost every major newspaper.

Although there is no way of knowing the impact on public opinion of this single story, the overall effect of the Tet Offensive in early 1968 was to deepen doubts about the war and destroy confidence in the Johnson administration's handling of it. Public support for the war did not suddenly vanish during Tet. Throughout 1967 more people had disliked Johnson's war policies than endorsed them, although the president won back some support during the "progress campaign" late in the year. The first public response to Tet was to rally behind the war effort, but that reaction lasted only briefly. By the time the enemy attacks had waned, 50 percent of the American people thought it had been a mistake to send troops to Vietnam, an increase of 5 percent over December 1967. Public support for the administration's management of the war plummeted from 39 percent in January 1968 to 26 percent by late March. Even more startling, those who thought that the United States was making progress in the war declined from half the population to less than one-third.

The shift in attitudes toward the war, some observers maintain, occurred because the American people were misinformed about Tet. These critics blame the news media for reporting so sensational, inaccurate, or distorted that it prevented the public from realizing that the Tet Offensive was an American victory. The most influential of these critics is Peter Braestrup, a former war correspondent for the *New York Times* and *Washington Post,* who has argued that American journalists were so overwhelmed during Tet that they got the story wrong. "Essentially, the dominant themes of the words and film from Vietnam . . . added up to a portrait of defeat" for the United States and South Vietnam, Braestrup has written, when in fact Tet was "a severe military-political setback for Hanoi."

Making sense of the welter of events during Tet was difficult, but television journalists were not overwhelmed. They dutifully reported official reactions in Washington and Saigon, which usually emphasized that enemy successes were transient and casualties enormous. Sometimes, though, they took issue with those interpretations, as when David Brinkley, in reaction to General Westmoreland's statement about heavy Vietcong losses, commented tersely, he "did not say it [the Tet Offensive] was not effective." Editorial comments, many of them openly skeptical of official pronouncements, were far more numerous in the nightly newscasts than before Tet. Often, journalists expressed the shock and disbelief so many people felt, as when ABC news analyst Joseph C. Harsch asserted that Tet was at odds with "what the government had led us to expect." CBS's Robert Schakne expressed the same idea more vividly when he exclaimed that Tet had turned the world upside down. Journalists occasionally tried to discern the long-term effects of Tet by projecting current developments into the future. Thus, Schakne declared that there could be another major offensive and warned that "our troubles in Vietnam may be just beginning." As the current wave of attacks waned, NBC's Douglas Kiker reported that U.S. intelligence authorities feared another Vietcong assault, this one even more effective. Yet these predictions were no more pessimistic than General Wheeler's private assessment of the situation for Johnson. "The enemy . . . has the will and capability to continue," Wheeler found after visiting in South Vietnam in late February. The Tet Offensive, the general concluded, was "a very near thing."

Although pessimism was common, television journalists did not declare that Tet was a victory for the North Vietnamese and Vietcong. "First and simplest, the Vietcong suffered a military defeat," Walter Cronkite reported from Saigon on 14 February. Their suicidal attacks had produced staggering losses, and they had not succeeded in persuading large numbers of South Vietnamese to support their cause. Yet Cronkite also found that Tet had caused severe political problems by widening the Johnson administration's credibility gap and weakening the South Vietnamese government. "Pacification," he believed, "may have been set back by years, certainly months." Cronkite reiterated these conclusions two weeks later in a special evening program. "To say that we are closer to victory today is to believe, in the face of the evidence, the optimists who have been wrong in the past," he declared. "To suggest we are on the edge of defeat is to yield to unreasonable pessimism. To say that we are mired in stalemate seems the only realistic, yet unsatisfactory, conclusion." No other television journalist offered such a full evaluation of Tet. Yet the brief, fragmentary comments of other reporters and anchors did not fundamentally conflict with this assessment.

The results of the Tet Offensive were by no means as clear as Braestrup has insisted. By the standards of conventional war—those that shaped the U.S. army's strategy of attrition—Tet was indeed a defeat for the North Vietnamese and the Vietcong. The attackers had absorbed huge losses and had failed to maintain control of the cities and towns they had seized. By the standards of revolutionary war, however, the North Vietnamese and Vietcong seem to have been victorious. The attack proved the vulnerability of practically every South Vietnamese city or hamlet. It set back pacification, and it dealt U.S. morale a withering blow. "At the time of the initial attacks, the reaction of our military leadership approached panic," reflected Clark Clifford, who took over as secretary of defense in March 1968. "There was, for a brief time, something approaching paralysis, and a sense of events spiraling out of the control of the nation's leaders." The Johnson administration was bitterly divided over how to react to the enemy initiative. Not until 31 March—two months after the Tet Offensive began—did Johnson make a major statement on Vietnam. Then he announced a partial bombing halt, a new peace initiative, and his own withdrawal from the presidential race. The administration sealed its own fate with misleading optimism, ineffective war making, and inaction. At the very least, then, Tet represented a major psychological triumph for the North Vietnamese and Vietcong.

After Tet, TV reporting of the war in many ways followed earlier patterns. Most stories contained no editorial comments; again, television focused on American soldiers in the field. The portrayal of the war though, was far less heroic than before. American troops began going home in 1969 under President Richard M. Nixon's strategy of Vietnamization. Really the mirror image of attrition, Vietnamization was no strategy at all; it consisted of pulling American troops out, hoping for peace, and seeing what happened. Those U.S. forces that remained frequently expressed their dissatisfaction with the war, and news stories reflected this disillusionment. CBS's Gary Shepard, for example, reported in October 1969 from Saigon about the use of marijuana in Vietnam, while on the same night NBC's Fred Briggs covered an antiwar protest in Fayetteville, North Carolina, by Vietnam veterans. Six months later, NBC's Kenley Jones did a story about soldiers in the Twenty-second Infantry who were "near revolt" over their orders to invade Cambodia. The troops complained that they did not understand what the United States was doing in Cambodia or, for that matter, Vietnam. "This is a different war," Jones concluded, and these soldiers wanted no part of it. Neither did a majority of the American people.

Did it matter that the Vietnam War was covered on television? How did TV reporting affect public attitudes toward the war? These are important questions, but they cannot be answered as precisely as we might wish. Television did affect public understanding of the war, since by 1970 a majority of Americans got most of their news from television. Yet what they learned from nightly newscasts is by no means clear. Studies have revealed that most viewers have trouble remembering anything from news programs that they just finished watching. Perhaps that is because, as one scholar has observed, television "is designed to be watched intermittently, casually, and without full concentration. Only the commercials command and dazzle." Even if one does watch intently, the meaning one extracts from a news report is a product of individual values and attitudes. NBC's George Page recalled reporting on a battle in a way that he thought might create "a dovish attitude" among viewers. Then he got a letter from someone who had doubts about U.S. goals in Vietnam but who reacted to Page's story by saying, "Go, Marines. Go."

Yet even if it cannot be precisely measured, television's influence during the Vietnam War was important. Images do have powerful effects, however much the reaction varies among individual viewers. It is no accident that Morley Safer's Cam Ne report created such a stir while similar stories in newspapers went almost unnoticed. The reporting of the Tet Offensive on television undoubtedly shocked many people, especially after previous coverage of the war had been comparatively tame. Walter Cronkite's declaration that the war was a stalemate had a profound effect on at least one viewer, Lyndon Johnson, and, nearly a quarter century later, on George Bush. Certain that unrestricted reporting from Vietnam had undermined popular support of the war, Pentagon officials in the Bush administration restricted reporters' access to troops in the Persian Gulf and censored their reports.

While the Bush administration vastly oversimplified the "lessons" of Vietnam, it does seem that nightly news coverage did contribute to popular dissatisfaction with the war. Television presented a war that was puzzling and incoherent—a series of disjointed military operations that were often individually successful but collectively disastrous. Night after night, television slowly exposed the illogic of attrition. If viewers grew weary or discontent or outraged, it was partly because television just happened to show them an important part of the Vietnam War "the way it was."

SUGGESTIONS FOR FURTHER READING

A short and readable interpretive survey that describes and attacks Americans' moralistic approach to foreign policy is George F. Kennan, *American Diplomacy, 1900–1950* (Chicago, 1953). A scholar and career diplomat, Kennan played an instrumental role in American policy formation after World War II; he is the author of the containment policy. Kennan's book is often called a "realist" interpretation because he argues that the United States is not unique, has a moral vision no better than other nations, and must understand the realities of power. Kennan's influence is clearly reflected in a number of other studies of American diplomacy. See, for example, John Spanier, *American Foreign Policy Since World War II*, 11th ed. (Washington, D.C., 1988) and Hans J. Morgenthau, *In Defense of the National Interest* (New York, 1951). Robert E. Osgood, *Ideals and Self-Interest in America's Foreign Relations* (Chicago, 1953) perceptively considers notions of idealism and realism in American diplomacy.

---

*Available in paperback edition.

An approach to foreign policy quite different from Kennan's is William Appleman Williams, *The Tragedy of American Diplomacy* (New York, 1959). Sometimes called the founder of the "revisionist" school, Williams argues that economic concerns are the driving forces behind foreign policy. Two general accounts, both influenced by the Williams thesis, are Stephen Ambrose, *Rise to Globalism*, 5th ed. (New York, 1988) and Walter LaFeber, *The American Age* (New York, 1989).

The war in Vietnam has already inspired a torrent of books and articles, including fiction, memoirs, and history, and the flow shows no signs of abating. A general and balanced account written to accompany a television series is Stanley Karnow, *Vietnam: A History* (New York, 1983). A convenient collection of documents with interpretive essays is William Appleman Williams, Thomas McCormick, Lloyd Gardner, and Walter LaFeber, eds., *America in Vietnam* (Garden City, N.Y., 1985). Other useful collections are Robert J. McMahon, *Major Problems in the History of the Vietnam War* (Lexington, Mass., 1990); Harrison E. Salisbury, ed., *Vietnam Reconsidered* (New York, 1984); and Andrew J. Rotter, ed., *Light at the End of the Tunnel: A Vietnam War Anthology* (New York, 1991).

Some of the contemporary disillusionment with the war can be followed in Arthur M. Schlesinger, Jr., *The Bitter Heritage: Vietnam and American Democracy* (Boston, 1967); David Halberstam, *The Best and the Brightest* (New York, 1972); and Frances Fitzgerald, *Fire in the Lake* (Boston, 1972). Leslie H. Gelb with Richard K. Betts, *The Irony of Vietnam: The System Worked* (Washington, D.C., 1979) criticizes policymakers in Washington for their rigidity and failure to adjust policies to changing needs. Gabriel Kolko, *The Roots of American Foreign Policy* (New York, 1969) is a more radical approach, viewing the Vietnam War as a logical result of the American containment policy. George C. Herring, *America's Longest War: The United States and Vietnam*, 2nd ed. (New York, 1986) is a more moderate example of the same thesis. Patrick J. Hearden, *The Tragedy of Vietnam* (New York, 1991) is in the Williams school and sees American involvement in Vietnam stemming from economic needs of business. Two other recent books trace the origins of the war to the era of World War II and describe the gradual involvement of the United States in the Vietnamese civil war: James S. Olson and Randy Roberts, *When the Domino Fell: America and Vietnam, 1945–1995* (New York, 1996); and Marilyn B. Young, *The Vietnam Wars, 1945–1990* (New York, 1991).

A group of writers, some of them former Army officers and politicians, believe the war could have been won. Included in this group, sometimes called the "new revisionists," are Guenter Lewy, *America in Vietnam* (New York, 1978) (a portion of which is reprinted here); Timothy J. Lomperis, *The War Everyone Lost—and Won* (Baton Rouge, La., 1984); Harry G. Summers, Jr., *On Strategy* (Navato, Calif., 1982); Richard M. Nixon, *No More Vietnams* (Garden City, N.Y., 1976); and William C. Westmoreland, *A Soldier Reports* (Garden City, N.Y., 1976). A convenient collection of four very different views of the Vietnam War may be found in Patrick J. Hearden, ed., *Vietnam: Four American Perspectives* (West Lafayette, Ind., 1990).

Charles DeBenedetti and Charles Chatfield, *An American Ordeal* (Syracuse, N.Y., 1990) deals sympathetically with the antiwar movement. Tom Wells, *The War Within: America's Battle over Vietnam* (Berkeley, Calif., 1994) calls the opposition to the war the most successful antiwar movement in history. But Adam M. Garfinkle, *Telltale Hearts: The Origins and Impact of the Vietnam Antiwar Movement* (New York, 1995) argues that the antiwar movement did not end the war and, indeed, may have prolonged it. Todd Gitlin, *The Whole World Is Watching* (Berkeley, Calif., 1980) discusses the impact of television on the war and the antiwar movement. Andrew Martin, *Receptions of War: Vietnam in American Culture* (Norman, Okla., 1993) discusses television productions, films, and novels about the war. Christian G. Appy, *Working-Class War: American Combat Soldiers and Vietnam* (Chapel Hill, N.C., 1993) and Myra MacPherson, *Long Time Passing* (Garden City, N.Y., 1984) discuss the psychological effects of the war. Michael Herr, *Dispatches* (New York, 1977) and Philip Caputo, *A Rumor of War* (New York, 1977) are among the best of many personal accounts.

Discussion and debate about the Vietnam War, its causes, and its legacy show no sign of abating. A recent discussion of the debate among historians is Gary R. Hess, "The Unending Debate: Historians and the Vietnam War," *Diplomatic History,* 18 (Spring 1994), 239–264.

Unity or Disunity: The Multicultural Debate

No question has intrigued Americans more than that asked in 1782 by J. Hector St. John de Crevecoeur: "What then is the American, this new man?" Crevecoeur, a Frenchman who chose to settle in New York, answered that the new nation, built from a bewildering array of people from different backgrounds, was forging a new consensus. He marveled at the diversity of the settlers, "a mixture of English, Scotch, Irish, French, Dutch, Germans, and Swedes." But they did not remain loyal to their old countries. "Here individuals of all nations are melted into a new race of men," he decided. The Latin motto of the new nation, *E Pluribus Unum* (out of many, one), seemed to affirm Crevecoeur's idea that the United States could build a unity out of diversity.

Over the course of American history there often seemed to be ample reasons to challenge Crevecoeur's idea that Americans could create and maintain a consensus out of diversity. Crevecoeur did not mention the blacks in the United States, most of whom were slaves when he wrote. Nor did he write of Native Americans, whom he did not consider part of the ethnic mix in his day. He also did not anticipate the massive immigration of the nineteenth century that would constantly threaten the idea of assimilation. Anti-Catholicism, Anti-Semitism, racism, and prejudice against Asians and eastern and southern Europeans sometimes led to conflicts, often to bloody riots, and to regular calls for immigration restriction.

Despite such conflicts, the idea survived that American democracy and the American way of life were stronger and better because they were built on diversity. But if many agreed on the value of diversity, not everyone agreed on the exact way that unity could be achieved from the ethnic and racial mix. Some, taking their clue from Israel Zangwill, a Jewish immigrant and playwright, thought of the United States as a great "melting pot" where the cultures and beliefs of various nationalities, races, and ethnic groups were melted down, resulting in an amalgam that was American. Others borrowed from Horace Kallen, another Jewish immigrant, who wrote on the eve of World War I about a "national fellowship of cultural diversity" or what became labeled "cultural pluralism." Immigrants retained some of their ethnic identity, some of their diversity, even as they achieved unity by becoming Americans.

There was always some debate over how much ethnic diversity newcomers could legitimately retain and still become Americans, but the emphasis was always on unity, on the need to abandon old world ways, on the need to become Americanized. By the mid-twentieth century, however, this emphasis changed, at least among some, as political and cultural movements helped to stimulate racial and ethnic pride that led to what became labeled "multiculturalism." Historians began to rewrite the story of the American past to include the lives of ordinary people, women, and various ethnic groups and to give more attention to African-Americans and Native Americans. Ethnic festivals and museum exhibits fostered pride in peoples' ancestry, creating a recognition of what was called "hyphenated Americans"—Irish-Americans, Italian-Americans, African-Americans, Mexican-Americans, and so on. Textbook writers tried to make their accounts of American history more multicultural, and by emphasizing Africa and Asia they diminished the traditional emphasis on Europe and Western Civilization. Those who taught literature sought to add novels, poetry, and other literary (as well as non-literary) texts to the curriculum, replacing those works that had been part of the traditional canon. Some went so far as to condemn the emphasis on the canon as part of a conspiracy to deprive women and minorities of their cultural heritage and to impose upon them the alien ideas of white men. Many states and local school boards mandated multilingual education and the provision of other public services, including the courts, in languages other than English for immigrants and other non-English speakers.

Opposition to all or parts of the emphasis on multiculturalism arose immediately and increased in the 1980s and 1990s. Some feared that the liberalized immigration policies begun in 1965 had attracted too many immigrants, both legal and illegal, and that newcomers would soon overwhelm the "natives." Once again, as in the 1890s, there were campaigns launched to restrict immigration and to make English the official language of the country. Some denounced many of the programs enacted in the 1960s, especially welfare and affirmative action, charging that they gave unfair favored treatment to women and some minorities in government, industry, and the universities. In many of the nation's universities, critics accused supporters of multiculturalism of demeaning the importance of the Western tradition and of undermining free speech and academic freedom by prohibiting certain kinds of talk and behavior; students had to be "politically correct" or be punished for "improper" talk and behavior. These controversies and disagreements, sometimes labeled the "culture wars," were not confined to universities but were fought out on television, in the popular press, and in political campaigns. Patrick Buchanan, advisor to Richard Nixon and Ronald Reagan and sometime conservative presidential candidate himself, announced in 1992: "There is a religious war going on in this country, a cultural war as critical to the kind of nation we shall be as the cold war itself, for this is war for the soul of America."

At the end of the twentieth century the debate over multiculturalism raised once again the question: What does it mean to be an American? The selections that follow reveal at least part of the debate as it has emerged in recent years.

In the first selection, Ronald Takaki begins with a personal experience and uses it to defend a multicultural perspective as the only way to understand the American experience and to preserve a meaningful and accurate picture of American identity. We must recognize the existence of racial and ethnic diversity and conflict, and this recognition of differences must become part of the way we view what American is. "What is needed," he concludes, "is a fresh angle, a study of the American past from a comparative perspective."

Arthur M. Schlesinger, Jr., in the second selection, describes the forces that he claims are "disuniting America." He fears that the revolt against the notion of the melting pot and the recognition of the diversity among Americans have gone too far, leading to the failure to recognize the existence of a "common culture and a single society." He argues that "the cult of ethnicity" cannot be allowed to destroy the "assimilation process" that historically has successfully created "an acceptance of the language, the institutions, and the political ideals that hold the nation together."

In the third selection, Michael Lind reviews the debate historically and in rather different terms. He asks the question, "Are we a nation?" to which he answers "a resounding and unequivocal Yes." A nation, he writes, is "a concrete historical community, defined primarily by common language, common folkways, and a common vernacular culture," and he insists that "most Americans," irrespective of race and ethnicity, share a common national identity and "most immigrants and their descendants will be assimilated into it."

Why has multiculturalism in the textbooks and the universities been so controversial? Do you agree with Patrick Buchanan's apocalyptic evaluation that the issue at stake is the "soul of America"? Does the existence of ethnic and racial diversity and cultural differences among Americans endanger unity? Can the country achieve a workable consensus out of what seems to be a bewildering diversity? Or will the United States experience the kind of ethnic divisions and conflict that have undermined national unity in other parts of the world?

Are those who debate the issue really arguing with one another? For example, does Takaki call for an end to the study of Western Civilization, as Schlesinger argues is the agenda of the multiculturalists? Does Schlesinger in his fears of a "disuniting of America" call for us to ignore the existence and the contributions of minority ethnic and racial groups as Takaki argues? Or, to put the question in a less confrontational manner: Is there a necessary contradiction between a recognition and appreciation of the importance of the Western tradition in American culture and a recognition and appreciation of the contributions of people from other traditions? Are the two positions necessarily irreconcilable? If we Americans are not all identical racially, ethnically, culturally, or in terms of gender and class, does it follow that there is nothing that unites us, that there is nothing that we share and which differentiates us from others?

RONALD TAKAKI

A Different Mirror

I had flown from San Francisco to Norfolk and was riding in a taxi to my hotel to attend a conference on multiculturalism. Hundreds of educators from across the country were meeting to discuss the need for greater cultural diversity in the curriculum. My driver and I chatted about the weather and the tourists. The sky was cloudy, and Virginia Beach was twenty minutes away. The rearview mirror reflected a white man in his forties. "How long have you been in this country?" he asked. "All my life," I replied, wincing. "I was born in the United States." With a strong southern drawl, he remarked: "I was wondering because your English is excellent!" Then, as I had many times before, I explained: "My grandfather came here from Japan in the 1880s. My family has been here, in America, for over a hundred years." He glanced at me in the mirror. Somehow I did not look "American" to him; my eyes and complexion looked foreign.

Suddenly, we both became uncomfortably conscious of a racial divide separating us. An awkward silence turned my gaze from the mirror to the passing landscape, the shore where the English and the Powhatan Indians first encountered each other. Our highway was on land that Sir Walter Raleigh had renamed "Virginia" in honor of Elizabeth I, the Virgin Queen. In the English cultural appropriation of America, the indigenous peoples themselves would become outsiders in their native land. Here, at the eastern edge of the continent, I mused, was the site of the beginning of multicultural America. Jamestown, the English settlement founded in 1607, was nearby: the first twenty Africans were brought here a year before the Pilgrims arrived at Plymouth Rock. Several hundred miles offshore was Bermuda, the "Bermoothes" where William Shakespeare's Prospero had landed and met the native Caliban in *The Tempest*. Earlier, another voyager had made an Atlantic crossing and unexpectedly bumped into some islands to the south. Thinking he had reached Asia, Christopher Columbus mistakenly identified one of the islands as "Cipango" (Japan). In the wake of the admiral, many peoples would come to America from different shores, not only from Europe but also Africa and Asia. One of them would be my grandfather. My mental wandering across terrain and time ended abruptly as we arrived at my destination. I said good-bye to my driver and went into the hotel, carrying a vivid reminder of why I was attending this conference.

Questions like the one my taxi driver asked me are always jarring, but I can understand why he could not see me as American. He had a narrow but widely shared sense of the past—a history that has viewed American as European in ancestry. "Race," Toni Morrison explained, has functioned as a "metaphor" necessary to the "construction of Americanness": in the creation of our national identity, "American" has been defined as "white."

But America has been racially diverse since our very beginning on the Virginia shore, and this reality is increasingly becoming visible and ubiquitous. Currently, one-third of the American people do not trace their origins to Europe; in California, minorities are fast becoming a majority. They already predominate in major cities across the country—New York, Chicago, Atlanta, Detroit, Philadelphia, San Francisco, and Los Angeles.

This emerging demographic diversity has raised fundamental questions about America's identity and culture. In 1990, *Time* published a cover story on "America's Changing Colors." "Someday soon," the magazine announced, "white Americans will become a minority group." How soon? By 2056, most Americans will trace their descent to "Africa, Asia, the Hispanic world, the Pacific Islands, Arabia—almost anywhere but white Europe." This dramatic change in our nation's ethnic composition is altering the way we think about ourselves. "The deeper significance of America's becoming a majority nonwhite society is what it means to the national psyche, to individuals' sense of themselves and their nation—their idea of what it is to be American."

Indeed, more than ever before, as we approach the time when whites become a minority, many of us are perplexed about our national identity and our future as one people. This uncertainty has provoked Allan Bloom to reaffirm the preeminence of Western civilization. Author of *The Closing of the American Mind,* he has emerged as a leader of an intellectual backlash against cultural diversity. In his view, students entering the university are "uncivilized," and the university has the responsibility to "civilize" them. Bloom claims he knows what their "hungers" are and "what they can digest." Eating is one of his favorite metaphors. Noting the "large black presence" in major universities, he laments the "one failure" in race relations—black students have proven to be "indigestible." They do not "melt as have *all* other groups." The problem, he contends, is that "blacks have become blacks": they have become "ethnic." This separatism has been reinforced by an academic permissiveness that has befouled the curriculum with "Black Studies" along with "Learn Another Culture." The only solution, Bloom insists, is "the good old Great Books approach."

Similarly, E. D. Hirsch worries that America is becoming a "tower of Babel," and that this multiplicity of cultures is threatening to rend our social fabric. He, too, longs for a more cohesive culture and a more homogeneous America: "If we *had* to make a choice between the *one* and the *many*, most Americans would choose the principle of unity, since we cannot function as a nation without it." The way to correct this fragmentization, Hirsch argues, is to acculturate "disadvantaged children." What do they need to know? "Only by accumulating shared symbols, and the shared information that symbols represent," Hirsch answers, "can we learn to communicate effectively with one another in our national community." Though he concedes the value of multicultural education, he quickly dismisses it by insisting that it "should not be allowed to supplant or interfere with our schools' responsibility to ensure our children's mastery of American literate culture." In *Cultural Literacy: What Every American Needs to Know*, Hirsch offers a long list of terms that excludes much of the history of minority groups.

While Bloom and Hirsch are reacting defensively to what they regard as a vexatious balkanization of America, many other educators are responding to our diversity as an opportunity to open American minds. In 1990, the Task Force on Minorities for New York emphasized the importance of a culturally diverse education. "Essentially," the *New York Times* commented, "the issue is how to deal with both dimensions of the nation's motto: 'E pluribus unum'—'Out of many, one.' " Universities from New Hampshire to Berkeley have established American cultural diversity graduation requirements. "Every student needs to know," explained University of Wisconsin's chancellor Donna Shalala, "much more about the origins and history of the particular cultures which, as Americans, we will encounter during our lives." Even the University of Minnesota, located in a state that is 98 percent white, requires its students to take ethnic studies courses. Asked why multiculturalism is so important, Dean Fred Lukermann answered: As a national university, Minnesota has to offer a national curriculum—one that includes all of the peoples of America. He added that after graduation many students move to cities like Chicago and Los Angeles and thus need to know about racial diversity. Moreover, many educators stress, multiculturalism has an intellectual purpose. By allowing us to see events from the viewpoints of different groups, a multicultural curriculum enables us to reach toward a more comprehensive understanding of American history.

What is fueling this debate over our national identity and the content of our curriculum is America's intensifying racial crisis. The alarming signs and symptoms seem to be everywhere—the killing of Vincent Chin in Detroit, the black boycott of a Korean grocery store in Flatbush, the hysteria in Boston over the Carol Stuart murder, the battle between white sportsmen and Indians over tribal fishing rights in Wisconsin, the Jewish-black clashes in Brooklyn's Crown Heights, the black-Hispanic competition for jobs and educational resources in Dallas, which *Newsweek* described as "a conflict of the have-nots," and the Willie Horton campaign commercials, which widened the divide between the suburbs and the inner cities.

This reality of racial tension rudely woke America like a fire bell in the night on April 29, 1992. Immediately after four Los Angeles police officers were found not guilty of brutality against Rodney King, rage exploded in Los Angeles. Race relations reached a new nadir. During the nightmarish rampage, scores of people were killed, over two thousand injured, twelve thousand arrested, and almost a billion dollars' worth of property destroyed. The live televised images mesmerized America. The rioting and the murderous melee on the streets resembled the fighting in Beirut and the West Bank. The thousands of fires burning out of control and the dark smoke filling the skies brought back images of the burning oil fields of Kuwait during Desert Storm. Entire sections of Los Angeles looked like a bombed city. "Is this America?" many shocked viewers asked. "Please, can we get along here," pleaded Rodney King, calling for calm. "We all can get along. I mean, we're all stuck here for a while. Let's try to work it out."

But how should "we" be defined? Who are the people "stuck here" in America? One of the lessons of the Los Angeles explosion is the recognition of the fact that we are a multiracial society and that race can no longer be defined in the binary terms of white and black. "We" will have to include Hispanics and Asians. While blacks currently constitute 13 percent of the Los Angeles population, Hispanics represent 40 percent. The 1990 census revealed that South Central Los Angeles, which was predominantly black in 1965 when the Watts rebellion occurred, is now 45 percent Hispanic. A majority of the first 5,438 people arrested were Hispanic, while 37 percent were black. Of the fifty-eight people who died in the riot, more than a third were Hispanic, and about 40 percent of the businesses destroyed were Hispanic-owned. Most of the other shops and stores were Korean-owned. The dreams of many Korean immigrants went up in smoke during the riot: two thousand Korean-owned businesses were damaged or demolished, totaling about $400 million in losses. There is evidence indicating they were targeted. "After all," explained a black gang member, "we didn't burn our community, just *their* stores."

"I don't feel like I'm in America anymore," said Denisse Bustamente as she watched the police protecting the firefighters. "I feel like I am far away." Indeed, Americans have been witnessing ethnic strife erupting around the world—the rise of neo-Nazism and the murder of Turks in Germany, the ugly "ethnic cleansing" in Bosnia, the terrible and bloody clashes between Muslims and Hindus in India. Is the situation here different, we have been nervously wondering, or do ethnic conflicts elsewhere represent a prologue for America? What is the nature of malevolence? Is there a deep, perhaps primordial, need for group identity rooted in hatred for the other? Is ethnic pluralism possible for America? But answers have been limited. Television reports have been little more than thirty-second sound bites. Newspaper articles have been mostly superficial descriptions of racial antagonisms and the current urban malaise. What is lacking is historical context; consequently, we are left feeling bewildered.

How did we get to this point, Americans everywhere are anxiously asking. What does our diversity mean, and where is it leading us? *How* do we work it out in the post–Rodney King era?

Certainly one crucial way is for our society's various ethnic groups to develop a greater understanding of each other. For example, how can African Americans and Korean Americans work it out unless they learn about each other's cultures, histories, and also economic situations? This need to share knowledge about our ethnic diversity has acquired new importance and has given new urgency to the pursuit for a more accurate history.

More than ever before, there is a growing realization that the established scholarship has tended to define America too narrowly. For example, in his prize-winning study *The Uprooted*, Harvard historian Oscar Handlin presented—to use the book's subtitle—"the Epic Story of the Great Migrations That Made the American People." But Handlin's "epic story" excluded the "uprooted" from Africa, Asia, and Latin America—the other "Great Migrations" that also helped to make "the American People." Similarly, in *The Age of Jackson*, Arthur M. Schlesinger, Jr., left out blacks and Indians. There is not even a mention of two marker events—the Nat Turner insurrection and Indian removal, which Andrew Jackson himself would have been surprised to find omitted from a history of his era.

Still, Schlesinger and Handlin offered us a refreshing revisionism, paving the way for the study of common people rather than princes and presidents. They inspired the next generation of historians to examine groups such as the artisan laborers of Philadelphia and the Irish immigrants of Boston. "Once I thought to write a history of the immigrants in America," Handlin confided in his introduction to *The Uprooted*. "I discovered that the immigrants *were* American history." This door, once opened, led to the flowering of a more inclusive scholarship as we began to recognize that ethnic history was American history. Suddenly, there was a proliferation of seminal works such as Irving Howe's *World of Our Fathers: The Journey of the East European Jews to America*, Dee Brown's *Bury My Heart at Wounded Knee: An Indian History of the American West*, Albert Camarillo's *Chicanos in a Changing Society*, Lawrence Levine's *Black Culture and Black Consciousness*, Yuji Ichioka's *The Issei: The World of the First Generation Japanese Immigrants*, and Kerby Miller's *Emigrants and Exiles: Ireland and the Irish Exodus to North America*.

But even this new scholarship, while it has given us a more expanded understanding of the mosaic called America, does not address our needs in the post–Rodney King era. These books and others like them fragment American society, studying each group separately, in isolation from the other groups and the whole. While scrutinizing our specific pieces, we have to step back in order to see the rich and complex portrait they compose. What is needed is a fresh angle, a study of the American past from a comparative perspective.

While all of America's many groups cannot be covered in one book, the English immigrants and their descendants require attention, for they possessed inordinate power to define American culture and make public policy. What men like John Winthrop, Thomas Jefferson, and Andrew Jackson thought as well as did mattered greatly to all of us and was consequential for everyone. A broad range of groups has been selected: African Americans, Asian Americans, Chicanos, Irish, Jews, and Indians. While together they help to explain general patterns in our society, each has contributed to the making of the United States.

African Americans have been the central minority throughout our country's history. They were initially brought here on a slave ship in 1619. Actually, these first twenty Africans might not have been slaves; rather, like most of the white laborers, they were probably indentured servants. The transformation of Africans into slaves is the story of the "hidden" origins of slavery. How and when was it decided to institute a system of bonded black labor? What happened, while freighted with racial significance, was actually conditioned by class conflicts within white society. Once established, the "peculiar institution" would have consequences for centuries to come. During the nineteenth century, the political storm over slavery almost destroyed the nation. Since the Civil War and emancipation, race has continued to be largely defined in relation to African Americans—segregation, civil rights, the underclass, and affirmative action. Constituting the largest minority group in our society, they have been at the cutting edge of the Civil Rights Movement. Indeed, their struggle has been a constant reminder of America's moral vision as a country committed to the principle of liberty. Martin Luther King clearly understood this truth when he wrote from a jail cell: "We will reach the goal of freedom in Birmingham and all over the nation, because the goal of America is freedom. Abused and scorned though we may be, our destiny is tied up with America's destiny."

Asian Americans have been here for over one hundred and fifty years, before many European immigrant groups. But as "strangers" coming from a "different shore," they have been stereotyped as "heathen," exotic, and unassimilable. Seeking "Gold Mountain," the Chinese arrived first, and what happened to them influenced the reception of the Japanese, Koreans, Filipinos, and Asian Indians as well as the Southeast Asian refugees like the Vietnamese and the Hmong. The 1882 Chinese Exclusion Act was the first law that prohibited the entry of immigrants on the basis of nationality. The Chinese condemned this restriction as racist and tyrannical. "They call us 'Chink,' " complained a Chinese immigrant, cursing the "white demons." "They think we no good! America cuts us off. No more come now, too bad!" This precedent later provided a basis for the restriction of European immigrant groups such as Italians, Russians, Poles, and Greeks. The Japanese painfully discovered that their accomplishments in America did not lead to acceptance, for during World War II, unlike Italian Americans and German Americans, they were placed in internment camps. Two-thirds of them were citizens by birth. "How could I as a 6-month-old child born in this country," asked Congressman Robert Matsui years later, "be declared by my own Government to be an enemy alien?" Today, Asian Americans represent the fastest-growing ethnic group. They have also become the focus of much mass media attention as "the Model Minority" not only for blacks and Chicanos, but also for whites on welfare and even middle-class whites experiencing economic difficulties.

Chicanos represent the largest group among the Hispanic population, which is projected to outnumber African Americans. They have been in the United States for a long time, initially incorporated by the war against Mexico. The treaty had moved the border between the two countries, and the people of "occupied" Mexico suddenly found themselves "foreigners" in their "native land." As historian Albert Camarillo pointed out, the Chicano past is an integral part of America's westward expansion, also known as "manifest destiny." But while the early Chicanos were a colonized people, most of them today have immigrant roots. Many began the trek to El Norte in the early twentieth century. "As I had heard a lot about the United States," Jesus Garza recalled, "it was my dream to come here." "We came to know families from Chihauhua, Sonora, Jalisco, and Durango," stated Ernesto Galarza. "Like ourselves, our Mexican neighbors had come this far moving step by step, working and waiting, as if they were feeling their way up a ladder." Nevertheless, the Chicano experience has been unique, for most of them have lived close to their homeland—a proximity that has helped reinforce their language, identity, and culture. This migration to El Norte has continued to the present. Los Angeles has more people of Mexican origin than any other city in the world, except Mexico City. A mostly mestizo people of Indian as well as African and Spanish ancestries, Chicanos currently represent the largest minority group in the Southwest, where they have been visibly transforming culture and society.

The Irish came here in greater numbers than most immigrant groups. Their history has been tied to America's past from the very beginning. Ireland represented the earliest English frontier: the conquest of Ireland occurred before the colonization of America, and the Irish were the first group that the English called "savages." In this context, the Irish past foreshadowed the Indian future. During the nineteenth century, the Irish, like the Chinese, were victims of British colonialism. While the Chinese fled from the ravages of the Opium Wars, the Irish were pushed from their homeland by "English tyranny." Here they became construction workers and factory operatives as well as the "maids" of America. Representing a Catholic group seeking to settle in a fiercely Protestant society, the Irish immigrants were targets of American nativist hostility. They were also what historian Lawrence J. McCaffrey called "the pioneers of the American urban ghetto," "previewing" experiences that would later be shared by the Italians, Poles, and other groups from southern and eastern Europe. Furthermore, they offer contrast to the immigrants from Asia. The Irish came about the same time as the Chinese, but they had a distinct advantage: the Naturalization Law of 1790 had reserved citizenship for "whites" only. Their compatible complexion allowed them to assimilate by blending into American society. In making their journey successfully into the mainstream, however, these immigrants from Erin pursued an Irish "ethnic" strategy: they promoted "Irish" solidarity in order to gain political power and also to dominate the skilled blue-collar occupations, often at the expense of the Chinese and blacks.

Fleeing pogroms and religious persecution in Russia, the Jews were driven from what John Cuddihy described as the "Middle Ages into the Anglo-American world of the *goyim* 'beyond the pale.' " To them, America represented the Promised Land. This vision led Jews to struggle not only for themselves but also for other oppressed groups, especially blacks. After the 1917 East St. Louis race riot, the Yiddish *Forward* of New York compared this anti-black violence to a 1903 pogrom in Russia: "Kishinev and St. Louis—the same soil, the same people." Jews cheered when Jackie Robinson broke into the Brooklyn Dodgers in 1947. "He was adopted as the surrogate hero by many of us growing up at the time," recalled Jack Greenberg of the NAACP Legal Defense Fund. "He was the way we saw ourselves triumphing against the forces of bigotry and ignorance." Jews stood shoulder to shoulder with blacks in the Civil Rights Movement: two-thirds of the white volunteers who went south during the 1964 Freedom Summer were Jewish. Today Jews are considered a highly successful "ethnic" group. How did they make such great socioeconomic strides? This question is often reframed by neoconservative intellectuals like Irving Kristol and Nathan Glazer to read: if Jewish immigrants were able to lift themselves from poverty into the mainstream through self-help and education without welfare and affirmative action, why can't blacks? But what this thinking overlooks is the unique history of Jewish immigrants, especially the initial advantages of many of them as literate and skilled. Moreover, it minimizes the virulence of racial prejudice rooted in American slavery.

Indians represent a critical contrast, for theirs was not an immigrant experience. The Wampanoags were on the shore as the first English strangers arrived in what would be called "New England." The encounters between Indians and whites not only shaped the course of race relations, but also influenced the very culture and identity of the general society. The architect of Indian removal, President Andrew Jackson told Congress: "Our conduct toward these people is deeply interesting to the national character." Frederick Jackson Turner understood the meaning of this observation when he identified the frontier as our transforming crucible. At first, the European newcomers had to wear Indian moccasins and shout the war cry. "Little by little," as they subdued the wilderness, the pioneers became "a new product" that was "American." But Indians have had a different view of this entire process. "The white man," Luther Standing Bear of the Sioux explained, "does not understand the Indian for the reason that he does not understand America." Continuing to be "troubled with primitive fears," he has "in his consciousness the perils of this frontier continent. . . . The man from Europe is still a foreigner and an alien. And he still hates the man who questioned his path across the continent." Indians questioned what Jackson and Turner trumpeted as "progress." For them, the frontier had a different "significance": their history was how the West was lost. But their story has also been one of resistance. As Vine Deloria declared, "Custer died for your sins."

By looking at these groups from a multicultural perspective, we can comparatively analyze their experiences in order to develop an understanding of their differences and similarities. Race, we will see, has been a social construction that has historically set apart racial minorities from European immigrant groups. Contrary to the notions of scholars like Nathan Glazer and Thomas Sowell, race in America has not been the same as ethnicity. A broad comparative focus also allows us to see how the varied experiences of different racial and ethnic groups occurred within shared contexts.

During the nineteenth century, for example, the Market Revolution employed Irish immigrant laborers in New England factories as it expanded cotton fields worked by enslaved blacks across Indian lands toward Mexico. Like blacks, the Irish newcomers were stereotyped as "savages," ruled by passions rather than "civilized" virtues such as self-control and hard work. The Irish saw themselves as the "slaves" of British oppressors, and during a visit to Ireland in the 1840s, Frederick Douglass found that the "wailing notes" of the Irish ballads reminded him of the "wild notes" of slave songs. The United States annexation of California, while incorporating Mexicans, led to trade with Asia and the migration of "strangers" from Pacific shores. In 1870, Chinese immigrant laborers were transported to Massachusetts as scabs to break an Irish immigrant strike; in response, the Irish recognized the need for interethnic working-class solidarity and tried to organize a Chinese lodge of the Knights of St. Crispin. After the Civil War, Mississippi planters recruited Chinese immigrants to discipline the newly freed blacks. During the debate over an immigration exclusion bill in 1882, a senator asked: If Indians could be located on reservations, why not the Chinese?

Other instances of our connectedness abound. In 1903, Mexican and Japanese farm laborers went on strike together in California: their union officers had names like Yamaguchi and Lizarras, and strike meetings were conducted in Japanese and Spanish. The Mexican strikers declared that they were standing in solidarity with their "Japanese brothers" because the two groups had toiled together in the fields and were now fighting together for a fair wage. Speaking in impassioned Yiddish during the 1909 "uprising of twenty thousand" strikers in New York, the charismatic Clara Lemlich compared the abuse of Jewish female garment workers to the experience of blacks: "[The bosses] yell at the girls and 'call them down' even worse than I imagine the Negro slaves were in the South." During the 1920s, elite universities like Harvard worried about the increasing numbers of Jewish students, and new admissions criteria were instituted to curb their enrollment. Jewish students were scorned for their studiousness and criticized for their "clannishness." Recently, Asian-American students have been the targets of similar complaints: they have been called "nerds" and told there are "too many" of them on campus.

Indians were already here, while blacks were forcibly transported to America, and Mexicans were initially enclosed by America's expanding border. The other groups came here as immigrants: for them, America represented liminality—a new world where they could pursue extravagant urges and do things they had thought beyond their capabilities. Like the land itself, they found themselves "betwixt and between all fixed points of classification." No longer fastened as fiercely to their old countries, they felt a stirring to become new people in a society still being defined and formed.

These immigrants made bold and dangerous crossings, pushed by political events and economic hardships in their homelands and pulled by America's demand for labor as well as by their own dreams for a better life. "By all means let me go to America," a young man in Japan begged his parents. He had calculated that in one year as a laborer here he could save almost a thousand yen—an amount equal to the income of a governor in Japan. "My dear Father," wrote an immigrant Irish girl living in New York, "Any man or woman without a family are fools that would not venture and come to this plentyful Country where no man or woman ever hungered." In the shtetls of Russia, the cry "To America!" roared like "wild-fire." "America was in everybody's mouth," a Jewish immigrant recalled. "Businessmen talked [about] it over their accounts; the market women made up their quarrels that they might discuss it from stall to stall; people who had relatives in the famous land went around reading their letters." Similarly, for Mexican immigrants crossing the border in the early twentieth century, El Norte became the stuff of overblown hopes. "If only you could see how nice the United States is," they said, "that is why the Mexicans are crazy about it."

The signs of America's ethnic diversity can be discerned across the continent—Ellis Island, Angel Island, Chinatown, Harlem, South Boston, the Lower East Side, places with Spanish names like Los Angeles and San Antonio or Indian names like Massachusetts and Iowa. Much of what is familiar in America's cultural landscape actually has ethnic origins. The Bing cherry was developed by an early Chinese immigrant named Ah Bing. American Indians were cultivating corn, tomatoes, and tobacco long before the arrival of Columbus. The term *okay* was derived from the Choctaw word *oke,* meaning "it is so." There is evidence indicating that the name *Yankee* came from Indian terms for the English—from *eankke* in Cherokee and *Yankwis* in Delaware. Jazz and blues as well as rock and roll have African-American origins. The "Forty-Niners" of the Gold Rush learned mining techniques from the Mexicans; American cowboys acquired herding skills from Mexican *vaqueros* and adopted their range terms—such as *lariat* from *la reata, lasso* from *lazo,* and *stampede* from *estampida.* Songs like "God Bless America," "Easter Parade," and "White Christmas" were written by a Russian-Jewish immigrant named Israel Baline, more popularly known as Irving Berlin.

Furthermore, many diverse ethnic groups have contributed to the building of the American economy, forming what Walt Whitman saluted as "a vast, surging, hopeful army of workers." They worked in the South's cotton fields, New England's textile mills, Hawaii's canefields, New York's garment factories, California's orchards, Washington's salmon canneries, and Arizona's copper mines. They built the railroad, the great symbol of America's industrial triumph. Laying railroad ties, black laborers sang:

> Down the railroad, um-huh
> Well, raise the iron, um-huh
> Raise the iron, um-huh.

Irish railroad workers shouted as they stretched an iron ribbon across the continent:

> Then drill, my Paddies, drill—
> Drill, my heroes, drill,
> Drill all day, no sugar in your tay
> Workin' on the U.P. railway.

Japanese laborers in the Northwest chorused as their bodies fought the fickle weather:

> A railroad worker—
> That's me!
> I am great.
> Yes, I am a railroad worker.
> Complaining:
> "It is too hot!"
> "It is too cold!"
> "It rains too often!"
> "It snows too much!"
> They all ran off.
> I alone remained.
> I am a railroad worker!

Chicano workers in the Southwest joined in as they swore at the punishing work:

> Some unloaded rails
> Others unloaded ties,
> And others of my companions
> Threw out thousands of curses.

Moreover, our diversity was tied to America's most serious crisis: the Civil War was fought over a racial issue—slavery. In his "First Inaugural Address," presented on March 4, 1861, President Abraham Lincoln declared: "One section of our country believes slavery is *right* and ought to be extended, while the other believes it is *wrong* and ought not to be extended." Southern secession, he argued, would be anarchy. Lincoln sternly warned the South that he had a solemn oath to defend and preserve the Union. Americans were one people, he explained, bound together by "the mystic chords of memory, stretching from every battlefield and patriot grave to every living heart and hearthstone all over this broad land." The struggle and sacrifices of the War for Independence had enabled Americans to create a new nation out of thirteen separate colonies. But Lincoln's appeal for unity fell on deaf ears in the South. And the war came. Two and a half years later, at Gettysburg, President Lincoln declared that "brave men" had fought and "consecrated" the ground of this battlefield in order to preserve the Union. Among the brave were black men. Shortly after this bloody battle, Lincoln acknowledged the military contributions of blacks. "There will be some black men," he wrote in a letter to an old friend, James C. Conkling, "who can remember that with silent tongue, and clenched teeth, and steady eye, and well-poised bayonet, they have helped mankind on to this great consummation. . . ." Indeed, 186,000 blacks served in the Union Army, and one-third of them were listed as missing or dead. Black men in blue, Frederick Douglass pointed out, were "on the battlefield mingling their blood with that of white men in one common effort to save the country." Now the mystic chords of memory stretched across the new battlefields of the Civil War, and black soldiers were buried in "patriot graves." They, too, had given their lives to ensure that the "government of the people, by the people, for the people shall not perish from the earth."

Like these black soldiers, the people in our study have been actors in history, not merely victims of discrimination and exploitation. They are entitled to be viewed as subjects—as men and women with minds, wills, and voices.

> In the telling and retelling
>   of their stories,
> They create communities
>   of memory.

They also re-vision history. "It is very natural that the history written by the victim," said a Mexican in 1874, "does not altogether chime with the story of the victor." Sometimes they are hesitant to speak, thinking they are only "little people." "I don't know why anybody wants to hear my history," an Irish maid said apologetically in 1900. "Nothing ever happened to me worth the tellin'."

But their stories are worthy. Through their stories, the people who have lived America's history can help all of us, including my taxi driver, understand that Americans originated from many shores, and that all of us are entitled to dignity. "I hope this survey do a lot of good for Chinese people," an immigrant told an interviewer from Stanford University in the 1920s. "Make American people realize that Chinese people are humans. I think very few American people really know anything about Chinese." But the remembering is also for the sake of the children. "This story is dedicated to the descendants of Lazar and Goldie Glauberman," Jewish immigrant Minnie Miller wrote in her autobiography. "My history is bound up in their history and the generations that follow should know where they came from to know better who they are." Similarly, Tomo Shoji, an elderly Nisei woman, urged Asian Americans to learn more about their roots: "We got such good, fantastic stories to tell. All our stories are different." Seeking to know how they fit into America, many young people have become listeners; they are eager to learn about the hardships and humiliations experienced by their parents and grandparents. They want to hear their stories, unwilling to remain ignorant or ashamed of their identity and past.

The telling of stories liberates. By writing about the people on Mango Street, Sandra Cisneros explained, "the ghost does not ache so much." The place no longer holds her with "both arms. She sets me free." Indeed, stories may not be as innocent or simple as they seem to be. Native-American novelist Leslie Marmon Silko cautioned:

> I will tell you something about stories. . .
> They aren't just entertainment.
>   Don't be fooled.

Indeed, the accounts given by the people in this study vibrantly re-create moments, capturing the complexities of human emotions and thoughts. They also provide the authenticity of experience. After she escaped from slavery, Harriet Jacobs wrote in her autobiography: "[My purpose] is not to tell you what I have heard but what I have seen—and what I have suffered." In their sharing of memory, the people in this study offer us an opportunity to see ourselves reflected in a mirror called history.

In his recent study of Spain and the New World, *The Buried Mirror,* Carlos Fuentes points out that mirrors have been found in the tombs of ancient Mexico, placed there to guide the dead through the underworld. He also tells us about the legend of Quetzalcoatl, the Plumed Serpent: when this god was given a mirror by the Toltec deity Tezcatlipoca, he saw a man's face in the mirror and realized his own humanity. For us, the "mirror" of history can guide the living and also help us recognize who we have been and hence are. In *A Distant Mirror,* Barbara W. Tuchman finds "phenomenal parallels" between the "calamitous 14th century" of European society and our own era. We can, she observes, have "greater fellow-feeling for a distraught age" as we painfully recognize the "similar disarray," "collapsing assumptions," and "unusual discomfort."

But what is needed in our own perplexing times is not so much a "distant" mirror, as one that is "different." While the study of the past can provide collective self-knowledge, it often reflects the scholar's particular perspective or view of the world. What happens when historians leave out many of America's peoples? What happens, to borrow the words of Adrienne Rich, "when someone with the authority of a teacher" describes our society, and "you are not in it"? Such an experience can be disorienting—"a moment of psychic disequilibrium, as if you looked into a mirror and saw nothing."

Through their narratives about their lives and circumstances, the people of America's diverse groups are able to see themselves and each other in our common past. They celebrate what Ishmael Reed has described as a society "unique" in the world because "the world is here"—a place "where the cultures of the world crisscross." Much of America's past, they point out, has been riddled with racism. At the same time, these people offer hope, affirming the struggle for equality as a central theme in our country's history. At its conception, our nation was dedicated to the proposition of equality. What has given concreteness to this powerful national principle has been our coming together in the creation of a new society. "Stuck here" together, workers of different backgrounds have attempted to get along with each other.

> People harvesting
> Work together unaware
> Of racial problems,

wrote a Japanese immigrant describing a lesson learned by Mexican and Asian farm laborers in California.

Finally, how do we see our prospects for "working out" America's racial crisis? Do we see it as through a glass darkly? Do the televised images of racial hatred and violence that riveted us in 1992 during the days of rage in Los Angeles frame a future of divisive race relations—what Arthur Schlesinger, Jr., has fearfully denounced as the "disuniting of America"? Or will Americans of diverse races and ethnicities be able to connect themselves to a larger narrative? Whatever happens, we can be certain that much of our society's future will be influenced by which "mirror" we choose to see ourselves. America does not belong to one race or one group, the people in this study remind us, and Americans have been constantly redefining their national identity from the moment of first contact on the Virginia shore. By sharing their stories, they invite us to see ourselves in a different mirror.

Arthur M. Schlesinger, Jr.

The Disuniting of America

The attack on the common American identity is the culmination of the cult of ethnicity. That attack was mounted in the first instance by European Americans of non-British origin ("unmeltable ethnics") against the British foundations of American culture; then, latterly and massively, by Americans of non-European origin against the European foundations of that culture. As Theodore Roosevelt's foreboding suggests, the European immigration itself palpitated with internal hostilities, everyone at everybody else's throats—hardly the "monocultural" crowd portrayed by ethnocentric separatists. After all, the two great "world" wars of the twentieth century began as fights among European states. Making a single society out of this diversity of antagonistic European peoples is a hard enough job. The new salience of non-European, nonwhite stocks compounds the challenge. And the non-Europeans, or at least their self-appointed spokesmen, bring with them a resentment, in some cases a hatred, of Europe and the West provoked by generations of Western colonialism, racism, condescension, contempt, and cruel exploitation.

I

Will not this rising flow of non-European immigrants create a "minority majority" that will make Eurocentrism obsolete by the twenty-first century? This is the fear of some white Americans and the hope (and sometimes the threat) of some nonwhites.

Immigrants were responsible for a third of population growth during the 1980s. More arrived than in any decade since the second of the century. And the composition of the newcomers changed dramatically. In 1910 nearly 90 percent of immigrants came from Europe. In the 1980s more than 80 percent came from Asia and Latin America.

Still, foreign-born residents constitute only about 7 percent of the population today as against nearly 15 percent when the first Roosevelt and Wilson were worrying about hyphenated Americans. Stephan Thernstrom doubts that the minority majority will ever arrive. The black share in the population has grown rather slowly—9.9 percent in 1920, 10 percent in 1950, 11.1 percent in 1970, 12.1 percent in 1990. Neither Asian-Americans nor Hispanic-Americans go in for especially large families; and family size in any case tends to decline as income and intermarriage increase. "If today's immigrants assimilate to American ways as readily as their predecessors at the turn of the century—as seems to be happening," Thernstrom concludes, "there won't be a minority majority issue anyway."

America has so long seen itself as the asylum for the oppressed and persecuted—and has done itself and the world so much good thereby—that any curtailment of immigration offends something in the American soul. No one wants to be a Know-Nothing. Yet uncontrolled immigration is an impossibility; so the criteria of control are questions the American democracy must confront. We have shifted the basis of admission three times this century—from national origins in 1924 to family reunification in 1965 to needed skills in 1990. The future of immigration policy depends on the capacity of the assimilation process to continue to do what it has done so well in the past: to lead newcomers to an acceptance of the language, the institutions, and the political ideals that hold the nation together.

II

Is Europe really the root of all evil? The crimes of Europe against lesser breeds without the law (not to mention even worse crimes—Hitlerism and Stalinism—against other Europeans) are famous. But these crimes do not alter other facts of history: that Europe was the birthplace of the United States of America, that European ideas and culture formed the republic, that the United States is an extension of European civilization, and that nearly 80 percent of Americans are of European descent.

When Irving Howe, hardly a notorious conservative, dared write, "The Bible, Homer, Plato, Sophocles, Shakespeare are central to our culture," an outraged reader ("having graduated this past year from Amherst") wrote, "Where on Howe's list is the *Quran,* the *Gita,* Confucius, and other central cultural artifacts of the peoples of our nation?" No one can doubt the importance of these works nor the influence they have had on other societies. But on American society? It may be too bad that dead white European males have played so large a role in shaping our culture. But that's the way it is. One cannot erase history.

These humdrum historical facts, and not some dastardly imperialist conspiracy, explain the Eurocentric slant in American schools. Would anyone seriously argue that teachers should conceal the European origins of American civilization? or that schools should cater to the 20 percent and ignore the 80 percent? Of course the 20 percent and their contributions should be integrated into the curriculum too, which is the point of cultural pluralism.

But self-styled "multiculturalists" are very often ethnocentric separatists who see little in the Western heritage beyond Western crimes. The Western tradition, in this view, is inherently racist, sexist, "classist," hegemonic; irredeemably repressive, irredeemably oppressive. The spread of Western culture is due not to any innate quality but simply to the spread of Western power. Thus the popularity of European classical music around the world—and, one supposes, of American jazz and rock too—is evidence not of wide appeal but of "the pattern of imperialism, in which the conquered culture adopts that of the conqueror."

Such animus toward Europe lay behind the well-known crusade against the Western-civilization course at Stanford ("Hey-hey, ho-ho, Western culture's got to go!"). According to the National Endowment for the Humanities, students can graduate from 78 percent of American colleges and universities without taking a course in the history of Western civilization. A number of institutions—among them Dartmouth, Wisconsin, Mt. Holyoke—require courses in third-world or ethnic studies but not in Western civilization. The mood is one of divesting Americans of the sinful European inheritance and seeking redemptive infusions from non-Western cultures.

III

One of the oddities of the situation is that the assault on the Western tradition is conducted very largely with analytical weapons forged in the West. What are the names invoked by the coalition of latter-day Marxists, deconstructionists, poststructuralists, radical feminists, Afrocentrists? Marx, Nietzsche, Gramsci, Derrida, Foucault, Lacan, Sartre, de Beauvoir, Habermas, the Frankfurt "critical theory" school—Europeans all. The "unmasking," "demythologizing," "decanonizing," "dehegemonizing" blitz against Western culture depends on methods of critical analysis unique to the West—which surely testifies to the internally redemptive potentialities of the Western tradition.

Even Afrocentrists seem to accept subliminally the very Eurocentric standards they think they are rejecting. "Black intellectuals condemn Western civilization," Professor Pearce Williams says, "yet ardently wish to prove it was founded by their ancestors." And, like Frantz Fanon and Léopold Senghor, whose books figure prominently on their reading lists, Afrocentric ideologues are intellectual children of the West they repudiate. Fanon, the eloquent spokesman of the African wretched of the earth, had French as his native tongue and based his analyses on Freud, Marx, and Sartre. Senghor, the prophet of Negritude, wrote in French, established the Senegalese educational system on the French model and, when he left the presidency of Senegal, retired to France.

Western hegemony, it would seem, can be the source of protest as well as of power. Indeed, the invasion of American schools by the Afrocentric curriculum, not to mention the conquest of university departments of English and comparative literature by deconstructionists, poststructuralists, etc., are developments that by themselves refute the extreme theory of "cultural hegemony." Of course, Gramsci had a point. Ruling values do dominate and permeate any society; but they do not have the rigid and monolithic grip on American democracy that academic leftists claim.

Radical academics denounce the "canon" as an instrument of European oppression enforcing the hegemony of the white race, the male sex, and the capitalist class, designed, in the words of one professor, "to rewrite the past and construct the present from the perspective of the privileged and the powerful." Or in the elegant words of another—and a professor of theological ethics at that: "The canon of great literature was created by high Anglican assholes to underwrite their social class."

The poor old canon is seen not only as conspiratorial but as static. Yet nothing changes more regularly and reliably than the canon: compare, for example, the canon in American poetry as defined by Edmund Clarence Stedman in his *Poets of America* (1885) with the canon of 1935 or of 1985 (whatever happened to Longfellow and Whittier?); or recall the changes that have overtaken the canonical literature of American history in the last half-century (who reads Beard and Parrington now?). And the critics clearly have no principled objection to the idea of the canon. They simply wish to replace an old gang by a new gang. After all, a canon means only that because you can't read everything, you give some books priority over others.

Oddly enough, serious Marxists—Marx and Engels, Lukacs, Trotsky, Gramsci—had the greatest respect for what Lukacs called "the classical heritage of mankind." Well they should have, for most great literature and much good history are deeply subversive in their impact on orthodoxies. Consider the present-day American literary canon: Emerson, Jefferson, Melville, Whitman, Hawthorne, Thoreau, Lincoln, Twain, Dickinson, William and Henry James, Henry Adams, Holmes, Dreiser, Faulkner, O'Neill. Lackeys of the ruling class? Apologists for the privileged and the powerful? Agents of American imperialism? Come on!

It is time to adjourn the chat about hegemony. If hegemony were as real as the cultural radicals pretend, Afrocentrism would never have got anywhere, and the heirs of William Lyon Phelps would still be running the Modern Language Association.

IV

Is the Western tradition a bar to progress and a curse on humanity? Would it really do America and the world good to get rid of the European legacy?

No doubt Europe has done terrible things, not least to itself. But what culture has not? History, said Edward Gibbon, is little more than the register of the crimes, follies, and misfortunes of mankind. The sins of the West are no worse than the sins of Asia or of the Middle East or of Africa.

There remains, however, a crucial difference between the Western tradition and the others. The crimes of the West have produced their own antidotes. They have provoked great movements to end slavery, to raise the status of women, to abolish torture, to combat racism, to defend freedom of inquiry and expression, to advance personal liberty and human rights.

Whatever the particular crimes of Europe, that continent is also the source—the *unique* source—of those liberating ideas of individual liberty, political democracy, the rule of law, human rights, and cultural freedom that constitute our most precious legacy and to which most of the world today aspires. These are *European* ideas, not Asian, nor African, nor Middle Eastern ideas, except by adoption.

The freedoms of inquiry and of artistic creation, for example, are Western values. Consider the differing reactions to the case of Salman Rushdie: what the West saw as an intolerable attack on individual freedom the Middle East saw as a proper punishment for an evildoer who had violated the mores of his group. Individualism itself is looked on with abhorrence and dread by collectivist cultures in which loyalty to the group overrides personal goals—cultures that, social scientists say, comprise about 70 percent of the world's population.

There is surely no reason for Western civilization to have guilt trips laid on it by champions of cultures based on despotism, superstition, tribalism, and fanaticism. In this regard the Afrocentrists are especially absurd. The West needs no lectures on the superior virtue of those "sun people" who sustained slavery until Western imperialism abolished it (and, it is reported, sustain it to this day in Mauritania and the Sudan), who still keep women in subjection and cut off their clitorises, who carry out racial persecutions not only against Indians and other Asians but against fellow Africans from the wrong tribes, who show themselves either incapable of operating a democracy or ideologically hostile to the democratic idea, and who in their tyrannies and massacres, their Idi Amins and Boukassas, have stamped with utmost brutality on human rights.

Certainly the European overlords did little enough to prepare Africa for self-government. But democracy would find it hard in any case to put down roots in a tribalist and patrimonial culture that, long before the West invaded Africa, had sacralized the personal authority of chieftains and ordained the submission of the rest. What the West would call corruption is regarded through much of Africa as no more than the prerogative of power. Competitive political parties, an independent judiciary, a free press, the rule of law are alien to African traditions.

It was the French, not the Algerians, who freed Algerian women from the veil (much to the irritation of Frantz Fanon, who regarded deveiling as symbolic rape); as in India it was the British, not the Indians, who ended (or did their best to end) the horrible custom of *suttee*—widows burning themselves alive on their husbands' funeral pyres. And it was the West, not the non-Western cultures, that launched the crusade to abolish slavery—and in doing so encountered mighty resistance, especially in the Islamic world (where Moslems, with fine impartiality, enslaved whites as well as blacks). Those many brave and humane Africans who are struggling these days for decent societies are animated by Western, not by African, ideals. White guilt can be pushed too far.

The Western commitment to human rights has unquestionably been intermittent and imperfect. Yet the ideal remains—and movement toward it has been real, if sporadic. Today it is the *Western* democratic tradition that attracts and empowers people of all continents, creeds, and colors. When the Chinese students cried and died for democracy in Tiananmen Square, they brought with them not representations of Confucius or Buddha but a model of the Statue of Liberty.

V

The great American asylum, as Crèvecoeur called it, open, as Washington said, to the oppressed and persecuted of all nations, has been from the start an experiment in a multiethnic society. This is a bolder experiment than we sometimes remember. History is littered with the wreck of states that tried to combine diverse ethnic or linguistic or religious groups within a single sovereignty. Today's headlines tell of imminent crisis or impending dissolution in one or another multiethnic polity—the Soviet Union, India, Yugoslavia, Czechoslovakia, Ireland, Belgium, Canada, Lebanon, Cyprus, Israel, Ceylon, Spain, Nigeria, Kenya, Angola, Trinidad, Guyana. . . . The list is almost endless. The luck so far of the American experiment has been due in large part to the vision of the melting pot. "No other nation," Margaret Thatcher has said, "has so successfully combined people of different races and nations within a single culture."

But even in the United States, ethnic ideologues have not been without effect. They have set themselves against the old American ideal of assimilation. They call on the republic to think in terms not of individual but of group identity and to move the polity from individual rights to group rights. They have made a certain progress in transforming the United States into a more segregated society. They have done their best to turn a college generation against Europe and the Western tradition. They have imposed ethnocentric, Afrocentric, and bilingual curricula on public schools, well designed to hold minority children out of American society. They have told young people from minority groups that the Western democratic tradition is not for them. They have encouraged minorities to see themselves as victims and to live by alibis rather than to claim the opportunities opened for them by the potent combination of black protest and white guilt. They have filled the air with recrimination and rancor and have remarkably advanced the fragmentation of American life.

Yet I believe the campaign against the idea of common ideals and a single society will fail. Gunnar Myrdal was surely right: for all the damage it has done, the upsurge of ethnicity is a superficial enthusiasm stirred by romantic ideologues and unscrupulous hucksters whose claim to speak for their minorities is thoughtlessly accepted by the media. I doubt that the ethnic vogue expresses a reversal of direction from assimilation to apartheid among the minorities themselves. Indeed, the more the ideologues press the case for ethnic separatism, the less they appeal to the mass of their own groups. They have thus far done better in intimidating the white majority than in converting their own constituencies.

"No nation in history," writes Lawrence Fuchs, the political scientist and immigration expert in his fine book *The American Kaleidoscope,* "had proved as successful as the United States in managing ethnic diversity. No nation before had ever made diversity itself a source of national identity and unity." The second sentence explains the success described in the first, and the mechanism for translating diversity into unity has been the American Creed, the civic culture—the very assimilating, unifying culture that is today challenged, and not seldom rejected, by the ideologues of ethnicity.

A historian's guess is that the resources of the Creed have not been exhausted. Americanization has not lost its charms. Many sons and daughters of ethnic neighborhoods still want to shed their ethnicity and move to the suburbs as fast as they can—where they will be received with far more tolerance than they would have been 70 years ago. The desire for achievement and success in American society remains a potent force for assimilation. Ethnic subcultures, Stephen Steinberg, author of *The Ethnic Myth,* points out, fade away "because circumstances forced them to make choices that undermined the basis for cultural survival."

Others may enjoy their ethnic neighborhoods but see no conflict between foreign descent and American loyalty. Unlike the multiculturalists, they celebrate not only what is distinctive in their own backgrounds but what they hold in common with the rest of the population.

The ethnic identification often tends toward superficiality. The sociologist Richard Alba's study of children and grandchildren of immigrants in the Albany, New York, area shows the most popular "ethnic experience" to be sampling the ancestral cuisine. Still, less than half the respondents picked that, and only one percent ate ethnic food every day. Only one-fifth acknowledged a sense of special relationship to people of their own ethnic background; less than one-sixth taught their children about their ethnic origins; almost none was fluent in the language of the old country. "It is hard to avoid the conclusion," Alba writes, "that ethnic experience is shallow for the great majority of whites."

If ethnic experience is a good deal less shallow for blacks, it is because of their bitter experience in America, not because of their memories of Africa. Nonetheless most blacks prefer "black" to "African-Americans," fight bravely and patriotically for their country, and would move to the suburbs too if income and racism would permit.

As for Hispanic-Americans, first-generation Hispanics born in the United States speak English fluently, according to a Rand Corporation study; more than half of second-generation Hispanics give up Spanish altogether. When *Vista,* an English-language monthly for Hispanics, asked its readers what historical figures they most admired, Washington, Lincoln, and Theodore Roosevelt led the list, with Benito Juárez trailing behind as fourth, and Eleanor Roosevelt and Martin Luther King Jr. tied for fifth. So much for ethnic role models.

Nor, despite the effort of ethnic ideologues, are minority groups all that hermetically sealed off from each other, except in special situations, like colleges, where ideologues are authority figures. The wedding notices in any newspaper testify to the increased equanimity with which people these days marry across ethnic lines, across religious lines, even, though to a smaller degree, across racial lines. Around half of Asian-American marriages are with non-Orientals, and the Census Bureau estimates one million interracial—mostly black-white—marriages in 1990 as against 310,000 in 1970.

VI

The ethnic revolt against the melting pot has reached the point, in rhetoric at least, though not I think in reality, of a denial of the idea of a common culture and a single society. If large numbers of people really accept this, the republic would be in serious trouble. The question poses itself: how to restore the balance between *unum* and *pluribus?*

The old American homogeneity disappeared well over a century ago, never to return. Ever since, we have been preoccupied in one way or another with the problem, as Herbert Croly phrased it 80 years back in *The Promise of American Life,* "of preventing such divisions from dissolving the society into which they enter—of keeping such a highly differentiated society fundamentally sound and whole." This required, Croly believed, an "ultimate bond of union." There was only one way by which solidarity could be restored, "and that is by means of a democratic social ideal. . . ."

The genius of America lies in its capacity to forge a single nation from peoples of remarkably diverse racial, religious, and ethnic origins. It has done so because democratic principles provide both the philosophical bond of union and practical experience in civic participation. The American Creed envisages a nation composed of individuals making their own choices and accountable to themselves, not a nation based on inviolable ethnic communities. The Constitution turns on individual rights, not on group rights. Law, in order to rectify past wrongs, has from time to time (and in my view often properly so) acknowledged the claims of groups; but this is the exception, not the rule.

Our democratic principles contemplate an open society founded on tolerance of differences and on mutual respect. In practice, America has been more open to some than to others. But it is more open to all today than it was yesterday and is likely to be even more open tomorrow than today. The steady movement of American life has been from exclusion to inclusion.

Historically and culturally this republic has an Anglo-Saxon base; but from the start the base has been modified, enriched, and reconstituted by transfusions from other continents and civilizations. The movement from exclusion to inclusion causes a constant revision in the texture of our culture. The ethnic transfusions affect all aspects of American life—our politics, our literature, our music, our painting, our movies, our cuisine, our customs, our dreams.

Black Americans in particular have influenced the ever-changing national culture in many ways. They have lived here for centuries, and, unless one believes in racist mysticism, they belong far more to American culture than to the culture of Africa. Their history is part of the Western democratic tradition, not an alternative to it. Henry Louis Gates Jr. reminds us of James Baldwin's remark about coming to Europe to find out that he was "as American as any Texas G.I." No one does black Americans more disservice than those Afrocentric ideologues who would define them out of the West.

The interplay of diverse traditions produces the America we know. "Paradoxical though it may seem," Diane Ravitch has well said, "the United States has a common culture that is multicultural." That is why unifying political ideals coexist so easily and cheerfully with diversity in social and cultural values. Within the overarching political commitment, people are free to live as they choose, ethnically and otherwise. Differences will remain; some are reinvented; some are used to drive us apart. But as we renew our allegiance to the unifying ideals, we provide the solvent that will prevent differences from escalating into antagonism and hatred.

One powerful reason for the movement from exclusion to inclusion is that the American Creed facilitates the appeal from the actual to the ideal. When we talk of the American democratic faith, we must understand it in its true dimensions. It is not an impervious, final, and complacent orthodoxy, intolerant of deviation and dissent, fulfilled in flag salutes, oaths of allegiance, and hands over the heart. It is an ever-evolving philosophy, fulfilling its ideals through debate, self-criticism, protest, disrespect, and irreverence; a tradition in which all have rights of heterodoxy and opportunities for self-assertion. The Creed has been the means by which Americans have haltingly but persistently narrowed the gap between performance and principle. It is what all Americans should learn, because it is what binds all Americans together.

Let us by all means in this increasingly mixed-up world learn about those other continents and civilizations. But let us master our own history first. Lamentable as some may think it, we inherit an American experience, as America inherits a European experience. To deny the essentially European origins of American culture is to falsify history.

Americans of whatever origin should take pride in the distinctive inheritance to which they have all contributed, as other nations take pride in their distinctive inheritances. Belief in one's own culture does not require disdain for other cultures. But one step at a time: no culture can hope to ingest other cultures all at once, certainly not before it ingests its own. As we begin to master our own culture, then we can explore the world.

Our schools and colleges have a responsibility to teach history for its own sake—as part of the intellectual equipment of civilized persons—and not to degrade history by allowing its contents to be dictated by pressure groups, whether political, economic, religious, or ethnic. The past may sometimes give offense to one or another minority; that is no reason for rewriting history. Giving pressure groups vetoes over textbooks and courses betrays both history and education. Properly taught, history will convey a sense of the variety, continuity, and adaptability of cultures, of the need for understanding other cultures, of the ability of individuals and peoples to overcome obstacles, of the importance of critical analysis and dispassionate judgment in every area of life.

Above all, history can give a sense of national identity. We don't have to believe that our values are absolutely better than the next fellow's or the next country's, but we have no doubt that they are better *for us,* reared as we are—and are worth living by and worth dying for. For our values are not matters of whim and happenstance. History has given them to us. They are anchored in our national experience, in our great national documents, in our national heroes, in our folkways, traditions, and standards. People with a different history will have differing values. But we believe that our own are better for us. They work for us; and, for that reason, we live and die by them.

It has taken time to make the values real for all our citizens, and we still have a good distance to go, but we have made progress. If we now repudiate the quite marvelous inheritance that history bestows on us, we invite the fragmentation of the national community into a quarrelsome spatter of enclaves, ghettos, tribes. The bonds of cohesion in our society are sufficiently fragile, or so it seems to me, that it makes no sense to strain them by encouraging and exalting cultural and linguistic apartheid.

The American identity will never be fixed and final; it will always be in the making. Changes in the population have always brought changes in the national ethos and will continue to do so; but not, one must hope, at the expense of national integration. The question America confronts as a pluralistic society is how to vindicate cherished cultures and traditions without breaking the bonds of cohesion—common ideals, common political institutions, common language, common culture, common fate—that hold the republic together.

Our task is to combine due appreciation of the splendid diversity of the nation with due emphasis on the great unifying Western ideas of individual freedom, political democracy, and human rights. These are the ideas that define the American nationality—and that today empower people of all continents, races, and creeds.

"What then is the American, this new man? . . . Here individuals of all nations are melted into a new race of men." Still a good answer—still the best hope.

MICHAEL LIND

Are We a Nation?

"Are we a nation?" The question was raised, in an address of that title, by Senator Charles Sumner of Massachusetts after the Civil War. At the end of the twentieth century, the question of whether America is a nation has arisen again. Unlike Sumner, that great champion of Union and racial integration, proponents of the leading schools of thought about American national identity today—multiculturalism and democratic universalism—tend to answer the question in the negative.

Are we a nation? No, say the multiculturalists, who are found predominantly though not exclusively on the left. The United States, they say, is not a nation-state. Rather, it is a nation of nations, a federation of nationalities or cultures sharing little or nothing but a common government: a miniature UN. How the cultures that compose the multinational American citizenry are to be defined is the subject of dispute among those who think of America in this way. Contemporary multiculturalists usually identify the nations or cultures of the United States with five races defined by descent: white, black or African-American, Hispanic, Asian-Pacific Islander, and American Indian/Inuit. In contrast, a small but eloquent band of old-fashioned cultural pluralists (in the tradition of the early-twentieth-century American thinkers Horace Kallen and Randolph Bourne) tends to identify the nations of America with ethnic groups, particularly white ethnic groups: English, German, Irish, Italian, Polish, and so on. Though they may disagree about how many American cultures there are, multiculturalists and cultural pluralists agree that the United States is not a nation-state like France or Poland or China or even Brazil, but a multinational federation, like Canada and Switzerland and the former Soviet Union and Yugoslavia. The philosopher Michael Walzer has summarized this view, common to multiculturalists and cultural pluralists: "It isn't inconceivable that America will one day become an American nation-state, the many giving way to the one, but that is not what it is now; nor is that its destiny."

A multiculturalism of the right is conceivable, as a response by conservatives who wish to preserve cultural or racial "purity" through a policy of voluntary ethnic or racial segregation; something like this is promoted by the French right of Jean Marie Le Pen, and there are American parallels in some of the proposals of the Ku Klux Klan. To date, however, most multiculturalists and cultural pluralists in the United States have been on the political left. They have tended to share an antipathy to the mainstream culture of the American majority. Denying or ignoring the black and Latin American elements of American vernacular culture, multiculturalists tend to misdescribe it as "white" culture. Compounding the confusion, theorists of multiculturalism, like many conservatives, often identify this white middle American culture—rather implausibly, it must be said—with "western civilization."* The confusion only deepens when multiculturalists count among the supposed victims and enemies of "western civilization" immigrants from Spanish-speaking, Catholic Latin America, whose traditions exhibit greater continuity with ancient Rome and Latin Christendom than does the culture of Protestant, English-speaking North Americans. The confusion arises from the equation—as spurious in the case of Latin American mestizos as in the case of black Americans—of nonwestern with nonwhite. If one rejects this assumption, if one assumes that Americans of different races can, and in fact do, share, not only a common civilization but a common nationality, then the multicultural enterprise simply collapses.

The major opposition to multiculturalism today comes from democratic universalists, who are mostly, though not exclusively, on the political right. *Are we a nation?* The democratic universalists answer No as well. Universalists reject the multicultural celebration of racial-cultural identities, fearing it will encourage the "Balkanization" of America; however, they do not counter it with an inclusive American nationalism of their own. By their own theory, they cannot; for democratic universalists agree with multiculturalists that the United States is not a conventional nation-state. The United States, according to universalists, is not a nation-state at all, but an idea-state, a nationless state based on the philosophy of liberal democracy in the abstract. There is no American people, merely an American Idea. Someone who believes ardently in this founding idea (variously defined as human equality or natural rights or civil liberty or democracy or constitutional government) is a genuine American, even if he shares little or nothing of the prevalent culture, mores and historical memories of the American cultural majority. Americanness, in this view, is less akin to membership in a national community than to belief in a secular political faith—the religion of democracy. In the

---

*Whether the diverse societies of the ancient Mediterranean, Latin Christendom, and modern Western Europe and its lands of settlement and colonies really can be spoken of as a single civilization or culture is open to question. Even if they could, the United States, and all of the English-speaking countries, would be best understood as atypical offshoots of a continental civilization in which the cultural leaders for the longest periods were Italy and France, and which is based on a shared legacy of Roman law and Catholicism.

words of the late Theodore H. White, "Americans are not people like the French, Germans, or Japanese. . . .Americans are held together only by ideas." Another journalist, Cokie Roberts, has written, "We have nothing binding us together as a nation—no common ethnicity, history, religion, or even language—except the Constitution and the institutions it created." (The fact that nowadays conservatives tend to espouse democratic universalism is surprising, inasmuch as this doctrine confuses the American *nation* with its *government*—a point lost on everyone on the right except for a few "paleoconservatives").*

The democratic universalist's characterization of the United States as a nonnational idea-state usually comes as part of a package with American exceptionalism—the belief that the United States is not only different in kind from other countries but superior in its morality and institutions. House Speaker Newt Gingrich has called for Americans to reject multiculturalism and "reassert American exceptionalism." The British writer Paul Johnson even claims that the future of humanity depends on the geopolitical power of the United States, "a great and mighty nation which is something more than a nation, which is an international community in itself, a prototype global community, but which at the same time is a unity, driven by agreed assumptions, accepting a common morality and moral aims, and able therefore to marshal and deploy its forces with stunning effect."

These, then, are the two schools of thought that have almost monopolized recent discussions of American identity. Both agree that the United States has never been a conventional nation-state, and differ only as to what kind of nonnational state it is or should be. Is the United States, as the multiculturalists claim, a federation of races, or is it—as the democratic universalists argue—a postnational idea-state?

The answer is: neither. The multiculturalists and the democratic universalists are both wrong. The United States is not, and never has been, either a multinational democracy or a nonnational democracy. The United States has been, is, and should continue to be a liberal and democratic nation-state.

The multiculturalists are mistaken in equating the conventionally defined American races with cultures, and identifying those cultures, in turn, with nationalities. By the usual criteria of nationality, most of the Americans who are labeled white, black, Hispanic, and Asian—as well as American Indians and Inuit who have assimilated to the mainstream culture—are members of a single national community, the American nation. That nation is not homogeneous; it is divided into subcultures, some of which, like the historic black American subculture, more or less correspond to race ("Hispanic" and "Asian and Pacific Islander," though, are bureaucratic categories that do not correspond to genuine ethnic subcultures). A people does not have to be as homogeneous as, say, the Japanese in order to constitute a nation; Italians are members of a single nation, in spite of their enormous regional variety, and the racial diversity of Brazil and

---

*It can be argued, to be sure, that democratic universalism on the right is a rather thinly camouflaged popular nationalism, with "democracy" and "Western civilization" really understood, by advocates and audience alike, to refer to what used to be called the American way of life, not to Norwegian parliamentary procedure or Italian literature.

Mexico does not mean that those countries lack distinctive national heritages and identities.

While the multiculturalists and their cousins the cultural pluralists are wrong to think of the United States as a federation of racial cultures, the democratic universalists are mistaken in thinking that American national identity can be founded on an idea. The very notion of a country based on an idea is absurd. What if two countries are founded on the same idea—say, individual rights, or the rule of law? Does that mean they are the same country? The communist states all professed to be founded on the ideas of Marx and Lenin—and yet Russian, Chinese, and Vietnamese communists remained not only distinct from each other but often mutually hostile. At best, a political or religious dogma is merely one—and not the most important—element of the culture that distinguishes one nationality from another.

A nation may be *dedicated* to a proposition, but it cannot *be* a proposition—this is the central insight of American nationalism, the doctrine that is the major alternative to multiculturalism and democratic universalism. To the question, *Are we a nation?* the American nationalist answers with a resounding and unequivocal Yes. A straightforward American nationalism, in one form or another, is *the* alternative to the fissioning that the multiculturalists celebrate as pluralism and the democratic universalists condemn as Balkanization.

A genuine nation is not a mere citizenry, a mere collection of individuals who share nothing other than common rulers and common laws. If a common government alone were sufficient, then the Soviet and Romanov and Hapsburg and Ottoman Empires would have been nations themselves, rather than "prison-houses of the nations" (as Tsarist Russia was described).* A real nation is a concrete historical community, defined primarily by a common language, common folkways, and a common vernacular culture.† Such an extrapolitical American nation exists today, and has existed in one form or another for hundreds of years. Most Americans, of all races, are born and acculturated into the American nation; most immigrants and their descendants will be assimilated into it. The American nation is different in detail from the Chinese and Russian and Mexican and French nations. It is not, however, different in kind.

Not only does the transracial American majority constitute a single nation, but that majority is deeply nationalist in its sentiments. Few Americans are consistent liberals or conservatives; most are nationalists, by reflex if not reflection.

---

*The language of international law confuses matters, by referring to subjects or citizens of a state as its nationals whether the state corresponds to an actual nation or not. The United Nations really should be called the United Regimes or the United States (the United States, conversely, might more accurately be called the United Nation of America).

†For the nationalist, as for some opponents of nationalism, there is a difference between patriotism and nationalism. Patriotism is allegiance to a particular government or constitution; nationalism is loyalty to the interests of the cultural nation. The nationalist is willing to sacrifice patriotic duty to national loyalty, if necessary—as in 1776, when the American Patriots decided that the needs of the American nation had to prevail over their patriotic allegiance to the British empire. Governments should serve nations, not nations governments.

American nationalism, however, is the political doctrine that dares not speak its name.

American nationalism is almost never represented in public discussions of American identity, which as I have noted tend to be dominated by multicultural-ism and democratic universalism. Since World War II, nationalism has been con-sidered by many to have been discredited by its association with German Na-tional Socialism, Italian Fascism, and Japanese militarism (which were of course three quite different phenomena). American intellectuals have also been deeply influenced by political philosophies hostile to nationalism. On the left, antina-tionalism has been fed by Marxism, which viewed nationalism as an ephemeral phase of political development destined to be superseded in the era of cosmopoli-tan socialism (ironically, Marxism has proven to be an ephemeral phase of na-tionalism in Russia and China). The antinationalists of the right tend to be nos-talgic for multinational empires like the Hapsburg and the British, and to associate nationalism with the overthrow of European rule over nonwhite na-tions, something of which a certain kind of conservative disapproves. Although nationalism around the world has often been liberal and democratic rather than authoritarian or totalitarian, American politicians, intellectuals, and journalists continue to indulge in the old-fashioned practice of treating nationalism as a *malum in se.* The world, we are told again and again, is threatened by a resur-gence of nationalism (as though there had ever been a great era of selfless inter-nationalism). Adjectives like "aggressive" and "sinister" and "dark" are often af-fixed to nationalism in order to make the term seem even more frightening. The critics of nationalism in the abstract seldom trouble themselves to ask whether it makes any sense to view things as different and incompatible as the eighteenth-century philosopher J. G. Herder's tolerant aesthetic pluralism and Hitler's mur-derous racist imperialism as aspects of the same phenomenon—in this case, "German nationalism."

The pejorative connotations that hover around the subject of nationalism—ours and everyone else's—in conventional American public discourse do not mean that nationalism is weak or nonexistent in the American body politic. Indeed, na-tionalism in one form or another is probably the conception of American identity with the greatest influence among Americans as a whole, particularly among the majority who do not have college educations. Outside of a small educated elite, hardly any Americans think of their country as a minature UN or as an abstract idea-state. Though they may be trained to repeat these formulas, most Americans do not really believe them. The patriotism of ordinary Americans is no different in kind from that of Italians or Indians or Russians; it has more to do with family, neighborhood, customs, and historical memories than with constitutions or polit-ical philosophies. It may very well be, indeed, that popular nationalism as a senti-mental attachment to people and customs and country, is much stronger in the United States than in Western Europe, where "post-patriotic" attitudes, at least among the more educated, are much more prevalent.

The American people, then, constitute a genuine nation; with its own nation-state, the U.S.A., and with its own genuine, if largely inarticulate, nationalism. The really interesting argument, it turns out, is not the stale debate between multiculturalists and democratic universalists about what kind of nonnational state the United States is: multi- or post? It is another controversy, a less familiar dispute, over how the "nation" in the American "nation-state" is to be defined. In this debate among nationalists, the two sides are nativists and liberal nationalists.

Nativists tend to impose racial and/or religious tests on membership in the national community. To be American, in the nativist view, is to be white and/or Christian or a member of "the Judeo-Christian tradition" (a euphemism that really means Christian). The racial and religious definitions of Americanness are not always joined; there are secular racists, and there are conservative nativists who envision a multiracial but pan-Christian American national community. The latter option—a pan-Christian but not white-supremacist American nativism—is the more or less overt goal of right-wing Christian political activists like Pat Robertson, leader of the Christian Coalition. Old-fashioned Anglo-American or even Euro-American nativism will have diminishing appeal in a country in which a growing percentage of the population is nonwhite; however, the potential attractiveness of a nonracist, pan-Christian religious nativism to Americans of all races should not be underestimated.

Liberal nationalists share an unapologetic American nationalism with nativists—but that is about all that they share. The liberal nationalist rejects racial or religious tests for membership in the American nation. A nonwhite American is as genuine an American as a white American (indeed, black Americans can make a better claim for their "Americanness" than most of the descendants of European immigrants). One can despise and reject Christianity and Judaism and be not merely a fine citizen but a member in good standing of the American cultural nation. Insofar as American nationality is a matter of vernacular culture, rather than race or beliefs, a radical black lesbian atheist who grows up in Chicago is more "American" than a white English conservative who immigrates in adulthood and who, though he is an expert on the Founding Fathers, is unfamiliar with the American idiom.*

For the liberal nationalist, then, the American nation is defined by language and culture, not by race or religion. The national language is American English, in its various regional and subcultural dialects. The national culture is not the high culture of the art galleries and civics classes, but rather the vernacular culture that has evolved in the United States in the past several centuries, and continues to evolve, from the unsystematic fusion of various regional and racial customs and traditions. The liberal nationalist argument, it must be stressed, is not that a transracial American nationality is something that will emerge in the future, from the mingling of today's conventionally defined American racial and ethnic groups. Such mixing, rather, merely reinforces a common cultural nationality that already exists.

---

*Liberal nationalism and nativism tend to be found on the "liberal" and "conservative" sides of the contemporary American political spectrum. It is possible, however, to be a liberal nationalist with many conservative political views ("liberal" in liberal nationalism refers to the liberal-democratic constitution of the state, not to particular policies). It is also possible to imagine an American racial or religious nativism that is "left-wing" with respect to economics, like the populism of William Jennings Bryan.

The American cultural nation, properly defined, has included Americans of different races for centuries. White supremacists and black nationalists to the contrary, black Americans were members of the American cultural nation for generations before they were granted U.S. citizenship. Indeed, the transracial American nation is considerably older than the United States itself; for several generations before 1776, a distinct, unique, English-speaking North American nationality, including slaves born and raised on American soil, had begun to diverge from other parts of the English-speaking world.* Even if the federal government were abolished tomorrow, the American cultural nation would endure. The American nation is older than its government, and will almost certainly outlive the United States, which like all regimes will prove mortal. States and constitutions come and go; cultural nations, though they are not eternal, last a very long time.

Of the two rival versions of American nationalism, nativism has the greatest antiquity, for the simple reason that most Americans, until well into the twentieth century, thought of the American people as a white Christian nation (something that is hardly surprising, insofar as most Americans for generations to come will be conventionally white and at least nominally Christian). Even though it rejects the venerable traditions of white supremacy and Protestant/Christian hegemony, the liberal nationalist philosophy . . . has deep roots in the American heritage—in the strong-state nationalism of George Washington, Alexander Hamilton, Daniel Webster, Abraham Lincoln, and Theodore Roosevelt; in the New Deal liberalism of Franklin Roosevelt, Harry Truman, and Lyndon Johnson that created and sustains a middle class that would be destroyed by unchecked capitalism; and, most important of all, in the tradition of color-blind racial integrationism descending from abolitionists like Frederick Douglass to civil rights reformers like Martin Luther King, Jr. Liberal nationalism might be most simply defined as yesterday's "melting-pot" nationalism updated to favor the cultural fusion and genetic amalgamation not just of white immigrant groups but of Americans of all races.

In civil rights law, the natural corollary to the liberal nationalist conception of the American nation as a cultural and (in time) genetic melting pot is the rejection of any distinctions based on biological race. Race is an arbitrary category that is bound to grow more arbitrary, as intermarriage produces growing numbers of Americans with ancestors in several of today's officially defined racial groups. In civil rights, liberal nationalists favor a return to the original, color-blind vision that animated the leaders of the Civil Rights Revolution like Martin Luther King, Jr., Bayard Rustin, Hubert Humphrey, and Lyndon Johnson. Since the 1960s, this vision has been betrayed on the left by multiculturalists, with

---

*The linguistic and cultural definition of nationality, it should be noted, is an objective anthropological test that does not depend on subjective perceptions. If subjective beliefs defined nationality, then Swedes, say, might decide they were all really Portuguese, and the actual Portuguese would have no grounds for objecting.

their defense of racial quotas and their conception of the United States as a federation of genetically defined nationalities. It is time for the American center-left to reclaim the color-blind idealism that should never have been ceded to the reactionary right.

Liberal nationalism provides not merely a different vision of the American people, but a different understanding of the American past. American exceptionalism, the belief in American uniqueness that is so important to democratic universalism, is rejected by liberal nationalists, whose American patriotism does not depend on overblown claims about American uniqueness or superiority. One should cherish one's nation, as one should cherish one's family, not because it is the best in the world, but because, with all its flaws, it is one's own.

The exceptionalist interpretation of American history holds that American politics from 1776 to the present has consisted of the gradual, painful, but progressive working out of the ideas of the Founding Fathers. Exceptionalism, in other words, is both *idealist* and *gradualist*. The liberal nationalist conception of the American past, in contrast, is *realist* and *catastrophist*. It is realist, insofar as it sees American society as the result of power struggles and inherited cultural legacies, not just abstract philosophical debates. It is catastrophist, insofar as it views American history not as the smooth and logical unfolding of an argument about liberty or democracy, but as a sequence of racial, cultural, and political regimes, each assembled by the victors in a cataclysmic and violent struggle.

Though the word "revolution" is easily tossed about today, in fact there have been only three genuine revolutions in U.S. history—the War of Independence and its violent aftermath (including the suppression of Shays' Rebellion and the Whiskey Rebellion); the Civil War and Reconstruction; and the Civil Rights Revolution from the 1950s to the 1970s. American revolutions are violent. More Americans died in the Civil War than in all of America's foreign wars combined. During the Civil Rights era, the United States was convulsed by the most extensive domestic political violence since the end of Reconstruction. American revolutions are also disruptive. Since 1789, the French have had five republics (along with several monarchies, one directory, a consulate, and a couple of empires). By contrast, the United States, since 1789, has had only one federal constitution; the two dominant parties have had the same names since the 1860s; even the boundaries of the states, unlike political jurisdictions in other democracies, are fixed in America. The formal constitutional and political continuity that we Americans cherish disguises the fact that there have been three "republics" of the United States since the War of Independence: Anglo-America (1789–1861); Euro-America (1875–1957) and Multicultural America (1972–present).

Each of these three republics has put the basic building blocks of the nation-state—race, culture, and citizenship—together in a different way.* At the risk of

---

*I do not deny that American history can be divided into periods on the basis of different criteria—for example, political party systems, or profound changes in the distribution of power between the state and federal governments (like the New Deal). Changes in the rules governing race and citizenship are not the only changes defining eras in American history; they are merely the most important.

oversimplification (a risk inseparable from any attempt to discuss major issues of public importance), I argue that each of these American "republics" has had its own consensus, its own threefold national formula, describing the national community, the civic religion, and the political creed. At any given time, there have been dissident views; but in every era, a particular national formula has tended to prevail.

In the national formula of the First Republic of the United States, Anglo-America, the national community was identified with the Anglo-Saxon or Anglo-Germanic element of the population; the civic religion, Protestant Christianity; and the political creed, federal republicanism. There was considerable doubt as to whether Irish-American Catholics—to say nothing of Jews or black Americans—could ever be "real Americans." The Civil War and Reconstruction created a Second Republic, Euro-America, which peaked in the middle of the twentieth century. The Euro-American national formula, redefined to accommodate the European immigrants of the late-nineteenth and early-twentieth century, was somewhat more inclusive than the Anglo-American. To be a "genuine American," according to the popular consensus in the Second Republic, was to be of European descent and to be Christian (Protestant or Catholic) in religion (the Eisenhower-era phrase "Judeo-Christian" was, in practice, a polite euphemism for pan-Christian). The antebellum elimination of most restrictions on white male suffrage and the post–Civil War nationalization of basic civil rights turned the Anglo-American political creed of federal republicanism into a creed of federal democracy; even in the 1950s, however, the U.S. remained a highly decentralized federal state.

The Third Republic is the one in which we live. Multicultural America was born in the turmoil of the Civil Rights Revolution between the 1950s and the 1970s. The New Deal liberals who led the first, color-blind stage of the Civil Rights Revolution, which dismantled white supremacy, lost control during the second phase, which saw the triumph of group-consciousness and racial preference programs. A revolution that began as an attempt to purge law and politics of racial classifications and to enlarge the middle class to include the disadvantaged ended, ironically, with a renaissance of race-conscious government and the political triumph of economic conservatism. Multicultural America is not the Third Republic that the color-blind liberals intended in the early sixties; it is the Third Republic that emerged later, from the intersection of black-power radicalism and white-backlash conservatism. Its patron saints are not Martin Luther King, Jr., and Lyndon Johnson, but Stokely Carmichael and Richard Nixon.

Unlike the First and Second American Republics, which were clearly nation-states, the Third Republic has the outward trappings of a multinational state. According to the quasi-official ideology of the Third Republic, there is no coherent American national community, but rather five national communities, defined by race—white, black, Hispanic, Asian and Pacific Islander, and Native American. The civic religion, to the extent that there is one, is a secular philosophy, an ideal of authenticity, that stresses conformity to particular racial or sexual or religious subcultures. The political creed of post-sixties America has been centralized multicultural democracy—the replacement of territorial federalism by a kind of

Washington-centered racial federalism (exemplified by federally coerced racial gerrymandering of electoral districts).

The basic elements of Multicultural America came together by the early seventies; since then, its institutions and even its rhetoric ("multiculturalism," "affirmative action," "diversity") have been relatively stable. Multicultural America is built on the repudiation of white supremacy (common to the first two American republics) in favor, not of color-blind liberalism, but of an elaborate system of racial preferences for citizens who are officially designated as nonwhite by government bureaucracies. These racial preferences in education, hiring, contracting, and political redistricting are available not only to descendants of the victims of American white supremacy, but also to recent immigrants from Latin America, the Caribbean, Asia, and the Indian subcontinent. The high level of legal immigration from Latin America and Asia means that the category of Americans eligible for racial preference programs and subsidies at the expense of white Americans, whether native or naturalized, grows by almost a million every year.

Far from being a challenge to the post-sixties American power structure, or an inevitable response to changing demography, the ideology of multiculturalism is, in practice, a rationalization for the racially based tokenism that has ramified throughout American society since the 1960s. Multiculturalism is not the wave of the future, but an aftershock of the black-power radicalism of the sixties. Nor is multiculturalism, in the broadest sense, to be blamed entirely on the left. From the beginning, conservatives have been as instrumental as liberals in promoting racial preference politics, for tactical reasons. The Nixon administration pioneered the imposition of racial quotas in the workforce, in order to pit unionized white workers against black workers; with equal cynicism, the Reagan and Bush administrations promoted the ghettoization of black and Hispanic voters in racially gerrymandered congressional districts, thereby undermining Democratic Congressmen and helping the Republican party to capture the House of Representatives in 1994. While the influence of multicultural ideology on campus may appear to give credence to conservative charges that the left is in control, it can be argued that racial preference programs in politics and the workplace actually help the right. Tokenism provides a suitably "progressive" camouflage for a system of divide-and-rule politics in which the homogeneous American social and economic elite—the white overclass—benefits from racial divisions among the American majority. Without the political division of wage-earning white, black, and Hispanic Americans along racial lines—a division exacerbated, though not caused, by racial preferences and multicultural ideology—it is doubtful that the white overclass in the United States, in the last generation, would have been able to carry out its agenda of destroying unions, reducing wages, cutting worker benefits, replacing full-time workers with temps, and shifting the burdens of taxation from the rich to the middle and working classes, with so little effective popular opposition.

If Multicultural America endures for another generation or two, the future for the United States is a bleak one of sinking incomes for the transracial American majority and growing resentment against the affluent and politically dominant white oligarchy. The Balkanization of America, in the form of civil war along racial lines, is unlikely. American vernacular culture is so powerful in its appeal that it will break down even the strongest immigrant cultures, and interracial marriage is already undermining racial categories. The real threat is not the Balkanization but the Brazilianization of America, not fragmentation along racial lines but fissioning along class lines. Brazilianization is symbolized by the increasing withdrawal of the white American overclass into its own barricaded nation-within-a-nation, a world of private neighborhoods, private schools, private police, private health care, and even private roads, walled off from the spreading squalor beyond. Like a Latin American oligarchy, the rich and well-connected members of the overclass can flourish in a decadent America with Third World levels of inequality and crime.

Such a grim future cannot be averted by trivial reforms, like the pseudo-populist gimmicks of the plutocratic right (tax cuts, term limits) or the techno-cratic panaceas of the neoliberals (worker retraining, reinventing government). Renewing the American nation-state will require a real, not merely metaphorical, revolution in politics and society, a revolution as sweeping—though, we may hope, not as violent—as the Civil Rights Revolution. The goal of liberal nationalism, as a political movement, must be to dismantle Multicultural America and replace it with a Fourth Republic of the United States—let us call it Trans-America.

In Trans-America, a color-blind, gender-neutral regime of individual rights would be combined with government activism promoting a high degree of substantive social and economic equality. The racial and gender quotas of the left, and the educational and political privileges of the wealthy oligarchy defended by the right, would be rejected in favor of a new union of cultural and economic nationalism in the interest of the transracial middle class. A truly representative political system, purged both of racial gerrymandering and of campaign finance practices that favor corporations and the rich; a new system of middle-class-friendly capitalism, in which today's growing economic inequality has been checked and reversed by selective government intervention in the marketplace; and a color-blind society, in which cultural fusion is accompanied, in time, by racial amalgamation—these are the goals of American liberal nationalism at the end of the twentieth century and the beginning of the twenty-first.

SUGGESTIONS FOR FURTHER READING

A good place to begin to explore multiculturalism is Lawrence H. Fuchs, *The American Kaleidoscope: Race, Ethnicity, and Civic Culture* (Hanover, N.H., 1990). He surveys the ethnic scene from the beginning of the nation and argues that American civic culture will survive despite sharp ethnic and racial conflict. Other books that offer a broad perspective are Philip Gleason, *Speaking of Diversity: Language and Ethnicity in Twentieth Century America* (Baltimore, 1992) and David H. Hollinger, *Postethnic America: Beyond Multiculturalism* (New York, 1995). Ellen Carol DuBois and Vicki L. Ruiz, eds., *Unequal Sisters: A Multicultural Reader in U.S. Women's History*, 2nd ed. (New York, 1994); David Riemers, *Still the Golden Door* (New York, 1985); and Sanford J. Ungar, *Fresh Blood:*

---

*Available in paperback edition.

The New American Immigrants (New York, 1995) deal with controversies raised by recent immigrants.

The debate over multiculturalism has produced a varied and often, but not always, stridently confrontational literature. The clearest and perhaps the most controversial defense of Afrocentrism may be found in the works of Molefi Kete Asante; a good place to start is *The Afrocentric Idea* (Philadelphia, 1987). Stanley Fish, *There's No Such Thing as Free Speech and It's a Good Thing, Too* (New York, 1994) considers problems concerning speech codes in the fight for multiculturalism, emphasizing the relationship between language and power. Todd Gitlin, *The Twilight of Common Dreams: Why America is Wracked by Culture Wars* (New York, 1995) sympathizes with multiculturalism and supports the fight for diversity in school curriculums and hiring practices, but he is also concerned with the growing lack of unity in the fight to solve common problems. Christine E. Sleeter and Peter L. McLaren, *Multicultural Education, Critical Pedagogy, and the Politics of Difference* (Albany, N.Y., 1995) considers multiculturalism in the classroom. David T. Goldberg, *Multiculturalism: A Critical Reader* (Cambridge, Mass, 1994) is a series of essays discussing a wide range of issues concerning race and ethnic diversity.

For sharply critical comments on Afrocentrism and other aspects of multiculturalism and their effects see Richard Bernstein, *Dictatorship of Virtue: Multiculturalism and the Battle For America's Future* (New York, 1994). Other influential critiques of various aspects of multiculturalism are: Allan Bloom, *The Closing of the American Mind: How Higher Education Has Failed Democracy and Impoverished the Souls of Today's Students* (New York, 1987); Lynne V. Cheney, *Telling the Truth: Why Our Culture and Our Country Have Stopped Making Sense and What We Can Do About It;* Paul Craig Roberts and Lawrence M. Stratton, *The New Color Line: How Quotas and Privilege Destroy Democracy* (Washington, 1995); Roger Kimball, *Tenured Radicals: How Politics Has Corrupted Our Higher Education* (New York, 1990); and Dinesh D'Souza, *Illiberal Education: The Politics of Race and Sex on Campus* (New York, 1991).

For a brief general introduction to the debate, or at least some aspects of it, see John Higham, "Multiculturalism and Universalism: A History and a Critique," along with comments from other scholars and Higham's rejoinder in *American Quarterly,* 45 (June 1993), 195–255. The debate over "political correctness" can be followed in Harold K. Bush, Jr., "A Brief History of PC, with Annotated-Bibliography," *American Studies International,* 33 (April 1995), 42–64.

Conflict and Consensus
in American History